The Encyclopedia of
TV Game Shows

Third Edition

The Encyclopedia of
TV GAME SHOWS

Third Edition

David Schwartz
Steve Ryan
Fred Wostbrock

Foreword by
Merv Griffin

Facts On File, Inc.

The Encyclopedia of TV Game Shows, Third Edition

Checkmark Books
An imprint of Facts On File, Inc.
11 Penn Plaza
New York NY 10001

Library of Congress Cataloging-in-Publication Data

Schwartz, David.
   The encyclopedia of TV game shows / David Schwartz, Steve Ryan, Fred Wostbrock ; foreword by Merv Griffin. — 3rd ed.
     p.   cm.
   Includes bibliographical references and index.
   ISBN 0-8160-3846-5 (hardcover). — ISBN 0-8160-3847-3 (pbk.)
   1. Game Shows—Dictionaries. I. Ryan, Steve. II. Wostbrock, Fred. III. Title.
PN1992.8.Q5S38   1999
791.45'6—dc21   98-24891

Checkmark Books are available at special discounts when purchased in bulk quantities for businesses, associations, institutions or sales promotions. Please call our Special Sales Department in New York at 212/967-8800 or 800/322-8755.

You can find Facts On File on the World Wide Web at
http://www.factsonfile.com

Cover design by Joanna Riesman and Steve Ryan

This book is printed on acid-free paper.

Printed in the United States of America

VB BVC 10 9 8 7 6 5 4 3 2 1
(pbk)   10 9 8 7 6 5 4 3 2 1

CONTENTS

FOREWORD

I have always found quiz and game shows to be a fascinating part of the history of both radio and television. As a young man I was a fan of "Winner Take All," "Truth or Consequences," and "Doctor I.Q.," among others.

Even though my career thoughts were directed toward singing and acting, I was always a fan of radio quizzes and of the early panel and early game shows.

In 1958 (on June 30, 1958, to be exact) a fellow San Franciscan, Mark Goodson, called and asked if I'd be interested in hosting his newest game creation for CBS. In one deep breath I answered with a fast yes. The game was a cute series titled "Play Your Hunch," and I was delighted to be part of the world of game shows.

"Play Your Hunch" was a very exciting experience, and it helped to make Merv Griffin a household name. I also realized that the ingredients of a successful game show were twofold. First, and perhaps most important, you must have an interesting concept that an audience can easily follow and be part of. The other is to find a perfect host that gels to perfection with the show. A few examples of that would be Alex Trebek on "Jeopardy!", Pat Sajak on "Wheel of Fortune," the late great Allen Ludden hosting the different versions of "Password," and the late Garry Moore hosting the classic, "I've Got a Secret."

While hosting a show appears easy, it is one of the most difficult jobs to do. The host must at all times keep the show moving, never allowing the excitement or drama to miss for a moment, know the game inside and out . . . and look like every mother's favorite son-in-law.

After "Play Your Hunch," I went on to host my own talk show, first on NBC then later in syndication. In September 1963 I created my first game show "Word for Word," which I also hosted. Then on March 30, 1964 "Jeopardy!" with the great Art Fleming was born.

Throughout the 1960s I created several game shows, and in 1975 my love of words and crossword puzzles turned into a show called "Wheel of Fortune," based on the game hangman my sister and I would play in the back of the car on long summer trips.

Both shows, "Jeopardy!" and "Wheel of Fortune," have stood the test of time. As of this writing, both are the top-two syndicated shows in the history of television. Who ever thought that my love of those radio quiz shows when I was a boy would develop into both "Jeopardy!" and "Wheel of Fortune"? And as I write this foreword for David, Steve, and Fred, I realize that I've been either hosting or creating game shows for four decades, including our latest quiz show "Click" in syndication.

Please sit back, relax, and enjoy the third edition of *The Encyclopedia of TV Game Shows*. I know I will.

—Merv Griffin
Beverly Hills, California

Merv Griffin.

INTRODUCTION

Game shows . . . since the dawn of radio and television, they've been a part of our way of life. Game shows have entertained us, made us laugh, educated us, and even touched us. The names, faces, and games immediately ring bells and buzzers. The fun is contagious, and memorable.

The Encyclopedia of TV Game Shows, Third Edition, is the result of many years of intense research. If there's anything you want to know about game, quiz, and panel shows, it's probably in this book. Working as a team, we have put together the most comprehensive listing of network, syndicated, and cable game shows that have been broadcast since 1946. If you weren't around in the early days, here's an exclusive front row seat in which to recall the glorious past of television.

Did you know that Johnny Carson, Walter Cronkite, Merv Griffin, Jackie Gleason, Regis Philbin, Rod Serling, and Mike Wallace were all game show emcees at one time? Did you spot Kirstie Alley when she was a contestant on both ''Match Game'' and ''Password Plus''? Or Phyllis Diller when she was a contestant on ''You Bet Your Life'' with Groucho Marx? Do you recall when Vanna White was asked to ''Come on down!'' as a contestant on ''The Price Is Right''? Remember the times Burt Reynolds and Tom Selleck lost on ''The Dating Game''? We'll bet you didn't know that Jimmy Carter, Gerald Ford, Richard Nixon, and Ronald Reagan were all guests on game shows. These magical memories and countless others are all detailed in this book.

The book features exclusive photos of your favorite emcees and models, as well as the sets on which they held court. Can you recall what the original ''Let's Make a Deal'' and ''The Price Is Right'' sets looked like? Both of these descriptions, and more, can be found in the pages that follow.

For this third edition, we've updated *The Encyclopedia of TV Game Shows* to include all of the new game shows that have reached the small screen since the appearance of the second edition. We've also dusted off old scrapbooks to bring you a bonanza of new classic game show photographs, many of which have never been published. And, as an added bonus you'll also find an updated history of game shows over the past fifty plus years and many new nuggets of trivia spread throughout the book.

Please read the acknowledgments because these special people—many of whom are personal friends—are the real heroes of this book. Without their unique talents for hosting, announcing, creating new ideas, producing, writing, and designing brilliant new sets there wouldn't be any game shows. These few hundred or so people who work in the game show industry are indeed a special breed, and we as authors and also co-workers are proud to have chosen such a career path.

—David Schwartz, Steve Ryan, and Fred Wostbrock
Hollywood, California

ACKNOWLEDGMENTS

The authors would like to thank the following people, production companies, networks, and photo services for helping us gather the information and pictures used in the book.

ABC Television, ABR Entertainment, Ginger Adams, Art Alisi, Marty Allen, Paul Alter, Cheryl Anderson, Ralph Andrews Productions, Kathleen Ankers, George Ansbro, Bill Armstrong, Associated Press, Portia Badham, Ron Baldwin, Barbara Barnard, Chuck Barris Productions, Barry and Enright Productions, Jack Barry, Shirley Bawidamann, Orson Bean, Mark Becker, Joe Behar, John Behrens, Ellie Bendes, Bern Bennett, Peter Berlin, Mike Bevan, Stu Billett, Dennis Biondi, Blair Entertainment, Leona Blair, Howard Blumenthal, Caroline Bock, Lin Bolen, Cindy Bonsall, Phyllis Borea, Mark Bowerman, Frank Bresee, Michael Brockman, Richard Brockway, Fred Bronson, Jean De Vivier Brown, Lorraine Brown, Buena Vista Television, Gloria Burke, Anne Burkhimer, CBS Television, California State University—Northridge, Charles Cappleman, Bill Carruthers, Dena Carruthers, Peter Carruthers, Tim Carruthers, Waipehe Carruthers, Johnny Carson, Joe Cates, Heidi Cayn, Century Towers Productions, Bill Chastain, Norman Checkor, Roxanne Checkor, Erik Christensen, Lisa Ciulik, Dick Clark, Gail Clark, Jack Clark, Mike Clark, Bob Clayton, Cleveland Press, Yoko Coleman, Columbia Pictures Television, Brian Conn, Ted Cooper, Grover Crisp, Dan Cross, Ann Cullen, Bill Cullen, Jean Cummings, Dresser Dahlstead, Kay Daly, Joe Daniel, Michael Davies, Richard Dawson, Lisa Dee, Milton DeLugg, Phyllis Diller, The Disney Channel, Verna Dittamo, Roger Dobkowitz, Phil Donahue, Don Pitts Voices, Dick Dudley, Geoff Edwards, Ralph Edwards Productions, Dan Einstein, Dan Enright, Susan Epstein, Frank Esopi, Joyce Estrin, Bob Eubanks, George Faber, Gil Fates, Chester Feldman, George Fennaman, Ray Ferry, Rob Fiedler, Art Fleming, Michael Fleming, Ed Flesh, Rex Fluty Jr., Food Network, Four Star Entertainment, Dan Fox, Sonny Fox, Ladd Framer, Howard Frank, Steve Friedman, Ester Furst, Game Show Network, Mike Garguilo, Lloyd Gaynes, Alan Gilbert, Johnny Gilbert, Jerry Gilden, Michael Gilman, Pat Gleason, Andrew Golder, Jeff Goldstein, Jonathan Goodson, Mark Goodson, Frank Gorshin, Berni Gould, Chet Gould, Charlene Grayson, Ron Greenberg, Don Gregory, Merv Griffin, Merv Griffin Productions, Darris Gringeri, John Guedel, Michael Gwartney, Frank Hagan, Monty Hall, David Hammett, Ed Hammond, Kiiana Hampton, Mae Hampton, Lon Harding, John Harlan, Ron Harris, William Harris, Stefan Hatos, Michael Hawks, Johnny Hayes, Mike Hayes, Merrill Heatter, Franklin Heller, Art Hellyer, Kay Henley, Marilu Henner, Shelley Herman, Mike Hill, Bill Hillier, Bob Hilton, Howard Hinderstein, Donna Holden, Larry Hovis, Wayne Howell, Tina Hummel, Barbara Hunter, Marty Ingels, Jerita Ingle, Dan Ingram, Stacy Jackson (Lifetime Television), Frank Jacoby, Chris Jacquish, Art James, Dennis James, Bert Jayasekera, Allan Jeffreys, Jim Victory Television, Gabrielle Johnston, Romain Johnston, Gary Jonke, Ed Jubert, KCAL-TV, KCOP-TV, KMPC Radio, KRLA Radio, KTLA-TV, KTTV-TV, Rick Kates, Harris Katleman, Cynthia Kazarian, Mary Kellogg, Bob Kennedy, Tom Kennedy, Richard Kline, King World, Allan Koss, Jerry Kupcinet, Jim Lange, Joel Lawrence, Richard Lawrence, Vicki Lawrence-Schultz, Steve LeBlang, Jean Lewis, Frank Liberman, Library of Congress, Charles Lisanby, Lorimar-Telepictures, Delilah Loud, Glenn Lowney, Allen Ludden, Gary Lycan, John "Ted" Lyman, MTV Networks, Sue MacIntyre, Dave Mackey, Sheila MacRae, Lori Marshall, Peter Marshall, Sandy Martindale, Wink Martindale, Nick Martino, Perry Massey, Mark Maxwell-Smith, Philip Mayer, Bill McCord, Joel McGee, Paul McGuire, Matt McKenzie, Jim McKrell, Lisa McKrell, Kevin Meagher, Jeff Merkin, Carol Merrill, Mike Metzger, David Michaels, Ann Miller, Jonathan Miller (Television Index), James Monaco, Jaye P. Morgan, Don Morrow, Gregg Moscoe, Roger Muir, John Mula, Jan Murray, Museum of TV & Radio, Russ Myerson, NBC Television, Dave Nagel (ESPN), Jeff Nagler, Jack Narz, Mike Narz, Jim Newton, Cathi Nicholson, Marilyn Nicholson, Robert Noah, Charlie O'Donnell, Odyssey Channel, Karen Osmer (The Family Channel), Matt Ottinger, Gary Owens, Betsy Palmer, Betty Panos, Don Pardo, Dean Parker, Lillian Parker, Marty Pasetta, Jim Peck, Erin Perry, Jim Perry, Personality Photos Inc., Susan Petracca, Chuck Pharis, Stuart Phelps, Don Pitts, Gail Pitts, Playboy Enterprises, Beverly Pomerantz, Steve Radosh, Mark Ragonese, Gene Rayburn, Reeves Entertainment, Don Reid, Richard Reid, Charles Nelson Reilly, John Rhinehart, Ray Richmond, Geraldo Rivera, Joan Rivers, Claudine Roberts, Brian Robinette, Rod Roddy, Heidi Rotbart, Michele Roth, Stephanie Ryan, Saban Productions, Anthony Sabatino, Soupy Sales, Theresa Savage, George Schlatter, Murray Schwartz, Screen Gems Television, John Seekings, Jeremy Shamos, Stephanie Sheeran, Frances Siddon, K. Mathy Simon, Ron Simon, Susan Simons, Nancy Sinatra, Ira Skutch, Bill Smith, Lillian M. Smith, Alan Solomon, Aaron Solomon, David Sparks, Roger Speakman, Pamm Spencer, Robert Stahl, Willie Stein, Herb Stemple, Scott Sternberg, Bob Stewart, Bob Stewart Productions, Jay Stewart, Sande Stewart, Bunny Stivers, Mike Stokey, Scott Stone, Suzanne Stone, Stone-Stanley Productions, Ralph Story, Milt Suchin, Marc Summers, Mark Surface, Bob Synes, Syracuse University, Joel Tator, Jake Tauber, Lori

ix

Tellez, Lloyd Thaxton, Geoff Theobald, Alan Thicke, Vicky Tiffany, Peter Tomarken, Ryan Tredinnick, Tom Trimble, 20th Century-Fox Television, UCLA, UPI, USA Cable Network, USC Archives, John Vackrinos, Marge Van Ostrand, Viacom, Lee Vines, Keenie Voigt, WABC-TV, WNEW-TV, WPIX-TV, WQED-TV, WWOR-TV, Mike Wagner, Richard Wagoner, Waldwick High School, Dale Walsh, Rolanda Watts, Phillip Wayne, Harfield Weedin, Bill Wendell, Adam West, Randy West, Betty White, Paul Winchell, William Paterson College, Dave Williger, Jay Wolpert, Gene Wood, Worldvision, and special thanks to fellow TV historian Bob Boden.

MARK GOODSON TRIBUTE

July 1998 marks the fiftieth anniversary of the first Mark Goodson game show to appear on network television. That show, "Winner Take All," was hosted by Bud Collyer and premiered on CBS July 1, 1948.

Mark Goodson set the standard for style and excellence in an industry where he accumulated ten prestigious Daytime Emmy Awards for outstanding game or audience participation shows. Today, Mark Goodson's name is synonymous with game shows. He is recognized by the *Guinness Book of Records* as the most prolific producer in television history, with a lifetime total of 39,312 shows totaling an unprecedented 21,831.5 hours. If you tried to view all of Mark Goodson's work it would take more than two and a half years to watch every episode back-to-back if you watched twenty-four hours a day nonstop.

Mark Goodson is one of the most respected and successful television producers of all time. Since February 1950, a Mark Goodson–produced show has appeared on national television at least once a week every week to the present.

It was on Thursday, February 2, 1950 that the granddaddy of all panel shows, "What's My Line?", premiered. It proved so popular that it was soon moved to Sunday evenings, where it remained on the CBS schedule for seventeen years, with John Daly as host. Over the broadcast history of the show many prominent mystery guests appeared, including Marlon Brando, Johnny Carson, Clint Eastwood, Paul Newman, Ronald Reagan, Eleanor Roosevelt, Carl Sandburg, Frank Sinatra, Barbra Streisand, Elizabeth Taylor, and, of course, Mark Goodson. By the time "What's My Line?" left the air in 1967 it had become the second-longest-running primetime show in television, right behind "The Ed Sullivan Show."

During the early 1950s, Mark Goodson also developed other classic game formats, which included "I've Got a Secret," hosted by Garry Moore, and "Beat the Clock," with Bud Collyer.

In 1956, Mark Goodson developed one of his most successful programs, "To Tell the Truth" (his personal favorite, as well), which was telecast both primetime and daytime on CBS. Its format, which Mark Goodson has called the best game concept he ever devised, was a variation of "What's My Line?" and consisted of a panel of quick-witted celebrities cross-examining three people who claimed the same identity.

In 1961, Mark Goodson gave us another long-running hit, "Password," with Allen Ludden as its host. This show has been described as the most cerebral and ingenious of all his formats.

Mark Goodson also created "Family Feud," a resounding network hit since its original introduction on ABC. "Family Feud" has also had the distinction of being one of television's highest-rated first-run syndicated properties.

Over the years, Mark Goodson's creativity introduced many features now standard in game show programming. He innovated the strategem of having contestants compete against each other; he introduced the "bell and buzzer" to see who could answer first in a contest; and he was the first to keep champion contestants on the show until they met defeat at the hands of a challenger. All of these innovations came to television for the first time in 1948 with "Winner Take All."

Mark Goodson once said, "The greatest challenge in the world is to invent a new game." One might ask, "What makes a good game show?" This is how Mark Goodson explained the process. "A good game show must actively involve the viewer. A good game show seeks the simplest, sparest framework. A good game show will have the viewer talking out loud to the TV."

Mark Goodson was a perfectionist who looked at an idea from all possible perspectives. He wasn't content until a concept was absolutely flawless, declaring "I hate to fail even more than I like to succeed." Mark Goodson was a man of enthusiasm, incredible energy, and unparalleled imaginative skills.

Mark Goodson enters and signs in on "What's My Line?"

Jonathan Goodson on the set of "Family Feud," with the top-ten longest running game shows from Mark Goodson Productions on the survey board.

It was this kind of dedication that led to other game show favorites such as "Blockbusters," "Card Sharks," "Child's Play," "Classic Concentration," and many others that spanned the 1940s, 50s, 60s, 70s, 80s, and 90s. That's six decades of historical television! And possibly most significant, his astute helmsmanship of the extensive Goodson-Todman empire assured that no aspect of its operations was ever implicated in the quiz show scandals of the late 1950s.

The longest-running game show in TV history is Goodson's creation "The Price Is Right," which began back in 1956 as a quiet panel show hosted by another game show legend, Bill Cullen. It left the airwaves in 1965 and came back in 1972 bigger, louder, and more colorful than ever. Since then the new host, Bob Barker, has shepherded the program through its fourth decade as daytime's most popular and loved game show.

Referring to his creative drive, Mark Goodson once commented, "How do I explain to you what I can't quite explain to myself: my lifetime romance with TV games? I think they seduced me. Like tall mountains, they were there, and dared me to climb them. Or, more accurately, they weren't there—and dared me to create them."

Mark Goodson died in 1992, shortly after becoming the first game show producer to be inducted into the Academy of Television Arts and Sciences Hall of Fame. Today, his legacy lives on, and his son Jonathan Goodson carries on the family tradition as a creative and powerful television entity.

OWNER'S MANUAL

There are four types of game shows. First are the "quiz shows," in which the emphasis is on the ability of the contestants to answer various questions. Second are the "panel" shows, in which celebrity participants try to guess some sort of secret that a guest holds. Third are the "audience participation" shows, in which stunts are performed for the entertainment of the audience, both in the studio and at home. Finally there are the "game shows," in which the players must learn the rules of a specific game and try to master that show's particular skill.

For each show entry we have included the following easy-to-read information: the show's premiere date, debut guests, the packager, the broadcast history (which includes the first and last broadcast dates for every network run), host, announcer, model, producers, directors, set designers, music directors, as well as a concise description of the show's format and notable panelists. Special notes have been provided to supply little-known pieces of information that might be of interest to buffs. Cross-references to another entry within the text are indicated by small capital letters.

The appendixes consist of a categorical list of personalities with their credits, a chronology, game shows by network, award winners and nominees, top-rated shows, unusual facts about game show hosts, and game show miscellany. The book also contains a bibliography and a comprehensive index.

We have tried to be as complete and accurate as possible, but omissions and errors may occur. We welcome hearing suggestions from you to help make future editions even better!

THE HISTORY OF GAME SHOWS

Over the years, millions of dollars have been won by thousands of contestants on hundreds of our favorite game shows. Before you is a fifty-year time capsule of memories, trivia, and data filled with magical moments and television treasures.

Quiz shows, as they were first called, achieved great acceptance and popularity on American radio in the 1930s and 40s. The first radio quiz show to gain national popularity was "Uncle Jim's Question Bee" with Jim McWilliams, in 1936. In 1939 big-money quiz shows hit radio, and among the most popular were "Pot O'Gold" with host Ben Grauer, Horace Heidt and his Musical Knights, and "Take It or Leave It," which featured the famous $64 question. In 1940 Ralph Edwards and "Truth or Consequences" came to radio, bringing humor and stunts to the quiz show craze. Edwards dominated the 1940s and 50s. His creation "Truth or Consequences" became a television classic. Ralph Edwards went on to create and host another television classic, "This Is Your Life," which began as a stunt on "Truth or Consequences."

Led by "Stop the Music," a show created by Mark Goodson, Harry Salter, and Louis G. Cowan, radio quiz shows dampened the enthusiasm for network comedy programs. Each member of this talented trio went on to leave his distinctive trademark on the game show industry. Mark Goodson teamed up with Bill Todman to create a game show dynasty. Harry Salter created "Name That Tune," and Louis G. Cowan gave us the "Quiz Kids," "The $64,000 Question," and others. "Stop the Music" was responsible for knocking one of radio's leading comics, Fred Allen, off the air.

Television broadcasting in the United States began at the New York World's Fair in 1939. Commercial television officially began on July 1, 1941 as two stations signed on the air, WNBT Channel 1 and WCBW Channel 2 in New York. On the very first day of programming NBC/WNBT broadcast two game shows, "Uncle Jim's Question Bee" and "Truth or Consequences" with Ralph Edwards. These shows were one-time special broadcasts to inaugurate the arrival of the new medium. One day later, July 2, 1941, CBS/WCBW added the first regularly scheduled game show to their lineup, "The CBS Television Quiz" with host Gil Fates. This weekly show ran for over a year and was broadcast live from their studios above Grand Central Station in the heart of New York City.

During the early forties, U.S. involvement in World War II put television broadcasting on hold for the duration of the war. Television would not get back on track until 1946, when a peacetime economy could encourage more development in this new medium.

In April 1946, the DuMont Television Network began broadcasting on a regular basis in New York and Washington, D.C. on a two-station network. Only a few thousand fortunate households had television sets and programming was extremely limited. On June 20, 1946, DuMont added their first game show, "Cash and Carry," a question-and-answer show played in a grocery store setting, making it historically the first network game show. (By FCC definition a program is considered network only if it is seen on two different stations in different cities at the same time.) Hosting the show was Dennis James, who began working for DuMont on experimental broadcasts back in 1938. Dennis James would go on to host a variety of game shows that spanned five decades. These shows would include "Chance of a Lifetime," "High Finance," "Name That Tune," "The Name's the Same," "PDQ," "People Will Talk," and a syndicated version of "The Price Is Right," among others.

Prior to "Cash and Carry," several other quiz shows had been seen on the other two New York networks, but only on one station. CBS carried "Missus Goes-A-Shopping" from 1944 to 1946. It was telecast live from different supermarkets in the Manhattan area.

"Missus Goes-A-Shopping" was the first network radio show to make the transition to a weekly television series, where it had several modest runs and set the stage for a plethora of audience-participation shows that were to come.

By the end of 1947, there were twelve television stations on the air, broadcasting to approximately 14,000 households. On May 1, 1948, AT&T opened the coaxial cable between New York City and Washington, D.C., making network television an actuality. Prior to this time, the networks shared one cable, with each network having two or three days to feed their programs. Now all the networks could feed programs back and forth every day of the week.

CBS began regular network programming on a continual basis on May 3, 1948. Two months later they selected a radio quiz show, "Winner Take All," created by the team of Goodson and Todman, as their first true network television game show. Bill Cullen was the radio host of "Winner Take All" and would later follow Bud Collyer and Barry Gray to host his own (and his first) television game show. Bill Cullen would go on to set the record for hosting more game shows than any other host in television history.

Legendary game show icons turn out to salute fifty years of game shows: (standing from left to right) Charlie O'Donnell, Jack Smith, Ralph Story, Ralph Edwards, Tom Kennedy, Jack Narz, Bob Eubanks, Betty White, Ed McMahon, Charles Nelson Reilly, Alex Trebek, Peter Marshall, Bill Armstrong, and Gene Wood. Kneeling (from left to right) are the authors of **The Encyclopedia of TV Game Shows,** *David Schwartz, Steve Ryan, and Fred Wostbrock.*

By the late 1940s and early 50s, this powerful new medium called television was taking America by storm. It was clear that television was destined to replace the radio as the number-one source of entertainment in the home. Sales of televisions skyrocketed and radio giants such as Jack Benny, Bob Hope, and Burns and Allen found new fame and fortune on the small screen. America was fascinated with the tube and our interests soared, particularly with the newest innovation . . . The Game Show!

Game shows had two important factors that contributed to their prosperity. First of all, they were inexpensive to produce, and secondly, they had been a popular form of programming on radio for at least a decade. The only stumbling block for game shows at this time occurred in August 1949, when the FCC proposed a ban on quiz shows and giveaways on television, claiming this form of programming was a violation of the criminal lottery laws. In late September, the FCC suspended its ban and the rest is history. To date, nearly fifty years later, more than five hundred game shows have aired nationally on network, syndication, and cable TV.

In 1950, two of the networks (NBC and CBS) began daytime programming. On November 16, 1950, NBC added the first daytime game show, "Remember This Date," seen Tuesday and Thursday afternoons with Bill Stern as host and Don Pardo as announcer. CBS countered by adding their first daytime game on February 12, 1951, a morning version of "Winner Take All" with host Barry Gray.

Many of America's favorite television game shows began on radio. There was "Beat the Clock," "Name That Tune," "Queen for a Day," "Twenty Questions," "You Bet Your Life," and others. Some shows began on radio with titles that were updated when the shows made the transition to television. Radio listeners remember "The $64,000 Question" as "Take It or Leave It." In just a short time, most of the popular radio quiz and panel shows were adapted for television, along with a multitude of new and exciting variations.

In the 1950s, America developed a voracious appetite for a regular ration of game, panel, and quiz shows. Network executives recognized America's enormous hunger for fun and games, and television viewers embraced their newfound friend, the game show emcee. Throughout the 1950s it was not uncommon to see these "leading men" on numerous shows: Jack Barry, Bill Cullen, Bud Collyer, John Daly, Ralph Edwards, Dennis James, Garry Moore, Jan

Murray, Bert Parks, Gene Rayburn, and others. It wasn't long before the channels were filled with a cornucopia of new shows in which contestants tried to "Think Fast," "Play the Game," "Stop the Music," "Beat the Clock," "Break the Bank," and "Strike It Rich."

A show that took a more serious approach was "G.E. College Bowl," hosted by Allen Ludden. Because of his association with this show, Ludden became identified as a scholarly sort and later his name became synonymous with television's most intellectual word game, "Password." "G.E. College Bowl" made an effort simultaneously to entertain and educate us as we watched two teams of students representing their schools engage in a battle of knowledge. Even more scholastic was the approach of "What in the World?" hosted by Dr. Froelich Rainey, director of the University of Pennsylvania Museum. In this show, panelists were presented with objects and artifacts of archaeological derivation and were asked to identify and establish their origins. Today, shows of this caliber are more likely to appear on public broadcasting or specialized cable channels. In the early days of television, if a game show concept played well and appeared flawless it made it to the home screen. Today, with more targeted marketing and a more serious approach to program development, most game shows go through a gauntlet of testing before reaching the airwaves.

Panel shows were abundant in the early days of television. Without a doubt, the granddaddy of all panel shows was "What's My Line?" moderated by the ever-sophisticated John Charles Daly. It premiered on CBS in 1950 and would continue to entertain audiences for three decades in a row. Packagers Mark Goodson and Bill Todman were masters at assembling the definitive panel. They constructed their panels with a variety of celebrities and dignitaries who were articulate, amusing, and always entertaining. Their panels often included publishers, poets, politicians, actors, comedians, and writers, among others. Who can forget Arlene Francis, Dorothy Kilgallen, and Bennett Cerf as the nucleus of America's favorite panel show? The format of "What's My Line?" was simple and pure—guessing the occupation of average citizens—and the producers realized that the quips and witticisms of the panelists were as important as the game itself. High stakes weren't necessary either, with the winning player receiving a whopping fifty bucks.

As a tribute to "What's My Line?", over the years there have been myriad clones, but few have attained the success and longevity of the original. "What's My Line?" proved "bigger than a bread box" and its staying power ranks it second, behind "The Price Is Right," on the list of all-time longest-running game shows. It should be noted that Mark Goodson and Bill Todman also had mega-hits in the 1950s with two other panel shows, "I've Got a Secret," originally hosted by Garry Moore, and "To Tell the Truth," originally hosted by Bud Collyer, making them the undisputed champions of panel shows.

Like panel shows, stunt shows were also a popular form of programming in the 1950s. Once again the creative genius of Mark Goodson and Bill Todman brought us the first television stunt format. That game show was "Beat the Clock," hosted by Bud Collyer and assisted by Roxanne. "Beat the Clock" was actually a blend of stunts and slapstick. The stunts were imaginative and wacky, even by today's standards.

To illustrate its popularity and audience appeal, an entire episode of "The Honeymooners," starring Jackie Gleason, centered around Ralph Kramden as a clumsy "Beat the Clock" contestant. You can imagine the slapstick humor that resulted.

"Truth or Consequences" was actually the first radio stunt show, masterfully emceed by its creator Ralph Edwards. Ralph Edwards would bring "Truth or Consequences" to the television airwaves six months after the debut of "Beat the Clock." Both shows would span the 1950s, 60s, 70s, and 80s under numerous incarnations and hosts. Do you recall Jack Bailey, Steve Dunne, Bob Barker, Bob Hilton, and Larry Anderson all hosting "Truth or Consequences"? And how about Jack Narz, Gene Wood, and Monty Hall all hosting "Beat the Clock"?

Another form of game show that surfaced in the 1950s could be described as agony shows. Without a doubt, the best example of an agony show would be "Queen for a Day," hosted by Jack Bailey. In this show, poor souls appeared on camera to tell their often painful, heartbreaking, embarrassing, and tearful tales of personal tragedy and misfortune. At the end of each show, one of these contestants would be voted the winner and be crowned "Queen for a Day." Another popular agony show was "Strike It Rich," hosted by Warren Hull.

By 1955, America had entered the era of big-money quiz shows. On radio, one of the biggest prizes was $64 on "Take It or Leave It." That show grew to become the very popular "The $64,000 Question," hosted by Hal March. In the mid-1950s, $64,000 was indeed a fortune. To put it in better perspective, Charles Van Doren was earning less than $5,000 a year as a college instructor when he competed and won the top prize on an even bigger money show, "Twenty-One," hosted by Jack Barry. Van Doren accumulated $129,000 in fourteen appearances on that show.

With the large cash rewards for both contestants and producers came a scandalous era in the history of game shows. In the beginning, there was no manipulation of contestants. The deception and deceit evolved slowly. The earliest signs appeared when various sponsors started to apply pressure to the producers. This was a time when a handful of producers were drawn in by the temptation to manipulate the outcome of shows. Numerous producers fell into the trap of scripting contests to create an arena in which only the underdogs or contestants most favored by the audience would be allowed to advance or even win. Producers of these tainted shows tried to justify tampering with contests by explaining that they were simply seeking to entertain television viewers to the best of their ability. In other words the more dramatic the contest, the greater the popularity of the show. Keeping the sponsors and the networks happy meant a longer run for their shows. It's not difficult to understand why some quiz show producers succumbed to the pressures and secretly briefed those contestants whom they hand-selected to win. Contestants who were considered dull or uninteresting were unknowingly offered as sacrificial lambs. It was this brand of inequity and godlike behavior that would lead to the downfall of the big-money quiz shows of this era. All of the quiz shows involved in the scandals conducted business on the premise that struggling contestants trying to amass awesome amounts of cash would capture the imagination of the television viewing audience. The producers were indeed correct, as big winners became overnight celebrities and national heros. "The $64,000 Question" was so popular that it became the only primetime game show to beat "I Love Lucy," "The Ed Sullivan Show," and "The Jack Benny Show" in the ratings war. Even losers on "The $64,000 Question" who reached the $8,000 level were rewarded with brand-new Cadillacs. It was no surprise that these programs achieved staggering heights of popularity.

Three years after the fraudulent practices began, like Jack and Jill, game shows all came tumbling down. The knockout punch was delivered in 1958 when a former "Dotto" contestant came forward with concrete evidence that the show was fixed. A "Twenty-One" contestant followed suit with a no-holds-barred description of how "Twenty-One" was rigged. These accusations led to investigations and hearings by a New York grand jury and by a congressional subcommittee.

Here's a thought to ponder: Where did contestants on the quiz shows "The $64,000 Question" and "Twenty-One" answer their most difficult questions? Answer: In the studios, contestants answered the toughest questions from glass-enclosed isolation booths, but the toughest questions of all were answered before the New York Grand Jury, where many of the contestants who testified perjured themselves. The charges brought forth were eventually proven to be true. The scandal that followed led to the swift demise of all the big-money quiz shows.

The big-money quiz shows fell like the mighty Goliath, leaving a black eye on the face of game shows that would remain for years to remind us that the carefree, innocent age of the 1950s was not so innocent after all. The most famous contestant to emerge from the scandals was Charles Van Doren, who would eventually admit to receiving answers on "Twenty-One." President Dwight D. Eisenhower referred to the scandals as "A terrible thing to do to the American public." It was the sullying of Charles Van Doren's clean-cut image that may have stunned Americans the most. His short-lived hero status had elevated him to such great heights that he appeared on the cover of *Time* magazine and became a regular personality on the NBC "Today" show.

The reputation of an industry was permanently scarred by the quiz show scandals, which rocked the very foundation of trust that television was built upon. Federal regulations were enacted to watch over the industry and prevent further fraud in broadcasting. In May 1959, Congress passed a law making it illegal to rig a game show, and the networks set up a standards and practices department. Networks subsequently took control away from program sponsors. Careers

were destroyed, quiz producers were unofficially blacklisted from television for years, and many other participants went into hiding. Although the careers of Jack Barry and Dan Enright of "Twenty-One" fame were severely damaged, by the mid-1970s they had teamed up once again and returned to television with the highly successful "The Joker's Wild," emceed by Barry himself. Network executives denied any and all knowledge of their shows being fixed and no one from the networks was ever implicated.

Also, not all contestants participated in the scandals, nor were they even aware of the deception. Famed television psychologist Dr. Joyce Brothers was an honest contestant who went on to win $64,000 on the show of that name. Dr. Brothers surprised both the producers and the television viewers with her expertise in the field of boxing.

The scandal left America feeling betrayed, but television and game shows recovered and came back stronger than ever. In fairness to most game and quiz show producers, there were only a few producers who were guilty of fixing shows. It is a tribute to the most prolific creator of game shows, Mark Goodson, that no aspect of his operations was involved or implicated in the quiz show hanky-panky that rocked the industry and the country in the late 1950s.

It should be pointed out that the vast majority of game and quiz shows operated with the utmost integrity. One such production that took quiz shows in an entirely different direction was "You Bet Your Life." This show, hosted by the one and only Groucho Marx, was more about comedy and laughs than quizzes and big bucks. This classic, which ran on NBC from 1950 to 1961, featured the nonstop wisecracks and witticisms of Groucho. A stuffed duck that bore a striking resemblance to Groucho appeared whenever a contestant said the "secret word." There were also contestants with colorful personalities, such as the young aspiring comedienne Phyllis Diller, making her network television debut. Other shows from that decade were played for laughs as well. Some of these were "Funny Boners," "It Pays to Be Ignorant," "Pantomime Quiz," "Make Me Laugh," and "Who Do You Trust?" with the young Johnny Carson as host. In fact, there was a variety of game shows. By the summer of 1958 there were twenty-three game shows in primetime and fifteen in daytime.

In the 1960s, the networks moved their game shows to daytime, a new playground for a new, primarily female audience. As game shows survived on daytime television, they all but disappeared from primetime. A new decade and a new daytime viewing audience brought new emcees. Newcomers such as Bob Eubanks, Art Fleming, Monty Hall, Art James, Tom Kennedy, Jim Lange, Allen Ludden, Peter Marshall, and Wink Martindale became instant winners with the large female viewing audience. This elite group of emcees would continue to dominate the small screen for some four decades. And, many of our favorites from the 1950s achieved even greater popularity. It was not uncommon to see Bob Barker, Bill Cullen, Dennis James, Jack Narz, and Gene Rayburn hosting several different shows throughout the 1960s as well as the 70s and 80s.

Daytime television would be the primary venue for the next generation of audience participation shows. The shift from primetime to daytime required networks and producers to rethink the established rules for success and create a new blueprint that would appeal to daytime audiences.

In general, primetime television was viewed in a relaxed atmosphere, after the day's work was complete. By contrast, daytime programming had to compete with regular housework and viewing was interrupted by such things as floor washing, dish washing, and clothes washing. It's no wonder that a wide variety of soap and cleaning products became major sponsors for the daytime game shows. It was obvious that the programming had to be modified for the more hectic pace of daytime viewers.

It's only logical that the 1960s game shows would be redesigned to include more dazzling sets, livelier audiences, attention-grabbing music, wacky sound effects, and hyperactive contestants all meant to draw us back to the television after we had been pulled away to answer the doorbell or change baby's diaper.

Even though daytime television meant smaller viewing audiences and lower budgets, game shows would become as profitable for the networks as primetime television programs. In some cases, they outperformed their primetime counterparts. Game shows once again demonstrated their attraction as a source of entertainment, information, and amusement. Those 1960s game shows captured our imagination with a blend of fantasy and reality that would prove to be incredibly diverse. Many visually enticing game shows featuring larger-than-life sets were introduced, including "Treasure Isle," "Video Village," and others.

Another visually exciting show was "Concentration," with its bigger-than-life mechanical game board. Although "Concentration" was born in 1958 and was an instant hit for its network, NBC, it really took off like a rocket in the 1960s. Throughout its original network run, "Concentration" often dominated its time slot. The reasons were simple. The show had a solid format and the producers were certain that viewers enjoyed the challenge of solving those rebus puzzles.

"Password," introduced in 1961, was innovative in that it was the first successful daytime game show to team celebrity players with contestants from the general public. Allen Ludden was the host of this word-association game that still reigns as the quintessential word game. "Password" was also one of the first game shows to introduce a bonus round. The show and its celebrities proved to be so popular with television viewers that in 1962 it went primetime on CBS. Such celebrities as Lucille Ball, Jack Benny, Carol Burnett, Henry Fonda, Mary Tyler Moore, Elizabeth Montgomery, Burt Reynolds, Adam West, Betty White, and others enjoyed playing "Password" as much as we enjoyed watching them.

Celebrities proved to be a valuable addition to game shows. A variety of shows was introduced in which celebrity humor and wit appeared to be more important assets than the game itself. The very popular and long-running "The Hollywood Squares," hosted by five-time Emmy winner Peter Marshall, featured celebrities who were encouraged to give clever and humorous answers to a broad range of obscure and intrigu-

ing questions. Who could forget the playful quips and witticisms of regular celebrities Wally Cox, Rose Marie, Charley Weaver, and, of course, Paul Lynde in the center square? "The Hollywood Squares" proved to be so popular that it was a fourteen-and-a-half-year hit on NBC daytime, as well as a hit in syndication for the production team of Merrill Heatter and Bob Quigley. The creative team of Heatter and Quigley would bring television viewers and game show fans to new levels of game playing and entertainment. While "The Hollywood Squares" would be their biggest success in the 1960s, they enjoyed other successes in the 70s and 80s with "Gambit," hosted by Wink Martindale, and "High Rollers," hosted by Alex Trebek. Along the way, Heatter and Quigley would garner four prestigious Emmy Awards. As a team they were responsible for more than twenty different game shows.

Another popular celebrity show from the 1960s was "You Don't Say!" packaged by Ralph Andrews and partner Bill Yagemann and hosted by Tom Kennedy. Ralph Andrews would go on to give us other game shows that included "Celebrity Sweepstakes," "It Takes Two," "It's Your Bet," and "Liars Club."

In the celebrity word game "You Don't Say!" as the title suggests, "It's not what you say that counts, it's what you don't say!" Frequent guest stars included Don Adams, Pat Carroll, Michael Landon, June Lockhart, Lee Marvin, and Betty White. Other celebrity game shows in the 1960s were "Call My Bluff," "The Celebrity Game," "The Match Game," "Missing Links," "Name Droppers," "PDQ," "People Will Talk," "Snap Judgment," "What's This Song?", and others.

By the mid-1960s, television was changing almost as rapidly and dramatically as our American society. Enter Chuck Barris. In 1965 Barris sold "The Dating Game" with emcee Jim Lange to the ABC daytime lineup. "The Dating Game" exemplified 1965 television, complete with psychedelic flowers, beautiful bachelorettes, and handsome bachelors. The prize here was not a big cash jackpot, but instead a great date at an exotic location. The show was such an instant hit that it was soon on the ABC primetime schedule as well. It seems that America fell in love with Jim Lange and "The Dating Game."

Barris' new approach to game shows aroused this generation of television viewers with a new style of relationship show. So popular was "The Dating Game" that it inspired another Barris hit, "The Newlywed Game," with host Bob Eubanks. Like its sister show, "The Newlywed Game" would also find a place on the ABC daytime and primetime schedules. Barris would continue to push the envelope of titillation and produce game shows throughout the 1960s and 70s. His biggest and most controversial hit, "The Gong Show," was yet to come.

Also in the 1960s, we saw the teaming of emcee Monty Hall and producer Stefan Hatos. Together Monty and Stefan created one of America's best-loved game shows, the classic "Let's Make a Deal." Since its debut in 1963, a single decade hasn't gone by in which American audiences haven't been entertained by Monty and those cleverly costumed contestants. Monty Hall and Stefan Hatos would continue to create game shows throughout the 1960s, 70s, and 80s. A few of those shows were "Chain Letter," "Split Second," and "Three for the Money." More than thirty years after the debut of "Let's Make a Deal," the show is still as popular as ever, playing in countless foreign markets, as well as in rerun syndication here in the United States.

In the mid-1960s, we tuned in to watch "Jeopardy!", with the original emcee Art Fleming. "Jeopardy!" featured a twist on classic quiz shows by giving the answers and requiring the contestants to provide the questions. It would run for more than a decade and this set the stage for "Jeopardy!" to become one of the hottest syndicated properties of the 1980s and 90s. An ex-game-show host himself, Merv Griffin was the creator of this timeless classic. Merv Griffin had previously hosted "Keep Talking," "Play Your Hunch," and "Word for Word" and was soon to host his own Emmy-winning syndicated talk show, "The Merv Griffin Show." However, his biggest success, "Wheel of Fortune," was yet to come.

We also saw the first show premiered by Bob Stewart Productions in 1966. That show was "Eye Guess," with host Bill Cullen. Bob Stewart hit a home run for himself and NBC, and this show ran solidly for three years. Stewart would go on to create other classics throughout the 1960s, 70s, 80s, and 90s. His greatest success to date has been the various incarnations of "The $10,000 Pyramid," hosted separately by Dick Clark, Bill Cullen, and John Davidson. Stewart's shows included "Jackpot," "Personality," "Three on a Match," "Winning Streak," and "Chain Reaction," among others. It's interesting to note that Bill Cullen emceed eight different game shows for Bob Stewart. Most of the other shows Bob Stewart created were hosted by either Geoff Edwards or Dick Clark, and all but a handful were produced in New York City. Bob Stewart was the last of the major game show producers to leave New York City for Los Angeles.

Other notable shows during the 1960s included "Dream House," "The Movie Game," "Sale of the Century," "Say When!!", "Supermarket Sweep," and "The Who What or Where Game."

By the end of the 1960s, game shows and television in general were changing once again, for the better. Color came to television toward the mid-1960s, and for the first time audiences could see, in living color, the superb sets where their favorite emcees held court each weekday (or weeknight).

Showing color required having color to show. The creative game show set designers began to add bright carpets, multicolored podiums, dazzling lights that chased and flashed, and carefully crafted set pieces that moved and turned to give us that ever-changing look. Before the late 1960s and early 70s, game show set designers had never utilized lights as part of the set design. Remember Heatter-Quigley's 1973 entry "Baffle"? If you do, you saw the first game show to make use of neon lights.

As the free-spirited 1960s came to a close, the 70s would bring us even more new and exciting shows and innovations. One of the changes to affect game shows was the distribution by syndication instead of network. The FCC defines syndication as "any program sold, licensed, distributed or offered to television stations in more than one market for non-interconnected television broadcast exhibition." That, teamed with the 1971 primetime access rule, which stated that the TV networks had to return a half hour of time to the local stations, opened the door for game shows in the early evening hours on local stations and expanded the opportunities for syndication. The concept of syndication had been around since the 1950s, but now the door was wide open for the revival of the classic game shows from past decades. Remember these familiar and successful shows that were being syndicated in the 1970s? They were "Beat the Clock," "Break the Bank," "Concentration," "The Dating Game," "I've Got a Secret," "Let's Make a Deal," "Match Game PM," "The Newlywed Game," "Tic Tac Dough," "To Tell the Truth," "Truth or Consequences," "What's My Line?", and more than twenty-five others.

In the years that made up 1970s television, viewers and game show fans alike saw the first shows of a thirty-three-year-old Canadian named Alex Trebek; young country singer-songwriter turned emcee Chuck Woolery; veteran actor and television star Richard Dawson; and game show creator Chuck Barris, who moved from behind the camera to host "The Gong Show." Other favorites such as Bob Barker, Jack Barry, Dick Clark, Bill Cullen, Bob Eubanks, Art Fleming, Monty Hall, Art James, Dennis James, Tom Kennedy, Jim Lange, Allen Ludden, Peter Marshall, Wink Martindale, Garry Moore, Jack Narz, and Gene Rayburn continued to dominate the small screen. At times, it was not unusual to see several of our favorites hosting more than one game show at a time. The 1970s saw game shows reach a new peak of popularity. Not since the 1950s had so many flourished on television.

Even though the 1970s would prove to be a lucrative decade for game shows, they actually started out slowly. In 1970, television viewers only saw the premiere of two game shows, "Can You Top This?" and "Words and Music." Both were hosted by Wink Martindale, who went on to host Heatter-Quigley's "Gambit" for more than four years and, later, Barry and Enright's "Tic Tac Dough" for seven years.

In 1972, we saw the return of "The Price Is Right" to the CBS daytime lineup with host Bob Barker. "The Price Is Right" has the distinction of being the longest-running daytime game show in television history, earning Bob Barker a record-breaking seven Emmys along the way. If it were not for the insight of Mark Goodson and Bill Todman to return with an updated version of "The Price Is Right," we would never have heard Johnny Olson or his successor Rod Roddy yell that now familiar phrase "Come on down!" Bob Barker and the models who appeared with him proved to be so popular with the American public that in 1975 the show was expanded to become the first successful hour-long program in game show history.

By 1973, game shows were in full swing on the three major networks. "The Price Is Right" with Bob Barker was a year old, as was Wink's "Gambit" and "The Joker's Wild" with Jack Barry, and they were all on CBS. A newcomer to the CBS lineup was a celebrity word-communication game, "The $10,000 Pyramid," with host Dick Clark. And Dick

Clark was certainly not a newcomer to television. Best known for his "American Bandstand" series dating back to 1957, Clark had also hosted several other game shows, including "The Object Is" and "Missing Links." Dick Clark would go on to win three Emmys for his hosting duties on "Pyramid."

Although "The Match Game" was a hit in the 1960s, Gene Rayburn returned in 1973 to host an ever popular "Match Game" series for six years on CBS and seven years in syndication. Each week millions of viewers tuned in to watch contestants trying to "match" their favorite celebrities. During its CBS run, "The Match Game" received some of daytime's highest ratings, thanks to the puckish Gene Rayburn and those playful celebrities.

A show that ran back-to-back with "The Match Game" for more than four years was Goodson-Todman's "Tattletales," hosted by Bert Convy. This show was an updated version of the 1969 Goodson-Todman show "He Said, She Said." This new version achieved even greater success in the 1970s by mixing celebrity humor into the format as Hollywood couples shared their intimate and private secrets for all of America to hear. Convy later went on to host three other celebrity game shows, "Super Password," "Win, Lose or Draw," and "3rd Degree."

Other celebrity shows were "Break the Bank," "Celebrity Sweepstakes," "Hollywood Connection," "Hollywood's Talking," and "Liars Club."

Over at NBC, Art Fleming was going full speed with "Jeopardy!" and another Art, Art James, was wrapping up a four-year run on "The Who What or Where Game." Art James would quickly resurface on NBC with "Blank Check" and later with "The Magnificent Marble Machine." "Concentration" was wrapping up its incredible fourteen-and-a-half-year run on NBC. ABC was leading the pack with creations from Hatos-Hall, Chuck Barris, and Goodson-Todman. Those shows were "Let's Make a Deal" (which switched over from NBC), "Split Second," "The Dating Game," "The Newlywed Game," and "Password." These were the hot shows to beat in the ratings in the early 1970s.

By the mid-1970s, game shows were experiencing a plateau of success with over twenty-five different shows on the air in both network and in syndication. Among them was 1975's "Musical Chairs," hosted by singer Adam Wade, the first African American to host a game show.

By the summer of our nation's bicentennial in 1976, we saw the debut of two classic formats that took America by storm. Those shows were "The Gong Show," hosted by creator/producer Chuck Barris, and "Family Feud," hosted by Richard Dawson.

"The Gong Show" was the most successful spoof of amateur talent shows to hit television. It ran for two years on the NBC daytime schedule and four years in syndication, first hosted by Gary Owens and later by Chuck Barris. Jaye P. Morgan was a regular "gonger" on both versions of the show.

"Family Feud," which revealed answers to questions that surveyed one hundred average Americans, would prove to be an even bigger success for ABC. The unique hosting style of Richard Dawson of "Hogan's Heroes" and "Match Game" fame would soon capture the daytime audience, making "Family Feud" a household viewing staple. Its enormous popularity would span the 1970s, 80s, and 90s.

Viewers saw other popular game forms in the 1970s as well. As the original "Jeopardy!" with Art Fleming was coming to the end of an era, we saw Alex Trebek host his first American game show, "The Wizard of Odds," and we met Chuck Woolery and Susan Stafford for the first time on "Wheel of Fortune," long before Pat Sajak and Vanna White.

The look of daytime game shows was indeed changing. It seemed that big money and big prizes were in vogue once again. Each day Wink Martindale could give away a car on "Gambit" as could Tom Kennedy on "Split Second." Monty Hall would give away as much as $35,000 a day on "Let's Make a Deal" if a contestant was lucky enough to win "the big deal of the day." On several 1970s shows we saw the return of the isolation booth and, of course, the big bucks to go with it. Remember Tom Kennedy hosting "50 Grand Slam" and Alex Trebek hosting "Double Dare" and "The $128,000 Question"? Contestants from this era could win fortunes if they had Lady Luck on their side.

Several game shows went on location . . . meaning the shows were not taped in either Los Angeles or New York. Being produced on location often gave a show a more exciting and distinct look. "Dealer's Choice" was taped at the Tropicana Hotel in Las Vegas with emcee Jack Clark and "The Diamond Head Game" was taped on the beach at the Kuilima Hotel in Oahu, Hawaii with host Bob Eubanks.

When game shows weren't being taped on location, producers were changing the look of game shows inside the studios. Some twenty years earlier game shows were low-budget, to say the least; now in many cases the sets were the largest single expense.

In the late 1970s game shows began to dwindle on daytime television as soap operas were expanded to one-hour shows. As the 1970s came to a close, one thing became clear; these were possibly the best ten years game shows had ever seen.

By 1980 the game show genre was turning forty. Unlike in the previous decade, game shows really didn't flourish in the 1980s. There are only a handful of truly successful game shows. On daytime network TV, "The Price Is Right," with Bob Barker, was still at the top of the ratings. Both "Jeopardy!", with Alex Trebek, and "Wheel of Fortune," with Pat Sajak, reigned as the kings of syndication for their distributor King World. And, Vanna White was the queen of game shows with "Vanna-Mania" sweeping the nation by 1985; a phenomenon that has continued for more than a decade.

Cable became a hot item in the 1980s. Although HBO launched the very first cable network in 1975, it wasn't until 1981 that the first game shows were introduced by a cable network. The Playboy Channel led off with "Everything Goes," hosted by comic Kip Addotta. This game show was a spicy competition in which players lost items of clothing for incorrect responses to questions. Later that same year, CBS Cable debuted a remake of a 1950s classic, "Quiz Kids," with "All in the Family" producer Norman Lear as host. Yes, the same Norman Lear who gave us "All in the Family," "The Jeffersons," and "Maude." In 1983, The Nashville Network introduced a country music trivia game show, "Fandango," with host Bill Anderson. This country music singer-songwriter had hosted his first game show, "The Better Sex," back in 1977, with Sarah Purcell as his cohost. Also in 1983 the Disney Channel launched its first game show "Contraption," tailor-made just for kids. And in 1986, Nickelodeon gave us "Double Dare," with host Marc Summers. It appeared that all the cable networks were jumping on the bandwagon to create their own highly specialized game shows for their own demographics.

In the following year the USA Network began running a block of repeat game shows, including "Bullseye," "Chain Reaction," "The Gong Show," "The Joker's Wild," "Let's Make a Deal," and "Liars Club." Later in the 1980s, MTV would introduce the very hip cult classic about TV trivia, "Remote Control," hosted by Ken Ober, complete with a silly life-size Bob Eubanks Pez dispenser.

And many of our old favorites were still hosting game shows. We saw Bert Convy, Bob Eubanks, Monty Hall, Art James, Tom Kennedy, Jim Lange, Peter Marshall, Wink Martindale, and Gene Rayburn still going strong with a potpourri of game show fun. Bill Cullen started off the decade by hosting "Blockbusters," a successful question-and-answer show from the Mark Goodson stable. This show was cocreated by one of the coauthors of this book, Steve Ryan.

"Card Sharks" was another popular Mark Goodson game show that began in the late 1970s and carried over into the early 80s with host Jim Perry. Perry would also have a successful run with "Sale of the Century" later in the decade.

Also in 1983, Betty White hosted her first game show, "Just Men!", and won an Emmy for her work. We also saw another outstanding female game show host in the 1980s. That lady was Vicki Lawrence, hosting "Win, Lose or Draw." In 1993 and 1994, on her own talk show, "Vicki!", she saluted game shows and some of our favorite emcees, including Bob Eubanks, Monty Hall, Tom Kennedy, Jim Lange, Peter Marshall, Gary Owens, Gene Rayburn, and Betty White. And, if you think female game show hosts are an innovation, you're wrong. Back in 1949, long before there was a "Studs" or "The Dating Game," Arlene Francis hosted her own game show, "Blind Date." Arlene Francis found her greatest fame as a regular panelist on "What's My Line?"

In the 1980s television was still changing with the times. The new age of computer graphics brought dynamic new images to many game shows. For example, the life-size mechanical "Concentration" board was replaced by state-of-the-art computer graphics. And players now explained their solution to each rebus in front of a chroma-key screen, in a manner similar to that used by the weather personalities in reporting the weather. "Jeopardy!" also jumped into the computer age by replacing the answer cards with electronically generated computer lettering. "Catch Phrase," hosted by veteran Art James, was the very first game show to introduce computer animation—generating thousands of "Catch Phrase" puzzles. This show was created by Steve Radosh for

Marty Pasetta Productions and the puzzles for this show were created by coauthor Steve Ryan, who also created the "Classic Concentration" rebus puzzles.

As we button up the 1980s, the home computer has become a household staple, inspiring software for the classic game show formats that have remained. Those top shows of the 1980s were "Classic Concentration," "Family Feud," "Jeopardy!", "The Price Is Right," and "Wheel of Fortune."

In the 1990s, television in general appears to be ever-changing and game shows are outnumbered by both talk and tabloid news shows. However, game shows have continued to become even more exciting. It seems the catch phrase for 1990s television is "interactive" and game shows will be at the head of the pack, along with home shopping channels and pay-per-view feature-film viewing. Interactive television is in its infancy, and it appears to have great potential for game shows, since it allows for direct viewer participation. Many television visionaries believe interactive television will come into its own by the end of the decade when a generation of young videogame players and computer wizards come of age. Some of these visionaries include Jonathan Goodson Productions, Merv Griffin Productions, Merrill Heatter Productions, Wink Martindale Productions, and Stone-Stanley Productions.

Martindale, in 1993, became the first emcee (as well as executive producer) to host television's first interactive game show, "Trivial Pursuit." This show allowed home viewers to play along live with Wink by calling a 900 number. At various points in the show, the home winners from across the United States were announced.

In 1994 Wink Martindale and partner Bill Hillier would create three other interactive games, "Boggle," "Jumble," and "Shuffle," all hosted by Wink, for the Family Channel game show block.

TV game shows entered a new era on December 1, 1994 when Sony Pictures launched the first cable TV network devoted exclusively to TV game shows.

The Game Show Network features over 50,000 episodes of programs originally produced by Mark Goodson and Bill Todman, Chuck Barris, Merv Griffin, Bob Stewart, Jack Barry and Dan Enright, and Columbia Television. Shows on the initial schedule included "Beat the Clock," "Blockbusters," "The Dating Game," "I've Got a Secret," "Jeopardy!", "The Joker's Wild," "Match Game," "The Newlywed Game," "Password," "Tic Tac Dough," "To Tell the Truth," "What's My Line?", and "Wheel of Fortune."

Original programming in the first season included "Club A.M.," a morning show hosted by former game show announcer Steve Day ("Just Men!", "Caesars Challenge") and game show contestant coordinator Laura Chambers, and "Prime Games," a nighttime series that gave viewers at home a chance to participate in a series of interactive games. Peter Tomarken, best known for hosting "Press Your Luck," emceed "Prime Games." The off-camera announcer on the Game Show Network was Los Angeles veteran radio personality and program director of KRLA radio Mike Wagner.

In celebration of launching the new network many game

show favorites such as Bob Eubanks, Tom Kennedy, Jim Lange, Peter Marshall, Jack Narz, Gene Rayburn, Ann Cullen (Mrs. Bill Cullen), and others were recruited to reminisce about their game show experiences.

By early 1998, Game Show Network had passed the cable penetration level of twelve million homes. Original programming continued to expand to include new interactive game shows such as "Super Decades" and "Trivia Track"; "Game World," a daily show that featured great moments in the previous day's TV game shows; and "Game TV," a weekday magazine that featured interviews, home-viewer games, and weekly visits from "Mr. Game Show" (coauthor Fred Wostbrock), who answers viewer questions on the world of game shows.

Fresh and familiar faces were seen hosting the new programming on Game Show Network, including Larry Anderson, Marianne Curan, Dave Nemeth, and Nancy Sullivan. Game Show Network began running current episodes of "The Dating Game," "The Newlywed Game," and "Wheel of Fortune 2000" in the fall of 1997. In January 1998, Game Show Network introduced "Jep!", a junior version of the classic quiz show "Jeopardy!"

Game shows continued their comeback on other cable TV channels as well. MTV had great success with the dating game "Singled Out" that made hostess Jenny McCarthy a household name. Networks such as the Food Network, the Odyssey Channel, and MSNBC added game shows to their schedules.

The Family Channel added an entire block of new game shows to their afternoon schedule while Lifetime Television brought in game show favorite Wink Martindale to host their new series, "Debt." The combination of Wink Martindale and "Debt" proved to be a successful one. "Debt" became a CableAce winner. Lifetime's partner in "Debt" was Buena Vista Television, which in 1997 resurrected "Make Me Laugh," as well as creating the offbeat "Win Ben Stein's Money" for Comedy Central. Nickelodeon continued to produce game shows for kids with great success.

Game shows continued to dominate the top-two spots among all syndicated programs: "Wheel of Fortune" and "Jeopardy!" have held their lock on these positions for over a decade. "The Dating Game" and "The Newlywed Game" returned for new runs in syndication, and both "The Holly-wood Squares" and "The Match Game" were scheduled to return to the airwaves in fall 1998.

It's clear to see that game shows have come a long way since the days of "Uncle Jim's Question Bee." In the last fifty-plus years, we have seen more than five hundred game shows hosted by hundreds of friendly faces. Perhaps the friendliest belongs to Bill Cullen, who hosted more than twenty different game shows in an incredible career that spanned five decades.

Not only have game shows become a phenomenon in the United States, but their appeal stretches worldwide. Formats created by American packagers are currently experiencing enormous success in foreign markets. Among these are "Blockbusters," "Family Feud," "The Hollywood Squares," "Jeopardy!", "Let's Make a Deal," "Press Your Luck," "The Price Is Right," and "Wheel of Fortune."

While it still remains a mystery why some game show formats succeed while others fail, over the decades packagers, producers, and network executives have tried to pinpoint the precise reasons for the success of game shows as a genre. In a nutshell, here are some explanations:

- Perhaps it's the fantasy of being a winner or identifying with the pressure and excitement of the moment.
- Could it be the parade of ordinary everyday people that grace the small screen to entertain us?
- Maybe it's the dream of instant riches.
- Or, the ability to participate in an entertaining manner from our own armchairs.

Whatever the conclusion, it goes without saying that we love the . . .

- Surprises,
- Tension,
- Energy,
- Voracity,
- Excitement,
- Riches,
- Yippees,
- Academia, and
- Nonsense . . .

that game shows give us. And always will.

ABOUT FACES

premiere: January 4, 1960   *packager:* Ralph Edwards Productions   *broadcast history:* ABC daytime January 4, 1960–June 30, 1961   *host:* Ben Alexander   *announcer:* Tom Kennedy   *producer:* Joe Landis   *director:* Joe Landis   *music director:* Irv Orton   *origination:* Studio E, ABC Television Center, Hollywood

Actor Ben Alexander (who played Detective Frank Smith on "Dragnet" during its TV run in the 1950s) emceed "About Faces," this live daytime entry. Contestants, selected from the studio audience, played various games with the goal of reuniting long separated friends and relatives.

In one game a contestant tried to recognize a face from his or her past. The player was given a clue at the start of the game, and three minutes to question a guest who answered with yes or no responses.

In another game, a pair of contestants were placed opposite each other and presented with clues concerning incidents in their lives. The first player to correctly associate his or her relationship with the person opposite was the winner.

In other games members of the studio audience were shown celebrity baby pictures and had to determine which one was that of the celebrity present on the show.

Did you know . . . "About Faces" had a home participation segment titled "Place the Face," which was inspired by PLACE THE FACE, another Ralph Edwards game show that aired during the 1950s?

ACROSS THE BOARD

premiere: June 1, 1959   *packager:* Bob Stivers Productions   *broadcast history:* ABC daytime June 1, 1959–October 9, 1959   *host:* Ted Brown   *announcer:* George Ansbro   *executive producer:* Bob Stivers   *producer:* Hal Davis   *director:* Hal Tulchin   *origination:* Elysee Theater, New York

New York radio personality Ted Brown hosted "Across the Board," this short-lived daytime series that had two players attempting to complete a crossword puzzle from a series of picture and word clues. The player with the most correct identifications won merchandise prizes.

Did you know . . . "Across the Board" host Ted Brown was Buffalo Bob Smith's replacement on "Howdy Doody" when Bob had a heart attack in 1954? Ted's character was called "Bison Bill."

THE AD-LIBBERS

premiere: August 3, 1951   *packager:* Persons Productions   *broadcast history:* CBS primetime August 3, 1951–August 31, 1951   *host:* Peter Donald   *producers:* Hal and Ted Persons   *director:* Hal Persons   *origination:* New York   *debut guests:* Charles Mendick, Patricia Hosley, Joe Silvers, Jack Lemmon, Cynthia Stone, Earl Hammond

This five-week summer series replaced "Mama" in 1951. On "The Ad-Libbers," a brief outline of a situation was given to the panelists, who then ad-libbed dialogue to fit the scenario. The panelists worked without a script or rehearsal. For each suggestion used, a home viewer received a case of Maxwell House coffee supplied by the sponsor.

Did you know . . . "The Ad-Libbers" was actor Jack Lemmon's first steady job in television? Years later he would jump from the small screen onto the silver screen, winning two Academy Awards.

ALL ABOUT FACES

premiere: August 30, 1971   *packager:* Screen Gems Television   *broadcast history:* Syndicated August 30, 1971–September 1972   *host:* Richard Hayes   *executive producer:* Dan Enright   *producer:* David Fein   *directors:* Bill Burrows (studio), Dan Enright (film)   *music:* John Hill, Gordon Fleming   *origination:* CFTO–TV, Toronto, Canada

This daily syndicated comedy-game show was produced in Canada for American television. On "All About Faces," each program consisted of situations in which a hidden camera recorded an unsuspecting citizen who was forced into making a decision. Sample challenges included a woman sitting in a restaurant and ordering a meal and the waiter bringing out something totally different. Does the woman send the food back or eat it?

At the moment of decision the film clip was stopped and two teams, each composed of a celebrity couple, tried to guess the outcome. Each team, which began with $50, could bet any or all of their money on the outcome. The team with the most money at the end of the show was the winner.

Do you remember the 1971 game show "All About Faces"? If not, here's a full set shot of the show that was taped in Canada for American TV stations.

Did you know . . .   Richard Hayes, the show's host, was a winner on ARTHUR GODFREY'S TALENT SCOUTS? As a result of the appearance, he signed a recording contract with Mercury Records and had a top-five hit in 1949 with "The Old Master Painter." "All About Faces" was revived in 1984 as ANYTHING FOR MONEY.

ALL ABOUT THE OPPOSITE SEX

premiere: June 18, 1990   *packager:* Barry and Enright Productions   *broadcast history:* Syndicated June 18, 1990–August 17, 1990   *host:* David Sparks   *announcer:* Larry Van Nuys   *executive producer:* Dan Enright   *producer:* Gary Jonke   *director:* Tom Maguire   *set designers:* Rob Sangrillo, George Petersen   *music:* Ed Lojeski   *origination:* Santa Fe Communications Studios, Los Angeles

In this syndicated series men were pitted against women in a contest to see who knew more about the opposite sex.

Seven studio contestants of each sex competed for a daily cash prize of $1,000, with both teams staying on for a full week of shows, in "All About the Opposite Sex." In addition, twenty-five members of each sex from the audience were used as a voting section on some questions.

In the first round, a romantic situation was presented to one team with three possible responses. The members of the team and their audience voting section chose one of the responses. One player from the opposing team tried to predict

how they voted. They scored one point for each person who voted that way (a maximum of thirty-two points possible). A member of the voting team was briefly interviewed before his or her vote was revealed. If they voted the same way, the point score for the guessing team was doubled. Two questions, one to each team, were played in this round.

Round two was similar to round one, with one situation and three possible responses presented. This time one member of the guessing team tried to pick one of the seven he or she felt had voted the same as the majority would have voted. A correct judgement doubled the team's score.

In the final round, another situation was presented and there were only two possible responses. A player from the guessing team tried to predict how the majority of the seven voted. If correct, his or her team's score was doubled. A second question was played with the teams reversing roles. The high scoring team at the end of this round won the game.

ALL AMERICAN ULTRA QUIZ
See ULTRA QUIZ.

THE ALL NEW DATING GAME
See THE DATING GAME.

ALL STAR BLITZ
premiere: April 8, 1985   *packager:* Peter Marshall Enterprises/Merrill Heatter Productions   *broadcast history:* ABC

daytime April 8, 1985–December 20, 1985; USA (cable) March 31, 1986–December 26, 1986 (repeats of ABC series) *host:* Peter Marshall *announcer:* John Harlan *executive producers:* Merrill Heatter, Noreen Conlin *producers:* Art Alisi, David Greenfield *director:* Jerome Shaw *set designer:* John C. Mula *origination:* Studio 55, ABC Television Center, Los Angeles *debut guests:* John Byner, Abby Dalton, Leslie Uggams, Robert Mandan

Four years after his fifteen-year association with THE HOLLYWOOD SQUARES ended, Peter Marshall returned to hosting game shows with "All Star Blitz."

In this show, two studio contestants and four celebrity guests attempted to solve a word phrase puzzle.

Players, in turn, chose a star from among twelve possible game board stars that corresponded to the four celebrity guests. Each celebrity was connected to three of these stars and, depending on which star was chosen, a celebrity gave an answer to a question. The player either agreed or disagreed with the answer given and, if correct, won the star. A player kept control of the game and chose stars until he or she made an incorrect judgment.

When a series of four stars formed a square around a celebrity, words, or portions of words making up a phrase, were

Peter Marshall is happy to be hosting another star-studded game show after his long and successful run with "The Hollywood Squares."

revealed. The first player to complete the phrase won. The first player to solve two puzzles correctly became the champ.

The champ played a bonus round called the "Blitz Bonanza." The player spun a wheel to uncover up to four parts of a six-part puzzle of a name or a well-known phrase. The player and each of the four celebrities guessed parts of the phrase. The player won $250 for each correct word or words, and $10,000 for solving the puzzle.

Did you know . . . Peter Marshall, the host of "All Star Blitz," was a contract player at 20th Century–Fox during the 1950s and appeared in the films *Ensign Pulver* and *The Cavern"?*

ALL STAR SECRETS
premiere: January 8, 1979 *packager:* Hill-Eubanks Group *broadcast history:* NBC daytime January 8, 1979–August 10, 1979 *host:* Bob Eubanks *announcers:* Charlie O'Donnell, Tony McClay *creator:* Mike Hill *executive producers:* Mike Hill, Bob Eubanks *producer:* Walt Case *directors:* Bill Carruthers, Chris Darley *set designers:* Ed Flesh, Dennis Roof, Molly Joseph *music:* Lee Ringuette *origination:* NBC Studios 2 and 3, Burbank *debut guests:* McLean Stevenson, Pat Boone, Phyllis Diller, Greg Morris, Mary Ann Mobley.

Three contestants attempted to match a "secret" with one of five guest celebrities on "All Star Secrets." A secret was read about one of the five stars. One of the stars was eliminated and that star then chose one of the other four celebrities he or she thought the secret was about. The contestants had the option of either taking that celebrity's advice or choosing for themselves who they believed was the subject of the secret. For every correct answer, the contestants received money. The player with the most money at the end of the show kept his or her winnings and received merchandise prizes.

Did you know . . . this show was almost called "Celebrity Secrets," but was changed to "All Star Secrets" at the last minute?

Bob Eubanks appeared as himself in two episodes of "The Adventures of Ozzie and Harriet" in 1964. At that time he was a radio personality at Los Angeles station KRLA and had just finished promoting the 1964 Beatles concert at the Hollywood Bowl.

Were you watching when . . . Arnold Schwarzenegger was a guest during the week of July 23, 1979? His secret? To become a major movie star within ten years. His secret came true!

ALMOST ANYTHING GOES
premiere: July 31, 1975 *packager:* Bob Banner–Robert Stigwood Productions *broadcast history:* ABC primetime July 31, 1975–August 28, 1975; ABC primetime January 24, 1976–May 2, 1976; ABC weekend mornings September 11, 1976–September 4, 1977; Syndicated September 16, 1977–September 1978

1975–1976 primetime version ''Almost Anything Goes''
hosts: Charlie Jones, Lynn Schackelford, Dick Whittington, Regis Philbin **announcer:** Sam Riddle **executive producers:** Bob Banner, Beryl Vertue **producers:** Jeff Harris, Bernie Kukoff, Sam Riddle **directors:** Mac Hemion, Kip Walton **set designer:** Archie Sharp
1976–1977 weekend version ''Junior Almost Anything Goes''
host: Soupy Sales **announcer:** Eddie Alexander **producer/director:** Kip Walton **set designer:** Archie Sharp
1977–1978 syndicated version ''All Star Almost Anything Goes''
host: Bill Boggs **commentator:** Jim Healy **score girl:** Judy Abercrombie **producer:** Sam Riddle **director:** Louis V. Horvitz **origination:** California State University, Fullerton

Three teams, consisting of members representing small communities, competed on this show in a series of zany and competitive athletic events. Points were awarded to the winner of each event. In the end the top scoring team won and returned to play in quarter-final and championship rounds.

On the first telecast of ''Almost Anything Goes,'' one stunt included contestants carrying loaves of bread while sliding across a greased pole suspended over a pool. In another, each had to balance an egg on his or her head, while riding down an obstacle course in a golf cart.

Did you know . . . in the fall of 1976 a weekend version called ''Junior Almost Anything Goes'' was added to the ABC Saturday morning lineup? The same type of stunts were used with children competing instead of adults.

During the 1977–1978 season a syndicated version called ''All Star Almost Anything Goes'' was seen with teams representing various television shows.

''Almost Anything Goes'' was based on a similar European show called ''It's a Knockout.''

ALUMNI FUN

premiere: January 20, 1963 **packager:** Cleary-Moses-Reid Productions **broadcast history:** ABC Sundays January 20, 1963–April 28, 1963; CBS Sundays January 5, 1964–April 5, 1964; CBS Sundays January 10, 1965–March 28, 1965; CBS Sundays January 23, 1966–May 1, 1966 **hosts:** John K. M. McCaffery, Clifton Fadiman, Peter Lind Hayes **announcers:** Bill Shipley, Joe King **creator:** Don Reid **executive producer:** John Cleary **producer:** John A. Aaron **directors:** Ron Winston, Earl Dawson, Kirk Alexander, Lamar Caselli **set designers:** Robert Bright, John Ward **music:** Don Reid **origination:** CBS Studio 52, New York **debut guests:** Tulane: Howard K. Smith, Charles DeFour, Hamilton Richardson; George Washington University: Jacob Rosenthal, Eva Adams, Eddie LeBarron

In this question-and-answer game, prominent college alumni competed on two teams of three players. The goal was to win scholarship money for their alma maters. The teams competed in a season-long elimination tournament, with the winning team receiving $15,000 and the second place team $10,000. In the first season of ''Alumni Fun,'' teams stayed on until they were defeated.

The teams tried to answer questions in seven categories (places, literature, the arts, history, people, business, and sports) from the ''tree of knowledge.''

The game consisted of three rounds, with questions worth one hundred points in each of the first two rounds. Teams, in turn, selected a category and had to answer two of the three possible questions correctly to win the points. In round three, each team had one minute and fifteen seconds to answer fifty-point questions. The team with the most points won the game.

Did you know . . . John K. M. McCaffery was the host for the 1963 season, Clifton Fadiman handled the 1964 season, and Peter Lind Hayes was the emcee for the 1965 and 1966 seasons?

Among the prominent alumni who appeared on the show were Vice President Hubert Humphrey, Los Angeles Dodgers president Walter O'Malley, Dr. Charles Mayo of the Mayo Clinic, NBC ''The Tonight Show'' and ''Today'' creator Sylvester ''Pat'' Weaver, pitcher Sandy Koufax, columnist Art Buckwald, ABC newscaster Howard K. Smith, Olympic athlete Jesse Owens, sports broadcaster Red Barber, politician Franklin D. Roosevelt Jr., and astronaut Gus Grissom.

''Alumni Fun'' was produced by the same company that produced ''G.E. College Bowl'' (see COLLEGE BOWL) and was sponsored by American Cyanamid, the organization that awarded the financial grants.

AMATEUR'S GUIDE TO LOVE

premiere: March 27, 1972 **packager:** Merrill Heatter–Bob Quigley Productions **broadcast history:** CBS daytime March 27, 1972–June 23, 1972 **host:** Gene Rayburn **announcer:** Kenny Williams **executive producers:** Merrill Heatter, Bob Quigley **producers:** Robert Noah, Art Alisi **location producers:** Ray Horl, Les Roberts, John Carsey **director:** Jerome Shaw **set designer:** Robert Tyler Lee **music:** Mort Garson **origination:** Studio 43, CBS Television City, Los Angeles **debut guests:** Michael Landon, Barbara Eden, Charles Nelson Reilly

On ''Amateur's Guide to Love'' guest celebrities involved unsuspecting people on the street in comedy situations. The results were recorded on location in Southern California by a hidden camera.

The person in each situation was faced with the need to make one of two possible decisions on a matter related in some way to sex, marriage, or love. A celebrity panel located in the studio discussed the situation and voted upon which move would be the wisest. The subject received $200 if the celebrities were correct in the prediction of the outcome, $100 if incorrect.

AMERICAN GLADIATORS

premiere: September 9, 1989 **packager:** Four Point Entertainment/Trans World International/Samuel Goldwyn Television **broadcast history:** Syndicated September 9, 1989–September 14, 1997; USA (cable) January 4, 1993–October 8, 1993; USA (cable) June 27, 1994–September 8, 1995; USA (cable) July 1, 1996–September 13, 1996 (USA broadcasts were repeats of syndicated series) **hosts:** Mike Adamle, Joe Theismann, Todd Christensen, Larry Csonka, Lisa Malosky, Dan ''Nitro'' Clark **referees:** Bob McElwee, Larry Thompson *announcer:* John Harlan   *creators:* Dan Carr, Jon C. Ferraro *executive producers:* Barry Frank, Ron Ziskin   *producers:* Chuck Howard, Eytan Keller, J. Brian Gadinsky   *directors:* Ken Fouts, Andy Young, Bob Levy   *set designers:* Archie Sharp, Bill Bohnert   *music:* Bill Conti, Dan Milner   *origination:* Universal Studios, Hollywood 1989–1991; CBS/MTM Studios, Studio City 1991–   *Gladiators: (1989–1990) male:* Nitro, Gemini, Malibu, Titan, Laser—*female:* Sunny, Lace, Zap, Gold, Blaze   *(1990–1991) male:* Nitro, Gemini, Thunder, Turbo, Laser—*female:* Lace, Gold, Blaze, Diamond, Ice   *(1991–1992) male:* Gemini, Laser, Nitro, Thunder, Turbo, Tower—*female:* Blaze, Gold, Ice, Lace, Zap, Diamond, Storm   *(1992–1993) male:* Laser, Sabre, Tower, Turbo, Viper—*female:* Diamond, Elektra, Siren, Sky, Storm, Zap *(1993–1994) male:* Hawk, Laser, Sabre, Tower, Turbo—*female:* Ice, Jazz, Siren, Sky, Zap   *(1994–1995) male:* Hawk, Laser, Nitro, Sabre, Turbo—*female:* Ice, Jazz, Siren, Sky, Zap

A new genre of athletic competition game shows hit the small screen in the fall of 1989 with the appearance of the "American Gladiators." Each week male and female amateur athletes, chosen from rigorous tryouts in cities around the United States, took on the Gladiators—mostly professional athletes and bodybuilders—in a series of physically demanding sporting events. The Gladiators were given names such as "Tower," "Thunder," and "Ice."

Two men and two women challenged Gladiators of the same sex. The amateur players received points if they were successful in various competitions. The highest scoring player of each sex returned to compete in quarter-final, semi-final, and championship rounds. The yearly winners received cash and prizes, including a new automobile.

The overall winners from the first season were Brian Hutson, an office furniture buyer who played football at Mississippi State, and Bridget Venturi, an options trader who was a three-sport star in high school.

Events in the first season included: "the Joust," in which the challengers and the Gladiators were outfitted with padded pugel sticks and had to knock their opponents off their perches; "Powerball," in which two contenders attempted to get as many balls as possible into containers guarded by three Gladiators; and "the Eliminator," in which the teams went head to head in a timed obstacle course to determine the day's winner.

New events were introduced each season. In the second season "Atlasphere" and Hang Tough made their debut. In Atlasphere two Gladiators and two contenders of the same sex competed from inside large metal spheres. The contenders attempted to score points by rolling their sphere onto one of four goal areas on a large playing field while the Gladiators tried to prevent them from scoring. Hang Tough featured one contender and one Gladiator within a playing area of sixty feet by twenty feet consisting of hanging rings. Each player started at one end and in a sixty-second time limit tried to swing from one end of the area to the other, trying to avoid the Gladiator who started out at the opposite end.

In the 1991–1992 season the show moved from Universal Studios, Hollywood to a larger studio, dubbed "Gladiator Arena," at CBS/MTM Studios in Studio City. New events that

season included "Swingshot" and "The Maze." In Swingshot two contenders and two Gladiators were attached to bungee cords hanging from the ceiling. The object of the event was for each contender to jump to the ground from his or her platform, bounce towards a center column that was covered with balls attached by Velcro, and bounce back to his or her individual platform with the balls while the Gladiators tried to block their progress. In The Maze the contender tried to find his or her way through a maze loaded with dead ends and Gladiators in a forty-five second time limit.

The 1992–1993 season featured an event played on the ceiling of the studio. In "Skytrack" both contenders and one Gladiator were harnessed to an upsidedown track elevated twenty feet in the air. Using Velcro gloves and shoes to move along the track, the contenders raced each other and the Gladiator to the end of the track and back.

In the fifth season, 1993–1994, "Gauntlet," "Pyramid," "Tug-o-war," and "Whiplash" were introduced as new events. In Gauntlet each contender had twenty-five seconds to battle his or her way through an eighty-foot-long field, avoiding Gladiators armed with blocking pads trying to prevent each contender from completing the event. In Pyramid both contenders tried to climb a thirty-five-foot-high padded pyramid while avoiding two Gladiators who tried to prevent them from succeeding. One contender took on one Gladiator in Tug-o-war. Both stood on a tilting platform fifteen feet above the ground and the contender had sixty seconds to either pull the rope away or knock the Gladiator off their platform. Whiplash also featured one contender versus one Gladiator in an attempt to thrust the Gladiator outside the boundaries of a circular playing ring.

The 1996–1997 season consisted of episodes of "International Gladiators," featuring shows taped in Australia.

Did you know . . . former football stars Mike Adamle and Joe Theismann were the original hosts of "American Gladiators" when the show premiered? Theismann was replaced by another football star, Todd Christensen, after the first thirteen shows. Christensen was replaced by another former football star, Larry Csonka, when the show began its second season. Entering the fifth season, Csonka was replaced by sports reporter Lisa Malosky.

The overall winners from the first season were Brian Hutson, an office furniture buyer who played football at Mississippi State, and Bridget Venturi, an options trader who was a three-sport star in high school. As the popularity of the show increased, a series of toys based on the show was introduced, along with a fan club, a soundtrack album of music from the show, and a live tour featuring the stars of this show began traveling the United States.

AMERICANA

premiere: December 8, 1947   *packager:* Martin Stone Productions/NBC Television   *broadcast history:* NBC prime-time December 8, 1947–July 4, 1949   *hosts:* John Mason Brown, Deems Taylor, Ben Grauer   *substitute hosts:* John K. M. McCaffery, Ed Herlihy, Andre Baruch   *cohost:* Vivian

America went ape over "Animal Crack-ups," hosted by Alan Thicke.

ANIMAL CRACK-UPS

premiere: August 8, 1987   *packager:* Vin Di Bona Productions   *broadcast history:* ABC primetime August 8, 1987–September 12, 1987; ABC Saturday morning September 12, 1987–December 30, 1989; ABC Saturday morning June 2, 1990–September 1, 1990   *host:* Alan Thicke *assistant:* Debbie Bartlett *voice of "Reggie the Heggie":* Susan Blu *executive producer:* Vin Di Bona   *producer:* Bill Armstrong *directors:* Jeff Goldstein, Ron de Moraes   *set designer:* Bill Bohnert   *theme song:* "Animals Are Just Like People Too" sung by Alan Thicke and written by Alan Thicke, Todd Thicke, Gary Pickus   *origination:* Studio 57, ABC Television Center, Hollywood

A panel of four celebrity guests answered questions to see how much they knew about the world of animals on "Animal Crack-ups." The program made extensive use of film footage of animal antics to illustrate the questions. After a question was asked, each member of the panel gave an answer. For each correct answer, a player received a toy monkey. The player with the most monkeys won $2,500 for his or her favorite charity.

Did you know . . .   Alan Thicke wrote the theme song for the first American game show hosted by fellow Canadian Alex Trebek, THE WIZARD OF ODDS?

ANIMAL PLANET ZOOVENTURE

premiere: March 31, 1997   *packager:* Zooventure Entertainment, Inc.   *broadcast history:* Animal Planet (cable) March 31, 1997– ; Discovery (cable) April 6, 1997–   *host:* JD Roth *executive producer:* Robert Noah   *producers:* Bianca Pino, Gabrielle Johnston, David Greenfield   *director:* James Marcione   *production designer:* Bill Bohnert   *art director:* Jin Kim   *music supervisor:* Steve Love; theme composed and performed by Mark Waldron, Nancee Kahler McCraw   *origination:* San Diego Zoo, San Diego

The San Diego Zoo is the setting for this game show about animals, seen simultaneously on the Animal Planet and Discovery cable channels. Kids compete for the chance to be zookeeper for a day at the San Diego Wild Animal Park. Throughout the show, animals are brought on camera, and facts about them are presented.

Four kids compete on each show, two in the first game and two in the second game. Both winners compete against each other in a final round.

The games consist of ten- and twenty-points stunts, such as having each player act like a "tiger mom" (getting down on their hands and knees) and move their "cubs" (stuffed animals) with their teeth from one part of the set to another across a "slippery marsh." There are ten-point questions about animals.

In the final round, the two remaining players compete. A question is asked; the answer is displayed on a screen, with a blank space for every letter in the answer. Letters pop up on the screen, and players buzz in to answer. Each correct response earns one point, and the player with the most points at the end of sixty seconds is the day's winner.

Ferrer   *announcers:* Dick Dudley, Hugh James *producers:* Martin Stone, Gordon Duff   *directors:* Ted Mills, Frederick Coe   *origination:* NBC Studio 8G, New York   *debut guests:* Bennett Cerf, Millicent Fenwick, Lewis Gannett, and Linda Nisan. First guests in new format (1949): Mary Margaret McBride, Lewis Gannett, and Colonel Stoopnagle (F. Chase Taylor)

One of the first network television quiz shows, "Americana" dealt with American history and folklore and featured questions submitted by viewers. Each program opened with a shot of a little red school house and a bugler blowing to announce assembly. The most interesting question of the week won a set of the *Encyclopedia Americana* worth $212.

Originally, questions were posed to a celebrity panel, which was replaced on February 4, 1948 by a panel of five high school students, known as the "board of experts."

The format changed again on June 6, 1949 with three students now playing against three celebrity guests in a question and answer session on America and its history.

Did you know . . .   John Mason Brown hosted "Americana" for its first month on the air? Then Deems Taylor took over for two weeks in January 1948. Ben Grauer, who had joined NBC in 1930 as a special events reporter, became the new host on February 4, 1948. Vivian Ferrer was added as a cohost in 1949.

Ben Grauer was on hand to broadcast the beginning of television when NBC covered the 1939 New York World's Fair. For over twenty years Grauer covered the New Year's ceremonies at Times Square in New York for NBC before retiring in 1977.

ANNIVERSARY GAME

premiere: January 27, 1969 *packager:* Circle Seven Productions *broadcast history:* Syndicated January 27, 1969–September 1970 *host:* Alan Hamel *announcer:* Dean Webber *creator:* Larry Miller *producers:* David Beiber, John Reed King *director:* Ajar Jacks *set designer:* Jim Stringer *origination:* KGO-TV, San Francisco

In this daily syndicated show, three married couples competed for points and prizes by performing stunts and answering questions.

The first round in "Anniversary Game" consisted of each spouse predicting how his or her mate would react to a practical joke or a gag. In the second round all three couples competed against each other to complete a stunt. In the third and final round all the couples answered general knowledge questions for points to determine the day's champions. The winning team received a merchandise prize called "the anniversary surprise."

ANSWER YES OR NO

premiere: April 30, 1950 *packager:* West Hooker Productions *broadcast history:* NBC primetime April 30, 1950–June 23, 1950 *host:* Moss Hart *announcer:* William Lazar *producers:* Wayne Wirth, West Hooker *directors:* Joe Cavalier, Doug Rodgers *origination:* NBC Studio 6B, New York *debut guests:* Russell Crouse, Leveen McGrath, Arlene Francis, Mr. and Mrs. Bennett Cerf

This late-night Sunday show, "Answer Yes or No," hosted by playwright Moss Hart, was a psychological game with a panel of celebrity experts and two guests. The emcee posed a situation to one of the guests, and then the panel was given the opportunity to question the guest to determine how he or she responded and why. Viewers received $5 if their questions were used on the show, and the author of the most intriguing question of the week received an Emerson radio.

Did you know . . . host Moss Hart was married to longtime TO TELL THE TRUTH panelist Kitty Carlisle?

ANYBODY CAN PLAY

premiere: July 6, 1958 *packager:* John Guedel Productions *broadcast history:* ABC primetime July 6, 1958–December 8, 1958 *host:* George Fennaman *assistant:* Judy Bamber *scorekeeper:* Andy Stewart *announcer:* Ed Chandler *producer:* John Guedel *game supervisor:* Walter Guedel *director:* John Alexander *set designer:* James Trittipo *origination:* Studio B, ABC Television Center, Los Angeles

Four studio contestants competed in different kinds of tests for cash and prizes on "Anybody Can Play." Among the challenges were identifying movie stars in disguise, identifying unusual items such as a cornucopia or a blunderbuss—guessing the age and weight of a bathing beauty and unscrambling words. A popular game involved listening to a song and associating it with one of two possible news events that occurred the same year.

Players received ten points for correct answers and lost five points for wrong guesses. They stayed on the show for four

George Fennaman and assistant Judy Bamber invite contestants to take the money and run on "Anybody Can Play."

weeks and the high scoring contestant at that time won $5,000. Second place earned $2,000; third place, $1,000; and fourth place, $500.

Home viewers competed for $10,000 in cash and merchandise prizes such as a vacation in Paris, a mink coat, an organ, and a home soda fountain. To qualify, they had to send in postcards predicting the order in which the studio contestants would finish and guessing their ages and weights. The ten closest viewers won prizes, while the closest guess also won money.

ANYONE CAN WIN

premiere: July 14, 1953 *packager:* Bernard Prockter Productions *broadcast history:* CBS primetime July 14, 1953–September 1, 1953 *host:* Al Capp *model:* Shirley Cabot *announcer:* Joe O'Brien *executive producer:* Everett Rosenthal *producer/director:* Sylvan Taplinger *music director:* Wladmir Selinsky *origination:* New York *debut guests:* Ilka Chase, Patsy Kelly, Jimmy Dykes

This summertime game show, "Anyone Can Win," was seen on alternating weeks with another game show, FOLLOW THE LEADER. A panel of four celebrities competed in a general-knowledge quiz. Three of the celebrities were fully visible to the audience, while the fourth wore the mask of an Al Capp comic strip character, "Hairless Joe."

Before the show began, all members of the studio audience picked the celebrity they thought would answer the most questions correctly. The members of the audience who picked the right celebrity divided $2,000.

Celebrity panelists were chosen at random to answer questions. Each player started the game with ten points and gained one point for a correct answer, a point would be lost for a wrong guess.

Periodically throughout the show, telephone calls were placed to home viewers, who were given the opportunity to identify the masked panelist.

Did you know . . . host Al Capp was better known as the cartoonist for the comic strip "Lil' Abner"?

ANYTHING FOR MONEY

premiere: September 17, 1984 *packager:* Gary Bernstein–Larry Hovis Productions for Paramount Television *broadcast history:* Syndicated September 17, 1984–September 1985; USA (cable) September 29, 1986–June 24, 1988 (repeats of syndicated series) *host:* Fred Travalena *announcer:* Johnny Gilbert *executive producers:* David Fein, Tracy Goss *producer:* Eythan Keller *directors:* Paul Miller, Jeff Goldstein *segment director:* Kevin Meagher *set designers:* Anthony Sabatino, William H. Harris *origination:* TAV Vine Street Studios, Los Angeles

Two studio contestants tried to predict the outcome of pre-filmed situations. They were asked, "Would a lady sell a basket of groceries she just purchased, to a stranger?" The players on "Anything for Money" had to determine whether or not the subject would agree or refuse to do what was asked. Each correct prediction won money for the contestants.

Three rounds were played, with the contestants playing for $200 in round one, $300 in round two, and $500 in round three.

ANYTHING YOU CAN DO

premiere: September 13, 1971 *packager:* Don Reid Productions *broadcast history:* Syndicated September 13, 1971–September 1974 *hosts:* Gene Wood, Don Harron *assistants:* Wendy Owens, Margaret Zobeck, Kerry O'Brien, Lee Beauchamp *announcer:* Bill Luxton *executive producer:* Don Reid *producers:* Lorne Freed, Allan Reid, Richard Reid, Alan Shalieck *directors:* Bill McKee, Lorne Freed *set designer:* John Richard *music:* composed by Don Reid *music coordinator:* Alan Moorhouse *origination:* Ottawa, Canada

In "Anything You Can Do," this "battle of the sexes," two teams of three players (men vs. women) competed to see who could complete stunts in the fastest time.

A team selected a stunt from the board, but the opposing side got the first chance to perform it. Four rounds of stunts were played on each show, with both teams attempting them, in each event.

In one stunt, players put on pairs of panty hose, locked arms, and attempted to kick in unison like a chorus line.

Another stunt required that the players ride children's bicycles down a predetermined line and attempt to toss newspapers through a window.

Both teams also played a "Brain Game" round, in which all three players worked together to spell a complicated word by putting letters on a board in a faster time than their opponents. The team using the least time in all five rounds won the day's competition and received merchandise prizes.

Did you know . . . Gene Wood emceed the first year of "Anything You Can Do," then left to host BEAT THE CLOCK? Don Harron, a regular on "Hee Haw," became the new host in September 1972.

ARE YOU KIDDING?

premiere: June 8, 1990 *packager:* Pye-Ross Productions/CBS Entertainment Productions *broadcast history:* CBS primetime special June 8, 1990 *host:* John Mulrooney *announcer:* John Harlan *executive producers:* Jeremy Fox, Chris Pye *producer:* Gregory Ross *director:* Barry Glazer *set designer:* Jimmy Cuomo *music:* Spike Jones *origination:* CBS Television City, Los Angeles *debut guests:* G. Gordon Liddy, Cathy Ladman, Vic Dunlop

This one-time special, "Are You Kidding," featured a celebrity panel who attempted to discern which of three stories was true and which two were fraudulent.

The stories were viewed with video clips. In the show's first segment, the stories included one about a wig with a hidden pocket for money, one about flavor-coated spoons for kids, and another about a cardboard fan for overheated passengers.

ARE YOU POSITIVE

premiere: July 6, 1952 *packager:* Lester Lewis–Allan Lawrence Productions *broadcast history:* NBC early evening July 6, 1952–August 24, 1952 *hosts:* Bill Stern, Frank Coniff *announcers:* Dick Dudley, Gene Hamilton *producers:* Lester Lewis, Allan Lawrence *director:* Warren Jacober *origination:* New York *debut guests:* Jimmy Cannon, Lefty Gomez, Frank Frisch

This early evening sports quiz, "Are You Positive," which aired on Sundays, was originally called "Bill Stern's Sports Quiz." Host Bill Stern was a sportscaster for NBC television. He was replaced as host on July 27 by Frank Coniff, a columnist for the New York *Journal American.*

The panel of three sports experts were asked to identify a famous sports personality from photographs taken when the individual was a child. The viewing audience was encouraged to send in suggestions. If the viewer's suggestion was used, he or she received $5. If a suggestion stumped the panel, the contributor received $10 more and a book—either *All Sports Record Book* or *The Official Encyclopedia of Baseball.*

Did you know . . . host Bill Stern called the play-by-play of the first baseball broadcast on television? The date was May 17, 1939, as NBC covered the game between Columbia and Princeton from Baker Field in Manhattan.

ART FORD SHOW

premiere: July 28, 1951 *packager:* Art Ford Productions
broadcast history: NBC primetime July 28, 1951–September
15, 1951 *host:* Art Ford *assistants:* Arlene Cunningham,
Pat Hall *announcer:* Jack Costello *producer:* Ray Buffum
director: Jac Hein *music:* Archie Koty Trio *origination:*
NBC Studio 8H, New York *debut guests:* Hal Moore (KYW
Radio, Philadelphia), Fred Robbins (WINS New York),
Johnny Syms (Radio America Brazil)

New York radio personality Art Ford hosted this Saturday
night summer series in which three disc jockeys from radio
stations around the country comprised the panel, and each
competed to guess composers, vocalists, and orchestras of
various records. The panelist with the most correct answers
at the end of the ''Art Ford Show'' received a special ''Disc
Jockey Oscar.'' The records were played by hostess Arlene
Cunningham, who also kept score. She was replaced by Pat
Hall on August 11.

Another feature on this show was a performance by a
guest recording artist. Eileen Barton appeared on the first
show and other shows featured Toni Arden, Fran Warren,
Mary Mayo, Kay Armen, and Rosemary Clooney.

Did you know . . . in addition to the debut jockeys listed
above, others who appeared on the panel included Bill Randall of WERE Cleveland, Ted Brown of WMGM New York,
Joe Franklin of WJZ Schnectady, and Bob Clayton of WHDH
Boston? Years later both Ted Brown and Bob Clayton would
become game show emcees.

ART LINKLETTER SHOW

premiere: February 18, 1963 *packager:* Artel Productions
broadcast history: NBC primetime February 18, 1963–
September 16, 1963 *host:* Art Linkletter *announcer:* Jack
Slattery *executive producer:* Wilbur Stark *producer:* Irvin
Atkins *director:* Hal Cooper *art director:* E. Jay Krause
music director: Bob Walters *origination:* NBC Studio 4,
Burbank *debut guest:* Debbie Reynolds

Television personality Art Linkletter returned to primetime after a two-year absence with this audience-
participation series. Contestants on the ''Art Linkletter
Show'' were asked to guess the outcome of situations filmed
with a hidden camera that involved people in awkward circumstances, comical emergencies, or dealing with life's
everyday problems. Players received cash for participating in
the show.

Did you know . . . on April 1, the format was changed
to use celebrity judges instead of contestants? Among the
regular judges were Jayne Meadows and Carl Reiner.

Also appearing on the show were the ''Linkletter Players,''
a group that included Ken Berry, Buck Henry, Carol Merrill,
Arte Johnson, and Richard Dawson.

ASK ME ANOTHER

premiere: July 3, 1952 *packager:* Louis Cowan Productions
broadcast history: NBC primetime July 3, 1952–September
25, 1952 *host:* Joe Boland *executive producer:* John Lew-
ellan *producer:* Jay Sheridan *director:* Don Meier *orig-

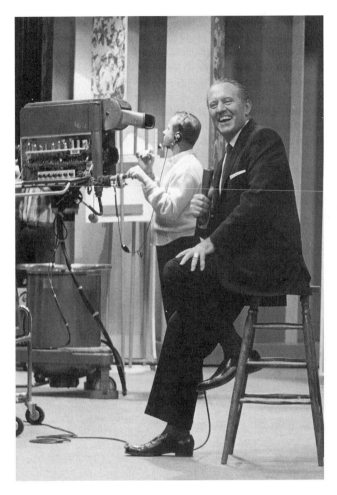

*Always jovial Art Linkletter takes a break behind the scenes on the
''Art Linkletter Show.''*

ination:* Studebaker Theater, Chicago *debut panelists:*
Johnny Lujack, Lonny Lunde, Fran Allison, Warren Brown;
debut guests: Johnny Coulon, Fred Merkel, and Gertrude
Ederle

A celebrity panel of four tried to guess the identity of three
famous sports personalities on ''Ask Me Another.'' Athletes
stood behind a curtain while the panel asked questions to
determine who they were. On each show one of the three
sports figures performed his or her specialty while being
questioned.

Did you know . . . host Joe Boland was a former college
football coach for both Purdue and Notre Dame? ''Ask Me
Another'' took its title from a book of the same name.

AUCTION-AIRE

premiere: September 30, 1949 *packager:* Masterson-
Reddy-Nelson Productions *broadcast history:* ABC
primetime September 30, 1949–June 23, 1950 *host:* Jack
Gregson *assistant:* ''Rebel'' (Charlotte) Randall *announc-
ers:* Kenny Williams, Glenn Riggs *executive producers:*
John Reddy, John Masterson, John Nelson *producer:*

Donald Hirsch   *director:* Edward Nugent   *origination:* Ritz Theater, New York

This early audience participation show, seen on ABC networks on the East Coast and in the Midwest, featured viewers competing in an auction using labels from Libby's food products.

On "Auction-Aire," members of the home and studio audiences phoned in their bids for merchandise to one of the stations that carried the show, and these were relayed to the Ritz Theater where the show was broadcast. At the end of each auction, both the highest bidding viewer and the highest bidding member of the studio audience received the merchandise.

Each program also featured one auction in which a bidder needed the most labels from one particular product to win and another in which a bidder had to have the greatest variety of Libby labels to win.

Viewers could also win a new car by correctly guessing the numbers in "The Mystery Chant," a bunch of auctioneer's gibberish.

THE BABY GAME

premiere: January 1, 1968 *packager:* Bob Stivers Productions *broadcast history:* ABC daytime January 1, 1968–July 12, 1968 *host:* Richard Hayes *announcer:* Chet Gould *producers:* Eric Leiber, Bob Synes *director:* Mike Garguilo *set designer:* Ron Baldwin *origination:* ABC Studio TV–15, New York

Two couples competed on "The Baby Game," a game designed to test their knowledge of childhood behavior. A specific situation involving a child was explained. Players earned points on their ability to predict what the child would do. A previously filmed sequence was shown and the results were determined. The team with the highest score won merchandise prizes.

Each game began with an event that featured both teams competing against each other and a time limit. (Example: "Quick Picker Uppers," where each child was put in a blanket and then "rolled" by his parents over a floor covered with pieces of material. In a forty-five–second time limit, the child tried to pick up as many pieces of material as possible with their blanket.)

Three other rounds were played with each player trying to guess how kids would react in different situations, such as in "Ring Toss." In this game teams tried to guess how many of three sets of children would move closer to each other to make the toss easier. In the "Baby Game Bakery," three kids were shown how to make a multilevel layer cake and then had to attempt to duplicate the feat.

Rounds two and three were worth a potential ten points for correct predictions and round four, twenty-five points.

Did you know . . . host Richard Hayes was known as "America's Favorite Babysitter"? During the six-month run of "The Baby Game," a $15,000 college education was offered as a prize in an "America's cutest kid" contest. Viewers entered by submitting photos of their kids. Five additional runners-up won new 1968 Pontiac station wagons.

BABY RACES

premiere: September 12, 1993 *packager:* Robert Sherman Productions/Family Productions *broadcast history:* Family Channel (cable) September 12, 1993–August 27, 1994 *host:* Fred Travalena *announcer:* Gene Wood *executive producer:* Robert Sherman *producer:* Jerry Cardwell *director:* George Choderker *set designer:* Tim Duffy *origination:* Disney-MGM Studios, Orlando

Young children and their parents competed together in a variety of events and stunts on "Baby Races" in order to win toys for the kids and merchandise for the parents.

Each game began with teams competing against each other within a time limit. Teams also played three individual events, including: "sandbox golf," in which they tried to knock plastic balls into a large hole with a miniature golf club; "cow catcher," in which the children rode on their dads' backs—who were dressed in horse costumes—picked up toy cows and placed them in a corral; and "anteater antics," in which each kid wore a mask with a magnet in it and tried to move toy metal ants from a hill to a basket. All events were played in a forty-five–second time limit.

Both teams received prizes, with each child selecting a toy from a large display in the toy room and the parents receiving a $300 gift certificate and other prizes.

Points of various totals were awarded to each team after every event, but the game was played more for fun than actual competition.

BACK THAT FACT

premiere: October 22, 1953 *packager:* Barry-Enright-Friendly Productions *broadcast history:* ABC primetime October 22, 1953–November 26, 1953 *host:* Joey Adams *assistants:* Hope Lange, Al Kelly *announcer:* Carl Caruso *producers:* Jack Barry, Dan Enright, Ed Friendly, Jack Farren *director:* Mickey Trenner *music director:* John Gart *origination:* New York

On "Back That Fact," this short-lived series, contestants were interviewed and asked questions about their backgrounds. Players could either answer truthfully or bluff. If it was believed that a false statement was made, an off-stage voice (announcer Carl Caruso) interrupted and asked the player to "back that fact." If the player could give proof of the statement, he or she won a prize; otherwise the player was defeated.

Did you know . . . assistant Hope Lange is best remembered for her later starring role in the 1968 TV series "The Ghost and Mrs. Muir"?

BAFFLE

premiere: March 26, 1973 *packager:* Merrill Heatter–Bob Quigley Productions *broadcast history:* NBC daytime March 26, 1973–March 29, 1974 *host:* Dick Enberg *announcer:* Kenny Williams *executive producers:* Merrill Heatter, Bob Quigley, Robert Noah *producers:* Art Alisi, Ken Williams *director:* Jerome Shaw *set designer:* Jim Newton *music:* Mort Garson *origination:* NBC Studio 4, Burbank *debut guests:* Arte Johnson, Barbara Feldon

Two celebrities, each teamed with a studio contestant, competed to guess well-known phrases or names from letter clues.

One member of a team was shown a phrase and put three letters—but not the first three, of the first word—on a board for his or her teammate to see. The teammate had to guess the phrase from the letters showing or have letters added one at a time until the phrase was identified. The team using the least amount of time on each phrase won that round.

After four rounds were played, the winning team played a bonus game in which the contestants attempted to guess

Could this be Dick Enberg, advertising that he just earned his Bachelor of Arts degree from the University of Florida? Actually not, he's just promoting his new game show "Baffle" in 1973.

words from three-letter clues with the possible grand prize of a new car.

On September 29, 1973 the format was changed to feature only celebrity teams.

Did you know . . . "Baffle"—an updated version of the 1965 syndicated game show PDQ—replaced CONCENTRATION, NBC's longest-running daytime game show?

Host Dick Enberg has called the play-by-play for six Super Bowl contests.

John Davidson held the record for having formed the answer to a scrambled word problem in the shortest amount of time: four seconds. He came up with "Kiss Me," with the three letters *k, s,* and *m* as his only clues.

Were you watching when . . . Bill Bixby, Barbara Feldon, Marty Ingels, Arte Johnson, Gary Owens, and Peter Marshall appeared as celebrity players on "Baffle"?

BALANCE YOUR BUDGET

premiere: October 18, 1952 *packager:* Louis Cowan–Alfred Hollander–Peter Arnell Production *broadcast history:* CBS primetime October 18, 1952–May 2, 1953 *host:* Bert Parks *assistant:* Lynn Connor *announcer:* Lee Vines *producer:* Peter Arnell *director:* Sherman Marks *set designer:* Robert Rowe Paddock *origination:* New York

"Balance Your Budget" was a Saturday night quiz show designed to help contestants cope with the problem of staying "in the black." Players described what caused their household budgets to slip "into the red."

Emcee Bert Parks, keeper of the "horn of plenty," asked the contestants questions to help them win what they needed to solve their problems. Winners were also given a chance to win the "Treasure Chest" by choosing a key to see if it opened the lock. The value of the chest started at $1,500 and increased in $500 increments until the right key was picked.

Did you know . . . assisting Parks was seventeen-year-old Lynn Connor, who had been selected from over six-hundred applicants as "Miss Posture Perfect" by Sealy Mattress, the sponsor of "Balance Your Budget"?

BANK ON THE STARS

premiere: June 20, 1953 *packager:* Masterson-Reddy-Nelson Productions *broadcast history:* CBS primetime June 20, 1953–August 8, 1953; NBC primetime May 15, 1954–August 21, 1954 *hosts:* Jack Paar, Bill Cullen, Jimmy Nelson *announcers:* Olin Tice (CBS), Bill McCord (NBC) *executive producer:* Marlo Lewis *producers:* John Nelson, Ric Eyrich *directors:* Dave Rich, Craig Allen, Al DeCaprio *set designers:* Robert Gundlack, Richard Senie *music directors:* Ivan Ditmars, Mack Shopnick *origination:* NBC Studio 3B, New York (1954)

During the summer of 1953, "Bank on the Stars" was seen on CBS on Saturday nights, with Jack Paar as emcee and Olin Tice as announcer.

Teams consisting of two members answered questions based on their observation of film clips. If one member of the team gave a correct answer and the other answered incorrectly, that team received $50. If both members of the team answered correctly, that team collected $100. If neither player came up with the right response, the team was eliminated. Each team could win up to $300 and an opportunity to try for a $500 bonus. Losing players were allowed to dip one hand into a barrel of silver dollars.

The bonus round, called the "Bank Night Bonus," consisted of a single question about a scene from a movie that was heard but not seen by the players.

Did you know . . . "Bank on the Stars" returned for a second season in the summer of 1954 on NBC? Bill Cullen hosted from May 15 to July 10 and was replaced by ventriloquist Jimmy Nelson from July 17 to August 21. NBC staff announcer Bill McCord was the announcer and Cynthia Price joined as the assistant to the host on May 29.

Jack Paar was discovered by Jack Benny during World War II, performing as a G.I. entertainer at Guadalcanal. After the war he was a summer replacement on radio for Jack Benny and later appeared with Marilyn Monroe in the movie *Love Nest*.

BARGAIN HUNTERS

premiere: July 6, 1987   *packager:* Merrill Heatter Productions/Josephnson Communications   *broadcast history:* ABC daytime July 6, 1987–September 4, 1987   *host:* Peter Tomarken   *announcer:* Dean Goss   *executive producer:* Merrill Heatter   *producers:* Art Alisi, Steve Friedman, Paul Gilbert   *director:* Jerome Shaw   *set designer:* Anthony Sabatino   *music:* Score Productions   *origination:* Hollywood Center TV Studios, Los Angeles

"Bargain Hunters" was network television's first combination game show/home shopping series. Six contestants competed daily in a test of their ability to spot merchandise bargains.

Three games were played with two contestants competing in each one. The winner from each game returned at the end of the show to play in the "Super Saver" to determine the day's champion.

The first game played was the "Bargain Quiz," in which a prize was shown together with its price. Each player decided if that price was a bargain or not. Correct guesses were worth one point and three points determined a winner.

In the second game, "Bargain Trap," five prizes were shown with prices; one item overpriced (the trap). Two players, in turn, chose items they felt were bargains, trying to avoid the trap. If they chose the trap, they automatically lost. In the event of a tie (both players avoiding the trap), each player guessed how much markup the overpriced item was, with the player coming closest winning.

The third game was "Bargain Busters," in which a prize was shown with three prices. Each player picked the price he or she felt was correct. The player with the most correct guesses after three rounds was the winner.

The three winners returned to play in the "Super Savers Round." Seven items of merchandise with their prices were shown, and each player had to choose the three that were being offered at the best bargain prices. The player choosing the items comprising the biggest bargains won the game and those items.

Throughout the show, merchandise was offered at special prices, to the home viewers.

BATTLE OF THE AGES

premiere: January 1, 1952   *packager:* ATV Films   *broadcast history:* DuMont primetime January 1, 1952–June 17, 1952; CBS primetime September 6, 1952–November 29, 1952   *hosts:* John Reed King, Morey Amsterdam   *announcers:* Norman Brokenshire, Arthur Van Horn   *producer:* Norman Livingston   *directors:* Mendo Brown, Frank Bunetta, Andrew McCullough   *set designer:* Manuel Essman   *music directors:* Al Finelli, Milton DeLugg   *theme song:* "They're Either Too Young or Too Old"   *origination:* New York   *debut guests:* Will Mahoney, Harold & Lola, Teresa Brewer, Zola Mae, Peggy Jane Shaulis

Two teams of professional performers competed for audience applause in "Battle of the Ages," to determine which act was better. One team, called "the veterans," was made up of people over the age of thirty-five who played for the Actors Fund of America, while the other team, "the youngsters," under the age of thirty-five, played for the scholarship fund of the Professional Children's School.

Guests on the first CBS telecast were Will Mahoney with his famous dance on a xylophone, and Harold & Lola with their dance of the cobra for the "veterans" team. The "youngsters" team was composed of songstress Teresa Brewer and piano prodigies Zola Mae, age eleven, and Peggy Jane Shaulis, age eight.

Did you know . . . when the show premiered on DuMont, John Reed King was the host and Al Finelli conducted the orchestra? In the fall of 1952 the show moved to CBS and Morey Amsterdam took over as host, with Milton DeLugg taking over the band.

Morey Amsterdam cowrote the 1945 hit song "Rum and Coca-Cola" for the Andrews Sisters and was one of the original hosts on "Broadway Open House," the first late-night television show.

BATTLESTARS

premiere: October 26, 1981   *packager:* Merrill Heatter Productions   *broadcast history:* NBC daytime October 26, 1981–April 23, 1982; NBC daytime April 4, 1983–July 1, 1983
1981–1982 version
host: Alex Trebek   *announcer:* Rod Roddy   *executive producer:* Merrill Heatter   *producers:* Robert Noah, Art Alisi   *director:* Jerome Shaw   *set designer:* James Agazzi   *music:* Mort Garson   *origination:* NBC Studio 3, Burbank   *debut guests:* Betty White, Dean Butler, Nell Carter, Joan Van Ark, Dick Van Patten, Garry Shandling
1983 version "The New Battlestars"
host: Alex Trebek   *announcer:* Charlie Tuna   *executive producer:* Merrill Heatter   *producers:* Jay Redack, Art Alisi   *director:* Jerome Shaw   *set designer:* Molly Joseph   *music:* Mort Garson   *origination:* NBC Studio 3, Burbank   *debut*

guests: Tom Wopat, Vicki Lawrence, Erik Estrada, Jim J. Bullock, Debbie Reynolds, Glen Scarpelli

Two studio contestants and six celebrity guests were featured on ''Battlestars,'' this weekday game show.

Each of the stars sat inside a triangle, surrounded by three points of light. A contestant selected a celebrity to answer a question by pulling a plunger that selected randomly. The player could agree or disagree with the answer given and, if correct in his or her judgement, a point of light was eliminated in that person's favor. When all three points of light were eliminated, the star was captured by the player. The first to capture three stars won the game.

In the bonus game of the 1981 version, the player tried to guess the identity of a famous person in a photo covered by sixteen squares. Three of the squares, chosen at random, were revealed and the player could take a guess to win a possible $5,000. If the person was unsuccessful another piece was revealed, the dollar value went down and he or she could call on a celebrity for additional help.

In the bonus game of the 1983 version, the winner tried to come up with three correct answers, with each of the first two worth $500, and the third worth a $10,000 jackpot. A question was read with three suggested answers. One celebrity gave an answer, which the player could agree with or not. If he or she didn't, the player chose the correct answer from the two remaining possibilities.

Were you watching when . . .   a young unknown comic named Jerry Seinfeld was booked on ''Battlestars'' as a celebrity guest star? Other celebrity comic bookings were Phyllis Diller, Martin Mull, Joan Rivers, and Rip Taylor.

BEACH CLASH
premiere: September 19, 1994   *packager:* Taylorvision/First Media Entertainment/All American Television   *broadcast history:* Syndicated September 19, 1994–September 17, 1995   *hosts:* David Hirsch, Alison Armitage   *hardbodies:* Kirstin Ekman, Devon Jenkin, Rich Macdonald, Robert Monterrosa   *creator:* Bryan Taylor   *executive producers:* Bryan Taylor, Len Depanicis   *coordinating producer:* Rita Cash   *director:* Bruce Gowers   *set designer:* Bill Bohnert   *theme:* Gareth Young, Treana Morris (performed by ''Tag'')   *origination:* Will Rogers Beach, Malibu

''Beach Clash'' was a weekly one-hour competition, taped on the beach at Malibu, California, that tested the skill, strength, and endurance of two teams of players.

Each team was made up of four players, two contenders (one male and one female) and two ''hardbodies,'' show regulars with names like ''Sandy,'' ''Breeze,'' ''Ripper,'' and ''Zuma.''

David Hirsch, who had replaced Dick Clark as host on ''American Bandstand,'' and Alison Armitage of the TV series ''Acapulco H.E.A.T.'' cohosted, with Olympic Gold Medalist Sherri Howard serving as referee.

The teams competed in ten events staged on the sand and in the water including ''Hot Air Climb,'' ''Bungee Basketball,'' ''King of the Raft,'' ''Beach Bout,'' and a ''Crash and Burn'' finale that included a variety of challenges such as a hill climb, a two-person kayak maneuvering a wave-runner around a course, a sprint and sand-crawl, and a rope-swing into a pool.

The team with the most points won the week's competition. The winning team of the year was awarded $10,000 and a Hawaiian vacation.

BEAT THE CLOCK
premiere: March 23, 1950   *packager:* Mark Goodson–Bill Todman Productions   *broadcast history:* CBS primetime March 23, 1950–February 23, 1958; CBS daytime September 16, 1957–September 12, 1958; ABC daytime October 13, 1958–January 30, 1961; Syndicated September 15, 1969–September 20, 1974; CBS daytime September 17, 1979–February 1, 1980
1950–1961 version
host: Bud Collyer   *substitute hosts:* Bob Kennedy, Sonny Fox, Win Elliott, Frank Wayne, Bill Hart, John Reed King   *announcers:* Bern Bennett (1950–1958), Dirk Fredericks (1958–1961)   *commercial announcer:* Bill Shipley (Sylvania)   *substitute announcers:* Lee Vines, Bob Shepard, Hal Simms, Dick Noel   *assistants:* Roxanne Arlen (1950–1955), Beverly Bentley (1955–1956), Joanne Jordan (1956–1957), Madeline Tyler, Bette Calvin, Nancy Kovack, Louise

Man your battlestations for the star-studded ''Battlestars,'' hosted by Alex Trebek.

King, Toby Dean *producers:* Gil Fates, Bud Collyer, Jean Hollander *directors:* Byron Paul, Jerome Schnur, Franklin Heller, Paul Alter, Ira Skutch, Lloyd Gross *stunts:* Frank Wayne, Bob Howard, Neil Simon *set designers:* Grover Cole (CBS), Neil DeLuca (CBS), Robert Rowe Paddock (CBS), Hy Bley (ABC), Dick Bernstein (ABC) *origination:* Maxine Elliott Theater (Studio 51), New York (1950–1958); Ritz Theater, New York (1958–1961)

1969–1974 version

host: Jack Narz (1969–1972), Gene Wood (1972–1974) *announcers:* Gene Wood (1969–1972), Nick Holenreich (1972–1974) *assistant:* Gail Sheldon *producers:* Frank Wayne, Gene Wood *directors:* Paul Alter, Ira Skutch, Stuart Phelps, Trevor Evans *set designers:* Ted Cooper, Steve Yuranyi *music:* Dick Hyman *origination:* Little Theater, New York (1969–1970), CFCF-TV, Montreal, Canada (1970–1974)

1979–1980 version

host: Monty Hall *announcer:* Jack Narz *assistants:* Cindee Appleton, Autumn Hargis, Lisa Parkes *executive producer:* Frank Wayne *producer/director:* Paul Alter *set designers:* Romain Johnston, Jack Hart *music:* Score Productions *music direction:* Arthur B. Rubinstein *origination:* Studio 31, CBS Television City, Los Angeles

One of the most durable television game shows, "Beat the Clock" made its debut on CBS radio on January 5, 1949 and moved to TV on March 23, 1950.

Contestants chosen from the studio audience attempted to perform stunts in a given time limit (usually sixty seconds or less). A large clock on stage ticked off the seconds so the players and audience could see how much time was left as the stunt progressed. Prizes were awarded for completing the stunt within the time limit.

During the 1950s, contestants were usually families (husband, wife, and children), with one or both of the parents participating in the stunt. At that time there was a $100 clock round, a $200 clock round, and a jackpot round, in which the wife had twenty seconds to unscramble a series of words into a famous quotation or saying.

Most of the stunts were created by staff writers Frank Wayne and Bob Howard and frequently involved the use of custard pies, whipped cream, breakable dishes, and exploding balloons. Each stunt was thoroughly tested before being used on the air. In the early 1950s future playwright Neil Simon was one of the stunt writers and actor James Dean was a stunt tester.

Each program also featured a bonus stunt that was more difficult. The value started at $100 and increased by $100 each week until successfully completed. One of the longer-running bonus stunts involved getting two toupees (suspended from the ceiling) at a time into a top hat worn by the player. The stunt was introduced in December 1953 and it ran thirty-two weeks before someone accomplished it.

By 1956, with big-money quiz shows in vogue, the weekly bonus stunt was revamped into the "Super Jackpot Stunt." It was played by each couple that completed the $100 and $200 clock stunts. The value started at $5,000 and was increased by $1,000 until it was won.

In October 1957, "Beat the Clock" gave home viewers a chance to win a trip to New York by drawing their ideas of what they thought the show's announcer Bern Bennett looked like. Over 21,000 people submitted drawings with Edward Darnell of Columbus, Indiana winning the grand prize, which also included an appearance as a contestant. Bennett, who was also Bud Collyer's announcer on WINNER TAKE ALL and TO TELL THE TRUTH, was introduced on camera on December 2, 1957. (His next on-camera appearance would be twenty-four years later on "To Tell the Truth.")

Veteran game show host Bud Collyer emceed "Beat the Clock" from 1950 to 1961. His original assistant was Roxanne, who became a celebrity in her own right. Roxanne introduced the contestants, showcased the prizes, and took pictures of the players after they completed a messy stunt. A "Roxanne" doll, complete with toy camera, was introduced in the fall of 1952. She appeared on the cover of *TV Guide* twice, in August 1954 and a year later, in August 1955. She left the show in August 1955 and was replaced by Beverly Bentley. Bette Calvin and Madeline Tyler were assistants who helped in the stunts.

When "Beat the Clock" began on TV it was seen as a forty-five minute sustaining (no commercials) show on Thursday nights. In March 1951, the show had moved to Saturday night at 7:30 P.M., picked up Sylvania as its sponsor, and found its following.

A daytime version was added by CBS in September 1957. A year later the show moved over to ABC, where it continued until the end of January 1961.

In the fall of 1969, "Beat the Clock" was revived as a first-run syndicated series with the addition of a celebrity guest each week to help the contestants. The first year the show was taped in New York City, then it moved production to Montreal, Canada for the remaining four years. ("Beat the Clock" was the only Mark Goodson game show ever to be produced in Canada.)

Veteran emcee Jack Narz handled the first three seasons and "Beat the Clock" announcer Gene Wood moved on-camera to host the final two years.

Each show featured two couples who competed against the clock to complete stunts. If they were successful they went to the "cash board" to choose a letter in the show's title that revealed a cash amount between $25 and $200.

If they completed a stunt quickly they were given a chance to earn extra money by attempting to repeat their actions.

Celebrities also had their own solo stunts to perform. Each team could win $50 by betting on either the star or the clock. Among the celebrities who tried their hand at the stunts were William Shatner, Cab Calloway, Bob Denver, Jim Backus, Marty Allen, Peggy Cass, and Betty White.

CBS revived "Beat the Clock" again in September 1979, adding the words "All New" to the title and moving production to CBS Television City in Los Angeles. Monty Hall, best known as host of LET'S MAKE A DEAL, emceed the new version with former "Beat the Clock" host Jack Narz returning as announcer and associate producer.

In this incarnation, two couples competed against each other and the clock. Each stunt was worth $500 with the

Bud Collyer and assistant Roxanne (in polka dots), on the original set of "Beat the Clock" in 1952. Note the famous clock in the background.

team completing the first stunt getting a chance for an additional $500 on the next stunt.

After two rounds were played (four stunts) both teams competed in the "Bonus Shuffle." Teams got two disks each, with the disk that landed on the highest cash amount ($300 to $1,000) advancing that team to the "Bonus Stunt" round for a chance to earn ten times the cash amount.

On November 5, 1979 the show became "All New All Star Beat the Clock" with the format altered to two teams of two celebrity guests playing for sections of the studio audience. Values of the stunts were worth $250, with the rest of the format remaining the same.

Did you know . . . "Beat the Clock" host Bud Collyer graduated from Fordham University with a degree in law and during the 1940s was the voice of Superman on radio?

During the 1950s, an episode of "The Honeymooners" featured Jackie Gleason, Audrey Meadows, and Art Carney in their roles as Ralph and Alice Kramden and Ed Norton appearing as contestants on "Beat the Clock."

Roxanne appeared in the 1956 films *Bundle of Joy* and *The Best Things in Life Are Free.*

Each show opened with announcer Bern Bennett introducing Bud Collyer as "America's Number One Clock Watcher." Every summer Collyer went on vacation and was replaced by "America's Number Two Clock Watcher." They were Bill Hart in 1951, John Reed King in 1952, "Beat the Clock" stunt creator Frank Wayne in 1953, Bob Kennedy in 1954, and Win Elliott in 1955.

Were you watching when . . . on WHAT'S MY LINE? on April 7, 1957, "Beat the Clock" stunt creators Frank Wayne and Bob Howard stumped the panel, who couldn't guess their occupation?

These game show hosts were all celebrity contestants on the syndicated version of "Beat the Clock": Steve Allen, Bert Convy, Dick Clark, Richard Dawson, Tom Kennedy, Allen Ludden, Gene Rayburn, and Gene Wood.

BEAT THE ODDS

premiere: December 16, 1968 *packager:* Bill Derman Productions for Bing Crosby Productions **broadcast history:** Syndicated December 16, 1968–September 1969 **host:** Johnny Gilbert *announcer:* Bill Baldwin *creator:* Bill Derman *producer:* Alan Neuman *origination:* Studio 4, KCOP Television, Los Angeles

In "Beat the Odds" two contestants tried to form words from only the first and last letters of the word and its number of letters.

Contestants scored ten points for each acceptable word. A player could freeze his or her score at any time, protecting points earned up until that point. A player lost control of the board to an opponent when unable to form a word. A turn and all points accumulated were lost if Mr. Whammie (a cartoon character) appeared on one of the two screens instead of a letter. The first player to reach one hundred points won the game.

Did you know . . . "Beat the Odds" made its first appearance on July 17, 1961 on Los Angeles TV station KTLA? Mike Stokey (of PANTOMIME QUIZ) was host, with longtime KTLA personality Stan Chambers as announcer. Stokey was replaced by Dennis James as host in July 1962, who continued for the rest of its run. "Beat the Odds" ran until August 23, 1963.

In the fall of 1968, "Beat the Odds" reappeared as a first-run series for national syndication. Longtime TV announcer Johnny Gilbert made one of his rare appearances as a game show host on this new version.

BEDROOM BUDDIES

premiere: August 10, 1992 *packager:* Lighthearted Entertainment in association with United Entertainment Group/Chris-Craft Television **broadcast history:** Syndicated August 10, 1992–September 18, 1992 **host:** Bobby Rivers *executive producer:* Howard Schultz *producer:* Barry Kaplan *director:* Glenn Weiss *set designer:* John Gilles *theme:* Def Jef *origination:* Studio 42, CBS Television City, Los Angeles

Three couples, either married, engaged, or just living together, competed in "Bedroom Buddies," this adult-oriented game from Howard Schultz, the producer of the relationship show STUDS. On this program couples had to prove how well they knew the person they were sleeping with.

The game began with a statement read and three possible responses revealed. One player had to recognize which of the three answers his or her partner had given. If correct, that team received a pillow. A second couple then played. One player had to guess which of the remaining two statements

were made by his or her mate. Six questions were played but only two couples could respond to any one question.

A round of "romantic choices" was played, in which each couple was given a question like "What was your most exciting encounter?" One mate had to guess what his or her partner said from between two choices.

The final round, "Double Score or Nothing," involved the male partner trying to guess where his "bedroom buddy" would like to spend her bedroom fantasy. If their answers matched, their score was doubled and the team with the highest score won a trip to locations such as Boston, Lake Tahoe, or Las Vegas.

BEDTIME STORIES

premiere: June 18, 1979 *packager:* Merrill Heatter–Bob Quigley Productions **broadcast history:** Syndicated June 18, 1979–August 1979 **hosts:** Al Lohman and Roger Barkley *announcer:* Kenny Williams *executive producers:* Merrill Heatter, Jay Redack *producers:* Robert Noah, Art Alisi *director:* Bob Loudin *music:* Stan Worth *origination:* Studio 6, KTTV Television, Los Angeles

Los Angeles radio personalities Al Lohman and Roger Barkley hosted this short-lived series, "Bedtime Stories." Two married couples, interviewed in their bedrooms, discussed their secrets for a successful relationship. Later in the show, these couples competed against each other as they tried to guess how many out of one hundred people responded to a sex type question. Each correct prediction was worth $500. Three questions were played in each match-up.

After ten shows (in two weeks) were taped, the format was changed. In the new version, two married couples tried to guess how the other couple responded to a question in a prerecorded segment. Correct guesses were worth $500.

THE BETTER SEX

premiere: July 18, 1977 *packager:* Mark Goodson–Bill Todman Productions **broadcast history:** ABC daytime July 18, 1977–January 13, 1978 **hosts:** Bill Anderson and Sarah Purcell *announcer:* Gene Wood *executive producer:* Ira Skutch *producer:* Robert Sherman *director:* Paul Alter *set designer:* Ed Flesh *origination:* Studio 54, ABC Television Center, Los Angeles

A team of six men competed against a team of six women. A team member given a question either responded correctly or bluffed on "The Better Sex." Two members of the opposing team either agreed or disagreed with the answer. An incorrect choice resulted in two of a team's members being eliminated. If a team chose the right answer, two members of the opposing team were eliminated. The game continued until one team lost all of its members.

The winning team played against thirty members of the studio audience of the opposite sex. The team had to try to outbluff all thirty, using six questions. If successful, the team divided $5,000. If not, each member of the audience left standing after all six questions were asked, divided $500.

Did you know . . . Emcee Bill Anderson had over seventy-five hit singles on the Billboard country music charts

Have we got your attention yet? "The Better Sex," hosted by Bill Anderson and Sarah Purcell, lasted only six months—maybe because it had nothing to do with sex.

since 1958? In 1963 his number-one country classic, "Still," crossed over and became a top-ten hit on the pop music charts. In 1983, he became host of the first country music quiz show, FANDANGO, on the Nashville Network.

This show marked the national television debut of Sarah Purcell. Years later she would find greater fame on NBC's "Real People."

BID 'N' BUY

premiere: July 1, 1958   *packager:* Stivers-Atkins Productions   *broadcast history:* CBS primetime July 1, 1958–September 23, 1958   *host:* Bert Parks   *announcer:* Bill Rogers   *producers:* Robert Stivers, Irv Atkins   *director:* Seymour Robbie   *set designer:* John Ward   *origination:* New York

Four contestants were given $10,000 in cash on "Bid 'N' Buy," the auction game show that replaced THE $64,000 QUESTION during the summer of 1958. The show was sponsored by Revlon.

A silhouette or picture puzzle was flashed on a screen as the first clue to a major prize. The contestants were allowed a guess each, and, if no one was correct, bid against each other for word clues given in the form of a rhyming couplet. Any contestant who bought three clues during a show was allowed to keep whatever remained of their original $10,000 stake, whether they won any prizes or not.

On the first program, prizes included an $11,000 Mercedes-Benz sports convertible, an $11,000 Bergdorf Goodman wardrobe, and a trip for two to London to see the musical production of *My Fair Lady* plus an amount equalling the total of an evening's box office receipts for the show.

Did you know . . . at age nineteen Bert Parks was signed as a singer and straight man on radio's "Eddie Cantor Show"?

THE BIG DATE

premiere: June 17, 1996   *packager:* Lighthearted Entertainment   *broadcast history:* USA (cable) June 17, 1996–September 19, 1997   *host:* Mark Walberg   *executive producer:* Howard Schultz   *supervising producer:* Michael Maddocks   *coordinating producer:* Linda Lea   *producer:* Lisa Kridos   *director:* Lenn Goodside   *set designer:* Kelly Van Patter   *music:* Will Anderson   *origination:* Studio 4, Hollywood Center Studios, Hollywood

"The Big Date" was USA cable's attempt at a first-run dating show in their afternoon lineup, which also included repeats of "LOVE CONNECTION."

The format of the game was to pair up contestants for the "big date." At the beginning one player was introduced along with three members of the opposite sex. After listening to the three talk about themselves briefly, the player chose one as a possible match. Then this pair of players tried to match answers to questions, and if they matched twice they moved on to the next round. Throughout this round players were given the option to swap their potential dates after a question was played. Whenever two players made two matches they became a couple and moved on to the final round. This process was repeated a second time with additional players to unite a second couple to compete with the first couple in the final round.

In the final round the two couples competed to see which pair was most compatible by trying to match answers to statements like "I once had a crush on one of my teachers" by holding up cards that said "Me" or "Not Me." The couple with the most matches won and moved on to the daily bonus round.

The winning couple of the day was asked six questions, for which one player predicted his or her date's behavior on true/false statements. They received $50 toward their date, and if they got at least four right they returned at the end of the week to compete for a trip.

BIG DEAL!

premiere: September 1, 1996   *packager:* Stone-Stanley Productions/New World Entertainment   *broadcast history:* Fox primetime September 1, 1996–October 6, 1996   *host:* Mark DeCarlo   *announcer:* John Cramer   *field announcer:* Tom Kelly   *dancers:* Lindsley Allen, Robin Antin, Joie Shettler, Stella Angelova   *executive in charge of production:* Heidi Cayn   *executive producers:* Scott Stone, David Stanley   *producers:* Gary Auerbach, Mark Cronin   *director:* Sandi Fullerton   *production designers:* Joe Stewart, John Shaffner, Scott Storey   *origination:* Studio 2, Disney Studios, Burbank

"Big Deal!" was one of the few attempts to bring game shows back to primetime network television in the 1990s. Inspired by the long-running "LET'S MAKE A DEAL," this one-hour series with former "Studs" host Mark DeCarlo as emcee had a brief six-week run on the Fox network in fall 1996.

Members of the studio audience were selected to participate in various stunts and games. Among the stunts featured on the first show were a cow milking contest and a family throwing baseballs through the windows of their house to win a vacation.

If a player succeeded, he or she won a prize, which could be swapped for another prize before the first gift was revealed. Like the original "Let's Make a Deal," there was always the chance that the player was trading a valuable prize for a worthless one.

At the end of the show, two players were given the opportunity to trade what they had won on the show for a chance at the Big Deal, their choice of one of three video walls and what was behind it.

THE BIG GAME

premiere: June 13, 1958   *packager:* Jackson Stanley Productions   *broadcast history:* NBC primetime June 13, 1958–September 19, 1958   *host:* Tom Kennedy   *announcers:* Wendell Niles, Johnny Jacobs   *producer:* Jackson Stanley   *directors:* Bill Bennington, Dick Weinberg   *set designer:*

Big game hunter Tom Kennedy in search of the extremely exotic double-breasted bush turkey.

Raphael Bretton   *music director:* Ivan Ditmars   *origination:* NBC Studio 4, Burbank

This game show was based on the game "Battleships." On "The Big Game," two contestants answered various questions. Correct responses allowed a player to take a shot at a pegged translucent animal on the opponent's board. Bagging the animal earned the player cash.

Each contestant was called a "hunter" and was given three magnetic animals to place in his or her "jungle"—which was visible only to the player and the audience. Each jungle game board had twenty-five spaces in which the player could hide the animals. A rhino covered two spaces; a lion, three; and a crocodile, four.

Players were asked questions worth three to six shots. The kinds of questions included spelling words and naming songs. Knocking out the first animal was worth $100; the second, $400; and the third, $1,500. The first player to bag all of his opponent's animals won the game.

Did you know . . .   Tom Kennedy made his network debut as a game show host on this program?

Producer Jackson Stanley was a long-time writer on the PEOPLE ARE FUNNY radio and TV series.

THE BIG PAYOFF

premiere: December 31, 1951   *packager:* Walt Framer Productions   *broadcast history:* NBC daytime December 31, 1951–March 27, 1953; NBC primetime June 29, 1952–September 14, 1952; CBS daytime March 30, 1953–October 16, 1959; NBC primetime June 21, 1953–September 27, 1953   *hosts:* Randy Merriman, Robert Paige, Bert Parks   *substitute hosts:* Bobby Sherwood, Warren Hull, Ralph Paul, Bob Haymes, Jimmy Blaine   *hostess:* Bess Myerson   *substitute hostesses:* Hollis Burke, Sydney Smith   *question girl:* Susan Sayers   *models:* Pat Conlon, Nancy Walters, Marion James, Pat Conway, Fran Miller   *singers:* Betty Ann Grove, Denise Lor, Judy Lynn   *announcers:* Ralph Paul, Mort Lawrence   *producers:* Walt Framer, Joseph Gottlieb, Sid Tamber   *directors:* Paul Alter, Mike Case, Jeff Hayden, Ken Whelan   *music:* Burt Buhrman Trio   *origination:* Roof of Amsterdam Theater, New York; Colonial Theater, New York; CBS Studios 62 and 50, New York

Colgate-Palmolive sponsored this popular daytime series that was part quiz show, part fashion show. On "The Big Payoff," contestants were selected on the merit of the letters sent in by men who told why the women in their lives deserved the wonderful prizes offered. The men then had to answer three questions correctly to receive the prizes. If a man could answer a fourth question, he won a mink coat and a trip anywhere in the world that Pan American Airways (later KLM Royal Dutch Airlines) flew.

Preceding each payoff question was a fashion show with a commentary by hostess Bess Myerson. Questions were delivered on a silver tray by Susan Sayers. Among the many models who appeared on the show were Nancy Walters, Marion James, and Pat Conway.

Music was provided by the Burt Buhrman Trio. In February 1953, singer Betty Ann Grove joined the show. She stayed until March 22, 1957 and was replaced by vocalist Judy Lynn.

Other regular features included: "Little Big Payoff," in which children played; "Turn About Payoff," in which women played for the men in their lives; "Bridal Payoff," which was for engaged couples; "Blessed Payoff," which was for expectant mothers; and "Knight in Shining Armor," which was for single women.

Did you know . . .   original host Randy Merriman left the show in December 1957 to return to Minneapolis? He was replaced by actor-singer Bob Paige who stayed until September 1959. Game show veteran Bert Parks took over on September 28, 1959 as "The Big Payoff" revised its format. Three couples now competed against each other in a guessing game, with the highest score after three questions going for the jackpot of a mink coat and a trip. Three weeks later, CBS dropped the show.

"The Big Payoff" was also seen on Sunday evenings during the summers of 1952 and 1953 as a replacement for the "Colgate Comedy Hour."

The show was recreated for the 1958 Columbia Pictures movie *Miss Casey Jones.*

Hostess Bess Myerson, Miss America for 1945, would later serve as New York City commissioner of consumer affairs.

THE BIG SHOWDOWN

premiere: December 23, 1974 *packager:* Don Lipp–Ron Greenberg Productions *broadcast history:* ABC daytime December 23, 1974–July 4, 1975 *host:* Jim Peck *assistant:* Heather Cunningham *announcer:* Dan Daniels *executive producers:* Ron Greenberg, Don Lipp *producer:* Shelley Dobbins *director:* Dick Schneider *set designer:* Ron Baldwin *origination:* ABC Studio TV–15, New York

In "The Big Showdown," three contestants competed in a question-and-answer game. In order to win, the contestant had to reach a target number established at the beginning of the game. To begin the game a toss-up question was read. The first player to buzz in got a chance to answer. If correct, the player received one point and control of the board that contained six numbers, each worth between one and six points. The first player to reach the target number exactly won the money and another round began. The two highest scoring players moved on to compete in "Final Showdown."

In the Final Showdown round, a target number of seven was established and questions worth one, two, or three points were revealed. The player who answered a question correctly controlled the choice of the next question and point value. The first player to reach the target number won the game, $250 in cash, and a chance to win $10,000.

The winner of the second round was then escorted to a dice board. Two dice, one of which contained the word "Show" on one face and the other with the word "Down" on one face were used. The player was given one roll to throw the dice and have the words Show and Down appear for $10,000. If he or she failed, the player was given thirty seconds to roll the dice as many times as possible to have the words appear for $5,000.

A contestant just won $10,000 for rolling "Show Down!" Assistant Heather Cunningham shares in his excitement.

Did you know . . .   A pilot of "The Big Showdown" was taped in 1973 and was just known as SHOWDOWN? A year later, in 1974, another pilot was ordered from ABC and that second version made it to the ABC daytime schedule. Emcee Jim Peck was creator Ronnie Greenberg's choice to host both pilots.

THE BIG SURPRISE

premiere: October 8, 1955 *packager:* Louis Cowan Productions/Entertainment Prod. Inc. *broadcast history:* NBC primetime October 8, 1955–June 9, 1956; NBC primetime September 18, 1956–April 2, 1957 *hosts:* Jack Barry, Mike Wallace *assistant:* Lorraine Rogers *"easy question girl":* Sue Oakland *"hard question girl":* Mary Gardner *announcers:* Lee Vines, Jack Clark *executive producers:* Steve Carlin, Harry Fleishman *producers:* Joe Cates, Seymour Robbie, David Lowe, Merrill Heatter *directors:* Joe Cates, Seymour Robbie, David Lowe, Frederick Carr *set designer:* Eddie Gilbert *music director:* Norman Leyden *origination:* NBC Studio 6A, New York

NBC jumped onto the big-money quiz show bandwagon with "The Big Surprise" in the fall of 1955. Contestants answered questions in a chosen category in their quest to win up to $100,000.

During the first six months on the air the program underwent numerous format changes. Originally, contestants were people who had performed some worthy deed. They appeared with their "reporters" who came along to tell why they had suggested the contestant. The game consisted of questions based on the contestant's family, friends, hometown, hobbies, and special interests, with correct answers taking the player from $1 to $100,000. If a contestant missed one of the first four questions, the game was over.

At one point during the game, a contestant could be "rescued" if he or she missed a question by having someone else correctly answer a substitute question. The rescuer then got ten percent of the winnings.

Another innovation was the use of "easy" and "hard" questions. If players missed easy questions they lost all of their winnings, while if they missed hard questions, they only lost half. Easy questions were brought in by Sue Oakland and hard ones by Mary Gardner.

On March 10, 1956 Mike Wallace replaced Jack Barry as host of the show. By this time, the format had evolved into a quiz where the contestant chose a category and then answered ten questions ranging in value from $100 to $100,000. The contestant could also answer two insurance questions that would guarantee all of the winnings up to that time even if he or she missed a subsequent question.

All questions above the $2,000 level were prepared under the supervision of James Colvin of the *Encyclopedia Britannica* editorial board.

During the summer of 1956 "The Big Surprise" was replaced by another Louis Cowan game show, DOWN YOU GO.

Here's a shot of Mike Wallace hosting "The Big Surprise" as he greets a young contender some twelve years before "60 Minutes."

Were you watching when . . . movie superstar Errol Flynn was a celebrity contestant on the version Mike Wallace hosted?

THE BILL GWINN SHOW
premiere: February 5, 1951   *packager:* Bill Gwinn–Jesse Martin Productions   *broadcast history:* ABC primetime February 5, 1951–April 21, 1952   *host:* Bill Gwinn *announcer:* Lou Cook   *producers:* Jesse Martin, Stuart Phelps   *director:* Stuart Phelps   *set designers:* Herbert O. Phillips, Al Goodman   *music director:* Rex Koury *theme:* "The Song Is You," sung by Bill Gwinn   *origination:* Studio A, ABC Television Center, Los Angeles

On "The Bill Gwinn Show," couples came on and told their love story on a set reminiscent of where they met, and related a song that best exemplified their relationship and the role of that song in their lives. The studio audience then selected the couple with the best story for prizes.

This program began on Los Angeles TV station KECA in January 1951 under the title "It Could Happen to You." When it went to the network a month later the title became IT COULD BE YOU. A few weeks later it became "This Could Be You" and by April it was called "The Bill Gwinn Show." In the last month on the air the title was again changed, this time to "This Is My Song."

Host Bill Gwinn was better known to Los Angeles audiences as emcee of the musical quiz show "What's the Name of That Song?", which was seen in Southern California from 1948 to 1959.

BLACKOUT
premiere: January 4, 1988   *packager:* Jay Wolpert Productions/Taft Entertainment   *broadcast history:* CBS daytime January 4, 1988–April 1, 1988   *host:* Bob Goen *announcers:* Johnny Gilbert, Jay Stewart   *creator/executive producer:* Jay Wolpert   *producers:* Randy Neece, Joel Hecht   *director:* John Dorsey *set designer:* Ed Flesh *music:* Middle C Productions, Chip Lewis   *origination:* Studio 33, CBS Television City, Los Angeles   *debut guests:* Markie Post, Charles Siebert

On "Blackout," two celebrity contestant teams tried to complete a pun that had four words missing, which they attempted to guess. One member of a team attempted to describe one of the missing words to his or her partner within a twenty-second time limit. The description was recorded and during the playback the opposing team could "blackout" up to seven seconds. If one team couldn't correctly guess the clue, the opposing team had a chance to guess the answer. The first team to solve two puns won the game.

The winning team could earn up to $10,000 in the bonus round by guessing five subjects from an assortment of clues in a seventy-second time limit. One team member was shown clues that appeared one at a time. When the contestant felt enough clues had been revealed for their partner to guess the subject, it was then presented to the partner for him or her to solve.

BLADE WARRIORS

premiere: October 1, 1994   *packager:* Blade Warrior Productions/Select Media **broadcast history:** Syndicated October 1, 1994–April 30, 1995   *hosts:* Mac Maki, Jim Davidson, Kiana Tom **warriors:** (male) Cory Miller, Alan Vano, Pat Parnell, Eric Wylie, Chris Mitchell, A. J. Jackson (female) Kim Bowie, Kati Blumer, Donna Dennis, Deanna Wilshire **executive producers:** Mitch Gutkowski, Marc Juris, Michael Haigney **coordinating producer:** Keiren Fisher **games creator:** John Troxtel   **set designer:** Tom Buderwitz **music:** Ronnie Lawson, Larry Jurvis **origination:** Barker Hanger, Santa Monica Airport

"Blade Warriors" was a weekly one-hour competition featuring players who tested their athletic ability by completing stunts as they skated. Competition was held between two male players and two female players and the team with the highest point score at the end of the show moved on to another round in a thirteen-week elimination series. At the end of the season the winners of each of the two thirteen-week competitions played for a grand prize of $100,000.

Some of the six events that were featured on each show were "Bladeball," "Techno-Tag," "Slam Shot," and "Full Tilt." Each player competed against the show's regulars, called "warriors," for points that varied from event to event.

The final event was the "Steeple Skate," an obstacle course worth thirty-five points to the player who completed it in the fastest time.

"Blade Warriors" was the first athletic competition game show to feature "in-line skating," often called rollerblading. The term refers to the wheels of the skate, which are set in a line. The sport became popular in the 1980s but its origins can be traced back about two hundred years.

BLANK CHECK

premiere: January 6, 1975   *packager:* Jack Barry Productions **broadcast history:** NBC daytime January 6, 1975–July 4, 1975   *host:* Art James **assistant:** Judy Rich **announcers:** Johnny Jacobs, Johnny Gilbert **creators:** William T. Naud, Rich Jeffries **executive producer:** Jack Barry **producer:** Mike Metzger **director:** Richard Kline **set designer:** Ed Flesh **origination:** NBC Studios 2 and 4, Burbank

Six contestants, playing on a week's worth of programs, competed in a game of second-guessing. The object of "Blank Check" was to successfully complete a four-digit check from five randomly selected numbers, thereby winning that amount.

To begin the game, one contestant became the check writer and the other five vied for the opportunity to replace the check writer by first answering a riddle. The player who answered the riddle correctly then guessed which of five randomly selected numbers the check writer had picked to begin his or her check. If correct, the challenger became the new check writer, but if incorrect, the writer added the number to his or her check.

A check writer completing three digits on a check was then challenged by a member of the studio audience to guess what the fourth digit would be. Contestants won whatever checks they completed during the week and a bonus prize was awarded to the contestant who wrote the highest check.

BLANKETY BLANKS

premiere: April 21, 1975   *packager:* Bob Stewart Productions **broadcast history:** ABC daytime April 21, 1975–June 27, 1975   *host:* Bill Cullen **announcer:** Bob Clayton **executive producer:** Bob Stewart **producers:** Anne Marie Schmidt, Donald Epstein **director:** Mike Garguilo **set designer:** Warren Clymer **music:** Score Productions **origination:** Elysee Theater, New York **debut guests:** Anne Meara, William Shatner

Four contestants competed in this humorous word game "Blankety Blanks." A subject category was revealed along with six numbers which concealed clues to the subjects identity. The host selected a card from a spinning wheel and placed it in an electronic machine that pinpointed one of the four players and revealed a dollar amount, from $10 to $100.

The player selected a clue and received a chance to identify the subject. If correct, the player received the money. If not, another player was selected in the same manner and the game continued.

After each subject was guessed, that player's money could be doubled by solving a "Blankety Blank," a nonsense riddle (example: "The bird who spoke up in prison was a real ———"). If the player guessed correctly (answer: "stool pigeon"), he or she won the money. The first player to score $2,000 was the winner.

The four contestants were divided into two teams of two, with each team having one celebrity partner.

Did you know . . . during 1975, Bill Cullen was seen on three different game shows? In addition to hosting "Blankety Blanks" for ABC, he emceed the syndicated "The $25,000 Pyramid" and was a panelist on TO TELL THE TRUTH.

BLIND DATE

premiere: May 5, 1949   *packager:* Bernard Shubert Productions **broadcast history:** ABC primetime May 5, 1949–June 8, 1950; ABC primetime August 31, 1950–September 20, 1951; NBC primetime June 7, 1952–July 19, 1952; DuMont primetime June 9, 1953–September 15, 1953   *hosts:* Arlene Francis, Jan Murray **announcers:** Walter Herlihy, Rex Marshall, Terry O'Sullivan **creator:** Tom Wallace **producers:** Bernard Shubert, Richard Lewis, Mike Dutton **directors:** Fred Carr, Richard Lewis, Ed Nugent, Alan Neuman, Lawrence Schwab **set designer:** Beulah Frankel **music directors:** Glenn Osser, Ray Bloch **origination:** New Amsterdam Theater, New York (1952)

Six men, known as the "Hunters," from various colleges tried to win dates from three women, known as the "Hunted," for expense-paid dates on the town including invitations to the Stork Club in New York.

On "Blind Date," the men were seated on one side of a wall and telephoned one of the women seated on the other side. Each man attempted to talk her into accepting a date. On the basis of answers to specially prepared questions and the sound of his voice, the woman chose the man who impressed her the most.

From the theater balcony, a bird's-eye view of celebrity guests Anita Gillette and Soupy Sales participating in the fun of "Blankety Blanks," hosted by Bill Cullen.

"Blind Date" began as a radio series on NBC, premiering on July 8, 1943.

When the show returned in May 1953, it was called YOUR BIG MOMENT with host Melvyn Douglas. After three weeks, Jan Murray became the new host and the title went back to "Blind Date."

Did you know . . . Arlene Francis made her Broadway debut in the play *One Good Year* at the Fulton Theater in February 1936?

BLOCKBUSTERS

premiere: October 27, 1980   *packager:* Mark Goodson–Bill Todman Productions   *broadcast history:* NBC daytime October 27, 1980–April 23, 1982; NBC daytime January 5, 1987–May 1, 1987
1980–1982 version
host: Bill Cullen   *announcer:* Bob Hilton, Johnny Olson, Rich Jeffries   *executive producer/director:* Ira Skutch   *producer:* Robert Sherman   *set designer:* Dennis Roof   *music:* Bob Cobert   *origination:* NBC Studios 2 and 3, Burbank
1987 version
host: Bill Rafferty   *announcer:* Rich Jeffries   *executive producer:* Robert Sherman   *producer:* Diane Janaver   *director:* Marc Breslow   *set designer:* Dennis Roof   *music:* Music Design Group, Stanley Blits   *origination:* NBC Studios 3 and 4, Burbank

In the original 1980 version of "Blockbusters," a team of two related players were pitted against a single player in a question-and-answer game. Correct answers enabled a team to link blocks vertically or horizontally on a game board. The first team to connect a path of their blocks from one side of the board to the other won the game and $250.

The winning team played a similar type of game for bonus money. In the "Gold Run" they tried to connect a series of blocks from one side to the other by answering rapid-fire questions in a sixty-second time limit. They won $100 for each block and $5,000 if they completed the "gold run."

When the show returned in 1987, the following changes were made. The teams were eliminated and only two players competed, with a best two-out-of-three match determining the winner. The players got $100 for each game won and played for $5,000 in the bonus round.

Did you know . . . a coauthor of this book, Steve Ryan, was cocreator of this popular NBC game show?

After more than four decades of game show hosting, Bill Cullen received his first Emmy nomination for best game show host, for his hosting duties on "Blockbusters."

In the 1998 film *Great Expectations*, starring Ethan Hawke and Gwyneth Paltrow, a clip of "Blockbusters" (featuring Bill Cullen) was seen in the movie. This was the first time "Blockbusters" was featured in a blockbuster movie.

BOARDWALK AND BASEBALL'S SUPER BOWL OF SPORTS TRIVIA

premiere: January 28, 1988   *packager:* Ohlmeyer Communications   *broadcast history:* ESPN (cable) January 28, 1988–May 16, 1988; ESPN (cable) April 3, 1989–September 18, 1989; ESPN-2 (cable) October 4, 1993–January 7, 1994

After three decades of hosting some of America's favorite game shows, Bill Cullen received his first Emmy nomination for best game show host of "Blockbusters," a show cocreated by puzzle master Steve Ryan.

(repeats of 1988 and 1989 series)   *host:* Chris Berman   *producer:* Gary Cox   *director:* Robert Katz   *set designer:* Jimmy Cuomo   *origination:* Boardwalk & Baseball Amusement Park, Orlando

ESPN sportscaster Chris Berman hosted this sports-trivia quiz that featured students representing thirty-two colleges, competing for a top prize of $10,000. On each show of "Boardwalk and Baseball's Super Bowl of Sports Trivia," two teams of three players competed in a single elimination match.

In round one, a question ("the kick-off") was asked and the first player to buzz in could earn five points for a correct answer and five additional bonus points on the "extra point" questions. Players could confer with their teammates on the extra point questions.

In round two, the point values were doubled to ten points with the same question format as in round one.

In round three, each team chose a category from four possible choices. Teams alternated answering questions valued at ten points each from their chosen categories. If a team came up with the wrong answer, the opposing team could pick up those points by answering the question correctly.

The final round was a hundred-second race against the clock called the "lightning round." In this rapid-fire series of questions, teams received ten points for right answers and lost ten points for wrong guesses. The team with the most points at the end of this round moved on to the next round of competition.

BODY LANGUAGE

premiere: June 4, 1984   *packager:* Mark Goodson Productions   *broadcast history:* CBS daytime June 4, 1984–January 3, 1986   *host:* Tom Kennedy   *announcers:* Johnny Olson, Gene Wood, Bob Hilton   *executive producer:* Chester Feldman   *producer:* Mimi O'Brien   *director:* Paul Alter   *set designer:* Jack Hart   *music:* Score Productions   *origination:* Studio 33, CBS Television City, Los Angeles   *debut guests:* Vicki Lawrence, Jamie Farr

Two teams, each composed of a celebrity guest and a contestant competed on "Body Language." One player became the "guesser," the other the "actor." The guesser tried to come up with the five words pantomimed by the actor in sixty seconds. Each correct guess placed that word in a puzzle with seven blanks. The guesser who solved the puzzle won $100. The value of the following rounds increased in value and the first team to score $500 won the game.

In the bonus round, one player tried to guess ten words at $100 each, acted out by his partner in sixty seconds. If the player could guess three more words in an additional twenty seconds, the number of correct guesses was multiplied by $1,000.

Were you watching when . . . America's favorite funny lady, Lucille Ball was a guest on ''Body Language''? She guested on the show several times. The reason? Physical comedy, of course!

BOGGLE—THE INTERACTIVE GAME

premiere: March 7, 1994 *packager:* Martindale-Hillier Productions/Fiedler-Berlin Productions **broadcast history:** Family Channel (cable) March 7, 1994–November 18, 1994 *host:* Wink Martindale *announcer:* Randy West *executive producers:* Wink Martindale, Bill Hillier **supervising producers:** Peter Berlin, Rob Fiedler *producer:* Gary Johnson *director:* Rob Fiedler *set designer:* Scott Storey *music:* Ed Lojeski *origination:* Glendale Studios, Glendale

The board game ''Boggle'' became part of the second series of interactive game shows introduced by the Family Channel. Premiering in March 1994, along with SHUFFLE—THE INTERACTIVE GAME, home viewers with touch-tone telephones were given a chance to play a specially designed version of ''Boggle'' during ''Shuffle Play Breaks'' for prizes.

In the studio game, four players participated in a series of elimination rounds, playing a hidden word game. Each player had a grid resembling a telephone key pad of twelve numbers with a series of letters next to each number. A series of four- and five-letter words were hidden among the letters available on the pad. After a clue was given, each player had ten seconds to punch in the correct number sequence to create the word. Each clue appeared after three seconds when the first letter of the answer was revealed. Each word was worth up to one thousand points and the players' scores were determined by how fast they punched in their answers.

Each of the three rounds in the game consisted of five questions with the low-scoring player eliminated after each round until only one player remained. The remaining player received the trip of the day.

A new combination of letters was revealed at the beginning of each round (though each time, the lowest scoring player from the previous round was eliminated) and all other players' scores returned to zero at the same time.

BORN LUCKY

premiere: October 5, 1992 *packager:* Stone-Stanley Productions **broadcast history:** Lifetime (cable) October 5, 1992–April 2, 1993; Lifetime (cable) July 5, 1993–December 31, 1993 *host:* Bob Goen *announcer:* Jonathan Coleman *creator:* Tony McLaren *executive producers:* Scott Stone, David Stanley *producer:* Stephen Brown *director:* Bob Loudin *set designers:* Joe Stewart, John Shaffner *music:* Gary Scott *origination:* various malls around the country

Four contestants competed in a stunt game show taped at various shopping malls for a chance at $2,000 in mall money. The first week's shows of ''Born Lucky'' were taped at the Glendale Galleria in California.

Each player had a chance to win up to $100 in the first round by participating in a stunt, such as trying to follow a sequence of commands, moving an item through a maze using a magnet held in the mouth, in sixty seconds, or solving

a series of brainteasers. The top two highest scoring players moved on to the second round.

In the second round, the ''challenge round,'' the two remaining players bid against each other to see who could accomplish a particular stunt, like putting on several jackets in sixty seconds. If the player who won the challenge accomplished the stunt, he or she became the winner, otherwise the opponent became the victor.

The winning player then got a chance to win $2,000 in mall money by accomplishing a series of five additional stunts in ninety seconds.

Did you know . . . Bob Goen began his broadcasting career as a disc jockey for KFOX–AM in Long Beach, California in 1977? He later became a sports anchor for a TV station in Palm Springs before hosting his first game show, PERFECT MATCH, in 1986. Goen is currently the cohost of ''Entertainment Tonight.''

BRAINS AND BRAWN

premiere: September 13, 1958 *packager:* Ile de France International Productions *broadcast history:* NBC primetime September 13, 1958–December 27, 1958 *hosts:* Fred Davis and Jack Lescoulie *announcer:* Bill Wendell *producer:* Herb Moss *directors:* Paul Bogart, Craig Allen *set designer:* Maurice Gordon *music director:* Louis Geristo *origination:* NBC Studio 8H, New York and on location *debut guests:* Sam Snead, Tommy Bolt, Kurt Stehling, Willy Ley

Two teams, each composed of a professional expert (''brains'') and a top sports athlete (''brawn''), competed against each other in ''Brains and Brawn,'' test of mental and physical skills for cash prizes of up to $30,000. The losing team received a Lark Studebaker station wagon as a consolation prize.

The ''brains'' segment was broadcast from NBC Studios in New York City and the ''brawn'' segment on location depending on the type of athletic contest. By November 1, the entire show was done on location.

Based on a European game show created by Pierre Bellemare, ''Brains and Brawn'' consisted of five rounds of competition. Round one was worth $2,000; round two, $4,000; round three, $6,000; round four, $8,000; and round five, $10,000. Each round was broken down into two parts, with each team member competing for half of the available prize money. The brains competed against each other in the quiz segment, while the brawns were pitted against each other in an athletic contest in their own sport.

The questions were authenticated by the *Encyclopedia Americana* and the sporting events were designed by *Sports Illustrated* magazine.

The premiere program featured the team of golfer Tommy Bolt and missile-and-space expert Willy Ley competing against golf legend Sam Snead and chief of the rocket group for the U.S. Navy's Operation Vanguard, Kurt Stehling. The brains answered questions on rockets and space while the golfers competed in putting and approaching the green on location, at the Winged Foot Golf Club in Mamaroneck, New York. (The ''Bolt-Ley'' team won the day's events.)

Among the other celebrities and athletes who were contestants on ''Brains and Brawn'' were basketball stars Bob Cousy and Bob Pettit, Olympic champs Bob Mathias and the Reverend Bob Richards, show biz experts Gypsy Rose Lee and actor Burt Wheeler, and baseball players Willie Mays and Jackie Jensen, who competed in a test of base-running, ball-throwing, and home-run hitting at the Polo Grounds in New York.

Did you know . . . co-host Jack Lescoulie was the original announcer on NBC's ''Today'' show? Announcer Bill Wendell was Ernie Kovacs' announcer in the 1950s and has been David Letterman's announcer since 1982.

BRAINS & BRAWN

premiere: July 10, 1993 *packager:* NBC Productions *broadcast history:* NBC Saturday morning July 10, 1993–October 16, 1993 *host:* Mark-Paul Gosselaar *cohosts:* Danielle Harris, Tatyana Ali *executive producer:* Gary Considine *director:* Rob Katz *set designers:* Josee Lemonnier, Ron Olsen *music:* Scott Gale, Rich Eames *origination:* Universal Studios, Hollywood

In the 1990s version of ''Brains & Brawn'' two teams of teenagers competed against each other in a test of mind and body. Mark-Paul Gosselaar of the TV show ''Saved by the Bell'' emceed the weekly competition with Danielle Harris of ''Roseanne'' and Tatyana Ali of ''The Fresh Prince of Bel-Air'' alternating as cohosts.

Each team, consisting of three players, including a celebrity captain, competed in six rounds of academic and physical challenges.

The game began with a two-minute drill of multiple choice questions. Each of the six players locked in their answers and earned ten points for their team for correct responses.

Round two was called ''Slamball.'' One player hit balls, within a thirty-second time limit, trying to score ten points for each goal knocked through the basket, while a member of the opposing team tried to block his or her shots.

The third round, ''Shoot to Kill,'' tested the basketball skills of the players. In thirty seconds, two players tried to shoot free throws while a member of the opposing team tried to block their shots. Ten points were earned for each basket and both teams got a chance to play.

In round four the teams tried to pick out the nonmatching name from a series of three words. In round five, the teams played a form of volleyball. Each player was connected by a bungee cord and had to hit balls over a net that was blacked out to hide the opposing team. Each team scored twenty points for each win in this three-minute round.

The sixth and last round featured an obstacle course which concluded the day's contest on ''Brains & Brawn.'' The team with the most points got a one-second head start for each ten-point advantage they had over the other team. The first team to cross the finish line won the game and received the prizes.

BREAK THE BANK

premiere: October 22, 1948 *packager:* Wolf Productions *broadcast history:* ABC primetime October 22, 1948–September 23, 1949; NBC primetime October 5, 1949–January 9, 1952; CBS primetime January 13, 1952–February 1, 1953; NBC daytime March 30, 1953–September 18, 1953; NBC primetime June 23, 1953–September 1, 1953; ABC primetime January 31, 1954–June 20, 1956; NBC primetime October 9, 1956–January 15, 1957

1948–1953 primetime version

host: Bert Parks *cohost:* Bud Collyer *substitute hosts:* Peter Donald, Johnny Olson *assistant (''the paying teller''):* Janice Gilbert *announcers:* Bob Shepard, Win Elliott *producers:* Ed Wolf, Herb Wolf, Jack Rubin *directors:* Marshall Dirkin, Craig Allen, Lloyd Gross *set designer:* Bob Markell *music director:* Peter Van Steeden *origination:* NBC Studio 8H, New York (1949–1952)

1953 daytime version

host: Bud Collyer *assistant:* Janice Gilbert *announcer:* Win Elliott *producers:* Jack Rubin, Herb Wolf *director:* Craig Allen *music:* Ernestine Holmes at the organ *origination:* NBC Studio 6B, New York

1954–1956 version

host: Bert Parks *substitute host:* Bill Cullen *assistant:* Janice Gilbert *announcer:* Johnny Olson *commercial announcer:* Rex Marshall *producers:* Herb Wolf, Jack Rubin *directors:* Lloyd Gross, Matt Harlib *music director:* Peter Van Steeden *origination:* New York

1956–1957 version ''Break the $250,000 Bank''

host: Bert Parks *assistant:* Janice Gilbert *announcer:* Johnny Olson *final authority:* Joseph Nathan Kane *executive producer:* Ed Wolf *producer:* Jack Rubin *director:* Lloyd Gross *music director:* Peter Van Steeden *origination:* Century Theater, New York; Ziegfeld Theater, New York

One of the first successful TV game shows, ''Break the Bank'' came from radio, where it first aired on July 5, 1946. The show made the transition to the small screen in the fall of 1948. Bert Parks emceed the radio version and was joined by Bud Collyer when the show came to television. In addition to the primetime version, NBC aired a daytime version during 1953 with Bud Collyer as sole host.

To begin the game, contestants from the studio audience selected a category and were asked a series of questions with values beginning at $25 increasing to $500. One wrong answer was permitted, but two wrong answers eliminated the player, whose winnings were then forfeited to the bank. If, the player successfully completed the $500 question (''the gateway to the bank'') he or she had a chance to ''break the bank'' by correctly answering one more question. The value of the bank depended on how long it had been since the last contestant ''broke the bank.'' The bank's minimum value was $1,000. During the summer of 1950 a record bank of $8,870 was won.

A regular feature during 1950 was the ''wish bowl,'' where viewers sent in penny postcards for a chance at being called and invited to New York to be on the show. The lucky viewer received a three-day stay for two at the Statler Hotel and $150 for spending money.

Ten years after the success of "The Hollywood Squares" came a revival of "Break the Bank," with nine celebrities and an even bigger game board.

During 1953 another feature was the "bank holdup," where a camera panned the studio audience until an alarm went off. The person on whom the camera stopped was given the opportunity to win a special prize.

Among the guest hosts who filled in during the vacations of Bert Parks and Bud Collyer were "Break the Bank" announcer Johnny Olson, Bill Cullen, Bob Shepard, Win Elliott, Walter O'Keefe, Edward Arnold, and Buddy Rodgers. Also featured on the show was "the paying teller" Janice Gilbert, daughter of creator Ed Wolf.

When the show returned in the fall of 1956 the big-money quiz craze was the rage and "Break the Bank" became "Break the $250,000 Bank."

Competing on the new version of "Break the Bank" were contestants with specialized knowledge in specific categories. They were asked five $100 questions and, if successful, a $5,000 question. Upon reaching that plateau they appeared on the next program to answer questions worth $10,000. Prize money increased with additional appearances on the show.

On the show, the contestant's immediate family and close friends sat in an area on stage called the "family circle." The player who couldn't answer a particular question could call on a member of the circle for help.

All questions at the $5,000 level and above were answered on a part of the stage called the "Hall of Knowledge." "Break the $250,000 Bank" did not last long enough for anyone to reach the maximum. The record winning was $60,000, by Dr. Harry Duncan, a seventy-nine-year-old dentist whose category was religion.

BREAK THE BANK

premiere: April 12, 1976 *packager:* Jack Barry and Dan Enright Productions *broadcast history:* ABC daytime April 12, 1976–July 23, 1976; Syndicated September 18, 1976–September 11, 1977 *hosts:* Tom Kennedy, Jack Barry *announcers:* Johnny Jacobs, Ernie Anderson *producers:* Jack Barry, Dan Enright *director:* Richard Kline *set designer:* John C. Mula *music:* Stu Levin *origination:* Studio 55, ABC Television Center, Los Angeles *debut guests:* Lynda Carter, Jo Ann Pflug, Jan Murray, Liz Torres, Dick Gautier, Alice Ghostly, Marjoe Gortner, Abe Vigoda, Robert Hegyes

Two contestants competed on this "Break the Bank," an updated version of the 1950s game show of the same name. Squares, numbered from one to twenty, were located on a large playing board and one player selected a square. Two celebrities, each represented by that square, gave their response to a question. One celebrity gave the correct answer, the other an incorrect answer. The contestant who picked the celebrity giving the right answer, won the box and continued to play. To win the game, a player had to acquire three boxes with the same money amount. To break the bank, a player had to find three special boxes scattered throughout the board.

Tom Kennedy was host of this ABC network version of "Break the Bank," and Jack Barry emceed the syndicated edition.

BREAK THE BANK

premiere: September 16, 1985   *packager:* Kline and Friends for Blair Entertainment   *broadcast history:* Syndicated September 16, 1985–September 12, 1986   *hosts:* Gene Rayburn, Joe Farago   *assistant:* Julie Hayek   *announcer:* Michael Hanks   *executive producer/director:* Richard Kline   *producer:* Gary Cox   *set designer:* John C. Mula   *music:* Hal Hidey   *origination:* Hollywood Center TV Studios

Another version of "Break the Bank" appeared in syndication in the 1985–1986 season, this one completely different from the two earlier versions.

Two couples played against each other to answer general knowledge questions. Each question was worth a different value of time (from five to one hundred seconds), and each team received a clue to a puzzle for each correct answer. (Example: clues . . . Fire-Butler-Mitchell-O'Hara-Atlanta-Book—answer . . . *Gone With the Wind*.) The first team to solve two puzzles won the game.

Using the time won in the main game, the winning team attempted to win merchandise prizes by completing a variety of stunts. Stunts ranged from correctly guessing what sport a mime was performing, to correctly guessing faces on a tic-tac-toe board, to identifying popular songs played on a xylophone. The team earned a bank card for each event they successfully completed. At the end of the game, the teams used their accumulated bank cards to try to open a vault, if the card worked, the team won its contents.

In December, Joe Farago became the new host of "Break the Bank," and soon after the format was altered. Players simply guessed puzzles from up to six clues and a corresponding bonus round featured another puzzle. Each team could win up to ten bank cards but for every clue they used in their attempt to solve the puzzle, they forfeited their bank cards. Each card was worth cash or prizes, with one card bankrupting them and another card breaking the bank.

Did you know . . . after his stint as host of "Break the Bank," Joe Farago made the switch to the lucrative career of hosting television infomercials?

BROADWAY TO HOLLYWOOD HEADLINE CLUES

premiere: July 4, 1949   *packager:* DuMont Television   *broadcast history:* DuMont daytime July 4, 1949–May 4, 1951; DuMont primetime July 20, 1949–July 15, 1954   *hosts:* George F. Putnam, Don Russell, Bill Slater, Conrad Nagel   *producers:* Ted Hammerstein, Jerry Gross, Edgar Higgins Jr., Marion Glick   *director:* Pat Fay   *origination:* New York

This combination magazine news program and quiz show made its debut under the title "Headline Clues" in July 1949. The primetime version adopted the "Broadway to Hollywood Headline Clues" title on October 21, 1949 with the daytime version keeping the shorter title.

The program opened with a summary of the day's news. Then in the quiz show segment of the program viewers were telephoned and asked questions on the news stories, for prizes. By 1951, the quiz segment was dropped and the show became a news and feature show.

Did you know . . . George Putnam, who would later achieve greater recognition as a newscaster in the Los Angeles area during the 1950s and 60s, was the original host of the primetime version? He later became a radio talk show host in Southern California and frequently rode his horse in the annual Tournament of Roses Parade. Putnam left the show in February 1951 and was replaced by Bill Slater.

DuMont network announcer Don Russell emceed the daytime version.

BRUCE FORSYTH'S HOT STREAK

premiere: January 6, 1986   *packager:* Reg Grundy Productions   *broadcast history:* ABC daytime January 6, 1986–April 4, 1986   *host:* Bruce Forsyth   *announcers:* Gene Wood, Marc Summers   *executive producer:* Robert Noah   *producer:* Pam Meerson   *director:* James Marcione   *set designers:* Anthony Sabatino, William H. Harris   *music:* Marc Ellis, Ray Ellis   *origination:* Studio 54, ABC Television Center, Los Angeles

Two teams of five players competed on this thirteen-week daytime series. On "Bruce Forsyth's Hot Streak," one team consisted of five men, the other of five women. Each team was given forty seconds to communicate a word (examples: ticket or fortune cookie) from one member to another without repeating any words said by the previous player. For each successful pass, a team received $100 with a maximum of $400 possible.

The game consisted of three rounds. One hundred dollars a pass was awarded in rounds one and two, and $200 in round three. The team with the most money earned, won the game. Only those on the winning team received their earnings.

In the bonus round, the winning team tried to earn as much as $10,000. The captain of the team was given a subject (examples: Florida or Tarzan) and gave four words or names associated with the topic. The captain's team members were given twenty seconds (five seconds apiece) to guess the words. The team won $200 for each word correctly guessed. They then played a second round with a new subject, for $300 a correct guess, and could win five times their bonus-round earnings on a final-round subject, but only if they guessed all four words.

BULLSEYE

premiere: September 29, 1980   *packager:* Jack Barry and Dan Enright Productions   *broadcast history:* Syndicated September 29, 1980–September 24, 1982; USA (cable) April 1, 1985–June 26, 1987 (repeats)   *host:* Jim Lange   *announcers:* Jay Stewart, Charlie O'Donnell   *producers:* Ron Greenberg, David Fein   *director:* Richard Kline   *set designer:* John C. Mula   *music:* Hal Hidey   *origination:* NBC Studios, Burbank (1980); CBS Television City, Los Angeles (1981–1982)

Two players competed on "Bullseye," with one pushing a button that stopped three spinning wheels. One wheel revealed a category, a second revealed a money amount, and the third revealed a number between one and five. That number represented the number of questions to be answered in the chosen category in order to win that amount of money. When one player finished a round, his or her opponent got a chance to play. The first player to reach $1,000 won the game.

In January 1982, the show became "Celebrity Bullseye" with weekly guest stars playing instead of contestants.

Did you know . . . while "Bullseye" was a syndicated show, it was taped at the NBC studios in Burbank just across the hall from "The Tonight Show" set? One day, Johnny Carson (who himself was an ex-game-show emcee) walked onto the "Bullseye" set and commented to emcee Jim Lange and producer Ronnie Greenberg on how he liked the very large and very stylish set. Back in the 1950s when Johnny Carson was a top game show emcee, the sets were rather small and lacked the bright neon lights that the "Bullseye" set had to offer.

Contestants tried to hit the "Bullseye" on this syndicated question-and-answer game show hosted by Jim Lange.

Producers Jack Barry and partner Dan Enright were among the leaders in game show syndication back in the 1980s. At one time they had "Bullseye" with Jim Lange, THE JOKER'S WILD with Jack Barry, and TIC TAC DOUGH with Wink Martindale.

BUMPER STUMPERS
premiere: June 29, 1987 *packager:* Jack Barry and Dan Enright Productions/Wink Martindale Enterprises/Global Television Network *broadcast history:* USA (cable) June 29, 1987–December 28, 1990 *host:* Al DuBois *announcer:* Ken Ryan *creator:* Wink Martindale *developed by:* Mark Maxwell-Smith *executive producer:* Wink Martindale *supervising producers:* Jeff Loseff, Michael Bevan, Bob Boden *producers:* Doug Gahm, Gary Jonke *director:* William G. Elliott *set designers:* Anthony Sabatino, David Timmons *music:* Ed Lojeski *origination:* Global Television Studios, Toronto, Canada

"Bumper Stumpers" was the second new game show created for the USA cable network (the first was LOVE ME LOVE ME NOT) and featured two teams of two contestants who attempted to guess the meaning behind personalized license plates.

The object of the game was to solve the "Super Stumper," a personalized license plate whose seven letters or numbers were revealed one at a time. To earn the right to have another blank filled in, both teams competed against each other to solve a "Jump-in."

The Jump-ins consisted of two license plates and a question that pertained to one of those two plates. The team that guessed which plate the question pertained to, received a chance to spell out its meaning. (Example: "Which of these plates belongs to a wig maker . . . G8RAD or 2PAS4U?"—the correct answer: number two, meaning "Toupees for you.")

The team that solved the "Super Stumper" won $500 and played a two-part bonus round. In part one the team tried to decipher up to seven plates in thirty seconds winning $100 for a correct guess.

In the second part the team tried to double their winnings by collecting $500 hidden behind five of the seven letters comprising the word "Stumper." Behind the other two letters were "Stop" signs which automatically ended the bonus game.

Did you know . . . Wink and his wife Sandy are animal lovers? They seem to name their pets after Wink's shows. Their first puppy was named Gambit (after Wink's GAMBIT) and their next two puppies were named Bumper and Miss Stumper (after Wink's show BUMPER STUMPERS).

BY POPULAR DEMAND
premiere: July 2, 1950 *packager:* Mark Goodson–Bill Todman Productions *broadcast history:* CBS primetime July 2, 1950–September 22, 1950 *hosts:* Robert Alda, Arlene Francis *announcer:* Bern Bennett *producer:* Frank Satenstein *director:* Herbert Sassan *music director:* Harry Sosnik *origination:* CBS Studio 50, New York

This summertime replacement from Mark Goodson and Bill Todman featured four entertainment acts competing with each other in an elimination competition to determine which act would return the following week. The first two acts competed, with the winner determined by studio audience applause. That winner took on the next competitor and the last winner of the day returned on the following show.

Original host Robert Alda left in the beginning of September, replaced by WHAT'S MY LINE? panelist and BLIND DATE hostess Arlene Francis, who emceed the final three telecasts.

BZZZ!

premiere: January 22, 1996 *packager:* Ralph Edwards–Stu Billett Productions *broadcast history:* Syndicated January 22, 1996–March 8, 1996; Syndicated September 9, 1996–September 5, 1997 *host:* Annie Wood *executive producers:* Ralph Edwards, Stu Billett, John Rhinehart *producers:* Tim Crescenti, Lynne Speigel, Annie Wood *supervising producers:* Mike Metzger, Jeffrey Mirkin *director:* Bob Loudin *set designer:* Scott Storey *origination:* Studio 4, Hollywood Center Studios

"Buzz!" made its debut as a limited-run syndicated series on a select number of stations in January 1996. It returned for a full season on many more stations in fall 1996.

One player was designated as the "buzzer," and four players of the opposite sex were designated as contestants. The four contestants were introduced via silhouette and the buzzer asked each a question. The buzzer then eliminated one of the four, and the remaining three were called out, one at a time, to be interviewed by the buzzer in a two-minute round.

At any time in this "Compatibility Round," the buzzer could either buzz the contestant (thereby eliminating him or her from the game) or "ring the bell," which indicated selection of that player as the buzzer's date. If the buzzer eliminated all three players or did not make a selection in two minutes, the contestant eliminated in the silhouette round became the buzzer's date.

Two games were played on each show, and the couples from each game played in the "Simpatico Round," where they tried to match answers to five questions (originally seven questions when the show first aired). Each match was worth $100, and all five right earned the couple $1,000.

The couple with the most matches in the Simpatico Round won a prize and played the "Final Buzz," in which the contestant who was chosen by the buzzer was given the option of accepting the date or taking a prize package of gifts.

CAESARS CHALLENGE

premiere: June 14, 1993 *packager:* Rosner Television/Stephen J. Cannell Productions *broadcast history:* NBC daytime June 14, 1993–January 14, 1994; USA (cable) June 27, 1994–November 4, 1994 (repeats) *host:* Ahmad Rashad *assistants:* Dan Doherty, Zack Ruby *announcer:* Steve Day *creators:* Rick Rosner, Mike Dubelko *executive producer:* Rick Rosner *producer:* Harry Friedman *director:* Steve Grant *set designer:* Ed Flesh *music:* Stormy Sacks *origination:* Caesars Palace, Las Vegas

Three contestants competed in a game of answering questions and unscrambling words on "Caesars Challenge." After a category was revealed, a scrambled word appeared and the players tried to answer a toss-up question. The player with the right answer collected $100 and earned the right to move one letter of the word into its correct position and then guess the word. If the contestant could not solve it, another question was played and another letter moved. The player who correctly guessed the word received $100 for each letter that had not been moved into its proper place. Each round had at least two words and the values of the letters and questions increased in the second ($200) and third ($300) round.

A "lucky slot" worth at least $500 was included in each game. The player who picked the letter that was supposed to be in that slot won the jackpot for guessing the word on that turn. The value of the lucky slot increased $500 after each game until a contestant won.

The player with the most cash after three rounds won the game and played the bonus game. In the bonus game, letters were selected at random from a cage containing two hundred letters. Players continued to select letters until a nine-letter word could be formed from the available letters. The player could move one letter into its proper place on the game board and was given ten seconds to guess the word for a grand prize. If unable to solve the problem, the player returned on the next show and if successful at winning the game that time, was given the chance to move two letters of another randomly selected word.

On November 22, 1993 the bonus game for "Caesars Challenge" was changed. In the new bonus round, the champion tried to unscramble five words within thirty seconds to win a new car. The first word had five letters; the second word, six letters; the third word, seven letters; the fourth word, eight letters; and the fifth word, nine letters. As time elapsed, letters moved into their correct order in the word. Winning players remained on the show for up to three days.

A weekend edition of "Caesars Challenge" was seen on Los Angeles TV station KCAL from September 18, 1993 to December 25, 1993.

CALL MY BLUFF

premiere: March 29, 1965 *packager:* Mark Goodson–Bill Todman Productions *broadcast history:* NBC daytime March 29, 1965–September 24, 1965 *host:* Bill Leyden *announcers:* Johnny Olson, Wayne Howell *executive producer:* Robert Noah *producer:* Jack Farren *director:* Mike Garguilo *word editor:* Eric Lieber *set designer:* Tom Trimble *origination:* NBC Studio 6A, New York *debut guests:* Peggy Cass, Orson Bean

Two teams, each composed of two contestants and one celebrity guest, competed in a game to determine the correct definition of obscure words on "Call My Bluff."

One team was given a word and each player presented a definition of the word, with only one player giving the real definition, and the other two bluffing. The opposing team had to choose the real definition from the three possibilities. If they guessed correctly they received one point, and the first team to score two points won the game and $100.

Both teams participated in the bonus round. In the bonus round a guest with an interesting story was introduced and briefly gave clues to his or her own story. The members of the winning team were then given three cards, one with the actual story and the others blank. The two players with the blank cards came up with bluffs. The opposing team tried to find out the true story by asking questions. If they were successful they earned the right to play another game and $200 was added to the jackpot for the next bonus game. If the team that was bluffing was successful they won the jackpot and their opposing team was replaced.

Were you watching when . . . emcees Bill Cullen, Art James, and Gene Rayburn were all guests on "Call My Bluff"?

Ahmad Rashad and contestants look on as centurion Dan Doherty brings up the letters for the next round of play.

In May 1965 actress Lauren Bacall made a rare game show appearance as a panelist for a week.

CAMOUFLAGE

premiere: January 9, 1961   *packagers:* Camouflage Inc. Jerry Hamer Productions 1961–1962; Chuck Barris Productions 1980   *broadcast history:* ABC daytime January 9, 1961–November 16, 1962; Syndicated February 4, 1980–April 1980

1961–1962 version

host: Don Morrow   *announcers:* Johnny Gilbert, Chet Gould   *executive producer:* Herbert Gottlieb   *producers:* Gil Cates, Ron Greenberg   *director:* Gil Cates   *set designer:* John Dapper   *drawings:* Republic Graphics Inc.   *music:* Paul Taubman   *origination:* Elysee Theater, New York

1980 version

host: Tom Campbell   *announcer:* Johnny Jacobs   *producers:* Steve Friedman, Mike Metzger   *director:* John Dorsey   *set designer:* Romain Johnston   *music:* Milton DeLugg   *origination:* Sunset Gower Studios, Los Angeles

The object of "Camouflage" was to locate and trace a hidden object (like a thumbtack or a dragon) hidden in a cartoon-type drawing. Two contestants competed to answer true-false questions with a correct answer providing the opportunity to look at the drawing. The first player to spot and trace the object won the game. Any player who attempted to trace the object and failed gave his opponent a free chance.

When a player reached the thirty-point level on the question segment of the game they were given a look at what the object looked like.

A player won the game when they successfully traced the object. Their prize was determined by adding the value of the puzzle to their point score earned in the questioning.

The top-scoring player of the day got a chance to win a new car by finding a bonus hidden object in another drawing in fifteen seconds.

Almost twenty years after its original debut, "Camouflage" returned for a brief thirteen-week run. The game still featured two players trying to trace the outline of a concealed item in a drawing, but players now earned $50 for each correct answer in a general knowledge quiz. Each game had a predetermined value, from $200 to $1,000 and the bonus game was played for a new car.

Did you know . . .   host Don Morrow was the narrator of the record album *Grimm's Hip Fairy Tales*, released by Roulette Records in 1961?

CAMPUS ALL-STAR CHALLENGE

premiere: April 14, 1990   *packager:* College Bowl Productions   *broadcast history:* BET (cable) April 14, 1990–June 2, 1990; BET (cable) June 1, 1991–July 20, 1991; BET (cable) June 6, 1992–July 25, 1992; BET (cable) September 5, 1992–October 24, 1992 (repeats); BET (cable) June 12, 1993–July 31, 1993; BET (cable) September 4, 1993–October 23, 1993 (repeats); BET (cable) June 11, 1994–July 30, 1994; BET (cable) September 10, 1994–October 29, 1994 (repeats); BET (cable) June 24, 1995–August 12, 1995   *host:* Clint Holmes *announcer:* Burton Richardson   *creator:* Don Reid   *executive producers:* Don Reid, Richard Reid, Nelson Davis   *producer:* Mary Oberembt   *director:* Dennis Rosenblatt   *set designer:* Don Wallschlaeger   *music:* Don Reid *origination:* Studio 5, Hollywood TV Center, Los Angeles

America's historically black colleges competed in this 1990s update of the quiz show COLLEGE BOWL. Each week on "Campus All-Star Challenge" two teams of four students participated in a game of quick recall and general knowledge.

The game was structured like a basketball game with two eight-minute halves. The match began with a "toss-up" question worth ten points that any player could ring in to answer. If correct, their team could earn bonus points, with a stated value, by answering "free throw" questions.

The team with the most points at the end of the game won and moved on to the next round of competition.

Teams in the yearly competition, seen each summer on the Black Entertainment Television (BET) cable channel, competed in a single elimination tournament. The televised portion consisted of the competition between the final eight teams. The final program of the season was an all-star match between the top students from the east and the west.

The winning school received $50,000 in institutional grants. In 1990, West Virginia State College won the championship. The following year Florida A&M took the crown, and in 1992 Norfolk State University was the victor. Tuskegee was the first team to win the competition two years in a row, winning in 1993 and 1994. Jackson State was the winner in 1995, the last time it was telecast on BET.

The first season (1990) was taped at BET studios in Washington, D.C. The following seasons originated at Hollywood Center Studios in Los Angeles.

Did you know . . . "Campus All-Star Challenge" host Clint Holmes had a top-ten hit in 1973 with the song "Playground in My Mind?" Announcer Burton Richardson was best known to late-night audiences as the announcer on "The Arsenio Hall Show."

CAN DO

premiere: November 26, 1956   *packager:* Phillip Productions   *broadcast history:* NBC primetime November 26, 1956–December 31, 1956   *host:* Robert Alda   *announcer:* Bill Wendell   *creators:* Joe Cates, Elroy Schwartz   *executive producer:* John Greenhut   *producer:* Thomas Naud   *director:* Joe Cates   *stunt director:* Snag Werris   *music director:* Ted Raph   *origination:* NBC Studio 6B, New York   *debut guests:* Gypsy Rose Lee, Sal Mineo, Rocky Graziano, Polly Bergen, Martha Raye

In this game, "Can Do," contestants tried to determine whether or not celebrity guests could perform stunts. After a series of question-and-answer rounds between the contestants and celebrities, the contestants made their decisions in an isolation booth. The first round was worth $1,500 and the value doubled on each following round. An incorrect guess left the player with ten percent of his or her winnings.

CAN YOU TOP THIS?

premiere: October 3, 1950   *broadcast history:* ABC primetime October 3, 1950–March 26, 1951; Syndicated January 26, 1970–September 1970

Morey Amsterdam is center stage as he tries to tell the best joke on "Can You Top This?" From left to right are host Wink Martindale and panelists Dick Gautier, Jack Carter, and Stu Gilliam.

1950–1951 version

host: Ward Wilson   **announcer:** Ed Michaels   **"joke teller":** "Senator" Edward Ford   **producer:** "Senator" Edward Ford   **directors:** Marshall Diskin, Roger Bower   **origination:** New York   **debut guests:** Harry Hershfield, Joe Laurie Jr., Peter Donald, Senator Edward Ford

1970 version

packager: Four Star Television   **host:** Wink Martindale   **"joke tellers":** Dick Gautier, Richard Dawson   **executive producer:** Morey Amsterdam   **producers:** Sheldon Brosky, Perry Cross   **director:** Martin Kane   **set designer:** E. Jay Krause   **origination:** Studio 33, CBS Television City, Los Angeles   **debut guests:** Danny Thomas, Stu Gilliam, Morey Amsterdam, Richard Dawson

"Can You Top This?" was a popular radio series, making its debut on December 9, 1940 and running until 1954. In the fall of 1950, the show began a brief television run. "Senator" Edward Ford was the resident "joke teller" who told jokes submitted by home viewers. The studio audience responded with results that showed up on a laugh meter that registered from zero to one hundred. A panel of three celebrity comedians then tried to beat that score with jokes of their own in the same category. The home viewers who submitted the joke each received $25 every time the comedians couldn't top their scores. Regular panelists included Harry Hershfield, Joe Laurie Jr., and Peter Donald.

"Can You Top This?" was revived in 1970 as a daily show for syndication. Dick Gautier and Richard Dawson were some of the celebrity "joke tellers" during the run of the show. Morey Amsterdam appeared as the only regular panelist, with two guest celebrities appearing each week. Some of the celebrity joke tellers included Milton Berle, Jack Carter, Monty Hall, Gary Owens, Danny Thomas, and Paul Winchell.

Did you know . . .   "Can You Top This?" regular Morey Amsterdam cowrote the Andrews Sisters 1945 hit "Rum and Coca-Cola"?

Recognize these famous faces? From left to right are "Card Sharks" emcee Jim Perry playing host to contestants Jim Lange, Alex Trebek, Jack Clark, and Tom Kennedy, from a week honoring game show greats.

CARD SHARKS

premiere: April 24, 1978 *packager:* Mark Goodson–Bill Todman Productions *broadcast history:* NBC daytime April 24, 1978–October 23, 1981; CBS daytime January 6, 1986–March 31, 1989; Syndicated September 8, 1986–September 1987

1978–1981 version

host: Jim Perry *card dealers:* Ann Pennington, Janice Baker, Lois Areno, Kristin Bjorklund, Melinda Hunter, Markie Post *announcers:* Gene Wood, Jack Narz, Charlie O'Donnell, Johnny Olson, Jay Stewart, Bob Hilton *executive producer:* Chester Feldman *producer:* Jonathan Goodson *directors:* Marc Breslow, Paul Alter *set designer:* James Agazzi *music:* Score Productions *origination:* NBC Studios 3 and 4, Burbank

1986–1989 version

hosts: Bob Eubanks, Bill Rafferty *card dealers:* Lacey Pemberton, Suzanna Williams *announcers:* Gene Wood, Bob Hilton, Charlie O'Donnell *executive producers:* Jonathan Goodson, Chester Feldman *producer:* Mimi O'Brien *director:* Marc Breslow *set designer:* Dennis Roof *music:* Edd Kalehoff *origination:* Studio 33, CBS Television City, Los Angeles

On "Card Sharks" two contestants competed to complete a block of five consecutive playing cards by guessing whether the next card to be unveiled would be higher or lower than the last one.

To earn control of the board, one player predicted how many people out of one hundred would answer a question a certain way. An opponent then predicted whether the actual number would be higher or lower. The player whose prediction was closest to the correct number played the cards. The first player to win two games with the cards became the champ and played the "Money Cards."

A player started the bonus round with $200 and was shown a base card. The player then wagered some or all of the money on whether the next card was higher or lower. They played seven cards, with the last wager a minimum bet of at least half their money.

Jim Perry was the host of the NBC daytime version, Bob Eubanks emceed the CBS daytime version, and Bill Rafferty did the syndicated edition.

Were you watching when . . . it was "game show emcee" week on "Card Sharks"? Among the hosts who played the game were Jack Clark, Bill Cullen, Tom Kennedy, Jim Lange, Allen Ludden, Wink Martindale, Gene Rayburn, and Alex Trebek.

CASH AND CARRY

premiere: June 20, 1946 *packager:* Carr-Stark Productions *broadcast history:* DuMont primetime June 20, 1946–July 1, 1947 *host:* Dennis James *producer:* Charles Stark *director:* Tom Carr *set designer:* Robert Bright *origination:* Wanamaker's department store, New York

"Cash and Carry" was one of the first network television

Here's game show television pioneer Dennis James as he takes a sit-down break on the set of his 1946 entry "Cash and Carry."

Art James looks on as an excited contestant wins big on "Catch Phrase."

game shows seen on the two-station DuMont network. This series was presented in a grocery store setting lined with shelves of Libby's food products with questions worth $5, $10, and $15.

Other features of the show were stunts for the players to complete, and a home viewer contest where viewers tried to guess what was under a barrel.

Did you know . . . "Cash and Carry" originated from DuMont's TV studios at Wanamaker's department store at Ninth Avenue and Broadway in New York City. Part of the store was an auditorium that was converted in 1946 into three TV studios at a cost of $500,000. During the day shoppers could watch the cast and crew rehearsing.

CATCH PHRASE

premiere: September 16, 1985   *packager:* Marty Pasetta Productions   *broadcast history:* Syndicated September 16, 1985–January 10, 1986   *host:* Art James   *model:* Shana Forman (Mary Poms)   *announcer:* John Harlan   *producer:* Steve Radosh   *director:* Marty Pasetta   *puzzles:* Steve Ryan   *set designer:* Rene Lagler   *music:* Marc Ellis, Ray Ellis   *origination:* Studio 1, Metromedia Studios, Los Angeles

Two studio players attempted to solve visual puzzles from an animated drawing, on "Catch Phrase." Each correct guess put money into a pot and revealed one of nine parts of a super catchphrase puzzle giving the player a chance to guess the phrase. The first player to correctly guess the super catchphrase won all the money in the pot. Dollar values for each catchphrase increased in each round and were selected at random.

The player with the most money after several rounds (the number varied depending on the length of the game) won and then played for a bonus prize. The winning player tried to solve five catchphrases in a row on a game board of twenty-five squares in sixty seconds or less for $5,000. Any less than the five in a row paid off at $200 per puzzle.

Director Marty Pasetta was best known as director of the Academy Award telecasts for many years as well as numerous variety specials. Shana Forman was the featured model on the game shows TEMPTATION and THE WIZARD OF ODDS, under the name Mary Poms.

Did you know . . . a coauthor of this book, Steve Ryan, created the puzzles used on "Catch Phrase?"

CBS TELEVISION QUIZ

premiere: July 2, 1941   *packager:* CBS Television   *broadcast history:* CBS primetime July 2, 1941–Fall 1942   *host:* Gil Fates   *assistant:* Frances Buss   *producer/director:* Worthington Miner   *origination:* Grand Central Studios, New York

"CBS Television Quiz" was the first regularly scheduled continuing game show on commercial television since the Federal Communications Commission (FCC) authorized the beginning of commercial television in the spring of 1941. Both CBS and NBC began broadcasting on their New York stations on July 1, 1941.

Gil Fates, who went on to host many of the CBS telecasts of the 1940s and later produce WHAT'S MY LINE? for twenty-five years, was emcee of this show that featured a wide variety of quizzes, games, and stunts.

CELEBRITY BILLIARDS

premiere: September 27, 1967   *packager:* Almaro Productions for Medallion TV   *broadcast history:* Syndicated September 27, 1967–September 1968   *host:* Ted Travers   *featuring:* Minnesota Fats (Rudolph Wanderone Jr.)   *creator/producer:* Allan David   *director:* John Dorsey   *set designer:* Herman Zimmerman   *origination:* KTLA-TV, Los Angeles

"Celebrity Billiards" was a weekly series featuring celebrity guests, among them Don Adams, Morey Amsterdam, Milton Berle, Bill Cosby, Phyllis Diller, and James Garner, who took on Minnesota Fats in a best two-out-of-three billiards match. The winner received $1,000 for his or her favorite charity and the loser $500.

CELEBRITY BOWLING

premiere: January 16, 1971   *packager:* Seven-Ten Productions   *broadcast history:* Syndicated January 16, 1971–September 1978   *host:* Jed Allan   *assistants:* Bill Buneta, Bobby Cooper, Dave Davis, Sherry Kominsky   *producers:* Don Gregory, Joe Seigman   *director:* Don Buccola   *set designer:* Anthony Sabatino   *bowling equipment:* Brunswick and AMF   *origination:* KTTV Studios, Los Angeles

Four celebrities, on teams of two, played members of the studio audience in a ten-frame best-ball bowling match on "Celebrity Bowling." Using two alleys specially constructed in a TV studio, each team member bowled his first ball. The player who knocked down the fewest pins bowled his second bowl in his partner's alley in an effort to knock down the most possible pins.

Among the celebrity bowlers who appeared on the show were Steve Allen, Richard Dawson, Michael Douglas, Virginia Graham, Tom Kennedy, Wink Martindale, Jayne Meadowns, Gary Owens, William Shatner, Brenda Vaccaro, and Adam West.

CELEBRITY CHARADES

premiere: January 1979   *packager:* Fein-Schwartz Productions/Columbia Television   *broadcast history:* Syndicated January 1979–September 1979   *host:* Jay Johnson and "Squeaky"   *announcer:* Dick Patterson   *executive producers:* David B. Fein, Allan B. Schwartz   *producer:* Don Segall   *director:* Ron Kantor   *set designer:* C. Murawski   *music:* Score Productions   *origination:* TAV Studios, Hollywood

"Celebrity Charades" was the 1979 attempt to revive PANTOMIME QUIZ, one of the most popular game shows of the 1950s. The new version was emceed by ventriloquist Jay Johnson and his friend "Squeaky."

Two teams, each comprised of four celebrity guests, competed in this daily game of charades. One member of a team was given a phrase and pantomimed it for the other three teammates. The teammates had to guess the phrase in a seventy-five-second time limit. Each team played four charades per show and the team using the least time overall won $500 for their favorite team charity.

Did you know . . . host Jay Johnson was one of the stars of the TV sitcom "Soap"?

THE CELEBRITY GAME
premiere: April 5, 1964 *packager:* Merrill Heatter–Bob Quigley Productions/Four Star Television *broadcast history:* CBS primetime April 5, 1964–September 13, 1964; CBS primetime December 20, 1964–January 24, 1965; CBS primetime April 8, 1965–September 9, 1965; CBS Sunday afternoons October 1, 1967–January 7, 1968 (repeats of earlier shows) *host:* Carl Reiner *announcer:* Kenny Williams *executive producers:* Merrill Heatter, Bob Quigley *director:* Seymour Robbie *consultant:* Dr. Joyce Brothers *set designer:* Robert Tyler Lee *music:* Arlo *origination:* Studio 41, CBS Television City, Los Angeles *debut guests:* William Bendix, James Darren, Troy Donahue, Suzanne Pleshette, Eartha Kitt, Dorothy Malone, Robert Morse, Agnes Moorehead, Cliff Robertson

Three studio contestants tried to predict how a celebrity panel of nine guest stars would answer questions like "Do plain women make better wives than beautiful women?" and "Should a man be forced to wear a wedding ring?" Each player picked a celebrity and tried to guess if he or she

Emcee Carl Reiner playing host to some of our favorite television and film stars on the elegant set, designed by Robert Tyler Lee, of "The Celebrity Game," in 1964. Clockwise, from top left: Dale Robertson, Zsa Zsa Gabor, Jim Backus, Gisele MacKenzie, Frankie Avalon, Shelley Winters, Paul Lynde, Eden Marx, Groucho Marx.

answered yes or no. The celebrities revealed their answers and often gave humorous explanations of their views.

If only one player predicted correctly the player, won $100, if two were correct the payoff was $50 per player, and if all three chose correctly each received $25.

In the final round of each week's show, each contestant tried to predict whether the majority of the celebrities voted "Yes" or "No" on a final question. The payoffs were $100 if all three chose the right response, $150 if only two players were correct, and $300 if only one player could correctly predict the outcome.

Did you know . . . Carl Reiner originally played the role of Rob Petrie in the pilot of what would later become "The Dick Van Dyke Show"? (Reiner wound up playing the role of Rob's boss Alan Brady.)

Were you watching when . . . the following television and film superstars anxiously awaited their turns to do this primetime Merrill Heatter–Bob Quigley hit? They were Steve Allen, Lauren Bacall, Phyllis Diller (Diller was so funny on the show that she became a very popular semi-regular), Merv Griffin, Art Linkletter, Jayne Mansfield, Lee Marvin, Groucho Marx, Ronald Reagan, Nancy Sinatra, Gloria Swanson, and Elaine Stewart (long before she co-hosted "Gambit" with Wink Martindale).

CELEBRITY GOLF

premiere: September 25, 1960   *packager:* Jerry Fairbanks Productions/Bob-o-Links Productions **broadcast history:** NBC weekends September 25, 1960–May 21, 1961 **host:** Sam Snead **announcer/commentator:** Harry Von Zell **executive producer:** Norman Blackburn **director:** Norman McLeod **origination:** Desert Inn and Country Club, Las Vegas

Celebrities like Bob Hope and Harpo Marx took on golf legend Sam Snead in a nine-hole match on "Celebrity Golf," this Sunday afternoon weekly series. The show, sponsored by Kemper Insurance, was filmed at the Desert Inn and Country Club in Las Vegas. The celebrity won $1,000 for beating Snead in the overall match, $250 for each par, $500 for each birdie, and $10,000 for a hole in one. All the money won was given to charity.

CELEBRITY SWEEPSTAKES

premiere: April 1, 1974   *packager:* Ralph Andrews Productions/Burt Sugarman Productions **broadcast history:** NBC daytime April 1, 1974–October 1, 1976; Syndicated September 9, 1974–September 1975; Syndicated September 20, 1976–September 1977 **host:** Jim McKrell **announcers:** Bill Armstrong, Dick Tufeld, John Harlan **producers:** Bill Armstrong, Tom Cole, Neil Marshall, Larry Hovis, George Vosburgh, Joe Seiter, Terry Kyne, Scott Sternberg **director:** Dick McDonough **set designer:** Ed Flesh **music:** Stan Worth **origination:** NBC Studios 3 and 9, Burbank **debut guests:** Johnny Mathis, Fannie Flagg, Telly Savalas, Jo Ann Pflug, Pat Harrington Jr., Shelley Winters

Six celebrities (positioned in a setting resembling a race track starting gate), two contestants, and a studio audience who determined the odds on each question for each celebrity were involved in this question-and-answer game, "Celebrity Sweepstakes."

After a question was asked of the celebrity panel, the studio audience "bet" which of the six they felt would know the correct answer. When the odds were established, the on-stage contestants selected a celebrity. If that celebrity answered correctly, the contestant won the amount of cash determined by the odds. The player with the most cash at the end of the day returned on the next show and whoever won three days in a row received a new car.

Were you watching when . . . announcer Bill Armstrong was featured as a celebrity panelist for one week—a last-minute replacement for the booked celebrity who took ill? Armstrong announced the entire five shows, on camera, sitting in the number-one starting gate.

CELEBRITY TENNIS

premiere: September 1973   *packager:* 7/10 Productions **broadcast history:** Syndicated September 1973–September 1974 **hosts:** Tony Trabert, Jed Allan, Bobby Riggs **producers:** Joe Seigman, Don Gregory **director:** Don Buccola

This weekly series from the producers of CELEBRITY BOWLING featured two teams, each composed of two celebrities, who played a two-set doubles match. In "Celebrity Tennis," teams played for prizes given to members of the studio audience.

Each set had a time limit of seven minutes, with each player serving four points. Service alternated between teams after each four points were played. Fifteen points won the game (or whoever was leading when time ran out) won the game.

CELEBRITY TIME

premiere: April 3, 1949   *packager:* World Video **broadcast history:** ABC primetime April 3, 1949–March 26, 1950; CBS primetime April 2, 1950–June 27, 1950; CBS primetime October 1, 1950–September 21, 1952 **host:** Conrad Nagel **announcer:** Bill Hamilton **producers:** Martin Ritt, Richard Lewine **directors:** Fred Carr, Tom DeHuff, Alan Dinehart, Danny Mann, Ralph Nelson **set designer:** Paul Sylbert **music:** Alvy West Orchestra **origination:** New York

"Celebrity Time" began as a battle-of-the-sexes in which celebrity guests played various games and answered quizzes. By June of 1952, the quiz segment was dropped and the show became a variety show with Nagel continuing as emcee.

CHAIN LETTER

premiere: July 4, 1966   *packager:* Stefan Hatos–Monty Hall Productions **broadcast history:** NBC daytime July 4, 1966–October 14, 1966 **host:** Jan Murray **announcer:** Wendell Niles **executive producers:** Stefan Hatos, Monty Hall **director:** Joe Behar **set designer:** Mary Weaver **music:** Ivan

Which celebrity would you have placed your bet with?

Ditmars *origination:* NBC Studio 3, Burbank *debut guests:* Betty White, Hans Conreid

On "Chain Letter," two teams competed, each composed of a celebrity captain and a studio contestant. A category, such as "items you might find in a lady's handbag" or "gifts for the boss's birthday," was given and the first player named a word pertaining to that category. The next player had to give a word in that same category using the last letter of the previous word as the first letter of the new word. Each player had ten seconds to come up with an answer or the chain would be broken, thus giving the opposing team a point.

The team with the most points after a three-minute round won the game and $100. They then went on to play a "fast money" bonus round in which the contestant received $20 for each word he or she and the celebrity partner could form from a chain word. The bonus round continued until the chain was broken.

Did you know . . . Jan Murray appeared in a Tarzan movie? In 1967 Jan appeared in *Tarzan and the Great River*, in which Mike Henry played Tarzan.

CHAIN REACTION
premiere: January 14, 1980 *packager:* Bob Stewart Productions (1980); Bob Stewart–Sande Stewart Productions (1986–1991) *broadcast history:* NBC daytime January 14, 1980–June 20, 1980; USA (cable) September 29, 1986–December 27, 1991

1980 version

host: Bill Cullen *substitute host:* Geoff Edwards *announcer:* Johnny Gilbert *executive producer:* Bob Stewart *producer:* Sande Stewart *directors:* Mike Garguilo, Bruce Burmester *set designer:* Ed Flesh *music:* Bob Cobert *origination:* NBC Studios 2 and 4, Burbank *debut guests:* Fred Grandy, Nipsey Russell, Patty Duke, Joyce Bulifant

1986–1991 version

hosts: Geoff Edwards, Blake Emmons **cohost/announcer:** Rod Chalabois **executive producer:** Tom Froundjian **producer:** Sande Stewart **director:** Lucian Albert **set designer:** Andy Wilson **origination:** CFCF-TV, Montreal, Canada

On "Chain Reaction," two teams, each composed of two celebrities and one contestant, played a word association game in which they tried to complete a chain of words associated with each other.

The first and last words of the chain were revealed, and teams alternated at guessing the connecting words. Letters were revealed one at a time. A correct guess earned one point for each letter in the unknown word. Fifty points won the game and $250. Example of a chain: Felix . . . Oscar . . . Hollywood . . . Squares . . . Rounds . . . Boxing . . . Trunks . . . Beach.

The winning team played a bonus round where the two celebrities constructed, one word at a time, sentences for their partners to decipher in ninety seconds. Each correct answer was worth $100 and ten correct won $10,000.

"Chain Reaction" was revived as a first-run show in 1986 for the USA cable network. The new edition, produced in Montreal, Canada, featured only studio contestants, eliminating the role of the celebrity teammates. Blake Emmons hosted the first weeks of the new "Chain Reaction" shows but was replaced by Geoff Edwards. When the show began running on USA, the series began with the shows hosted by Edwards.

The game was basically the same as the NBC version, with only the scoring system changed. Guessing a word was worth ten points, with twenty points awarded for coming up with the last word in the chain. Point values increased as teams played the second and third chains. The first team to reach 200 points won the game. In the new bonus round, the winning team tried to complete a chain of words in sixty seconds for a possible $3,000.

In January 1991 the show became "The $40,000 Chain Reaction," with the weekly champ earning $7,500 and the big winners returning for a championship round at the end of the season for a $40,000 first prize. The bonus game was revised and became the "Missing Link" game, where the daily winner could win $300 by guessing the middle word in a three-word chain with only the first letter revealed. The addition of a second letter dropped the value to $200 and a third letter cut the potential winnings to $100.

THE CHALLENGERS

premiere: September 3, 1990 **packager:** Ron Greenberg Productions/Dick Clark Productions/for Buena Vista Television **broadcast history:** Syndicated September 3, 1990–August 31, 1991 **host:** Dick Clark **judge:** Gary Johnson **announcers:** Don Morrow, Bob Hilton **executive producers:** Dick Clark, Ron Greenberg **coproducer:** Janet Markowitz **directors:** Morris Abraham, Chris Darley **set designers:** Bente Christensen, John Ivo Gilles **music:** Al Kasha, Joel Hirschhorn, Michael Lloyd **origination:** Studio 9A, Hollywood Center Studios, Los Angeles

Three contestants competed for cash in this daily quiz show based on recent news events. "The Challengers" began each day's program with a sixty-second sprint round of rapid-fire questions. Players started with $200 in their banks and received $100 for correct answers.

The player with the most money after the sprint round chose from six possible categories. Each category had three questions, valued at $150, $200, and $250. Each player selected the category he or she wished to answer questions from. If two or more players picked the same category they competed against each other to answer it. If all three players selected the same question the value doubled and the contestant who answered correctly was given a chance to answer the two remaining questions in the category. Players lost money for wrong answers, and the contestant who successfully answered the last question, worth the most, selected the next category to be played.

A second round of six categories were played with the value of the questions worth $300, $400, and $500. All the players participated in the "final challenge" to determine the day's winner. Players selected one of three questions in a final category. They could risk any part of their day's earnings to answer questions worth the same as, double, or triple their wager. The higher the odds, the harder the question. The highest bidder for each question earned the right to answer, with the top-scoring player returning on the next show.

CHANCE FOR ROMANCE

premiere: October 13, 1958 **packager:** Irving Mansfield–Peter Arnell Productions **broadcast history:** ABC daytime October 13, 1958–December 5, 1958 **host:** John Cameron Swayze **announcer:** Joel Crager **producers:** Irving Mansfield, Peter Arnell **production supervisor:** Allan Wallace **director:** Clay Yurdin **music director:** Henry Sylvern **origination:** New York

"Chance for Romance" was a short-lived audience participation show that attempted to match young men and women. Three men or three women, each seeking friendship, were introduced to members of the opposite sex. The contestants were chosen by members of a board of experts in human relations that included a sociologist, a marriage counselor, and a psychologist, with the intention of sparking romance between the two.

Did you know . . . host John Cameron Swayze was the first anchorman on the NBC nightly news? Swayze was the host of the "Camel News Caravan" from 1948 to 1956. In later years, he was best known as the commercial spokesman for Timex watches.

CHANCE OF A LIFETIME

premiere: September 6, 1950 **packager:** Robert Jennings Productions **broadcast history:** ABC primetime September 6, 1950–November 28, 1951 **host:** John Reed King **assistant:** Janie Ford **announcer:** Ken Roberts **producer:** Robert Jennings **director:** Charles Harrell **set designer:** James McNaughton **music director:** Joseph Biviano **origination:** New York

Contestants selected two lucky letters of the alphabet—contained in the sponsor's name (B-E-N-D-I-X) on "Chance of a Lifetime." Each letter corresponded to a button that either buzzed or rang and which determined the value of the prize. Buzzers were worth prizes from $200 to $500 in value and bells worth $500 to $1,000. Players had to answer questions or participate in stunts, such as watching an Olympic gymnast perform on the parallel bars and then attempting to repeat the routine, or perform a scene from a famous movie and then identify the film.

Celebrity guests appeared on the show from time to time, and a home viewer contest was featured, where viewers were called and asked to identify a celebrity from clues.

"Chance of a Lifetime" left the air in November 1951 after a little more than a year, but returned six months later with a new host (Dennis James) and a new format.

CHANCE OF A LIFETIME

premiere: May 8, 1952   *packager:* Robert Jennings Productions   *broadcast history:* ABC primetime May 8, 1952–August 20, 1953; DuMont primetime September 11, 1953–June 24, 1955; ABC primetime July 3, 1955–June 23, 1956   *host:* Dennis James   *announcers:* Jay Simms, Ken Roberts, Kenny Williams   *producer:* Herbert Moss   *director:* Lou Sposa   *set designers:* Willis Connor, Norman Davidson   *music directors:* John Gart, Bernie Leighton   *origination:* DuMont Adelphi Theatre, New York

Dennis James took over as host of "Chance of a Lifetime" when the show returned to ABC in May 1952 with the format changing to that of a talent competition. Two professional performers competed against each other in the first half of the show, with studio audience applause determining the winner.

In the second half of the show, the winner from the first half competed against the winner from the previous week's show. The winner, again determined by applause from the studio audience, received $1,000 and a week's engagement at a nightclub, as well as $500 for a home viewer partner.

Did you know . . . among the distinguished discoveries on "Chance of a Lifetime" were Diahann Carroll, Roger Williams, and Dick Van Dyke?

CHARADE QUIZ

premiere: December 4, 1947   *packager:* Telamuse Productions/Stanley Catcher Productions   *broadcast history:* DuMont primetime December 4, 1947–June 23, 1949   *host:* Bill Slater   *producers:* Victor Keppler, Gertrude Catcher   *directors:* Henry Alexander, David Lewis   *origination:* Adelphi Theater, New York   *debut guests:* Minnabess Lewis, Herb Polesie, Bob Shepard

This early DuMont quiz show featured charades submitted by home viewers for the show's repertory company to act out. On "Charade Quiz" the panel had ninety seconds to guess each charade. Each viewer received $10 if his or her suggested charade was used and another $15 if it stumped the panel.

The repertory company was composed of Allan Frank, Richard Seff, and Ellen Fenwick. Regular panelists included Minnabess Lewis, Herb Polesie, Bob Shepard, and Jackson Beck.

Did you know . . . Bill Slater was the narrator of the Paramount newsreels?

THE CHEAP SHOW

premiere: September 1978   *packager:* Payson-Odin Productions/20th Century Fox TV   *broadcast history:* Syndicated September 1978–September 1979   *host:* Dick Martin   *assistants:* Janelle Price ("Wanda the hostess"), Shirl Bernheim ("Polly the prize lady"), Joe Baker and Billy Beck ("Purveyors of punishment"), Roger Chapline ("Roger the security guard")   *announcer:* Charlie O'Donnell   *executive producers:* Chris Bearde, Robert D. Wood   *creators:* Chris Bearde, Rick Kellard, Bob Comfort   *producers:* Terry Kyne, Kathe Connolly   *director:* Terry Kyne   *set designer:* Jack McAdam   *music:* John Phillips   *origination:* Metromedia Studios, Los Angeles

Two couples and two guest celebrities participated in "The Cheap Show," a comedy game show. A question was asked of the celebrities, one of whom gave the correct answer, the other a false response. If a player picked the celebrity with the right answer, they won a cheap prize (valued under $16) and their opponents were punished (doused with water, hit with a cream pie, etc.). If a player picked the wrong celebrity, his or her partner was punished. After three rounds, the highest scoring team was asked to predict what number hole "Oscar the Wonder Rodent" would enter when placed on a board with numbered holes. The team then won a decent prize in accordance with whatever hole Oscar entered.

Gary Owens awaits the arrival of fellow panel members Barbi Benton and Richard Nixon on the spoof game show "The Cheap Show." Producers regularly teased the audience by announcing guests who were no-shows. Guess what? Richard Nixon was the no-show that week.

Did you know . . . both Bob Newhart and Truman Capote were such fans of this game show spoof that they asked to be guests on the show?

CHILD'S PLAY

premiere: September 20, 1982 *packager:* Mark Goodson Productions *broadcast history:* CBS daytime September 20, 1982–September 16, 1983 *host:* Bill Cullen *announcers:* Gene Wood, Bob Hilton, Johnny Gilbert *executive producers:* Jonathan Goodson, Chester Feldman *producer:* Mimi O'Brien *director:* Ira Skutch *set designer:* James Agazzi *music:* Score Productions *origination:* Studio 33, CBS Television City, Los Angeles

On ''Child's Play,'' two contestants attempted to guess words from definitions given by children ages five to nine. Each player, in turn, was given a chance to guess the word after each of three definitions had been given. A second round, ''Fast Play,'' featured players trying to guess words on a ''jump-in'' basis. The contestant with the most points after two rounds won $500 and played the bonus round called ''Triple Play.''

The champion was given forty-five seconds to guess six words from a maximum of three written definitions at $100 for a correct guess or $5,000 for all three.

Playing host to America's favorite game shows was ''Child's Play'' to the talented Bill Cullen.

A new bonus game, ''Turnabout,'' was introduced in the spring of 1983. In it, the day's winner tried to describe seven words to five kids in a time limit of forty-five seconds. The contestant earned $100 for each word the kids guessed and $5,000 if they got all seven. The kids divided up $100 for each word they said and $1,000 if they came up with all of them.

CHOOSE UP SIDES

premiere: January 7, 1956 *packager:* Mark Goodson–Bill Todman Productions *broadcast history:* NBC Saturday morning January 7, 1956–March 31, 1956 *host:* Gene Rayburn *announcer/''Mr. Mischief'':* Don Pardo *team captains:* Tommy Tompkins, Roger Peterson *producer:* Jean Kopelman *director:* Lloyd Gross *stunts:* Frank Wayne, Bob Howard *set designer:* Bob Wightman *origination:* Hudson Theater, New York

In ''Choose Up Sides,'' two teams of four children competed in a stunt game show similar to BEAT THE CLOCK. The teams, called the ''Bronco Busters'' and the ''Space Pilots,'' tried to outperform each other in a series of stunts and games.

Two teams of four kids, each of whom was given the opportunity to compete against someone on the other team, vied to see who could complete a stunt faster. The winner received two hundred points, while the loser was given a chance to win one hundred points by completing another stunt.

Halfway through the show, ''Mr. Mischief'' (announcer Don Pardo) would announce a date and the child in the studio audience whose birthday was closest to that date would get a chance to try the ''Sooper Dooper Doo'' stunt. In Sooper Dooper Doo the contestant tossed fifteen large cards at a sticky beach ball. The child who was able to get the most number of cards to stick in a four-week period won a special prize.

''Choose Up Sides'' was the only Goodson-Todman game show produced as a kids-only series.

Did you know . . . host Gene Rayburn was the original announcer on ''The Tonight Show'' when it premiered in 1954 with Steve Allen as host?

CLASH

premiere: May 1, 1990 *packager:* Four Cats Productions *broadcast history:* Ha! (cable) May 1, 1990–March 31, 1991; Comedy Central (cable) April 1, 1991–December 28, 1991 *host:* Billy Kimball *announcer:* Dave Levin *creators:* Tim Disney, Billy Kimball *producers:* Dana Calderwood, Laurie Rich *director:* Dana Calderwood *set designer:* Bill Groom *music:* Carter Burwell *origination:* New York

In ''Clash,'' the lighthearted game show, two opposing teams from different walks of life competed in a question-and-answer game. Sample contests included ''nudists vs. fashion designers,'' ''butchers vs. vegetarians,'' and ''nuns vs. strippers.''

Each team consisted of three players and in round one they tackled four categories, each containing four questions. Three possible answers were shown. Correct choices were

Host Alex Trebek ponders over one of Steve Ryan's "Classic Concentration" rebuses. (The answer is "Torn Between Two Lovers.") Steve Ryan created all of the rebuses for the show.

worth ten points. The player with the correct response chose the next category to be played.

The questions in round two were worth twenty points each and behind one of the questions was a grudge match, where one player from each team was tested in a bizarre stunt, such as building a statue of playing cards.

Round three contained the big questions worth fifty, one hundred, and one hundred fifty points. Players competed, losing points for wrong answers. The high-scoring team at the end of the round won the game.

A player on the winning team with the most correct answers spun the "oval of odds" wheel to determine which of six categories the team would play for a bonus prize. Five categories contained questions virtually impossible to answer, while the last category contained a question almost impossible to answer wrong.

CLASSIC CONCENTRATION

premiere: May 4, 1987   *packager:* Mark Goodson Productions   *broadcast history:* NBC daytime May 4, 1987–September 20, 1991; NBC daytime October 28, 1991–December 31, 1993 (repeats of 1987–1991 shows)   *host:* Alex Trebek   *models:* Diana Taylor, Marjorie Goodson-Cutt   *announcers:* Gene Wood, Art James   *executive producers:*

Chester Feldman, Howard Felsher   *producer:* Gabrielle Johnston   *director:* Marc Breslow   *rebus designs:* Steve Ryan   *graphic artists:* Bernard Schmittke, Vern Jorgensen, Carolyn Hughes, Suzanne Morales   *set designers:* James Agazzi, Diane O'Connell, Molly Joseph, R. Brandt Daniels   *music:* Score Productions, Stanley Blits   *based on a concept by:* Buddy Piper   *origination:* NBC Studio 3, Burbank

After a fourteen-year absence from network daytime television, CONCENTRATION returned as "Classic Concentration," with an updated version based on the original series.

Two contestants competed against each other to solve a rebus puzzle by matching pairs of prizes on a twenty-five-square game board. With each match, two parts of the puzzle were revealed. The first player to correctly identify the puzzle won the game and all prizes credited to him or her. Also on the board were "wild cards," which formed automatic matches with whatever prizes were behind the number called. (The original "Concentration" was played on a thirty-square board with additional pieces called "Forfeit One Gift" and "Take One Gift" mixed into the game.)

The winner played a bonus matching game for a new car. Hidden behind fifteen numbers were seven matching prize cards for different cars and one card that did not match. The object was to match all seven cars in the allotted time, with the last matched being the car won. There was a base time of thirty-five seconds to complete the matching, with an additional five seconds added for each time the car was not won. (In the original version, there was no bonus game.)

In November 1987, the Take One Gift was returned to the main game and in February 1988 a second Take was added. Players had the option of using the Take after they made the match or holding it and using it after they made any other match in the game.

From July 4, 1988 to June 1990, contestants played a best two-out-of-three puzzle game match to determine who got a chance to play the bonus game for a new car. Beginning with the June 30, 1990 show, the winner of each puzzle game played for a new car. There were two car games each day. Players remained on the show until they won a new car or lost two games.

A "cash pot" prize was added to one game on each show in November 1989. The value of the pot started at $500, with $100 added each day until it was won.

Did you know . . .   Steve Ryan, a coauthor of this book, was the creator of all the rebus puzzles used on "Classic Concentration"? In 1991, Sterling Books published a volume on the history of the show as well as many of the puzzles.

Announcer Gene Wood took ill in July 1991 and was replaced for a month by the original announcer of "Concentration," Art James. James had last announced on "Concentration" in January 1961.

CLICK

premiere: September 6, 1997   *packager:* Merv Griffin Productions   *broadcast history:* Syndicated September 6, 1997–   *host:* Ryan Seacrest   *cohost/announcer:* Amber Bonasso   *executive producers:* Merv Griffin, Ernest Chambers *supervising producer:* Peter Marino   *producer:* John Lauderdale   *director:* Kevin McCarthy   *production designer:* Bob Rang   *original music:* Steve Lindsey   *origination:* The Production Group Studios, Hollywood

"Click" was one of two new 1997 syndicated game shows oriented to a teen audience. (The other was "Peer Pressure.") It was the first new game show from Merv Griffin, creator of "JEOPARDY!" and "WHEEL OF FORTUNE," in over five years.

On a set with a computer motif, three teams, each consisting of two teenagers, play a game of knowledge by competing in three rounds (called "levels") of questions. In the first level, each team competes against the "Motherboard," where they have sixty seconds to click on the mouse and answer as many questions as they can. Questions are selected by mouse; each icon reveals a dollar amount ($25 to $100) and a category. Categories on the game board include "Word Wizard," where the contestants play Spell Check, Definitions, and Funetics; "Web Site," where questions are augmented with the use of audio, video, or e-mail messages; and "Double Click," where the value of a question doubles.

In level two, one team keeps control of the game board until they miss a question or hit a "virus," at which point control to goes to the other teams.

All questions in level three are worth $100 with one player from each team positioned at one of three sites on stage (web site, word wizard, or game board) with the host controlling the mouse. When clicked, the mouse determines the next

"Click," the game show that teaches teens what they should know based on what they do know, was created by Merv Griffin and is hosted by Ryan Seacrest.

site to play a question. Questions answered incorrectly are tossed up for the players remaining at their podiums to answer. After several questions, teammates switch positions, and the team with the most money at the conclusion of this round wins the game.

COLLEGE BOWL

premiere: January 4, 1959   *packagers:* Moses-Reid-Cleary Productions (1959–1984); Richard Reid Productions/College Bowl Company (1987)   *broadcast history:* CBS Sunday afternoon January 4, 1959–June 28, 1959; CBS Sunday afternoon October 4, 1959–June 26, 1960; CBS Sunday afternoon October 2, 1960–June 11, 1961; CBS Sunday afternoon September 24, 1961–June 17, 1962; CBS Sunday afternoon September 23, 1962–June 16, 1963; NBC Sunday afternoon September 22, 1963–June 14, 1964; NBC Sunday afternoon September 20, 1964–June 13, 1965; NBC Sunday afternoon September 19, 1965–June 12, 1966; NBC Sunday afternoon September 18, 1966–June 4, 1967; NBC Sunday afternoon September 23, 1967–June 9, 1968; NBC Sunday afternoon September 28, 1968–June 8, 1969; NBC Sunday afternoon October 11, 1969–June 14, 1970; Syndicated special June 3, 1978; NBC primetime special May 23, 1984; Disney Channel (cable) September 13, 1987–December 20, 1987
1959–1970 version

hosts: Allen Ludden, Robert Earle   *announcers:* Don Morrow, Jerry Damon, Mel Brandt, Alan Berns   *creator:* Don Reid   *producer:* John Cleary   *directors:* Lamar Caselli, Robert Hultgren   *set designer:* Willis Conner   *theme written by:* Don Reid   *origination:* From 1959 to 1961 the show was broadcast from various college campuses; in the fall of 1961 the show moved to CBS Studio 59 in New York. From the 1963 to 1970 the show was telecast live from either NBC Studio 6A or 8H in New York.
1978 version

host: Art Fleming   *announcer:* Nelson Davis   *executive producer:* Don Reid   *producers:* Allan Reid, Richard Reid   *director:* Allan Reid   *origination:* Konover Hotel, Miami Beach
1984 version

host: Pat Sajak   *announcer:* Mel Brandt   *executive producer:* Don Reid   *producer/director:* Walter C. Miller   *set designer:* Ed Flesh   *origination:* St. John's Arena at Ohio State University
1987 version

host: Dick Cavett   *announcer:* Jim McKrell   *executive producers:* Don Reid, Richard Reid   *producer:* Mary Oberembt   *director:* Dennis Rosenblatt   *set designers:* Anthony Sabatino, William H. Harris   *origination:* Walt Disney World, Orlando

Two varsity scholar teams, each consisting of four undergraduates representing colleges and universities, competed in a question-and-answer game of knowledge and quick recall known as "The Varsity Sport of the Mind." On "College Bowl," the questions covered liberal arts subjects such as science, literature, world affairs, government, mathematics, history, and performing arts.

Allen Ludden, hosting his very first television game show, "G.E. College Bowl," back in 1959.

Each round began with a "toss-up" question worth ten points. Any of the eight players could ring in to answer and if correct, that player's team got a chance to answer bonus questions, each worth from twenty to forty points. The game was divided into twelve-minute halves and the team with the most points at the end of the game won. The winning team received $1,500 in scholarship grants while the runners-up were awarded $500. By the end of the network run, the scholarship prizes were increased to $3,000 for the winners of each match and $1,000 for the runners-up. Any team that won five games in a row retired as undefeated champion.

"College Bowl" began on the NBC radio network on October 10, 1953 with Allen Ludden as host. In the first game, Northwestern beat Columbia one hundred thirty-five to sixty. The moderator was in a New York studio, the students on their own campuses, and everybody was connected by means of a three-way radio hookup.

When it came to television in January 1959, the show was renamed "G.E. College Bowl" after its sponsor General Electric. "College Bowl" was seen from September until June each year, taking the summers off.

At first the show was broadcast from the various college campuses, but later the program moved into the studio at the network. The first show was broadcast from Faunce Hall Auditorium at Brown University in Providence, Rhode Island. Competing on the show were a team from Brown University and Pembroke of Rhode Island against a team from Northwestern University of Illinois. Northwestern won a close match, one hundred forty-five to one hundred thirty-five. The same two teams met on the tenth anniversary show.

On the last network program in June 1970, Old Dominion College beat Albright College of Pennsylvania. "G.E. College Bowl" was the last live game show on network television, when it ended its original run.

Allen Ludden left the show in June 1962 and when the program returned in the fall, Robert Earle became the new emcee. In September 1963, "G.E. College Bowl" moved from CBS to NBC and began color broadcasts from Studio 8H at Rockefeller Center in New York.

In 1978 a championship match was televised from the Konover Hotel in Miami and featured a championship match between Yale, Oberlin, Stanford, and Cornell. Art Fleming emceed the show. He also hosted the radio version of "College Bowl," heard over the CBS Radio Network in the 1970s.

A 1984 "College Bowl" special celebrated the series' thirtieth anniversary with a primetime telecast on NBC from St. John's Arena at Ohio State University. Pat Sajak hosted as teams battled for $20,000 in scholarship money.

The Disney Channel brought "College Bowl" back as a weekly series on cable in the fall of 1987. It originated from Disney World in Orlando, Florida, with talk show personality Dick Cavett as host. The top sixteen collegiate teams competed in a single elimination competition in the yearly National Championship Tournament.

"College Bowl" returned again to cable television on the Black Entertainment Television network (BET) under the title CAMPUS ALL-STAR CHALLENGE in 1990.

Did you know . . . "G.E. College Bowl" was the first game show to be awarded the George Foster Peabody award for outstanding achievement in broadcasting in 1960? The award, established in 1940, is considered among the most prestigious in broadcasting. "College Bowl" also won an Emmy Award for outstanding achievement in the field of panel, quiz, and audience participation programs in 1963.

College Bowl announcer Alan Berns, a staff announcer for CBS since 1959, was the voice that identified the network ("This is CBS") on their station breaks from 1988 to 1995. He was also heard as the announcer on the daytime serial "Guiding Light."

COLLEGE MAD HOUSE

premiere: September 9, 1989   *packager:* Stone Television Productions/Lorimar   *broadcast history:* Syndicated September 9, 1989–September 1, 1990   *host:* Greg Kinnear   *referees:* Donna Wilson, Richard MacGregor   *announcer:* Beau Weaver   *executive producers:* Bob Synes, Scott Stone

That's Greg Kinnear hosting his first and only game show, in 1989, titled "College Mad House."

producers: Stephen Brown, Randolph Gale *director:* Joe Behar *set designers:* Anthony Sabatino, William H. Harris *music:* Gary Scott *origination:* Hollywood Center Studios, Los Angeles

Greg Kinnear, who went on to host "Talk Soup" for E! Entertainment cable channel and "Later" for NBC-TV, emceed "College Mad House," the spin-off of the kids' game show FUN HOUSE during the 1989–1990 season.

Two teams of college students from rival universities competed in a series of sloppy stunts and trivia questions. Teams consisted of four players, two men and two women, who participated in stunts like "Pillow Pole." While standing four feet above the ground on a slippery surface, players tried to knock their opponents off by using pillows. In "Human Nut Bars" the contestants competed in a race to roll their bodies through a series of candy bar ingredients.

The team with the highest point total earned a trip to the "Mad House," a three-story maze of rooms, tunnels, and stairways. The winning team had two minutes to grab prizes while trying to avoid obstacles such as spinning tunnels, slippery surfaces, and cream pies and seltzer, flung at them by the losing team.

COLLEGE OF MUSICAL KNOWLEDGE

premiere: December 1, 1949 *packagers:* MCA 1949–1950 NBC Television 1954 *broadcast history:* NBC primetime December 1, 1949–June 29, 1950; NBC primetime October 5, 1950–December 28, 1950; NBC primetime July 4, 1954– September 12, 1954

1949–1950 version

host: Kay Kyser *announcers:* Verne Smith, Ben Grauer, Ted Brown *regulars:* Ish Kibbible, Liza Palmer, Sue Bennett, Michael Douglas, The Honeydreamers, Dr. Roy K. Marshall, Diane Sinclair, Ken Spaulding *producers:* Earl Ebi, Seymour Kulik *directors:* Earl Ebi, Seymour Kulik, Robert Wilbor, Jack Heim *casting:* David Susskind *set designer:* Larry Goldwasser *music director:* Carl Hoff *theme song:* "Thinking of You" *origination:* International Theater, New York

1954 version

host: Tennessee Ernie Ford *announcer:* Jack Narz *regulars:* The Cheerleaders *producers:* Howard Reilly, Perry Lafferty, Paul Phillips *director:* Jim Hobson *music director:* Frank DeVol *origination:* NBC Studio 1, Burbank

Big-band leader Kay Kyser was host of "College of Musical Knowledge," the musical quiz–variety show, based on his 1940s radio show. Kyser, garbed in cap and gown and called "The Professor," recruited contestants from the studio audience and asked musical questions that were based on performances by members of the band and special guests.

Three bearded judges, dressed in tails and resembling the Smith Brothers ("Smith Brothers cough drops"), sat behind a desk and comically judged the answers.

Among the writers on this show were Bob Quigley, who would later team up with Merrill Heatter to produce THE HOLLYWOOD SQUARES and many other game shows during the 1960s and 70s.

The 1954 summer version of "College of Musical Knowledge" was hosted by country singer Tennessee Ernie Ford

Tennessee Ernie Ford can clearly see that his show stacks up a winner.

("Sixteen Tons") and consisted of two groups of contestants who tried to identify songs for prizes. The winning contestants tried to guess the $100 bonus song, which increased in value each week until it was identified.

COME CLOSER

premiere: September 20, 1954 *packager:* Robert Jennings– Herbert Moss Productions *broadcast history:* ABC primetime September 20, 1954–December 13, 1954 *hosts:* Jimmy Nelson with Danny O'Day, Humphery Higby and Farfel the Dog *announcer:* Johnny HIcks *creator:* Robert Jennings *producer:* Herbert Moss *director:* Lou Sposa *set designer:* Romain Johnston *music director:* Alan Roth *origination:* New York

On the quiz show, "Come Closer," ventriloquist Jimmy Nelson and his dummies asked comic questions of members of the studio audience. The contestant coming closest to the correct answer won cash and prizes. A jackpot prize based on a clue given in song by dummy Danny O'Day was also featured.

Did you know . . . host Jimmy Nelson, accompanied by his dog Farfel, was best known as the spokesman for Nestle's Quik, the chocolate powdered drink mix, in a series of TV commercials during the 1950s? Do you remember the jingle

. . . "N-E-S-T-L-E-S, Nestle's makes the very best chhhho-
colate"?

CONCENTRATION

premiere: August 25, 1958   *packagers:* Jack Barry and Dan
Enright Productions (1958); NBC Productions (1958–1973);
Mark Goodson–Bill Todman Productions (1973–1978)
broadcast history: NBC daytime August 25, 1958–March 23,
1973; NBC primetime October 30, 1958–November 20, 1958;
NBC primetime April 24, 1961–September 18, 1961; Syndicated September 10, 1973–September 1978
1958–1973 daytime version
hosts: Hugh Downs, Bob Clayton, Ed McMahon   *substitute
hosts:* Art James, Jim Lucas, Bill Mazer   *model:* Paola Diva
announcers: Art James, Jim Lucas, Bob Clayton, Wayne
Howell   *substitute announcers:* Bill McCord, Vic Roby, Don
Pardo   *executive producers:* Robert Noah, Roger Muir   *producers:* Jack Farren, Norman Blumenthal   *directors:* Van
Fox, Ted Nathanson, Gertrude Rosenstein, Lynwood King
set designer: Otis Riggs Jr.   *graphic artists:* Bernie
Schmittke, Charles Brio, Jean Masse, Lou Cuveas   *music directors:* Paul Taubman, Milton Kaye   *music conductor:* Al Finelli   *origination:* NBC Studios 3A and 8G, New York

*It's no wonder that Hugh Downs and Art James look bewildered.
These perplexing rebuses puzzled a lot of contestants and viewers
over the years.*

1958 primetime version
host: Jack Barry   *announcer:* Bill McCord   *executive producer:* Roger Muir   *producer:* Jack Farren   *director:* Bob
Hultgren   *set designer:* Otis Riggs Jr.   *music director:* Paul
Taubman   *origination:* Studio A, NBC 67th Street Studios,
New York
1961 primetime version
host: Hugh Downs   *substitute host:* Art James   *models:* Annette Cash, Liz Gardner, Marilyn Grey, Pat White   *announcer:* Jim Lucas   *producer:* Jack Farren   *director:* Ted
Nathanson   *set designer:* Hjalmar Hermanson   *music director:* Milton Kaye   *origination:* Ziegfeld Theater, New York
1973–1978 syndicated version
host: Jack Narz   *announcer:* Johnny Olson   *producers:*
Howard Felsher, Buck D'Amore, Allen Koss   *director:* Ira
Skutch   *set designer:* Ted Cooper   *origination:* Metromedia
Studios, Los Angeles

"Concentration" was NBC-TV's longest-running game
show, spanning more than fourteen years in daytime. During
that period, there were also two primetime versions, a four-
week run in 1958 with Jack Barry as host that was a quick
fill-in when TWENTY-ONE was suddenly canceled and a five-
month run in 1961 with Hugh Downs as host that was
broadcast in color. The daytime version was the last NBC
show to make the switch to color on November 7, 1966.

"Concentration" had the unique distinction of being
broadcast from two different locations at the same time. During 1961, the daytime version called NBC Studio 3A in
Rockefeller Center, home, while the Monday night edition
was telecast from the Ziegfeld Theater at 54th Street and
Sixth Avenue. During its long network run, "Concentration"
was taped in just about every NBC studio, with Studio 8G
called home most often.

Based on the children's card game of the same name, the
object of the television version was to solve a rebus puzzle
by matching pairs of prizes that hid the puzzle.

Two players, in turn, called out a pair of numbers (from
one to thirty), which appeared on a three-sided wedge on a
game board. If the prizes (or information such as "forfeit one
gift" or "take one gift") matched, the player was credited
with the prize. "Wild Cards" were instant matches with
whatever else was called.

The third part of the wedge was shown when a match was
made, and revealed two portions of a slowly building rebus
(word-picture). The player was given a chance to guess the
answer and if correct, they won the game and all prizes credited to them. If not, they called out two more numbers and
tried to make another match. When the pieces did not reveal
a match, the opposing player got a chance to call numbers.

The winning player continued to play against new challengers until he or she was defeated, or until winning twenty
games. In the fifteen-year network run, only two players,
Mrs. Ruth Horowitz of Huntington Station, Long Island, New
York (July–August 1966), and Terri Lee Coffin of Balston
Spa, New York (January–February 1973), retired as undefeated champions.

The first puzzle used on the network show was "It Happened One Night" and the last puzzle was "You've Been

More Than Kind." Among the regular features introduced during its run were "The Cash Wheel" in 1960, "The Envelope and its Unknown Contents" in 1962, and the annual Challenge of Champions in 1963.

The Challenge of Champions featured the top four winners of the most games from the previous year, competing in a tournament to crown a grand champion. The winner received, in addition to all the prizes in the regular game, a trip for two around the world and a trophy, nicknamed "The Connie," which was based on "The Thinker," Rodin's famous sculpture. The first champion was Arthur Levine, a lawyer from Washington, D.C.

"Concentration" was the number-one-rated daytime game show on television from 1958 to 1962. In 1969 Hugh Downs received an Emmy nomination for his hosting duties on the show.

"Concentration" also featured special theme shows honoring the different countries of the world, yearly salutes to the Boy Scouts and Girl Scouts, its own anniversary specials, and a Christmas show with celebrities dressed up in Santa Claus costumes playing the game for CARE, the nonprofit organization which sent packages of food and clothing to needy people overseas.

Original announcer Art James left the show in December 1960 to host his own series, "Say When!!", and was replaced by Jim Lucas. Lucas stayed for three years until he was replaced by Bob Clayton on December 30, 1963. When Hugh Downs relinquished his duties as emcee in January 1969, Clayton moved up to host and longtime NBC staff announcer Wayne Howell joined as the new announcer.

From March to September 1969, "The Tonight Show" sidekick Ed McMahon emceed "Concentration," but when he left Bob Clayton returned as permanent host.

"Concentration" ended its run on NBC on March 23, 1973, after some 3,796 shows. Six months later it returned as a daily syndicated series produced by Mark Goodson–Bill Todman Productions in Hollywood with Jack Narz as host. The new version of "Concentration" featured the addition of a bonus game, "Double Play," in which the winner of the main game got a chance to win a new car. To win the car the player had to solve two fully revealed rebuses in ten seconds.

"Concentration" returned to network television in May 1987 with an updated edition called CLASSIC CONCENTRATION.

Did you know . . . Hugh Downs began his career as a staff announcer for NBC in Chicago in 1943 after serving in the U.S. Army? He transferred to New York in 1954 to join Arlene Francis and the "Home" show. In July 1957 he joined Jack Paar as his sidekick on the "The Tonight Show." When Paar left the "The Tonight Show" in 1962, Downs moved over to host "Today" for nine years. In 1985 Downs was recognized by the *Guinness Book of World Records* for holding the record for the greatest number of hours on network commercial television.

Gene Rayburn, of THE MATCH GAME fame, auditioned for the role of emcee of "Concentration" back in 1958. He didn't get the job, but did land another NBC series, DOUGH RE MI.

In 1961, when NBC was planning the nighttime version of "Concentration," the network wanted Hal March to host. But the sponsor insisted on Hugh Downs and it was Downs who was seen at night.

Bob Clayton, who emceed the last four years of "Concentration" on NBC, went to announce many shows for Bob Stewart in the 1970s, including THE $10,000 PYRAMID, BLANKETY BLANKS, PASS THE BUCK, and SHOOT FOR THE STARS.

Were you watching when . . . these celebrities stopped by and played "Concentration": Johnny Carson, Bill Cullen, Phyllis Diller, Dave Garroway, Merv Griffin, Burt Reynolds, Joan Rivers, Soupy Sales, and Betty White?

CONQUER FORT BOYARD

premiere: March 20, 1993 *packager:* Jacques Antoine Et Cie/Vin Di Bona Productions *broadcast history:* ABC primetime special March 20, 1993 *hosts:* Chris Berman and Cathy Lee Crosby *executive producers:* Vin Di Bona, Eytan Keller *coordinating producers:* Mark Fetterman, Grant Johnson *director:* Louis J. Horvitz *set designer:* Bill Bohnert *music:* Dennis McCarthy *origination:* Fort Boyard, off the coast of France

ESPN sportscaster Chris Berman and actress Cathy Lee Crosby hosted "Conquer Fort Boyard," the one-time special that was taped at Fort Boyard, a stone fortress located off the coast of France and dating back to the days of Napoleon.

Teams competed against each other in various physical and mental activities, including a visit to a room inhabited by snakes; bungee jumping into the center of the fort; and swimming through an underwater tunnel. The winning team got the chance to receive $15,000 in a treasure room guarded by two Bengal tigers.

CONTRAPTION

premiere: April 18, 1983 *packager:* Acme Game Show, Inc. *broadcast history:* Disney Channel (cable) April 18, 1983–January 9, 1988; Disney Channel (cable) March 8, 1989–October 25, 1989 *host:* Ralph Harris *announcer:* Miranda Frederick *team coaches:* Robin Shaw, Kevin Bickford *executive producers:* Peter Locke, Donald Kushner, Larry Gottlieb, Jonathan Debin *producer:* Barry Cahn *director:* Kip Walton *set designer:* Peter Clemens *music:* Robin Frederick

On "Contraption," six children on two teams of three watched scenes from Walt Disney films and answered questions about them. One member of each team played at a time and for each correct answer the child received a "contraptile." At the end of each round of questioning, the two kids competed in a "mini-race" for additional contraptiles. The team with the most contraptiles won the game.

COUCH POTATOES

premiere: January 23, 1989 *packager:* Saban Productions/Group W *broadcast history:* Syndicated January 23, 1989–September 8, 1989; USA (cable) September 11, 1989–March 23, 1990 (repeats of 1989 syndicated version) *host:* Marc Summers *announcers:* Joe Alaskey, Jim McKrell *creators:* David Greenfield, Ellen Levy *executive producers:* Haim Saban, Robert Unkel *producer:* Allen Koss *director:* Dennis

If you were a couch potato, you'd know why Lois Lane had a really big crush on this Man of Steel.

Rosenblatt *set designers:* Anthony Sabatino, William H. Harris *origination:* Studio 4, Fox Television Center, Los Angeles

On "Couch Potatoes," a daily syndicated show, two teams of contestants tested their knowledge of TV past and present. Each team was composed of three friends each of whom took the name of one of his or her favorite TV shows.

Each round began with a "tune-in" question, worth twenty-five rating points, and the team that answered correctly could earn additional points by answering three "spin-off" questions. Team members could answer only one of the spin-off questions and a wrong answer gave their opponents control.

After four rounds of questions, teams were given a chance to earn additional points in the "couch-up round." One member of each team participated at a time, trying to answer a trivia question with the point value determined at random. Points ranged from fifty to two hundred points to an automatic couch-up, where a team could catch up to their opponents' score if they were behind. This round consisted of each player answering two questions. The team with the most points after this round won the game and $1,000.

The winning team played the "channel roulette" bonus round for an additional $5,000. The goal was to accumulate one thousand points in thirty seconds by choosing a channel (2 to 13) and identifying the TV show pictured on the screen. Each channel had a different point value and players alternated in calling out the channels. Behind one of the twelve channels was "pay TV," which, if chosen, caused the team to lose all points accumulated. If they didn't reach the thousand points before the time elapsed they received $1 for each point earned.

Were you watching when . . . these game show favorites were all surprise guests on "Couch Potatoes": Bob Eubanks, Jim Lange, Wink Martindale, and Gary Owens?

Marc Summers' mother, Lois, was a special guest on "Couch Potatoes." She suprised her son on a Mother's Day theme show.

COUNTY FAIR
premiere: September 22, 1958 *packager:* Gale-Gernannt Productions *broadcast history:* NBC daytime September 22, 1958–September 25, 1959 *host:* Bert Parks *substitute hosts:* Keefe Brasselle, Danny Dayton, Pat Harrington Jr. *announcer:* Kenny Williams *"Miss County Fair":* Christy Logan, Linda Fields, Betty Martin, Linda Cristal, Zeme North,

The one and only Bert Parks with Miss County Fair Christie Logan, from his 1958 game show "County Fair."

Sandra Wirth   *executive producers:* Herb Landon, Joe Cates *producers:* Perry Cross, Carl Jampel, Bob Quigley   *director:* Joe Durand   *set designer:* Don Shirley Jr.   *music:* Bill Gale and his Fairgrounds Philharmonic   *origination:* NBC Studio 8H, New York

NBC's gigantic studio, 8H, was converted into a county fair setting for "County Fair," this daytime audience-participation show. Host Bert Parks was the "fairground impresario" and announcer Kenny Williams was the "barker."

With the studio audience sitting in a theater-in-the-round grandstand, contestants competed in a variety of stunts, skits, games, and contests. "County Fair" also featured a series of continuing stunts throughout its year-long television run.

Among the regular stunts was the "Punch Your Way Out of a Paper Bag," where contestants and guest celebrities tried to punch their way out of an eight-foot-high paper bag. A jackpot prize was offered to the player who was successful (only two contestants ever accomplished this feat). Among the celebrity contestants who made an attempt were football star Frank Gifford, basketball star Bob Cousy, baseball star Yogi Berra, actor Gene Barry, columnist Earl Wilson, and boxer Rocky Graziano.

"County Fair" was originally heard on the CBS radio network, debuting in 1945 with Jack Bailey and Win Elliott as hosts.

CROSS-WITS

premiere: December 15, 1975   *packagers:* Ralph Edwards Productions (1975–1980); Crossedwits Productions (1986–1987)   *broadcast history:* Syndicated December 15, 1975–September 1980; Syndicated September 8, 1986–September 1987

Here's guest celebrity Bill Cullen and his contestant partner, as host Jack Clark reads the "Cross-Wits" clues in the cross-fire round.

1975–1980 version

host: Jack Clark **assistant:** Jerri Fiala **announcers:** Jay Stewart, Jerry Bishop, John Harlan **creator:** Jerry Payne **producers:** Bruce Belland, Ed Bailey, Ray Horl **director:** Richard Gottlieb **set designers:** Anthony Sabatino, William H. Harris **music:** Ron Kaye, Buddy Kaye, Phillip Springer **origination:** Metromedia Studios, Los Angeles

1986–1987 version

host: David Sparks **announcer:** Michelle Roth **executive producers:** Norman Checkor, Phillip Mayer **producers:** Chris Pye, Roxann Checkor, Susan Mayer **director:** Barry Glazer **set designer:** Jimmy Cuomo **music:** Andrew Belling **origination:** Studio 33, CBS Television City, Los Angeles

Two teams of three players (one studio contestant and two guest celebrities) tried to guess words in "Cross-Wits," a crossword puzzle game. Teams played one at a time and tried to guess a crossword from a clue. Teams scored ten points for each letter in the crossword. Each crossword was also a clue to the identity of a person, place, or thing. The first team to solve the master puzzle earned extra points.

The top-scoring team of the day played the "cross fire" round and they had sixty seconds to guess ten crosswords from clues, for a bonus prize.

In the 1986 version (the title "Crosswits" was not hyphenated) the game was played in the same way as the earlier version, but with changes in the point scoring. In round one, a team got five points per letter of each word. In round two, the value doubled to ten points and in round three the values doubled again, to twenty points.

Were you watching when . . . Phyllis Diller celebrated her sixty-ninth birthday on the 1986 version of "Crosswits"? Also appearing on that version were comedians (and future talk show hosts) Arsenio Hall and Rosie O'Donnell.

In 1976 these game show emcees were all guest celebrities: Bill Cullen, Geoff Edwards, Art James, Dennis James, Allen Ludden, Peter Marshall, Wink Martindale, Jim McKrell, Jack Narz, Gary Owens, and Chuck Woolery.

THE DATING GAME

premiere: December 20, 1965 *packagers:* Chuck Barris Productions 1965–1989; Brian Graden Productions/Columbia Tri Star TV 1996–1997; Columbia Tri Star TV 1997– *broadcast history:* ABC daytime December 20, 1965–July 6, 1973; ABC primetime October 6, 1966–January 17, 1970; Syndicated September 10, 1973–September 1974; Syndicated September 4, 1978–September 1980; Syndicated September 15, 1986–September 8, 1989; Syndicated September 9, 1996–
1965–1980 version
host: Jim Lange *announcer:* Johnny Jacobs *executive producer:* Chuck Barris *producers:* Walt Case, Larry Gottlieb, Steve Friedman, Mike Metzger *directors:* Bill Carruthers, John Dorsey *set designers:* George Smith, Bill Morris, Bob Inkelas *music:* Lyn Barris, Frank Jaffe, Lee Ringuette *dancers (1965–1966):* Anita Mann, Ellen Friedman *featured Band (1965–1966):* The Regents: Craig Boyd, drums; John Harris, bass; Michael McDonald, lead guitar; Jerry Rosa, keyboards; Tom Baker, rhythm guitar *origination:* Studio 55, ABC Television Center, Los Angeles (1965–1966); ABC Vine Street Theater, Hollywood (1966–1974); KTLA Golden West Studios, Los Angeles (1978–1980)
1986–1989 ersion
hosts: Elaine Joyce, Jeff MacGregor *announcers:* Bob Hilton, Charlie O'Donnell *executive producers:* Chuck Barris, Jeff Wald, Scott Sternberg *producers:* Walt Case, Bruce Starin *directors:* John Dorsey, Linda Howard, Clay Jacobson *set designers:* Ed Flesh, John Shaffner *music:* Milton DeLugg, Lee Ringuette *origination:* Studio 7, Sunset Gower Studios, Los Angeles
1996–1997 version
host: Brad Sherwood *announcer:* Virginia Watson *executive producers:* Brian Graden, Lois Clark Curren, Jeff Olde *coordinating producer:* George David Monas *director:* Jerry Kupcinet *production designer:* Jimmy Cuomo *origination:* Hollywood Center Studios, Los Angeles
1997– version
host: Chuck Woolery *announcer:* John Cramer *executive producers:* Michael Canter, Lois Clark Curren *coordinating producer:* Rikk Greengrass *director:* Paul Casey *production designer:* Jimmy Cuomo *origination:* Hollywood Center Studios, Los Angeles

"The Dating Game" featured three young men who vied for a date with the young woman who was hidden from their view. She asked questions specially prepared to reveal the romantic nature of each man and later chose the one with whom she would like to have a date. The couple was given either a night on the town or an expense-paid trip to some fun locale. The game was also played with one bachelor choosing from among three young ladies, and with celebrity guests as the decision makers.

San Francisco radio personality Jim Lange had been the announcer on "The Tennessee Ernie Ford Show" prior to taking on "The Dating Game" hosting duties. Lange also hosted a local television show over KGO-TV in San Francisco titled "Bright and Early."

"The Dating Game" returned to the fall of 1996 as one-half of "The Dating Newlywed Hour." The new version featured a new host, comedian Brad Sherwood, and a new format.

The show began with one player, called the "chooser," watching on a video screen, while the three eligible bachelors or bachelorettes enter, each wearing headphones so that they couldn't hear any comments. After viewing all three, the chooser made a selection based on looks.

The second round of the game was based on the contestants' personality. The chooser was given interesting or unusual facts about the contestants and then selected the items he or she wanted to know more about. The player who the fact related to then told the story behind it. At the end of this round, the chooser made a selection based on personality.

The chooser was then given the choice of going on a date with the person he or she had selected based on looks or the person selected based on personality. Occasionally the choice was pro forma, since the same person was selected for both looks and personality.

"The Dating Game" began its second season on September 8, 1997, with Chuck Woolery taking over as host and the show returning to its original format of the 1960s and 1970s.

Did you know. . . "The Dating Game" producer Chuck Barris was also a songwriter? In 1962, Barris wrote a top-ten hit for Freddy Cannon, called "Palisades Park."

Who will be the lucky guy? Bachelor number one? Bachelor number two? Or bachelor number three?

"The Dating Game" was so popular in the sixties that Baskin-Robbins named one of their thirty-one ice cream flavors "Dating Game." It was a pink ice cream with diced dates and butter toasted pecans.

The first celebrity on "The Dating Game" was Adam West, who appeared on January 10, 1996 to promote the premiere of the new "Batman" TV series. Some of the other celebrities who visited "The Dating Game" looking for love included Karen Carpenter (1970), Dick Clark (1973), Richard Dawson (1967), Phyllis Diller (1973), Farrah Fawcett (1969), Sally Field (1966), Mark Harmon (1972), Michael Jackson (1972), Don Johnson (1969), Lassie (1971), Steve Martin (1968), Lee Marvin (1966), Groucho Marx (1967), Willie Nelson (1967), Burt Reynolds (1967), Don Rickles (1967), Arnold Schwarzenegger (1973), Tom Selleck (1967), and Suzanne Sommers (1973). When both Burt Reynolds and Tom Selleck appeared on the show twice, neither was chosen by the young woman for a date. Burt Reynolds returned for a third time in 1971 and was given his choice to select a date from three young bachelorettes.

During the 1978–1980 syndicated season Oscar winner Cuba Gooding Jr. was a bachelor looking for love on "The Dating Game."

DEALER'S CHOICE
premiere: January 21, 1974 *packager:* Fishman-Freer Productions/Columbia Television *broadcast history:* Syndicated January 21, 1974–December 12, 1975 *hosts:* Bob Hastings, Jack Clark *assistant:* Jane Nelson *announcer:* Jim Thompson *executive producers:* Ed Fishman, Randall Freer *producer:* Dave Fishman *director:* Dan Smith *set designers:* Glenn Holsey, Ross Bellah *music:* John LaSalle *origination:* Tropicana Hotel, Las Vegas; The Burbank Studios

Three contestants each received one hundred chips as an initial stake with which to play various betting games on "Dealer's Choice." Prizes were awarded to each contestant according to the total number of chips accumulated. Games on the show included "Blackjack," "Any Pair Loses," "Aces Out," "Wheel of Chance," and "Dealer's Derby."

The big winner of the day got a chance at a bonus prize by rolling special bonus dice whose faces represented sums of money. One face also had a spade on it. To win the grand prize, the contestant rolled until $1,000 was reached. If on any roll the spade showed up, the game ended and the contestant lost the money accumulated. The contestant, however, could quit at any time and keep all earnings up to that point.

"Dealer's Choice" was originally taped at the Tropicana Hotel in Las Vegas, but later moved to The Burbank Studios in California. Actor Bob Hastings, best known for roles on "McHale's Navy" and "General Hospital" was host for only the first few weeks before being replaced by veteran game show host Jack Clark.

DEBT
premiere: June 3, 1996 *packager:* Faded Denim Productions/Buena Vista Television *broadcast history:* Lifetime (cable) June 3, 1996–August 14, 1998; Syndicated March 9, 1998–September 1998 *host:* Wink Martindale *announcer:* Julie Claire *security guard:* Kurt Engstrom *based on a concept by:* Sarah Jane West *executive in charge of production:* Julie Stern *senior producer:* Andrew Golder *producers:* Dean Young, David Greenfield *director:* James Marcione *production designer:* Jimmy Cuomo *music:* Alan Ett *origination:* Studio 9, Hollywood Center Studios (1996); Studio 1, Hollywood Center Studios (1997)

Three contestants compete in this question-and-answer game, with the winner getting a chance to have his or her debt paid off. The debts of the players are averaged together and staked to each contestant with that amount as the total to be reduced in the game.

Round one is called "General Debt," in which players try to answer questions in their choice of five categories. Each question has a value ranging from minus $50 to minus $250. If a player answers a question correctly, its value is deducted from the player's debt total. One category, the most difficult on the board, is called the "Debtonator," and the value of each question is doubled.

The game begins with a question worth $1, and the player who answers it gets control of the game board and determines the first category to be played.

The player who has the highest debt total at the end of this round is eliminated from the game and receives a $200 savings bond and a "Debt" piggy bank.

Round two, "Gambling Debt," features the two remaining players competing to wager who could answer the most

Wink Martindale is happy to be hosting his CableAce award-winning game show, "Debt."

questions (five is the maximum) in a series of five categories. One player bids, and the other can bid higher or challenge. The value of the categories in this round begins at $300 and goes to a maximum of $1,000. If the player answers all the questions correctly he or she has the value deducted from his or her score. If the player fails to complete his or her challenge, the opponent gets the value deducted from his or her score. The player with the smallest debt at the end of this round wins the game, while the other player receives a $500 savings bond and a Debt piggy bank.

The winning player moves on to the "Pay Off Your Debt" round, in which he or she tries to answer ten questions in sixty seconds. If he or she succeeds, the player's debt is reduced to zero, and he or she gets a chance to bet his or her entire debt, if so desired, by answering one question in a favorite subject in pop culture. A correct answer doubles the player's winnings. If answered incorrectly, however, the player loses all winnings from the show and returns home still in debt.

DESIGNATED HITTER

premiere: December 1, 1993   *packager:* William Carruthers Company   *broadcast history:* ESPN (cable) December 1,

The glitz and glamour of Las Vegas shines through on the set of "Dealer's Choice," with emcee Jack Clark.

1993—March 31, 1994 *host:* Curt Chaplin *announcer:* Rick Stern *executive producer:* Bill Carruthers *producers:* Tim Carruthers, Chris Ciaffa, Charlie Kolich *director:* Bill Carruthers *set designer:* Jerry Dunn *origination:* Empire Studios, North Hollywood

New York radio personality Curt Chaplin hosted "Designated Hitter," this daily game show that tested the sports knowledge of three studio contestants.

The players each selected five questions, in turn, from four possible categories . . . baseball, football, basketball, and one called curve ball, a category that covered all other sports. Each category had five questions, a "single" worth $25, a "double" worth $50, a "triple" worth $75, a "homer" worth $100, and a "pinch-hit" worth an undisclosed amount. Players competed on a jump-in basis on all except the pinch-hit question, which was available to only the player who selected it.

Each wrong answer was an "out" and any player who accumulated three outs lost $100 from their score. The top-two scoring players moved on to the second round.

In round two, the players each selected one sports category and then alternated answering four questions in that category. Questions were worth $25 (single), $50 (double), $75 (triple), and $100 (homer). If a player missed a question, his or her opponent could choose to answer and add the extra cash to that person's own bank. The player with the most money at the end of this round won the game and played the "Grand Slam" bonus for additional cash.

In the Grand Slam the winner had to answer four questions correctly, one from each category, for up to $3,000 cash. The first correct answer was worth $250; the second, an additional $500; the third, $750 more; and the final question, $1,500.

THE DIAMOND HEAD GAME

premiere: January 6, 1975 *packager:* Fishman-Freer Productions/Columbia Television *broadcast history:* Syndicated January 6, 1975–September 1975 *host:* Bob Eubanks *assistant:* Jane Nelson *announcer:* Jim Thompson *executive producers:* Ed Fishman, Randall Freer *producer:* Dave Fishman *director:* Terry Kyne *art director:* Richard Stiles *music:* Alan Thicke *origination:* Kuilima Hotel, Oahu

This one-season syndicated game show "The Diamond Head Game," was taped at the Kuilima Hotel in Oahu, Hawaii, the first game show to originate entirely from the fiftieth state. Members of the studio audience were divided into four sections, each representing one of the four islands of Hawaii. Each show used eight players, two from each section. Two players competed at a time in a question-and-answer game, with the winner moving on to a final round against the three winners from the next rounds.

In the final round, the four players were situated at the bottom of a three-step climb and were read a list of items. Each player, in turn, repeated item names until he or she missed one. The game continued until only one player remained and that player became the day's champ.

Bob Eubanks, back on the air with "The Diamond Head Game" from Hawaii. He appears to be delighted to receive a lei from his assistant, Jane Nelson.

The champion was put into a glass booth containing U.S. currency and slips of paper with prizes written on them, all blowing around the booth. The winner had fifteen seconds to gather up as much as possible for his or her winnings.

After the first thirteen weeks, "The Diamond Head Game" shows were taped, and the format was changed. The game now began with two teams, each made up of three players, competing in a question-and-answer quiz of three rounds. Each round had a category (e.g., card games) with five possible answers (e.g., poker, bridge, pinochle, blackjack, and hearts). A statement was read, and players tried to match the statement to one of the possible answers. Any player could buzz in, and if his or her answer was correct, the team received ten points. If the answer was wrong, the opposing team got a chance to answer.

Point values increased to twenty points in round two and to thirty points in round three. The team with the most points moved on to round four, in which the three team members now competed as individuals. A category and a list of items was given. Players alternated, trying to remember things on that list. Two wrong answers eliminated a player from the game and the last remaining player became the day's winner.

The champion was given fifteen seconds to enter the Diamond Head volcano to gather up slips of paper being blown around him or her and put them in a treasure bag. The first five slips pulled out of the bag by host Bob Eubanks became the player's prizes.

The player was given a chance to trade in the prizes he or she had collected for a chance to win a bonus prize. This consisted of choosing one of five bills: three of the bills were worth $100, a fourth was worth a $5,000 prize package, and the last one was a special grand prize.

Did you know . . . Bob Eubanks tried his luck as a singer in the 1960s. Among his singles were "Smoke, Smoke, Smoke That Cigarette" and "Heaven of the Stars."

DO YOU KNOW?

premiere: October 12, 1963 *packager:* CBS News *broadcast history:* CBS weekends October 12, 1963–April 25, 1964 *host:* Robert Maxwell *producer:* Joel Heller *director:* Martin Carr *origination:* New York

Children were quizzed about books they had been assigned to read on this Saturday afternoon series, "Do You Know?" Two teams made up of three nine- to-twelve-year-olds from different schools competed each week. The questions, accompanied by films, drawings, and assorted objects to be identified, were based on books the children were assigned to read beforehand.

Books were suggested by the American Library Association, the Child Study Association of America, and the National Education Association. The premiere broadcast featured *The Sea Around Us* by Rachel Carson. Other spotlighted books included *A Bridle for Pegasus* by Katherine Shippen; *Young Thomas Edison* by Sterling North; and *Wonderful World of Energy* by Lancelot Hogben.

"Do You Know?" was produced by the Public Affairs Department of CBS News.

DO YOU TRUST YOUR WIFE?

premiere: January 3, 1956 *packager:* Don Fedderson Productions *broadcast history:* CBS primetime January 3, 1956–March 26, 1957 *host:* Edgar Bergen with Charlie McCarthy, Mortimer Snerd, and Effie Klinker *announcers:* Ed Reimers, Bob Lamond *executive producer:* Fred Henry *producer:* Don Fedderson *directors:* Jim Morgan, Fred Henry *music director:* Frank Devol *origination:* The Republic Studios, Hollywood

On "Do You Trust Your Wife," married couples were chosen for their unusual backgrounds, and interviewed by ventriloquist Edgar Bergen and one of his dummies. They were then asked a series of four questions and the husband could answer them or trust his wife to. The first correct answer earned $100; the second, $200; and the third, $300. On the fourth question, the couple could risk all or any part of their winnings on their ability to answer it.

Three couples played each week and the top-scoring couple returned at the end of the week to play against last week's winner on the "Trust Fund Question," where they could win $100 a week for a year.

"Do You Trust Your Wife?" was seen Tuesday nights after THE $64,000 QUESTION and after its CBS run, it would return as part of the ABC daytime lineup in 1957 with new host Johnny Carson and new title "Who Do You Trust?"

Did you know . . . in 1937, Northwestern University awarded an honorary degree to Edgar Bergen's dummy Charlie McCarthy? The degree of "Master of Innuendo and Snappy Comeback" was given by the School of Speech. Edgar Bergen, a pre-med student at Northwestern, created Charlie McCarthy while in high school.

DOCTOR I.Q.

premiere: November 4, 1953 *packager:* ABC Television *broadcast history:* ABC primetime November 4, 1953–October 17, 1954; ABC primetime December 15, 1958–March 23, 1959

1953–1954 version

hosts: Jay Owen, James McClain *assistants:* Tom Reddy, Ed Michaels, Art Fleming, George Ansbro, Dirk Fredricks *announcer:* Bob Shepard *creator:* Lee Segall *producer:* Frederick Heider *director:* Charles Dubin *set designer:* Beulah Frankel *theme song:* "We're in the Money" *origination:* Elysee Theater, New York

1958–1959 version

host: Tom Kennedy *assistants:* Mimi Walters, Kay Christopher, Sue England, Carol Byron *announcer:* Bill Ewing *executive producer:* Selig J. Seligman *producer:* Harfield Weedin *director:* Hap Weyman *set designer:* George Smith *music:* Bobby Hammack *origination:* Studio D, ABC Television Center, Los Angeles

Tom Kennedy was billed as "Doctor I.Q.," the mental banker, on this primetime game show.

"Doctor I.Q." was one of the most successful quiz shows on radio during the 1940s. Its first attempt to make the transition to television came in the fall of 1953.

"Doctor I.Q." was a question-and-answer game, with the emcee known as "Doctor I.Q." on the stage and assistants with hand microphones roaming the studio audience looking for possible players. When they found one, they would call out "Doctor, I have a lady in the balcony!" Upon hearing a question answered correctly, the doctor would say, "Give that lady ten silver dollars."

The show was first heard in the Houston, Texas area with Ted Nabors as the first "Doctor." The program made its national debut on the NBC radio network on June 10, 1939 with Lew Valentine as host. James McClain became "Doctor I.Q." in 1942 and continued for the rest of the radio run. Jay Owen was the first TV "Doctor" and James McClain replaced him on January 18, 1954. Future "Jeopardy!" host Art Fleming was one of the doctor's assistants.

"Doctor I.Q." returned to ABC for a brief run during the 1958–1959 season. Tom Kennedy, hosting his second network game show, was joined by a quartet of female assistants.

DOLLAR A SECOND

premiere: September 20, 1953 *packager:* Trinity Tele-Productions *broadcast history:* DuMont primetime September 20, 1953–June 14, 1954; NBC primetime July 4, 1954–August 22, 1954; ABC primetime October 1, 1954–June 24, 1955; NBC primetime July 5, 1955–August 30, 1955; ABC primetime September 2, 1955–August 31, 1956; NBC primetime June 22, 1957–September 28, 1957; *host:* Jan Murray *assistants:* Patricia White, Bernard Martin, Stuart Mann, Evelyn Patrick *announcers:* Terry O'Sullivan, Ken Roberts, Tom Reddy *creator:* Jean Paul Blondeau *producers:* Mike Dutton, Jess Kimmel, Dave Brown, Bud Granoff *directors:* Frank Bunetta, Dave Brown, Phil Levens, Martin Magner *origination:* Hudson Theater, New York (NBC versions)

A team of two contestants tried to answer questions and complete stunts on "Dollar a Second," and for every second they remained on the show they received a dollar. They could quit at any time with their winnings, or risk the possibility of losing all of their money due to certain events out of their control. Some of the unexpected events employed included a fire alarm ringing in a particular fire station and a toy train completing a certain number of trips around a track.

Any time a player missed a question, his or her mate had to pay a penalty. Frequently the partner would be doused with water or hit with a cream pie.

"Dollar a Second" was based on a French quiz series, "Cent Francs La Seconde" (100 Francs a Second), and was sponsored by Mogen David Wine.

THE $1.98 BEAUTY SHOW

premiere: September 1978 *packager:* Chuck Barris Productions *broadcast history:* Syndicated September 1978–

Kooky comic Rip Taylor finally gets a chance to host his own game show. Here he embraces "The $1.98 Beauty Show" winner of the week.

September 1980 *host:* Rip Taylor *assistant:* Larry Spencer *announcer:* Johnny Jacobs *executive producer:* Chuck Barris *producer:* Gene Banks *director:* John Dorsey *set designer:* Romain Johnston *music director:* Milton DeLugg *theme song:* "Ain't She Sweet" *origination:* NBC Studios, Burbank

"The $1.98 Beauty Show," a Chuck Barris creation, spoofed beauty contests, with six women from eighteen to eighty years old competing in mock beauty contests. A celebrity panel rated the women on their beauty, their swimsuits, and how they performed in a talent competition, with the winner receiving $1.98 and a tacky crown.

Did you know . . . that female comic Sandra Bernhard was a contestant on "The $1.98 Beauty Show" in 1978?

DON ADAMS' SCREEN TEST

premiere: September 8, 1975 *packager:* Stacey Productions for Universal Television *broadcast history:* Syndicated September 8, 1975–September 19, 1976 *host:* Don Adams *announcer:* Dick Tufeld *executive producer:* Don Adams *producer/director:* Marty Pasetta *set designer:* Michael Baugh *music:* Hal Mooney *origination:* Los Angeles

Comedian Don Adams, best known for his role as Maxwell Smart on the TV series "Get Smart," emceed this weekly game show that featured two studio contestants reenacting scenes from famous movies with guest celebrities, after viewing clips from the original films. On ''Don Adams' Screen Test,'' the player whose performance was judged the best by a guest producer or director received a part in an upcoming movie or TV show.

Among the celebrities who dropped by to act with the contestants were James Caan, Phyllis Diller, Shirley Jones, and Don Rickles.

Did you know . . . announcer Dick Tufeld was the voice of the robot in the 1960s science fiction TV show ''Lost in Space,'' as well as in the 1998 feature film?

DOTTO

premiere: January 6, 1958 *packager:* Frank Cooper Productions/Sy Fischer Associates *broadcast history:* CBS daytime January 6, 1958–August 15, 1958; NBC primetime July 1, 1958–August 12, 1958 *host:* Jack Narz *announcers:* Ralph Paul (CBS), Wayne Howell (NBC) *creators:* Al Schwartz, Snag Werris *producer:* Ed Jurist *director:* Jerome Schnur *dotto drawings:* Jerry Hammer Associates *artist:* Eric Leiber *set designers:* Maurice Gordon, Charles Lisanby, Ron Baldwin *music director:* Hank Sylvern *orig-ination:* CBS Studio 62, New York; Colonial Theater, New York (NBC)

''Dotto'' featured two contestants trying to guess the identity of a famous person, place, or thing, outlined by a series of dots.

Contestants answered general knowledge questions to which point values were assigned. A question was worth five, eight, or ten dots. If a player answered correctly, the dots were connected. If they answered incorrectly, their opponent received the dots. When a player reached the level of twenty-five connected dots, he or she was given a clue. A second clue was given at the thirty-five dot level. The player won an amount of money that was determined by the number of unconnected dots.

''Dotto'' was the first game show dropped as a result of the quiz show scandal in 1958. It was dropped without warning after its August 15 broadcast and replaced on the following Monday with TOP DOLLAR.

Did you know . . . ''Dotto'' was one of the few shows to be seen on two different networks at the same time? CBS broadcast the daytime version, while NBC had the nighttime edition.

Were you watching when . . . game show hosts Hal March (THE $64,000 QUESTION) and Johnny Carson (WHO DO YOU TRUST?) competed in a special game of ''Dotto'' on July 15, 1958?

A shot of emcee Jack Narz holding the question cards on ''Dotto,'' from a 1958 broadcast.

DOUBLE DARE

premiere: December 13, 1976 *packager:* Mark Goodson–Bill Todman Productions *broadcast history:* CBS daytime December 13, 1976–April 29, 1977 *host:* Alex Trebek *announcers:* Gene Wood, Johnny Olson *executive producer:* Jay Wolpert *producer:* Jonathan Goodson *directors:* Marc Breslow, Paul Alter *set designer:* Henry Lickel *music supervisor:* Bart Eskander *origination:* Studio 33, CBS Television City, Los Angeles

In ''Double Dare'' two contestants attempted to identify people, places, and things from a series of clues. Contestants were in separate soundproof booths with lock-out devices that sealed their opponents' booths when they answered. The first player to come up with a correct answer got $50 and a chance to ''dare'' the other opponent to come up with the correct answer on the next clue. The opponent who succeeded got $50, the one who failed the challenger's dare received $100. The next clue was played for a ''double dare'' for double cash prizes. The first player to earn $500 won the game.

In the bonus round, the champion played against three Ph.D.s known as ''the spoilers.'' The champion gave the spoilers five clues out of a possible ten and hoped that the spoilers couldn't guess the subject. The champion won money for each wrong guess by a spoiler. The spoilers won $100 if they came up with the subject.

Did you know . . . ''Night Court'' costar Markie Post was an associate producer on ''Double Dare''?

This 1976 game show would mark Alex Trebek's first show for Goodson-Todman Productions. In 1987, he would return to host CLASSIC CONCENTRATION for six years, adding a short stint in 1991 when he emceed a revival of TO TELL THE TRUTH.

DOUBLE DARE

premiere: October 6, 1986 *packager:* MTV Networks *broadcast history:* Nickelodeon (cable) October 6, 1986–March 15, 1991; Syndicated February 22, 1988–September 8, 1989 *host:* Marc Summers *assistants:* Robin Marrella, Dave Shikiar, Jamie Bojanowski *announcer:* "Harvey" (John Harvey) *creators:* Geoffrey Darby, Michael Klinghoffer, Dee LaDuke, Bob Mittenthal *producers:* Michael Klinghoffer, Dana Calderwood, Angelika Bartenbach *directors:* Michael Klinghoffer, James Colistro, Hugh Martin *set designers:* James Fenhagen, Byron Taylor, Nancy Tobias *music:* Edd Kalehoff *origination:* WHYY–TV, Philadelphia (1986–1989); Universal Studios, Orlando (1989–1991)

"Double Dare" was the first game show to be broadcast on the Nickelodeon network, a cable service that specialized in programming for children. "Double Dare" was an instant hit

Marc Summers is about to get drenched, slimed, and sprayed by his assistants (left to right) Robin Marrella, Dave Shikiar, and Jamie Bojanski on the Nickelodeon set of "Double Dare."

and a syndicated version was made available to commercial television in the spring of 1988. On January 23, 1989 the title was changed to "Super Sloppy Double Dare."

The Fox Television Network added a primetime version in April 1988 that featured an entire family competing. The Fox edition ran until July 1988, and reappeared on Nickelodeon on August 13, 1990 combining new shows and reruns.

The kids-only version of "Double Dare" was seen on Nickelodeon until March 1991, leaving only the family version FAMILY DOUBLE DARE.

"Double Dare" featured two teams, each with two kids, competing by answering trivia questions and completing stunts.

In round one, one team controlled the board for as long as they were able to give correct answers. If the team didn't know the answer, they could dare their opponents to answer at double point value (they collected if their opponents were wrong). The opposing team could double dare the first team, forcing them either to answer the question or complete a physical challenge, such as bursting ten balloons filled with shaving cream in fifteen seconds, by sitting on them. This increased the score by four times the initial value of the question.

Point values for round one began at $10 for the initial response, $20 for the dare portion, and $40 for a double dare. The values were doubled in round two and the team with the most money when the time ran out won the game.

The winning team played the "Double Dare Obstacle Course" in which they tried to complete stunts, like finding a flag in a vat of styrofoam or climbing up a slide filled with chocolate pudding. Each stunt completed in sixty seconds earned the team a prize—with eight stunts completed winning the team a grand prize.

"Double Dare" received the first CableAce Award presented to a game show, in 1989.

DOUBLE EXPOSURE

premiere: March 13, 1961 *packager:* Merrill Heatter–Bob Quigley Productions *broadcast history:* CBS daytime March 13, 1961–September 29, 1961 *host:* Steve Dunne *assistant:* Judith Rawlins *models:* June Palmer, Betty Andrews *announcer:* Kenny Williams ("Mr. Rules") *executive producer:* Merrill Heatter *producer:* Bob Quigley *director:* Jerome Shaw *set designer:* Robert Tyler Lee *music director:* Sid Wayne *origination:* Studio 43, CBS Television City, Los Angeles

Two contestants tried to identify the picture of a famous person hidden behind a twelve-piece jigsaw puzzle overlay, on "Double Exposure." Each player had an identical puzzle and the players were isolated from each other so they could not see what the other had revealed. Each puzzle was also numbered differently, so what may have been piece number three on one person's puzzle could have been number seven on the opponent's puzzle.

Before each piece was revealed, an electronic wheel was spun, indicating either a merchandise prize or a cash amount ($10 to $60). Any player who accumulated over $100 au-

A cameraman's view of "Double Exposure" and its host, Steve Dunne.

tomatically lost the game. In order to win the prizes a player had to successfully solve the puzzle.

Did you know . . . Steve Dunne was the costar of the series ''The Brothers Branigan'' and emcee of TRUTH OR CONSEQUENCES in the mid-1950s?

DOUBLE OR NOTHING

premiere: October 6, 1952 *packager:* Walt Framer Productions *broadcast history:* CBS daytime October 6, 1952–July 2, 1954; NBC primetime June 5, 1953–July 3, 1953 *host:* Bert Parks *assistant:* Joan Meinch *announcer:* Bob Williams *producer:* Walt Framer *directors:* Rai Purdy, Matt Harlib *music director:* Ivan Ditmars *origination:* International Theater, New York

Contestants were asked a series of questions worth $10, $20, and $40 and a double-or-nothing question, for possible winnings of $140 per game. On ''Double or Nothing,'' all the day's contestants participated in the Red and White Sweepstakes (the colors of Campbell's Soup, the sponsor) at the end of the show. In the Red and White Sweepstakes another question was asked and each contestant wrote an answer down. The player with the first correct answer won the sweepstakes.

''Double or Nothing'' was based on the radio show of the same name that aired from 1940 to 1952. Among the hosts were Walter Compton, John Reed King, Todd Russell, and Walter O'Keefe.

DOUBLE TALK

premiere: August 18, 1986 *packager:* Bob Stewart Productions *broadcast history:* ABC daytime August 18, 1986–December 19, 1986 *host:* Henry Polic II *announcers:* Bob Hilton, Johnny Gilbert *executive producer:* Anne Marie Schmidt *producer:* David Stewart *director:* Bruce Burmester *set designer:* Ed Flesh *music:* Bob Cobert *origination:* Studio 54, ABC Television Center, Los Angeles *debut guests:* Betty White, Stuart Damon

''Double Talk'' consisted of two teams, each composed of a celebrity guest and a studio contestant, competing. One player attempted to solve the first half of a puzzle while his or her partner attempted to solve the other half. Examples of puzzles: ''Crack . . . the Cubes'' which translates into ''Break the Ice'' and ''The Price . . . of Survival'' which means ''The Cost of Living.''

If they were correct they earned ten points. If a team solved all four puzzles, they won a jackpot of $1,000. If they were incorrect, their opponents could win five points by solving a puzzle. The teams played four boards of four puzzles with the final board worth twenty points for each puzzle. The team with the highest score won the game and played for a possible $10,000 in the bonus game.

In the bonus round, one player was shown a set of initials (example: A———F———) and then tried to get his or her teammate to guess the words that made up that phrase by using incomplete sentences in the bonus game. The team was given sixty seconds and could win $100 for each correct answer and $10,000 for all ten.

DOUBLE UP

premiere: September 5, 1992   *packager:* Slam Dunk Productions/NBC Productions   *broadcast history:* NBC Saturday morning September 5, 1992–October 17, 1992   *host:* J. D. Roth   *assistant:* "Disco"   *creator:* Pat Jarvis   *executive producers:* J. D. Roth, Kurt Brendlinger   *director:* Kim Paul Friedman   *set designers:* Josee Lemonnier, Ron Olsen   *theme:* Dis Style Productions (lyrics by Jonte Ray)   *origination:* NBC Studios, Burbank

"Double Up," a Saturday morning kids' game show seen for only seven weeks, featured a real-life brother and sister trying to pick the ideal date for each other. If their selection matched the choice of the studio audience, they both enjoyed the "ultimate night out on the town," which included a limousine, a $500 shopping spree, dinner at a restaurant, and tickets to a rock concert.

The game began with the sister asking questions of three potential dates for her brother to determine who would make the best match. One question was posed to each girl. After the sister concluded her questioning, her brother asked questions of three potential dates for his sister. Two rounds of questions were played before each sibling made a choice and the audience voted for their own selection. The brother and sister both had to match the audience's selection in order to win the grand prize.

Host J. D. Roth, who also served as executive producer of "Double Up," had previously emceed the kids' game show FUN HOUSE and had appeared in the TV series "Charles in Charge" and "As the World Turns." In 1985 he was a finalist in the acting category on "Star Search."

DOUGH RE MI

premiere: February 24, 1958   *packager:* Jack Barry and Dan Enright Productions   *broadcast history:* NBC daytime February 24, 1958–December 30, 1960   *host:* Gene Rayburn   *substitute hosts:* Jack Barry, Roger Tuttle, Dayton Allen, Keefe Brasselle, Fred Robbins   *announcers:* Roger Tuttle, Wayne Howell   *executive producers:* Robert Noah, Ed Pierce   *producers:* Hugh Branigan, Fred Stettner   *directors:* Ted Nathanson, Dick Schneider, Dick Auerbach   *set designer:* Ted Cooper   *music director:* Paul Taubman   *origination:* NBC Studio 8H, New York

Three contestants competed for cash prizes in this daytime musical game show, "Dough Re Mi." Each game consisted of three songs, valued at $100, $300, and $500. At the start of the game, each of the players was given $200. The first three notes of a song were played and the bidding was opened for the fourth note. Players bid part of their bankrolls until a bell was rung or no one wished to go any further with the bidding. The first four notes were then played and the player who guessed the song's name correctly won the value of the song. The player who could not guess correctly would recoup half of the money lost by challenging another contestant. If the challenged player could guess the name of song, the challenger lost the entire bid and the challenged player won the value of the song.

From time to time, celebrity guests joined the panel to play for charity. The first celebrity guest to visit the show was Lou Costello on May 16, 1958. Other guest stars were Florence Henderson, Jaye P. Morgan, and Peter Marshall.

Did you know . . . host Gene Rayburn was half of the first two-person morning team in radio? In 1946 Gene was teamed up with Jack Lescoulie to host the morning show on WNEW radio in New York. Lescoulie was replaced by Dee Finch after six months and the Rayburn and Finch morning show became the top-rated show in New York City radio.

DOWN YOU GO

premiere: May 30, 1951   *packager:* Louis Cowan Productions   *broadcast history:* DuMont primetime May 30, 1951–May 20, 1955; CBS primetime June 11, 1955–September 3, 1955; ABC primetime September 15, 1955–June 14, 1956; NBC primetime June 16, 1956–September 8, 1956   *hosts:* Dr. Bergen Evans, Bill Cullen   *announcers:* Ed Cooper, Dick Stark, John Mallow, Don Hancock, Carol Brooke, Jim Coy   *executive producer:* Steve Carlin   *producers:* Gail Compton, Jay Sheridan, Roger Gerry, Polly Cowan, Shirley Bernstein   *directors:* Barry McKinley, Dick Sandwick, Jack Sameth, Joe Cates, Seymour Robbie   *set designer:* Norman Davidson   *origination:* WGN–TV, Chicago May 30, 1951–December 1, 1954; New York December 8, 1954–September 8, 1956; NBC Studio 6B (1956)   *debut guests:* Francis Coughlin, Toni Gillman, Carmelita Pope, Robert Breen

Four celebrity panelists played a game based on the parlor game, "Hangman." On "Down You Go," the panel tried to identify common phrases, song titles, and expressions submitted by home viewers. Before the guessing began, a clue was given and each panelist was allowed to ask a question about the phrase. Players then guessed letters in the words and a wrong guess eliminated that player from the round. Viewers received cash prizes for submitting phrases and additional money if their phrases stumped the panel.

The panelist with the highest number of "knockdowns" (times being eliminated) had to identify a penalty phrase drawn from a treasure chest, within a time limit. Failing to do so doubled the winnings of each viewer whose phrase had stumped the panel.

Dr. Bergen Evans, a professor of English at Northwestern University, was host of the show from its premiere in 1951 until June 23, 1956. When the show moved to NBC Bill Cullen took over as host. The NBC version of 1956 featured a panel of Arthur Treacher, Hildy Parks, ventriloquist Jimmy Nelson, and Jayne Mansfield.

At one time or another during its run, "Down You Go" was seen on all four commercial networks.

DRAW ME A LAUGH

premiere: January 15, 1949 *broadcast history:* ABC primetime January 15, 1949–February 5, 1949 *hosts:* Walter Hurley and Patricia Bright *cartoonist:* Mel Casson *producer:* Milton Krents *director:* Howard Cordery *origination:* New York

On "Draw Me a Laugh," this four-week game show series, cartoonist Mel Casson (who drew the newspaper comic strip "Jeff Crockett") sketched cartoons from ideas submitted by home viewers. At the same time, the gag line, but not the cartoon idea, was given to a studio contestant, who within a two-minute time limit drew his or her own sketch. A panel of four audience members then judged which of the two drawings was the funniest. Another feature of the show was music by folk singer Oscar Brand.

DRAW TO WIN

premiere: April 22, 1952 *packager:* O'Keefe-O'Brien Productions *broadcast history:* CBS primetime April 22, 1952–June 10, 1952 *host:* Henry Morgan *announcer:* Art Hannes *cartoonists:* Bill Holman, Abner Dean *producers:* Winston O'Keefe, Joel O'Brien, Marlo Lewis *director:* Joel O'Brien *set designer:* John Eberhardt *origination:* New York *debut guests:* Bill Holman, Abner Dean, Sidney Hoff, Eve Hunter

Comedian Henry Morgan emceed "Draw To Win," a short-lived picture charade show that featured four panelists trying to guess the caption of a cartoon drawn by a cartoonist. Home viewers who submitted the ideas received $5 for their submission and additional money if their drawing was not identified. Examples included phrases like "saved by the bell," where the picture showed a man being pulled out of the water by a Southern "belle."

Among the cartoonists who appeared on "Draw to Win" included Bill Holman, Abner Dean, Roger Price, Hilda Terry, and Ham Fisher. After this series left the air, host Henry Morgan became better known as a panelist on the long-running I'VE GOT A SECRET.

Did you know . . . "Draw To Win" announcer Art Hannes was a staff announcer for CBS from 1945 to 1969? He was heard every Sunday night as the announcer for "The Ed Sullivan Show" and on Mondays on "Studio One." He played a network announcer in the movie *The Night That Panicked America*, inspired by the Orson Welles Halloween broadcast of "The War of the Worlds."

DREAM GIRL OF '67

premiere: December 19, 1966 *packager:* Chuck Barris Productions *broadcast history:* ABC daytime December 19, 1966–December 29, 1967 *hosts:* Dick Stewart, Bob Barker, Wink Martindale, Paul Peterson *announcers:* Hank Simms, Johnny Jacobs *producer:* Gene Banks *directors:* Bill Howell, John Dorsey *set designer:* George Smith *fashion coordinator:* Barbara Rosenquest *music coordinator:* Lyn

Will this young woman be the "Dream Girl of '67"? Host Wink Martindale presents another contender to the viewing audience.

Barris *origination:* The Hollywood Palace Theater, Los Angeles

Five female contestants, ranging in age from eighteen to twenty-seven, were judged by a panel of celebrity bachelors on the basis of poise, personality, and fashion consciousness in this daily beauty pageant. The contestants also participated in a fashion show and were judged on their fashion sense. A different female celebrity served as fashion narrator each week.

Celebrity bachelors for the first week were Troy Donahue, Ross Martin, and Paul Peterson. Lee Meriweather was fashion narrator.

Each daily winner returned to compete on the Friday show to become "Dream Girl of the Week." All weekly winners returned at the end of the year to compete for the title "Dream Girl of '67." Kathy Austin was crowned with the title on the final broadcast on December 31, 1967.

Dick Stewart was the host for the first six months of the show. Bob Barker filled in for one week just prior to the premiere of his new show THE FAMILY GAME. Wink Martindale took the helm on June 26, 1967. When Martindale left to host HOW'S YOUR MOTHER-IN-LAW?, Paul Peterson, a regular on "The Donna Reed Show" became the new host.

Did you know . . . ABC Sports broadcaster Al Michaels was a production assistant on "Dream Girl of '67"?

DREAM GIRL USA

premiere: September 1986 *packager:* Dream Girl Enterprises (Chambers-Seligman Productions)/20th Century Fox Television *broadcast history:* Syndicated September 1986–September 1987 *host:* Ken Howard *announcers:* Danny Dark, Ernie Anderson *executive producers:* Ernest Chambers, Michael Seligman *director:* Louis Horvitz *set designer:* Bob Rang *music:* Kevin Kiner *origination:* Studio 55, ABC Television Center, Los Angeles

Four women competed each week in this beauty contest, "Dream Girl USA," hosted by actor Ken Howard, who had starred in the TV show "The White Shadow" from 1978 to 1981. The contestants were scored by four judges in four categories . . . beauty and style, figure and form, talent, and personality. Every fifth week there was a semifinal with the four previous weekly winners competing.

All of the semifinal winners returned for a special one-hour final competition to determine the "Dream Girl of 1987." The grand prize winner received $100,000 and the runner-up got a Pontiac Fiero automobile. A student from the University of Texas, Ursula Lawson was crowned "Dream Girl of 1987."

DREAM HOUSE

premiere: March 27, 1968 *packager:* Don Reid Productions *broadcast history:* ABC primetime March 27, 1968–September 19, 1968; ABC daytime April 1, 1968–January 2, 1970; NBC daytime April 4, 1983–June 29, 1984

1968–1970 version

host: Mike Darrow *announcer:* Chet Gould *producers:* Ron Greenberg, Ron Kweskin, George Vosburgh *directors:* Alan Mifelow, Dick Schneider *set designer:* Ron Baldwin *origination:* Colonial Theater, New York

1983–1984 version

host: Bob Eubanks *assistant:* Debbie Bartlett *announcer:* Johnny Gilbert *creators:* Don Reid, Richard Reid *executive producers:* Bob Rubin, Don Reid, Bob Synes *producers:* Charles Colarusso, Lee Goldstein, Peter Noah *director:* Jeff Goldstein *set designers:* Anthony Sabatino, William H. Harris, Molly Joseph *music:* Michael Malone *origination:* NBC Studio 3, Burbank

In this question-and-answer game, "Dream House," two husband-and-wife teams competed against each other for the grand prize, a new house worth more than $40,000.

Each game was played for a room of furniture. Seven wins were required to receive the grand prize (four wins were needed on the nighttime version).

Each question was worth five points. An incorrect response gave opponents a chance to earn ten points. The player who answered correctly was locked out of the next question. Two minutes before the end of the game the point value doubled.

Each team was given one last chance to win the game in the "catch-up round," where they could play for an additional ten to fifty points on one final question. The more points they played for, the harder the question. The team with the most points at the end of this round won the game.

An exclusive behind-the-scenes shot of Bob Eubanks taken during a rehearsal on the set of "Dream House."

"Dream House" had a two-year run on ABC, airing in both primetime and daytime. In 1983, NBC revived it as a daytime series with some changes in the game.

In this version, the game began with a true-false toss-up question and the team that answered correctly earned $50 and a chance to choose the topic of the next question. The value of each question was determined by the player stopping a "money machine" that set an amount between $50 and $150. Players could also earn an additional prize if it landed on a special space, or lose control of the board if it landed on "turnover." After a team answered a question by selecting one of two possible answers, their opponents could choose to challenge them if they felt they'd selected an incorrect response. If they were successful they won the cash. All four topics were played in round one and four additional topics were played in round two.

The team with the most money at the end of round two won the game and a room of furniture. If they had won the game by more than $500, they received a $500 bonus. If they had won by more than $1,000 they won a new car.

The winning team got a chance to win their dream house by correctly guessing the three-digit combination to unlock the door. The combination was contained in a series of three rows of four possible numbers. The team was given a chance to select one number in each row.

One number was removed from the twelve possible for each time a team won a game. The team got a chance to have three more numbers removed by answering three multiple choice questions. A team could also win the house by winning five consecutive games.

Did you know . . . Bob Eubanks began his broadcasting career as a disc jockey at KACY radio in Oxnard, California? In 1960 he joined the staff at KRLA, Pasadena where he remained for eight years. Among the other DJ's at KRLA during that era were Charlie O'Donnell, Wink Martindale, and Casey Kasem.

DREAM LEAGUE

premiere: February 1, 1993 *packager:* SPO Productions/ESPN *broadcast history:* ESPN (cable) February 1, 1993–May 27, 1993; ESPN (cable) September 1, 1993–September 29, 1994 *hosts:* John Naber, Dwight Stones *field commentators:* Gretchen Jensen, Adrian Karsten *referee:* Neil Hoffer *announcer:* Steve Kamer *creator:* Dave Williams *producer:* Michael Gannon *director:* Jim Frazier *set designers:* Expo Design *origination:* Caesars Palace, Las Vegas; Universal Studios, Hollywood; Atlanta

Two competing teams, each consisting of three studio contestants (later changed to two) and a sports celebrity captain, competed in a test of sports knowledge and athletic ability. Participating celebrities included Steve Garvey, Gaylord Perry, Michael Cooper, Dwight Stones, Franco Harris, and Nancy Lieberman-Cline.

The first series of programs was taped at the Sports Pavilion at Caesars Palace in Las Vegas. Former Olympic gold medal swimmer John Naber hosted with ESPN reporters Gretchen Jensen and Adrian Karsten assisting on the athletic action. A second series of shows was taped at Universal Studios Hollywood with only Naber and Jensen returning. In early 1994 a third series of "Dream League" shows originated from Atlanta, Georgia, the site of the 1994 Super Bowl. Dwight Stones took over as host for those programs.

The trivia portion of the game was modeled after a football game, with each team starting at the goal line and attempting to advance down the field to the other goal line by answering sports trivia questions. A correct response moved a team ten yards (twenty yards if they responded within three seconds).

A touchdown was worth one hundred points in the first five-minutes of a ten-minute game (two hundred points in the second half), and enabled a team to earn extra points by participating in one of four physical challenges. The first series of shows featured football-passing for accuracy, basketball field goals, golf-chipping, and softball-hitting for distance.

The team with the most points at the end of the game played the "dream cycle" for a grand prize of a weekend vacation. To win, each member of the team had to complete a specific sports challenge in a maximum of forty-five seconds.

DROODLES

premiere: June 21, 1954 *packager:* Frank Cooper Associates *broadcast history:* NBC primetime June 21, 1954–September 17, 1954 *host:* Roger Price *announcer:* Don Pardo *executive producer:* Sy Fischer *producer:* Alan Dinehart *director:* Craig Allen *origination:* Century Theater, New York *debut guests:* Marc Connelly, Denise Lor, Carl Reiner, Denise Darcel

On "Droodles," a celebrity panel tried to identify a droodle, or supply a caption to one of host Roger Price's "Droodle Picture Drawings." A droodle was a simple line drawing that depicted an object or scene from a strange or different perspective.

Home viewers could also send in their droodles and if the panel could not guess what they were in a four-minute time limit, the viewer won $100.

Many of Roger Price's "Droodles" were published in a series of books. Price, a one-time gag writer for Bob Hope, helped to create the party game "Madlibs."

DUELING FOR PLAYMATES

premiere: August 7, 1983 *packager:* Trikilis Productions *broadcast history:* Playboy Channel (cable) August 7, 1983–August 30, 1988 *host:* Lonnie Shorr *announcer:* John Harlan *executive producer:* Michael Trikilis *producer:* Ken Shapiro *director:* Barry Glazer *set designer:* Bill Bohnert *music:* Tom Bruner *origination:* Golden West Studios, Los Angeles

Two male contestants vied to win a date with a Playboy playmate and an evening on the town on "Dueling for Playmates," this first-run cable game show.

The players competed in four rounds of competition. In the first round, they tried to predict how the playmates responded to certain questions. The players scored twenty-five points if they were correct. In the second round, the players were put in a mud pit and tried to place as many balls as they could on a ledge in a specified time limit.

A film profile of each playmate was shown in round three and the two contestants were later asked questions about the film. In the final round, each of the two contestants did a strip tease before a panel of three playmates who rated them on personality, body, movement, and sensuality. The player with the most points won the game and the date with the playmate.

EARN YOUR VACATION

premiere: May 23, 1954 *packager:* CBS Television *broadcast history:* CBS primetime May 23, 1954–September 5, 1954 *host:* Johnny Carson *assistants ("airline hostesses"):* Jackie Loughery, Millie Sinclair *announcer:* Roy Rowan *producer:* Bill Brennan *director:* John Claar *music director:* Lud Gluskin *origination:* Studio 41, CBS Television City, Hollywood

Johnny Carson made his national television debut hosting this Sunday night summer replacement series "Earn Your Vacation." Contestants competed for an all-expense-paid trip to the city of their choice in any place in the world.

On "Earn Your Vacation" contestants answered questions about geography to win a trip. In order to win, the contestant had to answer four questions moving up a "step" with every correct answer. A contestant who missed a question was given a second chance in the "States Game."

In the States Game the contestant was given thirty seconds to place assorted cutouts of individual states on a map of the United States. A prize was given for each state put in its proper place, and a "dream vacation" if a predetermined state was among the correct guesses.

Assisting host Johnny Carson in the role of "airline hostesses" were Jackie Loughery, winner of the Miss United States title in the 1953 Miss Universe contest, and model Millie Sinclair.

"Earn Your Vacation" was heard as a radio series on CBS from June 5, 1949 to July 2, 1950 with Jay C. Flippen as host and Johnny Jacobs as announcer.

E.S.P.

premiere: July 11, 1958 *packager:* Providerence Productions *broadcast history:* ABC primetime July 11, 1958–August 22, 1958 *host:* Vincent Price *announcer:* Don Morrow *consultant:* Carroll B. Nash, director of parapsychology at St. Joseph's College in Philadelphia *creator:* George Wolf *producer:* Lou Morgan *director:* Lou Sposa *set designer:* Henry May *music director:* Richard Hayman *origination:* New York

Horror-film star Vincent Price hosted "E.S.P.", this weekly series that tested the sixth sense, extrasensory perception.

Little did Nebraskan Johnny Carson know that hosting "Earn Your Vacation" would lead him on the road to superstardom as the host of NBC's "The Tonight Show."

Two contestants were placed in separate isolation booths and experiments were conducted to see who had the higher degree of ESP.

The game format of this show was dropped after three weeks and the show continued for several weeks more as a series exploring people and the powers of ESP.

Did you know . . . host Vincent Price was a contestant on the big money quiz show THE $64,000 CHALLENGE? In October 1956 he battled actor Edward G. Robinson to a $32,000 tie on the subject of art.

EVERY SECOND COUNTS

premiere: September 17, 1984 *packager:* Charles Colarusso Productions/Group W *broadcast history:* Syndicated September 17, 1984–September 1985 *host:* Bill Rafferty *assistant:* Debbie Bartlett *announcer:* Johnny Gilbert *executive producer:* Charles Colarusso *producer:* Peter Noah *director:* Barry Glazer *set designers:* Anthony Sabatino, William H. Harris *origination:* Studio 7, KTTV Television, Los Angeles

Three couples competed in this daily show, "Every Second Counts," by answering nine questions in categories like "Thirty-one Flavors—are these ice cream flavors real or not?" and "Beauty Pageant—are these contests real or not?"

In the first round a correct answer earned two seconds for a team and in the second round four seconds. The team that accumulated the most time after playing three categories in each round won the game and played a bonus round.

Bill Rafferty encourages contestants to make every second count on his syndicated game show.

The bonus round featured four levels of prizes, the highest level being a new car. To win the prize on level one, the players had to answer four questions correctly; level two required five correct answers; level three, six correct; and level four, seven correct—all using the time earned in the main game. All the questions were from one category and could be answered with one of three possible answers.

EVERYBODY'S TALKING!

premiere: February 6, 1967 *packager:* Jerome Schnur Productions *broadcast history:* ABC daytime February 6, 1967–December 29, 1967 *host:* Lloyd Thaxton *announcers:* Wink Martindale, Charlie O'Donnell *executive producer:* Jerome Schnur *producers:* Bill Chastain, Jorn Winther *director:* Jorn Winther *set designer:* Henry Lickel *music:* Score Productions *origination:* Studio D, ABC Television Center, Los Angeles

Three studio contestants competed for cash on "Everybody's Talking!" by trying to guess the person, place, or thing that was being described by "people on the street" interviews that were prerecorded and edited into a series of short clips.

Each round was initially worth one hundred points and decreased in value as more of the film was shown. The first player to buzz in with a guess froze the value of that round. The game continued until the rest of the film was shown. The other two players were given a chance to guess the subject if they felt the first player had guessed incorrectly. The player with the correct answer won the points.

Additional rounds were played until one player passed one hundred points. That player won the game and his or her points were converted into dollars. The winner also played a bonus game in which it was necessary to identify another subject from a series of film clips. He or she buzzed in to stop the film and make a guess. If the guess was correct the score (again counted down from a starting point of one hundred) was tripled. The winner took on two new challengers in a new game.

After several weeks on the air, the show replaced the studio contestants with a weekly panel of celebrities who played for viewers at home.

Host Lloyd Thaxton was a popular TV dance show emcee in Los Angeles during the 1960s. In the 1980s he produced the consumer information series "Fight Back!"

Did you know . . . "Everybody's Talking!" marked the first game show that famed announcer Charlie O'Donnell would announce? Years later O'Donnell would be the voice of WHEEL OF FORTUNE, the annual Academy Awards ceremony, "The Miss America Pageant," countless Dick Clark specials, and other top game shows. He became the premiere voice for classy television specials.

Were you watching when . . . these TV favorites were all guest celebrities on "Everybody's Talking!" in 1967: Julie Newmar and Adam West ("Batman"), Barbara Eden ("I Dream of Jeannie"), and Phyllis Diller, the first lady of stand-up comedy?

EVERYTHING GOES

premiere: September 12, 1981   *packager:* Scott Sternberg Productions   *broadcast history:* Playboy Channel (cable) September 12, 1981–September 28, 1988   *host:* Kip Addotta   *announcer:* Jim Carson   *executive producer:* Scott Sternberg   *producers:* Mike Viseltear, Debbie Williams   *director:* Ian MacIntosh   *set designer:* Joe Hoffman   *origination:* Studio 55, ABC Television Center, Los Angeles

A three-member celebrity panel was joined by male and female contestants in a game show where players undressed each other when they gave a wrong answer.

Each show had a specific theme such as ''Romeo and Juliet'' or ''The Millionaire and Her Chauffeur.'' All contestants dressed in attire suitable to the theme.

EVERYTHING'S RELATIVE

premiere: February 1, 1965   *packager:* Merritt Enterprises for NBC Films   *broadcast history:* Syndicated February 1, 1965–August 27, 1965   *host:* Jim Hutton   *announcer:* Ed Brennan   *producers:* Roger Muir, Nick Nicholson   *director:* Tony Verdi   *origination:* WMAQ-TV, Chicago

This syndicated series, ''Everything's Relative,'' was produced initially for NBC owned and operated stations, and was a question-and-answer game with specific questions directed at members of a family (father, mother, and two children).

Two teams competed and questions were selected from a game wheel of seven categories. The object of the game was to get three correct answers in a row or be the first team to answer seven questions correctly.

''Everything's Relative'' was taped at WMAQ studios in the Merchandise Mart in Chicago.

EYE GUESS

premiere: January 3, 1966   *packager:* Bob Stewart Productions   *broadcast history:* NBC daytime January 3, 1966–September 26, 1969   *host:* Bill Cullen   *announcers:* Jack Clark, Don Pardo   *executive producer:* Bob Stewart   *producer:* Edyth Chan   *directors:* Lou Tedesco, Gene Waldstein   *set designer:* Rex Fluty Jr.   *music:* Bob Cobert   *origination:* NBC Studio 6A, New York

''Eye Guess'' was the first Bob Stewart Productions game show to air after Stewart left Mark Goodson–Bill Todman Productions. Stewart was involved with three of the Goodson classics, THE PRICE IS RIGHT, TO TELL THE TRUTH, and PASSWORD.

On this show, two contestants were shown eight answers and tried to memorize where they were on a game board. They then had to match a question with an answer by calling a number where they thought the correct answer was located. Calling out a wrong number could lead to some very funny answer.

The game consisted of two rounds, ten points for correct answers in round one, twenty points in round two. The first player to score one hundred points won the game, received $100, and played a bonus round.

In the bonus game, seven of the eight numbers revealed prizes and the last number revealed a stop sign. The player who cleared the entire board without hitting the stop sign

That's creator Bob Stewart and best friend Bill Cullen on the set of "Eye Guess." This NBC game show was a three-year hit for both men.

won a grand prize. For the first couple of weeks on the air, the bonus game consisted of trying to match celebrity spouses. Eight spaces on the game board were uncovered to reveal comedy pairs of humorously mismatched celebrity spouses, like Bette Davis–Ringo Starr. A name was read, and the contestant tried to find the right spouse among the mismatched pairs. Each correct guess was worth $25 and clearing the board earned a new car.

In the last year the show was on the air, the format was changed to one in which players received prizes instead of points in the main game, with seven prizes needed for a win. The bonus round was changed to playing with seven ''go'' signs and one ''stop'' sign. The player who could clear the board without hitting a stop won a new car.

Did you know . . .   Bill Cullen enrolled at the University of Pittsburgh as a pre-med student, but a shortage of funds forced him to drop out? He took a job as a mechanic and as a tow truck driver. He later went back to school and earned a bachelor's degree in fine arts. While Bill Cullen was hosting ''Eye Guess'' during the day for NBC, he was also a regular panelist on I'VE GOT A SECRET at night for CBS.

Michael King of King World, syndicators of JEOPARDY!, ''The Oprah Winfrey Show,'' and WHEEL OF FORTUNE, was a winning contestant on ''Eye Guess'' in 1968.

THE EYES HAVE IT

premiere: November 20, 1948   *packager:* NBC   *broadcast history:* NBC primetime November 20, 1948–January 27, 1949; NBC Sunday afternoon March 13, 1949–June 19, 1949 *host:* Ralph McNair   *producer:* Ralph McNair   *director:* Ted Ayers   *origination:* Washington, D.C.

Three guests on a panel were asked to identify familiar sights and famous people from photos disguised and altered in various ways—among them unusual angles, extreme close-ups, and bits and pieces of images.

This panel show, "The Eyes Have It," was broadcast from NBC's Washington, D.C. station WNBW, beginning as a local show on September 25, 1948 and joining the full network in November. After its primetime run, the show moved to Sunday afternoons and ran until June 19, 1949.

THE FACE IS FAMILIAR

premiere: May 7, 1966   *packager:* Bob Stewart Productions/ Filmways Television   *broadcast history:* CBS primetime May 7, 1966–September 3, 1966   *host:* Jack Whitaker   *announcer:* Jack Clark   *producer:* Bob Stewart   *director:* Lou Tedesco   *set design:* Charles Lisanby   *theme:* "Brasilia" by Herb Alpert and the Tijuana Brass   *origination:* Studio 41, CBS Broadcast Center, New York   *debut guests:* June Lockhart, Bob Crane

Two teams, each consisting of a celebrity guest and a studio contestant, tried to identify famous personalities from scrambled photographs, on "The Face Is Familiar."

The teams answered questions to earn the right to have a piece of the photo placed correctly. The game continued until one team identified the photo. They won $200 and a chance at an additional $500 by correctly recognizing famous people by only their eyes, noses, or lips. They were paid $50 for each correct guess and $500 for four correct answers.

During the season the show was on the air, the main game was changed. The revised format used a seven-piece game board with a scrambled photo of a famous person. One member of a team gave his or her opponent a piece of the puzzle. When the seven pieces were revealed, they were then switched to the right places in the photo, one at a time. The first team to guess correctly got $100, and the first team to win two games won the match and played the bonus game.

Did you know . . . host Jack Whitaker won an Emmy Award for Outstanding Sports Personality in 1978? While he was best known as a sports commentator, Whitaker was also the host of THE VERDICT IS YOURS during the summer of 1962.

FACE THE FACTS

premiere: March 13, 1961   *packager:* Impa Productions *broadcast history:* CBS daytime March 13, 1961–September 29, 1961   *host:* Red Rowe   *announcer:* Johnny Jacobs *producers:* Irving Mansfield, Peter Arnell   *director:* Joe Behar   *music director:* Kip Walton   *origination:* Studio 43, CBS Television City, Los Angeles

Los Angeles television personality Red Rowe hosted this daytime series, "Face the Facts," that featured four studio contestants trying to guess the outcome of criminal cases.

A case, based on a real incident that had been tried and judged in court, was reenacted using actors as plaintiffs and defendants. The contestants were given five hundred points to start with. Just prior to the verdict the action was stopped and the contestants would wager any or all of the five hundred points on their ability to predict the outcome. The player with the most points at the end of the show won merchandise prizes.

FACE THE MUSIC

premiere: January 1980   *packager:* Sandy Frank Productions   *broadcast history:* Syndicated January 1980–September 1981; USA (cable) January 2, 1989–September 8, 1989 (repeats of syndicated series); USA (cable) March 26, 1990–September 14, 1990 (repeats of syndicated series); Family Channel (cable) January 2, 1995–September 29, 1995 (repeats)   *host:* Ron Ely   *announcers:* Dave Williams, John Harlan, Art James   *creators:* Buddy and Beverly Piper, David Levy   *executive producers:* David Levy, Bruno Zirato Jr. *producers:* Ray Horl, Peggy Touchstone   *director:* Lou Tedesco   *set designer:* John C. Mula   *music:* Tommy Oliver *featured vocalist:* Lisa Donovan   *origination:* Studio 3, KTLA Television, Los Angeles; Studio 4, KTTV Television, Los Angeles

Three contestants competed in "Face the Music," this game of musical knowledge. The first two rounds featured the players trying to identify people, places, and things from song titles. The orchestra played a selection and the first player to identify it was given the opportunity to guess the subject it referred to. The two top winners moved to round three (played the same way) to determine the day's champ.

The winner played against the previous day's champ by trying to identify a mystery celebrity from a series of six pictures ranging from childhood to maturity. The faster the contestant could identify the celebrity the more he or she could win. The contestant who could correctly identify the celebrity after seeing just one photo won $10,000.

Did you know . . . host Ron Ely played Tarzan on the TV series of the same name from 1966 to 1968?

FACE TO FACE

premiere: June 9, 1946 *broadcast history:* NBC primetime June 9, 1946–January 26, 1947 *hosts:* Eddie Dunn and Bob Dunn

On "Face to Face," this early NBC game show that may not have been seen on the full network when it started, featured artist Bob Dunn sketching a picture of a person, using verbal clues. Viewers could see the person and make comparisons as the sketch progressed.

Eddie Dunn was the host of the show, which originated in NBC's first TV studio, 3H in New York.

FAMILY CHALLENGE

premiere: October 2, 1995 *packager:* Woody Fraser Productions/Maple Palm Productions *broadcast history:* Family Channel (cable) October 2, 1995–September 7, 1997 *hosts:* Ray Combs, Michael Burger *announcers:* Gene Wood, Charlie Glaize *creators/executive producers:* Woody Fraser, Dave Thomas *supervising producer:* Richard Crystal *producers:* Dave Garrison, David Greenfield, Damian Sullivan *directors:* Bob Loudin, Bob Levy *production designer:* Gene McAvoy *art director:* Henry L. Cota *theme music:* Wendy DeAugustine *origination:* Glendale Studios, Glendale (1995–1996); Universal Studios, Hollywood (1996–1997)

"Family Challenge" was a one-hour game show featuring two families competing in a series of stunts and games. Dur-

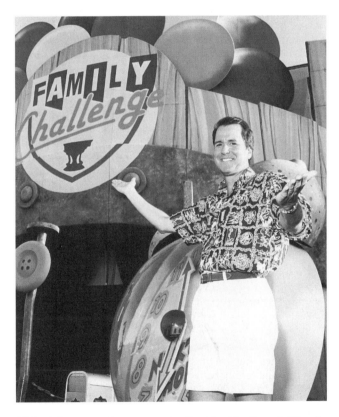

Michael Burger welcomes you to the big, big fun of "Family Challenge."

ing the first season, Ray Combs was the host; Gene Wood, the announcer. The series was taped at Glendale Studios. When the show began its second season, on September 30, 1996, the title was changed to "The New Family Challenge," and Michael Burger took over as host, with Charlie Glaize as announcer. The new season was taped outdoors at Universal Studios Hollywood.

The stunts and games changed on each show, as did the number of points a team could win for completing an event. Stunts included the "Slam Dunk Gunk Slide Game," "The Balloon Hug Bust," and "The Velcro Leap." The team with the most points at the end of the show received the "Family Challenge Cup."

FAMILY DOUBLE DARE

premiere: April 3, 1988 *packager:* MTV Networks *broadcast history:* FOX primetime April 3, 1988–July 23, 1988; Nickelodeon August 13, 1990– *host:* Marc Summers *assistants:* Robin Marrella, Chris Miles *announcers:* "Harvey" (John Harvey), Doc Holliday *executive in charge:* Scott Fishman *producers:* Angelika Bartenbach, Marc Summers *director:* Lexi Rae *set designers:* Byron Taylor, Kevin Sullivan *music:* Edd Kalehoff *origination:* Universal Studios, Orlando

"Family Double Dare," a spin-off of the kid's version, was a long-running feature on cable's Nickelodeon channel, first appearing for a brief run on the nighttime schedule of the Fox Television Network in the spring of 1988. On August 13, 1990 the repeats of the Fox series along with new episodes were added to Nickelodeon's schedule.

The format of "Family Double Dare" was the same as the kid's version, only this time an entire family competed in the stunts and in answering questions. The winning team of the day played for bonus prizes including trips and a new car.

Marc Summers was featured as host of both versions of DOUBLE DARE with Robin Marrella as his assistant throughout the entire run. The original announcer, "Harvey," left the show in 1992 and was replaced by Doc Holliday.

FAMILY FEUD

premiere: July 12, 1976 *packagers:* Mark Goodson–Bill Todman Productions (1976–1985); Mark Goodson Productions (1988–1995) *broadcast history:* ABC daytime July 12, 1976–June 14, 1985; Syndicated September 19, 1977–September 1985; ABC primetime (specials) May 8, 1978–May 25, 1984; CBS daytime July 4, 1988–September 10, 1993; Syndicated September 19, 1988–September 8, 1995
1976–1985 version

host: Richard Dawson *announcer:* Gene Wood *substitute announcer:* Johnny Gilbert *executive producer:* Howard Felsher *producer:* Cathy Dawson *director:* Paul Alter *set designer:* Henry Lickel *music:* Score Productions *origination:* Vine Street Theater, Los Angeles (1976); Studio 54, ABC Television Center, Los Angeles (1977–1985)
1988–1995 version

hosts: Ray Combs, Richard Dawson *announcer:* Gene Wood *substitute announcers:* Art James, Rod Roddy *senior executive producer:* Chester Feldman *executive*

The original star of "Family Feud," Richard Dawson!

producers: Howard Felsher, Gary Dawson *producer:* Gabrielle Johnston *directors:* Paul Alter, Marc Breslow, Andy Felsher *set designer:* Jack Hart *music:* Score Productions *origination:* Studio 33, CBS Television City, Los Angeles

One of the most successful game shows launched in the 1970s was "Family Feud." Within a year of its debut on ABC it was the number-one game show on daytime television and a primetime syndicated version was on its way to the top slot. The syndicated edition began as a weekly series in September 1977 and expanded to two nights a week in January 1979 and again, to five shows a week in September 1980. "Family Feud" was the number-one rated syndicated game show from 1978 until WHEEL OF FORTUNE eclipsed it in 1984. In 1977, "Family Feud" won an Emmy Award for "Outstanding Television Game Show."

Much of the success of "Family Feud" was credited to the easy-to-play game and the interaction of host Richard Dawson with the contestants. Dawson, a British comedian, had costarred in the TV show "Hogan's Heroes" during the 1960s. He was a regular panelist on the revived version of THE MATCH GAME in the 1970s.

On the original run of "Family Feud," two teams, each composed of five members from the same family, competed against each other to match answers with the results of a survey of one hundred people.

Two players, one from each team, faced off to answer a question (example: "Name the hour that you get up on Sunday mornings.") to earn the right to control the board. The player who came up with the most popular answer on the survey had the right to play or pass. The team playing the board was allowed three wrong answers (strikes). Points were awarded based on the number of people who responded. If a team failed to come up with all the answers, the opposing team could steal the points by coming up with one more unrevealed answer to the survey. The first team to score three hundred points won the game and played "Fast Money."

Only two members of the winning team participated in the Fast Money bonus round. Each person played separately and tried to come up with the most frequent response to five questions. The first player was given fifteen seconds, and the second player, twenty seconds. One point was given for each person in the survey who gave the correct answer and if the team could reach two hundred points they won $5,000. On the nighttime version (syndicated) they played for $10,000. If they scored fewer than two hundred points, they received $5 for each point.

ABC added "Family Feud" as a series of primetime specials on May 8, 1978. Each one-hour show featured five members of a cast of a television series competing for charity. The last special aired on May 25, 1984.

There were also celebrity weeks on the daytime version and from August 13, 1984 to October 4, 1984 ABC ran repeats of some of the celebrity shows on their daytime schedule in addition to the regular daytime edition of "Family Feud."

The original run of "Family Feud" ended its ABC series on June 14, 1985 and its syndicated version in September 1985. Three years later, in July 1988, CBS revived "Family Feud" for their daytime schedule, with a new syndicated edition premiering in September. The only change in the show was replacing host Richard Dawson with comedian Ray Combs.

On June 29, 1992 CBS expanded "Family Feud" to a one-hour format, adding the "Bullseye Round" to the show and renaming it The Family Feud Challenge. (The Bullseye Round was added to the syndicated version in September 1992.)

The Bullseye Round was played at the beginning of each program and determined how much money each family would play for in Fast Money if they won the game.

Each family began with a bank of $5,000 and one member at a time from each team tried to come up with the most popular answer to a survey question. Whoever came up with the number-one response had the value of the question added to the family bank. Five questions were played, with the first worth $1,000. The value of the other questions increased in increments of $1,000, up to $5,000 for the last Bullseye question.

On the daytime one-hour edition of "Family Feud," two new teams competed in the first half of the show, with the Bullseye bank beginning at $2,500 and the value of the five questions worth from $500 to $2,500. The winner of the game played Fast Money to try to win the bank and then meet the previous day's champion in the second half of the show. In the second half, the bank for each team started at $5,000 and the Bullseye questions ranged from $1,000 to $5,000.

The CBS version went into reruns on March 29, 1993 and continued until September 10, 1993 when the network returned the hour to their local stations.

In the fall of 1994, "Family Feud" underwent a series of changes that included the return of Richard Dawson as host of the show and the expansion of the syndicated version to an hour format.

The number of players on a team was reduced from five to four. Each game began with the "Bankroll Round" where one member from each team competed in a head-to-head competition to come up with the most popular response to a survey question. Three questions, with values of $500, $1,500, and $2,500, were asked as the teams try to increase their bankrolls from the original $2,500 stake.

The main game again consisted of the two teams answering survey questions with the first team to reach three hundred points winning the game and playing Fast Money to win their bankroll.

In the second half of the show, the winning team played a championship family from the original Richard Dawson version of "Family Feud." Values of the initial stake were doubled to $5,000 and the bankroll questions were increased to $1,000, $3,000, and $5,000.

Did you know . . . Richard Dawson played a futuristic game show host in the 1987 film *The Running Man*, starring Arnold Schwarzenegger and based on the novel by Stephen King?

"Family Feud" was not the first game show Richard Dawson hosted. In 1969 viewers in Southern California saw him host a program produced by Bob Barker called LUCKY PAIR. In 1974 Dawson emceed a new version of the 1950s panel show MASQUERADE PARTY.

Announcer Gene Wood began his career as part of a comedy duo in the early 1950s, teaming up with comedian Bill Dana (Jose Jimenez), who was his college roommate.

Were you watching when . . . On the very first "Family Feud," July 12, 1976, the Moseley family took on the Abramowitz family on the first "Family Feud"? The first question played was "Name a famous George." The six most popular replies of the survey of one hundred people were "George Washington" (74), "George Burns" (4), "George Gobel" (4), "George Jessel" (3), "Gorgeous George" (2), and "George Wallace" (2). It only took two hundred points to win the match. The Moseley family won the feud and collected $890 in fast money.

On a special "emcee week," these emcees played against each other. One team consisted of Bill Cullen, Bob Eubanks, Jim Perry, Nipsey Russell, and Betty White. The other team consisted of Tom Kennedy, Jim Lange, Peter Marshall, Bert Parks, and Leslie Uggams. Creator Mark Goodson made a rare cameo appearance as well!

Richard Dawson met his future wife Gretchen in the spring of 1981 when her family, the Johnsons, appeared as contestants on the show.

FAMILY FIGURES

premiere: October 16, 1990 *packager:* DLT Entertainment Productions *broadcast history:* BET (cable) October 16, 1990–December 29, 1990 *hosts:* Mario and Melvin Van Peebles *announcer:* John Greenwood *creator:* Mark Maxwell-Smith *producer:* Cathy Cambria *director:* Curtis Gadson *set designer:* Scott Perkins *music:* Terry Cummings, Pearcy Beatty *origination:* Washington, D.C.

The Black Entertainment Television (BET) cable network added this show to their lineup in the fall of 1990. "Family Figures" was hosted by actor Mario Van Peebles and his father Melvin.

Two teams, each composed of three members of a family, competed. A jump-in question that required two answers was read and the first team to correctly answer took control of the "figures" part of the question to earn points.

On the figures part of the question, each member of the team gave a numerical answer to a question (example: "The people of Africa make up what percent of the world's population?"). All three responses were averaged for a team answer. The team scored points if they were correct. If not, their opponents could steal the points by correctly predicting if the wrong answer was either too high or too low.

In round one, questions were worth one hundred points, in round two they were worth two hundred points, and in round three they were worth four hundred points. Each round had three questions and the team with the highest score after three rounds won the game.

The winning team played a bonus round for prizes. Four prizes were hidden behind three different numbers on a prize board of twelve squares. To earn picks on the board the team had to answer questions with three-part answers (example: "Name the three medals given in the Olympics."). Each member of the team answered one part and earned one pick for each correct answer. The contestants won any prize that was found twice on the board, but lost all they had won if they found the third match. A team could stop at any time in the bonus round.

THE FAMILY GAME

premiere: June 19, 1967 *packager:* Chuck Barris Productions *broadcast history:* ABC daytime June 19, 1967–December 29, 1967 *host:* Bob Barker *announcers:* Johnny Jacobs, Roy Rowan *producers:* Walt Case, Mike Metzger *directors:* Bill Carruthers, Seymour Robbie *set designer:* George Smith *music coordinator:* Lyn Barris *origination:* Studio D, ABC Television Center, Los Angeles

Parents and their children tried to predict and match answers to a series of questions à la THE NEWLYWED GAME format.

"The Family Game" featured three families—the parents and two of their children between the ages of six and eleven.

In the first round the younger children were asked four questions while their parents were off stage. The parents returned and the mothers responded to the same four questions. Their teams scored ten points for each answer they matched.

In the second round, the parents again left the stage and the older children answered four more questions. The first three were worth fifteen points and the fourth was a bonus question worth twenty-five points. When the parents returned, the fathers tried to match answers to the first three questions and both parents responded to the bonus question.

FAMILY SECRETS

premiere: March 22, 1993   *packager:* Dave Bell Associates *broadcast history:* NBC daytime March 22, 1993–June 11, 1993   *host:* Bob Eubanks   *announcer:* Dean Miuccio   *executive producers:* Dave Bell, Dennis Bogorad, Steve Radosh *director:* Marc Breslow   *set designer:* Ed Flesh   *music:* David Shapiro   *origination:* Studio 2, Walt Disney/MGM Studios, Orlando

Two teams, each composed of a mother, father, and child, competed against each other to see which family group knew themselves better on "Family Secrets." The teams competed for cash in each of four rounds with the high-scoring team playing for a family vacation in the bonus round.

In the first round, both parents were taken offstage and the children were asked two questions about their fathers. When the dads returned they tried to match the answer their children gave. Questions were worth $100 and the emphasis was on the humor in the responses, for example: "Given three possible choices, describe your father's eating habits."

In the second round the kids tried to match their answers to their moms', at $100 per correct match. In the third round, the children left the stage and their parents played to see how well they knew their kids. Values of the questions were doubled to $200.

The fourth round featured only one question, worth $500. Both teams tried to see how well they knew the average American family by trying to predict what percentage of the sample responded in a particular way. The team closest to the actual answer collected the money. The team with the most money at the end of this round won the game and received a merchandise prize.

The winning team also played a bonus round for a chance at a family vacation. To win the trip the parents had to answer three general knowledge questions correctly and were allowed to give three incorrect answers. Their child, after each category was revealed, decided which parent would answer.

FANDANGO

premiere: March 8, 1983   *packager:* Reid-Land Productions *broadcast history:* Nashville Network (cable) March 8, 1983–March 31, 1989   *host:* Bill Anderson   *assistant:* Blake Pickett   *announcer:* "Edgar the Talking Jukebox"   *creators:* Elmer Alley, Allan Reid   *executive producers:* Allan Reid,

Here's Bill Anderson and model Blake Pickett on the set of TNN's country music trivia game show "Fandango."

Mady Land   *producers:* Audrey Cain, Debbie Cothran, Ken Vincent   *directors:* Allen James, Ken Vincent   *set designers:* Ron Baldwin, Jim Stanley   *theme music:* Mike Johnson, performed by the Po'Folks Band   *origination:* Opryland, Nashville

Country singer Bill Anderson was the emcee for this country music game show broadcast on The Nashville Network (TNN), a cable network devoted to country music. Three contestants competed, with the player who correctly answered a "toss-up" question receiving ten points and the right to choose a bonus question from nine possible subjects for additional points. The point values doubled in round two and the player with the most points won the game.

In the bonus round, the day's champ tried to match one of two possible answers to a question about a famous country music star. Four successful matches won a contestant a bonus prize.

Blake Pickett joined the show in March 1987 as assistant.

FANTASY PARK

premiere: April 13, 1991   *packager:* Azoff Television/Brad Lachman Productions   *broadcast history:* Fox primetime April 13, 1991 (special)   *host:* Mark Thompson   *announcer:* John Driscoll   *executive producers:* Irving Azoff, Brad Lachman, Jim Cahill   *producer:* Bill Bracken   *director:* Michael Dimich   *set designers:* John Shaffner, Joe Stewart   *theme:* Patterson, Waiz and Fox   *origination:* Studio 7, Fox Television Center, Los Angeles

"Fantasy Park" was a one-time special that awarded select viewers who had previously called a special telephone number outlandish dream prizes such as a six-pack of classic automobiles (including a 1965 Mustang convertible, a 1957 Chevrolet, a 1959 Pink Cadillac, a 1969 G.T.O., a 1957 Thunderbird Roadster, and a 1963 Corvette Stingray), a job as a record company executive, $20,000 worth of tickets to concerts and sporting events, $10,000 in cash, or a condo on the beach in Hawaii.

Winners for each of the fantasies were selected by computer. Three people were chosen to vie for the condo in Hawaii and they were flown to the studio in Los Angeles in order to determine the winner. The contestants were shown two telephone numbers, only one of which was a direct line to Hawaii. The first player to get through won the home.

FAST DRAW

premiere: May 25, 1968 *packager:* Tele-Column Productions/Warner Brothers–7 Arts TV *broadcast history:* Syndicated May 25, 1968–Fall 1968 *host:* Johnny Gilbert *announcer:* Fred Scott *producer:* Howard Felsher *director:* Lee O'Farrel *origination:* WNEW-TV Studios, New York

"Fast Draw" featured two teams, comprised of a studio contestant and a celebrity partner, with one player from each team designated the artist and the other the guesser. The artists took turns drawing pictures to illustrate subjects such as Noah, Australia, and Valentine's Day. The timer started at sixty seconds and each artist had ten seconds to add to the picture so that his or her partner could wager a guess.

After one team correctly guessed the subject, the unused time was translated into points and the high-scoring team won $100 and a chance to earn a bonus prize. The celebrity had to draw a picture on a new subject and have it recognized by his or her partner, all within thirty seconds, in order for them to win the bonus prize.

Were you watching when . . .   Art James and Gene Rayburn were celebrity artists on "Fast Draw"?

FEATHER YOUR NEST

premiere: October 4, 1954 *packager:* William Esty Productions *broadcast history:* NBC daytime October 4, 1954–July 27, 1956 *host:* Bud Collyer *assistants:* Jean Williams, Janis Carter *substitute hosts:* Bob Kennedy and Kyle McDonnell *announcer:* Randy Kraft *producers:* Jeff Selden, Joseph Tinney *directors:* Kenneth Buckridge, Paul Alter, Cy Mann *set designer:* George Buckman *music:* Arlo *origination:* Hudson Theater, New York

Three couples competed in a question-and-answer quiz to win furnishings for their home in "Feather Your Nest," this daytime show sponsored by Colgate Palmolive. Each piece of furniture required a specific number of points to win it, and couples competed one at a time.

The quiz had three levels, each represented by colored feathers. The first level had red feathers worth one thousand points a question, the second level had yellow feathers worth two thousand points, and the third level had green feathers worth three thousand points.

A contestant had ten seconds to answer each question and tried to accumulate more than six thousand points within a predetermined time limit for a chance to play for a jackpot prize.

The couples had fifteen seconds to answer the jackpot question; if correct they won all of the room's furnishings.

Long before "Pictionary" and "Win, Lose or Draw," there was "Fast Draw" with Johnny Gilbert.

At the end of each show each couple drew a number from a box shaped like a miniature house. The team with the lowest number after thirteen weeks won a new home and a car (usually a Nash Rambler).

On January 3, 1956 the format changed so that only two couples competed, with one member of each team selecting a piece of merchandise and the questions attached to it. If that person's partner got the answer right, the couple won the gift. The couple with the highest score of the day could win an entire room of furniture by solving a final riddle about a famous personality.

Original assistant Jean Williams was replaced by Janis Carter shortly after the show premiered in October 1954. Bob Kennedy was a frequent replacement as host when Bud Collyer vacationed.

50 GRAND SLAM

premiere: October 4, 1976 *packager:* Ralph Andrews Productions *broadcast history:* NBC daytime October 4, 1976–December 31, 1976 *host:* Tom Kennedy *announcer:* John Harlan *assistants:* Debbie Bartlett, Judy Ovitz *executive producer:* Ralph Andrews *producer:* George Vosburgh *director:* Dick McDonough *set designer:* Ed Flesh *origination:* NBC Studios 3 and 4, Burbank

Allen Ludden looks on as Tom Kennedy impresses the audience with his mating call rendition of the double-breasted bush turkey on "50 Grand Slam."

"50 Grand Slam" was a short-lived game show that tested a person's expert knowledge of a subject and offered a grand prize of $50,000.

The competition began with two experts on a specific subject competing on the $200 level. To begin the game, one player was taken to a soundproof isolation booth on stage. Each expert was asked the same four-part question and the contestant with the most correct answers won the round. If the contestants tied they both returned to play on the next show. To earn money the contestants had to answer at least two questions correctly. If they were successful they moved on to the next money level ($500). Other steps up the money ladder were $1,000, $2,000, $5,000, $10,000, $20,000, and $50,000. Any player who reached the $50,000 level but failed to win the grand prize received a new car as a consolation prize.

There were nine players for each subject, with two selected at random to begin the game. The game continued until all the players were involved or one player won the $50,000. A player defeating the reigning champion won the amount on the first level and began his or her own climb to the top.

During the thirteen-week run of "50 Grand Slam" five players were successful in their quest for $50,000. They were Stanley Green ("American Musical Theater"), Wayne Bryant ("American Musical Theater"), Jonathan Colgate ("American History"), Richard McNeely ("The Bible"), and Louis Segal ("Shakespeare").

Did you know . . . STUMPERS, with host Allen Ludden, and "50 Grand Slam" both premiered on October 4, 1976 and both were canceled on December 31, 1976?

Were you watching when . . . Tom Kennedy surprised fellow emcee Allen Ludden by walking onto the "Stumpers" set to congratulate him on his new series? Then, when Tom Kennedy was hosting "50 Grand Slam," Allen Ludden walked onto Tom's "50 Grand Slam" set to congratulate him on his new series!

FIGURE IT OUT

premiere: July 7, 1997 *packager:* Nickelodeon Productions *broadcast history:* Nickelodeon (cable) July 7, 1997– *host:* Summer Sanders *announcer:* Jeffrey "J" Dumas *creators/executive producers:* Kevin Kay, Magda Liolis *producer:* Eileen Braun *director:* Kyle Flood *production designer:* Byron Taylor *original music:* Rick Witkowski *origination:* Universal Studios, Orlando

Olympic gold medalist Summer Sanders hosts this kids' panel game show, where four celebrities, mostly from Nickelodeon shows, try to guess the unique accomplishment of the guest contestant.

Panelists can only ask questions that result in a "yes" or "no" answer. A panelist can keep asking questions as long as they get "yes" responses.

The game is played in three one-minute rounds, with the contestant winning a prize if time runs out in a round without the panel guessing his or her accomplishment.

During these rounds, as the panelists say words in their questions that appear in the description of the contestant's accomplishment (e.g., National Pickle Juice Champion), the words appear as clues on a large game board called "Billy the Answer Head." Additional clues are "dropped in" from above or brought in on a toy train on tracks in front of the panel. If a guest stumps the panel for three rounds, he or she wins a grand prize.

A member of the studio audience can also win a prize in each game if a member of the panel performed a predetermined "Secret Slime Action" (e.g., putting one's hand up to one's mouth). The panelist who unwittingly performed this action gets slimed with a liquid dropped from above his or her head.

At the end of each game, the guest demonstrates his or her unique accomplishment.

FINDERS KEEPERS
premiere: November 2, 1987 *packager:* MTV Networks *broadcast history:* Nickelodeon (cable) November 2, 1987– September 11, 1988; Syndicated September 12, 1988–March 10, 1989; Nickelodeon (cable) March 13, 1989–June 30, 1990 *hosts:* Wesley Eure, Larry Toffler *announcers:* "Harvey" (John Harvey), Joe Conklin, Harry Stevens *creators:* Geoffrey Darby, Michael Klinghoffer, Dee LaDuke, Neil Krupnick, Bonni Grossberg *executive producer:* Geoffrey

Messenger Marilyn presents emcee Bill Nimmo with a postcard bearing the name of that day's home viewer to be called on the telephone and given a chance to play "For Love or Money."

Darby *producers:* Michael Klinghoffer, Roseanne Lopopolo *directors:* Dana Calderwood, Kevin Gill *set designer:* Byron Taylor *music:* Edd Kalehoff *origination:* WHYY-TV, Philadelphia

Two teams of two kids competed against each other on "Finders Keepers" to find hidden objects camouflaged in a picture. After finding an object, a team had thirty seconds to search for a mystery item in one of the rooms of a fantasy house. Teams won points by finding objects in both the pictures and the rooms, but their opponents scored the points if the objects were not found. After playing four "hidden pictures," the teams got the chance to search the rooms. A second set of four hidden pictures were played in the second half of the show and the team with the most points after both rounds won the game.

The winning team was given ninety seconds for the bonus round, where they played for bonus prizes by trying to find eight objects spread throughout the house. To assist in their search, a clue was given to help locate the item, and kids were allowed to trash the rooms as much as necessary to find the objects.

Wesley Eure emceed the original Nickelodeon version with "Harvey" featured as announcer. When the show was syndicated in the fall of 1988, Eure and "Harvey" were replaced by Larry Toffler as host and Joe Conklin and Harry Stevens as announcers. After a six-month syndicated run the show returned to Nickelodeon with repeats.

FOLLOW THE LEADER
premiere: July 7, 1953 *packager:* Harrison-Gould Productions/CBS-TV *broadcast history:* CBS primetime July 7, 1953–August 18, 1953 *host:* Vera Vague *announcer:* Roy Rowan *producers:* Berni Gould, Paul Harrison *director:* John Claar *music director:* Gaylord Carter *origination:* CBS Television City, Los Angeles

This summertime series, "Follow the Leader," was based on the children's game of the same name and broadcast on alternate weeks with ANYONE CAN WIN.

Two three-minute sketches were enacted by the host. Selected members of the studio audience attempted to reenact the same sketch but on a "loaded" set, one that had chairs that fell apart, windows that would not open, etc. Each routine had ten specific acts and for each one correctly performed the player got $10.

FOR LOVE OR MONEY
premiere: June 30, 1958 *packager:* Walt Framer Productions *broadcast history:* CBS daytime June 30, 1958–January 30, 1959 *host:* Bill Nimmo *announcer:* Frank Simms *executive producer:* Walt Framer *producer:* Bob Wald *director:* Ken Whelan *set designer:* Charles Lisanby *music director:* Arlo *origination:* CBS Studio 62, New York

Three players competed to answer questions on "For Love or Money," this CBS morning show. Each question was associated with a prize and the player giving the correct answer could choose to keep the prize or take an unknown sum of money that ranged from 2¢ to $9,999.

FRACTURED PHRASES

premiere: September 27, 1965 *packager:* Ben Joelson–Art Baer Productions *broadcast history:* NBC daytime September 27, 1965–December 31, 1965 *host:* Art James *announcers:* Lee Vines, Wayne Howell *producer:* Stu Billet *director:* Lloyd Gross *set designer:* Rex Fluty Jr. *theme:* Jacques Belasco *origination:* NBC Studio 8H, New York

On "Fractured Phrases," the object of the game was to recognize the meaning of a fractured phrase, a garbled line disguised by writing it as a pun, phonetically. (Example: La Fur Compact Tummy . . . or "Lover come back to me.")

Each team was composed of two players, and one player was given fifteen seconds to come up with the correct meaning of the phrase by repeating it to his or her partner. If successful, this person received two points. If this person failed, his or her partner had ten seconds to repeat the phrase. If both members failed to guess correctly, their opponents could guess for one point. The first team to score ten points won the game.

In the bonus round, the winning players tried to recognize fractured names for $25 per correct answer. They were given two columns of fractured names and had to match fractured first names with last names and then identify the people.

On November 22, 1965 the format was changed to feature two teams, each composed of a contestant and a celebrity guest. Vivian Vance and Phil Foster were the first celebrities to play.

FREE 4 ALL

premiere: June 27, 1994 *packager:* Stone-Stanley Productions/USA Cable *broadcast history:* USA (cable) June 27, 1994–November 4, 1994 *host:* Mark Walberg *executive producers:* Scott Stone, David Stanley *producers:* Kathy Cotter, Jed Cohen *director:* Bob Loudin *set designers:* Joe Stewart, John Shaffner *origination:* Studio 9B, Hollywood Center Studios, Los Angeles

Two teams of three players competed in "Free 4 All," this question-and-answer game that was one of two first-run game shows produced by Stone-Stanley Productions for USA cable in the summer of 1994.

In the first round the game started with a toss-up question and the team that answered correctly got to choose a bonus question from four possible categories. Correct answers were worth twenty-five points in this round and after a category was selected it was replaced on the game board with a new one.

Point values were doubled to fifty in round two, and the trailing team was given their choice of four categories to begin the round. The team who answered correctly selected the next category, and this new one was added to the game to replace the previous category.

The third round was a minute and a half of rapid-fire questions in a specific category. Correct answers were worth seventy-five points and the team with the most points at the end of this round won the game.

The winning team played a one-minute bonus round where each player, in turn, selected a category from ten possibilities and then answered a question from it. The team earned $100 for each correct answer with one of the categories concealing a bonus trip. The team won the prize if they answered that question correctly.

FREEDOM RINGS

premiere: March 2, 1953 *packager:* George F. Foley Productions *broadcast history:* CBS daytime March 2, 1953–August 27, 1953 *hosts:* John Beal, Rex Marshall *assistant:* Alice Ghostly *announcer:* Rex Marshall, Vince Williams *producer:* Richard Linkroum *directors:* Lloyd Gross, Don Appell *music:* Ben Ludlow *origination:* New York

"Freedom Rings," sponsored by Westinghouse Electric Corporation, was shown twice a week in the daytime, and featured both telephone contestants and members of the studio audience competing for prizes.

Two telephone contestants were chosen from entry blanks filled out at their local Westinghouse dealer. They received a Westinghouse product for each correct answer and two correct answers enabled them to play for a complete Westinghouse kitchen by answering a jackpot question.

"Freedom Rings" also featured members of the studio audience who appeared on stage and were then confronted with a problem or a chore that an average housewife faced during her daily housekeeping. If the contestant solved the problem or completed the chore within a predetermined time limit he or she won a prize.

John Beal starred as host and appeared as "father of the typical American family," whose problems were worked out onstage. Actress Alice Ghostley appeared as his wife. Beal was replaced by "Freedom Rings" announcer Rex Marshall on June 2.

FUN AND FORTUNE

premiere: June 6, 1949 *packager:* Mildred Fenton Productions *broadcast history:* ABC primetime June 6, 1949 (one broadcast) *host:* Jack Lescoulie *producer:* Mildred Fenton *director:* Marshall Diskin *origination:* New York

Jack Lescoulie, the original announcer/sidekick on NBC's early morning series "Today," hosted the one and only broadcast of "Fun and Fortune." Contestants tried to identify, within four clues, an item behind a curtain. The player earned $50 by guessing the item from the first clue. The prize money diminished as additional clues were revealed. Kirk Douglas was one of the "items" and the prize offered was a chance to act in a screen test with him.

THE FUN FACTORY

premiere: June 14, 1976 *packager:* Fishman-Freer Productions/Columbia Television *broadcast history:* NBC daytime June 14, 1976–October 1, 1976 *host:* Bobby Van *announcer:* Jim Thompson *regulars:* Betty Thomas, Debbi Harmon, Rhonda Bates, Doug Steckler, Dick Blasucci, Marty Barris, Buddy Douglas *executive producers:* Ed Fishman, Randall Freer *producers:* David Fishman, Mort Green *directors:* Walter C. Miller, Tom Trbovich *set designers:* Bill Camden, Hub Braden *music:* Stan Worth *origination:* NBC Studio 4, Burbank

Contestants were selected from the studio audience in "The Fun Factory," and they answered general knowledge

Elaine Joyce joins husband Bobby Van on "The Fun Factory." Ten years later, Elaine would host her own game show, "The All New Dating Game."

a diaper on a doll to hitting a football with a croquet mallet. Performance of each stunt constituted an inning of the game and the team with the most points won cash prizes and a chance to earn more by answering a jackpot question.

Did you know . . . Johnny Olson began his broadcasting career singing in 1928 at radio station WIBU in Poynette, Wisconsin as an unpaid singer calling himself "The Buttermilk Kid." After attending the University of Minnesota, where he studied pharmacy, Olson sang and managed a band called "The Hips Commanders," with whom he recorded such songs as "Wabash Moon" and "Walking My Baby Back Home."

FUN HOUSE
premiere: September 5, 1988 *packager:* Stone Television Productions/Lorimar-Telepictures *broadcast history:* Syndicated September 5, 1988–September 9, 1990; Fox Saturday morning September 10, 1990–April 13, 1991 *host:* J. D. Roth *announcers:* "Tiny" (John Hurley), Michael Chambers *cheerleaders:* Jacqueline and Samantha Forrest

questions for prizes. Musical numbers and comedy skits were interspersed between the questions. The three top winners of the day competed for a bonus jackpot. They answered three questions with numerical answers. These were totaled and the player who came the closest to the exact total won bonus prizes. If the winner came within ten numerals of the exact answer he or she also won a new car.

FUN FOR THE MONEY
premiere: June 17, 1949 *packager:* James L. Saphier Productions *broadcast history:* ABC primetime June 17, 1949–December 9, 1949 *host:* Johnny Olson *announcer:* Bob Cunningham *producers:* Stefan Hatos, James Saphier *director:* Ed Scotch *origination:* WENR Studios at Civic Opera House, Chicago

"Fun for the Money" was the only network game show that veteran TV announcer Johnny Olson emceed on a continuing basis. He guest-hosted several shows including PLAY YOUR HUNCH, but was best known for announcing numerous shows from the 1950s to the 80s.

On this show, set in a baseball atmosphere, members of four-person teams had to perform tasks ranging from putting

"Fun House" emcee J. D. Roth and cheerleader Jackie Forrest on the show's superb set, with two contestants.

creator: Bob Synes *executive producers:* Bob Synes, Scott Stone, Steven Goldberg, David Stanley *producers:* Stephen Brown, Randolph Gale, Deborah Williams *director:* Joe Behar *set designers:* Anthony Sabatino, William H. Harris *music:* Score Productions *origination:* Studios 3 and 8, Hollywood Center Studios, Los Angeles

In this daily syndicated show, two teams, consisting of two kids ages nine through thirteen, competed in physical stunts and answered trivia questions. The series was hosted by twenty-year-old JD Roth.

The teams, red and orange, consisted of a boy and a girl who participated in three different games of skill. The team that won each event received twenty-five points and could earn an additional twenty-five points by answering a question after each stunt.

Most of the stunts were geared to be messy and went by titles such as "Fill the Cavity," "Alien Faces," "Smashed Potatoes," and "Jungle Gold." Both teams competed in the "Fun House Grand Prix," a catch-up round where the teams earned additional points by racing around a track in vehicles ranging from giant vacuum cleaners to sandwiches on wheels.

The team with the highest point score won the game and had a chance to win prizes in the "Fun House." Once inside the house, the team had two minutes to grab prize tags scattered throughout an obstacle course. One player had to collect three tags before his or her partner got a chance. If either selected a predetermined "power prize," both won a grand prize trip to an exotic locale.

After two seasons in syndication, "Fun House" was picked up by the Fox Broadcasting Company for a seven-month run on their Saturday morning schedule.

Were you watching when . . . a very young Leonardo DiCaprio appeared on "Fun House"? One of the wacky tasks he was asked to perform was to go fishing in a small pool of water. To make the task just a little tougher, he could only catch the fish using his teeth. Little did young Leonardo

Remember emcee Lloyd Thaxton and those witty celebrity guests from "Funny You Should Ask"?

know that he would go from one water-logged adventure to another—starring in the greatest water-logged adventure of all time, *Titanic.*

FUNNY BONERS

premiere: November 20, 1954   *packager:* Ralph Edwards Productions   *broadcast history:* NBC Saturday morning November 20, 1954–July 9, 1955   *hosts:* Jimmy Weldon with Webster Webfoot   *announcer:* "Easy Marvin"   *executive producer:* Ralph Edwards   *producer:* Leslie Raddatz   *director:* Stuart Phelps   *origination:* NBC Studio E, Hollywood

This junior version of Ralph Edwards' TRUTH OR CONSEQUENCES featured children who were asked questions by host-ventriloquist Jimmy Weldon and his dummies, Webster Webfoot and Easy Marvin. If a child's answer was correct, he or she won points, but if incorrect the child had to perform a silly penalty stunt. The winners of the day won merchandise prizes.

FUNNY YOU SHOULD ASK!!

premiere: October 28, 1968   *packager:* Merrill Heatter–Bob Quigley Productions   *broadcast history:* ABC daytime October 28, 1968–June 27, 1969   *host:* Lloyd Thaxton   *announcers:* Kenny Williams, Mike Laurence   *executive producers:* Merrill Heatter, Bob Quigley   *producer:* Stan Dreben   *director:* Jorn Winther   *set designer:* Romain Johnston   *music:* Score Productions   *origination:* Studio D, ABC Television Center, Los Angeles   *debut guests:* Jan Murray, Paul Lynde, Judy Carne, Abby Dalton, Stu Gilliam

This daytime comedy game show, "Funny You Should Ask!!" featured five celebrity guests who gave answers to questions like "What's the first thing you would do if the one you loved didn't know how to kiss?" Two studio contestants then tried to match those answers to the celebrities who gave them. Four of the five answers given by the celebrities were played in each round.

The player with the most correct answers in a round won a $100 gift certificate (the players split the $100 if they tied), and a player won the "Funny Money" jackpot if he or she had a perfect round. The jackpot increased $100 each round until it was won.

The contestant with the most correct matches during a day's show won a bonus prize. Comedian Stu Gilliam was a regular panelist on the show.

GAMBIT

premiere: September 4, 1972 *packager:* Merrill Heatter–Bob Quigley Productions *broadcast history:* CBS daytime September 4, 1972–December 10, 1976 *host:* Wink Martindale *card dealer:* Elaine Stewart *announcer:* Kenny Williams *executive producers:* Merrill Heatter, Bob Quigley *producer:* Robert Noah *director:* Jerome Shaw *set designer:* Romain Johnston *music:* Mort Garson *origination:* Studios 41 and 43, CBS Television City, Los Angeles

Two husband-and-wife couples competed against each other by answering questions on "Gambit." A right answer gave them the option to keep or to give away a playing card from an oversized, but otherwise regulation deck, in a game of blackjack. The object was to score "21" exactly, or get as close as possible to 21 without going over before the opponent did.

Any team that hit 21 exactly, during the game or bonus round, won the "Gambit Jackpot," which started at $500 and increased by $500 each day until won.

A deck of fifty-two playing cards was used and the top card was revealed at the beginning of the game. A general knowledge question was read and the first team to answer correctly earned control of the card, and could either keep it or give it to their opponent. The game continued with another question and the team answering correctly got control of the next card, which was not revealed until awarded. A team could "freeze" if they felt another card would put them over 21. This forced their opponents to answer questions and get closer to 21 or go over in the attempt to win. The first team to win two games won the match, $200, and a chance to play the Gambit Board for merchandise prizes.

The Gambit Board consisted of twenty-one cards with prizes hidden behind each one. The winning team selected a card and added the prize to their winnings. They also received a "playing card" from the deck. The goal was to select prizes and keep their point total under 21. They could quit whenever they chose, but if they went over 21 all prizes accumulated were lost. Contestants won a new car if they hit 21 exactly.

Did you know . . . in 1959 Wink Martindale had a million-selling record titled, "Deck of Cards"? The song was so popular that Wink flew to New York City and appeared on "The Ed Sullivan Show" to perform the narrative. It has since become a perennial Christmas favorite.

In the early 1960s Wink hosted "The Wink Martindale Dance Party" for Los Angeles television station KHJ, and later for station KCOP. He also had the top-rated morning radio program in Los Angeles on KFWB.

While the Winker was hosting "Gambit" in the early 1970s he was also a top radio personality in Hollywood on KMPC Radio, along with fellow emcees Geoff Edwards, Jim Lange, and Gary Owens.

Wink Martindale points to the "Gambit" game board on which a contestant could win a new car.

82

"Gambit," THE PRICE IS RIGHT, and THE JOKER'S WILD all premiered on CBS on September 4, 1972.

Elaine Stewart, card dealer on "Gambit," was, and still is, married to game show creator and four-time Emmy winner Merrill Heatter.

GAMBLE ON LOVE

premiere: July 16, 1954   *packager:* Rockhill Productions *broadcast history:* DuMont primetime July 16, 1954–August 13, 1954   *hosts:* Denise Darcel, Ernie Kovacs *announcer:* Don Russell   *producer:* Robert Adams   *director:* Harry Coyle   *origination:* New York

Three couples who were "married, about to be married or just plain in love" were interviewed by the host regarding their "gamble on love." Each couple on "Gamble on Love" then had a chance at the wheel of fortune, with one partner spinning the wheel and the other answering questions for prizes.

Comedian Ernie Kovacs replaced Denise Darcel as host on August 6.

Did you know . . . Denise Darcel costarred with Lex Barker in the 1950 motion picture *Tarzan and the Slave Girl?*

THE GAME GAME

premiere: September 29, 1969   *packager:* Chuck Barris Productions   *broadcast history:* Syndicated September 29, 1969–September 1970   *host:* Jim McKrell   *announcer:* Johnny Jacobs   *producer:* Ira Barmak   *director:* John Dorsey   *set designer:* Archie Sharp   *music:* Frank Jaffe   *origination:* Studio 43, CBS Television City, Los Angeles

Three celebrity panelists and a studio contestant competed daily in the psychological game show "The Game Game." The show was billed as the program that revealed a little more about your favorite celebrities and yourself. Each day's game was built on a pivotal question, such as "How romantic are you?" or "How ambitious are you?" The show used tests validated by the Southern California Institute of Psychology.

The contestant could win cash by correctly predicting whether his or her total score at the end of the show would be lower or higher than the celebrities' scores. The contestant received $25 for each celebrity score correctly predicted and $100 if he or she outguessed all three celebrities. The celebrities remained on for a week's worth of shows and competed with a different contestant each day.

A quiz consisted of five questions, each of which had four possible responses. The players selected the responses they felt best suited their opinions; point scores, ranging from zero to fifteen, were revealed after the choices were made.

Did you know . . . this 1969 Chuck Barris entry was his first venture into the syndication market? Until this show, all of his shows were on the ABC Network.

GATERS

premiere: November 1, 1994   *packager:* Stone-Stanley Productions   *broadcast history:* ESPN (cable) November 1, 1994–December 30, 1994   *hosts:* Rob Blackman and Bill Guandolo   *executive producers:* Scott Stone, David Stanley *producer:* Brennan Huntington   *coproducer:* David Greenfield   *origination:* North Carolina

"Gaters" was an outdoor stunt show taped at various sports stadiums in North Carolina. A participant in the show was asked to compete by performing stunts such as catching oversized pretzels on the end of a plunger or hitting a paper plate tossed in the air, using a sling shot and plastic balls. Prizes for stunts completed ranged from T-shirts to "Gaters" caps.

G.E. COLLEGE BOWL

See COLLEGE BOWL.

GENERAL ELECTRIC GUEST HOUSE

premiere: July 1, 1951   *broadcast history:* CBS primetime July 1, 1951–August 26, 1951   *hosts:* Oscar Levant, Durward Kirby   *announcer:* Bob Hite   *producer:* Frank Telford *director:* Preston Wood   *music director:* John Gart   *origination:* New York   *debut guests:* Binnie Barnes, drama critic Whitney Bolton, producer Herman Levin, writer Don Ettinger

This hour-long summertime series, "General Electric Guest House," featured four celebrities, each representing a different facet of show business (a critic, a writer, a performer, and a producer), answering questions to see who was the most knowledgeable on the subject of entertainment.

Host Oscar Levant also performed musical numbers and stayed with the program through July 15. He was replaced by Durward Kirby for the rest of the run.

THE GENERATION GAP

premiere: February 7, 1969   *packager:* Castle-Drive Productions for Norton Simon/Talent Associates   *broadcast history:* ABC primetime February 7, 1969–May 23, 1969 *hosts:* Dennis Wholey, Jack Barry   *announcer:* Fred Foy *executive producer:* Daniel Melnick   *producer:* Chester Feldman   *director:* Mike Garguilo   *set designer:* Ron Baldwin *music director:* Norman Paris   *music:* Score Productions *origination:* Elysee Theater, New York

On "The Generation Gap," two teams of three players, with one team representing the younger generation (under thirty) and the other representing the older generation (over thirty), competed in a game of knowledge pertaining to each other's generations.

In the first round, questions were directed at individual members of each team. They scored twenty points if they were correct and members of the opposing team could each earn five points if they could predict whether the opposing players could answer the questions.

All players competed in the "cross-generation" round where questions were tossed up. Correct guesses earned ten points, while a team lost the points if a player answered incorrectly.

The team with the highest score at the end of the show won and each member of that team received that point score in cash. The point score of the losing team was divided among the members of that team.

Dennis Wholey, the original host, left "The Generation Gap" after two months and was replaced by Jack Barry on April 18. This was Barry's first return to network television after an eleven-year absence following the quiz show scandals.

Each program also featured guest performers of the past and present. Among the musical groups to perform were The Turtles, The Peppermint Rainbow, Jerry Butler, Wilson Pickett, and Jay and the Americans.

Did you know . . . "The Generation Gap" announcer Fred Foy was the legendary voice that narrated THE LONE RANGER series on both radio and television during the 1940s and 50s? Foy was also a staff announcer for the ABC Television Network from 1961 to 1985.

Were you watching when . . . Gene Wood was a contestant on "The Generation Gap"?

GET THE MESSAGE

premiere: March 30, 1964 *packager:* Mark Goodson–Bill Todman Productions *broadcast history:* ABC daytime March 30, 1964–December 25, 1964 *hosts:* Frank Buxton, Robert Q. Lewis *announcers:* Johnny Olson, Chet Gould *authority:* Dr. William Barnes *executive producer:* Robert Noah *producer:* Jack Farren *director:* Mike Garguilo *set designer:* Romain Johnston *origination:* Elysee Theater, New York *debut guests:* Abe Burrows, Orson Bean, Peggy Cass, Betty White

A female team of two celebrities and one studio contestant squared off against a male team of the same makeup on "Get the Message." The object of the game was for the contestants to guess expressions, titles, or names from one-word clues supplied by each of their teammates (example: the message was "Mickey Mouse" and the clues were "cartoon" and "rodent").

A correct guess was worth one point, and three points won the game. The studio contestant won $100 and played the "turnabout" bonus round in which he or she gave clues to the celebrity partner. If the celebrity partner guessed the message after one clue, the studio contestant won $100. Values diminished with each additional clue (two clues, $50; three clues, $25; and four clues, $10). Three words were played in the bonus round.

Frank Buxton was the original host and Robert Q. Lewis replaced him on September 28, 1964.

Were you watching when . . . these game show emcees guested on the show: Bill Cullen, Art James, and Gene Rayburn? They were all hosting Goodson–Todman shows at the time. Cullen was on THE PRICE IS RIGHT, James on SAY WHEN!!, and Rayburn on THE MATCH GAME.

GET THE PICTURE

premiere: March 18, 1991 *packager:* MTV Productions *broadcast history:* Nickelodeon March 18, 1991–March 13, 1993 *host:* Mike O'Malley *announcer:* Henry J *executive* *producers:* Andy Bamberger, Brown Johnson *creator/producer:* Marjorie Cohn *director:* Dana Calderwood *set designer:* Byron Taylor *music:* Dan Vitco *origination:* Universal Studios, Orlando

Two teams consisting of two kids, the orange team and the yellow team, competed in "Get the Picture," a game of identifying pictures by answering questions and connecting dots.

The game board consisted of sixteen squares, in four rows of four, and the match began with both teams trying to guess what a picture was, as squares were revealed one at a time. The team that guessed correctly earned twenty points.

The first round was called "Connect the Dots" and featured dots representing a picture. The team that answered a toss-up question earned twenty points and got to connect the dots in a square of their choice. The first team to correctly identify the picture collected an additional fifty points. A wrong guess cost a team twenty points.

Behind one of the squares was the "power surge" and the team that picked it could earn twenty points and have an actual piece of the picture revealed, by correctly guessing five pictures that were flashed one square at a time. The team had to do this in thirty seconds.

Round two was called "Dots" and teams answered questions by selecting from multiple choices. The number of correct answers determined the number of lines (out of twenty-five) a player could call. Each box on the game board was connected by four lines and when all were connected a box was revealed. Questions were worth forty points in this round and recognizing the picture was worth seventy-five points. The team with the most points at the end of this round won the game and played the "Mega Memory" bonus round.

Members of the winning team were given ten seconds to memorize the locations of nine pictures. Within a thirty-five second time limit, the contestants tried to match a clue with a photo by pressing the corresponding number on an oversized keypad on the studio floor. They won $100 for each of the first six correct answers and bonus prizes for additional correct responses.

GIANT STEP

premiere: November 7, 1956 *packager:* Entertainment Productions Inc/Harry Fleishman *broadcast history:* CBS primetime November 7, 1956–May 29, 1957 *host:* Bert Parks *announcer:* Mike Fitzmaurice *executive producer:* Steve Carlin *producer:* Ed Jurist *director:* Seymour Robbie *set designer:* Eddie Gilbert *music director:* Jerry Bresler *music adapted from:* Humperdinck's "Hansel and Gretel" *origination:* New York

Contestants, ages seven to seventeen, competed on "Giant Step" for a free college education and an all-expense-paid vacation anywhere in the world after graduation in this quiz show from the producers of THE $64,000 QUESTION.

The students picked their topics and attempted to complete the eight steps necessary to win the four-year scholarship. One question, containing two parts, was answered each week. If the students answered both parts they earned the right to move to the next step in the game. Answering at least one part of the question earned them merchandise prizes.

GIVE AND TAKE
premiere: March 20, 1952 *packager:* John Reed King Productions/CBS Television *broadcast history:* CBS daytime March 20, 1952–June 12, 1952 *hosts:* John Reed King, Bill Cullen *announcer/assistant:* Bill Cullen *producer:* Jack Carney *director:* Frank Satenstein *set designer:* Manuel Essman *music:* Fred Fiebel at the organ *origination:* CBS Studio 21, New York

"Give and Take" was a CBS daytime show seen on Thursday afternoons and was based on the CBS radio show of the same name that was first heard in 1945.

Five contestants were selected from the studio audience to compete for merchandise prizes. At the close of the show all the contestants returned for a final round of questions. In spelling-bee fashion, players were eliminated by a wrong answer, and prizes for that player were determined by the number of rounds that he or she survived.

GIVE-N-TAKE
premiere: September 8, 1975 *packager:* Carruthers Company/Warner Brothers Television *broadcast history:* CBS daytime September 8, 1975–November 26, 1975 *host:* Jim Lange *assistant:* Jane Nelson *announcer:* Johnny Jacobs *executive producer:* Bill Carruthers *producer:* Joel Stein *directors:* Bill Carruthers, John Dorsey *set designers:* George Smith, Spencer Davies *music:* Stan Worth *origination:* The Burbank Studios, Burbank

The object of the game was for players to build a prize package as close to $5,000 as possible, without going over. Four contestants, seated in a circle surrounding a large electronic spinning arrow, each received a merchandise gift of an unstated value on "Give-N-Take." Another prize was then revealed and a question read. The first player to correctly answer the question pressed a button to stop the arrow. The player the arrow pointed to could then keep the prize or give it to another player.

GLADIATORS 2000
premiere: September 17, 1994 *packager:* One World Entertainment/Four Point Entertainment/Samuel Goldwyn Company *broadcast history:* Syndicated September 17, 1994–September 14, 1997 *hosts:* Maria Sansone and Ryan Seacrest, Valarie Miller *voice of "Ben":* Pamela Segall *producer:* Garry Bormet *director:* Glenn Weiss *production designer:* Steve Graziani *theme music:* Richard Freeman Davis, John Arrin *origination:* Stage 3, CBS Studio Center, Studio City

"Gladiators 2000," a weekly spin-off of the popular AMERICAN GLADIATORS, made its debut in the fall of 1994, giving kids and teens a chance to compete in the same events as adults. Each event also included question-and-answer sessions to test the participants' knowledge of health, nutrition, and physical fitness.

Hosting "Gladiators 2000" were Maria Sansone, former host of ABC-TV's "Wide World of Sports for Kids" and Ryan Seacrest, who had emceed ESPN's "Radical Outdoor Challenge." When the show returned for its second season, in September 1995, Valarie Miller replaced Maria Sansone as cohost.

Each team was composed of two kids, ages ten to thirteen, assisted by two of the gladiators from the adult series, who acted as captains. Among the gladiators who appeared were Jazz, Ice, Nitro, Sabre, Siren, Hawk, Laser, Turbo, and Zap.

Each show consisted of three physical challenges with events like "Assault" where one team of contenders fired tennis balls at a moving target (a Gladiator coach from the opposing team) and "The Food Pyramid" where the challenge was to race up and down a thirty-foot-high foam pyramid, collecting items from each of the six basic food groups.

The day's competition concluded with "The Eliminator," where players completed an obstacle course that included climbing a rope ladder, crossing a row of hanging rings, climbing over a Plexiglas wall and running up a moving treadmill. Along the way the players had to answer questions in order to speed their way through the course.

Each event was worth points and the top-scoring team of the day won merchandise prizes.

First-run episodes were produced for two seasons. The 1996–1997 season consisted of repeat shows.

GLAMOUR GIRL
premiere: July 6, 1953 *packager:* Glamour Productions *broadcast history:* NBC daytime July 6, 1953–January 8, 1954 *hosts:* Harry Babbitt, Jack McCoy *announcers:* Frank Barton, Don Stanley *executive producer:* Jack McCoy *producer:* Don Ross *directors:* Bill Bennington, William Sterling *set designer:* Frank Swig *music director:* Gaylord Carter *origination:* NBC Studio 3, Burbank

Four contestants explained why they wanted to be glamorous on "Glamour Girl," this daytime series. The winner, selected by audience applause, was given a twenty-four-hour beauty treatment and returned to show off her new look on the next program.

Jack McCoy replaced Harry Babbitt as host on October 8, 1953.

GLOBAL GUTS See NICKELODEON GUTS.

GO
premiere: October 3, 1983 *packager:* Bob Stewart–Sande Stewart Productions *broadcast history:* NBC daytime October 3, 1983–January 20, 1984; CBN (cable) September 30, 1985–August 29, 1986 (repeats) *host:* Kevin O'Connell *announcer:* Johnny Gilbert *executive producer:* Bob Stewart *producer:* Sande Stewart *director:* Bruce Burmester *set designers:* Ed Flesh, Molly Joseph *music:* Bob Cobert *origination:* NBC Studio 2, Burbank *debut guests:* Richard Kline, Elaine Joyce

Two five-member teams sought to identify a word or phrase from clues supplied by their teammates. On "Go," the teams, each consisting of a celebrity guest and four other contestants, played one at a time. One player would attempt to identify the word or phrase as the others put together a question. Two players also participated by adding one word to the question. The active player moved down the line answering five questions as fast as he or she could. After one team played, the opposing team tried to beat their time. Round one was worth two hundred fifty points; round two, five hundred points; round three, seven hundred fifty points; and round four, one thousand two hundred fifty points. The first team to score one thousand five hundred points won the game.

The winning team played the jackpot round for $10,000; $20,000 if one team shut the other out in the main game. One player tried to answer seven questions in sixty seconds while his or her four teammates formulated the question by adding one word per player. Three of his or her teammates then formulated the second question, two created the third question, one created the fourth question, two again created the fifth question, three again created the sixth, and finally all four created the seventh and final question.

GO LUCKY

premiere: July 15, 1951   *packager:* Louis Cowan Productions   *broadcast history:* CBS primetime July 15, 1951–September 2, 1951   *host:* Jan Murray   *announcer:* Hal Simms   *producer:* Herb Moss   *director:* Jerome Schnur   *origination:* New York   *debut guests:* Janis Paige, Russell Nype

"Go Lucky" was a summertime quiz show based on the parlor game "Coffee Pot" and was sponsored by Lucky Strike cigarettes. Two contestants had two minutes to guess a common phrase that was acted out by a group of performers. The players could ask questions by substituting the word "lucky" in place of the phrase or word.

GOLF FOR SWINGERS

premiere: January 15, 1972   *packager:* Carruthers Company for McCann-Erickson Inc.   *broadcast history:* Syndicated January 15, 1972–September 1972   *host:* Lee Trevino   *producer/director:* Bill Carruthers   *origination:* Calabassas Country Club, Calabassas

In this weekly show, "Golf for Swingers," two guest celebrities played three holes of golf with professional Lee Trevino. Thirteen shows were filmed with guests including Bob Hope, Bing Crosby, Dean Martin, Glen Campbell, Monty Hall, Sammy Davis Jr., and Joey Bishop. The show was also known as "Lee Trevino's Golf for Swingers."

THE GONG SHOW

premiere: June 14, 1976   *packager:* Chuck Barris–Chris Bearde Productions   *broadcast history:* NBC daytime June 14, 1976–July 21, 1978; Syndicated September 1976–September 1980; USA (cable) October 1, 1984–October 9, 1987 (repeats); Syndicated September 12, 1988–September 15, 1989

1976–1980 version

hosts: Chuck Barris, Gary Owens   *assistant:* Siv Aberg

little man: Jerry Maren (confetti thrower)   *announcer:* Johnny Jacobs   *creators/executive producers:* Chuck Barris, Chris Bearde   *producer:* Gene Banks   *directors:* John Dorsey, Terry Kyne   *set designers:* E. Jay Krause, Lynn Griffin   *music director:* Milton DeLugg   *origination:* NBC Studios, Burbank; Sunset Gower Studios   *debut guests:* Phyllis Diller, Anson Williams, Jamie Farr

1988–1989 version

host: Don Bleu   *announcer:* Charlie O'Donnell   *executive producers:* Chris Bearde, Jeff Wald, Scott Sternberg   *producer:* Rac A. Clark   *directors:* Jeff Margolis, Steven Santos   *set designers:* Anthony Sabatino, William H. Harris   *music:* Joey Carbone   *origination:* Studio 41, CBS Television City, Los Angeles   *debut guests:* Argus Hamilton, Molly Cheek, Ramone Azteca

"The Gong Show" was the most successful spoof of amateur talent shows to hit television. Three celebrities—Phyllis Diller, Anson Williams, and Jamie Farr had the honor of being judges during the premiere week. The judges viewed variety acts performed by amateurs and each member of the panel rated the acts on a scale of one to ten, with ten being the best possible score. Any act that was deemed too awful (and there were many) to continue could be gonged at any time and be rejected immediately.

A sample of contestants who appeared on "The Gong Show" included a girl who whistled with her nose and a dentist who played "Stars and Stripes Forever" with his drill.

The top scorer of the day won the grand prize of $516.32 on the NBC daytime version and $712.05 on the nighttime edition. When the show was revived in 1988, the winner collected $701.

One of the biggest hits of the 70s, "The Gong Show." Chuck Barris hosted the NBC daytime show and radio-television superstar Gary Owens hosted the nighttime version.

In 1980, Universal Pictures released *The Gong Show Movie* starring Chuck Barris, Robin Altman, Mabel King, Jaye P. Morgan, Murray Langston, and Rip Taylor.

Did you know . . . that the original pilot of "The Gong Show" was taped at the KGO-TV Studios in San Francisco with Gary Owens as host? Original panel members on the pilot were Adrienne Barbeau, Richard Dawson (pre-FAMILY FEUD), Arte Johnson, and Jo Anne Worley.

In 1976, in addition to hosting "The Gong Show," Gary Owens was also hosting a national syndicated radio show, as well as his own top-rated daily radio show at station KMPC in California.

In 1994 and 1995, Gary Owens was inducted into three national Broadcasting Halls of Fame, joining such legends as Jack Benny, Carol Burnett, George Burns, Walter Cronkite, Red Skelton, and Orson Welles.

Comedian John Barbour was the original choice to host "The Gong Show" when it became a series on NBC. He taped five shows that never aired before being replaced by Chuck Barris. Barbour did go on to costar in the TV series "Real People" from 1979 to 1982.

Were you watching when . . . "The Gong Show's" semi-regular panel members were: Phyllis Diller, Jamie Farr, Arte Johnson, Soupy Sales, and Rip Taylor? Jaye P. Morgan was the only regular panel member and by far the most popular. Some eighteen years later both Jaye P. and Jamie would be photographed with emcee Chuck Barris for a photo that would make *People* magazine's twentieth-year edition in 1994. Other frequent semi-regulars were game show hosts Allen Ludden and Chuck Woolery.

"The Gong Show" made an appearance as a primetime TV special on NBC on April 26, 1977. The panel for the special included Arte Johnson, Jamie Farr, and Jaye P. Morgan, and the show featured Tony Randall singing, as well as appearances by Rosey Grier, Aretha Franklin, Ray Charles, and the UCLA Marching Band.

GRAND-PRIX ALL STAR SHOW

premiere: September 1982 *packager:* In Productions for American Television Syndication *broadcast history:* Syndicated September 1982–September 1983 *hosts:* Michael Young and Teri Ann Linn *announcer:* Mary Lou Sam *executive producer:* Lawrence P. O'Daly *producer:* John W. Coleman *director:* Sol Ehrich *origination:* Malibu Fun Center, Puente Hills

On "Grand-Prix All Star Show," this weekly game show taped at the Malibu Fun Center in Puente Hills, California, three celebrity guests were teamed with teenage contestants ages fourteen to sixteen to compete in athletic stunts.

Sample stunts included attempting to find a picture in a pile of foam rubber cubes before their opponents did, sliding down a water slide, having one partner take his or her clothing off, and then dress his or her teammate and racing miniature cars around a track.

Three rounds were played. First place in round one was worth ten points; second place, seven points; and third place,

three points. In round two, the point values jumped to twenty, fifteen, and five and in round three to thirty, twenty, and ten. The team with the highest score won prizes.

GRANDSTAND

premiere: July 9, 1988 *packager:* The Phoenix Communications Group *broadcast history:* Syndicated July 9, 1988–July 1989 *host:* Curt Chaplin *"Keeper of the Cards":* Deborah Johnston *announcer:* Dave Herman *executive producer:* Geoff Belinfante *supervising producer:* Richard Domich *producers:* Joseph M. Lavine, Helen Maier-Ruddick *director:* Mike Garguilo *set designer:* Ron Baldwin *music:* Bob Burke *origination:* National Video Center, New York

"Grandstand" was a weekly syndicated quiz show featuring three teams answering trivia questions, with each team consisting of a studio contestant and a celebrity guest from the sports world. Guests on the first show were basketball star Maurice Lucas, baseball manager Earl Weaver, and hockey star Bobby Hull.

The first round was called the "face-off round," where players demonstrated how much they knew about their celebrity partners. Against a sixty-second time limit, the teammate asked seven questions about the celebrity's career. The team scored twenty-five points for a correct answer and received a twenty-five point bonus for answering all seven questions correctly. The round concluded after each team played.

The second round was called the "fast break round" and teams competed against each other to answer questions worth twenty-five points. In the last two minutes of the round ("the two-minute drill"), point values doubled to fifty. The team with the most points at the end of this round won the game and received merchandise prizes.

In the bonus round ("touchdown round"), the winning team started at the twenty-yard line of a game board. They had sixty seconds to reach the end zone for a bonus prize. For each correct answer, the team moved ten yards and earned $200. If time started to run down, the team could call for "the bomb" and then risk all of their winnings on their ability to answer one final question.

Phoenix Communications is the official production company for Major League Baseball and the National Hockey League.

GREAT GETAWAY GAME

premiere: June 1, 1990 *packager:* Brockway Television Productions/Wink Martindale Productions *broadcast history:* Travel Channel (cable) June 1, 1990–April 1991 *host:* Wink Martindale *announcer:* Rick Sommers *creator:* Richard Brockway *executive producers:* Richard Brockway, Wink Martindale *producer:* Bill Maier *director:* Roy Dahl *set designer:* Ron Baldwin *music:* Graham Preskett *origination:* Times Square Studios, New York

Two contestants competed against each other to test their knowledge of travel trivia in the Travel Channel's first daily game show. On "Great Getaway Game," the winner of the day got a chance to win a trip.

The players competed to find a word hidden on a game board consisting of thirty squares (five rows of six). Behind each number was a letter, and the hidden word could be spelled out up, down, left to right, or right to left. A clue was read to start the game and each player selected two numbers to reveal the first letters in the game.

Players answered toss-up questions worth ten points to have additional letters revealed. The player who solved the puzzle earned one hundred points and a prize.

Points were doubled in game two and the player with the highest score won the match and a chance to try for a trip in the bonus game.

The object of the bonus game was to find five words related to a specific subject in thirty seconds. The letters of the words were hidden in seven rows consisting of seven columns of letters and could be spelled out up, down, left to right, or right to left. Winning players returned on the next show and continued to play until defeated.

THE GREATEST MAN ON EARTH

premiere: December 3, 1952   *packager:* Walt Framer Productions   *broadcast history:* ABC primetime December 3, 1952–February 19, 1953   *hosts:* Ted Brown, Vera Vague   *assistants:* Pat Conway, Fred Manners, Phyllis Hunt   *announcer:* Fred Mattis   *producer:* Walt Framer   *director:* Bob Doyle   *origination:* New York

In this weekly series, five women presented male candidates who competed for the title of "The Greatest Man on Earth." The men competed by answering questions and participating in stunts, culminating in the day's winner being named "Crown Prince." Winners from five shows returned on the sixth program to play for the title and a grand prize that included a new car and a trip to Switzerland.

Vera Vague replaced Ted Brown as host on January 15, 1953.

GRILL ME

premiere: September 9, 1996   *packager:* RPA Programming/Telescene/MCA-TV   *broadcast history:* USA (cable) September 9, 1996–September 15, 1996   *host:* Jordan Brady   *dancers:* Heather Marie, Melanie Taylor, Damian Perkins   *creators:* Bo Kaprell, Michael Klinghoffer   *executive producers:* Bo Kaprell, Michael Klinghoffer, Michael Yudin   *director:* Ron Kantor   *set designer:* John Gilles   *music:* Scooter Pietsch   *origination:* Empire Studios, Burbank

"Grill Me" was a one-show special, sponsored by American Honda, broadcast several times in one week on the USA cable network.

The show featured three celebrities, musician Dweezil Zappa, Susan Olsen of "The Brady Bunch," and Kristoff St. John of "The Young and the Restless," who played a question-and-answer game for charity. Set in a diner on stage, each round was named after the various courses of a meal.

Round one, the "Appetizer Round," featured categories with names like "A Knish called Wanda" and "The Brady Brunch." Value of the categories ranged from $9.95 to

$17.95, with that amount added to a player's score, and each category had three questions.

Players each began with $99.95 on their scoreboard, and the player who answered the first question, a toss-up, controlled the rest of the category. If a player didn't know the answer, he or she could challenge one of his or her opponents.

Round two, "All You Can Eat," featured questions worth $25 and had players trying to place names of people in one of three categories ("Surf," "Turf," or "Smurf").

"The Main Course," round three, was played the same way as the first round with values increased. The low-scoring player at the end of this round was eliminated from the rest of the game. The remaining two players competed in the sixty-second "Dessert Round." A player got $50 for each correct answer and kept control of the round until he or she missed a question. Then the opponent got to answer questions and build up his or her total.

The winning player won $5,000 for a chosen charity, while the other two players each earned $2,500 for their causes.

THE GRUDGE MATCH

premiere: September 7, 1991   *packager:* Richmel Productions/Genesis Entertainment   *broadcast history:* Syndicated September 7, 1991–September 6, 1992   *hosts:* Jesse Ventura, Steve Albert   *assistant:* Paula McClure   *announcer:* Steve Albert   *regulars:* Michael Buffer (ring announcer), John Pinette (referee), Theresa Ring (card girl), Andy and Pete Steinfeld (cornermen)   *creator/executive producer:* Rich Melcombe   *producer:* Mark Johnson   *director:* Bob Dunphy   *set designer:* Ed Flesh   *music:* Michael Cruz   *origination:* Universal Studios, Hollywood

"The Grudge Match" was a weekly one-hour show that gave contestants, two at a time, a chance to settle disputes by fighting it out in a boxing ring, using weapons like cream pies, ice cream, oversized boxing gloves, and water balloons.

Each player presented his or her dispute prior to the start of the match, which consisted of three one-minute rounds. The studio audience determined the winner at the conclusion of the final round.

One of the disputes settled revolved around a man who put his term paper on computer and his girlfriend who subsequently erased it. Another had to do with a woman who loaned her girlfriend an heirloom wedding gown, only to have her friend alter it into a miniskirt.

"The Grudge Match" featured wrestling's Jesse "The Body" Ventura and sports commentator Steve Albert as hosts, and Michael Buffer, boxing's premier ring announcer ("Let's Get Ready to Rumble").

GUESS AGAIN

premiere: June 14, 1951   *packager:* CBS Television   *broadcast history:* CBS primetime June 14, 1951–June 21, 1951   *host:* Mike Wallace   *announcer:* Art Hannes   *producer:* Al Span   *director:* Jerome Schnur   *origination:* New York   *debut guests:* Claire Luce, Victor Jury, Glenda Farrell and her son Tommy

This show lasted only two weeks and featured a stock company—Joey Faye, Mandy Kaye, and Bobbie Martin—who presented a series of vignettes followed by questions posed to a celebrity panel. Each of the panelists was aided by a playing partner from the studio audience and they each won $10 for answering the first question correctly, $15 for the second, $20 for the third, and $25 for the fourth. Each right answer gave the panelists a chance to answer the next question. Money won by the celebrity panelists was given to charity, while the audience player kept his or her winnings.

"Guess Again" was replaced on June 28 with the television debut of "Amos 'n' Andy."

GUESS WHAT?

premiere: July 8, 1952 *packager:* Larry White–Manny Rosenberg Productions *broadcast history:* DuMont primetime July 8, 1952–August 26, 1952 *host:* Dick Kollmar *producers:* Larry White, Manny Rosenberg *director:* Harry Coyle *origination:* New York *debut guests:* Quentin Reynolds, Virginia Peine, Mark Hanna

A celebrity panel tried to guess the subject of a film clip that was shown to the audience on "Guess What?" Each of the panelists asked questions with "yes" or "no" answers to determine the identity of the subject. Cash prizes were given to charities.

"Guess What?" was sponsored by Mogen David Wine.

THE GUINNESS GAME

premiere: September 17, 1979 *packager:* David Paradine Television Production/Hill-Eubanks Group/20th Century Fox TV *broadcast history:* Syndicated September 17, 1979–September 1980 *hosts:* Bob Hilton, Don Galloway *announcers:* Charlie O'Donnell, Tony McClay *developed by:* Michael Hill *executive producer:* Marvin Minoff *producer:* Walt Case *director:* Ron Kantor *set designers:* Ed Flesh, Jimmy Cuomo *music:* Lee Ringuette, Score Productions *origination:* Golden West Studios, Los Angeles

The best-selling book *The Guinness Book of Records* provided the inspiration for "The Guinness Game," this weekly syndicated game show that lasted one season.

Three studio contestants tried to predict if a record breaking stunt, performed live on the show, could be accomplished. Example: "Can five men change four tires on a car without a jack, in two minutes or less?"

Each player started with $1,000 and could bet up to ninety percent of his or her bankroll. The player with the most money after three rounds won the game and played a fourth round for a bonus prize.

Did you know . . . Don Galloway was a regular on the detective series "Ironside" from 1967 to 1975?

GUILTY OR INNOCENT

premiere: September 24, 1984 *packager:* Gannaway-Rubinstein Productions *broadcast history:* Syndicated September 24, 1984–December 1984 *host:* Melvin Belli *jury moderator:* John Shearin *announcer:* John Wells *creator:* Sherman Rubinstein *producer:* Mickey Grant *director:* Scott Redman *set design:* Herman Zimmerman *origination:* Dallas

On "Guilty or Innocent," twelve members of a studio jury watched a reenactment of an actual jury trial and then voted "guilty" or "innocent." After an initial sampling of the jurors' conclusions, deliberations were begun, and a final vote taken. If the studio jury's choice matched the actual verdict, they split $5,000. If they were unanimous in their voting and also correct, they split $10,000. The twelve players remained on the show for one week.

HAGGIS BAGGIS

premiere: June 20, 1958 *packager:* Rainbow Productions (Joe Cates Productions) *broadcast history:* NBC primetime June 20, 1958–September 29, 1958; NBC daytime June 30, 1958–June 19, 1959 *hosts:* Jack Linkletter, Fred Robbins, Dennis James *announcers:* Bill Wendell, Jerry Damon *executive producer:* Joe Cates *producers:* David Brown, Gil Cates *director:* Ted Nathanson *set designer:* Norman Davidson *music:* Murray Ross *theme:* Erwin Drake *origination:* Ziegfeld Theater, New York

Contestants played "Haggis Baggis" on a large game board that consisted of twenty-five squares, and the object was to guess the identity of a celebrity whose picture was revealed as the squares were uncovered. Players picked questions corresponding to a square and with every correct answer a portion of the celebrity photo was revealed.

The winner of the game had a choice of two groups of prizes. If the opponent in the previous game could correctly guess which group the winner took, the opponent won the other group of prizes.

Jack Linkletter was host of the nighttime edition of "Haggis Baggis" and New York radio personality Fred Robbins hosted the daytime edition. Dennis James replaced Robbins as emcee on February 9, 1959.

Did you know . . . Jack Linkletter emceed "Haggis Baggis" while still a student at the University of Southern California? In 1963 he returned to television as host of the folk music series "Hootenanny." In 1965 he hosted the game show THE REBUS GAME and in 1969 he joined his father Art as cohost of an afternoon variety show on NBC.

HAIL THE CHAMP

premiere: September 22, 1951 *packager:* GAM Productions *broadcast history:* ABC Saturday mornings September 22, 1951–June 14, 1952; ABC Saturday mornings December 27, 1952–June 20, 1953 *hosts:* Herb Allen, Howard Roberts *assistants:* Jim Andelin, Angel Casey *announcer:* John Dunham *producers:* Maurice Morton, Sheldon Kaplan *directors:* Grover Allen, Ivor McLaren *origination:* Civic Opera House, Chicago

This children's quiz show, "Hail the Champ," featured six youngsters on each program. Two players were used in each of three contests. The three finalists from each of the contests played in a final event to determine the day's winner. Prizes for the winner included a new bicycle.

"Hail the Champ" made its debut as a local series on Los Angeles television station KLAC on October 6, 1948 and ran until April 6, 1951. Herb Allen was the host and continued when the show moved to ABC in the fall of 1951. When the show returned in December 1952, Howard Roberts became the new host and Angel Casey his assistant.

HAVE A HEART

premiere: May 3, 1955 *packager:* Robert Jennings Productions *broadcast history:* DuMont primetime May 3, 1955–June 21, 1955 *host:* John Reed King *producer:* Morton Catok *director:* Frank Reeves *origination:* New York

Four contestants competed on teams of two in "Have a Heart," to answer general knowledge questions. Players received cash for correct answers and the winning team donated their earnings to hometown charities.

"Have a Heart" was one of the last shows produced for the DuMont network.

HE SAID, SHE SAID

premiere: September 15, 1969 *packager:* Mark Goodson–Bill Todman Productions *broadcast history:* Syndicated September 15, 1969–August 21, 1970 *host:* Joe Garagiola *announcer:* Johnny Olson *producers:* Howard Felsher, Ira Skutch *directors:* Ira Skutch, Paul Alter *set designers:* Ted Cooper, Kathleen Ankers *origination:* NBC Studio 8H, New York

Former baseball player Joe Garagiola made his debut as a game show host on "He Said, She Said," a daily program sponsored by Holiday Inn. Four celebrity couples, each playing for a married couple in the studio audience, tried to recognize a clue word given by their mates, related to an incident in their lives.

The first half of the game was played with the husbands on stage and their wives in a soundproof room offstage. Each round began with a topic, such as "A time you needed a tranquilizer" or "Something she didn't tell you about for a long time." Each of the men gave a one- or two-word clue and told about an incident in their lives that was related to the clue words.

Teams scored twenty-five points if the wives recognized the clue word given by their husbands and lost ten points if they guessed incorrectly or failed to recognize the clues.

Halfway through the show the husbands and wives exchanged places. The team with the most points at the end of the show won a week's vacation at a Holiday Inn for their audience partners.

"He Said, She Said" was revived in 1974 under the title TATTLETALES.

Did you know . . . creators Goodson and Todman had intended this husband-and-wife quizzer to bow on NBC as "It Had to Be You" in the fall of 1963. Instead, it ended up in syndication six years later as "He Said, She Said."

Were you watching when . . . Gene Rayburn and his wife Helen were playing against Bill Cullen and his wife Ann in 1969?

HEADLINE CHASERS

premiere: September 9, 1985 *packager:* Merv Griffin Productions/Wink Martindale Productions *broadcast history:* Syndicated September 9, 1985–September 1986 *host:* Wink Martindale *announcer:* Johnny Gilbert *executive producers:* Merv Griffin, Wink Martindale *producer:* John Tobyansen *director:* Kevin McCarthy *set designer:* Bob Rang *origination:* TAV Celebrity Theater, Los Angeles

Two couples competed in a game of guessing newspaper and magazine headlines on "Headline Chasers." Each puzzle started with a value of $500 and contained a headline with letters missing. As clues were given and letters added to the headline, the value decreased by $100. After one team correctly solved the headline, they got a chance to answer two bonus questions for an additional $100 each.

A second round was played for $500 and a third round for $1,000. The team with the most money after three rounds won the game and played the "headline extra" for $5,000.

The winning team was given a headline with letters missing and a chance to guess for a possible $5,000. They could buy up to four clues, each costing $1,000, and then guess for a reduced value.

Did you know . . . in 1985 Wink Martindale created "Headline Chasers" with his wife Sandy in the kitchen of their Malibu home while reading the LA *Times?* Wink was reading the paper and the idea for a game show featuring headlines was created. "Headline Chasers" was to become the first game show (of several) that Wink would create and also emcee.

HIGH FINANCE

premiere: July 7, 1956 *packager:* Jade Productions/Peter Arnell Productions *broadcast history:* CBS primetime July

Wink Martindale both created and hosted this 1985 game show titled "Headline Chasers."

7, 1956–December 15, 1956 *host:* Dennis James *announcers:* Jay Simms, Jack Gregson *creators:* Dennis James, Bob Jennings *producer:* Peter Arnell *director:* Lou Sposa *music director:* John Gart *origination:* Maxine Elliott Theater (CBS Studio 51), New York

"High Finance" was a primetime game show that could make a player's dream come true. The player became an investor with a goal to win as much as $75,000. Each contestant played for his or her own dream prize (example: a miniature golf course and driving range), and in the final round played for the $75,000.

All questions used on the show were taken from three newspapers that the contestants were asked to read before they appeared on the show.

In the first part of the game, the player tried to build a bank account by answering five $300 questions. The player had to answer three out of the five questions correctly in order to move on to the investment segment.

In the investment segment, one level was played each week. Each level had prizes that could be obtained by answering a question and spending part of the player's bankroll. When a contestant returned on the next show to play the second level, he or she was required to sell back part of the prize winnings. This increased the player's bankroll so that new merchandise could be obtained.

On the fourth level, the winner played for a dream prize and on the fifth level, for the grand prize of $75,000.

HIGH LOW

premiere: July 4, 1957   *packager:* Jack Barry and Dan Enright Productions   *broadcast history:* NBC primetime July 4, 1957–September 19, 1957   *host:* Jack Barry   *announcer:* Don Pardo   *executive producer:* Robert Noah   *producer:* Al Freedman   *director:* Charles Dubin   *set designer:* Ted Cooper   *music director:* Paul Taubman   *origination:* NBC Studio 6A, New York   *debut guests:* Burl Ives, John Van Doren, Patricia Medina

In "High Low," this summer replacement quiz show, contestants tested their knowledge while competing against a three-member celebrity panel. Both the player (who was stationed in an isolation booth) and the panel were asked a multipart question. The panelists indicated how many parts they could answer and the contestant could choose whether he or she wanted to triple the money and answer as many parts of the question as the "high" panelist had chosen or double the money and answer as many parts as the "low" panelist had chosen. The contestant who failed to answer all

A dapper looking Jack Barry makes last-minute adjustments before showtime.

the required parts correctly left with ten percent of his or her previous winnings.

Players began the game with $500 and the biggest winner during "High Low's" run was Terry Curtis, who won $76,000.

HIGH ROLLERS

premiere: July 1, 1974   *packager:* Merrill Heatter–Bob Quigley Productions (1974–1980); Merrill Heatter Productions/Century Towers Productions/Orion Television (1987–1988)   *broadcast history:* NBC daytime July 1, 1974–June 11, 1976; Syndicated September 8, 1975–September 19, 1976; NBC daytime April 24, 1978–June 20, 1980; Syndicated September 14, 1987–September 9, 1988; USA (cable) September 19, 1988–September 13, 1991 (repeats of 1987–1988 version)
1974–1976 version
host: Alex Trebek   *assistants:* Ruta Lee, Elaine Stewart, Leslie Uggams, Linda Kay Henning   *announcer:* Kenny Williams   *executive producers:* Merrill Heatter, Bob Quigley, Robert Noah   *producers:* Art Alisi, Ken Williams   *director:* Jerome Shaw   *set designer:* Jim Newton   *music:* Stan Worth   *origination:* NBC Studio 2, Burbank
1978–1980 version
host: Alex Trebek   *assistants:* Becky Price, Lauren Firestone   *announcer:* Kenny Williams   *executive producers:* Merrill Heatter, Bob Quigley   *producers:* Robert Noah, Art Alisi   *director:* Jerome Shaw   *set designer:* Jim Newton   *origination:* NBC Studio 3, Burbank
1987–1988 version
host: Wink Martindale   *assistants:* KC Winkler, Crystal Owens   *announcer:* Dean Goss   *executive producer:* Merrill Heatter   *producers:* Steve Friedman, Art Alisi   *director:* Jerome Shaw   *set designers:* Anthony Sabatino, William H. Harris   *music directors:* Lynne McCleerly, Lee Ringuette   *theme:* Michael Camilo   *origination:* Studio 41, CBS Television City, Los Angeles

The object of "High Rollers" was to eliminate all the numbers, one through nine, that appeared on a game board, by using any combination of numbers that appeared on the sum total of a pair of dice. The first player to roll a combination that was not available lost the game.

To gain control of the dice, the two contestants had to answer a toss-up question. The first to answer correctly gained control of the dice and had the option of rolling or passing them on to their opponent.

The first player to win two games played the "Big Board" and received $100 for each number he or she could remove by the roll of the dice, and a grand prize of $10,000 if all nine numbers were eliminated.

On April 26, 1976 the format of "High Rollers" was changed. Contestants now had to guess the identity of a celebrity photograph. Each photograph was covered with a nine-piece puzzle. Players still answered a toss-up question to gain control of the dice. The number of the roll was used to reveal pieces of the puzzle. Each piece of the puzzle also represented a prize for the contestant who guessed the celebrity. The first contestant to win two games won the match

Host Alex Trebek stands by as the lovely Ruta Lee prepares to roll the dice on NBC's "High Rollers."

and got a chance to play the "Big Numbers" for the $10,000 grand prize.

The show went back to its original format when it returned in 1978.

"High Rollers" began as a daytime show on NBC in 1974 with Alex Trebek as host and Ruta Lee as cohost. Elaine Stewart was the cohost on the 1975 syndicated version. During the initial run, 1974–1976, the cohost tossed the dice for the contestants.

In April 1978, "High Rollers" returned to NBC's daytime schedule. Alex Trebek returned as host, joined by models Becky Price and Lauren Firestone. Contestants were given the opportunity to roll the dice in this version.

"High Rollers" returned again to television in the fall of 1987 in a first-run syndicated version. Veteran game show emcee Wink Martindale took over as host and was joined by

models KC Winkler and Crystal Owens. The syndicated version lasted only one season in first-run production, but enjoyed a three-year run in repeats on the USA cable network.

Did you know . . . Howard Hughes offered "High Rollers" hostess Elaine Stewart a film contract but it was producer Hal Wallis who signed her? Metro-Goldwyn-Mayer acquired her contract and cast her in the movies *The Bad and the Beautiful, Take the High Ground,* and *Legs Diamond.*

Lucille Ball was once quoted as saying that Alex Trebek and "High Rollers" were her favorite game show duo. She made several guest star visits to the "High Rollers" set!

HIT MAN

premiere: January 3, 1983 *packager:* Jay Wolpert Productions *broadcast history:* NBC daytime January 3, 1983– April 1, 1983 *host:* Peter Tomarken *announcer:* Rod Roddy *executive producer:* Jay Wolpert *producers:* Roger Speakman, Randy Neece *director:* John Dorsey *set designer:* Jack Hart *origination:* NBC Studio 4, Burbank

Three contestants competed in "Hit Man" for the chance to take on the preceding day's champion and play for a grand prize of $10,000. A story (example: "The Making of *Star Wars*") was read and photographs were shown. When it was completed, questions based on the story were asked. When a player gave a correct answer, he or she was given a "hit man." An incorrect answer eliminated the player from the next question. The first two players to correctly answer six questions received $300 and moved into round two. The third player was eliminated from the game.

In round two, the two players competed against the previous day's champion. The champion received seven hit men and the first place winner from round one received four hit men and the second place player received three. Another story was read and questions were asked. When a player answered a question correctly, he or she eliminated one of his or her opponent's hit men. The first player to eliminate the other players' hit men won the game and went on to play the "Triple Crown" for a chance to win $10,000.

Did you know . . . this marked the first show that co-author Fred Wostbrock would work on? In the winter of 1982 packager and executive producer Jay Wolpert hired Fred and gave him his first break in the world of game shows. They have remained great friends since that winter afternoon in 1982.

HOLD EVERYTHING!

premiere: June 18, 1990 *packager:* Barry and Enright Productions *broadcast history:* Syndicated June 18, 1990–August 17, 1990 *host:* Pat Bullard *announcer:* Larry Van Nuys *executive producer:* Dan Enright *executive in charge of production:* Chris Sohl *field producers:* Joe Coppoletta, Gary Jonke *director:* Tom Maguire *set designers:* Rob Sagrillo, George Petersen *music:* Ed Lojeski *origination:* Sante Fe Communications, Burbank

Three celebrities, each playing for charity in "Hold Everything!", tried to predict how an unsuspecting person would react to various situations and problems. The pretaped event was shown to the panel and then stopped just before its conclusion. Each of the celebrity guests tried to predict how the participant would react.

Four rounds were played, with the first round worth one point; the second round, two points; the third round, three points; and the fourth round, four points. The top-scoring celebrity received $1,000 for his or her favorite charity.

HOLD IT PLEASE

premiere: May 8, 1949 *packager:* CBS Television *broadcast history:* CBS primetime May 8, 1949–May 22, 1949 *host:* Gil Fates *producer/director:* Frances Buss *music director:* Max Showalter *origination:* Grand Central Station Studios, New York

The short-lived quiz series "Hold It Please" featured weekly winners who returned on the following show to become assistant masters of ceremony. Emcee for the program was Gil Fates, who would later produce WHAT'S MY LINE? for twenty-five years. He was joined on "Hold It Please" by regulars Bill McGraw, an actor appearing on Broadway in *Angel in the Wings*, comedian Mort Marshall, and actress Cloris Leachman. Each program opened with a shot of a telephone switchboard and the operator (played by Eva Marie Saint) answering "Hold It Please."

The cast of regulars acted out questions for both studio contestants and viewers at home to answer. A contestant who answered correctly won a valuable prize and a chance at the $1,000 jackpot question.

During a player's tenure as assistant emcee, he or she could answer any missed questions and could thus win the prizes offered for those questions.

Did you know . . . "Hold It Please" emcee Gil Fates was the first quiz show host on CBS television? Commercial television began on July 1, 1941 and one day later CBS premiered their first quiz show, THE CBS TELEVISION QUIZ. Gil was the emcee and Frances Buss his on-camera assistant. Buss later became one of the first female directors in television.

HOLD THAT CAMERA

premiere: August 27, 1950 *packager:* West Hooker Productions *broadcast history:* DuMont primetime August 27, 1950–December 15, 1950 *hosts:* Jimmy Blaine, Kyle MacDonnell *producer:* Ted Kneeland *directors:* Ray Nelson, Alex Leftwich *music director:* Ving Merlin *origination:* New York

"Hold That Camera" originated as a game show where a home viewer, via telephone, gave directions to an on-camera partner who performed stunts for prizes. A second team attempted to do the same stunt and the team using the least time won.

After a month on the air, both the game format and its host, Jimmy Blaine, were dropped and the show became a variety program with Kyle MacDonnell.

Did you know . . . Jimmy Blaine was the host of the first Hanna-Barbera cartoon series for television? From December 1957 to September 1960, Jimmy was the host of "Ruff and Ready" airing Saturday mornings on NBC.

HOLD THAT NOTE

premiere: January 22, 1957 *packager:* Wolf Productions *broadcast history:* NBC primetime January 22, 1957–April 2, 1957 *host:* Bert Parks *assistant:* Janice Gilbert *announcer:* Johnny Olson *executive producers:* Herb Wolf, Ed Wolf *producer:* Jack Rubin *director:* Lloyd Gross *music director:* Peter Van Steeden *orchestra conductor:* Ernie Evans *origination:* Ziegfeld Theater, New York

"Hold That Note" appeared as a sudden and unannounced replacement on the NBC schedule for "Break the $250,000 Bank" (see BREAK THE BANK) on January 22, 1957.

Two contestants competed in a musical quiz where they attempted to identify songs as they were being played by the studio orchestra. The first to correctly guess three songs in a row won the game and a cash jackpot.

Each song began with a predetermined value of up to twenty-five notes, with the value decreasing as the tune was played. Each unplayed note was multiplied by $50 and added to the jackpot that was won by the player who correctly guessed three songs in a row. The losing player received ten percent of the jackpot as a consolation prize.

The champ could retire after any win, but if he or she decided to face another opponent and then lost, the new champion's winnings were deducted from the amount won by the former champion.

Did you know . . . Bert Parks replaced Eddie Albert in the Broadway production of *The Music Man* on June 27, 1960 in the role originally created by Robert Preston? Bert continued with the show for over three hundred performances.

HOLLYWOOD CONNECTION

premiere: September 5, 1977 *packager:* Jack Barry and Dan Enright Productions *broadcast history:* Syndicated September 5, 1977–Spring 1978 *host:* Jim Lange *announcers:* Jay Stewart, Johnny Gilbert *executive producers:* Stan Dreben, Dan Enright *producer:* Ron Greenberg *director:* Richard Kline *set designer:* John C. Mula *origination:* KTLA Television, Los Angeles *debut week guests:* Pat Carroll, Jan Murray, Anson Williams, Marcia Wallace, Buddy Hackett, Jaye P. Morgan

Six celebrity guests were asked questions intended to reveal a bit of their personalities on "Hollywood Connection." They answered by choosing from among three possible responses. Two contestants then tried to guess which answer was chosen. The contestants were awarded points and the player with the most points played a bonus round where all the celebrities associated a word with a given subject. Each of the contestants then wrote three possible answers and tried to match celebrities for $250 a match. If the winning player earned $750 (three correct matches), he or she won a bonus prize and could risk all of the prize money on double stakes.

THE HOLLYWOOD GAME

premiere: June 19, 1992 *packager:* Pasetta Productions/ Rastar/CBS Entertainment Productions *broadcast history:* CBS primetime June 19, 1992–July 10, 1992 *host:* Bob Goen *announcer:* John Cramer *executive producers:* Marty Pasetta, Ray Stark *producer:* Stephen Radosh *director:* Greg Pasetta *set designer:* Bill Bohnert *music:* Tim Hosman *origination:* Studio 33, CBS Television City, Los Angeles

In this four-week primetime summer series, "The Hollywood Game," two teams consisting of two contestants competed in a quiz about movie and television trivia. Each team played three rounds, choosing categories represented by the nine letters in the word "H-O-L-L-Y-W-O-O-D."

In the first round each team played two questions, worth $100 and $200. They viewed a film clip before hearing the question. If the team failed to answer correctly, their opponents got a chance to steal the money.

Round two consisted of three questions in a chosen category, worth $200, $400, and $800, and in round three values were increased to $500, $1,000, and $2,000.

The final round, called the "Double Feature," determined the day's winner. Each team was allowed to wager all, half, or none of their accumulated bankroll on a predetermined category. The high-scoring team at the end of this round moved to the bonus round.

The winning team played the "Fast Picture Round" for a chance to win $25,000. Each player was given fifteen seconds to identify nine pictures taken from a particular category (example: "men in uniform" or "Barbra Streisand films") of the player's choice. The payoff was $1,000 per correct guess and $25,000 for all nine guessed correctly in the allotted time.

THE HOLLYWOOD SQUARES

premiere: October 17, 1966 *packagers:* Merrill Heatter–Bob Quigley Productions (1966–1981); Century Towers Productions/Orion TV (1986–1989) *broadcast history:* NBC daytime October 17, 1966–June 20, 1980; NBC primetime January 12, 1968–September 13, 1968; Syndicated November 1, 1971–September 1981; Syndicated September 15, 1986–September 8, 1989; USA (cable) September 11, 1989–June 25, 1993 (repeats of 1986–1989 series)

1966–1981 version

host: Peter Marshall *announcer:* Kenny Williams *executive producers:* Merrill Heatter, Bob Quigley *producers:* Les Roberts, Bill Armstrong, Jay Redack, Art Alisi *director:* Jerome Shaw *set designers:* E. Jay Krause, Bente Christensen *original theme:* Jimmy Haskell (1966–1969), "Merrill and Bob's Theme" William Loose (1969–1981) *origination:* NBC Studio 3, Burbank (1966–1980); Versailles Theatre, Riviera Hotel, Las Vegas (1980–1981) *debut daytime guests:* Rose Marie, Morey Amsterdam, Wally Cox, Abby Dalton, Charley Weaver, Agnes Moorehead, Ernest Borgnine, Nick Adams, Pamela Mason *debut primetime guests (1968):* Edie Adams, Morey Amsterdam, Milton Berle, Raymond Burr, Wally Cox, Abby Dalton, Nanette Fabray, Buddy Hackett, Charley Weaver

1986–1989 version

host: John Davidson *substitute host:* Jim J. Bullock *announcers:* Shadoe Stevens, Richard Stevens *executive producer:* Rick Rosner *producers:* Scott Sternberg, E. V. DiMassa Jr., Harry Friedman *directors:* Bob Loudin, Steve Grant *set designers:* Dennis Roof, Rob Sagrillo *music:* Stormy Sacks *origination:* NBC Studios, Burbank (1986); ABC Television Center, Los Angeles (1987); Fox Television Center, Los Angeles (1987–1988); Stage 37, Universal Studios, Hollywood (1988–1989) *debut guests:* Betty White, Mariette Hartley, John Byner, Phylicia and Ahmad Rashad, Lorenzo Lamas, Itzhak Perlman, Emma Samms, Jackie Collins, Bronson Pinchot

"The Hollywood Squares" was one of the most popular and longest-running daytime game shows on NBC. Much of the success of the show was attributed to the humorous answers given to questions answered by the celebrities who made up the squares on the board.

One of the most popular celebrities on the show was Paul Lynde, who occupied the center square. Lynde did not become a regular on the show until the fall of 1968.

Celebrities on the final daytime show, June 20, 1980 were Rose Marie, Tom Poston, Michele Lee, Leslie Uggams, George Gobel, Marty Allen, Charlie Callas, Wayland Flowers and Madame, and Vincent Price.

The object of the game was for two contestants to play, and win, a game of celebrity tic-tac-toe. Players called upon a star to answer a question and could either agree or disagree with the star's answer. If they were correct in their judgement, their mark, an "X" or "O," was put on the celebrity's square. The first player to connect three squares in a row, either horizontally, vertically, or diagonally, won the game.

Players received $200 for a *win* and the player who won two out of three *games* became the champion. The second game of the day was the "secret square game" and the contestant who picked the predetermined star had a chance to win an assortment of prizes. A player retired as an undefeated champion after winning five matches.

A nighttime version of "The Hollywood Squares" was seen on Friday nights during 1968 and a Saturday morning edition called the STORYBOOK SQUARES, featuring celebrities dressed as literary characters from children's books such as "Tom Sawyer" and "Humpty Dumpty," aired on NBC in 1969.

A weekly, early-evening version of "The Hollywood Squares" premiered in the fall of 1981. When the daytime version left NBC in June 1980, this syndicated daytime version was expanded to five days a week and production moved to Las Vegas. The last episode of the version Peter Marshall hosted aired in September 1981.

In 1983, "The Hollywood Squares" returned to the NBC daytime schedule as part of the hour-long THE MATCH GAME–HOLLYWOOD SQUARES HOUR. Jon Bauman, a former member of the singing group Sha Na Na, was host.

In September 1986, "The Hollywood Squares" returned as an all-new five-day-a-week series produced for syndication. John Davidson was host and Joan Rivers was a regular panelist.

A true classic celebrating its 2,000th show. In the front row are Ruta Lee and Sandy Duncan. In the second row, from left to right, are Charley Weaver, Rose Marie, John Davidson (who later hosted "Hollywood Squares"), George Gobel, Kent McCord, host Peter Marshall, Vincent Price, and the center square, Paul Lynde.

Several changes were made for this version. The winner of each game received $500 and the top winner of the day got a chance to choose from among five keys for a chance to win a new car. If the key selected started the car, he or she won the car. Otherwise, the winner returned on the next show and if he or she won again, four keys were presented, thereby increasing the chances of winning the car.

Did you know . . .   Peter Marshall was not the original host for "The Hollywood Squares"? When the pilot was taped for CBS, veteran game show host Bert Parks was seen as "The Master of The Hollywood Squares." When NBC picked up the show, they chose Marshall, who had started his career at age fourteen as NBC's youngest page and was also part of a comedy team with Tommy Noonan. Peter Marshall won five Emmys for his emceeing style and creators/executive producers, Merrill Heatter and Bob Quigley won four Emmys. Peter won two Emmys in 1974, one for "Best Host in a Game Show" and the other for "Daytime Host of the Year."

When creators Merrill Heatter and Bob Quigley tried to sell "The Hollywood Squares," each of the three networks turned them down with a fast, flat "No!" However, Merrill Heatter knew that "The Hollywood Squares" would become a hit, and he repitched "The Hollywood Squares" to NBC. They finally said "yes," and "The Hollywood Squares" became a true game show classic.

The set for "The Hollywood Squares" was almost forty feet tall and once an earthquake hit the Hollywood and Burbank areas while the show was taping. Everyone ran out of their squares and out of the NBC Studios with the exception of the center square, Paul Lynde, who remained in his square during the entire (non-damaging) earthquake! Paul Lynde, who occupied the center square for most of the network and syndicated run, was not seen on the first or the last show. Ernest Borgnine was in the center square on the first show and George Gobel was seated there on the last show.

Oscar winner Jack Palance was once caught sleeping in his square during a taping!

In 1994, Peter Marshall would make numerous guest appearances on the hit FOX series "In Living Color." He played himself hosting the very hip "East Hollywood Squares," a parody of the original "The Hollywood Squares."

Were you watching when . . . television and film greats were sitting in the larger-than-life tic-tac-toe set? Among them were Wally Cox, Alice Cooper, Sammy Davis Jr., Phyllis Diller, Bob Hope, Marty Ingels, Shirley Jones, Mickey Mantle, Rose Marie, The Monkees, Roger Moore, Vincent Price, Burt Reynolds, Jimmy Stewart, Charley Weaver, and Adam West.

These game show emcees were also seen sitting in the squares: Dick Clark, Bob Clayton, Hugh Downs, Bob Eubanks, Art Fleming (who won a contestant over $11,000 while occupying the center square), Tom Kennedy, Art James, Dennis James, Wink Martindale, Jim McKrell, Jack Narz, Gene Rayburn, Alex Trebek, and Chuck Woolery!

O. J. Simpson first appeared on "The Hollywood Squares" as a contestant (while he was in college). Years later he appeared again, this time as a celebrity.

HOLLYWOOD'S TALKING

premiere: March 26, 1973 *packager:* Jack Barry Productions *broadcast history:* CBS daytime March 26, 1973–June 22, 1973 *host:* Geoff Edwards *announcer:* Johnny Jacobs *executive producer:* Richard Kline *producer/director:* Ken Johnson *set designer:* Don Roberts *origination:* Studio 31, CBS Television City, Los Angeles

In "Hollywood's Talking," numerous celebrities, shown in short film clips, commented about people, places, and things without actually naming the subjects. Three studio contestants tried to correctly identify these subjects. If they answered correctly before the first third of the tape had elapsed, they received $150; by the second third of the tape, $100; and before the tape ended, $50. The first player to collect $250 won the game and played a bonus film clip round.

HOME RUN DERBY

premiere: April 1960 *packager:* Homer Productions/ZIV Television *broadcast history:* Syndicated April 1960–October 1960; ESPN (cable) December 17, 1988–December 28, 1988; ESPN (cable) July 10, 1989–October 28, 1989 (the ESPN broadcasts were repeats of the 1960 series) *host:* Mark Scott *umpire:* Art Passarella *producer:* Lou Breslow *director:* Ben Stoloff *origination:* Wrigley Field, Los Angeles

"Home Run Derby" was a series that ran for twenty-six weeks and featured top baseball players competing in a home-run hitting contest. The series was filmed in the fall of 1959 at Wrigley Field in Los Angeles.

"Home Run Derby" was seen during the 1960 season on over 150 stations. Twenty-eight years later the series reappeared on the ESPN sports cable channel. The show was popular and was repeated during the summer of 1989.

Each week two players competed in a nine-inning contest. Hitting against batting practice pitchers, the players tried to hit home runs. Any ball not hit out of the park was an out and each player was allowed three outs per inning. Players who hit three consecutive home runs won an extra $500 (a fourth straight home run earned another $500 and each additional one beyond that earned $1,000). The winning player of the day received $2,000 and the loser $1,000, with the winner returning on the next show to take on another challenger.

Some nineteen players participated in the show. Hank Aaron won six times and collected $13,500. Mickey Mantle won four times and collected $10,000. Other players who competed included Willie Mays, Ernie Banks, Jackie Jensen, Harmon Killibrew, Rocky Colovito, Frank Robinson, and Duke Snider.

Jackie Jensen hit the most home runs in one game, with fourteen, and the most consecutive, with five in a row. Hank Aaron, baseball's all-time leading home run hitter with 755 career home runs, managed only nine home runs.

Did you know . . . there were two Wrigley Fields, both owned by William Wrigley? One was in Chicago and was home to the Chicago Cubs. The other was in Los Angeles and was the home of the Pacific Coast League's Los Angeles Angels until 1957. "Home Run Derby" was filmed there in 1959 and the American League's Los Angeles Angels played their first season there in 1961. The Los Angeles Wrigley Field was demolished in the 1960s.

HOME SHOPPING GAME

premiere: June 15, 1987 *packager:* Home Shopping Entertainment Production *broadcast history:* Syndicated June 15, 1987–September 11, 1987 *host:* Bob Goen *announcer/cohost:* Bob Circosta *model:* Debbie Bartlett *executive producers:* Ken Yates, Robert O. Kaplan *producers:* Chris Pye, Jeff Goldstein *director:* Jeff Goldstein *set designer:* Bill Bohnert *origination:* KHSC-TV, Ontario, California

Two contestants competed daily on the "Home Shopping Game," in a combination game show–home shopping series. In the game portion, the players tried to guess three words from a series of scrambled letters. Each word was used in a description of merchandise that had just been made available at a special price to home viewers.

To earn the right to guess the words and see them become unscrambled, players tried to answer general knowledge questions. A right answer corrected the placement of one letter of each word. A player got $100 for guessing the first word correctly, $200 for the second word, and $300 for the final word. The cash values doubled after two rounds to $200, $400, and $600. The player who identified at least two of the three words in each round also received the merchandise prize and the contestant with the most money after four rounds was the day's winner.

The winning player played a two-part bonus game. In the first half, he or she was given the first letter of every word in a well-known phrase. He or she won $2,000 if the phrase was correctly guessed. If not, more letters were revealed and the prize value dropped.

In the second part the player was given thirty seconds to make as many words of three letters or more as possible, from one of the "phrase" words. Winnings were determined by multiplying the number of new words formed by the cash amount won in the first part of the bonus game.

THE HONEYMOON RACE

premiere: July 17, 1967 *packager:* Talent Associates *broadcast history:* ABC daytime July 17, 1967–December 1, 1967 *host:* Bill Malone *announcer:* Richard Hayes *producer:* John Green *director:* Lloyd Gross *music:* Score Productions *origination:* Hollywood Mall, Hollywood, Florida

"The Honeymoon Race" was a spin-off of SUPERMARKET SWEEP, which it replaced on the ABC daytime lineup on July 17, 1967. Taped at the Hollywood Mall in Hollywood, Florida, the show featured three honeymooning couples who competed in a scavenger hunt in the stores of the shopping center.

The time allowed for the race was determined in a preliminary round where the couples guessed the value of four items in ascending order. The teams, using the time earned in the first round, then set off to find five specific items hidden in the different stores in the mall. Teams raced through the mall in electric golf carts driven by the wives and the couple that found the most items in the allotted time won merchandise prizes. Each show consisted of two games featuring a different set of contestants.

During its four-and-one-half-month run, "Honeymoon Race" altered its format to become more of a stunt show. The couples, with the wives driving, raced around the mall and the husbands tried to complete a series of five errands or stunts in the different stores. The first team to complete the run won the game and all teams received prizes that were determined by their finishing order.

HOT POTATO

premiere: January 23, 1984 *packager:* Jack Barry and Dan Enright Productions *broadcast history:* NBC daytime January 23, 1984–June 29, 1984; USA (cable) June 29, 1987–June 23, 1989 (repeats of 1984 series); USA (cable) September 10, 1990–December 28, 1990 (repeats of 1984 series) *host:* Bill Cullen *announcer:* Charlie O'Donnell *executive producer:* Dan Enright *producers:* Allen Koss, Mark Maxwell-Smith *director:* Richard Kline *set designer:* John C. Mula *music:* Hal Hidey *origination:* NBC Studio 2, Burbank

In the game of "Hot Potato," two teams of three players, all with something in common (for example, being dentists, mothers-to-be, or left-handed), tried to name the most popular response to a question that had been asked of a group of people. A team tried to come up with seven of the ten possible answers to win the round. A team lost control of the question on a wrong guess and the first team to win two rounds became the champions and received $1,000.

The winners could try to earn as much as $5,000 in the bonus round by answering another series of questions.

"Hot Potato" became "Celebrity Hot Potato" on May 14, 1984.

Singer Vanesa Williams and Los Angeles Dodgers baseball catcher Steve Yeager pose with Bill Cullen in 1984 on the set of "Hot Potato."

Did you know . . . announcer Charlie O'Donnell tried his hand at acting in the 1960s He appeared in an episode of "Batman" that featured Otto Preminger as Mr. Freeze and in the 1966 movie *Blindfold* that starred Rock Hudson and Claudia Cardinale.

The day "Hot Potato" premiered, Bill Cullen was featured on the cover of the national *TV Guide* with Bob Barker, Jack Barry, Monty Hall, Wink Martindale, and Pat Sajak.

Singer/actress Vanesa Williams made her game show debut as a celebrity contestant on "Celebrity Hot Potato."

HOT SEAT

premiere: July 12, 1976 *packager:* Merrill Heatter–Bob Quigley Productions *broadcast history:* ABC daytime July 12, 1976–October 22, 1976 *host:* Jim Peck *announcer:* Kenny Williams *executive producers:* Merrill Heatter, Bob Quigley, Robert Noah *producer:* Bob Synes *director:* Jerome Shaw *set designers:* Anthony Sabatino, Jim Newton *music:* Stan Worth *origination:* Studio 54, ABC Television Center, Los Angeles

In "Hot Seat," two married couples competed in a game where one team played at a time. One person tried to predict how his or her mate would respond to questions. Predictions were validated by having the emotions measured electronically (electrical charges in the skin predicted emotional re-

The pressure is on when you're in the "Hot Seat," but the rewards can be worth the heat.

sponse). Each team played three questions, worth $100, $200, and $400, and the team with the most money had the option of playing for either a bonus prize or an additional $500.

HOW DO YOU RATE?

premiere: March 31, 1958 *packager:* Entertainment Productions, Inc./Harry Fleishman *broadcast history:* CBS daytime March 31, 1958–June 26, 1958 *host:* Tom Reddy *announcer:* Jack Clark *executive producer:* Steve Carlin *producer:* Ronald Dubin *director:* Seymour Robbie *set designer:* Eddie Gilbert *tests prepared by:* Dr. Robert Goldenson *music director:* Nick Nicholson *origination:* New York

Participants were tested on aptitude rather than academic knowledge on "How Do You Rate?" The tests, similar to those used by psychologists, challenged a player's proficiency in the skills, aptitudes, and judgments used in everyday living. The first player to solve four problems won the game and $150. The tests were prepared by Dr. Robert Goldenson, professor of psychology at Hunter College.

HOW'S YOUR MOTHER-IN-LAW?

premiere: December 4, 1967 *packager:* Chuck Barris Productions *broadcast history:* ABC daytime December 4, 1967–March 1, 1968 *host:* Wink Martindale *announcers:* Johnny Jacobs, Hank Simms, Roy Rowan *producer:* Mike Metzger *director:* Gene Law *set designer:* George Smith *origination:* Studio D, ABC Television Center, Los Angeles *debut guests:* George Carlin, Richard Dawson, Larry Storch

In "How's Your Mother-in-Law," this thirteen-week comedy game show series, a trio of guest celebrities served as "defense attorneys" representing mothers-in-law. The celebrities presented their cases to a jury composed of five unmarried men and five unmarried women who decided which mother-in-law they would most like to have as their own. The winning mother-in-law received $100. Questions were formed based on information provided by each woman's son-in-law prior to the show.

Did you know . . . the original title for this show was "Here Come the Mother-in-Laws?"

IDENTIFY

premiere: February 14, 1949 *packager:* ABC Television *broadcast history:* ABC primetime February 14, 1949–May 9, 1949 *host:* Bob Elson *announcer:* Wayne Griffin *producer:* William Hollenbeck *director:* Greg Garrison *origination:* WENR Studios at Civic Opera House, Chicago

This Chicago-based sports picture quiz "Identify" featured three contestants who attempted to identify either scenes from classic moments in sports or famous sports personalities.

Did you know . . . host Bob Elson was the play-by-play voice of the Chicago White Sox from 1931 to 1970? In 1971 he joined the Oakland A's broadcasting team and in 1979 was inducted into the Baseball Hall of Fame. He was calling the play-by-play of the 1932 World Series between the New York Yankees and the Chicago Cubs when Babe Ruth hit his famous "called" home run shot.

IDIOT SAVANTS

premiere: December 9, 1996 *packager:* MTV Productions *broadcast history:* MTV (cable) December 9, 1996–April 25, 1997 *host ("Master of the Brain"):* Greg Fitzsimmons *announcer ("The Brain"):* Matt Price *"Savant Players":* Heather Blaze, Tom Cohen, Shonda Farr, Paul Kozlowski, Matt Price, Dave Attell, Emmy Laybourne *creators:* Michael Dugan, Chris Kreski *producer:* Michael Dugan *line producer:* Jacqueline French *coordinating producer:* Amy Bazil Beaumont *director:* Steve Paley *set designer:* Mitchell Greenberg *music supervisor:* Charlie Singer *original music:* Rob Friedman *band ("The Mentalists"):* Rob Friedman, Alex Alexander, Keith Golden, Guyora Kats, Marc Ribler *origination:* Hotel Pennsylvania, New York

Four contestants competed week-long in this question-and-answer quiz show seen on the MTV cable network. The weekly winner received a grand prize, such as a trip or a new car.

In round one, a player selected a category with the first question worth one hundred points. The player who answered correctly got a chance at the two hundred-point bonus question. If the person answered incorrectly, the other three players got a chance to answer. The player who answered correctly could then attempt the "Big Gamble Ques-

tion" worth three hundred points. Players who decided to answer the Big Gamble Question lost points if their answer was incorrect. The player with the lowest score at the end of this round was eliminated and sent to the "Dunce Corner." All players who were eliminated during the game returned for the following show, except for the Friday show.

Round two, the "Double Savant Round," was played the same way as the first round, except that the "Brain" selected the categories, and the value of the questions was increased to two hundred, four hundred, and six hundred points. Again, the player with the lowest score was eliminated from the game.

The two remaining players competed in the forty-five-second "Brainstorm" round, in which all questions were worth two hundred points. The player with the most points at the end of this round was the day's winner.

The winner moved on to the "Grand Savant Round" where he or she was placed in the "cylinder of shush." The person had sixty seconds to answer ten questions correctly in his or her category of expert knowledge in order to receive the daily grand prize.

Players accumulated their point values during the week.

On the Friday show of each week, the point value of questions in the first two rounds was doubled. Round three, the "Double Grand Savant Round," featured the two remaining players who had not been already eliminated that day. Questions in this round were worth one thousand points. The player in second place was placed in the cylinder of shush first and given sixty seconds to add to his or her point score. The other player was then given sixty seconds in the cylinder to add to his or her score. All questions asked in the cylinder were in a player's area of expertise, and the player with the most points at the end of this round was the weekly winner.

"Idiot Savants" lasted less than five months on the air but was awarded the CableAce award for Outstanding Game Show in 1997.

I'LL BET

premiere: March 29, 1965 *packager:* Ralph Andrews–Bill Yagemann Productions *broadcast history:* NBC daytime March 29, 1965–September 24, 1965 *host:* Jack Narz *announcer:* Roy Mitchell *executive producers:* Ralph Andrews,

Bill Yagemann *producer:* Tom Cole *director:* Dick Mc-Donough *music director:* Rex Koury *origination:* NBC Studios, Burbank *debut guests:* Patricia Blair, Dan Blocker

Two celebrity couples competed on "I'll Bet" to see how well each person knew his or her spouse's ability to answer general knowledge questions.

One team member was asked a question via a special telephone so his or her mate could not hear it. The mate then bet up to one hundred points on his or her partner's ability to answer the question. If the prediction was correct, the couple won the points. The first team to reach two hundred won the game, $200 for a member of the audience, and a chance to win additional money in the "preference round."

Did you know . . . "I'll Bet" host Jack Narz taught flying at Van Nuys Airport in California before beginning his career as an announcer? Narz was the announcer on the first network telecast of the Emmy Awards in 1955.

Before beginning its run on NBC, "I'll Bet" was seen locally in Los Angeles on television station KTLA. Jack Narz was the emcee for both versions. Among the hosts on the revived version, IT'S YOUR BET, was Jack's brother, Tom Kennedy.

I'LL BUY THAT
premiere: June 15, 1953 *packager:* Peter Arnell Productions *broadcast history:* CBS daytime June 15, 1953–July 2, 1954 *host:* Mike Wallace *model:* Betsy Palmer *announcer:* Hal Simms *producer:* Peter Arnell *directors:* Rai Purdy, Burt Shevelove *origination:* CBS Studio 60, New York *debut guests:* Vanessa Brown, Hans Conreid, Audrey Meadows, Albert Moorehead

A celebrity panel tried to identify an unseen object that was suggested by a home viewer in this daily audience participation show. "I'll Buy That" was the first daytime game show to feature a celebrity panel.

Viewers were asked to write in about something they would like to bring to the program to sell. Items ranged from a hula skirt to a Civil War uniform to a two-thousand-year-old Chinese egg.

The item was shown to the audience but not to the panel. The panel then attempted to identify the article by asking questions. Each question asked raised the purchase price of the item from its minimum of $5 to a maximum of $150.

Once an article was identified, the panel was asked three questions. If they answered them all correctly, the "purchase price" of the item was tripled.

ILLINOIS INSTANT RICHES
premiere: July 9, 1994 *packager:* Jonathan Goodson Productions *broadcast history:* WGN July 9, 1994– *hosts:* Mark Goodman and Linda Kollmeyer *announcer:* Bill Barber *executive producer:* Jonathan Goodson *producer:* Tommy Rivera *director:* Sarah Tucker Fisher *set designer:* Bente Christensen *music:* Score Productions *origination:* Studio 2, WGN-TV, Chicago

"Illinois Instant Riches," seen on superstation WGN, has the unique distinction of being the only state lottery game show currently being viewed on a national basis.

Contestants on the show must have purchased an Illinois Instant Riches scratch-off lottery ticket and uncovered three TV symbols to be eligible for the weekly contestant drawing. Fifteen contestants are drawn for each show's "contestant pool," from which three players are selected at random to play in three individual games.

Each prospective contestant is seated in a special section of the studio audience and is identified by an unlit lighting pole. Prior to each game, a wheel is spun causing the lights to chase randomly. When the wheel stops turning, one light remains lit, thereby selecting that contestant.

Modular games varied from show to show. On the premiere show, "Force Field," "Home Run," and "Double Dollars" were featured as main games, with "Knockout" used as the bonus game. The bonus game allowed all three players to compete against one another for a possible grand prize of $100,000.

Other popular games that have been played include "Vortex," "Thunderball," "Mismatch," and "Wrecking Ball." In 1995, the bonus game was changed to "Pot of Gold" and

Hosts Linda Kollmeyer and Mark Goodman are joined by coauthor Steve Ryan (center) on the set of "Illinois Instant Riches" with "Knockout," one of Steve's many game creations. The mysterious cube is first energized and then released into the arena for thirty seconds. Should a contestant's colored cylinder survive the wacky attack, he or she could go home with instant riches of up to $100,000.

pitted the top money winner of the day against the previous week's returning champion.

"Illinois Instant Riches" was created by Jonathan Goodson, the son of legendary game show producer Mark Goodson. Jonathan Goodson has also successfully launched other lottery game shows including "Bonus Bonanza" in Massachusetts, "Flamingo Fortune" in Florida, "New York Wired" in New York, and shows for Brazil, Hungary, and South Africa.

Did you know . . .   Steve Ryan, coauthor of *The Encyclopedia of TV Game Shows*, creates many of the modular games featured on "Illinois Instant Riches"? He currently heads new game development for the Jonathan Goodson produced lottery shows.

Host Mark Goodman was one of the original VJ's on cable channel MTV when it was started on August 1, 1981.

I'M TELLING

premiere: September 12, 1987   *packager:* Saban Productions/DIC Enterprises   *broadcast history:* NBC Saturday morning September 12, 1987–August 27, 1988; Family Channel (cable) September 9, 1989–September 8, 1990; Family Channel (cable) August 29, 1994–September 30, 1995; Family Channel (cable) October 30, 1995–March 29, 1996 (Family Channel broadcasts were repeats of NBC shows)   *host:* Laurie Faso   *announcer:* Dean Goss   *creator:* Ellen Levy   *executive producers:* Haim Saban, Andy Heyward   *producer:* David Greenfield   *director:* Jerome Shaw   *set designer:* Anthony Sabatino   *origination:* VIP Studios, Hollywood

Laurie Faso, the former star of the children's show "Marlo and the Magic Movie Machine," hosted "I'm Telling," a game show for kids.

Three brother-sister teams competed against each other to see how much they know about their siblings. In the first round, the brothers left the stage and each of their sisters were then asked three questions about their brothers. The brothers returned to the stage from a soundproof room and were asked the same questions. Points were scored if the answers matched.

In the second round, the sisters left the stage and their brothers answered the questions. When the sisters returned they tried to guess what their brothers said about them. The team with the highest point score won a $1,000 savings bond and played the "Pick-a-Prize Arcade" for merchandise prizes.

INFORMATION PLEASE

premiere: June 29, 1952   *packager:* Dan Golenpaul Productions   *broadcast history:* CBS primetime June 29, 1952–September 21, 1952   *hosts:* Clifton Fadiman, John K. M. McCaffery   *creator-producer:* Dan Golenpaul   *director:* Bruce Anderson   *set designer:* Jo Mielziner   *origination:* New York   *debut guests:* Franklin P. Adams, John Kiernan, James A. Michener

The popular radio show "Information Please" came to network television in the summer of 1952, when CBS scheduled it as a replacement for "The Fred Waring Show." "Information Please," a staple on radio from May 17, 1938 to April 22, 1951, had first appeared on the New York television station WOR on August 16, 1950.

Home viewers submitted questions to a panel of regulars including Franklin P. Adams and John Kiernan. They were joined each week by a guest panelist.

Viewers whose questions were used on the show received $10 gift certificates from the American Booksellers Association to be used toward the purchase of books or subscriptions to newspapers or magazines. Additional $50 gift certificates were awarded to those viewers whose questions stumped the panel.

"Information Please" radio host Clifton Fadiman emceed the first eight programs in the TV series and was followed by John K. M. McCaffery. The series was sponsored by General Electric.

INSPIRATION, PLEASE!

premiere: October 1, 1995   *packager:* Trinity Productions   *broadcast history:* Odyssey (cable) October 1, 1995–   *host:* Robert G. Lee   *announcer:* Donald Epstein   *creator/producer:* Donald Epstein   *executive producers:* Linda Hanick,

No fire and brimstone here, just a good old gospel game show hosted by Robert G. Lee.

Jeffrey Weber *director:* Bruce Burmester *set designers:* Ann Latham Cudworth, James Fenhagen, Erik Ulfers *origination:* Trinity TV Studios, New York

Three contestants compete for a grand prize of a trip for two to the Holy Land by answering questions on subjects and areas ranging from Bible trivia to art and zoology.

The game begins with questions worth ten points for correct answers and a chance at a bonus question in the same subject for an additional ten points. The first player to buzz in gets a chance to answer.

Point values of questions increase to twenty points in round two and thirty points in round three. An additional one hundred points can be won in round three if any player solves the "Inspiration Word." The first letter of each answer is a letter in the Inspiration Word, and the player who correctly guesses the word wins the points. The game ends when the word is solved.

The day's winner wins prizes and returns for other rounds in an elimination tournament to find the grand prize winner.

"Inspiration, Please!" is taped at the Trinity Studios at Trinity Church at Broadway and Wall Street in New York City.

The Odyssey Channel started in 1988 as the Visn (for Vision) Interfaith Satellite Network. It changed its name to the Faith & Values Channel in January 1994 and to the Odyssey Channel in September 1996.

IT COULD BE YOU

premiere: June 4, 1956 *packager:* Ralph Edwards Productions (Capricorn Productions) *broadcast history:* NBC daytime June 4, 1956–December 29, 1961; NBC primetime July 2, 1958–September 17, 1958; NBC primetime November 27, 1958–March 12, 1959; NBC primetime September 5, 1959–January 23, 1960; NBC primetime June 7, 1961–September 27, 1961 *host:* Bill Leyden *announcers:* Wendell Niles, Jay Stewart *executive producer:* Paul Edwards *producers:* Stefan Hatos, Steve Cates, Howard Blake, Richard Gottlieb *directors:* Stuart Phelps, Norman Abbott *set designer:* Bob Corrigan *music director:* Ivan Ditmars *theme:* "Who?" by Kearn, Hammerstein, and Harbach *origination:* NBC Studio D, Hollywood; NBC Studio 4, Burbank

Ralph Edwards created this show that involved members of the studio audience participating in different stunts and surprises. Reunions were frequent events on the show. Usually, three contestants were brought on stage and were given a series of clues to help them guess the identity of a person related to one of the contestants. The person was located behind a curtain.

Visits by celebrity guests were another feature on the show, and Bob Hope paid a visit on the first broadcast.

"It Could Be You" was hosted by Bill Leyden, who had emceed the Los Angeles segment of "Today" in the 1950s. In November 1960, Wendell Niles filled in as host and Jay Stewart as announcer.

"It Could Be You" returned to NBC's primetime schedule several times between 1958 and 1961, frequently as a summer replacement.

Creator Ralph Edwards points to his famous "This Is Your Life" book as he tells Bill Leyden it could be you.

Were you watching when . . . these celebrities dropped by NBC in Burbank to guest on "It Could Be You"? Visitors included Steve Allen, Bob Barker, Hugh Downs, Clint Eastwood, Bob Hope, Jayne Mansfield, Steve McQueen, Rod Serling, and the show's creator, Ralph Edwards.

IT PAYS TO BE IGNORANT

premiere: June 6, 1949 *packagers:* Tom Howard Productions (1949–1951); Stefan Hatos–Monty Hall Productions (1973–1974) *broadcast history:* CBS primetime June 6, 1949–September 19, 1949; NBC primetime July 5, 1951–September 27, 1951; Syndicated September 10, 1973–September 1974
1949–1951 version
host: Tom Howard *announcers:* Dick Stark (CBS), Ray Morgan (NBC) *creators:* Bob Howard, Ruth Howard *producers:* Tom Howard, Doug Coulter *directors:* Hugh Rogers, Ken Redford, Warren Jacober *music:* The Townsmen Quartet *origination:* NBC Studio 6B, New York (1951) *debut guests:* Lulu McConnell, Harry McNaughton, George Shelton

1973–1974 version

host: Joe Flynn   *announcer:* Jay Stewart   *executive producers:* Stefan Hatos, Monty Hall   *producer:* Charles Isaacs   *director:* Norman Abbott   *origination:* NBC Studio 4, Burbank   *debut guests:* Jo Anne Worley, Charles Nelson Reilly, and Billy Baxter.

Based on the popular radio show of the 1940s, ''It Pays to Be Ignorant'' was played more for laughs than prizes. It was seen on CBS television during the summer of 1949 as a replacement for ''Arthur Godfrey's Talent Scouts,'' and on NBC in the summer of 1951 as a replacement for YOU BET YOUR LIFE. Two decades later the show reappeared for one season as a weekly syndicated series.

Questions were chosen from the ''Dunce Cap'' and a panel of celebrities responded with ridiculous answers, jokes, and gags. Their goal was to make it impossible for a sensible answer to be heard. Tom Howard emceed both the radio and TV versions.

In the 1970s, comedian Joe Flynn (best known as Captain Binghampton on TV's ''McHale's Navy'') was befuddled by panelists Jo Anne Worley, Charles Nelson Reilly, and Billy Baxter.

IT PAYS TO BE MARRIED

premiere: July 4, 1955   *packager:* James Saphier Productions/H-F-H Enterprises   *broadcast history:* NBC daytime July 4, 1955–October 28, 1955   *host:* Bill Goodwin   *announcer:* Jay Stewart   *creators:* Stefan Hatos, Henry Hoople   *producers:* Stefan Hatos, Henry Hoople   *director:* Irving Lambrecht   *music director:* Gordon Kibbee   *origination:* NBC Studio 3, Burbank

Married couples were first interviewed to gain insight into their lives together and then they competed in a quiz. On ''It Pays to Be Married,'' merchandise and cash were awarded to the couple who used the least amount of time to answer the questions. Each couple were asked two personal questions, one directed at each mate.

Host Bill Goodwin was the long-time announcer on the ''Burns and Allen'' radio show.

IT TAKES TWO

premiere: March 31, 1969   *packagers:* Ralph Andrews Productions (1969–1970); Mark Phillips Philms & Telephission/MTM (1997)   *broadcast history:* NBC daytime March 31, 1969–July 31, 1970; Family Channel (cable) March 10, 1997–May 30, 1997

1969–1970 version

host: Vin Scully   *announcer:* John Harlan   *producers:* Bill Yagemann, Dick McDonough, Les Roberts   *directors:* Dick McDonough, Marc Breslow   *set designers:* E. Jay Krause, John Shrum, Bob Inkleas   *origination:* NBC Studios 2 and 4, Burbank   *debut week guests:* Shelley and Sarah Berman, Mike and Mary Lou Connors, Richard and Mara Long

1997 version

host: Dick Clark   *announcer:* Burton Richardson   *executive producer:* Mark Phillips   *line producer:* Rich de Michele   *coordinating producer:* Brian Conn   *director:* Barry Glazer   *set designer:* Jimmy Cuomo   *theme music:* Al Kasha, Mark

Hal Smith, alias ''Otis the drunk,'' from ''The Andy Griffith Show'' is really steamed at host Vin Scully. He's stuck in the hot box as three celebrity couples will try to estimate how many pounds he'll lose during the course of the program.

Phillips   *music:* Mark Northam   *origination:* Studio 5, Hollywood Center Studios, Los Angeles

Vin Scully, the broadcast voice of the Los Angeles Dodgers baseball team since 1950, emceed ''It Takes Two.'' This game show featured three celebrity couples answering questions with numerical answers and a member of the studio audience selecting the couple he or she felt was closest to the correct answer.

Questions on ''It Takes Two'' frequently involved humorous stunts or demonstrations, such as ''How many chicken legs could a college football team eat during the show?'' or ''How many pairs of shoes could be made from an alligator?'' to illustrate the problem.

Each celebrity player gave individual responses, which were then averaged to make one answer for each team. The studio player selected the team he or she felt was closest to the correct answer and, if correct, received $100. This was later changed to merchandise prizes. In January 1970 a rule was added so that an audience player could win a new car after selecting the right answer four times in a row.

After a twenty-seven-year absence from TV, ''It Takes Two'' returned for a brief twelve-week run on the Family

Channel. Dick Clark served as host, and this version did not use celebrity guests to play the game.

The game was basically the same, with three teams of two players coming up with numerical answers that were then averaged together. On the first question, the team coming closest to the correct answer received $100. The team that was next closest to the answer received $75. Cash values increased on four more questions that were played on the show, with values on the last question worth $1,000 for closest correct answer and $500 for second closest. The team with the most money at the end of the game received the money they had accumulated and played a bonus game for additional prizes.

The "Brainteaser" bonus round again asked a team to come up with a numerical answer and be within twenty-five percent of the actual answer, higher or lower, to win the bonus prize.

Did you know . . .   Vin Scully played centerfield while attending Fordham University as a communications major? In 1973, Scully was host of his own daytime variety show on CBS. And in 1982, for his outstanding broadcasting, he was elected to the Baseball Hall of Fame in Cooperstown, New York.

Where you watching when . . .   these emcees and their wives were all guests on "It Takes Two": Dick Clark, Tom Kennedy, Allen Ludden, Peter Marshall, and Jack Narz? Bob Clayton, who was not married at the time, appeared on the show with friend Jo Ann Pflug, who later married game show emcee Chuck Woolery.

IT'S A GIFT

premiere: January 29, 1946   *broadcast history:* CBS primetime January 29, 1946–July 6, 1946   *host:* John Reed King   *assistant:* "Uncle Jim"   *producer-director:* Frances Buss   *set designer:* James McNaughton   *origination:* New York

"It's a Gift" replaced MISSUS' GOES-A-SHOPPING on the CBS Tuesday schedule in January 1946, with host John Reed King, assistant "Uncle Jim," and producer/director Frances Buss moving from one show to the other. "It's a Gift" featured contestants answering questions for merchandise prizes.

The show was replaced by KING'S PARTY LINE on July 13, 1946.

IT'S A HIT

premiere: June 1, 1957   *packager:* C.M.C. Productions   *broadcast history:* CBS Saturday morning June 1, 1957–September 21, 1957   *host:* Happy Felton   *executive producer:* Pierson Mapes   *producers:* Happy Felton, Ted Westcott, Gene Schiess   *directors:* Ted Westcott, Harold Monroe   *origination:* New York

Two teams, each composed of youngsters ages seven to fourteen, and "managed" by a guest sports star, competed on a ball field constructed in a TV studio. On "It's a Hit," host Happy Felton was called "the umpire-in-chief" and the teams were drawn from organizations such as the Little League, the Boy Scouts, the Girl Scouts, and church groups.

Each contestant came to the plate, as in a regular baseball game, and swung at a baseball attached to a special shaft. When the ball was hit, a lighted scoreboard registered either a single, a double, a triple, or a home run. The batter was then asked a question, the difficulty of which was based on the value of the hit.

Each player moved around the bases as his or her teammates came to bat. When three outs were registered (for wrong answers) the opposing team came to bat. The players on the winning team received prizes, and additional prizes were given to their organization.

"It's a Hit" began on New York television station WABD in 1950 and was also seen on New York's WOR in 1954, prior to its network run.

IT'S ABOUT TIME

premiere: March 4, 1954   *packager:* Louis Cowan Productions   *broadcast history:* ABC primetime March 4, 1954–May 2, 1954   *host:* Dr. Bergen Evans   *announcer:* John Dunham   *producers:* Rachel Stevenson, Jay Sheridan, John Lewellen   *director:* Dan Schuffman   *origination:* Chicago   *debut guests:* drama critic Robert Pollak, "Quiz Kid" Ruth Duskin, housewife Shirley Stern, TV-radio pitchman Vin Gottschalk

"It's About Time" was a game show in which a celebrity panel tried to guess events and the years in which they occurred. To do so, they were provided with clues and were also able to ask the host questions.

"It's About Time" was the last primetime network game show to originate from Chicago.

IT'S ANYBODY'S GUESS

premiere: June 13, 1977   *packager:* Stefan Hatos–Monty Hall Productions   *broadcast history:* NBC daytime June 13, 1977–September 30, 1977   *host:* Monty Hall   *announcer:* Jay Stewart   *executive producers:* Stu Billet, Stefan Hatos   *producer:* Steve Feke   *director:* Joe Behar   *set designer:* Scott Ritenour   *music:* Stan Worth   *origination:* NBC Studio 3, Burbank

Two contestants tried to predict if five members of the studio audience would or would not come up with a predetermined answer to a question on "It's Anybody's Guess." They could play for one point if they believed one person in five would give the right answer (example: "Name a frequent guest on 'The Tonight Show'?" . . . answer: Don Rickles) or two points if they thought one person in three would give it. Members of the audience team won prizes if they came up with the predetermined answer. The first player to score five points won the game.

The winning contestant then played the bonus round in which the studio players were given a question with two predetermined answers. The champion received $300 for each response that was not one of the predetermined answers and a new car if none of the five players came up with the correct answers.

Monty Hall and a couple of contestants having a great time on "It's Anybody's Guess."

IT'S IN THE BAG

premiere: January 7, 1952   *packager:* Package Shows Inc. *broadcast history:* NBC daytime January 7, 1952–February 22, 1952   *hosts:* Jerry Toman, Bob Russell   *assistant:* Arlene James as "the cashier"   *announcer:* Don Pardo   *producer:* William Von Zehle   *director:* Frank Jacoby   *music:* Red Latham and The Jesters   *origination:* New Amsterdam Theater, New York

"It's in the Bag," one of the first game shows on daytime television, featured a set designed like a grocery store. Contestants were brought on stage by Arlene James, through a door with a bell that rang when it opened. Host Jerry Toman acted as proprietor of the store and asked the questions.

Each player was given an empty shopping bag, which could be filled by giving correct answers to questions. The first right answer was worth six cans of food; the second was worth twelve cans; and the third, twenty-four cans. The fourth question answered correctly won the player an appliance.

Cans of food were also put into the "Boodle Bag," a grand prize that was played for at the end of the show. The bag also included a major appliance and to win it a contestant's answer had to be ninety percent correct. If not, the prize carried over to the next show. The grand prize question on the first show was "What time was the sunrise in New York this morning?"

Some questions were acted out in skits by members of the cast or were sung by Arlene James or Red Latham and The Jesters.

Bob Russell replaced Jerry Toman as host on January 14, 1952 and the show was replaced by WINNER TAKE ALL on February 25.

"It's in the Bag" was seen on DuMont station WABD in New York from November 16, 1950 to June 7, 1951. Win Elliott was the host, with Florence Morris and Joy Kent as his assistants.

IT'S NEWS TO ME

premiere: July 2, 1951   *packager:* Mark Goodson–Bill Todman Productions   *broadcast history:* CBS primetime July 2, 1951–September 12, 1953; CBS primetime July 9, 1954–August 27, 1954   *hosts:* John Daly, Walter Cronkite   *announcers:* Art Hannes, Bill Hamilton, Bob Sherry, Bob Dixon *commercials:* Win Elliott, Margaret McKay   *producers:* Mark Goodson, Bill Todman   *director:* Jerome Schnur   *set designers:* Paul Sylbert, Ed Mitchell   *origination:* Mansfield Theater, New York   *debut guests:* Quincy Howe, Anna Lee, John Henry Faulk, Robin Chandler

On "It's News to Me," a celebrity panel was shown props, drawings, and photographs that were tied in with news events of the past and present and then asked to supply the story related to them. A member of the studio audience was given a chance to win cash by deciding whether the answer given by the panelist was right or wrong. The contestant was given $30 to start with, received $5 for each correct decision, and lost $5 for each incorrect guess.

"It's News to Me" was also visited by eyewitnesses or participants in important news events of the past. The panelists questioned the guest as they tried to determine the news event. The guest won $100 if the panel failed to correctly identify the event.

"It's News to Me" first appeared as a one-time special on Friday May 11, 1951 and returned as a weekly series begin-

Walter Cronkite hosted a game show? You bet! In the summer of 1954 he emceed "It's News to Me" for CBS.

ning on July 2, 1951, replacing WHO'S WHOSE, which was canceled after one broadcast.

WHAT'S MY LINE? host John Daly was the original emcee for "It's News to Me" from 1951 to 1953. When the show returned as a summer replacement in 1954 for Edward R. Murrow's "Person to Person," CBS newsman Walter Cronkite became the host.

The panel for the first program was Anna Lee, actress; Quincy Howe, professor of Journalism at the University of Illinois; Robin Chandler, hostess of CBS-TV's "Meet Your Cover Girl" and "Vanity Fair"; and John Henry Faulk, lecturer and former professor at the University of Texas.

Other regular panelists on "It's News to Me" were actress Nina Foch and writer Quentin Reynolds.

Did you know . . . John Daly was anchorman for the ABC evening news from 1953 to 1960 and vice president of ABC's news division? In 1954 he received an Emmy Award as "Best News Reporter or Commentator."

Were you watching when . . . on the special telecast of May 11, 1951, New York Yankee rookie Mickey Mantle made an appearance as a newsmaker? He was in the news because he had just hit his first major league home run.

IT'S YOUR BET

premiere: September 29, 1969 *packager:* Ralph Andrews Productions *broadcast history:* Syndicated September 29, 1969–September 1973 *hosts:* Hal March, Tom Kennedy, Dick Gautier, Lyle Waggoner *announcer:* John Harlan *producers:* Ken Johnson, Bill Yagemann, Ray Horl, Dick McDonough, Ray Simmons *directors:* Ken Johnson, Bill Yagemann *set designer:* Curt Nations *origination* NBC Studio 5, Burbank; Studio 2, KCST-TV, San Diego; KTTV Television, Los Angeles

"It's Your Bet" was a revised version of the NBC daytime game show I'LL BET that originally aired in 1965. When "It's Your Bet" began in September 1969 the show was emceed by Hal March, best known as host of THE $64,000 QUESTION. March was replaced by actor Dick Gautier in the spring of 1970. Tom Kennedy followed as host in 1971 and he was followed by Lyle Waggoner in 1972.

On "It's Your Bet" two celebrity couples played for members of the studio audience. One member of a team bet from twenty-five to one hundred points on his or her mate's ability to answer a question correctly. Questions were based on general knowledge or on the personal and professional lives of the players. If the answer was correct, the team won the points; if incorrect, the points went to their opponents.

The first team to score three hundred points won the game and played a "Preference Round" to win prizes for their audience partner. Each spouse played separately. One player was read a question and was shown three possible responses. He or she tried to predict which response would be given by his or her mate.

Were you watching when . . . Burt Reynolds was a featured guest on the version of "It's Your Bet" that was hosted by Tom Kennedy? Over the years Tom and Burt became good friends. Allen Ludden and his wife, Betty White, were also familiar faces on "It's Your Bet."

IT'S YOUR MOVE

premiere: September 18, 1967 *packager:* Ben Joelson–Art Baer Productions *broadcast history:* Syndicated September 18, 1967–December 1967 *host:* Jim Perry *announcer:* Dirk Fredericks *executive producers:* Ben Joelson, Art Baer *producer:* Howard Felsher *director:* Lloyd Gross *origination:* New York

"It's Your Move" was a short-lived game show featuring two teams each consisting of two contestants. The players bid against each other on how little time it would take to mime certain words to their partners.

I'VE GOT A SECRET

premiere: June 19, 1952 *packager:* Mark Goodson–Bill Todman Productions *broadcast history:* CBS primetime June 19, 1952–April 3, 1967; Syndicated September 11, 1972–September 1973; CBS primetime June 15, 1976–July 6, 1976

1952–1967 version

hosts: Garry Moore, Steve Allen *substitute hosts:* Dennis O'Keefe, Hal March, Bill Cullen, Henry Morgan, Don McNeil, Betsy Palmer, Bill Goodwin, Steve Allen, Arthur Godfrey *announcers:* John Cannon, Bern Bennett, Johnny Olson *executive producer:* Gil Fates *producers:* Allan Sherman, Howard Merrill, Chester Feldman *directors:* Frank Satenstein, Clarence Schimmel, Paul Alter, Franklin Heller, Ira Skutch *set designers:* Robert Rowe Paddock, Ron Baldwin, Henry May, Charles Lisanby *music directors:* Leroy Anderson, Norman Paris *origination:* Mansfield Theater (Studio 59), New York 1952–1960; CBS Studio 52, New York 1960–1967 *debut panelists:* Laura Hobson, Louise Albritton, Orson Bean, Melville Cooper

1972–1973 version

host: Steve Allen *announcer:* Johnny Olson *producer:* Ira Skutch *directors:* Stuart Phelps, Marc Breslow *set designer:* Romain Johnston *origination:* Metromedia Studios, Los Angeles *debut panelists:* Richard Dawson, Gene Rayburn, Pat Carroll, Meredith MacRae

1976 version

host: Bill Cullen *announcer:* Johnny Olson *executive producer:* Gil Fates *producers:* Chester Feldman *director:* Lloyd Gross *set designer:* Jim Ryan *music director:* Norman Paris *origination:* Ed Sullivan Theater, New York *debut panelists:* Richard Dawson, Henry Morgan, Elaine Joyce, and Pat Collins

One of the most popular and longest-running panel shows, "I've Got a Secret" was initially canceled by CBS after thirteen weeks. The network later reversed its decision and the show remained on the CBS primetime schedule for fifteen years.

Each week, four celebrity panelists tried to determine, by cross examination, each contestant's secret. Each panelist was given thirty seconds to quiz the guest and then attempt to guess the secret. The guest received $20 each time a

A true classic, "I've Got a Secret." Remember the panel? From left to right, emcee Garry Moore, and panel members Bill Cullen, Betsy Palmer, Henry Morgan, and Bess Myerson.

panelist failed to identify the secret and $80 if he or she stumped the entire panel.

The panel for the first telecast, on June 19, 1952, was comprised of screen actress Louise Albritton, comedian Orson Bean, Broadway actor Melville Cooper, and novelist Laura Hobson. Bill Cullen joined the panel as a regular on the third broadcast, July 3, 1952, and humorist Henry Morgan became a regular on November 13, 1952. They both remained with the show until the conclusion of the original network run. Other regular panelists were Faye Emerson, Jayne Meadows, Betsy Palmer, and Bess Myerson.

One of the regular features on "I've Got a Secret" was the visit of a celebrity guest with his or her own secret for the panel to guess. Boris Karloff was the first guest and presented his secret, "I am afraid of mice." Other memorable celebrity guests included Johnny Carson, who shot an arrow at host Garry Moore's head; Ronald Reagan, who made nine different entrances on the show; Paul Newman, who posed as a

vendor at a baseball game at Ebbets Field earlier in the day and sold Henry Morgan a hot dog; Fred Astaire, who played drums while Garry Moore danced; Rudy Vallee, who had just stolen panelist Faye Emerson's refrigerator; and Dave Garroway, who left the studio with Garry Moore during the questioning, leaving the blind-folded panel to finish the show by themselves.

Another classic moment occurred on September 17, 1962 when one set of guests was a Mr. and Mrs. Armstrong, whose secret was that their son Neil had just been selected to be an astronaut. After the secret was revealed, Garry Moore commented that it would really be something if their son Neil became the first man to walk on the moon. (A little less than seven years later, on July 24, 1969, Neil Armstrong became the first man to set foot on the moon.)

Garry Moore, a one-time radio partner of comedian Jimmy Durante during the 1940s, was the host of "I've Got a Secret" from its premiere until September 14, 1964, when he left the show to take a year-long trip around the world. He was replaced by Steve Allen, who continued as host for the rest of the original network run.

"I've Got a Secret" returned as a weekly syndicated series in 1972, with Steve Allen as host. In 1976, CBS broadcast a four-week series of shows taped at the Ed Sullivan Theater in New York, with Bill Cullen as host and featuring a rotating panel made up of Henry Morgan, Elaine Joyce, Phyllis George, Gene Rayburn, Pat Collins, and Richard Dawson, who would later host Goodson-Todman's new game show "Family Feud."

Did you know . . . Garry Moore made his debut on radio in 1939 as "Thomas Garrison Morfit" on the series "Club Matinee"? On one of the early broadcasts he offered listeners $50 to create a new name for him. One woman won the prize by cutting his last name in half, eliminating his first name and reconstructing "Garrison" into "Garry."

The cast of "I've Got a Secret" appeared on the cover of TV Guide magazine four times: January 15, 1955; August 22, 1959; August 18, 1962; and August 10, 1963.

Were you watching when . . . Bob Barker, George Burns, Monty Hall, Allen Ludden, and Rod Serling all guest-starred on the 1972 syndicated version? Game show favorite Paul Lynde was the first guest star to appear on the show, in 1972.

JACKPOT

premiere: January 7, 1974 *packager:* Bob Stewart Productions *broadcast history:* NBC daytime January 7, 1974–September 26, 1975; USA (cable) September 30, 1985–December 30, 1988; Syndicated September 18, 1989–March 16, 1990

1974–1975 version

host: Geoff Edwards *announcers:* Don Pardo, Wayne Howell *executive producer:* Bob Stewart *producer:* Bruce Burmester *director:* Mike Garguilo *set designer:* Warren Clymer *theme:* ''Jet Set'' by Mike Vickers *origination:* NBC Studio 8H, New York

1985–1988 version

packager: Bob Stewart Productions/Global Television Network *host:* Mike Darrow *announcers:* Ken Ryan, John Harris *producer:* Doug Gahm *directors:* William Elliott, Jack Sampson *set designer:* Ed Flesh *origination:* Toronto

1989–1990 version

packager: Bob Stewart/Sande Stewart Productions *host:* Geoff Edwards *announcers:* John Harlan, Johnny Gilbert *executive producer:* Bob Stewart *producer:* Sande Stewart *director:* Bruce Burmester *set designer:* Ed Flesh *origination:* Glendale Studios, Glendale

Sixteen contestants competed over the course of a week on ''Jackpot.'' One player occupied a box built like a pulpit on centerstage and answered riddles posed by the other fifteen players. Each riddle was worth money that accumulated until the jackpot riddle was located and solved. A player remained ''King of the Hill'' until missing a riddle. That player then swapped places with the player who had stumped him or her. A super jackpot was also located on the board and involved landing on a predetermined target number with the growing cash amount that could net the player up to $50,000.

After a ten-year absence, ''Jackpot'' returned with new shows on the USA cable network. Production moved from New York City to Toronto, Canada and Mike Darrow became host.

The basic game remained the same but several new features were added. Any player who could ''run the board'' by answering all fifteen riddles correctly won a new car. The player who answered the most riddles during the week won $10,000 and a player got a $1,000 bonus if he or she could go through the board without hitting the jackpot riddle until last.

In the fall of 1989, ''Jackpot'' jumped from cable to first-run syndication. Geoff Edwards, the original network host, returned, and production moved to Glendale, California.

Did you know . . . host Geoff Edwards appeared in the Paul Newman movie *W.U.S.A.* and in *The Comic* with

If you were good at solving riddles, ''Jackpot,'' hosted by Geoff Edwards, would be your kind of show.

Dick Van Dyke? Edwards was also a regular on NBC-TV's "The Bobby Darin Show" and appeared frequently on CBS's "Petticoat Junction."

While taping "Jackpot" in New York City each weekend, Edwards was also taping TREASURE HUNT some three thousand miles away in Hollywood for Chuck Barris Productions.

JACKPOT BOWLING

premiere: January 9, 1959 *packagers:* NBC Productions 1959–1960; Sagebrush Productions 1960–1961 *broadcast history:* NBC primetime January 9, 1959–June 24, 1960; NBC primetime September 19, 1960–March 13, 1961
1959–1960 version
hosts: Leo Durocher, Mel Allen, Bud Palmer *producer:* Barney Nagler *director:* Ted Nathanson *origination:* T-Bowl, Wayne, New Jersey; Hollywood Bowling Lanes, Queens, New York; Woodhaven Lanes, Queens, New York
1960–1961 version
host: Milton Berle *play-by-play:* Chick Hearn *"Bayuk Cigar Girl":* Laurie Brady *producer:* Buddy Arnold *director:* Dave Brown *set designer:* Jerry Decker *origination:* Hollywood Legion Lanes, Hollywood

This series, originally called "Phillies Jackpot Bowling" after its sponsor, was used as a filler program on Friday nights to bridge the time between the conclusion of boxing matches on "Cavalcade of Sports" and the 11 P.M. local news. "Jackpot Bowling" was first broadcast from a bowling alley in Wayne, New Jersey, and in May 1959 it moved to a bowling alley in Queens, New York.

The first host, Leo Durocher, lasted two weeks. Baseball broadcaster Mel Allen took over from January 23 to April 3, when Bud Palmer came on board. Palmer remained until October 1959, when Mel Allen returned. Allen left again at the beginning of the new baseball season in April 1960 and Bud Palmer returned as host.

On the show, two bowlers competed for a $1,000 weekly prize. Each attempted to make as many strikes as possible in nine rolls. Any player who could bowl six straight strikes won a jackpot of $5,000 plus $1,000 for each week the jackpot was not won.

When the show returned in September 1960, comedian Milton Berle became the host and Los Angeles Lakers basketball broadcaster Chick Hearn handled the play-by-play. In the 1970s, Hearn would host a local bowling show in Los Angeles, "Bowling for Dollars." On the show, broadcast from the Legion Lanes in Hollywood, California on Monday evenings, Berle welcomed celebrity guests each week who would bowl for their favorite charities.

THE JAN MURRAY SHOW
(Charge Account)

premiere: September 5, 1960 *packager:* Jantone Productions *broadcast history:* NBC daytime September 5, 1960–September 28, 1962 *host:* Jan Murray *substitute hosts:* Bill Wendell, Jim Lucas, Steve Lawrence, Hal March *assistants:* Maureen Arthur, Lorraine Rogers, Micki Marlo *models:* Marilyn Hannold, Paula Pardo *announcers:* Bill

Careful, Uncle Miltie! Don't get a split before you even roll the ball.

Wendell, Roger Tuttle, Don Pardo, Jerry Damon *word authority:* Professor Morgan Schmitter of Columbia University *producers:* Ed Pierce, Joseph Scibetta *directors:* Van Fox, Grey Lockwood, Bob Hultgren *set designers:* Tom Trimble, Ted Cooper *music director:* Milton DeLugg *origination:* NBC Studio 6B, New York

The game portion of "The Jan Murray Show" was known as "Charge Account," and was a game in which players tried to create words from letters called out at random.

Before beginning the competition, the two contestants were shown three prizes that were available for purchase with a player's winnings at special low prices (a living room set worth $2,500 for only $185 in winnings). Each player selected a prize to play for in the game.

A group of sixteen letters was selected and mixed in a cylinder and then the letters were called out one at a time. Each of the two players had a square gameboard divided into sixteen blank squares (four rows of four). As the letters were called out, the contestants put them in the squares in order to make the most three- and four-letter words. Players received $25 for each four-letter word created and $10 for each three-letter word. The player with the most money won the game.

Did you know . . . legendary NBC-TV announcer Don Pardo's daughter Paula appeared as a substitute model on the August 3, 1961 show of "Charge Account"?

JEOPARDY!

premiere: March 30, 1964 *packager:* Merv Griffin Productions (1964–1994); Columbia/Tri-Star Television 1994– *broadcast history:* NBC daytime March 30, 1964–January 3, 1975; Syndicated September 9, 1974–September 7, 1975; NBC daytime October 2, 1978–March 2, 1979; Syndicated September 17, 1984–

1964–1975 version

host: Art Fleming *announcer:* Don Pardo *producers:* Robert Rubin, Lynette Williams *directors:* Bob Hultgren, Eleanor Tarshis, Jeff Goldstein *set designers:* Tom Trimble, Merrill Sindler *theme song:* "Take Ten" by Julann Griffin *origination:* NBC Studios 8G and 6A, New York

1978–1979 version

host: Art Fleming *announcer:* John Harlan *producer* George Vosburgh *director:* Jeff Goldstein *set designers:* Henry Lickel, Dennis Roof *origination:* NBC Studio 3, Burbank

1984– version

host: Alex Trebek *announcer:* Johnny Gilbert *producers:* Alex Trebek, George Vosburgh, Harry Friedman *directors:* Dick Schneider, Kevin McCarthy *set designers:* Henry Lickel, Bob Rang, Ed Flesh, Naomi Slodki *music:* Merv Griffin *origination:* Studio 7, KTTV–TV, Los Angeles (1984–1985); Studio 4, KTLA–TV, Los Angeles (1985–1987); Studio 1, KTLA–TV, Los Angeles (1987–1991); Studio 9, Hollywood Center Studios (1991–1994); Studio 10, Sony Studios, Culver City (1994–)

Three studio contestants had to come up with questions to fit the answers given in their choice of categories in "Jeopardy!", television's most successful question-and-answer game.

"Jeopardy!" was a staple of NBC's daytime schedule for almost eleven years and made household names of host Art Fleming and announcer Don Pardo. The show was immortalized in a 1984 song by satirist Weird Al Yankovic, "I Lost on Jeopardy!"

The game began with the "Jeopardy!" round consisting of six categories, each containing five questions worth between $10 and $50. Players rang in after the answer was revealed and all replies had to be phrased in the form of questions. The player giving the last correct question took control of the board and determined the next answer to be revealed as well as its corresponding dollar amount. Players giving wrong answers had the value of the questions deducted from their scores. Behind one of the spaces on the board was a "Daily Double," in which players could risk any or all of their earnings based on their ability to come up with the question for the next answer revealed.

A second round, "Double Jeopardy!", featured six new categories again containing five questions. Values for this round

Were you watching the game show greats Bill Cullen, Peter Marshall, and Art James compete on "Jeopardy!" as announcer Don Pardo rolled out an anniversary cake for emcee Art Fleming?

doubled ($20 to $100) and the board held two "Daily Doubles."

In the third round, "Final Jeopardy!", all three players were given the opportunity to risk all or part of their day's earnings based on his or her ability to answer one final question. Contestants were given the category, made their wagers, and gave their final answers, making sure they were in question form. The top-scoring player returned to compete against two new players on the next show. Players who won for five consecutive days retired as undefeated champions.

On the first broadcast of "Jeopardy!", the categories in the first round were "Television," "Women," "Fictional Characters," "Odds and Ends," "American History," and "Science." The categories in "Double Jeopardy!" were "U.S. Geography," "Sports," "The Funnies," "Words," "Opera," and "Famous Names."

The first Final Jeopardy! category was "Famous Quotes," and the answer was " 'Good night sweet prince' was originally said to him." The correct question was "Who is Hamlet?" The first champion, Mary Eubanks (no relation to emcee Bob Eubanks) of North Carolina won $345.

To celebrate the two thousandth broadcast of "Jeopardy!" on February 21, 1972, comedian Mel Brooks appeared as the two-thousand-year-old man.

Announcer Don Pardo missed only one broadcast, on April 17, 1967, with substitute Wayne Morse taking Pardo's place. Host Art Fleming did not miss one show in the entire run of "Jeopardy!"

Prior to hosting "Jeopardy!", Art Fleming played Jeremy Pitt in the 1958 TV western "The Californians" and Ken Franklin in the 1959 series "International Detective." In 1954 he was seen as one of the assistants on DOCTOR I.Q., a popular quiz show.

In September 1974, "Jeopardy!" began airing once a week in a nighttime syndicated version. The only change in the show was the addition of a bonus round that the day's champion played after "Final Jeopardy!" He or she chose from among thirty numbers, each of which revealed a bonus prize and one number concealed a $25,000 jackpot.

"Jeopardy!" left NBC after 2,753 shows, on January 3, 1975. Merv Griffin's WHEEL OF FORTUNE premiered on NBC the following Monday. On October 2, 1978, "Jeopardy!" returned to NBC in an updated edition. The show moved from New York to Los Angeles, with Art Fleming continuing as host and John Harlan becoming the new announcer.

Changes were made in the way the game was played. Three players competed in round one, but only the top-two scoring players moved on to round two. The top scorer after two rounds became the champ and played a "Super Jeopardy!" round for a possible $5,000. He or she tried to correctly answer five consecutive questions in any row or column on the game board without getting three answers wrong. This version of "Jeopardy!" lasted only five months.

"Jeopardy!" made a successful return to television with a new daily syndicated version in September 1984. Distributed by King World, which had successfully launched WHEEL OF FORTUNE as a nighttime show a year earlier, "Jeopardy!" quickly became one of the top syndicated television programs.

Alex Trebek has been "Jeopardy!" 's perfect host for over ten years.

Alex Trebek became the new host and Johnny Gilbert the new announcer, and the format of the game remains the same as the original network version of the 1960s. Cash amounts are increased in the Jeopardy! round ranging from $100 to $500 and in the Double Jeopardy! round ranging from $200 to $1,000. Only the day's winner receives his or her money, and the other two players receive consolation gifts. Players who win five straight games retire as undefeated champions and become eligible to return for the yearly tournament of champions.

During the first ten years of the new "Jeopardy!", Jerome Vered of Studio City, California, set a one-day record, winning $34,000, the maximum possible in one show being $283,200. Frank Spangenburg, a New York City transit officer established a five-day record, winning $102,597 in January 1990.

On the January 19, 1993 broadcast, Air Force Lt. Colonel Daryl Scott of Washington, D.C. became the first player to win the championship with the least amount possible, $1. He returned on the next show and successfully defended his title, increasing his winnings to $13,402.

In the summer of 1990, ABC aired a primetime SUPER JEOPARDY! that featured former "Jeopardy!" winners competing for a $250,000 first prize.

A "Celebrity Jeopardy!" edition was introduced as an annual event in November 1992. Among the celebrities competing in the first year were Carol Burnett, Regis Philbin, Luke Perry, Cheech Marin, Donna Mills, and Emma Samms. Other celebrities who have appeared on "Jeopardy!" include Ed Asner, Kelsey Grammer, Kareem Abdul-Jabbar, Larry King, Bill Maher, Kathy Mattea, Leslie Nielsen, Rosie O'Donnell, Howard Stern's radio sidekick Robin Quivers, Tony Randall, General Norman Schwarzkopf, Sinbad, and Jay Thomas.

Did you know . . . announcer Don Pardo began his NBC career on June 15, 1944? He was the announcer on NBC's first daytime game show, REMEMBER THIS DATE, premiering in November 1950 with Bill Stern as host. On November 22, 1963 he read the first bulletin on NBC television, at 1:45 P.M. Eastern Time, on the shooting of President John F. Kennedy. The many shows Pardo has announced for include "Caesar's Hour," "The Mindy Carson Show," "The Jonathan Winters Show," WINNER TAKE ALL, THE PRICE IS RIGHT, "The Ford Fiftieth Anniversary Show," and starting with its debut in 1975, "Saturday Night Live." In 1987 he made his motion picture debut, playing a radio game show host in the Woody Allen film *Radio Days.*

The original title for "Jeopardy!" was to be "What's the Question?" but it was changed before the show premiered on NBC.

Art Fleming started his career in radio and was a World War II naval hero. He was the original announcer for Winston cigarettes ("Winston tastes good like a cigarette should"). He was also an usher at the wedding of Richard Nixon's daughter. Fleming was also among a select group of radio personalities who were part of the NBC Radio Network "Monitor" series. Among the other game show hosts heard on "Monitor" were Bill Cullen, Monty Hall, Garry Moore, and Gene Rayburn.

Game show creator Jay Wolpert (BLACKOUT, HIT MAN, RODEO DRIVE, SKEDADDLE, and WHEW!) won the 1969 "Jeopardy!" championship.

Before becoming one of America's top game show emcees, Alex Trebek was one of Canada's top television personalities. In 1961 he joined the Canadian Broadcasting Company (CBC) as a newsman. In 1963 he was signed to host "Reach for the Top" and from 1967 to 1972 he was host of one of Canada's top talk shows. In 1973, Trebek came to America to host his first U.S. game show, THE WIZARD OF ODDS, for NBC.

Were you watching when . . .   the authors of *The Encyclopedia of TV Game Shows* were featured as a "Jeopardy!" question and answer on March 13, 1991? The category was "Reference Books." The answer read, "Beat the Odds," "Music Bingo," and "Fast Draw" are entries in an encyclopedia of these by Schwartz, Ryan, and Wostbrock. If you said, "What are game shows?" (a "Jeopardy!" contestant did) you'd be absolutely correct. By the way, all three game shows were hosted by "Jeopardy!" announcer Johnny Gilbert.

Host Bob Bergen introduces a new generation of eager contestants to the fun and excitement of "Jep!", the Game Show Network's children's version of the hit show "Jeopardy!"

Original "Jeopardy!" emcee Art Fleming guest starred on these game shows: CONCENTRATION (for the show's twelfth anniversary), THE HOLLYWOOD SQUARES, I'LL BET, THE MATCH GAME, THE WHO WHAT OR WHERE GAME, and as the mystery guest on WHAT'S MY LINE? in 1973.

JEP!

premiere: January 30, 1998 **packager:** Scott Sternberg Productions/Columbia Tri Star TV **broadcast history:** Game Show Network (cable) January 30, 1998– **host:** Bob Bergen **executive producers:** Scott Sternberg, Harry Friedman **producer:** Pamela Corvais **coproducers:** Lisa Broffman, Gary Johnson, Rocky Schmidt **consultant:** Alex Trebek **director:** Kevin McCarthy **production designer:** Tom Buderwitz **music:** Steve Kaplan **origination:** Stage 11, Sony Pictures Studios, Culver City

Three contestants, ages ten to twelve, compete in this kids' version of the long-running question-and-answer game "JEOPARDY!" Like the original show, "Jep!" is played in three rounds during which the players try to come up with the correct question to match an answer in a particular category.

Round one, the "Jep! Round," has five categories, each with four answers. The player with the last correct question selects the next category and then hits a randomizer to determine the point value (from one hundred to five hundred) of the next answer to be revealed. Point values double and five new categories appear in the second round, called "Hyper Jep!"

These new features in "Jep!" include a "Jep!" prize on the game board that allows a player not only earn to points but also to win a bonus gift for coming up with the correct question. Another is a set of answers from members of the "Jep! squad," kids from various areas of the country who present prerecorded answers to the in-studio players.

In "Jep!" contestants who come up with incorrect questions to the supplied answers are subject to penalties. A player who has two incorrect replies has a large container of some object, such as rubber frogs, dumped on him or her from above, and a player who misses three questions has to sit out a question.

All players participate in the "Super Jep!" final round, in which one final category is revealed and each player wagers any or all of the day's earnings based on his or her ability to come up with the correct question before the answer is given. The player with the most points at the end of this round is the day's winner.

Each player is given the choice of two possible gifts to select as his or her prize. On the first broadcast, the winner of the day had to select between a Sony electronics package containing a TV, VCR, and Sony Play Station or a trip to a ski resort in White Fish, Montana.

Did you know . . . host Bob Bergen supplied voices to the animated characters Porky Pig and Tweety in the Warner Brothers film *Space Jam* that starred Michael Jordan?

JOE GARAGIOLA'S MEMORY GAME

premiere: February 15, 1971 **packager:** Merv Griffin Productions **broadcast history:** NBC daytime February 15, 1971–July 30, 1971 **host:** Joe Garagiola **announcer:** Johnny Olson **executive producer:** John Tobyansen **producers:** Robert Rubin, Les Roberts **director:** Jeff Goldstein **set designer:** Carden Bailey **origination:** NBC Studio 8G, New York

Five studio contestants, identified by the numbers one through five, were each given a packet containing some of the questions and answers to be used on that day's show and they had thirty seconds to study them. Emcee Joe Garagiola then collected all of the questions and answers and, beginning with a player selected at random, started the game.

On "Joe Garagiola's Memory Game," the first player could either answer the question or pass to another player by calling out his or her number (one through five). Contestants could keep passing the question around but had to answer when a buzzer rang. Players began with $50 bankrolls, earning $5 for correct answers and losing $5 for wrong answers. High scorer of the day was the winner.

Did you know . . . Joe Garagiola played professional baseball as a catcher for the St. Louis Cardinals, Pittsburgh

Funny and witty Joe Garagiola on the set of "Joe Garagiola's Memory Game" tries to remember what it was like to have hair.

Pirates, Chicago Cubs, and New York Giants from 1946 to 1954? His lifetime batting average was .257.

This was the only Merv Griffin–produced game show that famed announcer Johnny Olson announced. Their association began when they worked together on PLAY YOUR HUNCH in 1958. PLAY YOUR HUNCH was the first game show hosted by Merv Griffin and the first in a long series of Goodson-Todman shows that featured Johnny Olson as announcer.

THE JOKER'S WILD

premiere: September 4, 1972 *packagers:* Jack Barry Productions (1972–1975); Jack Barry and Dan Enright Productions (1977–1986); Kline and Friends/Jack Barry Productions (1990–1991) *broadcast history:* CBS daytime September 4, 1972–June 13, 1975; Syndicated September 1977–September 1986; Syndicated kids' version ("Joker! Joker! Joker!") September 1979–September 1981; USA (cable) April 1, 1985–April 24, 1987 (repeats of 1977–1986 version); Syndicated September 10, 1990–September 13, 1991; USA (cable) December 30, 1991–September 11, 1992 (repeats of 1990–1991 version); USA (cable) March 29, 1993–June 24, 1994 (repeats of 1990–1991 version)

1972–1975 version

host: Jack Barry *announcers:* Johnny Jacobs, Johnny Gilbert *executive producer:* John Tobyansen *producer:* Justin Edgerton *director:* Richard Kline *set designer:* Don Roberts *origination:* Studios 31 and 33, CBS Television City, Los Angeles

1977–1986 version

hosts: Jack Barry, Jim Peck, Bill Cullen *announcers:* Jay Stewart, Bob Hilton, Art James, Charlie O'Donnell *executive producer:* Dan Enright *producers:* Ron Greenberg, Gary Cox, Allen Koss *directors:* Richard Kline, Dan Diana *set designer:* John C. Mula *music:* Hal Hidey *origination:* KCOP Television, Los Angeles; The Production Group Studios, Los Angeles

1990–1991 version

host: Pat Finn *announcer:* Ed MacKay *executive producers:* Richard Kline, Douglas Barry, John Barry *producer:* Eric Warner *director:* Richard Kline *set designer:* John C. Mula *music:* Joe Manolakakis *origination:* Studio 33, CBS Television City, Los Angeles

Veteran game show producer-host Jack Barry made a successful comeback on network television with "The Joker's Wild," the daily question-and-answer show where "Knowledge is King and Lady Luck is Queen."

Barry had made two earlier attempts to return to the national spotlight. In 1969 he became host of THE GENERATION GAP when original emcee Dennis Wholey left and in 1971 Barry hosted a primetime quiz series for ABC called THE REEL GAME. Neither show lasted beyond their original thirteen week runs.

On "The Joker's Wild," two contestants answered questions from categories determined by a machine resembling a one-armed bandit that selected categories randomly. The machine projected three cards on a screen. A player then selected a category and the question asked was worth $50.

A joker card on the board doubled the value of the question, a pair of jokers increased it to $200, and three jokers were worth an automatic win. The first player to earn $500 won the game.

The winning contestant played a bonus game using the same machine, though it was now filled with cash and "devil" cards. The player stopped the spinning cards at will and, as long as cash amounts appeared in the three windows, he or she kept the accumulated money and could elect to continue the round. The player who accumulated $1,000 without a devil appearing won a bonus prize. The devil's appearance would cause the player to lose any winnings in the bonus round at that time, but the player had the option to quit at any time.

In the fall of 1976, Los Angeles TV station KHJ began broadcasting repeats of the CBS series, which paved the way for a new version of "The Joker's Wild" in September 1977.

In the fall of 1979, a children's version, "Joker! Joker! Joker!", aired with Jack Barry as host and Jay Stewart as announcer. Ron Greenberg produced and Richard Kline directed, in this version.

Jack Barry emceed "The Joker's Wild" until his death in 1984. In the fall of 1984, Bill Cullen became host and remained with the show until it was canceled in 1986.

Jack Barry on the set of "The Joker's Wild" from the first season back in 1972.

"The Joker's Wild" returned in the fall of 1990 with new shows and a revised format. Three contestants competed in round one, with control of the joker machine determined by the player who correctly answered a jump-in question. Dollar amounts ranging from $5 to $50 appeared in all three windows on the machine and were added together to determine the value of the questions in a particular category. If a joker appeared in the last window, the value of the category was tripled. The player in control answered questions until he or she missed one. His or her opponents would then try to answer the missed question. If successful, the opponent took control of the game board. This round ended when one player reached the $500 level. The player with the lowest score was eliminated and the remaining two players moved to the second round.

In round two, players continued to build their scores carried from round one, and the first to reach $2,000 won the game. The player in control spun the joker machine to determine the amount to be played for, chose one of two categories, and tried to answer as many questions as possible in fifteen seconds. The other player could steal control of the board by answering a missed question.

The day's winner played a bonus game for additional cash and prizes. He or she was given sixty seconds to play for spins on the joker machine by trying to guess words from three definitions. One spin was awarded for each correct answer. After the number of spins was determined the joker machine was put into motion. If three jokers appeared in the windows the player won the daily cash jackpot, which increased by $500 each day until won. If prizes were revealed, the player was allowed to freeze any of the windows and spin again to try to get the same prize to come up in the remaining windows.

Did you know . . . the original pilot for "The Joker's Wild" was taped in 1969 with Allen Ludden as host?

JUDGE FOR YOURSELF

premiere: August 18, 1953 *packager:* Mark Goodson–Bill Todman Productions *broadcast history:* NBC primetime August 18, 1953–May 11, 1954 *host:* Fred Allen *substitute host:* Herb Shriner *announcer:* Don Pardo *commercial announcer:* Dennis James for Old Gold Cigarettes *dancing cigarette packs:* Dixie Dunbar (Old Gold Regular), Floria Vestoff (Old Gold King Size) *featured singers:* Bob Carroll, Kitty Kallen, Judy Johnson, The Skylarks *producers:* Mark Goodson, Bill Todman *director:* Jerome Schnur *set designer:* Kathleen Ankers *music director:* Milton De-Lugg *origination:* NBC Studio 6B, New York *debut guests:* Broadway producer Cheryl Crawford, composer Jule Styne, *Varity* radio-TV editor George Rosen

With "Judge for Yourself," radio comedian Fred Allen, best known for his on-going "feud" with Jack Benny, moved to television in the 1953–1954 season.

In the original format, three professional acts (by singers, musicians, dancers, comedians) performed and were rated 1-2-3 by two panels of judges. One set of judges was composed of three celebrities, and the other set of three members of the studio audience. An audience-judge won $1,000 if his or her rating matched that of any of the celebrities.

The format was changed on January 5, 1954. Three contestants now listened to songs written by amateur songwriters that were performed by the show's regulars. The players tried to determine the one song that the audience liked best and any player who guessed correctly won part of the $1,000 jackpot.

Fred Allen later appeared as a semi-regular panelist on the Mark Goodson–Bill Todman game show WHAT'S MY LINE? from 1954 to 1956.

JUMBLE—THE INTERACTIVE GAME

premiere: June 13, 1994 *packager:* Martindale-Hillier Productions/Fiedler-Berlin Productions *broadcast history:* Family Channel (cable) June 13, 1994–September 2, 1994; Family Channel (cable) November 21, 1994–December 30, 1994 *host:* Wink Martindale *announcer:* Randy West *executive producers:* Wink Martindale, Bill Hillier *supervising producers:* Peter Berlin, Rob Fiedler *producer:* Gary Johnson *director:* Rob Fielder *set designer:* Scott Storey *music:* Ed Lojeski *origination:* Glendale Studios, Glendale

"Jumble," based on the popular newspaper feature created by Martin Dell, first appeared on June 7, 1954 and became a daily game show and interactive feature on the Family Channel in the summer of 1994. The show, "Jumble—The Interactive Game," was produced and hosted by Wink Martindale, who was also responsible for three other interactive shows for the Family Channel, BOGGLE, SHUFFLE, and TRIVIAL PURSUIT.

"Jumble" featured four contestants competing in an elimination match, with the day's winner receiving a trip as the prize. Each player had a keypad resembling a touch-tone telephone with numbers corresponding to letters of the alphabet.

A series of jumbled letters was revealed along with a clue. The players attempted to unscramble the correct sequence of letters by punching in their answers. They could earn as many as one thousand points depending on how fast they answered. Four words were played in this round and the low-scoring player was eliminated from the game.

The three remaining players moved on to round two, playing four new "Jumble" words. The low-scoring player was again eliminated and the remaining two contestants moved on to a final round to determine the day's winner.

JUST MEN!

premiere: January 3, 1983 *packager:* Century Tower Productions (Rick Rosner/Orion TV) *broadcast history:* NBC daytime January 3, 1983–April 1, 1983 *host:* Betty White *announcer:* Steve Day *executive producer:* Rick Rosner *producer:* Rickie Gaffney *director:* Bill Foster *set designer:* Bob Keene *music:* Stormy Sacks *origination:* NBC Studio 1, Burbank *debut guests:* Steve Sax, Leif Garrett, Josh Taylor, Jeff Altman, Tim Reid, David Hasselhoff, Dick Van Patten, Nels Van Patten

Two female contestants competed on this daytime show, "Just Men!", and tried to predict how a seven-member panel

Wow! A rare picture of Fred Allen hosting the 1953 Goodson-Todman game show "Judge for Yourself." Note the cue-cards near the studio monitor.

of male celebrities would respond to questions. Example: "Are you a grouch in the morning?"

A player selected a celebrity and questioned him for one minute. She then made her prediction and if she was right, won a car key. The player with the most car keys at the end of the show won the game and selected one of the keys in the hope that it would start a new car. If the car started, she won the prize; if not, she returned on the next show.

Did you know . . . Betty White won five Emmys for her acting: on "Life with Elizabeth" in 1953, "The Mary Tyler Moore Show" in 1975 and 1976, as a game show host for "Just Men!" in 1983, and in 1986 for "Golden Girls"?

In 1995 Betty White's autobiography was published. In it she talks about her game show career and her late husband, Allen Ludden.

KAY KYSER'S COLLEGE OF MUSICAL KNOWLEDGE See COLLEGE OF MUSICAL KNOWLEDGE.

KEEP IT IN THE FAMILY

premiere: October 12, 1957 *packager:* Frank Cooper Productions *broadcast history:* ABC primetime October 12, 1957–February 8, 1958 *host:* Bill Nimmo *announcer:* Johnny Olson *creators:* Leonard Stern, Roger Price *producer:* Art Stark *director:* Mickey Trenner *set designer:* Frank Volpel *origination:* New York

Two families, each composed of five members, answered general knowledge questions for merchandise prizes in "Keep It in the Family," this weekly quiz show. Each team began with two hundred points and then bid points to earn the right to answer a five-part question. One part of the question was designated for each member of the family and if all five parts of the question were answered correctly, the team then won a prize. Teams could bid up to one hundred points and the higher bid received the question.

The difficulty of the question was determined by the amount of the bid. The team lost the bid if any part of the question was missed and they were eliminated from the game if their score dropped below one hundred. The first team to reach three hundred fifty points won the game and then faced new challengers.

Keefe Brasselle was scheduled to emcee the show but was replaced before the premiere by Bill Nimmo.

Did you know . . . "Keep It in the Family" creators Leonard Stern and Roger Price formed the publishing house Price, Stern, and Sloan? Leonard Stern went on to produce numerous TV shows including "Get Smart" with Don Adams, while Roger Price is best remembered for his DROODLES puzzles and the game Mad Libs.

KEEP TALKING

premiere: July 15, 1958 *packager:* Wolf Productions *broadcast history:* CBS primetime July 15, 1958–October 28, 1958; CBS primetime November 9, 1958–September 2, 1959; ABC primetime October 29, 1959–May 3, 1960 *hosts:* Monty Hall, Carl Reiner, Vincent Price, Merv Griffin *announcers:* Bern Bennett, Johnny Olson *executive producer:* Lester Gottlieb *producers:* Herb Wolf, Alan Gilbert *directors:* Jerome Shaw, Lloyd Gross *set designers:* Sy Tomasoff, Gary Smith *origination:* CBS Studio 51, New York *debut guests:* Joey Bishop, Danny Dayton, Ilka Chase, Shari Lewis, Paul Winchell, Martyn Green

Two teams consisting of three celebrities competed on this comedy game show, "Keep Talking," by the producers of MASQUERADE PARTY. Regular panelists on "Keep Talking" included Orson Bean, Joey Bishop, Pat Carroll, Peggy Cass, Ilka Chase, Morey Amsterdam, Elaine May, Audrey Meadows, and Paul Winchell.

One team was called the "Chatterboxes" and the other the "Gabbers." Members of one team were given a secret phrase to work into an ad-libbed story. The emcee started the story and when a buzzer sounded, one member of a team picked up the story and tried to work the secret phrase in. Control of the story bounced back and forth between the players of one team. The team scored one point for getting the phrase in, and two points if the other team was unable to guess the phrase.

Monty Hall was the original emcee when "Keep Talking" premiered. Carl Reiner followed Monty Hall as host in November 1958, when the show moved into the slot previously held by THE $64,000 QUESTION. Reiner left in July 1959 and Vincent Price became host for the rest of the CBS run. "Keep Talking" moved to ABC in the fall of 1959 and Merv Griffin became emcee.

KING OF THE MOUNTAIN

premiere: July 28, 1990 *packager:* Fox Square Productions *broadcast history:* Fox primetime July 28, 1990 (special) *hosts:* John Mulrooney and Judy Cole *executive producer:* Kevin Bright *producer:* Larry Gotterer *director:* Louis Horvitz *set designer:* Joe Stewart *music:* Kevin Kiner

"King of the Mountain," an outdoor athletic contest based on a series that aired on the Tokyo Broadcasting System, featured ten contestants (five men and five women) competing for the "vacation of a lifetime." In the one and only broadcast, the vacation was a trip for two to Puerta Vallarta, Mexico, with a cash prize of $1,000.

The match began with all ten contestants competing in three events to earn points. In the first event, called the "suicide swamp," each player tried to cross a "swamp" by stepping on a series of stones. Some stones were anchored down, some were not, and a player who fell in the water was eliminated. The farther along a player got in an attempt to cross the swamp, the more points that player received. Any player who crossed the swamp without falling in received one hundred points.

Event two was the "human bowling" round, in which each player selected a number at random. This number determined the players' positions on an oversized bowling lane. A large two hundred pound bowling ball was rolled at the players who were dressed in protective bowling pin suits. They received twenty-five points if they were still standing after one ball was rolled and fifty points if still standing after two balls were rolled. The players rotated positions on the lane for the second frame with the position again determined by numbers selected at random. Any player who survived both frames received one hundred points.

The third event was called the "doors of deception," where each player tried to run through a series of four walls built of four doors by choosing the correct door in each wall. Some doors were just paper and allowed passage, while some were solid or filled with nets to prevent passage. Each player received twenty-five points for each wall conquered.

The four contestants with the highest point scores at the end of the third event moved on to "Boulder Mountain" to determine the day's winner. The players, in pairs of two, raced each other up a pass in order to reach the top of the mountain while also attempting to avoid man-made boulders that were tossed at them to slow their climb. The first player to reach the top raced the winner of the second match for the championship.

KING PINS

premiere: July 29, 1988   *packager:* MTV Networks   *broadcast history:* Nickelodeon (cable) July 29, 1988 (special)   *host:* George Siegal   *assistant:* Molly Scott   *announcer:* Al Rickman   *creator/producer:* Bob Mittenthal   *director:* Craig Coffman   *set designers:* Peet Foster, Robert Small   *organist:* Norman Weiss   *origination:* Mineola, New York

Two husband-and-wife teams competed in "King Pins," a one-broadcast show that combined answering general knowledge questions with bowling. Taped at the Sheridan Bowling Academy in Mineola, New York, the game began with the men answering a ten-point toss-up question. Their wives then bowled, attempting to knock down as many pins as they could. If a woman did not pick up a strike, she was presented with an obstacle to overcome during her next throw. The handicaps included making the woman bowl in oversized clown shoes, or having her throw the ball between her mates' spread-apart feet. After two questions and two chances at bowling, the players reversed positions.

A second round was played for twenty points a question, and both members of the team bowled. The husbands threw the first balls and their wives tried to knock down any leftover pins.

Between the first and second rounds, both teams played the "King Pins Golden Frame" for a bonus prize. Each woman was given two chances to knock down a gold headpin. Whoever did, won the prize; otherwise no points were scored in this event.

The game concluded with the "magic frame," where each team wagered any part of their score on the last frame. Each player tossed one ball. A strike doubled the team's wager. A spare earned the points originally bet and points were lost if the team failed to "mark."

The team with the most points won the game and their point score was multiplied by ten to represent a dollar value. They also competed in the "Big Bonus Bowling Round," where they tried to knock down six six-foot-tall pins with an oversized bowling ball. If they knocked them all down, they won a grand prize. If they did not, they received $100 for each pin knocked down.

KING'S PARTY LINE

premiere: July 13, 1946   *packager:* CBS Television   *broadcast history:* CBS primetime July 13, 1946–December 28, 1946   *host:* John Reed King   *assistant:* Jim Brown   *producer/director:* Frances Buss   *set designer:* James McNaughton   *origination:* CBS Grand Central Studios, New York

This early CBS quiz program was seen on WCBW, New York City as part of its Saturday night lineup and featured music, audience participation, stunts, and quiz questions. "King's Party Line" replaced another John Reed King series IT'S A GIFT.

KNIGHTS AND WARRIORS

premiere: September 19, 1992   *packager:* Welk Entertainment Group for Western International Syndication   *broadcast history:* Syndicated September 19, 1992–September 11, 1993   *host:* Joe Fowler   *hostess:* Lisa Canning   *announcer/"Lord of the Rules":* Bernard Earhard   *"Warriors":* "The Plague" (Jim Maniaci), "Pyro" (Douglas Rogel), "Chaos" (Benny Graham), "Knightmare" (Rodney Mitchell), "Lady Battleaxe" (Dot Jones), "The Steel Maiden" (Nancy Georges), "Venom" (Jessica Long), "Malice" (Cameo Kneuer)   *executive producer:* Jerry Gilden   *producers:* Paul Abeyta, John Latushko   *director:* Bob Bowker   *set designer:* Robert Rang   *music director:* Fred Lapides   *origination:* Stage 3, CBS/MTM Studios, Studio City

Four contestants, divided into two teams, competed in this weekly athletic sports fantasy series set in a medieval arena called the "Warriordome" (actually a stage at CBS Studio Center in Studio City, California). The contestants in "Knights and Warriors" were called "knights," and competed against eight costumed "warriors" with names like "Plague," "Lady Battleaxe," "Chaos," and "Princess Malice." The contestants in either the "purple" or the "gold" team participated in eight events, some played individually and some as a team.

In the first event, "Catapult," four of the warriors shot lightweight balls at two of the knights (one from each team), who attempted to field the balls and toss them through a ring of fire for either five, ten, or fifteen points (depending on the area from where they made the shot). There were two rounds in this one-minute event, one for the male contestants, the other for the female contestants.

The second event, "Battle Swords," featured the female contestants. Each player challenged one warrior on a pair of mechanical treadmills that were moving in opposite directions. To earn points they had to knock their opponents off the treadmill within thirty seconds.

Another individual event was the "Sorcerer's Wheel," where the men attempted to run around a twenty-foot revolving turntable that was spinning in the opposite direction. The players scored ten points for each lap they completed as they tried to elude a seventy-five pound swinging mace that was pushed at them by the warriors.

All the players competed in the fourth event, "The Volcano," where the knights tried to climb a thirty-foot structure while the warriors attempted to knock them off.

Another individual event for the men was the "Roller Joust." The contestants skated around a track to capture mounted rings on their lances while being pursued by the warriors.

The women competed one at a time against a single warrior in the "Tug-o-Warriors," where each woman tried to pull the warrior off a ten-foot pedestal.

In the final event, "Target Onslaught," one team member tried to earn time by hitting six floor-targets using a power crossbow. This person's teammate then took the time earned (plus a base time of thirty seconds) and tried to hit the warriors who were now sliding on pulleys mounted across the studio.

The team with the most points at the end of the show moved on to the next round of competition.

KNOCKOUT

premiere: October 3, 1977 *packager:* Ralph Edwards Productions *broadcast history:* NBC daytime October 3, 1977–April 21, 1978 *host:* Arte Johnson *announcers:* Jay Stewart, John Harlan *executive producer:* Ralph Edwards *producers:* Bruce Belland, Mark Maxwell-Smith *director:* Arthur Forrest *set designer:* Jim Newton *origination:* NBC Studio 2, Burbank

Comedian Arte Johnson, best known as a regular on "Rowan and Martin's Laugh-In" during the late 1960s, hosted "Knockout," this daytime game show that featured three contestants attempting to guess which one of four items was not related to the others.

Items were revealed one at a time on a game board and players buzzed in when they believed the unrelated item had been revealed. If he or she was correct, one letter of the word "K-N-O-C-K-O-U-T" was earned. Players could earn an additional letter by correctly guessing the category from the remaining items on the board or by challenging one of his or her two opponents. If the challenged player came up with the correct answer, he or she won two letters. If this person failed, the challenger received the letters and was now able to challenge his or her opponent for two additional letters. The first player to earn the eight letters to spell "Knockout" won the game and a prize.

The winning person played a bonus round for the chance to earn up to $5,000. The player tried to guess the category of three items. If he or she guessed correctly after one item was revealed, the answer was worth $500. After two clues the answer was worth $300 and $100 after all three were revealed. The player could increase his or her bankroll tenfold by choosing one of three possible clues in another puzzle and guessing the category.

Whoever won five games received a new car. Players remained on the show until they lost two games.

THE KRYPTON FACTOR

premiere: August 7, 1981 *packagers:* Alan Landsburg Productions/MCA Television (1981); Kushner-Locke Company for Western International (1990) *broadcast history:* ABC primetime August 7, 1981–September 4, 1981; Syndicated September 15, 1990–September 7, 1991
1981 version
host: Dick Clark *announcer:* John Harlan *creator:* Jeremy Fox *executive producers:* Alan Landsburg, Woody Frazer, Merrill Grant, Howard Lipstone *producer:* Fred Tatashore *director:* Arthur Forrest *set designers:* Bob Keene, Bente Christensen *music:* Roy Prendergast *origination:* Studio 59, ABC Television Center, Los Angeles
1990–1991 version
host: Willie Aames *announcer:* Laura Cody *producer:* Mike Metzger *director:* John Vogt *set designer:* John C. Mula *music:* Nigel Holten *origination:* Glendale Studios, Glendale

On this five-week summer series, "The Krypton Factor," four contestants competed each week for $5,000 in gold. The players were tested on knowledge, physical ability (obstacle course), reflex speed (video games), mental agility, and observation. The winners from each of the first four programs returned on the fifth show to compete for a grand prize of $50,000 in gold.

Round one had each of the players trying to complete a video game challenge, earning five points if successful.

Two tests of mental agility were asked of the players in the ten-point second round. In the first test, each player was read a series of five numbers (example: 10-6-17-3-8). To earn four points, they had to repeat the sequence but give the preceding number for each of the five given (answer: 9-5-16-2-7). The second test, worth six points, involved each player being read a series of six letters (example: J-R-W-A-H-O) and then the player repeated the sequence with the letter that followed it in the alphabet (answer: K-S-X-B-I-P). If a player made a mistake during one of the tests they earned no points for that particular test.

All four players earned points, depending on the order in which they had finished, in a pretaped obstacle-course race (featured in round three). Round four tested the player's powers of observation by asking them questions about a motion picture scene they had just been shown.

The game concluded with a three-minute round of general knowledge questions. Players earned two points for right answers and lost two points for incorrect answers. Halfway through the round, point values doubled to four points and the player with the most points at the end of this round became the day's winner.

"The Krypton Factor" returned as a weekly syndicated show in 1990 with kids competing in a year-long competition to attempt to win a $20,000 cash prize. Each week the players competed in tests of intelligence, observation, physical ability, and general knowledge.

The first round was an intelligence test and each player was individually asked two ten-point questions. All players had a chance to answer five-point bonus questions.

A specially edited scene from a classic film was viewed in round two. Each player was then asked ten-point questions about what they saw. A ten-point bonus round was also played and the players were asked to guess, with the help of five clues, the identity of an object from the film.

An obstacle course was featured in the "Physical Ability" round. The player who finished first received twenty points. Second place won fifteen points, third place won ten points, and fourth place won five points.

The final round was a two-minute round of general knowledge questions with all players competing against each other. Correct answers were worth five points and wrong answers cost a player two points. The player with the most points at the end of this round won the game, received merchandise prizes, and played in the next round of competition.

Did you know . . . host Willie Aames had been seen in the TV shows "Swiss Family Robinson," "Eight Is Enough," and "Charles in Charge"?

"The Krypton Factor" was based on a British series of the same name.

KWIK WITZ

premiere: September 20, 1996   *packager:* Beau & Arrow Productions   *broadcast history:* Syndicated September 20, 1996–   *hosts:* Andi Matheny, Jillian Hamilton   *creators:* Steve Belkin, Doug Singer   *developed by:* Mark Maxwell-Smith, Gary Shimokawa   *executive producer:* Steve Belkin   *supervising producer:* Mark Maxwell-Smith   *producers:* Ron West, Dan O'Connor, David Razowsky, Jules Belkin, Fran Belkin, Layton Kest   *director:* Gary Shimokawa   *set designers:* Bill Bartelt, Jim Bertram   *music:* John Tanner   *origination:* WMAQ-TV, Chicago

Two teams, each composed of two comedians, are presented a set of circumstances and then try to create comedy bits in this weekly game show that is usually aired Friday or Saturday nights.

Each show consists of a series of challenges, such as creating and singing a song that speaks to the children of today or staging an unlikely meeting between two people who made history.

Both teams try each challenge, and members of the studio audience rate the performances. One hundred points in each round are divided between the teams. The team with the most points at the end of the show receives a prize selected by the other team.

Andi Methany was host for the first season. She was replaced by Jillian Hamilton when the show began its second season in September 1997.

LADIES BE SEATED

premiere: April 22, 1949 *packager:* Tom Moore Productions *broadcast history:* ABC primetime April 22, 1949–June 10, 1949 *host:* Tom Moore *assistant:* Phil Patton *announcer:* Claude Kirshner *producers:* Greg Garrison, Phil Patton, Tom Moore *directors:* Greg Garrison, Tony Rizzo *music:* Buddy Weed Trio *origination:* WENR Studios at Civic Opera House, Chicago

The popular radio show "Ladies Be Seated" made a brief stop on television in the spring of 1949. The Chicago-based show, hosted by Tom Moore, featured quizzes and stunts that were performed mostly by female members of the studio audience.

A sample of stunts featured on the premiere telecast included three women competing in a quiz using a variety of noisemakers to give an answer, and two husbands in a race against time to put on ladies' clothing.

The radio version of "Ladies Be Seated" was heard on the ABC network from June 26, 1944 to July 20, 1950. Johnny Olson and his wife Penny were the hosts from 1944 to 1949 and Tom Moore hosted for the final year.

LAS VEGAS GAMBIT

premiere: October 27, 1980 *packager:* Merrill Heatter–Bob Quigley Productions *broadcast history:* NBC daytime October 27, 1980–November 27, 1981 *host:* Wink Martindale *card dealers:* Beverly Malden, Lee Menning *announcer:* Kenny Williams *executive producers:* Merrill Heatter, Bob Quigley *producer:* Robert Noah *director:* Jerome Shaw *set designers:* Bente Christensen, Jim Newton *music:* Stan Worth *origination:* Fountain Theatre, Tropicana Hotel, Las Vegas

NBC revived GAMBIT in 1980, renaming it "Las Vegas Gambit" and moving it to the Tropicana Hotel in Las Vegas. Wink Martindale returned as host and was joined by a new card dealer, Lee Menning. (Elaine Stewart was the card dealer on the original "Gambit.") During its yearlong run on NBC, Menning was replaced by Beverly Malden.

The game was unchanged from the original, with two couples still competing against each other to answer questions. A right answer gave a team the option of keeping or giving away an oversized playing card from an otherwise regulation deck in a game of blackjack. The object of the game was to score exactly twenty-one before your opponent did, or get as close as possible to twenty-one without going over.

The team that won the game played the "Gambit Bonus Board" with the added element of using members of the studio audience as "living playing cards." After a prize was revealed on the game board, a name was selected from the "Living Deck." The deck consisted of fifty-two people in the audience, each of whom was holding a concealed playing card. The members of the audience who were chosen received the same prizes won by the contestants on stage. The goal was to pick prizes and keep their point total under twenty-one. The team had the option of quitting at any time and keeping what they had won.

THE LAST WORD

premiere: September 18, 1989 *packager:* Merrill Heatter Productions *broadcast history:* Syndicated September 18, 1989–January 5, 1990 *host:* Wink Martindale *announcer/cohost:* Jennifer Lyall *executive producers:* Merrill Heatter, Art Alisi, Steve Friedman *director:* Henry Irizawa *set designer:* John Mula *music:* Score Productions *origination:* Vancouver, Canada *debut guests:* Ted Lange and Jill Whelan

Two teams, composed of a celebrity guest and a studio contestant, attempted to guess sets of words that had something in common, from randomly selected letters. On "The Last Word" the team that guessed the last word in a set of three won the game and prizes. The first team to win two games won the match.

One member from each team played at a time and the game began with spaces for three words revealed. Several free letters were filled in and the teams alternated in stopping a selector that revealed a letter in one of the three words. After a letter was revealed, a player could attempt to guess the word or pass control on to his or her opponent.

Correctly guessing a word earned the player a prize, but only the team that identified the last word was entitled to keep their prizes. If the selector stopped on a letter already revealed, the player had to choose a free letter for his or her opponent to see. If a player made an incorrect guess at a word, the computer typed in only the correct letters from the guess. It revealed the correct letters only and then stopped. This gave the opposing team a clue for their guess. The teams switched players for the second game and the first team that won two games became the champion.

The winning team played the "sixty-second challenge" for bonus prizes by trying to solve the last word in a series of ten puzzles in under one minute. They were shown two words and blank spaces for the letters of a third word related to the first two. Random letters were revealed one at a time in the third word until it was correctly guessed. The player received $100 for each word guessed and a prize package if he or she solved all ten in the allotted time.

LAUGH LINE

premiere: April 16, 1959 *packager:* SRO Productions *broadcast history:* NBC primetime April 16, 1959–June 11, 1959 *host:* Dick Van Dyke *announcer:* Tom Reddy *producers:* Frank Wayne, Mace Neufeld *director:* Seymour Robbie *set designer:* Ted Cooper *music director:* Elliott Lawrence *origination:* NBC Studio 6B, New York *debut guests:* Orson Bean, Elaine May, Mike Nichols, Dorothy Loudon

A celebrity panel created funny captions, known as "laugh lines," for living cartoons acted out by a stock company. Regular panelists included Elaine May, Mike Nichols, Dorothy Loudin, Pat Harrington Jr., and Roger Price.

The living cartoons on "Laugh Lines" were suggested by home viewers who described a humorous situation, positioned the actors and actresses, and created a caption. Each member of the panel repositioned the actors and actresses, changed their facial expressions, and used items on the set to create new captions. Audience applause determined how much money was awarded to the home viewer (from $5 to $25). Each member of the panel was given a chance to create a "laugh line" for each situation.

Did you know . . . this would be the last game show that Emmy-winning actor/comedian Dick Van Dyke would emcee? Soon after this show Van Dyke would star on Broadway in *Bye Bye Birdie*, move to the small screen with the award-winning "The Dick Van Dyke Show," and then to the big screen for roles in *Mary Poppins, Chitty-Chitty Bang Bang,* and *Cold Turkey.*

LEGENDS OF THE HIDDEN TEMPLE

premiere: September 11, 1993 *packager:* Stone-Stanley Productions *broadcast history:* Nickelodeon (cable) September 11, 1993– *host:* Kirk Fogg *announcer/voice of Olmec:* Dee Baker *executive producers:* David G. Stanley, Scott A. Stone, Stephen Brown *supervising producer:* Angelika Bartenbach *director:* Charles Ciup *production designer:* Byron Taylor *art director:* David Kahler *music:* The Music Machine *origination:* Nickelodeon Studios, Orlando

Six teams, each comprised of two kids, competed in a Mayan-ruin setting in a test of their physical and mental skills that included searching for legendary artifacts. Teams were eliminated throughout the game until only one remained.

Each game in "Legends of the Hidden Temple" consisted of three rounds, beginning with a race across a water-filled moat. The first four teams to complete the moat moved on to the second round.

In round two, "Olmec" told the legend of the day, and the teams competed in the "Steps of Knowledge." Teams tried to answer questions based on the information given and attempted to be one of the first two teams to reach the bottom step (three right answers).

The two remaining teams moved on to the "Temple Games," where they competed in three tests of physical strength and skill in order to acquire "Pendants of Life." Each game related to the day's legend and involved stunts and obstacle courses. The team with the most pendants won the game and got a chance to enter the temple to search for the day's artifacts.

The temple contained thirteen rooms of obstacles and games that the winning team had to maneuver through in less than three minutes to reach the treasure of the day. They could use their Pendants of Life to thwart temple guards (actors dressed as Mayan warriors).

LET'S CELEBRATE

premiere: December 15, 1946 *packager:* Young and Rubicam *broadcast history:* NBC primetime December 15, 1946 (special) *host:* Mel Allen *producer:* Wes McKee *director:* Edward Sobol *origination:* NBC Studio 8G, New York

Not much is known about "Let's Celebrate," this show that was seen as a one-time special. It was packaged by Young and Rubicam for their client Borden's. Members of the studio audience competed in stunts for prizes. New York Yankees baseball announcer Mel Allen was host.

Did you know . . . Mel Allen was the voice of the New York Yankees from 1939 to 1964? Broadcaster Red Barber and he were the first two baseball announcers inducted into the Baseball Hall of Fame in 1978.

LET'S GO BACK

premiere: July 6, 1991 *packager:* Scott Sternberg Productions *broadcast history:* Nostalgia Channel (cable) July 6, 1991–May 31, 1993 *host:* Scott Sternberg *announcer:* Charlie O'Donnell *creator/executive producer:* Scott Sternberg *producer:* Dave Williger *director:* Mark Corwin *set designer:* Tom Buderwitz *origination:* Studio 2, Glendale Studios in 1991; Empire Studios in Burbank in 1992

Three contestants competed in a test of their knowledge of the music, movies, and television of the 1950s, 60s, 70s, and 80s in "Let's Go Back." Each game board consisted of five categories with four questions in each category (one question for each decade).

In round one, the value of the questions was worth ten points and a player lost ten points for an incorrect guess. In the second round, the value of the questions was doubled. Each round also contained a "time capsule" question that was worth double-points and a bonus prize. Bonus prizes included a set of "I Like Ike" campaign buttons, a Ben Casey medical kit, and a John Travolta doll.

The scores after two rounds determined the player's position in round three, "The Decades Round." The player with the highest score needed only four correct answers to win the game, the next highest score needed five answers, and the last player six answers. All questions in this round were answered with the particular decade in which an event took place. The first player to reach zero won the game and $500.

LET'S MAKE A DEAL

premiere: December 30, 1963 *packager:* Stefan Hatos–Monty Hall Productions (1963–1986); Ron Greenberg–Dick Clark Productions (1990–1991) *broadcast history:* NBC daytime December 30, 1963–December 27, 1968; NBC primetime May 21, 1967–September 3, 1967; ABC daytime December 30, 1968–July 9, 1976; ABC primetime February 7, 1969–August 30, 1971; Syndicated September 13, 1971–September 1977; Syndicated September 22, 1980–September 1981; Syndicated September 17, 1984–September 1986; USA (cable) December 29, 1986–December 30, 1988 (repeats of the 1984–1986 series); NBC daytime July 9, 1990–January 11, 1991; Family Channel (cable) June 7, 1993–March 29, 1996 (repeats of the 1971–1977 series and 1984–1986 series)

1963–1977 version

host: Monty Hall *substitute hosts:* Geoff Edwards, Dennis James, Tom Kelly, Bill Leyden *models:* Carol Merrill, Claudia Brock, Barbara Lyon *announcer:* Jay Stewart *executive producer:* Stefan Hatos *producer:* Alan Gilbert *director:* Joe Behar *set designers:* Robert Kelly, John Shrum, Richard James *music director:* Ivan Ditmars *theme:* Sheldon Allman *origination:* NBC Studios 1 and 3, Burbank (1963–1968); Studio D, ABC Television Center, Los Angeles (1968–1976); Hilton Hotel, Las Vegas (1976–1977)

1980–1981 version

host: Monty Hall *announcer:* Chuck Chandler *producer:* Ian MacLennan *director:* Geoff Theobald *set designer:* Donald Halton *origination:* Panorama Studios, Vancouver

1984–1986 version

host: Monty Hall *models:* Melanie Vincz, Karen LaPierre *announcers:* Brian Cummings, Dean Goss *executive producer:* Stefan Hatos *producers:* Bob Synes, Alan Gilbert *directors:* Joe Behar, Hank Behar *set designers:* Ray Klausen, Molly Joseph, Bob Rappaport *music:* Todd Thicke, Sheldon Allman *origination:* NBC Studio 4, Burbank (1984–1985); Studio 6, Hollywood Center Studios, Los Angeles (1985–1986)

1990–1991 version

hosts: Bob Hilton, Monty Hall *models:* Georgia Sattelle, Diane, Elaine Klimaszewski *announcer:* Dean Miuccio *executive producers:* Dick Clark, Ron Greenberg *producers:* Bruce Starin, Paul Pieratt *directors:* Barry Glazer, Jim Marcione *set designers:* Anthony Sabatino, William H. Harris, Scott Storey *music:* Jerry Ray *origination:* Studio 1, Disney-MGM Studios, Orlando

"Let's Make a Deal" was one of the most popular television game shows of the 1960s. Thirty-three contestants were selected from the studio audience before air time and became the day's possible traders. They swapped items brought with them or played pricing games for gifts in oversized boxes or behind curtains, with the chance that the prize hidden might either be something more valuable or a worthless piece of junk called a "zonk."

Host Monty Hall might trade with one, two, or three people on each deal and give them several options during the deal. At the end of the show, two players were given a chance to trade once more for the "Big Deal of the Day," hidden behind one of three doors.

The contestants on the trading floor did not wear costumes until sometime in 1964 when one player wore a costume to attract Monty's attention. Before long, everyone was wearing outlandish costumes.

Announcer Jay Stewart was frequently seen on camera bringing items in on a tray or participating in the zonks. Carol Merrill was the model for the entire network run. Claudia Brock and Barbara Lyon filled in during Carol's absence in

Seeing Monty Hall and sidekick Jay Stewart without a studio audience of contestants wearing clever and colorful costumes was like seeing Dorothy in Kansas. Within a year of its 1963 debut, producer Stefan Hatos and Hall had evolved "Let's Make a Deal" into a magical form of entertainment equivalent to the land of Oz.

1967. Barbara Lyon was also seen on the 1967 primetime version.

"Let's Make a Deal" made two appearances in primetime. NBC ran a Sunday night version in the summer of 1967 and ABC carried the show from February 1969 to August 1971.

"Let's Make a Deal" returned to production as a syndicated series twice, in 1980 with a season of shows taped in Vancouver, Canada and in 1984, with Los Angeles–based shows. Carol Merrill and Jay Stewart made a surprise visit on the last first-run show in 1986.

NBC brought "Let's Make a Deal" back as a network show with a daytime edition that was seen from July 1990 to January 1991. Bob Hilton hosted this version that was taped at the Disney/MGM Studios in Orlando, Florida. Monty Hall followed Hilton as the host of "Let's Make a Deal" in the fall of 1990.

Repeats of "Let's Make a Deal" aired on the USA cable network from December 1986 to December 1988 and on the Family Channel starting in June 1993.

Did you know . . .   Monty Hall's career began in his native Canada where he emceed and produced the long-running "Who Am I?" and "Auctioneer"? He debuted on American television, serving as substitute for Warren Hull on STRIKE IT RICH. Monty was heard on NBC's radio series "Monitor" for over four years.

In the fourteen-year run of "Let's Make a Deal" as a network show, it broke all records for game show popularity with Monty Hall as host. In its first year "Let's Make a Deal" cut deeply into the audience of the CBS soap opera "As the World Turns." In 1967 (when "Let's Make a Deal" went primetime) it became the only show ever to compete successfully with "The Ed Sullivan Show" on CBS and "The FBI" on ABC.

When "Let's Make a Deal" left the NBC daytime schedule to move to the ABC (December 30, 1968) daytime schedule, NBC soon lost millions in daytime advertising revenue and ABC became the number-one daytime network.

Monty Hall is one of the select few game show emcees who has his star on the Hollywood Walk of Fame. Monty was also the Mayor of Hollywood for many years.

Monty Hall was featured on the national cover of *TV Guide*, January 21–27, 1984.

Monty Hall was named "Humanitarian of the Year" by Variety Club, and received other top honors from around the country and the world for his generous charity work.

Sheldon Allman, composer of the "Let's Make a Deal" theme, also wrote the theme to the classic cartoon series "George of the Jungle."

Were you watching when . . .   Monty Hall did several walk-ons on THE DATING GAME, DREAM HOUSE, and THE NEWLYWED GAME to promote the move of "Let's Make a Deal" to the ABC daytime schedule in 1968?

Monty Hall was the guest emcee of PASSWORD in 1972 when regular "Password" host Allen Ludden played against wife Betty White.

Monty Hall guest-starred on these top television shows: "The Odd Couple" (twice!), "That Girl" (playing a dentist treating Marlo Thomas's toothache), "The Wonder Years," "The Tonight Show," "The Hollywood Palace," both "Phil Donahue" and "Geraldo" (where Monty was saluted as a game show legend), "The Rosie O'Donnell Show," and other talk, game, and sitcom shows.

LET'S PLAY POST OFFICE

premiere: September 27, 1965   *packager:* Merv Griffin Productions   *broadcast history:* NBC daytime September 27, 1965–July 1, 1966   *host:* Don Morrow   *announcers:* Bill Wendell, Wayne Howell   *creator:* Louise Adamo   *producer:* Ron Greenberg   *director:* Dick Schneider   *set designer:* Tom Trimble   *music director:* Paul Taubman   *origination:* NBC Studio 6A, New York

In "Let's Play Post Office," three studio contestants were read "letters" written by a famous person and tried to guess the identity of the author from clues hidden in the letter. The faster the player guessed the identity of the author, the more money he or she could win.

The players were seated on a set that resembled the stamp windows in a post office and the letter was shown, one line at a time, on a game board shaped like a giant envelope.

When the game began, the stamp on the envelope showed the opening value of the letter, from $5 to $100, and the cancellation mark provided a clue by identifying the place the letter was written and the year it was composed. Contestants could momentarily interrupt the game when they felt they knew the identity of the writer. Play would continue until all players made their guesses. The value of the letter decreased as more of the letter was revealed. Those with correct answers received the value of the letter when they stopped the game.

The day's game concluded with a "zip round," in which five brief telegram-like messages were flashed on a screen and the contestants tried to buzz in and guess the "sender." Each correct guess was worth $25 and wrong answers cost a player $25. The high-scoring player at the end of the day returned on the next show.

Did you know . . .   host Don Morrow was the voice of the Shell Answer Man in Shell's commercials for eighteen years?

LET'S SEE

premiere: July 14, 1955   *packager:* John Reed King Productions   *broadcast history:* ABC primetime July 14, 1955–August 25, 1955   *host:* John Reed King   *announcer:* Al Owen   *producer:* John Reed King   *director:* Bob Springer   *origination:* Atlantic City

This weekly series, "Let's See," was broadcast from the Convention Hall on the Steel Pier in Atlantic City, New Jersey. A celebrity panel had up to four minutes to guess what a studio contestant had seen that day. Panelists on the debut show were singer Felix Knight, boxer Tony Canzoneri, and Miss America 1952, Colleen Hutchinson.

LETTERS TO LAUGH-IN

premiere: September 29, 1969 *packager:* Schlatter-Friendly-Romart Productions   *broadcast history:* NBC daytime September 29, 1969–December 26, 1969   *host:* Gary Owens   *producers:* Alan Neuman, Stan Dreben   *director:* Alan Levi   *set designer:* Ken Johnson   *music director:* Russ Freeman   *origination:* NBC Studio 2, Burbank   *debut week guests:* Ruth Buzzi, Jack Carter, Jill St. John, Dick Martin

This daytime game show, "Letters to Laugh-In," was emceed by "Laugh-In" regular and Los Angeles–based nationally known radio personality Gary Owens. Four celebrities, including a cast member of "Rowan and Martin's Laugh-In," told jokes submitted by home viewers before a "joke jury" of ten members of the studio audience who rated the performances on a scale from zero to one hundred. Prizes were awarded for the best and worst jokes of the day. The best and worst of the week also received grand prizes: a vacation to Hawaii for the best joke and seven days in downtown Burbank for the worst.

Did you know . . . in 1969 host Gary Owens was a regular on America's number-one rated television series, "Laugh-In," a regular on PBS's "Sesame Street" (as Letter Man), and a national radio personality with a successful syndicated radio series?

While hosting "Letters to Laugh-In," Gary Owens supplied his voice for countless successful national commercials, network specials, and dozens of classic cartoons. He was the voice of Roger Ramjet and the voice of Space Ghost. Today

It's "Letters to Laugh-In" and here's Gary Owens displaying thousands of jokes sent in by home viewers.

he is the voice of Powdered Toastman on the successful "Ren and Stimpy" cartoon and is also heard on a dozen other shows.

Were you watching when . . . these "Laugh-In" regulars were guest celebrities on "Letters to Laugh-In": Chelsea Brown, Judy Carne, Dick Martin, Dan Rowan, Alan Sues, and Jo Anne Worley?

LIARS

premiere: July 10, 1995   *packager:* Foxlab in association with Giant Bowling Pin Productions   *broadcast history:* Syndicated July 10, 1995–September 29, 1995   *host:* Fran Solomita   *lie detector expert:* Joe Paolella   *executive producer:* Kathy Cotter   *producers:* Seth Howard, Mashawn Nix, Wayne Waddell   *coordinating producer:* Rikk Greengrass   *director:* C. F. Bien   *art director:* John Ivo Gilles   *music:* Trey Parker   *origination:* Empire Studios, Burbank

On this daily syndicated series, one person accused another of some misdeed (e.g., "My brother is sleeping with my girlfriend").

Both players were interviewed by the host, and then a panel of three experts (the first show featured reporter Yolanda Gaskins, educator Dee Rubin, and Roger Clinton, brother of President Bill Clinton) voted on whether the accused player was telling the truth. The final test was administered by a polygraph expert who asked the accused four questions while that player was hooked up to a lie detector.

Did you know . . . Trey Parker, who wrote the theme music for "Liars," is the cocreator of the popular animated series "South Park," seen on Comedy Central?

LIARS CLUB

premiere: January 20, 1969   *packagers:* Ralph Andrews Productions (1969–1979); Four Star/Golden West Productions/Northstar Productions (1988–1989)   *broadcast history:* Syndicated January 20, 1969–June 13, 1969; Syndicated September 1976–September 1979; Syndicated October 3, 1988–June 30, 1989
1969 version
host: Rod Serling   *announcer:* Jim Isaics   *producers:* Ralph Andrews, Army Grant   *director:* Bill Chestnutt   *origination:* KTTV, Los Angeles
1976–1979 version
hosts: Bill Armstrong (1976), Allen Ludden (1977–1979)   *announcers:* Bill Berry, Joe Seiter   *executive producer:* Larry Hovis   *producers:* Joe Seiter, Sandy Lang   *directors:* Dick McDonough, Charlie Stark   *set designer:* John C. Mula   *origination:* KTLA Studio 6, Los Angeles
1988–1989 version
host: Eric Boardman   *announcer:* Bill Armstrong   *executive producers:* Bill Armstrong, Blair Murdoch, Jeff Simmons   *producer:* Blair Murdoch   *director:* Stan Litke   *origination:* Vancouver, Canada

Four contestants tried to guess which of four celebrity panelists was telling a true story about the function of a strange or unusual object, in "Liars Club." Players began with $100 and could bet up to half of their total in each of several

A rare shot of David Letterman as a celebrity liar on "Liar's Club." From left to right are Dick Gautier, Betty White, David Letterman, Larry Hovis, and emcee Allen Ludden.

rounds. Each round had different point values and if a player guessed right in every round he or she won a bonus prize.

"Liars Club" made its debut in January 1969 with "Twilight Zone" host Rod Serling as emcee. The second version of "Liars Club" appeared in September 1976 with TV producer Bill Armstrong as host. Allen Ludden followed Armstrong as host in the spring of 1977 and continued until the show ended in September 1979. Eric Boardman hosted the third version of "Liars Club," taped in Canada, that was seen in the 1988–1989 season.

Did you know . . . Bill Cullen, Bob Eubanks, Tom Kennedy, David Letterman, and Peter Marshall were all guest panelists on " Liars Club"?

Were you watching when . . . Charlton Heston made a surprise visit to the set of "Liars Club" to say hello to his pal Allen Ludden in 1978?

LIFE WITH LINKLETTER

premiere: October 6, 1950   *packager:* John Guedel Productions   *broadcast history:* ABC primetime October 6, 1950–April 25, 1952   *host:* Art Linkletter   *announcer:* Jack Slattery   *producers:* Irvin Atkins, John Guedel   *director:* Stuart

Phelps   *set designer:* Hank Gilbert   *music:* Muzzy Marcellino   *origination:* Studio E, ABC Television Center, Los Angeles

Radio personality Art Linkletter hosted his first television show, "Life with Linkletter," in this Friday night series that was based on his long-running radio series "House Party." The show featured members of the studio audience competing in stunts, as well as humorous interviews with children.

"House Party," which debuted on radio in 1944, came to television in September 1952 as a daytime series five months after "Life with Linkletter" left the air. It remained on the CBS schedule for seventeen years. Art Linkletter returned with another primetime series, PEOPLE ARE FUNNY, in 1954.

"Life with Linkletter" was also known as THE ART LINKLETTER SHOW.

Did you know . . . "Life with Linkletter" was broadcast from the same studio where the silent film classic *Phantom of the Opera* was filmed in the 1920s?

LINGO

premiere: September 28, 1987   *packager:* Ralph Andrews Productions/Bernstein-Hovis Productions   *broadcast his-*

tory: Syndicated September 28, 1987–September 1988 *hosts:* Michael Reagan, Ralph Andrews *hostesses:* Dusty Martell, Margaux McKenzie *executive producers:* Gary Bernstein, Larry Hovis, Ralph Andrews, William C. Elliott *producers:* Lou Valenzi, Heather Hawthorne-Doyle *directors:* Geoff Theobald, Michael Watt   *set designer:* Ed Flesh *origination:* Vancouver, Canada

"Lingo" aired for one season show and tested a player's knowledge of five-letter words. Two teams of two players competed and each team was given a "Lingo" card divided into five columns of five rows of numbers. The returning champs had even numbers, the challengers odd numbers. The object of the game was to cover one line on the card horizontally, vertically, or diagonally.

One team played at a time and was given the first letter of a five-letter word. If they failed to identify the correct word, a square was placed around any letters that were in the right place of the "Lingo" word. A circle was placed around letters that were in the word, but were not in their proper place. The team was given five chances to guess the word and, if successful, then covered two numbers on their game board. The numbers covered were determined after selecting two balls. The balls contained either a number on the game board, a bonus prize to play for, or a red ball, which caused the team to lose control of the game to their opponents. Control of the game also switched if the team could not guess the word in five tries. The first team to fill in a line won the game and $250. The losing team received $100.

The winning team played a bonus round with a new "Lingo" board and the chance to win $1,000. Sixteen numbers on the board were covered and thirty-five numbered balls were put in a hopper. The team was given two letters of a five-letter word and the number of balls to be selected was determined by the number of guesses needed to identify the word. The team won the money if they avoided filling in a line on their board.

Michael Reagan, son of President Ronald Reagan, was the original host of "Lingo." He was replaced for the last five weeks of the show by producer Ralph Andrews.

LIP SERVICE

premiere: February 22, 1992   *packager:* MTV Networks *broadcast history:* MTV (cable) February 22, 1992–January 3, 1993; MTV (cable) May 10, 1993–December 17, 1994 *hosts:* Jay Mohr, John Ales   *"DJ's":* T-Money, Spinderella (Dee Dee Roper) *announcer:* Laurie Allen *creators:* McPaul Smith, James Greenberg   *executive producer:* Lauren Corrao   *supervising producer:* Eileen Katz   *producers:* Risa Graubard, Gerri Bulion   *line producer:* Laurie Rich *directors:* Milton Lage, Richie Namm   *production designers:* James Fenhagen, Eric Ulfers, Mitchell Greenberg *music:* Anton Delano, Peter Balogh   *origination:* MTI Television City, New York

Two teams of three contestants lip-synched popular songs before a panel of celebrity judges. The teams in "Lip Service" competed in three rounds with the winning team of the season getting a chance to appear in their own video for the MTV network.

Round one, "The Deadly Medley," featured the players singing to excerpts from popular songs played in succession without the contestants knowing what song was coming up next. The players rotated as each new song was started. Each of three celebrity judges rated the teams after each round, on a scale of one to ten.

In round two, "The Flip Sync," the process was reversed. Each contestant sang one minute of the song while the superstar artist was seen lip-synching.

"The Scratch Factor" was the final round and each team performed a song that they had rehearsed in advance. The "scratch" catch was that the show's resident DJ could tamper with the recording by speeding it up, slowing it down, or altering the sound. The teams were scored on their ability to adapt to the changing soundtrack.

The team with the highest score of the day won a prize and the chance to return for the end-of-the-season competition.

The first season of "Lip Service" featured stand-up comedian Jay Mohr as host and "T-Money" as the resident DJ. They were replaced by John Ales and Spinderella in the second season.

LIVE LIKE A MILLIONAIRE

premiere: January 5, 1951   *packager:* Masterson-Reddy-Nelson Productions   *broadcast history:* CBS primetime January 5, 1951–March 14, 1952; ABC primetime October 18, 1952–February 7, 1953   *hosts:* Jack McCoy, John Nelson *announcers:* John Nelson, Jack Gregson, Michael Fitzmaurice *assistants:* Connie Clawson, Michael O'Halloran   *producer:* Jerry Browne   *director:* Ed Leftwich *music director:* Ivan Ditmars   *origination:* New York

On "Live Like a Millionaire," a family variety-talent show, children presented their parents, who then competed in a talent contest for the chance to win a week's interest on $1,000,000 and a vacation. Each child received a bicycle or camera for bringing his or her parents onto the show and audience applause determined the winner.

Jack McCoy was the original host and announcer John Nelson replaced him on March 30, 1951. Jack Gregson became the new announcer at that time. Michael O'Halloran was the original assistant and was later replaced by Connie Clawson.

LOVE AT FIRST SIGHT

premiere: June 1, 1992   *packager:* Action Time Productions/Paramount Television   *broadcast history:* Syndicated June 1, 1992–August 14, 1992   *host:* Jeff MacGregor   *creator:* Stephen Leahy   *producer:* Bruce Leddy   *director:* Robert Hersh   *set designers:* John Shaffner, Joe Stewart   *music director:* Stephen Trecasse   *origination:* Chelsea Television Studios, New York

Jeff MacGregor, who hosted "The All New Dating Game" from 1987 to 1989, was the emcee of "Love at First Sight," this summertime relationship show where six complete strangers matched wits, tried to strike sparks, and sought love at first sight. Two teams, one composed of three single men and the other of three single women, competed on this daily syndicated show that was seen on a limited number of stations in the summer of 1992.

The players competed in five rounds to learn more about each other. The first round was a word-association round, where two players, one from each team, bantered back and forth associating words, after the host started them off. In the second round, "Hot Line," two players left messages for a member of the opposing team corresponding to such situations as "You're bringing your new date home for the weekend. Leave a message for your mother about how much she will love your new date." In round three, players answered questions like "What are three things you're very good at?" to give insight into their personalities. After this round, each of the six players secretly indicated the member of the opposing team that they were most interested in dating.

The game continued with round four where players were given a chance to ask members of the opposite sex personal questions and in the final round each player described a talent they believed impressed the opposite sex. The women went first and the men chose one of them to display her talent. The situation was then reversed.

After the fifth round, each player chose the contestant he or she wanted to date. The couple won a trip if a match was made.

LOVE BETWEEN THE SEXES

premiere: September 15, 1992   *packager:* Black Entertainment Television   *broadcast history:* BET (cable) September 15, 1992–January 16, 1993   *host:* Harold McCoo   *announcer:* Connie Briley   *executive producers:* Cindy Mahmoud, Curtis Gadson, Lathan Hodge   *senior producer:* Dru Gibson   *director:* Ricardo Johnson   *set designer:* Scott Perkins   *theme music:* Khalid Keene, Brian Overton for K.O. Productions   *origination:* BET Studios, Alexandria

BET cable entered the relationship game show arena in September 1992 with "Love Between the Sexes," seen Tuesdays, Thursdays, and Saturdays. In the first part of the program, an unmarried woman met three eligible men. She was shown a short video profile of each man and then asked each of them questions to learn more about their personalities.

The members of the "peanut gallery" (six regular panelists—three men and three women who played for members of the studio audience) tried to predict who the woman would choose for her date. The panel received $200 for each time they guessed correctly.

In the second half of the show, the panel attempted to guess if there was a "love match" between a returning couple who were put together on an earlier show. Each member of the panel predicted "Yes" or "No" and received $200 for each time they judged correctly.

LOVE CONNECTION

premiere: September 19, 1983   *packager:* Eric Lieber Productions   *broadcast history:* Syndicated September 19, 1983–September 1994   *host:* Chuck Woolery   *announcers:* Rod Roddy, Gene Wood, Johnny Gilbert, Rich Jeffries, John Cervenka   *executive producer:* Eric Lieber   *producers:* Sid Marsh, Tom Weitzel, Louise Brooks, Tom McConnell, John

Love was in the air while Chuck Woolery hosted the long-running "Love Connection."

Ryder   *directors:* Paul Miller, Deborah Miller, Tom McConnell   *set designer:* Ray Klausen   *origination:* ABC Television Center, Los Angeles; TAV Theater, Hollywood; Hollywood Center Studios, Hollywood

"Love Connection" was the successful video dating game show that matched up couples who then went out on a first date and returned to the show to detail what happened. Over 2,000 episodes were produced between September 19, 1983 and July 1, 1994.

Potential contestants filled out questionnaires about their ideal dates and romantic tastes. They were then shown three videos of members of the opposite sex, from which they selected one person for a date. After the date, both players came back on the show to describe what happened on their first date.

The studio audience also selected from the three videos the person who they felt suited best the player. The player was then offered the opportunity to go out on a date with that person if he or she wished.

THE LOVE EXPERTS

premiere: September 18, 1978   *packager:* Bob Stewart Productions   *broadcast history:* Syndicated September 18, 1978–September 1979   *host:* Bill Cullen   *announcers:* Jack Clark, Jay Stewart   *executive producer:* Bob Stewart   *producer:* Anne-Marie Schmidt   *directors:* Bruce Burmester,

Geoff Edwards chuckles as host Bill Cullen gives his fatherly advice to a love-troubled contestant on "The Love Experts."

Mike Garguilo **set designer:** Henry Lickel **origination:** TAV Studios, Hollywood

A panel of four celebrities gave advice to contestants on matters of love and romance on "The Love Experts." At the end of the show, the four "love experts" selected the contestant who had the most unique or interesting love problem. The winning contestant won a prize or trip.

Among the regular celebrities who appeared on "The Love Experts" were Elayne Boosler, Jack Carter, Jamie Lee Curtis, Geoff Edwards, Anita Gillette, Elaine Joyce, Peter Lawford, David Letterman, and Soupy Sales.

LOVE ME, LOVE ME NOT

premiere: September 29, 1986 **packager:** Entertainment Planning Corporation/MGM Television **broadcast history:** USA (cable) September 29, 1986–September 11, 1987 **host:** Ross Shafer **cohost/announcer:** Marilyn Smith **creator:**

Steve Carlin **executive producers:** Steve Carlin, Blair Murdoch **producer:** Mark Phillips **director:** Stan Litke **set designer:** Ron Baldwin **origination:** CKVU-TV, Vancouver, Canada

Three men and two women were the players in this daily game show, "Love Me, Love Me Not," taped in Vancouver, Canada for the USA cable network. The object was for one of the two women to "catch" more men than her opponent could. Each male player gave a statement and each woman, playing one at a time, guessed if it was true or false. If the man fooled her he received $100, but if she guessed correctly he was captured. The female player with the most men and the male player with the most money won the game and played the bonus round.

The bonus round was played on an eight-petal daisy, with one player situated at petal number one and the other at petal number six. One player was given forty seconds to answer true-false questions. Correct responses enabled the player to move one step at a time until reaching his or her opponent. The player who reached an opponent in the allotted time won a bonus gift.

LOVE STORY

premiere: October 24, 1955 **packager:** Proctor and Gamble Productions **broadcast history:** CBS daytime October 24, 1955–March 30, 1956 **host:** Jack Smith **assistant:** Pat Meikle **announcer:** Fred Waldecker **producers:** Robert Quigley, Art Stark **director:** Freddie Batholomew **music director:** Paul Taubman **origination:** New York

"Love Story," this daytime series, began as a segment on the show "Welcome Travelers" and replaced it on October 24, 1955. Two people in love guested on the show and told their story. Host Jack Smith sang a song that had some special meaning for them and the couple tried to answer questions for $500 in cash and merchandise prizes. Any couple that answered all the questions attempted to answer the jackpot question for a trip for two to Paris, an automobile, and an additional $500.

LUCKY PARTNERS

premiere: June 30, 1958 **packager:** Martin and Allen Stone Productions **broadcast history:** NBC daytime June 30, 1958–August 22, 1958 **host:** Carl Cordell **hostesses:** Doris Wiss, Lynn Dollar, Karen Thorsell **announcer:** Fred Collins **executive producer:** Martin Stone **producer:** Carl Jampel **director:** Dick Schneider **set designer:** Otis Riggs Jr. **music directors:** John Gart, Billy Nale **origination:** NBC Studio 8H, New York

Contestants from the studio audience and players on stage tried to match serial numbers on dollar bills in "Lucky Partners," this short-lived series. Questions answered by five panelists determined which numbers on a large board of columns were put into play. To complete the required pattern and be eligible for prizes, viewers used bingo-type cards on which dollar serial-numbers were the key figures.

MADE IN AMERICA

premiere: April 5, 1964 *packager:* Steve Carlin Productions/MGM Television *broadcast history:* CBS primetime April 5, 1964–May 3, 1964 *host:* Hans Conreid *announcer:* Hal Simms *producer:* Steve Carlin *director:* Jerome Shaw *set designers:* Ron Baldwin, John Ward *origination:* CBS Studio 61, New York *debut guests:* Don Murray, Jan Sterling, Walter Slezak

A celebrity panel tried to guess in what manner the contestants made their fortunes on this short-lived Sunday night game show, "Made in America." All the contestants were self-made millionaires and they donated their winnings to charity (up to a possible $600) if they stumped the entire panel.

The millionaires were Martha Parks of Black Magic Inc., manufacturers of the first organic plant food for home use; James Caldwell of the Rubbermaid Corporation, manufacturers of household rubber products; and internationally known writer Fannie Hurst.

Each of the contestants was interviewed by host Hans Conreid to provide clues for the panel.

The show was called "I Made a Million" before its premiere, and it also had a different host. Broadcasting personality Bob Maxwell, who hosted DO YOU KNOW?, a children's informational series for CBS, was announced as host. Just before the first broadcast he was replaced by actor Hans Conreid. Conreid was best known as "Uncle Tonoose" on "The Danny Thomas Show" and as the voice of Snidley Whiplash in the Dudley Do-Right cartoons.

THE MAGNIFICENT MARBLE MACHINE

premiere: July 7, 1975 *packager:* Merrill Heatter–Bob Quigley Productions *broadcast history:* NBC daytime July 7, 1975–January 2, 1976; NBC daytime January 19, 1976–June 11, 1976 *host:* Art James *announcer:* Johnny Gilbert *executive producers:* Merrill Heatter, Bob Quigley, Robert Noah *producers:* Bob Synes, Art Alisi *directors:* Jerome Shaw, Lou Fusari *set designer:* Jim Newton *music:* Mort Garson *origination:* NBC Studio 4, Burbank *debut guests:* Florence Henderson, Roddy McDowell

Two teams, each composed of a celebrity guest and a contestant, guessed names and phrases from clues provided by an electronic printout on "The Magnificent Marble Machine." Players were told both the number of letters and words. Letters were revealed if neither team could guess correctly from the original clue; for example: "A Big Jungle Swinger" for "Tarzan"; "Sore Throat Advice" for "Gargle."

Emcee Art James and guest stars Jim McKrell and Chuck Woolery on the set of "The Magnificent Marble Machine."

The first team to score five points won the game and played an oversized pinball machine for cash and prizes. Each team member worked a "flipper" on the machine and tried to keep a ball in play for as long as possible. If a player could reach a score of fifteen thousand points after playing two balls, he or she won a grand prize.

Did you know . . . the giant pinball set took over sixty days to build? The machine contained two hundred fifty pounds of nails, four miles of wiring, thirty-eight gallons of glue, twenty-three coiled springs, enough glass for ten car windshields, twenty-five two-pound balls, and fourteen gallons of gold paint for the pinballs used.

Art James was one of a handful of successful emcees to have a show canceled on a Friday and on the next Monday have a brand-new series. His series, BLANK CHECK, was canceled by NBC on July 4, 1975 and on July 7, 1975 Art was hosting "The Magnificent Marble Machine."

Were you watching when . . . both Peter Marshall and Alex Trebek were celebrity guest stars and played opposite each other? Marshall was hosting the popular THE HOLLYWOOD SQUARES and Trebek was hosting HIGH ROLLERS. Both shows were created by Merrill Heatter and Bob Quigley, as was "The Magnificent Marble Machine." Throughout the 1970s the team of Heatter-Quigley often dominated the NBC daytime schedule.

MAJORITY RULES

premiere: September 2, 1949   *packager:* Dawson and Gingrich   *broadcast history:* ABC primetime September 2, 1949–July 30, 1950   *hosts:* Ed Prentiss, Tom Moore, Myron (Mike) Wallace   *announcer:* Jack Lester   *producers:* Anthony Rizzo, Stu Dawson, Harold Gingrich, Fred Killian   *directors:* Greg Garrison, Fred Killian   *origination:* WENR-TV, Chicago

This early ABC network game show is best known for introducing a young Mike (then known as Myron) Wallace to a national audience. He became host of "Majority Rules" on May 21, 1950.

Experts gave true or false answers to questions sent in by viewers. Every time the majority of the three panelists gave incorrect answers, the viewer sending in the question received $10. If all three panelists were wrong, the viewer won the amount contained in a treasure chest.

MAJORITY RULES

premiere: August 5, 1996   *packager:* Dream Works Television   *broadcast history:* Syndicated August 5, 1996–January 1997   *hosts:* Marc Summers, Arthel Neville   *creator/executive producer:* Mark Maxwell-Smith   *associate producer:* Leonard Koss   *director:* Glenn Weiss   *production designer:* Jimmy Cuomo   *music:* Scooter Pietsch   *origination:* NBC Studio 1, Burbank

"Majority Rules" was the first game show to come from Steven Spielberg's studio DreamWorks. It began as a test series on KPNX, Phoenix, Arizona on August 5, 1996. WWL,

New Orleans added the show to its schedule on October 7, 1996, but "Majority Rules" never expanded beyond those two stations. The show came to end in January 1997.

Four players competed in a game of second-guessing opinions of members of a studio audience, as well as those of other people polled in special surveys. Each player began with $500 and in round one tried to predict the opinions of other people. Correct answers were worth $100; incorrect guesses cost a player $100. Four questions, such as "Who is sexier? Antonio Banderas or Brad Pitt?" were played in this round.

In the second round, a question was read, and the first two players to ring in gave responses. The audience then chose the response they liked best, and that player got $100, while the other player lost $100. The last question of this round was worth $1,000. A question was read with three possible answers. Each player selected the answer they felt the majority of the audience would choose. Players who were correct in determining the answer of the majority divided the $1,000 and the top-two scoring players moved on to the "Speakers Face-off."

In the Speakers Face-off round, the two remaining players were each given fifteen seconds to convince the studio audience to choose their answer to a question like, "Which man or woman has done the most to change the course of history?" The player selected by the audience received $2,500, while the other player got $250.

The day's winner played the bonus round in which he or she tried to put three audience answers in order from highest to lowest percentage of response on a blank check. For example, if fifty-four percent, twenty-four percent, and twenty-two percent were the secret responses and the contestant had put them in the correct order, he or she could win $5,424.22. Before the answers were revealed, the player was given the option of taking $5,000 if he or she felt the order was not correct. If correct, the player got the value of the check plus a $10,000 bonus.

MAKE A FACE

premiere: October 2, 1961   *packagers:* TV Games Inc. (1961)/ Delta Productions (1962)   *broadcast history:* ABC daytime October 2, 1961–March 30, 1962; ABC Saturday morning September 29, 1962–December 22, 1962   *host:* Bob Clayton   *assistants:* Kathy Mitchell, Rita Mueller   *announcers:* Johnny Gilbert, Dirk Fredericks   *producers:* Herbert Gottlieb, Art Baer   *directors:* Seymour Robbie, Lloyd Gross   *set designer:* Romain Johnston   *music director:* Hank Sylvern   *origination:* Little Theater, New York

Two contestants, playing one at a time on "Make a Face," attempted to create the face of a character (boy scout, policeman, etc.) by stopping three revolving wheels on portions of a face. If they stopped the wheels in the correct positions, they were shown a portion of the face of a famous celebrity. The first player to correctly guess the identity of the celebrity won the game.

"Make a Face" premiered as a daytime series in October 1961 with adults competing as contestants. When the show

When asked to "Make a Face," emcee Bob Clayton and assistant Kathy Mitchell were all smiles.

returned in the fall of 1962, it was seen on Saturday mornings with children playing the game.

Kathy Mitchell was seen as assistant on the daytime edition of "Make a Face" and Rita Mueller was assistant on the Saturday morning version.

Did you know . . . Bob Clayton costarred with Jerry Lewis in the 1960 movie *The Bellboy*? After "Make a Face," Clayton joined CONCENTRATION as announcer in 1963 and in 1969 he replaced Hugh Downs as host of the long-running show.

Were you watching when . . . Bob Clayton sat in for Ed McMahon on "The Tonight Show" in the late 1960s. McMahon took ill that night and Clayton just finished taping CONCENTRATION when "The Tonight Show" producer rushed over and asked him to sit in with Johnny Carson. It was memorable; Clayton was still wearing his "Concentration" blazer.

MAKE ME LAUGH
premiere: March 20, 1958   *packagers:* Make Me Laugh Productions/Program Service Inc. (1958); Lukehill Productions/Paramount Television (1979); Dove/Four Point/Buena Vista TV (1997–   )   *broadcast history:* ABC primetime March 20, 1958–June 12, 1958; Syndicated January 15, 1979–February

29, 1980; USA (cable) October 2, 1984–September 26, 1986 (repeats of 1979–1980 series); Comedy Central (cable) June 2, 1997–
1958 version
host: Robert Q. Lewis   *hostess:* Penny Peterson   *announcers:* Ken Roberts, Glenn Riggs   *creators:* George Foster, Mort Green   *executive producers:* George Foster, Mort Green, Pat Weaver   *producer:* Johnny Stearns   *directors:* Johnny Stearns, Dave Brown   *set designer:* Al Brenner   *origination:* Little Theater, New York   *debut week guests:* Sid Gould, Buddy Lester, Henny Youngman
1979–1980 version
host: Bobby Van   *announcers:* Bill Berry, Johnny Gilbert   *producer:* George Foster   *directors:* Glenn Swanson, Tom Rickard   *set designer:* John Vallone   *music:* Artie Butler   *origination:* Studio 3, KTLA Television, Los Angeles
1997–   version
hosts: Ken Ober, Mark Cohen   *announcer:* Lou DiMaggio   *executive producers:* Ron Ziskin, Jim Mahoney, Andrew J. Golder, Mort Green, Reinette Heartstone-Foster   *line producer:* Linda Gaugel   *directors:* Ken Ceizler, James Marcione   *production designers:* David Morong, Matt Flynn   *music:* Mark Leggett   *origination:* The Production Group studios, Hollywood

Three comedians on a panel were each given one minute to make a contestant laugh in this comedy game show. A celebrity guest also appeared each week to act as a proxy for a viewer at home. The contestant received $1 for each second he or she did not laugh, up to a maximum of $180.

By the end of the original run on ABC, celebrity guests appeared each week to act as "proxy contestants" for home viewers who sent in postcards. The viewers received the money earned by the celebrity guest.

Twenty-one years after the network version, "Make Me Laugh" returned with a new series of shows for first-run syndication. The format was the same as the original 1958 version in which studio audience members were used as contestants. "Make Me Laugh" repeats aired on the USA cable network from 1984 to 1986.

"Make Me Laugh" returned for a third time with new shows, in summer 1997, for the cable network Comedy Central. The new version, hosted by comedian Ken Ober, who had previously emceed REMOTE CONTROL, added two new rounds to the original format.

After three contestants each faced the panel of three comedians, they were given the opportunity to risk any part of the money they had earned in the first round on predicting whether one of the comedians could make a new contestant laugh in one minute. After two tests in this round, the player with the highest score moved on to the bonus round.

In the bonus round, all three comedians got one final chance to make the player laugh in sixty seconds by alternating among themselves. The player won an additional $500 if they did not laugh.

Ken Ober was replaced by comedian Mark Cohen as host of "Make Me Laugh" in January 1998.

Were you watching when . . . comedians Gallagher, Howie Mandel, Bob Saget, Gary Shandling, and Yakov Smirnoff appeared on the 1979 version of "Make Me Laugh"?

MAKE THAT SPARE

premiere: October 8, 1960 *packager:* ABC Sports *broadcast history:* ABC primetime October 8, 1960–June 30, 1962; ABC primetime October 6, 1962–September 11, 1964; ABC weekend March 12, 1988 (special)

1960–1964 version

hosts: Johnny Johnston, Win Elliott *producer:* Jim Colligan *director:* Jack Sameth *origination:* bowling alleys in Paramus, New Jersey; Upper Saddle River, New Jersey; Queens, New York

1988 version

host: Chris Schenkel *analyst:* Nelson Burton Jr. *creators:* Jim Colligan, Frank Esposito *origination:* North Olmstead, Ohio

This live sports game was seen following the weekly primetime boxing matches on ABC. From 1960 to 1963, "Make That Spare" was seen on Saturday nights and from 1963 to 1964 on Friday nights. The length of each show varied, depending on how long the bowling matches lasted.

Each week, professional and amateur bowlers were given the chance to complete five classic spare patterns with different point values. The high scorer of each match received $1,000 and received the chance to win $5,000 by making a spare for a special sweepstakes.

Most of the matches were held at a bowling alley in Paramus, New Jersey. During the second season the show moved to Ridgewood Lanes in Queens, New York.

Johnny Johnston was host of "Make That Spare" during the 1960–1961 season and again from 1962 to 1964. Win Elliott was seen as host during the 1961–1962 season.

"Make That Spare" returned as a one-time special on March 12, 1988. ABC sportscaster Chris Schenkel called the action, with bowlers Walter Ray Williams Jr., Brian Voss, and all-time PBA champion Earl Anthony competing. The special was broadcast from the Buckeye Lanes in North Olmstead, Ohio.

MAKE THE CONNECTION

premiere: July 7, 1955 *packager:* Mark Goodson–Bill Todman Productions *broadcast history:* NBC primetime July 7, 1955–September 29, 1955 *hosts:* Jim McKay, Gene Rayburn *announcers:* Lee Vines, Durward Kirby *executive producer:* Gil Fates *producer:* Chester Feldman *director:* Jerome Schnur *music director:* Jack Shaindlin *origination:* Century Theater, New York *debut panel:* Betty White, Gloria DeHaven, Eddie Bracken, Gene Klavin

In "Make the Connection," this Thursday night summer replacement series, a panel of four celebrities tried to figure out the connection between two or more contestants. Some examples included a guest who had the hiccups for twenty-five years and the person who cured him; a lady naval officer and five men she recruited that day; and a teacher with several students from her class for expectant fathers.

Each panelist had thirty seconds to question the guests and come up with the connection. Each time the panel did not guess correctly the contestants received $25 and when the overall total reached $150 the contestants won the game.

Each week a celebrity guest also appeared with a connection for the panel to make. Comedian Wally Cox appeared on the first program and other celebrities who appeared included Jerry Colona, Hoagy Carmichael, Buster Keaton, George Jessel, and J. Fred Muggs, the chimp from "The Today Show."

Sponsored by Borden's, the show's regularly featured panelists included Betty White, Gloria DeHaven, Eddie Bracken, and New York radio personality Gene Klavin.

Original host Jim McKay left after four weeks and was replaced by "The Tonight Show" announcer Gene Rayburn, who made his debut as a network television game show host on August 4, 1955.

Did you know . . . "Make the Connection" host Gene Rayburn was half of the first two-man morning team in radio? In 1946 Rayburn teamed with Jack Lescoulie on New York radio station WNEW. Lescoulie left after six months and was replaced by Dee Finch. Rayburn and Finch remained a team for six years. When Rayburn left in 1952 to pursue a career in television, he was followed by future MAKE THE CONNECTION panelist Gene Klavin.

MAKE THE GRADE

premiere: October 2, 1989 *packager:* MTV Networks *broadcast history:* Nickelodeon (cable) October 2, 1989–December 29, 1991 *hosts:* Lew Schneider, Robb Edward Morris *announcer:* Maria Milito *creator:* Michael Klinghoffer *executive producers:* Geoffrey Darby, Kristin Martin, Andy Bamberger *producers:* Robert Mittenthal, Angelika Bartenbach *directors:* Bob Lampel, Thomas Williams *set designers:* Byron Taylor, David B. Ellis *music:* Edd Kalehoff *origination:* Universal Studios, Orlando

Three students in the same grade competed for cash prizes in this question-and-answer series, "Make the Grade," from Nickelodeon. Players answered questions in seven categories including math, home economics, social studies, the arts, English, science, and history. The questions were broken down into seven levels of difficulty: elementary and seventh grade through twelfth grade. To win the game a player had to answer one question from each category and one from each grade level. The first player to complete his or her board won the game and $500.

The winning player got a chance to win an additional $1,000 in the "Honors Round." He or she was given a choice of three categories, was asked to select one, and then answer seven questions in that category in forty-five seconds or less. He or she received $100 for each correct answer and $1,000 for correctly answering all seven.

Robb Edward Morris replaced Lew Schneider as host in 1990.

MASQUERADE PARTY

premiere: July 14, 1952 *packagers:* Wolf Productions (1952–1960); Stefan Hatos–Monty Hall Productions (1974–

1975) *broadcast history:* NBC primetime July 14, 1952–August 25, 1952; CBS primetime June 22, 1953–September 14, 1953; CBS primetime June 21, 1954–September 27, 1954; ABC primetime September 29, 1954–December 29, 1956; NBC primetime March 6, 1957–September 4, 1957; CBS primetime August 4, 1958–September 15, 1958; NBC primetime October 2, 1958–September 24, 1959; CBS primetime October 26, 1959–January 18, 1960; NBC primetime January 29, 1960–September 23, 1960; Syndicated September 9, 1974–September 1975

1952–1960 version

hosts: Bud Collyer, Douglas Edwards, Peter Donald, Eddie Bracken, Robert Q. Lewis, Bert Parks *timekeeper:* Renee Wolf *announcer:* Johnny Olson *commercial announcers:* Norman Brokenshire, Rex Marshall, Nelson Case, Don Morrow *producers:* Herb Wolf, Ed Wolf, Allan Sherman, Alan Gilbert *directors:* Craig Allen, Lloyd Gross *make-up:* George Fiala, Bill Herman *costumes:* Lou Eisle *music director:* Bobby Rosengarten *theme:* ''The Comedians'' by Kabalevsky *origination:* NBC Studio 8H, New York (1952); Ziegfeld Theater, New York (1957); Mansfield Theater (CBS Studio 59), New York (1959); Colonial Theater, New York (1960) *debut guests:* Peter Donald, Ilka Chase, John S. Young, Madge Evans

Actor, comedian, and dancer Eddie Bracken on the set of the only game show that he hosted, "Masquerade Party."

1974–1975 version

host: Richard Dawson *announcer:* Jay Stewart *producer:* Alan Gilbert *director:* Joe Behar *set designer:* Richard James *music:* Sheldon Allman *make-up:* Harry Blake, Stan Winston *costumes:* Robert Turturice *origination:* NBC Studios, Burbank *debut guests:* Bill Bixby, Lee Meriweather, Nipsey Russell.

On ''Masquerade Party,'' a celebrity panel attempted to identify guest celebrities who were disguised in elaborate costumes and make-up. Each member of the panel was permitted to ask up to five questions. The guests could win up to $300 each for their favorite charities by stumping the panel.

''Masquerade Party'' was one of the most successful panel shows during the 1950s. During its eight-year run on network television it bounced back and forth from NBC to CBS to ABC. A frequent summer replacement, ''Masquerade Party'' had six different hosts.

Bud Collyer was host when the show premiered in the summer of 1952. CBS newsman Douglas Edwards emceed the summer 1953 edition. When the show returned for a longer engagement in 1954 the host was Peter Donald, who had been a regular panelist. Actor Eddie Bracken was at the helm in the 1957 season and Robert Q. Lewis handled the summer 1958 cycle. Bert Parks became host in the fall of 1958 and remained for the rest of the network run.

The first telecast featured a panel with Ilka Chase, Peter Donald, Madge Evans, and John S. Young trying to recognize former CPA director Michael DiSalle, actress Anne Jeffreys, and baseball player Allie Reynolds.

Other regular panelists who appeared on the show included Lee Bowman, Buff Cobb, Dagmar, Faye Emerson, Sam Levenson, Audrey Meadows, Ogden Nash, Betsy Palmer, Bobby Sherwood, and Jonathan Winters.

On Sunday September 26, 1954, at 2 P.M., a special edition of ''Masquerade Party'' was broadcast on all three television networks. The show originated from both New York City and Washington, D.C., and among the guests was Vice President Richard Nixon.

''Masquerade Party,'' emceed by Richard Dawson, returned as a weekly syndicated show in 1974, featuring a panel of Bill Bixby, Lee Meriweather, and Nipsey Russell. The panelists continued to ask questions of the elaborately disguised guests, and members of the studio audience won prizes if the panelists could correctly guess the identity of the guest.

Were you watching when . . . these TV favorites were all guest stars in heavy make-up on the 1974 syndicated version: Steve Allen, Bob Barker, Phyllis Diller, Monty Hall (who, along with long time partner Stefan Hatos, acquired the rights to this new version), Ed McMahon, Leonard Nimoy, and William Shatner, among other favorites?

The Three Stooges received laughs on January 15, 1959, when they appeared on the show disguised as the famous Gabor sisters. Their antics failed to fool the panel of experts who quickly guessed their identity.

MASTERS OF THE MAZE

premiere: August 29, 1994 *packager:* Kline and Friends/Image Entertainment/Fenton Group *broadcast history:* Family Channel (cable) August 29, 1994–September 22, 1996 *hosts:* JD Roth, Mario Lopez *cast:* Renae Jacobs, Mark Maxwell-Smith, Barry Dennen, Clea Montville *executive producers:* Richard Kline, Hal Berger, Fenton Rosewarne, James M. Dowalby *producer/director:* Richard Kline *set designer:* John C. Mula *music:* Greg Edmonson *origination:* CBS Studio Center, Studio City

Three players competed against each other to earn up to fifty points apiece, with the two contestants earning fifty points moving on to race through a twenty-foot-high multi-level maze, in "Masters of the Maze."

The first player to correctly identify an out-of-focus picture earned ten points and a chance to answer a question about the picture for an additional five points. After one player reached fifty points, the remaining players competed in a "speed round" of identifying pictures for ten points until a second player earned fifty points.

The first player to earn fifty points had the option to race through the maze first or second. The player with the fastest time earned the chance to win numerous prizes in a final solo challenge.

The two highest-scoring players moved on to the "maze round," where they tried to work their way through the maze in the fastest time. They were guided through the maze by a partner and were equipped with a special suit that enabled one teammate to give directions to his or her partner.

Their goal was to find two "power sticks" and work their way through the "Mirror Maze," where they had to answer a question to proceed; the "Honeycomb Maze," where they had to rely on their partners' directions to get through; and the "Chamber of Knowledge," where they had to answer three true/false questions to open the gates to the finish line. Teams went through the maze one at a time and the fastest time won.

Mario Lopez became the new host when the show began its second season in October 1995.

Host J. D. Roth previously emceed the kid's game shows DOUBLE UP and FUN HOUSE.

THE MATCH GAME

premiere: December 31, 1962 *packagers:* Mark Goodson–Bill Todman Productions (1962–1982); Mark Goodson Productions (1990–1991) *broadcast history:* NBC daytime December 31, 1962–September 26, 1969; CBS daytime July 2, 1973–April 20, 1979; Syndicated September 8, 1975–September 1982; ABC daytime July 16, 1990–July 12, 1991
1962–1969 version
host: Gene Rayburn *announcer:* Johnny Olson *substitute announcer:* Wayne Howell *executive producer:* Robert Noah *producer:* Jean Kopelman *directors:* Jim Elson, Ira Skutch, Rodger Wolf, Mike Garguilo *set designer:* Otis Riggs Jr. *theme:* "Swingin' Safari" by Bert Kaempfert *origination:* NBC Studio 8H, New York *debut guests:* Arlene Francis, Skitch Henderson

A full-set shot from 1967 of the original "The Match Game," with emcee Gene Rayburn.

1973–1982 version

host: Gene Rayburn **announcer:** Johnny Olson **substitute announcer:** Bern Bennett **producer:** Ira Skutch **director:** Marc Breslow **set designer:** Jim Agazzi **music:** Score Productions **origination:** Studio 33, CBS Television City, Los Angeles **debut guests:** Richard Dawson, Anita Gillette, Jack Klugman, Michael Landon, Vicki Lawrence, Jo Ann Pflug

1990–1991 version

host: Ross Shafer **announcers:** Gene Wood, Bob Hilton **producers:** Jonathan Goodson, Chester Feldman **director:** Marc Breslow **set designer:** Jim Agazzi **music:** Score Productions **origination:** Studio 59, ABC Television Center, Los Angeles **debut guests:** Sally Struthers, Chris Lemmon, Ilene Graff, Daphne Maxwell Reid, Charles Nelson Reilly, Joe Alaskey

During the sixties, NBC introduced a series of new game shows that became audience favorites on their daytime schedule. On the last day of 1962, the new Mark Goodson–Bill Todman game show, "The Match Game," made its first appearance.

Two teams, each composed of a celebrity guest and two studio contestants, tried to match answers to a question for cash prizes. If two players matched, the answer was worth twenty-five points and if all three players matched, it was worth fifty points. The first team to reach one hundred points won the game and $100.

The winning team played the "Audience Match," where each correct guess about how the studio audience would respond earned $50.

Celebrity guests on the first week of "The Match Game" were Arlene Francis and Skitch Henderson. To celebrate the one thousandth broadcast on November 1, 1966, the celebrity captains were Mark Goodson and Phyllis Newman. Goodson's teammates were his daughter Jill and host Gene Rayburn's daughter Lynn.

On March 2, 1967 a home viewer game was introduced where a person at home was called on the telephone. The home viewer tried to match his or her response to one question with that of a player picked from the studio audience. If they matched, they split the jackpot, which started at $500 and increased by $100 each day it was not won.

In September 1969, NBC canceled "The Match Game" along with YOU DON'T SAY!, EYE GUESS, and PERSONALITY.

"The Match Game" returned to television four years later with a revised format. First called "Match Game '73" with annual numerical updates, this version featured two studio contestants and six guest celebrities. The premiere week welcomed Richard Dawson, Anita Gillette, Jack Klugman, Michael Landon, Vicki Lawrence, and Jo Ann Pflug.

Played with more of an emphasis on humor than the original NBC version, "Match Game '73" became the number-one daytime TV show within months.

The contestant with the most matches after playing two rounds of questions (trying to match each celebrity once) won the game and played the Audience Match where he or she tried to second guess the audience's response to a fill-in question for either $500, $250, or $100. Three celebrities were then chosen to give suggested answers. The contestant could either pick one or create a new one. The player was then given the opportunity to win ten times the money won on the first part of the audience match by matching one celebrity on another fill-in question.

A weekly primetime version, called "Match Game P.M.", was syndicated from September 1975 to September 1981. When CBS dropped the daytime version in April 1979, the show continued with new daily shows for syndication until September 1982.

"Match Game" returned for its third run on network television in October 1983 as part of THE MATCH GAME–HOLLYWOOD SQUARES HOUR. (See that title for more information.)

In July 1990, "Match Game" appeared on its third network with a new version for ABC. Ross Shafer was its new host and this edition also featured two contestants trying to match answers with six celebrities.

Each player chose one of two questions and tried to match as many celebrities as possible for $50 a match. After each player completed a question, they both participated in a new feature, "Match-Up."

Playing one at a time, each contestant selected one celebrity and in thirty seconds the celebrity tried to guess which of two possible answers the contestant had picked. (Example: wire———, either "tap" or "service.") Players received $50 for each successful guess.

A second round of questions was played at $50 a match against all six celebrities and a second round of Match-Up was played at $100 a match within a forty-five second time limit to determine the day's winner.

The winner of the day played the "Big Money Super Match" for additional cash. He or she was given an audience match fill-in, like "Treasure———." The player selected three celebrities for suggested answers. If the player guessed the most popular response, he or she won $500. The second most popular response paid $300 and the third $200.

The player then attempted to match one celebrity on one fill-in question for ten times the money won in the first half of the bonus round. The player spun a wheel to determine which celebrity to play against. If the wheel stopped on certain spots the contestant played for double winnings, as much as $10,000. The wheel was first introduced as an addition to the Gene Rayburn mid-70s version.

Did you know . . . Gene Rayburn was a page at NBC Studios at Rockefeller Center in 1936? In 1954, he was the original announcer on "The Tonight Show with Steve Allen" when it premiered on NBC's late-night schedule. In the summer of 1955, Rayburn made his debut as a game show host when he replaced Jim McKay as emcee of MAKE THE CONNECTION.

From 1958 to 1960, Gene Rayburn was the voice of Pontiac on their TV and radio commercials. In one of the TV commercials there was a dream sequence in which Gene Rayburn had to speak to himself. Since this was live television, a double was used. A young comic named Peter Marshall, who would later go on to host THE HOLLYWOOD SQUARES, played the double. To look like Rayburn, Marshall was fitted with a fake nose, fake cheekbones, and a hairpiece.

Long before Charles Nelson Reilly was a regular panelist on "Match Game" in the 1970s, he was Gene Rayburn's understudy on Broadway in *Bye Bye Birdie*.

Side-by-side Emmy winners: Allen Ludden and wife Betty White round out the panel on Gene Rayburn's "Match Game."

Gene Rayburn was one of New York's most successful radio personalities in the 1950s on top station WNEW. In the 1960s and into the 70s Gene was heard on the NBC radio series "Monitor."

Old Man Perriwinkle, a classic character that Rayburn created for the CBS and syndicated versions of "The Match Game," was a favorite of movie great Fred Astaire. Gene would often get calls and letters from the legendary entertainer.

Radio personality Howard Stern was a big fan of Gene Rayburn's as a kid growing up in New York City. Years later, Gene would guest on Howard Stern's television series, as well as be featured in Howard's best-selling book, *Private Parts.*

Were you watching when . . . Gene guest-hosted for Johnny Carson several times on "The Tonight Show" in the mid-sixties?

On January 5, 1967 Johnny Carson made a "surprise" visit to the set of "The Match Game." The purpose of his visit was to harass (in fun) Ed McMahon, who was appearing on the show all that week. On September 16, 1968 for an entire week Ed McMahon became the emcee to "The Match Game," when regular emcee Gene Rayburn acted as a guest celebrity.

These top emcees were all guests on "The Match Game" and "Match Game": Steve Allen, Bob Barker, Bill Cullen, Bob Eubanks, Art Fleming, Art James, Tom Kennedy, Allen Ludden, Peter Marshall, and Dick Martin.

Once, when Gene Rayburn was admiring a contestant's "dimples" he accidentally said that she had beautiful "nipples"!

THE MATCH GAME–HOLLYWOOD SQUARES HOUR

premiere: October 31, 1983 *packager:* Mark Goodson Productions/Orion Television *broadcast history:* NBC daytime October 31, 1983–July 27, 1984 *hosts:* Gene Rayburn and Jon Bauman *announcer:* Gene Wood *producer:* Robert Sherman *director:* Marc Breslow *set designer:* Dennis Roof *music:* Edd Kalehoff *origination:* NBC Studios, Burbank *debut guests:* Skip Stevenson, Barbi Benton, Jimmie Walker, Phil Proctor, Alison Arngrim, Tom Villard, Twyla Littleton, Bill Daily

NBC combined two of its most successful daytime game shows to make this daily one-hour show, "The Match Game–Hollywood Squares Hour." Gene Rayburn hosted "The Match Game" segment and former Sha Na Na singer Jon Bauman hosted "The Hollywood Squares" segment.

The show began with two new contestants playing "The Match Game." They each played three rounds of questions and tried to match as many of the six celebrities as they could. The player with the most matches moved on to play the previous day's champion in a game of "The Hollywood Squares." In the event of a tie, a "tiebreaker round" was played with another question. Four answers were shown to the players and each selected one. The first celebrity to give one of the two answers chosen determined the winner.

In the "The Hollywood Squares" segment, winning the game of tic-tac-toe was worth $100, with $25 awarded for each celebrity captured. The contestants played "The Hollywood Squares" until time ran out. The player with the most money was the day's winner and played the "Super Match" for additional cash.

Super Match offered up to $30,000 in additional cash with the player first trying to fill in the blank on the studio audience match for either $250, $500, or $1,000. The player selected three celebrities to give suggestions for possible matches.

The player then took the winnings from the audience match and tried to multiply it ten, twenty, or thirty times in a head-to-head match with one celebrity. The player selected one of the nine celebrities who each had concealed a card which contained the value of the round. The player then tried to match the celebrity to win the money.

When Gene Rayburn was hosting "The Match Game" segment, cohost Jon Bauman played on the panel. They reversed positions on the "The Hollywood Squares" segment.

MATCHES 'N MATES

premiere: March 20, 1967   *packager:* Nicholson-Muir Productions for 20th Century Fox TV   *broadcast history:* Syndicated March 20, 1967–September 1968   *host:* Art James   *announcers:* Bob McClain, Dave Michaels   *producers:* Roger Muir, Nick Nicholson   *director:* Jim Reynolds   *set designer:* Doug Lowe   *music director:* Nick Nicholson   *origination:* Cleveland; Atlanta

This one-season syndicated game show, "Matches 'N Mates," featured husband-and-wife teams trying to match questions to answers in order to reveal a letter of a word and to have the chance to guess that mystery word for prizes.

Two couples competed and each in turn called out a letter between "A" and "I" to hear a statement ("to paint a fence you would use . . ."). They tried to find the answer on a board which contained twelve answers. One mate called for the statement and the other tried to find the answer by randomly calling a number. If the answer matched the statement, a letter or blank space was revealed and placed on the hidden item board. Hidden items had a maximum of nine letters and the first team to identify three hidden items won the game and a bonus prize.

One hundred and thirty episodes of "Matches 'N Mates" were produced by Roger Muir and Nick Nicholson, who also created THE NEWLYWED GAME.

MATCHMAKER

premiere: September 14, 1987   *packager:* Kleinmann-Pollard-Hull Productions/Four Star Television   *broadcast history:* Syndicated September 14, 1987–September 1988   *host:* Dave Hull   *announcers:* Lou Hunt, Bill Armstrong   *producer:* John Tobyansen   *directors:* Jeff Goldstein, Arthur Forrest   *set designer:* Don Wallschlaeger   *music:* John Tobin, Jet 88   *origination:* Los Angeles

Los Angeles radio personality Dave Hull hosted "Matchmaker," a relationship game show, seen mostly in late-night time slots, where he tried to probe the psyches and explore the minds of six contestants (three men, three women) he could not see in an attempt to find the best possible match.

After a period of quizzing the players, Hull eliminated two contestants, one of each sex. He then resumed his questioning until two players were left.

The two players selected to be a couple could win a trip by trying to match answers on their likes and dislikes. Each player wrote down three responses to the first question. If they matched on one of those responses, they won a prize. On the second question, they tried to find one match from two responses and on the third question tried to match one response for the grand prize.

MAXIMUM DRIVE

premiere: August 29, 1994   *packager:* RPM Productions   *broadcast history:* Family Channel (cable) August 29, 1994–September 30, 1995   *host:* Joe Fowler   *cohosts:* Brian Vermeire, Mercedes Colon   *executive producers:* Vin DiBona, Eytan Keller   *producer:* Terry Moore   *supervising producers:* Grant Johnson, Melinda Zoldan   *director:* Eytan Keller   *set designer:* Bill Bohnert   *origination:* Universal Studios, Hollywood

Three teams of three players, ages twelve to fourteen, competed on an obstacle course racetrack using different kinds of motorized vehicles such as XR-80 motor scooters, all-terrain four-wheel vehicles, six-wheel "Argo" vehicles, and "Wave Runners," a motorized water vehicle. Vin DiBona, one of the producers of "Maximum Drive," is also the force behind "America's Funniest Videos."

The teams competed in five events using the different vehicles. The team finishing first in each race scored five points. Second-place finishers earned three points and third-place teams one point. The team with the most points at the end of the show won the game.

MEET YOUR MATCH

premiere: August 25, 1952   *packager:* Jantone Productions   *broadcast history:* NBC early evening August 25, 1952–September 5, 1952   *host:* Jan Murray   *announcer:* Wayne Howell   *producer:* Herbert Moss   *director:* Larry White   *origination:* International Theater, New York

This early evening TV game show, based on the radio show of the same name that was heard on NBC from July 8, 1952 to January 18, 1953, had a two-week television run. "Meet Your Match" lasted for six episodes and was seen on Mondays, Wednesdays, and Fridays.

The reigning champ selected his or her opponent from the studio audience. The two players then competed in a question-and-answer match with the game ending when one player missed a question. The winner received $25 and the loser $15. If a player won three straight rounds he or she attempted to answer a bonus question for a $500 bond.

MESSING PRIZE PARTY

premiere: December 6, 1948 *packager:* Marlo Lewis Productions *broadcast history:* CBS primetime December 6, 1948–June 17, 1949 *host:* Bill Slater *assistant:* Hugh Benson *announcer:* Joe O'Brien *producers:* Marlo Lewis, Minnabess Lewis, Bill Gillett, Kenneth Redford *directors:* Alan Dinehart, Bill Gillett, Kenneth Redford *music director:* Leon Blum *origination:* Maxine Elliott Theater (CBS Studio 51), New York

In "Messing Prize Party," contestants selected from the studio audience competed in charades, foot races, and other party games with prizes determined by spinning a wheel. Five-time winners received a Universal gas range and consolation prizes were provided by the sponsor, the Messing Bread Company.

Did you know . . . Bill Slater was headmaster of Brooklyn's Adelphi Academy? In 1936 he covered the Olympic Games in Berlin for NBC radio.

MIDWAY

premiere: May 28, 1952 *packager:* DuMont Television *broadcast history:* DuMont primetime May 28, 1952–September 3, 1952 *host:* Don Russell *producer:* Harry Coyle *director:* Barry Shear *origination:* Palisades Park

"Midway" was broadcast live from Palisades Park, an amusement park in New Jersey. Patrons were asked to participate in various games as host Don Russell strolled through the park.

MINDREADERS

premiere: August 13, 1979 *packager:* Mark Goodson–Bill Todman Productions *broadcast history:* NBC daytime August 13, 1979–January 11, 1980 *host:* Dick Martin *announcer:* Johnny Olson *executive producer:* Ira Skutch *producer:* Mimi O'Brien *director:* Ira Skutch *set designer:* Bente Christensen *music:* Score Productions *origination:* NBC Studio 4, Burbank *debut guests:* Patty Duke, Nipsey Russell

In "Mindreaders," a daytime game show, two teams, each composed of a celebrity captain and three contestants of the same sex, competed in second guessing their teammates' answers to provocative or funny questions.

A question was posed to a team, such as "Have you ever deliberately set out to seduce a member of the opposite sex?" with each player responding "Yes" or "No." The celebrity captain tried to predict how each player answered, earning $50 for each correct guess. If the celebrity predicted incorrectly, the opposing team captain could earn money by guessing the answers of the remaining players. Teams alternated on the questions posed and the first team to earn $300 won the game.

The winning team played against a jury of ten people selected from the studio audience. A question, such as "Have you ever eaten snails?" was asked with each jury member voting "Yes" or "No." A member of the winning team tried to predict how many of the ten voted a particular way. If the prediction was exact the team won $500. If the prediction was within two, either way, the team collected $200. Three questions were posed to the audience jury and each player second guessed on one.

The winning team tried to increase their bonus game winnings tenfold by predicting how their celebrity captain would answer another question. Each of the three players voted "Yes" or "No" with the majority determining the teams prediction. If they were right the winnings were increased, with a $15,000 jackpot possible.

Dick Martin was best known for his long association with partner Dan Rowan and their "Laugh-In" TV series of the late 1960s.

MISSING LINKS

premiere: September 9, 1963 *packager:* Mark Goodson–Bill Todman Productions *broadcast history:* NBC daytime September 9, 1963–March 27, 1964; ABC daytime March 30, 1964–December 25, 1964 *hosts:* Ed McMahon, Dick Clark *announcer:* Johnny Olson *producer:* Ira Skutch *directors:* Mike Garguilo, Alan Mifelow, Ira Skutch *set designer:* Romain Johnston *origination:* NBC Studio 6A, New York; Elysee Theater, New York (ABC) *debut guests:* Peggy Cass, Milt Kamen, Kitty Carlisle

Celebrity panelists on "Missing Links" tried to guess key words omitted from funny or embarrassing real-life stories narrated by studio contestants. Examples of stories included one told by a man who caught a home-run ball hit by Roger Maris (the man who broke Babe Ruth's one-season record) and one by a realtor who sold unusual homes.

As the studio guest reached the point in his or her story where a word was omitted, he or she paused and each member of the panel was given a chance to guess. The contestant received $50 if the panel determined the missing word on the first round. If they did not, they were given the first letter of the word and, if they guessed then, the contestant received $25.

Four missing words were played in each story and each program featured three stories. The last story of the day was told by a celebrity guest.

Did you know . . . Ed McMahon was host of "Missing Links" when it was on NBC and Dick Clark became host when the show moved to ABC in March 1964? "Missing Links" was replaced by JEOPARDY! on the NBC schedule.

Were you watching when . . . Johnny Carson made several of his rare guest-appearances on the Ed McMahon version of "Missing Links"?

MISSUS' GOES-A-SHOPPING

premiere: August 3, 1944 *packager:* CBS Television *broadcast history:* CBS primetime August 3, 1944–January 22, 1946; CBS daytime November 19, 1947–November 10, 1948 *host:* John Reed King *substitute host:* Gil Fates *assistants:* Paul Mowry, Jim Brown *producer:* Ralph Levy *directors:* Frances Buss, Ralph Levy *origination:* New York

By day, Ed McMahon hosted "Missing Links," and by night, he was Johnny Carson's announcer/sidekick. Joining Ed on the celebrity panel are Milt Kamen and Phyllis Newman.

"Missus' Goes-A-Shopping" was one of the first game shows produced by CBS to be seen on a continuing basis. Based on the show of the same name that was heard on CBS radio from February 17, 1941 to December 21, 1951, the TV edition first appeared on August 3, 1944. Seen only on CBS's New York affiliate, "Missus' Goes-A-Shopping" remained on the schedule until January 1946.

The show returned as a daytime series, was seen on Wednesday afternoons from 1:30 P.M. to 2 P.M., and originated from various supermarkets in the Manhattan area.

The first daytime show was telecast from a Big Ben's Supermarket and featured female shoppers competing in various contests including racing down an aisle while balancing cakes of soap in one hand.

Paul Mowry assisted host John Reed King on the 1944 edition of "Missus' Goes-A-Shopping" and Jim Brown replaced him for the 1947 broadcasts. When King left the show in the fall of 1948, the show was renamed THIS IS THE MISSUS' and Bud Collyer became host.

MONEY MAKERS

premiere: March 3, 1969 *packager:* Tele-Column Productions *broadcast history:* Syndicated March 3, 1969–May 30, 1969 *host:* Jim Perry *producer:* Howard Felsher *director:* Bill McKee *origination:* CJOH-TV, Ottawa, Canada

"Money Makers" was a thirteen-week syndicated series taped in Canada that featured contestants who answered general knowledge questions valued between one and nine points. After a player successfully answered a question, he or she could place the point value anywhere on a game board consisting of four rows and four columns. Upon completing a row, the contestant could win that amount in cash by answering one more question.

THE MONEYMAZE

premiere: December 23, 1974 *packager:* Don Lipp–Daphne Productions *broadcast history:* ABC daytime December 23, 1974–July 4, 1975 *host:* Nick Clooney *announcers:* Alan Kalter, Chet Gould *executive producer:* Don Lipp *producer:* Don Segall *consultant:* Ron Greenberg *director:* Arthur Forrest *set designer:* Ron Baldwin *music:* Score Productions *origination:* TV-1, ABC Television Center, New York

Two couples competed in "The Moneymaze," a game show in which they challenged each other's ability to answer questions. The top scorer after each round got a chance to find a prize in an oversized maze that covered most of the studio floor. One mate directed the other through the maze to the prize and they were bound by a fifteen-second time limit.

The top-scoring team of the day played the maze for a possible $10,000. One player had to go through the maze (with his or her spouse's assistance), touch as many pre-selected boxes as possible (five), and return to the starting point within sixty seconds. They could win $1, $10, $100, $1,000, or $10,000 depending on the number of boxes reached.

Did you know . . . Nick Clooney is the brother of singer Rosemary Clooney, and George Clooney from NBC's highly rated series "ER" is Nick's son?

In the 1980s announcer Alan Kalter was heard as the voice of the USA cable network and in September 1995 replaced Bill Wendell as announcer on the "Late Show with David Letterman."

MONOPOLY

premiere: June 16, 1990 *packager:* Merv Griffin Productions/King World *broadcast history:* ABC primetime June 16, 1990–September 1, 1990 *host:* Michael Reilly *hostesses:* Kathy Davis, Michelle Nicholas, Kathy Karges *announcer:* Charlie O'Donnell *producer:* Burt Wheeler *director:* Kevin McCarthy *set designer:* Ed Flesh *theme:* Merv Griffin, Mort Lindsey *origination:* Studio 4, Hollywood Center Studios, Los Angeles

The popular board game Monopoly became a weekly primetime game show in the summer of 1990. On "Monopoly," three studio contestants tried to collect as many properties as possible by solving puzzles.

To win a property, the players tried to solve puzzles with clues like "street lid" (answer: manhole) and "dog sled directive" (mush). The player who gave the right answer had the value of that property added to his or her bank. After a group of properties were claimed, one player could create a monopoly by answering a toss-up question to steal the

Host Nick Clooney greets a contestant as he climbs up from "The Moneymaze."

opponent's properties. The round continued until all twenty-two properties (eight sections) around the board were divided among the players.

Before the second round, the "Big Money Round," began, each player used his or her bankroll to buy houses (at $50 each) and hotels (at $250). Dice were then thrown and the players moved around the board until time ran out. A player who landed on free parking collected $500. At the end of the game, all the houses and motels were cashed in and the player with the most money won the game.

The winning player participated in the bonus round, where he or she attempted to go around the board for a possible $25,000. The player was given five rolls of the dice to circle the board, collecting $100 for each square passed. The player attempted to avoid five "go to jail" squares (one already existed on the board and the others were placed by the contestant—one on Second Street, one on Third Street, and two on the final street on the Monopoly board). If the player rolled "doubles" on the dice, he or she received an extra roll of the dice. Any player who completed the board won $25,000 ($50,000 if the run around the board ended exactly on "go.")

"Monopoly" was originally planned as a game show for syndication with Peter Tomarken as host. Not enough stations signed on, and the show teamed with a primetime version of JEOPARDY! for a summer run on ABC.

Did you know . . . host Michael Reilly was originally a contestant on the Alex Trebek version of "Jeopardy!" before becoming host of "Monopoly"?

MOTHER'S DAY

premiere: October 13, 1958   *packager:* Shamrock Productions   *broadcast history:* ABC daytime October 13, 1958–January 2, 1959   *host:* Dick Van Dyke   *assistants:* Betty Andrews, Dotty Mack   *announcer:* Bill Brophy   *producers:* Carl Jampel, Joe Gottlieb   *director:* Alex Leftwich   *origination:* The Latin Quarter, New York

"Mother's Day" was one of the first shows on ABC's daytime schedule when it started programming on October 13, 1958. Comedian Dick Van Dyke emceed this show, which featured three mothers, selected from letters sent in by their husbands, children, friends, or neighbors, competing for the title "Mother of the Day."

Broadcast from the Latin Quarter in New York City, the show tested the homemaking skills of the mothers in four rounds. The player scoring the greatest number of points won a mink coat and other merchandise prizes.

Among the skills tested were the ability to pick a hard boiled egg from among four possibilities, the ability to memorize a list of six items and then recall the items when asked about them, and the ability to choose a four-pound steak from among six steaks.

Dick Van Dyke hosted one more game show, LAUGH LINE, in 1959, before moving to a successful career as an actor in *Bye Bye Birdie* on Broadway, "The Dick Van Dyke Show" on TV, and *Mary Poppins* in the movies.

THE MOVIE GAME

premiere: September 8, 1969   *packager:* Henry Jaffe Enterprises   *broadcast history:* Syndicated September 8, 1969–February 1972   *hosts:* Sonny Fox, Larry Blyden   *cohost:* Army Archerd   *announcer:* Johnny Gilbert   *creator:* Ted Cott   *executive producers:* Bob Stivers, Robert Noah   *producers:* Bob Synes, George Vosburgh, Julian Bercovici   *directors:* Glen Swanson, Marc Breslow   *set designer:* Don Roberts   *origination:* Studio 6, KTLA Television, Los Angeles; Stage 9, Goldwyn Studios, Los Angeles

Questions on "The Movie Game" focused on the world of motion pictures. The original format had two teams of three players, each with two celebrity guests and a contestant, competing to see which team knew more about the movies.

The game began with rounds called "screen tests" that featured toss-up questions worth twenty points. The team that answered correctly could earn an additional ten points by answering two "close-up [bonus] questions."

During the first season on the air several changes were made on "The Movie Game." Original host Sonny Fox was followed by Larry Blyden and in-studio contestants were dropped in favor of two teams of three celebrities playing for home viewers.

Additional features included film-clip rounds and a bonus round where the losing team acted out a scene from a movie for the other team to identify. Two scenes were performed, and if the winning team got one right their prize money was doubled. If they recognized both scenes, their money was tripled.

The final round of the day was handled by longtime "Daily Variety" columnist Army Archerd. During part of the show's run, the round was a feature called "Portrait of a Star." Clues were given in a biography read by Army and the team that guessed the identity of the celebrity profiled earned fifty points. The team with the most points at the end of this round won the game, $250, and a chance at the bonus round. Later in the series, the final round was changed to a lightning round of ninety seconds of rapid-fire questions.

Among the movie stars who appeared as panelists on "The Movie Game" were Milton Berle, Carol Burnett, Joan Crawford, Carol Channing, Henry Fonda, Bob Hope, Gene Kelly, Dorothy Lamour, Dinah Shore, Phil Silvers, Ann Sothern, Jimmy Stewart, Rudy Vallee, John Wayne, and Adam West.

Did you know . . . "The Movie Game" was taped on the same lot where movie history was made? The first talking motion picture, *The Jazz Singer*, was filmed on the Warner Brothers Hollywood lot in the 1920s. Almost fifty years later, the same lot was in use as a television studio and "The Movie Game" originated from Stage 6.

The pilot of "The Movie Game" in 1966 was hosted by Jack Narz and one of the celebrities on the panel was Raquel Welch.

THE MOVIE MASTERS

premiere: August 2, 1989   *packager:* Chauncey Street Productions   *broadcast history:* American Movie Classics (ca-

Pitting their years of show business experience against a barrage of questions about movie trivia are Phyllis Diller, Hugh O'Brian, Dyan Cannon, and David Janssen. They join host Sonny Fox and columnist Army Archerd on "The Movie Game."

ble) August 2, 1989–January 19, 1990 *host:* Gene Rayburn *hostess:* Lori MacPherson *announcer:* Peter Pratt *creators:* Alan Goodman, Albie Hecht *consultant:* Norm Blumenthal *executive producers:* Fred Siebert, Alan Goodman *producers:* Nina Steiner, Albie Hecht *director:* Michael Bernhaut *production designer:* Jonathan Arkin *origination:* New York

Cable channel American Movie Classics broadcast this game show, "The Movie Masters," on an irregular basis in the fall of 1989. The program tested the ability of a celebrity panel to answer questions about motion pictures.

The object of the game was to identify what movie corresponded to a particular scene. The game board consisted of nine categories, each of which covered part of the scene. Panelists, in turn, selected a category and then tried to answer a question. If they were right, each received one point and got a chance to see a segment of the picture. If wrong, the other panelists then got a chance to answer.

The panelist who identified the movie that was illustrated by the scene won prizes for a member of the home audience. The other panelists received consolation prizes for their home audience partners.

The panel for the series was composed of actress Peggy Cass, film critic Clive Barnes, and long-time TO TELL THE TRUTH panelist Kitty Carlisle.

MOVIELAND QUIZ
premiere: August 12, 1948 *packager:* Lester Lewis Productions *broadcast history:* ABC primetime August 12, 1948–November 9, 1948 *hosts:* Arthur Q. Bryan, Ralph Dumke *assistant:* Patricia Bright *producer:* Lester Lewis *director:* Ralph Warren *origination:* WFIL-TV, Philadelphia

Contestants on "Movieland Quiz" were asked to identify titles and stars of motion pictures for cash prizes in this early ABC network quiz show broadcast from Philadelphia.

The studio set depicted the front of a movie theater, with Arthur Q. Bryan (once the voice of Elmer Fudd) as host and Patricia Bright as ticket seller. Ralph Dumke replaced Bryan during the run as host.

MUSIC BINGO
premiere: May 29, 1958 *packager:* Teletunes Productions *broadcast history:* NBC primetime May 29, 1958–September 11, 1958; ABC daytime December 8, 1958–January 1, 1960

host: Johnny Gilbert *announcers:* Wayne Howell (NBC), Allan Jeffreys (ABC) *executive producer:* Al Singer *producers:* Harry Salter, Johnny Stearns *directors:* Perry Lafferty, Lloyd Gross, Seymour Robbie *set designers:* Jesse Beers (NBC), John Dapper (ABC) *music director:* Ted Rapf *theme:* "So Long" by Russ Morgan, Irving Melsher, and Remus Harris *origination:* NBC Studio 8H, New York; Ritz Theater, New York (ABC); Elysee Theater, New York (ABC)

Longtime TV announcer Johnny Gilbert made his network television debut as host of "Music Bingo," a musical game show where two contestants competed against each other to guess song titles.

Using a bingo game board consisting of five rows of five columns, the players attempted to fill five spaces (either horizontally, vertically, or diagonally) before their opponents did. One player used the "sharp" as his or her mark, the other the "flat."

The band played a song and the first player to buzz in tried to name that song and if correct placed his or her mark in any available space on the game board. The game board contained four free spaces that were revealed at the beginning of each game. Also included in the game was the "Magic Melody," and the contestants who correctly identified the songs in it could replace their opponents' marks with their own.

The winning player collected $500 and the runner-up received $50 for each mark he or she had on the board.

Created by Harry Salter, who also conceived NAME THAT TUNE, "Music Bingo" was seen as a summer replacement on NBC during 1958. It returned for a one-year run on ABC daytime beginning in December 1958.

"Jeopardy!" announcer Johnny Gilbert hosting his own game show, "Music Bingo," in 1958.

Host Johnny Gilbert, who sang on this show and recorded an album of popular songs, later hosted FAST DRAW and BEAT THE ODDS during the 1960s, but his voice is better known to television audiences as the announcer on over thirty different game shows.

Did you know . . .   Johnny Gilbert studied opera and was a singer in Shelley Harmon's big band in his hometown of Newport News, Virginia?

MUSICAL CHAIRS

premiere: July 9, 1955 *packager:* Ross-Danzig Productions *broadcast history:* NBC primetime July 9, 1955–September 17, 1955 *host:* Bill Leyden *announcer:* Arch Presby *exutive producer:* Bob Masson *producers:* Frank Danzig, Bart Ross *director:* William Bennington *set designer:* Charles Myall *music director:* Bobby Troup *vocal group:* The Cheerleaders *origination:* NBC Studios, Hollywood *debut guests:* Johnny Mercer, Mel Blanc, Bobby Troup, Denise Darcel

"Musical Chairs," the Hollywood-based summer game show for the NBC network, had been seen in the Los Angeles area since 1953. Viewers sent in musical questions that a panel of four experts attempted to answer. The viewer whose question was used received an RCA Victor radio, and if the question stumped the panel he or she won a twenty-one inch television set.

The regular panel consisted of Mel Blanc, Johnny Mercer, and Bobby Troup. They were joined each week by a celebrity guest.

Some of the questions required the panelists to guess occupations from song titles ("I've Got a Crush on You" for wrestler; "After You're Gone" for mortician) or make up a song using viewer-suggested topics with each panel member adding a line. Other questions required that two members of the panel act out a song title for the other two members to guess, and one question had a viewer challenging Bobby Troup to come up with one-word song titles for each letter in the name "Heidi."

MUSICAL CHAIRS

premiere: June 16, 1975 *packager:* Don Kirshner–Jerome Schnur Productions *broadcast history:* CBS daytime June 16, 1975–October 31, 1975 *host:* Adam Wade *announcer:* Pat Hernon *executive producers:* Jerome Schnur, Don Kirshner *producer:* Bill W. Chastain Jr. *director:* Lynwood King *set designer:* Tom John *music director:* Derek Smith *origination:* Ed Sullivan Theater, New York

Adam Wade became the first African American to host a network game show with this short-lived series in 1975. In "Musical Chairs," four contestants vied to identify missing lyrics in a song and were able to select from three possible choices. The music and possible answers were provided by weekly musical guests.

Guests for the first week included Kelly Garrett, Ernestine Jackson, and the pop group The Tokens. Other musical performers who appeared on the show included Sister Sledge,

The Spinners, Bobby Rydell, Lou Rawls, Sheila MacRae, and Phyllis Newman.

In round one, correct answers earned $50; round two, $75; and round three, $100. A song, either sung by host Adam Wade or one of the weekly musical guests, was stopped at some point, and three possible lines of lyrics were sung. Each of the players chose the line he or she felt was right. Cash was awarded to the players who picked the right words. Other musical questions about the song or composers were also asked of the players.

Three rounds, each consisting of three songs, were played. In each round the first three correct answers to the first question were worth cash; on question two the first two correct answers were worth cash; and on question three only the first answer was worth a cash amount. In round three, the lowest scoring player was eliminated after each question until only one player remained and then became the day's champion.

Did you know . . . host Adam Wade received a basketball scholarship to Virginia State College? In 1957, he was hired by Dr. Jonas Salk as an assistant on the polio virus research team. On February 25, 1960, he was the "central subject" on "To Tell the Truth."

Host Adam Wade had three top-ten hits in 1961 ("Take Good Care of Her," "The Writing on the Wall," and "As If I Didn't Know"). Producer Don Kirshner was the music supervisor on the TV show "The Monkees" during the 1960s and producer/host of "Rock Concert" during the 70s.

MY GENERATION

premiere: March 8, 1998 *packager:* VH1 *broadcast history:* VH1 (cable) March 8, 1998– *host:* Craig Shoemaker *announcer:* Lindsey Stoddart *executive producers:* Gary Marks, Jeff Gaspin, Laureen Zalanick *producers:* Paul Raff, Rick Rosner *supervising producer:* Jane Lipsitz *coordinating producer:* George David Monas *director:* Paul Casey *production designer:* Scott Lelieur *virtual set designer:* Design Visual Partners *theme:* Matt McCartie, Andy Blunda *origination:* Stage 1, Production Group Studios, Hollywood

On "My Generation" two different generations of players compete in a game that tests their knowledge of music trivia.

Each team is composed of two players from the same graduating year. The first show featured two members from the class of 1988 taking on two alumni of the class of 1977.

In round one, the "Singles Round," teams attempt to answer questions in five categories. A player can choose to answer questions from either his or her generation or the opponents' generation. Categories range from guessing the title of an album from a list of song titles to guessing the real names of famous rock and roll stars. The first question is worth fifty points; the second question, one hundred points; and a bonus question, two hundred points. Teams compete against each other to answer the first question. One player answers the first question and his or her teammate has the choice of answering the next question or choosing another category. If they answer the second question correctly, the team can try the bonus question. If a team misses a question, the opposing team can steal the points by answering correctly. A team can win a bonus prize by answering a question from the other team's generation.

Five new categories are played in round two, the "CD Round," with point values doubled to one hundred, two hundred, and four hundred. The final "Speed Round" has both teams trying to guess a common word that is missing in a series of song titles. Correct answers are worth two hundred points and the team with the highest score at the end of this thirty-second round wins the game.

The winning team plays the "My Generation Time Warp" for a grand prize. One player attempts to guess the names of recording artists or groups from two-word clues given by his or her partner. If they come up with seven (out of ten possible) names in sixty seconds they win the daily grand prize.

"My Generation" is taped on a computer-generated 3D virtual set at the Production Group Studios in Hollywood. The show made its debut on VH1 with a five-and-a-half-hour marathon of episodes on March 8, 1998. It began its daily run on March 9.

Did you know . . . host Craig Shoemaker won the 1997 American Comedy Award for Stand-Up Comedian? In 1998 he became the cohost to Magic Johnson on "The Magic Hour," a one-hour syndicated talk show.

NAME DROPPERS

premiere: September 29, 1969 *packager:* Merrill Heatter–Bob Quigley Productions *broadcast history:* NBC daytime September 29, 1969–March 27, 1970 *hosts:* Al Lohman and Roger Barkley *announcer:* Kenny Williams *executive producers:* Merrill Heatter, Bob Quigley *producer:* Art Alisi *director:* Jerome Shaw *set designer:* Archie Sharp *origination:* NBC Studio 3, Burbank *debut guests:* Glenn Ford, Michael Landon, Meredith MacRae

Los Angeles radio personalities Al Lohman and Roger Barkley were cohosts of this daily game show, "Name Droppers," that featured a celebrity panel of three, with twenty studio contestants who played for a week and a "name dropper"—a person who in some way had a connection to one of the three celebrities. Examples were: a maid, first grade teacher, or mechanic.

The celebrities told stories about how they were related to the "name dropper." The contestants voted for the celebrity whose story they believed. If they were correct they each received $10. The "name dropper" collected $10 for each incorrect vote. In addition, in each game two contestants got a chance to explain why they chose as they did and then played for a bonus prize. The contestant with the greatest number of correct guesses on a week's worth of shows won a bonus of $1,000.

NAME THAT TUNE

premiere: July 6, 1953 *packagers:* Tel-o-tune Productions/Harry Salter Productions (1953–1959); Ralph Edwards Productions (1974–1981); Sandy Frank Productions (1984–1985) *broadcast history:* NBC primetime July 6, 1953–June 14, 1954; CBS primetime September 2, 1954–March 24, 1955; CBS primetime September 27, 1955–October 19, 1959; NBC daytime July 29, 1974–January 3, 1975; Syndicated September 9, 1974–September 1981; NBC daytime January 3, 1977–June 10, 1977; Syndicated September 10, 1984–September 1985; USA (cable) January 2, 1989–September 13, 1991 (repeats of 1984 series); Family Channel June 7, 1993–March 29, 1996 (repeats of 1984 series)
1953–1959 version

hosts: Red Benson, Bill Cullen, George DeWitt *announcers:* Stan Sawyer, Bob Kennedy, Wayne Howell, Johnny Olson

creator: Harry Salter *producers:* Harry Salter, Al Singer, Art Stark *director:* Perry Lafferty *set designer:* Hal Gardiner *music directors:* Harry Salter, Ted Rapf *featured vocalist:* Vicki Mills *theme song:* "Love Bird" *origination:* NBC Studio 6B, New York (1953–1954); CBS Studio 52, New York (1954–1959)
1974–1981 version

hosts: Tom Kennedy, Dennis James *announcer:* John Harlan *executive producers:* Ralph Edwards, Bruce Belland

Long before her work with Regis Philbin or her marriage with Frank Gifford, Kathie Lee Johnson was Tom Kennedy's "La La Girl" on "Name That Tune."

producers: Ray Horl, John Rhinehart, Richard Gottlieb, Bianca Pino *directors:* Terry Kyne, John Dorsey, Richard Gottlieb *set designer:* Ed Flesh *musicologist:* Harvey Bacal *music directors:* Bob Alberti, Stan Worth, Tommy Oliver *featured vocalists:* Steve March, Monica Burns, Kathie Lee Johnson *origination:* NBC Studio 2, Burbank; KTLA-TV, Los Angeles

1984–1985 version

host: Jim Lange *announcer:* John Harlan *executive producer:* Nelson Davis *producers:* Ray Horl, Peggy Touchstone *director:* Kip Walton *set designer:* Jack McAdam *music director:* Tommy Oliver *origination:* KTLA-TV, Los Angeles

"Name That Tune" was one of the most popular musical quiz shows in TV history. The original version in the 1950s aired on CBS for five seasons. "Name That Tune" began as a radio series on NBC on December 20, 1952. Red Benson hosted the radio version, which ran until April 10, 1953. In July 1953 the show moved to NBC television with Benson continuing as host. A year later "Name That Tune" moved to CBS and Bill Cullen became emcee. A year later Cullen was followed by George DeWitt. Stan Sawyer, Wayne Howell, and Bob Kennedy were the announcers during its year-long run on NBC. When the show moved to CBS, Johnny Olson became the new announcer.

Created by music director Harry Salter, "Name That Tune" featured two contestants who stood approximately twenty feet from two bells (one for each player) that were hung from the ceiling. The band played a musical selection and the first player to recognize it ran to the bell and rang it.

Four songs were played in each game, with the first worth $5; the second, $10; the third, $20; and the fourth, $40. The player with the most money won the game and played the "Golden Medley" round for additional cash.

In the Golden Medley round, the player was given thirty seconds to guess seven songs, with the first correct answer worth $25 and the winnings doubling with each subsequent answer to a possible $1,600. Songs for the Golden Medley round were selected by home viewers, who won the same amount of money as the studio contestant participating in the round.

If a player named all seven songs correctly in the Golden Medley round, the home viewer was flown to New York and these two were teamed up to play the "Golden Medley Marathon" for a possible $25,000 each. They were given thirty seconds to name five songs for $5,000 each. If they were successful, they returned for additional weeks and won $25,000 each if they completed five marathons.

Producer Ralph Edwards, best known for TRUTH OR CONSEQUENCES and "This Is Your Life," brought "Name That Tune" back to television in 1974. The new version aired for seven years, appearing twice as a daytime show on NBC and also in a nighttime syndicated version.

Dennis James was host of the first daytime version that was seen from July 1974 to January 1975. Tom Kennedy was doing double duty, as he emceed the nighttime edition as well as the 1977 daytime entry.

In the 1970s "Name That Tune," two contestants competed in a series of musical guessing games. Winning a round earned them points and the player with the most points after three rounds won the game.

Round one, called "Melody Roulette," was worth ten points, and the players competed against each other to guess the titles of five songs. Round two, "Bid-a-Note," had the players bidding against each other to see who could guess a song from the fewest notes. In round three, the players competed against the clock to guess song titles in order to determine the day's winner.

The winner played the Golden Medley, where it was necessary to guess seven songs in thirty seconds, with an incorrect guess stopping the game. In September 1976 the show became "The $100,000 Name That Tune" with weekly winners returning to play for a grand prize of $100,000.

Former THE DATING GAME host Jim Lange hosted the 1984–1985 daily version of "The $100,000 Name That Tune." Produced by Sandy Frank Productions, that series was repeated on USA cable from January 1989 to September 1991. The Family Channel aired the series as part of its game block introduced in the summer of 1993.

Did you know . . . "Name That Tune" vocalist Kathie Lee Johnson later starred in the TV series "Hee Haw Honeys"? Married to former football star Frank Gifford, she is now seen with Regis Philbin on "Live With Regis and Kathie Lee."

Were you watching when . . . Ralph Edwards surprised emcee Tom Kennedy on "The $100,000 Name That Tune"? Ralph, along with Tom Kennedy, presented a $100,000 check to the winning contestant.

THE NAME'S THE SAME

premiere: December 5, 1951 *packager:* Mark Goodson–Bill Todman Productions *broadcast history:* ABC primetime December 5, 1951–August 31, 1954; ABC primetime October 25, 1954–October 7, 1955 *hosts:* Robert Q. Lewis, Dennis James, Bob Elliott and Ray Goulding, Clifton Fadiman *substitute host:* Brian Aherne *announcers:* Lee Vines, Bob Shepard, Lee Goodman, Glenn Riggs *commercials:* John Reed King, Jean Sullivan *executive producers:* Mark Goodson, Bill Todman *producer:* Peter Arnell *directors:* Jerome Schnur, Herbert Hirshman *origination:* Elysee Theater, New York *debut guests:* Abe Burrows, Meredith Willson, Joan Alexander

A celebrity panel tried to guess the identities of guests who had the same names as famous people, famous places, or famous objects in the weekly show "The Name's the Same," from the creators of WHAT'S MY LINE? Each panelist could ask up to ten "yes" or "no" questions of the guests. A panelist could pass to a teammate without asking all of the allotted questions but had to pay $20 if he or she failed to identify the guest after using all of the allotted number of questions.

A regular feature of each show was an appearance of a celebrity guest with a secret wish for the panel to guess. When actress Yvonne De Carlo appeared on December 13, 1954, she teamed up with panelist Gene Rayburn. Their wish was for panelist Bess Myerson to wear Yvonne's famous "Salome" costume, which she did at the end of the show.

Remember the panel members on "The Name's the Same"? From left to right are Gene Rayburn, Bess Myerson, host Dennis James, Joan Alexander, and Arnold Stang from 1954.

Circus clown Emmett Kelly appeared on the April 25, 1955 show and turned cohost Ray Goulding into a clown while a blindfolded panel asked questions.

The panelists for the debut week were actress Joan Alexander, playwright Abe Burrows, and musician Meredith Willson. Other regular panelists on "The Name's the Same" included Audrey Meadows, Bess Myerson, Roger Price, Gene Rayburn, and Bill Stern.

Robert Q. Lewis was the host for the original run of "The Name's the Same." When the show returned on October 25, 1954, Dennis James became the new host. He was replaced by radio personalities Bob Elliott and Ray Goulding on April 11, 1955, and they were followed by Clifton Fadiman on June 28, 1955. Actor Brian Aherne filled in as host during Robert Q. Lewis' vacation in 1953.

Lee Vines was the program announcer from 1951 to 1954 with Jean Sullivan as spokesperson for Swanson and John Reed King pitching for Bendix. When the show returned in the fall of 1954, Bob Shepard took over as announcer and spokesperson for the new sponsor, Ralston Purina. Lee Goodman replaced him in 1955. Glenn Riggs filled in as substitute announcer.

THE NEIGHBORS

premiere: December 29, 1975 *packager:* Carruthers Company–Warner Brothers Television *broadcast history:* ABC daytime December 29, 1975–April 9, 1976 *host:* Regis Philbin *assistant:* Jane Nelson *announcer:* Joe Seiter *executive producer:* Bill Carruthers *producer:* Joel Stein *director:* John Dorsey *set designer:* George Smith *music:* Stan Worth *origination:* Vine Street Theater, Los Angeles

Five females, who were neighbors in real life, competed on this daytime show. Two were selected as players and the others formed a panel. Each player on "The Neighbors" was asked a question and had to decide if it referred to her or to one of her neighbors. The answers were based on a survey of the panel and if the player's choices matched, she received $25.

The second round worth $100 showcased the player's ability to pinpoint which neighbor made a statement about her. In the third round, the host read a statement and the players tried to determine who the statement was about. The player with the highest score at the end of three rounds was the winner.

Did you know . . . long before Regis Philbin teamed with Kathie Lee Gifford he was Joey Bishop's sidekick/announcer on Joey's late-night ABC talk show from 1967 to 1969?

THE NEWLYWED GAME

premiere: July 11, 1966 *packagers:* Chuck Barris Productions (1966–1980); Barris Industries (1985–1989); Columbia Tri Star TV (1996–) *broadcast history:* ABC daytime July 11, 1966–December 20, 1974; ABC primetime January 7, 1967–August 30, 1971; Syndicated September 5, 1977–September 1980; ABC daytime February 13, 1984–February 17, 1984; Syndicated September 16, 1985–September 8, 1989; Syndicated September 9, 1996–
1966–1980 version

host: Bob Eubanks *announcers:* Johnny Jacobs, Tony McClay *creators:* Nick Nicholson, Roger Muir *executive producer:* Chuck Barris *producers:* Bill Carruthers, Walt Case, Mike Metzger *directors:* Bill Carruthers, John Dorsey *set designers:* Sherman Loudermilk, George Smith, Lyn Griffin, Archie Sharp *music:* Frank Jaffe, Lynn Barris *origination:* Studio D, ABC Television Center, Los Angeles (1966–1974); Golden West Studios, Hollywood (1977–1980)
1984 version

host: Jim Lange *announcer:* Rod Roddy *producer:* Walt Case *director:* John Dorsey *set designer:* Ed Flesh *music:* Milton De Lugg *origination:* Los Angeles
1985–1989 version

hosts: Bob Eubanks, Paul Rodriguez *announcers:* Bob Hilton, Charlie O'Donnell *producers:* Walt Case, Scott Sternberg, Bruce Starin *directors:* John Dorsey, Jeff Goldstein *set designers:* Ed Flesh, Jimmy Cuomo, John Shafner *music:* Milton DeLugg, Lee Ringuette *theme song:* "Book of Love" (1988–1989) *origination:* Studio 7, Sunset Gower Studios, Los Angeles
1996–1997 version

host: Gary Kroeger *announcer:* Ellen K *executive producer:* Michael Canter *coordinating producer:* Rikk Greengrass *supervising producer:* April Benimowitz *director:* Paul Casey *set designer:* Jimmy Cuomo *music:* Jim Lattham *origination:* Hollywood Center Studios, Los Angeles; Caesars Palace, Las Vegas (special shows)
1997– version

host: Bob Eubanks *announcer:* John Cramer *executive producer:* Stephen Brown *coordinating producer:* Linda Lea *supervising producer:* Walt Case *director:* Rob Fiedler *set designer:* Jimmy Cuomo *music:* Steve Kaplan *origination:* Studio 2, Hollywood Center Studios

"The Newlywed Game" was one of the most popular game shows of the 1960s and early 70s and was created by Nick Nicholson and Roger Muir, who also created PAY CARDS! and MATCHES 'N MATES. It was the second Chuck Barris production to reach the small screen, appearing approximately six months after THE DATING GAME. Like "The Dating Game," "The Newlywed Game" quickly became a hit in the daytime and a primetime version was added in January 1967.

The format of the show presented four recently married couples answering questions designed to reveal what they knew or did not know about each other.

In the first part of the game, the husbands responded to questions while their wives were off-stage in a soundproof room. The wives then returned to the stage and tried to guess their husbands' answers. A right answer was worth five points. In the second round, the husbands tried to guess what their wives said, with ten points awarded for each correct answer. The game concluded with a twenty-five point bonus question and the high-scoring team received a bonus prize.

The format remained the same for over twenty years until the fall of 1988. At that time, the questions were valued at $25 in round one and $50 in round two. In the final round, the husbands could bet any or all of their winnings on their ability to guess their wives' responses.

Comedian Paul Rodriguez replaced Bob Eubanks as host in December 1988 and "The Newlywed Game" began using the 1958 hit record "Book of Love" as its theme song.

After a seven-year absence from TV, "The Newlywed Game" returned in fall 1996, packaged with "The Dating Game" in an hour block for first-run syndication.

Gary Kroeger hosted the first season of the new version, which featured three couples, married two years or less, trying to see how well they knew each other. The game consisted of four rounds.

In the first round, one mate tried to complete a statement made by his or her partner in a prerecorded video. If the

Were you watching talk show favorite Regis Philbin in 1975 when he hosted "The Neighbors"?

A great marriage: Bob Eubanks and "The Newlywed Game."

person was correct in guessing the ending, the team scored ten points.

Round two featured one player trying to guess which one of three answers was given by his or her mate. A correct guess was again worth ten points.

In round three, a "secret" was read about one of the wives. If a husband felt that the statement was about his wife, he held up a sign indicating "That's my wife!" If the first husband holding up the sign was correct, the team earned ten points. If he was wrong, the team lost ten points.

The final round consisted of ten questions, valued in increments of ten, from ten to one hundred points. The wives chose between two statements about their husbands. If their respective husband picked the same answer, the points were added to their score. The couple with the most points at the end of this round won the game and received a second honeymoon as their prize.

After one season of this new format, longtime "Newlywed Game" host Bob Eubanks returned, and the show went back to its original format.

Did you know . . . Bob Eubanks, who lauched a string of young adult clubs called "The Cinnamon Cinder" in the 1960s, was responsible for bringing The Beatles to Los Angeles in 1964 for their first concerts on the West Coast at the Hollywood Bowl?

Bob Eubanks was one of Los Angeles's top radio personalities on radio station KRLA in the 1960s. KRLA was home to future game show announcer Charlie O'Donnell.

The day "The Newlywed Game" debuted, a press conference held by then Secretary of Defense Robert McNamara pre-empted PASSWORD and millions of game show fans turned their dials to ABC and discovered a good-looking Bob Eubanks and a naughty show called "The Newlywed Game."

Both Nicholson and Muir were also involved with "Howdy Doody" in the 1950s. Muir was the producer of the show and Nicholson appeared as Clarabell the Clown from 1952 to 1955.

"The Newlywed Game" and emcee Bob Eubanks were so popular that from 1967 to 1971 the show and its host were seen in primetime as well as in daytime on ABC.

For close to two decades game show favorite Bob Eubanks has been hosting two holiday parades, the Rose Bowl Parade and the Santa Claus Lane Parade, which originates from Hollywood, California, each Christmas.

Were you watching when . . . fellow ABC emcee Monty Hall dropped by "The Newlywed Game" to wish Bob Eubanks a successful 1968 season?

Bob Eubanks guested on these top shows: "Mike Douglas," "Dinah!", "The Merv Griffin Show," THE HOLLYWOOD SQUARES, LIARS CLUB, "Nashville Now," REMOTE CONTROL (MTV's hip game show), "The Tonight Show" (with Jay Leno), "Live With Regis and Kathie Lee," and "The Rosie O'Donnell Show."

THE NEWS HOLE
premiere: October 26, 1994   *packager:* Century of Progress Productions   *broadcast history:* Comedy Central (cable) Oc-

tober 26, 1994–November 19, 1994   *host:* Harry Shearer *executive producers:* Harry Shearer, Harriet Sternberg, Kevin Bright   *producer:* Kevin Berg   *director:* Kent Weed   *set designer:* Joe Stewart   *origination:* Studio A, KCET-TV, Los Angeles

Cable TV network Comedy Central attempted to spoof news-based quiz shows with the short-lived "The News Hole." Hosted by Harry Shearer, who was part of the comedy group "The Credibility Gap" during the 1970s and cocreator of the offbeat "This Is Spinal Tap," the program featured a panel of four attempting to come up with answers, both comical and factual, to questions posed by the host. Points were awarded as the host deemed appropriate.

The final round of each show featured the four panelists pitted against video images of four famous people who were competing via satellite. The clips included Secretary of State Warren Christopher, Senator George Mitchell, sportscaster Bob Costas, and Haitian president Jean-Bertrand Aristide.

The panel for the debut show included "The Simpsons" creator Matt Groening; founding editor of *Spy* magazine, Susan Morrison; comedian Andy Kindler; and commentator Ian Sholes.

NFL TRIVIA GAME

premiere: September 5, 1988   *packager:* NFL Films (1988), ESPN (1989)   *broadcast history:* ESPN (cable) September 5, 1988–January 21, 1989; ESPN (cable) September 11, 1989–December 25, 1989

1988 version

host: Gabe Kaplan   *announcer:* Jeff Kaye   *producer:* Bob Rubin   *director:* Doug Schustek   *set designer:* Jesse Rosenthal   *origination:* New York

1989 version

host: David Sparks   *announcer:* Art James   *producer:* John Tobyansen   *set designer:* Don Wallenschlager   *origination:* KADY-TV, Oxnard, California

Sports cable channel ESPN presented "NFL Trivia Game," a weekly game show that aired during football season and tested the football knowledge of two teams each consisting of three studio players. The show was hosted by actor Gabe Kaplan, best known as star of TV's "Welcome Back Kotter."

The game was divided into four quarters and began with a coin toss. The challenging team called the coin and had the option of keeping control of the game or passing control to their opponents.

The team answering questions scored a "touchdown" worth six points if they answered three questions in a row correctly. Players alternated answering and only one could respond to a particular question. If they scored a touchdown, they played the extra point question. A team lost control of the game when they missed a question or after they scored.

The last part of the fourth quarter of the game was called "the two-minute drill" and all questions had true or false answers.

The team with the most points won the game, $500, and returned to face new challengers. Teams that won for three weeks in a row returned for the "playoff round" and the winner of that round won a trip to an upcoming Super Bowl.

NICKELODEON ARCADE

premiere: January 3, 1992   *packager:* MTV Networks *broadcast history:* Nickelodeon (cable) January 3, 1992–September 28, 1997   *host:* Phil Moore   *announcer:* Andrea Lively   *executive producers:* Geoffrey Darby, Brown Johnson, Andy Bamberger   *creators/producers:* James Bethea, Karim Miteff   *supervising producer:* Scott Fishman   *director:* Bob Lampel   *production designer:* Byron Taylor   *art director:* David Ellis   *music:* Dan Vitco, Mark Schultz, Dean Friedman   *origination:* Universal Studios, Orlando

Two teams, each composed of two kids, competed for prizes in "Nickelodeon Arcade," a video arcade game show. One player from each team played the "face-off," a thirty-second match on a video game, and the high-scoring player received twenty-five points and control of "Mikey."

The object of the game was to move Mikey, an animated video character, from one side of the game board to a predetermined goal. The team in control decided which way to move. Each square they landed on contained either a prize, bonus points, puzzles to solve, a video challenge, or a pop-quiz question.

A team lost control of the game board when it landed on a "game over" square or when it missed a question. The first team to reach the goal could earn fifty points by answering a question chosen from three possible categories by their opponents.

A second round was played with the same rules as the first. Point values were doubled and the team with the most points after this round won the game and played for bonus prizes.

The winning team entered the "Video Zone" and tried to complete three levels of a video game in sixty seconds. Each level had three parts to be completed, with $50 earned on each level. One player tried the first level, the other player tackled the second, and both attempted the final level.

NICKELODEON GUTS

premiere: September 19, 1992   *packager:* Chauncey Street Productions   *broadcast history:* Nickelodeon (cable) September 19, 1992–   *host:* Mike O'Malley   *referee:* Moira Quirk   *creators:* Albie Hecht, Scott Fishman, Byron Taylor   *executive producer:* Albie Hecht   *supervising producer:* Magda Liolis   *studio producer:* Christine Woods *international producer:* Sue Dreghorn   *director:* Jim Dusel   *production designer:* Byron Taylor   *art director:* David Ellis   *music:* Rick Witkowski   *origination:* Universal Studios, Orlando

Three teenaged players competed in this action sports show, "Nickelodeon Guts," where kids lived out their sports fantasies. Players competed in five athletic events with the winner receiving a glowing piece of the "aggro-crag."

Among the events featured were the "slam dunk," where contestants, with elastic bands around them, jump from a seven-foot platform to an eleven-foot-high hoop trying to shoot as many baskets as they could in sixty seconds; "basic training," where they tried to work their way through an obstacle course in the fastest time; "the longest yard," where they tried to broad jump for distance with elastic bands around them; and "white water rafting," where they tried to paddle a raft from one end of a pool to the other while manuevering around several buoys. First place in each event was worth three-hundred points; second place, two hundred points; and third place, one hundred points.

The final event was scaling the "aggro-crag," a man-made obstacle-laden mountain. The first to reach the top earned seven hundred twenty-five points; the second, five hundred fifty points; and the third, three hundred seventy-five points.

The player with the most points won the game and medals were presented in an Olympic-style ceremony.

In the second season of "Guts," the show was expanded from weekends to a daily series on Nickelodeon and new events such as "Jump Ball," "Tornado Run," "Waverunner," and "Hang Ten" were introduced.

On September 5, 1995 the title of the show was changed to "Global Guts" when the program started featuring players representing different countries. The game and the hosts remained the same.

"Nickelodeon Guts" was taped at Nickelodeon Studios in Orlando, Florida, on a stage called the "Extreme Arena."

NIGHT GAMES

premiere: October 14, 1991   *packager:* CBS Entertainment Productions/Kushner-Locke   *broadcast history:* CBS late night October 14, 1991–June 12, 1992   *host:* Jeff Marder   *announcer:* Luann Lee   *executive producers:* Peter Locke, Donald Kushner   *supervising producer:* Jonathan Debin   *producers:* Mike Metzger, Lorrie Shapiro, David Z. Sacks   *director:* Bob Levy   *set designer:* Don Wallschlaeger   *music:* Scott Harper   *origination:* Studio 42, CBS Television City, Los Angeles

Six single contestants, three men and three women, participated in "Night Games," where they rated each other on how much they liked each other's answers to various questions. The two players, one male and one female, with the highest scores won a romantic dinner date and a chance at a trip.

Round one was called "He Said She Said" and players rated each other on a scale of one to ten on their opinions and attitudes about men, women, dating, and relationships. A question, such as "In TV terms is your current sex life 'top-rated,' 'into reruns,' or 'canceled'?" was asked of one player and the members of the opposite sex rated the answer.

In round two, "Love Secrets," players rated each other on a scale of one to twenty on questions like "What road sign should be posted on your bedroom door?" or "Tell us about the one that got away." The man and woman having the highest scores at the end of this round won a romantic dinner date with each other and a chance at a trip.

In the bonus game, the two players won a trip if they matched answers on two out of three questions. Each question had three possible responses and each player picked one.

"Night Games" was one of three relationship game shows CBS presented in their late night time slot during the 1991–1992 season. The others were PERSONALS and A PERFECT SCORE.

NO RELATION

premiere: August 12, 1996   *package:* Dick Clark Productions   *broadcast history:* FX (cable) August 12, 1996–February 8, 1998   *host:* Mike Rowe   *announcer:* Jennifer Martin   *executives in charge of production:* Don Wollman, Fran LaMaina   *executive producer:* Dick Clark   *producer:* Thomas F. Frank   *director:* Steve Grant   *set designer:* Bill Eigenbrodt   *music:* Scooter Pietsch   *origination:* Studio 33, CBS Television City, Los Angeles

Three celebrity panelists tried to guess which member of a family of five was actually an impostor. Prior to the taping, the impostor was briefed by the family with the real-life fifth member off-stage during the game.

The game consisted of two rounds of questioning. In round one, each celebrity panelist had thirty seconds to question individually each member of the family. While one family member was being questioned, the others were taken off-stage where they couldn't hear the questioning.

The entire family was on-stage for round two. Each panelist had forty-five seconds to question the family members about each other. At the end of this round, each panelist decided who the impostor was, and the family won a trip if they stumped the entire panel.

NOW YOU SEE IT

premiere: April 1, 1974   *packagers:* Mark Goodson–Bill Todman Productions (1974–1975); Mark Goodson Productions (1989)   *broadcast history:* CBS daytime April 1, 1974–June 13, 1975; CBS daytime April 3, 1989–July 14, 1989
1974–1975 version
host: Jack Narz   *announcers:* Johnny Olson, Gene Wood   *executive producer:* Frank Wayne   *producer:* Buck D'Amore   *director:* Paul Alter   *set designer:* James Agazzi   *theme:*

Here's Jack Narz behind his podium, on the contemporary set of "Now You See It."

"Chump Change" by Quincy Jones *origination:* CBS Studio 33, Television City, Los Angeles

1989 version

host: Chuck Henry *announcers:* Mark Driscoll, Don Morrow *executive producer:* Jonathan Goodson *producers:* Gary Dawson, Andrew Felsher *director:* Andrew Felsher *set designer:* James Agazzi *music director:* Stanley Blits *theme:* "Chump Change" *origination:* Studio 33, CBS Television City, Los Angeles

In "Now You See It," contestants competed for cash prizes by trying to figure out the answers hidden in lines of scrambled letters. The game started with four contestants divided into two teams of two (later changed to only two players). In the first round, two players swung their chairs around so that they could not see the game board. Questions were posed to the other two players who could see the game board. They were read a question, and after one player signaled in, his or her partner turned around and called off the position of the answer on the game board (row number and column). Points were awarded based on adding the row and column numbers of the first letter of the answer. Players changed positions midway through the round, and the team with the most points moved on to the next round.

In round two, the players were given a clue and shown one letter at a time on a letter board. Players signaled in to guess, each right answer was worth one point and four points won the game.

The winner of round two played the previous day's champion in round three, which was played the same way as the first round. The player with the most points at the end of this round won the game and played the "Solo Game" bonus round.

In the Solo Game the winner of the day had sixty seconds to find ten answers on the game board of scrambled letters. After a clue was given, the player tried to find the answer by circling it with an electronic pen. The person received $100 for each correct answer and the cash bonus if he or she found all ten in the allotted time. The cash bonus started at $5,000, with $1,000 added each time it was not won. If the player won the bonus round, he or she retired as champion and the day's runner-up returned to play on the next show.

Beginning with the one hundred eighty-sixth show, the format was changed, eliminating the preliminary round with two teams of two players. Instead, two players competed in the "Qualifying Round." They were given a clue and had to reveal the answer as a series of letters were displayed. Correct guesses were worth one point, and five points won the game.

The winner of the Qualifying Round played the previous day's champion in the "Championship Round," where players looked for answers on the "big board," which had four rows, each with fourteen letters. After a question was read, players buzzed in and answered with the line number and position of the answer. Scoring was determined by adding the line number and position number together. When one player reached the fifty-point level, point values were doubled, and the first player to reach one hundred points won the game.

The bonus game in the revised version remained unchanged from the original version.

Fourteen years after leaving television, "Now You See It" returned as a daytime series on CBS. Los Angeles newscaster Chuck Henry emceed the new version, which featured some changes in the game.

In the first game between the two new contestants, the scoring system was changed. In the second game (between the winner of the first game and the previous champion) the players were supposed to find an answer in a particular category (e.g., a word for being drunk). In the bonus round, the winner of the day played the "Solo Round" in which they were given sixty seconds to find answers to general knowledge questions hidden on another game board.

NUMBER PLEASE

premiere: January 31, 1961 *packager:* Mark Goodson–Bill Todman Productions *broadcast history:* ABC daytime January 31, 1961–December 29, 1961 *host:* Bud Collyer *hostesses:* Reggie Dombeck, Suzanne Storrs, Nancy Kovack

Back in the early days of television, Bud Collyer says, "Please ask for Chiffon dishwashing liquid."

announcer: Ralph Paul　*producer:* Jean Kopelman　*directors:* Don Bohl, Glenn Swanson　*set designers:* Romain Johnston, John Dapper　*music director:* Don Elliott　*origination:* Ritz Theater, New York

In "Number Please," two contestants faced a game board consisting of two rows of twenty spaces—one row per player. The object of the game was for a player to be the first to guess the identity of the prize (for example, "Pottery Corn Dishes") in his or her row.

The game began with each player choosing three spaces that were revealed to show letters of the prize. Players then alternated calling out spaces (identified by number) until the the puzzle was solved. To win the game, a player had to correctly guess both puzzles.

Did you know . . .　The debut of "Number Please," originally scheduled for January 30, was delayed one day because of President John F. Kennedy's State of the Union address?

Hostess Reggie Dombeck, whose real name was Penny Wright, was also seen as the weather girl on New York TV station WABC in the early sixties.

THE OBJECT IS

premiere: December 30, 1963 *packager:* The Object Is, Inc. *broadcast history:* ABC daytime December 30, 1963–March 27, 1964 *host:* Dick Clark *announcer:* Mike Laurence *producer:* Wilbur Stark *director:* Hal Cooper *set designer:* Sherman Loudermilk *origination:* Studio D, ABC Television Center, Los Angeles *debut guests:* Dwayne Hickman, Yvonne Craig, Hans Conreid

In "The Object Is," a panel of three celebrities and three contestants tried to identify a famous personality from clues describing objects associated with that personality. Each contestant played with two of the celebrities, one who received a clue and another who gave a clue.

The game began with a celebrity giving the first clue. (Example: the famous person is "Charles Lindbergh" and the clue is "transatlantic airplane.") If the player answered correctly he or she earned ten points. If not, the player gave a clue to the second celebrity for seven points. Guessing after the third clue was worth five points and after the fourth clue, three points. The player scored points if the celebrity answered correctly. The celebrity then received a new subject and gave the next player a clue. The game continued until one player reached fifteen points. That player won the game, $75, and a chance to earn additional money in the "Winner's Game."

In the Winner's Game the champ teamed up with one celebrity. They were given an object (example: "a baby rattle") along with a category ("nursery rhyme characters"). They had thirty seconds to name famous people associated with that object, earning $5 for each acceptable answer.

During its three-month run, the show's format changed and the number of celebrities and contestants was reduced to two each, with one celebrity and one contestant working as a team.

The name of a famous person was given to one member of each team and he or she tried to get his or her partner to come up with the identity of the famous person by offering a clue in the form of an object. Guessing the famous person's name from the first clue was worth ten points and the value of a correct guess decreased with each succeeding clue.

If the first team failed to identify the famous person after one clue, the opposing team got a chance to give another clue from one partner to the other. Teams alternated, with each team given the opportunity to give up to three clues. Fifteen points won the game and $100. The first player who won two games won the match, played a bonus game with his or her celebrity partner, and met a new challenger.

"American Bandstand" host Dick Clark made his debut as a game show emcee on this short-lived series. Clark later hosted the replacement series for "The Object Is," the panel game MISSING LINKS. That show ran for only nine months. Clark did not host another game show until THE $10,000 PYRAMID in 1973.

Did you know . . . Dick Clark played the murderer in the last episode of the original "Perry Mason" TV series? The show was "The Case of the Final Fadeout" and it was broadcast May 22, 1966.

Dick Clark has appeared on the cover of *TV Guide* four times.

Monty Hall and his classic "Let's Make a Deal" premiered on NBC the same day "The Object Is" premiered on ABC.

OH MY WORD

premiere: September 1966 *packager:* Circle Seven Productions for Seven Arts Television *broadcast history:* Syndicated September 1966–September 1967 *host:* Jim Lange *announcer:* Jay Snyder *creator:* Dr. Arthur Hough *producer/director:* Ajar Jacks *origination:* KGO-TV, San Francisco

"Oh My Word" was created by Dr. Arthur Hough, a professor at San Francisco State College, and was first broadcast as a local show on KGO in San Francisco in March 1965. In the fall of 1966, Seven Arts Television produced it as a weekly syndication show.

Two guest celebrities attempted to determine which of four panelists was giving the correct definition of various wild and wacky words. Only one panelist was giving the real definition and the other responses were made up.

"Oh My Word" was seen for one season in syndication in the 1960s but was revived as TAKE MY WORD FOR IT in 1982.

America's favorite, Dick Clark, on the set of his very first game show, "The Object Is," with guest celebrities Nick Adams and Yvonne Craig.

ON YOUR ACCOUNT

premiere: June 8, 1953 *packager:* Proctor and Gamble Productions *broadcast history:* NBC daytime June 8, 1953–July 2, 1954; CBS daytime July 5, 1954–March 30, 1956 *hosts:* Win Elliot, Dennis James *announcers:* Bob Warren, Bill Rogers, Bob Dixon *executive producer:* Tom McDermott *producer:* Bob Quigley *directors:* Larry White, Charles Fisher *music director:* Paul Taubman *origination:* Hudson Theater, New York (1953–1954)

When "On Your Account" began its run, contestants came on the show to earn money for charity. Host Win Elliot served as the "friendly banker" who interviewed the person "applying" for the money. For example, a man wanted to reward an anonymous girl who returned his lost wallet or a person appeared to raise money for a favorite charity.

Players then went to the "safe deposit vaults" that contained questions worth $10, $20, $30, and $40. At the conclusion of the show the studio audience selected one of the day's contestants to receive a bonus jackpot of $100.

By 1955, the format had changed to more of a straight quiz. Three contestants each began with $50 and then answered questions worth from $25 to $100. Correct answers led to the big bonus worth $1,500 and merchandise prizes.

Host Win Elliott was replaced by Dennis James on October 4, 1954. Game show creator Merrill Heatter was a researcher on this show that was produced by his future partner Bob Quigley.

ON YOUR MARK

premiere: September 23, 1961 *packager:* Sonny Fox Productions *broadcast history:* ABC Saturday morning September 23, 1961–December 16, 1961 *host:* Sonny Fox *announcer:* Johnny Olson *executive producer:* Sonny Fox *producer/director:* Lloyd Gross *origination:* TV-1, ABC Television Center, New York

Three children, ages nine to thirteen, competed on this weekly series in question-and-answer rounds, based on the contestants' career potentials. For example, on "On Your

Even though "Oh My Word" was Jim Lange's first game show hosting job, the producers liked to keep him comfortable. They knew he was destined for stardom.

Mark" kids who wanted to be astronauts were tested in the areas of concentration, coordination, and leadership, for the grand prize of a trip to Cape Canaveral.

Did you know . . . Sonny Fox would achieve greater success as host of "Wonderama," a local children's show seen over WNEW television in New York City? "Wonderama" was seen each Sunday morning from 7 A.M. to 11 A.M. for over a decade.

ON YOUR WAY

premiere: September 9, 1953   *packager:* Larry White Productions   *broadcast history:* DuMont primetime September 9, 1953–January 20, 1954; ABC primetime January 23, 1954–April 17, 1954   *hosts:* Bud Collyer, John Reed King and Kathy Godfrey   *announcers:* Walter Raney, Don Morrow   *executive producer:* Lawrence White   *producers:* Bud Collyer, Mike Dutton   *directors:* Martin Magner, Richard DePew   *music director:* Marty Ames   *origination:* New York

Contestants on this question-and-answer show, "On Your Way," wanted to get to their particular destinations. Each correct answer got them one-fourth of the way there and the contestant who answered the most questions correctly won a trip to his or her destination.

On January 23, 1954 "On Your Way" moved from the DuMont network to ABC and John Reed King and Kathy Godfrey (Arthur Godfrey's sister) became the new hosts. On February 6 the format was changed to a talent show with the audience determining the winner of cash awards.

100 GRAND

premiere: September 15, 1963   *packager:* Larry-Thomas Productions   *broadcast history:* ABC primetime September 15, 1963–September 29, 1963   *host:* Jack Clark   *announcer:* Scott Vincent   *executive producer:* Bob Stivers   *producer:* John B. Green   *directors:* Bill Foster, Jerome Shaw   *set designer:* John Dapper   *music director:* Milton DeLugg   *origination:* Studio A, ABC 66th Street Studios, New York

ABC unsuccessfully tried to revive the big-money quiz shows of the 1950s with "100 Grand."

One contestant, possessing knowledge in a specific field, was quizzed by a panel of five professional authorities for cash prizes. Players who survived without missing a question then had to answer five questions submitted by home viewers for a grand prize of $100,000.

Did you know . . . "100 Grand" was featured in a 1963 *Look* magazine article about the return of big-money quiz shows?

A dapper Dennis James and the beautiful Pat Meikle from "On Your Account" in the mid-1950s.

THE $128,000 QUESTION

premiere: September 18, 1976   *packager:* Cinelar Associates/Viacom Television   *broadcast history:* Syndicated September 18, 1976–September 1978   *hosts:* Mike Darrow, Alex Trebek   *assistants:* Lauri Locke, Cyndi Reynolds, Sylvie Garnet, Patti Lee   *security:* Michael O'Rourke   *announcers:* Alan Kalter, Sandy Hoyt   *executive producers:* Steve Carlin, Jerry Appleton   *producers:* Willie Stein, Candy Cazau, Greg Harper, Ron Thornbury   *directors:* Dick Schneider, George Choderker, William G. Elliott   *set designers:* Kathleen Ankers, C. M. Zahurak   *music:* Guido Basso   *origination:* Ed Sullivan Theater, New York (1976–1977); Global TV, Toronto, Canada (1977–1978)

This weekly series, "The $128,000 Question," was based on THE $64,000 QUESTION. Contestants, selected because of their knowledge in specific fields, answered questions on their areas of expertise. The value of the questions started at $64 and doubled until a maximum of $64,000 was reached. Players risked their winnings on their ability to answer successive questions and wrong answers eliminated them. The top winners of the season competed for an additional $64,000.

The first season of shows was taped in New York City with Mike Darrow as host, while the second season was taped in Toronto with Alex Trebek as emcee. Michael O'Rourke was the security guard in charge of the questions.

ONE IN A MILLION

premiere: April 10, 1967   *packager:* Merv Griffin Productions   *broadcast history:* ABC daytime April 10, 1967–June 16, 1967   *host:* Danny O'Neill   *announcer:* Chet Gould   *creator:* Don Lipp   *producer:* Stu Billet   *directors:* Garth Dietrick, Alvin Mifelow   *set designers:* Tom Trimble, Rene D'Auriac   *origination:* Elysee Theater, New York

This short-lived panel show, "One in a Million," featured four guests, each with a story to tell, and a contestant who tried to determine if the stories were fact or fiction. If the contestant judged correctly, he or she won $25 and a clue to help guess the identity of the panelist whose unique accomplishment made him or her one in a million. Correctly selecting that person won the contestant an additional $250. Among the guests who appeared on one show were a kite-flying champion and a woman who was kidnapped in Berlin, Germany and forced to become a spy.

Did you know . . . producer Stu Billet teamed with Ralph Edwards in the 1980s to produce the long-running "The People's Court" with Judge Wapner?

$1,000,000 CHANCE OF A LIFETIME

premiere: January 6, 1986   *packager:* Lorimar–Telepictures Productions   *broadcast history:* Syndicated January 6, 1986–September 11, 1987   *host:* Jim Lange   *assistant:* Karen Thomas   *announcer:* Johnny Gilbert   *executive producers:* Bob Synes, Jay Feldman, Scott Stone   *producer:* Joel Stein   *directors:* Jerome Shaw, Joe Carolei   *set designers:* Anthony Sabatino, William H. Harris   *origination:* Studio 5, KTLA–TV, Hollywood

In "$1,000,000 Chance of a Lifetime," two couples competed in word-puzzle games with a jackpot prize of $1 million. One member from each team competed at a time. A clue was given and letters appeared one at a time until one player guessed the word. That word became a clue to the main puzzle and the player then chose one of the possible letters in the main puzzle. The letters appeared in their places in the phrase and the player was given a chance to guess. One extra letter (the "stinger") was among the available letters and if the player selected that one he or she lost a turn. The player could choose up to two letters on each turn.

In round one, players received $25 for each clue successfully interpreted, and each letter they revealed in the main puzzle added $25 to a pot that was won by the player who guessed the puzzle. The values doubled to $50 in round two and $100 in round three. The team with the most money after three rounds won the game.

The day's winning team played the bonus round for $5,000. The team chose from three categories (examples: sweet tooth, Arctic Circle, Middle Eastern cities) and had to guess six items in that category, in a maximum of sixty seconds, with letters revealed one at a time.

If they were successful, they could leave with their winnings or come back, risk their money, and try again to win the game and go for another $5,000. If they won three days in a row, they won $1 million.

Jim Lange handed out $1 million to nine lucky couples on the "$1,000,000 Chance of a Lifetime."

During its two-season run, nine couples won the grand prize.

ONE MINUTE PLEASE

premiere: July 6, 1954 *packager:* Harry S. Goodman Productions *broadcast history:* DuMont primetime July 6, 1954–February 17, 1955 *hosts:* John K. M. McCaffery, Allyn Edwards *announcer:* Don Russell *producer/director:* David Lowe *origination:* New York *debut guests:* Hermione Gingold, Cleveland Amory, Anne Burr, Jimmy Cannon, Ernie Kovacs, Alice Pearce

"One Minute Please" was based on a BBC-TV series. Two teams, each composed of three celebrities, were given a topic such as "How Peter Piper picked a peck of pickled peppers" or "How to Begin the Beguine" and each panelist had to incorporate it into a conversation for one minute without unduly repeating, hesitating, or straying from the point. Prizes were awarded to members of the studio audience.

Allyn Edwards replaced John K. M. McCaffery as host on November 19, 1954. Among the regular panelists were Cleveland Amory, Anne Burr, Jimmy Cannon, Marc Connelly, Hermione Gingold, Ernie Kovacs, and Alice Pearce.

PANTOMIME QUIZ

premiere: July 3, 1950 *packager:* Mike Stokey Productions
broadcast history: CBS primetime July 3, 1950–September 25, 1950; CBS primetime July 2, 1951–August 20, 1951; NBC primetime January 2, 1952–March 26, 1952; CBS primetime July 4, 1952–September 26, 1952; CBS primetime July 10, 1953–August 28, 1953; DuMont primetime October 20, 1953–April 13, 1954; CBS primetime July 9, 1954–August 27, 1954; ABC primetime January 22, 1955–March 6, 1955; CBS primetime July 8, 1955–September 30, 1955; CBS primetime July 6, 1956–September 7, 1956; CBS primetime July 5, 1957–September 6, 1957; ABC primetime April 8, 1958–September 2, 1958; ABC daytime May 18, 1959–October 9, 1959; ABC primetime June 8, 1959–September 28, 1959 *host:* Mike Stokey *timekeeper/assistants:* Sandra Spence, Virginia Dwyer, Spring Mitchell *announcers:* Ed Reimers, Ken Niles, Art Gilmore, Don Russell, Don Morrow, Art Fleming, Jimmy Blaine, Terry O'Sullivan, Charles Woods *producer:* Mike Stokey *directors:* A. C. Jones, Stuart Phelps, Philippe De-Lacy, Bill Bennington, Bud Cole, Harry Coyle, Alan Reisner, Eddie Nugent, Alan Dinehart, Joe Dachow, William Ayers *music director:* Frank DeVol *theme song:* ''Huckleberry Duck'' by Raymond Scott *origination:* Los Angeles (1950–1953); New York (1953–1959) *debut daytime guests:* Dick Van Dyke, Cliff Norton, Howard Morris, Jeff Donnell

''Pantomime Quiz'' was an annual summer replacement series during the 1950s. During its ten-year run it was seen on all four of the commercial networks (NBC, CBS, ABC, DuMont).

While attending Los Angeles City College in 1939, Mike Stokey and other students began playing ''The Game'' (charades) on experimental TV station W6XAO from a small studio over a car dealer's garage. On November 13, 1947 ''Pantomime Quiz'' began as a local series seen in the Los Angeles area on KTLA-TV, which had begun commercial broadcasting earlier in the year.

On October 4, 1949 WCBS New York began broadcasting a series of ''Pantomime Quiz'' shows and the following summer CBS picked it up as a summer replacement for ''The Goldbergs.'' Celebrities who appeared as the ''home team''

for the first season included Hans Conreid, Frank DeVol, Vincent Price, and Adele Jurgens.

Hosting ''Pantomime Quiz'' for its entire TV run was its creator Mike Stokey. Sandra Spence was the original scorekeeper, appearing on the show from 1950 to 1953. She later costarred in the TV series ''The Whirlybirds'' in the 1950s.

Chief Mike Stokey shows off his totem of talent, which includes (from top to bottom) Milt Kamen, Carol Burnett, Stubby Kaye, Denise Darcel, Tom Poston, and Howard Morris.

Virginia Dwyer was the scorekeeper in 1954. In 1955 she was replaced by Spring Mitchell.

Based on the parlor game charades, two teams consisting of four members each, competed against each other to pantomime famous phrases, quotes, or names. The team using the least time to guess the phrase was the winner. Home viewers sent in phrases and won cash if their phrases were used and bonus prizes if the panel could not identify the phrases in two minutes.

Among the celebrities who were regulars in later seasons were Carol Burnett, Robert Clary, Jackie Coogan, Dorothy Hart, Angela Lansbury, Vincent Price, Robert Stack, Judy Tyler, Dick Van Dyke, and Dave Willock.

"Pantomime Quiz" was the first Los Angeles–based quiz show to be picked up for network television, having first appeared on KTLA in November 1947. CBS picked it up for national exposure as a summer replacement in July 1950. The show became a summer staple throughout the 1950s and made stops at all four commercial networks. In 1953, during its run on the DuMont network, the show moved to New York City where it remained for the rest of the 1950s.

In 1962, "Pantomime Quiz" was renamed STUMP THE STARS and returned for a one-year run on CBS. Two syndicated versions of "Stump the Stars" were produced, one in 1964 and the other in 1969–1970. "Pantomime Quiz" was revived as CELEBRITY CHARADES in 1979.

Did you know . . . "Pantomime Quiz" was the first television program to receive an Emmy Award? In 1948 it was named "Most Popular Program on Television."

THE PARENT GAME

premiere: September 4, 1972   *packager:* Chuck Barris Productions   *broadcast history:* Syndicated September 4, 1972–September 1973   *host:* Clark Race   *announcer:* Charlie O'Donnell   *creators:* Barry Abel, Gary Jonke   *producer:* Gary Jonke   *director:* John Dorsey   *set designer:* Archie Sharp   *music:* Frank Jaffe   *authority:* Dorothy Thompson, U.S.C.   *origination:* ABC Vine Street Theater, Los Angeles

Radio personality Clark Race hosted this weekly show where three married couples matched their ideas about raising children with those of a child psychologist.

Five questions were featured on each show, with the first two worth five points each. The third question was worth ten points; the fourth, fifteen points; and the final question, thirty points.

Each player responded to the first four questions individually and then teamed up with his or her mate for a joint answer on the final question.

Included on the show were questions about situations, like, "You were at a barbershop reading a men's magazine when you saw a photo of your eighteen-year-old daughter in her 'birthday suit' . . . how would you react?" Four choices were given (would you ask her to explain, ask her to autograph it, do nothing about it, or forget you saw it) and each player selected the one he or she felt was right. Child

psychologist Dorothy Thompson of the University of Southern California made comments about the responses.

PARTY LINE

premiere: June 8, 1947   *broadcast history:* NBC primetime June 8, 1947–August 31, 1947   *host:* Bert Parks   *assistant:* Mimi Walters   *origination:* NBC Studio 3H, New York

"Party Line," this early television series, was broadcast on NBC's two-station network of WNBT, New York and WPTZ, Philadelphia. The format consisted of questions being asked, sometimes illustrated with a film clip or a demonstration, followed by a call placed to a home viewer. A correct answer earned $5 and a box of the sponsor's (Bristol Myers) products.

"Party Line" was originally broadcast on CBS with John Reed King. The show was dropped when CBS discontinued live studio programming in 1947.

PASS THE BUCK

premiere: April 3, 1978   *packager:* Bob Stewart Productions   *broadcast history:* CBS daytime April 3, 1978–June 30, 1978   *host:* Bill Cullen   *announcer:* Bob Clayton   *executive producer:* Bob Stewart   *producer:* Sande Stewart   *director:* Mike Garguilo   *set designer:* Jim Ryan   *origination:* Ed Sullivan Theater, New York

Four contestants competed in a game to come up with multiple answers to particular questions (example: What is something a person does to keep cool?), in "Pass the Buck." The bank started at $100 and $25 was added for each answer given. Players were eliminated when they gave unacceptable answers and the game continued until only one player was left. The remaining player received all the cash in the bank and a chance to win an additional $5,000.

The winner tried to name items in a particular category in fifteen seconds, receiving $100 for each answer on the board. Naming all the items in a particular row or one item in each of the four rows meant winning the $5,000.

Did you know . . . "Pass the Buck," "The $128,000 Question," and others were taped at the Ed Sullivan Theater, which in 1993 became the new home of David Letterman and his successful CBS late-night talk show?

PASSWORD

premiere: October 2, 1961   *packager:* Mark Goodson–Bill Todman Productions   *broadcast history:* CBS daytime October 2, 1961–September 15, 1967; CBS primetime January 2, 1962–September 9, 1965; CBS primetime December 25, 1966–May 22, 1967; ABC daytime April 5, 1971–June 27, 1975

1961–1967 version

host: Allen Ludden   *substitute host:* Jack Clark   *announcers:* Bob Marcato, Jack Clark, Frank Wayne, Bern Bennett, Lee Vines, Gene Wood, Bob Kennedy   *executive producer:* Bob Stewart   *producer:* Frank Wayne   *directors:* Lou Tedesco, Mike Garguilo   *set designers:* Ted Cooper, Bill Bohnert   *word authorities:* Professor David H. Greene of New

Veteran game show host Bill Cullen leads the fast-paced festivities on "Pass the Buck."

word using a one-word clue. If he or she could not, the opposing team received a chance to try. The point value started at ten and decreased by one until the word was guessed. The first team to score twenty-five points won the game and played the "Lightning Round," where one player tried to convey five words to his or her partner in one minute at $50 a word.

In the updated 1971 version the winning team played the "Betting Word," after the Lightning Round. The contestant was given the opportunity to risk any or all winnings on the ability to get his or her partner to say the word in fifteen seconds thereby doubling their bet.

The format was changed to "Password All-Stars" on November 18, 1974 and only celebrities played the game. On February 18, 1975 "Password" returned to the contestant format with several alterations. An elimination round was now played before the main game, a player was given the option of going for double points by trying to get his or her teammate to say the password on one clue, and a three-step lightning round was used in the bonus game.

Milton Bradley marketed twenty-five editions of the "Password" home game. In 1962, its first year on the market, over two million games were sold.

Kitty Carlisle and Tom Poston were the first celebrity guests on "Password" when it premiered on the CBS daytime schedule in October 1961. Carol Burnett and Garry Moore were the first nighttime celebrities when the show aired in primetime in January 1962. Other celebrities who appeared on the show included Marty Allen and Steve Rossi, Jack Benny, Henry Fonda, Bill Cullen, Phyllis Diller, Jane Fonda, Fred Gwynne, Jayne Mansfield, Lee Marvin, Ginger Rogers, Mickey Rooney, Jimmy Stewart, Danny Thomas, Mel Torme, and Mrs. Allen Ludden, Betty White.

"Password" was revived in 1979 under the title PASSWORD PLUS and in 1984 as SUPER PASSWORD.

Did you know . . . Allen Ludden was a Phi Beta Kappa with a master's degree in English from the University of Texas? Before beginning his broadcasting career, Ludden won a Bronze Star in World War II and served as personal manager for noted Shakespearean actor Maurice Evans. Ludden taught at Austin High School in Austin, Texas, before moving to New York in 1949 to host a local teenage discussion show entitled "Mind Your Manners."

Allen Ludden met Betty White during a 1962 summer stock production of "Critic's Choice." They enjoyed playing husband and wife on stage and soon followed suit in real life.

Ludden opened each "Password" show with "Hi Doll." He was referring to Betty White's mother and he said hello to her each day.

Allen Ludden's star on the Hollywood Walk of Fame is sandwiched between Gary Owens' and Betty White's. In May 1976, Allen Ludden received the Emmy Award for "Outstanding Game Show Host" and seven years later Betty White won an Emmy for her emceeing role on "Just Men!"

Were you watching when . . . Allen Ludden and Betty White appeared on "The Odd Couple" just as Felix (Tony

York University, Dr. Reason A. Goodwin, editor of the dictionary of the *World Book Encyclopedia* **music:** Bob Cobert **origination:** CBS Studios 50 and 52, New York; Studio 33, CBS Television City, Los Angeles; Studio 43, CBS Television City, Los Angeles **debut guests:** Kitty Carlisle, Tom Poston; **primetime debut guests:** Carol Burnett, Garry Moore
1971–1975 version
host: Allen Ludden **announcer:** John Harlan **executive producer:** Frank Wayne **producer:** Howard Felsher **directors:** Stuart Phelps, Ira Skutch **set designer:** Henry Lickel **music:** Score Productions **word authorities:** Dr. Robert Stockwell, Dr. Carolyn Duncan **origination:** ABC Television Center, Los Angeles; Vine Street Theatre, Los Angeles

On "Password," two teams, each composed of a celebrity guest and a contestant, competed in a game to guess words from one-word clues. One member of each team was given the "password" and tried to get his or her partner to say the

Randall) and Oscar (Jack Klugman) appeared as contestants on "Password?"

Jack Benny and his daughter Joan appeared as celebrities on "Password" and one of the words Jack had to give clues to was "miser."

Over the years "Password" featured numerous game show hosts as celebrity guest players, including Steve Allen, Bill Cullen, Monty Hall, Art James, Dennis James, Tom Kennedy, Peter Marshall, Garry Moore, Jack Narz, and Gene Rayburn.

Monty Hall took over "Password" in the early 1970s as its emcee while Allen Ludden played opposite Betty White. Monty hosted "Password" for one special week while Allen and Betty battled it out on the "Password" set.

Bob Cobert, composer of the "Password" theme, also wrote the theme music for THE $10,000 PYRAMID, THE $25,000 PYRAMID, "Dark Shadows," and "The Winds of War" mini-series.

PASSWORD PLUS

premiere: January 8, 1979 *packager:* Mark Goodson–Bill Todman Productions *broadcast history:* NBC daytime January 8, 1979–March 26, 1982 *hosts:* Allen Ludden, Bill Cullen, Tom Kennedy *announcers:* Gene Wood, Rich Jeffries *executive producer:* Howard Felsher *producer:* Robert Sherman *director:* George Choderker *set designer:* Bente Christensen *origination:* NBC Studio 3, Burbank *debut guests:* Elizabeth Montgomery, Robert Foxworth

In "Password Plus," the updated version of PASSWORD, two teams, each consisting of a celebrity guest and a contestant, again guessed words from one-word clues given by their partners. Each "password" in the new version was a clue to the password puzzle (the name of a person, place, or thing) and the first player to correctly guess the puzzle won the round. The first two puzzles played were worth $100 each and others after that were worth $200. The first team to collect $300 won the match.

Three television legends on the set of "Password," from the first nighttime telecast in January 1962. That's emcee Allen Ludden, with Garry Moore and Carol Burnett.

Tom Kennedy was a heavenly host on "Password Plus."

The winning team played "Alphabetics," where one player tried to communicate ten words in sixty seconds to his or her partner using one-word clues for $100 a word or a jackpot of $5,000 for all ten.

Bill Cullen filled in for Allen Ludden as a guest host from April 14, 1980 to May 12, 1980. On October 27, 1980, Tom Kennedy became the new host when Allen Ludden became too ill to continue. (Ludden passed away on June 9, 1981). The show was revived again in the fall of 1984 as "Super Password."

Did you know . . . Allen Ludden moved to New York in 1953 to be moderator of the radio quiz show "College Bowl"? In 1954 he hosted a morning show for WABC radio in New York that was produced by future NBC chairman Grant Tinker.

"Password Plus" was originally planned to be titled "Password '79."

Were you watching when . . . Kirstie Alley appeared as a contestant? On August 20, 1980 she teamed with celeb-rities Lucille Ball and Dick Martin. In her two days on the show, Kirstie won $800.

Jack Narz guest starred on "Password Plus" with his brother Tom Kennedy. During a taping, Jack mentioned to Tom how much easier it was being a host, rather than a guest celebrity. Tom jokingly disagreed, and Jack suggested they switch roles to see who was right. So for one day Jack Narz guest-emceed "Password Plus."

PAY CARDS!

premiere: September 9, 1968   *packager:* Nicholson-Muir Productions   *broadcast history:* Syndicated September 9, 1968–September 1969   *host:* Art James   *announcers:* Fred Collins, Glenn Rhyle, Jerry Thomas   *executive producers:* Nick Nicholson, Roger Muir   *producers:* Jim Reynolds, Robert Rushing   *directors:* Jim Reynolds, Mike Garguilo   *set designer:* Murl Rush   *origination:* New York; Cincinnati

Three contestants competed in "Pay Cards!", this daily game show based on the card game poker. The players attempted to build better hands than their opponents by selecting cards at random from a game board of twenty cards. The deck of cards consisted of single cards, which couldn't be paired, two of a kind, three of a kind, and four of a kind.

Each player selected three cards and kept them if they included a pair. A player could call a fourth card to try to complete a hand. If a player decided not to keep the fourth card or if he or she did not find a pair in the first three cards called, the next player selected cards. Play continued until all three persons completed their hands.

Players were awarded $10 for each pair, $30 for three of a kind, $50 for a full house, $100 for four of a kind, and $50 for the player with a high hand.

Three rounds were played with variations on the basic idea. A "wild card" round gave the players a chance to get five of a kind and earn $150. In the "strategy" round the four corner cards were revealed before the round began. The players called two additional cards on each of their first two turns (one card on their third turn) and then selected two from the six cards showing.

The player with the highest cash score won the game and played a jackpot round for bonus prizes. Twelve cards were revealed for twelve seconds for the champion to study. A wheel was spun to indicate a card to be called by the player, who would win the prizes if he or she found the card on the game board.

Celebrity guests appeared on many of the shows and played for members of the studio audience.

"Pay Cards!" was revived in 1981 as SUPER PAY CARDS!

PDQ

premiere: August 30, 1965   *packager:* Merrill Heatter–Bob Quigley Production   *broadcast history:* Syndicated August 30, 1965–September 26, 1969   *host:* Dennis James   *announcer:* Kenny Williams   *producers:* Merrill Heatter, Bob Quigley   *directors:* Larry White, Jerome Shaw, Stuart Phelps   *set designer:* Mary Weaver   *music:* Arlo   *origina-*

*The password is **longevity**. "Password" is Mark Goodson's fourth longest running game show of all time. Joining in on the fun are celebrity guests Carol Burnett and Monty Hall.*

tion: NBC Studio 1, Burbank   *debut guests:* Morey Amsterdam, Rose Marie, Gisele MacKenzie

On "PDQ," three celebrities and one contestant competed on two teams of two (one team consisted of two celebrities) to guess words or phrases from letter clues. One member of each team was placed in a soundproof booth. The other was shown a phrase and then put three letters, including the phrase's first letter, on a game board for his or her partner to see. The partner had to guess the word or have letters added, one at a time, until they both came up with the answer. After one team played, the opposing team played the same phrase.

The team using the least number of letters to guess the word won the round and scored points based on the difference in scores between the teams. Players on each team changed positions when one team reached the five-point level and the first team to score ten points won the game.

The contestants who won the game received $100 for every point they beat their opponents by. The contestants also received a chance to win additional cash by guessing ten words from three-letter clues in sixty seconds, for $50 a word.

"PDQ" was originally created for NBC owned and operated stations and was syndicated to other stations by Four-Star Television.

That's Morey Amsterdam, Rose Marie, emcee Dennis James, and Gisele MacKenzie on "PDQ."

''PDQ'' was revived as BAFFLE by NBC for their daytime schedule in 1973.

Did you know . . . Dennis James made his debut on television in 1938 hosting a pair of programs, ''Television Roof'' and ''Dennis James Sports Parade,'' for the DuMont station in New York? In the late 1940s he became well known as a sportscaster for DuMont's wrestling matches and frequently used his famous catch phrase ''Okay mother.''

PEER PRESSURE

premiere: September 6, 1997   *packager:* Wheeler-Sussman Productions   *broadcast history:* Syndicated September 6, 1997–   *hosts:* Nick Spano, Valarie Miller   *executive producers:* Burt Wheeler, Sharon Sussman   *producers:* Gary Ponticello, Lynne Spiegel Spillman   *director:* Joe Carolei   *production designer:* Last Design   *theme music:* Jon Ernst   *origination:* The Production Group Studios, Hollywood

''Peer Pressure'' is a weekly syndicated series, seen mostly on weekends. It consists of three teenage contestants who work their way around a game board spread out on a studio floor.

Players alternate turns, and their moves are determined by a giant Magic 8 Ball, which reveals the number of spaces they can move and one of four categories, with a stunt or question, that they need to complete to advance on the board.

Categories include ''Temptation,'' in which they must choose between taking a prize and moving back on the board or continuing to progress forward; ''Odd Job,'' where they have to perform a stunt like tossing newspapers on a porch; ''Fast Track,'' another physical stunt round; and ''Decision,'' in which they try to guess how a studio audience of their peers responds to a teenage dilemma. At the end of this round, the two players farthest along the game board move on to the ''Pressure Cooker'' round.

In the Pressure Cooker round, the two remaining players alternate in trying to match their answers to teenage dilemmas to the responses of a peer group (a section of the audience behind them). The first player to successfully match with his or her group three times wins the game and receives prizes.

PENNY TO A MILLION

premiere: May 4, 1955   *packager:* Wolf Productions   *broadcast history:* ABC primetime May 4, 1955–October 19, 1955   *host:* Bill Goodwin   *announcers:* George Ansbro, Jay Stewart   *executive producer:* Herb Wolf   *producer:* Alan Gilbert   *director:* Matt Harlib   *music directors:* Glenn Osser, Rex Koury   *origination:* Ritz Theater, New York (May–June, 1955); ABC Television Center, Los Angeles (July–Oct, 1955)

The game show ''Penny to a Million'' was hosted by Bill Goodwin, one-time announcer on the George Burns and Gracie Allen radio series. Two sets of contestants competed in a question-and-answer game with the value of the jackpot doubling with each correct answer and escalating from one penny to one million pennies ($10,000).

Four contestants competed at a time and each was given five seconds to come up with the answer to a question. A right answer doubled the cash in the jackpot and a wrong answer eliminated the player from the game. The last remaining player won a $50 bond and moved to a playoff round to face the winner from the second set of contestants.

The two winners competed in a playoff round to determine the day's champion. The champ received seventy-five percent of the total jackpot of both earlier rounds, and the runner-up twenty-five percent. If they both missed questions they divided the total evenly.

''Penny to a Million'' was originally broadcast from the Ritz Theater in New York City with Bill Goodwin as host, George Ansbro as announcer, and Glenn Osser as music director. On July 5, 1955 the show moved to Los Angeles with Goodwin continuing as host. Jay Stewart became the new announcer and Rex Koury the music director.

PEOPLE ARE FUNNY

premiere: September 19, 1954   *packagers:* John Guedel Productions (1954–1961); Roadblock Productions (Ohlmeyer Communications) (1984)   *broadcast history:* NBC primetime September 19, 1954–April 16, 1961; NBC primetime March 24, 1984–July 21, 1984

1954–1961 version

host: Art Linkletter   *announcer:* Pat McGeehan   *producer:* John Guedel   *directors:* George Foxe, Irving Atkins   *theme:* Bill Bates   *origination:* Linkletter Playhouse, NBC Studio D Hollywood

1984 version

host: Flip Wilson   *announcer:* Dick Tufeld   *executive producer:* Don Ohlmeyer   *producer/director:* Perry Rosemond   *set designer:* Ed LaPorta   *music director:* Milton DeLugg   *origination:* NBC Studios,Burbank

''People Are Funny,'' one of the most popular radio shows of the 1940s and 50s, made a successful transition to television in the fall of 1954. The radio series had begun on NBC in 1942 as ''Pull Over Neighbor'' with Art Baker as host. Art Linkletter became host on October 1, 1943 and continued with the show when it moved to television.

''People Are Funny'' was filmed at the NBC Studios at Sunset and Vine in Hollywood and 150 of the 246 shows produced were syndicated after the show left NBC in 1961.

Contestants were picked from the studio audience just prior to the start of each show. On the air, they were interviewed by Art and then were asked to become involved in a stunt to prove that ''people are funny.'' Some stunts were executed in the studio during the show and some took a week to complete.

A frequent stunt used was picking a name at random from a telephone book and then having the contestant call that person and try to keep him or her on the line for two or three minutes. Other stunts involved asking several players on stage to refrain from yawning while the entire studio audience yawned; having a man call his best friend and try to borrow his wife; and playing an anagram game.

On September 15, 1956 the Univac computer was introduced on the show. Couples, matched by the computer, got to know each other while answering questions in a quiz segment.

The last first-run episode of "People Are Funny" was seen on April 1, 1960. For the next year, the show was seen in reruns on NBC.

Art Linkletter was also seen hosting "House Party" on CBS while also hosting "People Are Funny."

In 1984, Flip Wilson hosted a three-month revival of "People Are Funny." Contestants were selected to perform outrageous stunts for laughs. Filmed mostly on the streets of Los Angeles, the show featured sample gags including two men trying to get a passerby to join them "fishing" in a manhole and a little girl trying to get a restaurant patron to eat her vegetables before her mother came back to the table.

Did you know . . . Art Linkletter was radio program manager at the San Francisco World's Fair in 1937? Linkletter costarred in the 1950 film *Champagne for Caesar* with Ronald Coleman, Celeste Holm, and Vincent Price. In 1969 he won a Grammy Award for "Best Spoken Word Recording" and in 1980, his autobiography, *I Didn't Do It Alone*, was published.

PEOPLE WILL TALK

premiere: July 1, 1963   *packager:* Merrill Heatter–Bob Quigley Productions/Four Star Television   **broadcast history:** NBC daytime July 1, 1963–December 27, 1963   **host:** Dennis James   *announcer:* Kenny Williams   *producers:* Merrill Heatter, Bob Quigley   *director:* Joe Behar   *music director:* Arlo   *origination:* NBC Studio 3, Burbank

Two contestants argued opposite sides of a question and then tried to find support for their opinions among a panel of fifteen judges representing a cross-section of the American public.

Each game of "People Will Talk" opened with the show's roving reporter conducting a filmed people-on-the-street interview on topics such as "Should bald men wear toupees?" and "Should a woman lie about her age?" Contestants representing each side of the issue were brought to the studio to debate it.

The panel voted for one of the two points of view. The contestants attempted to select panel members who they felt agreed with their opinions. If the panelist agreed with the contestant the contestant earned $25. If the panelist voted against the contestant, the opponent received $25. The first person to collect $100 won the game and a merchandise prize.

The original pilot for "People Will Talk" was taped for CBS with Arthur Godfrey as host.

Did you know . . . Dennis James appeared as "Chet Cumley" and Allen Ludden appeared as "David Dooley" on the November 2, 1966 episode of "Batman"?

THE PERFECT MATCH

premiere: September 18, 1967   *packager:* Bill Derman Productions/Screen Gems Television   **broadcast history:** Syndicated September 18, 1967–September 13, 1968   **host:** Dick Enberg   *announcer:* John Hilliard   *creator:* Bill Derman   *executive producer:* Harry Koplan   *producer:* Bill Derman, Larry Rosen   *directors:* Robert Robb, Bill Rainbolt   **set design:** Jim Fox   *theme*: Helen Miller, Howard Greenfield   *origination:* KTLA-TV, Los Angeles

NBC Sportscaster Dick Enberg hosted "The Perfect Match," which featured two three-member teams (men vs. women) who tried to discover which mates an IBM system 360 computer had selected as their perfect matches. The computer chose three matches for each of the six players. Each player received $50 if he or she chose the match the computer had selected, and if both players picked each other they won $200.

In round one, the men were presented with a romantic situation, such as "You're sitting on a bus next to an attractive young woman who has her eyes closed. Suddenly she slumps over, fast asleep on your shoulder, just as you are coming to your stop. How would you go about awakening her?" Each of the male players responded and the women then questioned them. A second situation was presented to the women and the men followed with questions.

In the second round, the players each responded "Yes" or "No" to questions read to them. Samples included "Do you think men should wear long hair?" and "Do you think a woman will use any means to catch a man?"

The third and final round was a free association with the host reading the beginning of a sentence and players finishing it with the first thoughts that entered their heads. At the conclusion of this round, players made their guesses as to who was selected for them.

Did you know . . . Dick Enberg was the play-by-play voice of the California Angels from 1969 to 1977? Before beginning his broadcasting career, Enberg was a professor teaching health science, as well as an assistant baseball coach at California State University, Northridge. He graduated Indiana University with a Ph.D. in health science in 1961.

PERFECT MATCH

premiere: January 13, 1986   *packager:* Lorimar-Telepictures   **broadcast history:** Syndicated January 13, 1986–September 12, 1986   **host:** Bob Goen   *announcer:* Johnny Gilbert   *executive producers:* Bob Synes, Scott Stone, Jay Feldman   *producer:* Scott Sternberg   *director:* Joe Behar   **set designers:** Ray Klausen, Randy Blom   **music:** Score Productions   *origination:* Studio 2, KTLA-TV, Los Angeles

Three married couples competed on "Perfect Match" to see which mate knew more about the other. The teams began with $200 each and the husbands bet part of their bankrolls on their ability to guess how their wives responded to a situation like "You're in the middle of a romantic encounter, the doorbell rings and it's your mother-in-law. What would you do?" Three questions were played with both mates trying to guess what the other said.

The final part of the game was the "Perfect Match" round where one mate read a "love note" to his or her spouse, leaving blanks for the other to fill in. The first completed love note was worth $100 and the second love note earned $200.

The team with the most money won the game and an additional $1,000. If a team matched on every question they won a $5,000 bonus.

THE PERFECT MATCH

premiere: October 3, 1994   *packager:* Bilkistar Productions *broadcast history:* ESPN (cable) October 3, 1994–December 30, 1994 *host:* Ken Ober *cohost:* Challen Cates *announcer:* Lou Dimaggio *executive producers:* Bob Seizer, Stephen Bilkis, Terry Cashman *producer:* Alan Winter *director:* Harold Reiser *set designer:* Gene McAvoy *music:* Terry Cashman *origination:* Empire Studios, North Hollywood

"The Perfect Match" joined the ESPN lineup in October 1994 as their first game show to offer an interactive segment for home viewers to participate in. The daily series was hosted by Ken Ober, who had emceed the offbeat TV trivia quiz show REMOTE CONTROL for MTV.

"The Perfect Match" consisted of four rounds, two rounds with two female contestants and two with male contestants. The top-scoring player of each sex participated in the bonus round for a grand prize.

In each round a player was given thirty seconds to match as many answers as he or she could to twelve possible matches revealed on a game board. Sample games included matching rival teams in different sports. Players scored three points for correct matches in round one and seven points in round two. The player with the highest point score won and teamed up with the winner of rounds three and four to play the bonus round.

In the bonus round, the teams had forty-five seconds to clear the board of twelve answers by matching the correct items given by the host. If they were successful they won a grand prize.

The interactive segment, played twice per show, gave the home viewers a chance to play "The Perfect Match" using their touch-tone telephones. They attempted to match answers given on the screen with one of nine responses, each connected to a corresponding number or sign on the phone dial. Players had six seconds to punch in their responses and the caller with the most correct answers using the least amount of time won the prize of the day. All daily winners competed at the end of the month in a game for a $2,500 grand prize.

Did you know . . .   "The Perfect Match" producer Terry Cashman produced singer Jim Croce's records during the 1970s and as a performer, recorded the popular baseball song "Talkin' Baseball (Willie, Mickey and The Duke)"?

A PERFECT SCORE

premiere: June 15, 1992   *packager:* Go For Productions *broadcast history:* CBS late night June 15, 1992–December 8, 1992 *host:* Jeff Marder *announcer:* David Greenfield *executive producers:* Jerry Golod, Larry Forsdick *producer:* David Greenfield *director:* Wally Benson *set designer:*

Gene Abel *music:* Steve Wylymz *origination:* Schulman Video Center, Los Angeles

A player put the fate of his or her love life into the hands of three close friends on this late-night game show "A Perfect Score." The friends attempted to find him or her the perfect date by questioning three potential candidates.

The player was seated behind a partition where the questions could be heard, as well as the answers of his or her potential date, but the player could not see the choice of dates until his or her friends selected one of the three.

Each candidate was questioned one at a time with questions like "After you date a woman, how long until you call her again?" and "What's the most dangerous location you ever made love in?"

After all three candidates were interviewed, the friends made their choices. The couple was then introduced and was sent on a romantic date.

The final part of the show was taped a week later with the contestant returning to reflect on the date and answer questions asked by his or her friends about the night out.

PERSONALITY

premiere: July 3, 1967   *packager:* Bob Stewart Productions/ Filmways Television   *broadcast history:* NBC daytime July 3, 1967–September 26, 1969 *host:* Larry Blyden *announcers:* Jack Clark, Bill Wendell *executive producer:* Bob Stewart *producer:* Anne Marie Schmidt *director:* Lou Tedesco *set designer:* Rex Fluty Jr. *music:* Bob Cobert *origination:* NBC Studio 6A, New York *debut guests:* Marty Allen, Joan Fontaine, Phyllis Newman

On "Personality," a celebrity panel of three, each playing for a member of the audience, tried to predict how other

A behind-the-scenes view of the hit game show "Personality" with emcee Larry Blyden. Can you spot celebrity guest Marty Allen?

celebrities responded to questions asked in prerecorded interviews.

In the first two rounds the panelists were given three possible responses for each question and after they chose, the correct answer was shown. In the third round, each celebrity panelist tried to guess how a sample of people responded to questions related to the celebrity.

The panelists received points for correct guesses and the top-scoring player of the day won $100 and a vacation for his or her audience partner.

Did you know . . . before hosting game shows Larry Blyden starred in the TV sitcoms "Joe and Mabel" in 1956 and "Harry's Girls" in 1963?

Were you watching when . . . these celebrities were guests on "Personality": James Brown, Bill Cullen, Phyllis Diller, Peter Fonda, Dustin Hoffman, Tom Kennedy, Jerry Lewis, Ann-Margret, Garry Moore, Leonard Nimoy, Gene Rayburn, and Adam West?

PERSONALITY PUZZLE

premiere: March 19, 1953 *packager:* Alan Pottash Productions *broadcast history:* ABC primetime March 19, 1953–June 25, 1953 *hosts:* John Conte, Robert Alda *announcer:* Don Morrow *producer:* Alan Pottash *director:* Ed Nugent *origination:* New York *debut panel:* Mischa Auer, Lisa Ferraday, Tony Canzoneri *debut guests:* John Carradine, Freddie Bartholomew, swimmer Florence Chadwick

"Personality Puzzle" featured a celebrity panel trying to guess the identities of famous guests by using clues and also by examining the guest's personal possessions, such as clothing and props.

The show was previewed as a one-time special on February 26, 1953 with John Conte as host, and a panel consisting of Tony Canzoneri, Lisa Ferraday, and Henry Morgan. Identified guests were Gabby Hayes and Mickey Spillane. The series returned on a biweekly basis, alternating with QUICK AS A FLASH, on March 19, 1953 with Robert Alda as host.

PERSONALS

premiere: September 16, 1991 *packager:* Rosner Television/Stephen J. Cannell Productions *broadcast history:* CBS late night September 16, 1991–December 23, 1992 *host:* Michael Burger *announcers:* Michael Carrington, Jennifer Martin *creators:* Rick Rosner, Mike Dubelko *executive producer:* Rick Rosner *producer:* Harry Friedman *director:* Steve Grant *set designer:* Don Wallschlaeger *music:* Stormy Sacks *origination:* Sheraton Hotel, Los Angeles International Airport

CBS was the first television network to bring game shows to late-night television with the premiere of "Personals" in September 1991.

Contestants for "Personals" were drawn from personal ads in magazines, newspapers, and viewer-submitted videotapes. A male contestant tried to determine with which of three female contestants he was most compatible.

In the first round, the females tried to predict how the male player would answer specific questions. Four questions were

asked, each with two possible choices. The female player with the most matches became the male's date. In the event of a tie, the male player guessed which female gave a specific response to a question and she became his date.

The winning couple played against a previous day's couple in the "Love Thermometer" bonus round to determine where the winners would be going on a romantic trip.

Sitting with their backs to each other so they could not see how their dates reacted, the players were asked questions to measure their compatibility. Each time they agreed in this ninety-second round they moved up a step. If they did not agree on any question, they dropped back to zero. When time ran out, their positions on the love thermometer determined where they would go, from Pink's Hot Dog Stand in Hollywood, to Las Vegas or to the grand prize destination, Europe.

Did you know . . . "Personals" was one of a trio of late-night game shows that CBS experimented with in the 1991–1992 season? The others were NIGHT GAMES and A PERFECT SCORE.

"Personals" host Michael Burger would later be one of the hosts on the daily ABC talk show "Mike and Maty," as well as on "The Home and Family Show" for the Family Channel on cable.

PICK YOUR BRAIN

premiere: September 18, 1993 *packager:* Marc Summers Productions/Summit Media Group *broadcast history:* Syndicated September 18, 1993–September 1994 *host:* Marc Summers *announcer/voice of 2XL:* Greg Berg *executive producers:* Marc Summers, Randy Rissman, Roger Shiffman *supervising producers:* Alan Silberberg, Jean Wiegman *director:* Richard S. Kline *set designers:* Bill Bohnert, Laurie Fraser *music:* Rick Phillips *origination:* Hollywood Center Studios, Los Angeles

Three kids competed in a question-and-answer game for a $5,000 savings bond, in "Pick Your Brain." In round one, two categories were revealed and each player selected one. Majority ruled in deciding which category was played. A short film was presented with information for the players to remember and seven questions, each worth twenty-five points, were asked.

The player in the lead at the end of round one began the second round. Each kid was then joined by either a relative or teacher as a partner. Three new categories were revealed and one was selected by each player. Categories included "phys quiz," where one partner had to decide whether the name of a music group was real or not; "2×2," with one player choosing from among two categories and his or her partner answering a question; and "XL's extra," where players alternated answering multiple choice questions. Questions were worth fifty points with a maximum of two hundred fifty points possible.

The final round was a question-and-answer session with all players competing against each other. The player with the highest score was given two brains (points), the player in

The dynamic duo of host Alan Thicke and guest star Adam West ham it up on the set of "Pictionary."

second place, one brain. The first player to reach five brains won the game and a $5,000 bond.

The winning player also played a bonus round where he or she was shown two prizes. One half of each prize was hidden behind four numbers, which were called out by contestants, and the first prize matched was the one won by the player.

PICTIONARY

premiere: June 12, 1989   *packagers:* Jack Barry and Dan Enright Productions/Quantum Media/MCA Television (1989); Kline & Friends/Worldvision (1997–)   *broadcast history:* Syndicated June 12, 1989–September 8, 1989; Syndicated September 22, 1997–September 1998

1989 version

host: Brian Robbins   *announcer:* Harry Stevens   *"The Judge":* Rick Zumwalt   *"Felicity":* Julie Friedman   *creators:* Bob Pittman, Brian Bedol   *executive producers:* Dan Enright, Brian Bedol   *supervising producers:* Bob Boden, Michael Bevan, Gary Jonke   *producer:* David Michaels   *director:* Michael Dimich   *set designers:* John C. Mula, Kevin Pfeiffer   *origination:* Studio 1, The Production Group, Los Angeles

1997–1998 version

host: Alan Thicke   *announcer:* Joe Cipriano   *executive producers:* Richard S. Kline, Rob Angel, Terry Langston, Richard

Gill   *producers:* Nancy Jones, Mark Maxwell-Smith   *director:* Richard S. Kline   *set designer:* John C. Mula   *music:* Greg Edmonson   *origination:* Studio 33, CBS Television City, Los Angeles   *debut guests:* Kelly Packard, Michael Gellman, Caroline Ray, Brian Austin Green

The popular board game Pictionary became a TV game show for kids in the summer of 1989 with Brian Robbins of "Head of the Class" as host and Barry and Enright Productions, producers of TIC TAC DOUGH and THE JOKER'S WILD, as packagers.

In the game, two teams of three pre-teenaged contestants competed to communicate words and phrases to their teammates by drawing pictures on an electronic device called a "telestrator."

The team with the most points after three rounds advanced to the "Water Works" bonus game, where a team competed in a relay race against the clock to uncover an artist's sketch of a famous person, place, or thing. If they uncovered the sketch they won the grand prize of the day.

Supervising the activity on the show was the ominous presence of "The Judge" (former professional arm wrestler Rick Zumwalt, complete with black robe and gavel), who acted as clock-watcher and official scorekeeper. He was aided by Julie Friedman in the role of "Felicity," playing a stereotypically dumb blonde who maintained the scoreboard.

"Pictionary" returned as a first-run syndicated show in September 1997, this time using two teams, each composed of one studio contestant and two celebrity guests, guessing words and phrases from clues drawn by one player.

In round one, each celebrity is given forty-five seconds to draw while his or her two teammates guess. Each word puzzle had a common link, and correct guesses earn a player $100 and one point.

Each team has three minutes to draw and guess puzzles in round two. Players alternate at the drawing board, with correct guesses again worth $100 and one point. The team with the most points at the end of this round wins the game.

The winning team plays the bonus round for additional cash. In a ninety-second time limit, the contestant draws words while his or her two celebrity teammates guess. The first three words are worth $100 each; the second set of three words, $300; and all words after that, $1,000.

Did you know . . .   the board game Pictionary was created in 1981 by Seattle waiter Robert Angel who borrowed $35,000 from his uncle? He manufactured several thousand games and sold them locally. The popularity of the game prompted the Nordstrom department store chain to pick it up for their stores. In 1986, Pictionary sold over 350,000 units. By the end of the 1980s almost ten million units of the game were shipped to stores.

Were you watching when . . .   these celebrities were guests on the Alan Thicke version: Rosie O'Donnell, Geraldo Rivera, Ben Stein, and Adam West?

PICTURE THIS

premiere: June 25, 1963   *packager:* Ben Joelson–Art Baer Productions   *broadcast history:* CBS primetime June 25,

1963–September 17, 1963 *host:* Jerry Van Dyke *announcer:* Lee Vines *producers:* Art Baer, Ben Joelson *director:* Gil Cates *set designers:* Tom John, Ed Mitchell; drawings supervised by Charles Colarusso *origination:* Studio 52, CBS-TV New York *debut guests:* Orson Bean, Gretchen Wyler

"Picture This" was the 1963 summer replacement series for the "Jack Benny Program" and featured two teams of players composed of a celebrity guest and a studio contestant with one player drawing, and then guessing an object from his or her partner's instructions. The opposing team selected what the other team would draw from five possible items that were listed, each within a specified time limit, without actually describing the object. A sample week of pictures to draw included "eye glasses" (sixty seconds), "dog" (one hundred fifteen seconds), "watermelon" (seventy seconds), "rocket" (ninety seconds) and "camera" (eighty-five seconds).

If the player drawing the picture could not identify the object, the opposing team received one point. The first team to score three points won the game. The final picture of the day was auctioned to the team who felt they could draw it in the shortest amount of time. The winning contestant received $200; the runner-up, $100.

The winning team also played a bonus round where the celebrity tried to draw six pictures in sixty seconds for his or her partner to guess. The player received $50 for each one correctly guessed.

Other celebrities who appeared on "Picture This" included Jim Backus, William Bendix, Dick Clark, Phyllis Diller, Allen Funt, Allan Sherman, and Alan Young.

PITFALL

premiere: September 14, 1981 *packager:* Catalena Productions *broadcast history:* Syndicated September 14, 1981–September 1982 *host:* Alex Trebek *announcer:* John Barton *executive producer:* Bill Armstrong *producers:* Ian MacLennan, John Barton *director:* Geoff Theobald *origination:* Panorama Studios, Vancouver, British Columbia

Two contestants competed in "Pitfall," this one-season syndicated show taped in Vancouver, Canada. The studio audience was asked a question and given four possible responses. Each member of the audience chose an answer and each contestant selected the answer he or she felt the majority of the audience chose. A player scored one point for picking the right answer. The first player to score five points (or the player who was ahead after five minutes of playing) won the game.

The winner played a pitfall round, where eight questions had to be answered in one hundred seconds in order for the contestant to cross an eight-section bridge. Each correct answer earned $100 and after completely crossing the bridge the player won a bonus prize.

Three of the sections of the bridge had pitfalls that could stop or slow the progress of the contestant unless he or she used a "pitpass" won in the main game. Passes were won by reaching certain levels of points. Before the pitfall round began, the pitfall sections were lighted once and the safe sec-

tions twice (in a random order) to help the player locate the pitfalls and use his or her passes to advantage. If the player failed to use the pitpasses at the right time, the section lowered and the player remained there until answering another question correctly.

PLACE THE FACE

premiere: July 2, 1953 *packager:* Ralph Edwards Productions (Target Productions) *broadcast history:* NBC primetime July 2, 1953–August 20, 1953; CBS primetime August 27, 1953–August 26, 1954; NBC primetime September 18, 1954–December 25, 1954; NBC primetime June 28, 1955–September 13, 1955 *hosts:* Jack Smith, Jack Bailey, Bill Cullen *announcers:* Jack Narz, Bob Warren *executive producer:* Paul Edwards *producers:* Ed Bailey, Joe Landis *director:* Joe Landis *set designers:* Al Goodman, Bob Corrigan *music director:* George Wyle *origination:* NBC Studio D, Hollywood (1953); Studio 41, CBS Television City, Los Angeles (1953–1954); El Capitan Theater, Los Angeles (1954–1955)

A player tried to guess the identity of a guest with whom he or she had had some previous connection (example: a grade school teacher or a longtime friend he or she had not

Bill Cullen listens intently as a contestant tries to identify the face in the frame from his recent or distant past on "Place the Face."

seen in years) on this weekly primetime series, "Place the Face."

The player had three minutes to guess the relationship, with clues given during the questioning. The "face," situated behind a picture frame, gave only "yes" or "no" answers. The faster the player came up with the connection, the bigger the cash prize received.

Each week also featured a celebrity guest who had to identify a face from his or her past.

Jack Smith was the original host on "Place the Face." He left to fulfill a nightclub engagement and was followed by Jack Bailey on a temporary basis on December 3, 1953. On January 28, 1954 Bill Cullen became the new permanent host.

Did you know . . . show announcer Jack Narz was Bill Cullen's brother-in-law at the time? Jack married Bill Cullen's wife's sister!

PLAYBOY'S LOVE & SEX TEST

premiere: August 7, 1992   *packager:* Little Joey Productions *broadcast history:* Playboy (cable) August 7, 1992–September 26, 1994   *host:* Bruce Gold   *costar:* Steve Blacknell *executive producer:* Michael Hill   *producer:* Allen Koss   *director:* Chris Tyner   *set designer:* Jimmy Cuomo   *music supervisor:* Lee Ringuette   *origination:* The Production Group, Hollywood

Cable TV's The Playboy Channel added this half-hour game show to their schedule in August 1992. Usually seen once a week in different time slots, "Playboy's Love & Sex Test" featured two teams, one with three women and the other with three men, playing to see who knew more about love and sex.

Teams started off with five hundred points and competed in five rounds of questions. The first round was based on people's responses to questions about love and sex. A sample of public opinion was shown via a prerecorded tape and an estimate was given as to how people responded. Each team had to decide if the real percentage was higher or lower than the original estimate. Teams scored 100 points if they were right.

Round two, "Fact or Fantasy," included a story told about something related to love or sex. Each of the panelists tried to guess if the story presented was true or not, with one hundred points awarded for each correct guess.

Round three profiled two Playboy Playmates and videos of them were screened. The players were then read a true statement about one of the playmates and had to decide which one it concerned.

After another round of Fact or Fantasy the game concluded with a five-hundred point final test. Each team tried to predict how a person responded when placed in a practical joke situation. The team with the most points at the end of this round was the winner.

PLAY THE GAME

premiere: September 24, 1946   *packager:* ABC   *broadcast history:* DuMont primetime September 24, 1946–December

17, 1946; ABC primetime August 20, 1948–November 6, 1948   *hosts:* Dr. Harvey Zorbaugh, Irene Wicker, Joe O'Brien   *producers:* Harvey Marlowe, Edward Sobol   *directors:* Harvey Marlowe, Edward Sobol, Richard Goggin *origination:* WRGB–TV, Schenectady (1946); New York City (1948)

"Play the Game" was one of the first continuing game shows on television. This charade game was produced by ABC in 1946 but was broadcast on the two-station DuMont network (WABD in New York, WTTG in Washington, D.C.). The ABC network did not begin full-time network broadcasting until 1948.

Hosted by Dr. Harvey Zorbaugh, a professor of educational sociology at New York University, the show featured guest stars pantomiming well-known names and phrases for home viewers to guess. Viewers called the studio with their answers and if correct won money.

Irene Wicker and Joe O'Brien were the hosts of the 1948 version that was seen on the ABC network.

PLAY THE PERCENTAGES

premiere: January 7, 1980   *packager:* Jack Barry and Dan Enright Productions/Colbert Television   *broadcast history:* Syndicated January 7, 1980–September 12, 1980; USA (cable) April 27, 1987–June 23, 1989 (repeats of 1980 series) *host:* Geoff Edwards   *announcers:* Jay Stewart, Bob Hilton *executive producer:* Dan Enright   *producer:* Ron Greenberg *director:* Richard Kline   *set designer:* John C. Mula   *music:* Hal Hidey   *origination:* KTTV Television, Los Angeles

Two contestants competed in a general knowledge game where they selected questions whose difficulty was determined by the percentage of people who missed the question in a recent survey. In "Play the Percentages," each game consisted of questions from three possible categories, one chosen by each player, and a "pot luck" category. The category to be played in each round was selected at random and the category chosen determined which player answered the first question. That player also determined the point value by choosing the difficulty of the question. "Pot Luck" was a jump-in category where either player could answer. Different categories were selected after two questions were played.

The first player to score two hundred fifty points won the game and $500. The winner played a bonus round and tried to find the five most popular responses to a question. Each question had six possible answers, with percentages attached to them. One answer had a zero percentage and if it was selected the bonus round ended. The others were multiplied by ten to give the player a cash jackpot. Any player who won five games in a row won a new car.

PLAY YOUR HUNCH

premiere: June 30, 1958   *packager:* Mark Goodson–Bill Todman Productions   *broadcast history:* CBS daytime June 30, 1958–January 2, 1959; ABC daytime January 5, 1959– May 8, 1959; NBC daytime December 7, 1959–September 27, 1963; NBC primetime April 15, 1960–September 23, 1960; NBC primetime June 20, 1962–September 26, 1962 *hosts:* Merv Griffin, Richard Hayes, Gene Rayburn, Robert Q.

Lewis *substitute host:* Johnny Olson *announcers:* Johnny Olson, Wayne Howell, Roger Tuttle *assistants:* Lynn Dalton, Suzanne Storrs, Liz Gardner, Thelma Tadlock *producers:* Bob Rowe, Ira Skutch *directors:* Lloyd Gross, Mike Garguilo *set designers:* Charles Lisanby, Frank Schneider *music director:* Joe Harnell *origination:* Mansfield Theater (CBS Studio 59), New York (1958–1959); Elysee Theater, New York (1959); NBC Studio 6B, New York (1959–1963)

In this game of observation and deduction, two teams of two contestants, usually husbands and wives, were asked to guess which of three possible solutions would solve a problem or answer a question.

In "Play Your Hunch," sketches were often performed with three participants, "X," "Y," and "Z." One team either tried to guess which one of the three was performing a task normal to that person, or they attempted to answer a question. A typical problem might have included discovering which of three girls was a judo expert, or which of three pairs of lips belonged to Marilyn Monroe.

If the team was correct they earned one point and $50 ($100 on the nighttime version). If they were incorrect, the opposing team guessed from the two remaining solutions. The first team to score three points won the game and faced new challengers.

When "Play Your Hunch" started on CBS in June 1958 the show featured a bonus game for the winning team to play. Called the "Last Straw Board," it consisted of seven straws, five long and two short. The husband-and-wife team received $100 for each long straw selected and if all five were

found before selecting a short straw they won a new car. By the time "Play Your Hunch" moved to NBC in December 1959 the bonus round had been discontinued.

Merv Griffin, who had been a San Francisco disc jockey and singer with Freddy Martin's big band, made his debut as a game show host on "Play Your Hunch." He left the show on September 28, 1962 to host his own talk variety show for NBC. He was replaced by Robert Q. Lewis for two weeks, followed by Gene Rayburn for the next month. On November 19, 1962, Robert Q. Lewis returned as permanent host.

Lynn Dalton and Suzanne Storrs were Merv's assistants on the CBS edition of "Play Your Hunch" in 1958. When the show moved to NBC, Liz Gardner became the new assistant. She was replaced by Thelma (Tad) Tadlock on February 26, 1960. Tadlock remained with the show until February 24, 1961.

"Play Your Hunch" was also the first Goodson-Todman game show to feature announcer Johnny Olson. During his 27-year association with Goodson-Todman, Olson was heard as announcer on over fifteen of their shows. Olson made a rare appearance as emcee of a Goodson-Todman game show by subbing for Merv Griffin on "Play Your Hunch" on December 29, 1961 and on March 6, 1962.

Did you know . . . as a singer with Freddy Martin's big band, Merv Griffin had a top-ten hit in 1949 with "I've Got a Lovely Bunch of Coconuts"? In 1962 Griffin guest-hosted "The Tonight Show" for a week. This led to a six-month daytime talk show on NBC and a long-running syndicated

Merv Griffin hosting the ABC daytime version of "Play Your Hunch" in 1959.

talk series that premiered in April 1965. His show aired in CBS's late-night slot in 1969 and in 1972 he returned to his syndicated series which ran until 1986.

Were you watching when . . . a young actor named Robert Redford was a demonstrator on "Play Your Hunch"? His payment? A new fishing pole. He had much better luck as an actor and later as a director.

These celebrities all guested on "Play Your Hunch": Bud Collyer, Phyllis Diller, Bob Hope, Boris Karloff, Gene Rayburn, and The Three Stooges.

THE POP 'N' ROCKER GAME

premiere: September 17, 1983   *packager:* Alan Landsburg Productions/Ron Greenberg Productions   *broadcast history:* Syndicated September 17, 1983–September 1984   *host:* Jon Bauman   *announcers:* Phil Hartman, Machine Gun Kelly *executive producer:* Ron Greenberg   *executive in charge of production:* Howard Lipstone   *producer:* David Yarnell   *director:* Arthur Forrest   *set designer:* Ed Flesh   *theme:* Bruce Gary and Berton Averre   *origination:* Studio 55, ABC Television Center, Los Angeles

Three contestants competed in this weekly game show "The Pop 'n' Rocker Game," hosted by Jon Bauman, onetime member of the rock group Sha Na Na. In round one of the game, music-oriented questions, coupled with visuals, were read. The first player to buzz in with the correct answer was awarded $50.

In round two, a sixty-second rapid-fire question-and-answer session was held. The value of the first question was $50 and increased by $10 with each question until time ran out.

The player with the highest cash score won and played the bonus round within a thirty-second time limit. A player was shown the scrambled letters of a rock music artist's name. The player was given a clue and in most cases came up with three correct answers, to win bonus prizes before time ran out.

Performances by two musical groups were also weekly features of the show. Among the talent who appeared on the show were Huey Lewis and the News, Irene Cara, Culture Club, and The Bangles.

Did you know . . . announcer Phil Hartman went on to greater fame as one of the "Not Ready for Primetime Players" on "Saturday Night Live" in 1986? At the time of his death, in 1998, he was starring in his own primetime series "News Radio."

PRESS YOUR LUCK

premiere: September 19, 1983   *packager:* Carruthers Company Production   *broadcast history:* CBS daytime September 19, 1983–September 26, 1986; USA (cable) September 14, 1987–April 1, 1995 (repeats); USA (cable) April 17, 1995–October 13, 1995 (repeats)   *host:* Peter Tomarken *announcers:* Rod Roddy, John Harlan   *executive producer/director:* Bill Carruthers   *producer:* Bill Mitchell   *set designer:* Ed Flesh   *"whammy" designer:* S. Steve Holland *music:* Lee Ringuette   *origination:* Studio 41, CBS Television City, Los Angeles

Three contestants tried to earn "spins" by answering questions on "Press Your Luck." After a question was read, the

"Press Your Luck" was one of the durable shows of the 1980s. Here emcee Peter Tomarken stands in front of the game board.

first player to buzz in was given a chance to win three spins depending on whether or not he or she gave a correct answer. This answer plus two others were then listed as three possibilities from which the other two players chose. A player received one spin for a correct answer. Four such questions were asked in each half of the game.

Each player then used the spins to earn cash and prizes located on a rotating game board, while trying to avoid a "whammy" that served to bankrupt the players. The player could give remaining spins to his or her opponent at any time. Four whammys eliminated a player from the game. The player with the most cash after two rounds won. A player retired after reaching the $25,000 limit.

In the first round the board had cash amounts up to $1,500 and in the second round up to $5,000.

Did you know . . . host Peter Tomarken was a clothing editor for *Women's Wear Daily*? Announcer Rod Roddy began his career as the narrator on "Soap," a soap opera satire.

Talk show host Jenny Jones was a contestant on "Press Your Luck."

THE PRICE IS RIGHT

premiere: November 26, 1956   *packagers:* Mark Goodson–Bill Todman Productions; Mark Goodson Productions *broadcast history:* NBC daytime November 26, 1956–

September 6, 1963; NBC primetime September 23, 1957–September 6, 1963; ABC daytime September 9, 1963–September 3, 1965; ABC primetime September 18, 1963–September 11, 1964; CBS daytime September 4, 1972–   ; Syndicated September 11, 1972–September 1979; Syndicated September 9, 1985–September 5, 1986; CBS primetime August 14, 1986–September 18, 1986; Syndicated September 12, 1994–January 27, 1995

1956–1965 version

host: Bill Cullen *substitute hosts:* Jack Clark, Bob Kennedy, Johnny Gilbert, Sonny Fox, Sam Levenson, Merv Griffin, Robert Q. Lewis, Jack Narz, Arlene Francis, Don Pardo *announcers:* Don Pardo, Johnny Gilbert *substitute announcers:* Roger Tuttle, Dick Dudley, Ed Jordan, Jack Clark, Vic Roby, Edward Haeffor *models:* Beverly Bentley, Toni Wallace, June Ferguson, Carolyn Stroupe, Maryann James, Gail Sheldon *producers:* Bob Stewart, Willie Stein, Beth Hollinger, Michael Graham *directors:* Max Miller, Don Bohl, Lou Tedesco, Paul Alter, Michael Graham *set designers:* Frank Schneider, Richard Senie, Willis Connor, Hjalmar Hermanson *music director:* Bob Cobert *tote machines:* The American Totalizer Company *origination:* Hudson Theater, New York (NBC); Colonial Theater, New York (NBC); Ziegfeld Theater, New York (NBC); Century Theater, New York (NBC); Ritz Theater, New York (ABC)

1972– version

hosts: Bob Barker, Dennis James, Tom Kennedy *announcers:* Johnny Olson, Gene Wood, Bob Hilton, Rod Roddy

Bill Cullen, host of the original "The Price Is Right" with show models June Ferguson on the left and Toni Wallace on the right.

models: Janice Pennington, Anitra Ford, Dian Parkinson, Holly Hallstrom, Kyle Meriweather, Kathleen Bradley, Gina Lee Nolin, Chantel Dubay *executive producers:* Frank Wayne, Bob Barker *producers:* Jay Wolpert, Barbara Hunter, Phillip Wayne Rossi, Roger Dobkowitz *directors:* Marc Breslow, Paul Alter *set designers:* Don Roberts, James Agazzi, Jack Hart, Bente Christensen *theme:* Edd Kalehoff, Score Productions *music director:* Stanley Blits *origination:* Studio 33, CBS Television City, Los Angeles

1994–1995 syndicated version

host: Doug Davidson *announcer:* Burton Richardson *models:* Julie Cialini, Ferrari Farris, Lisa Stahl *senior executive producer:* Jay Wolpert *executive producer/director:* Andy Felsher *producers:* Kathy Greco, Phil Wayne *set designer:* Jack Hart *music:* Score Productions *origination:* Studio 33, CBS Television City, Los Angeles

"The Price Is Right" has been part of the television landscape for almost forty years. It became the longest-running game show in television history, having been part of the CBS daytime schedule from 1972 on. It also became the number-one game show on daytime television, starting with the 1979–1980 season.

"The Price Is Right" premiered on NBC on November 26, 1956 (replacing "NBC Bandstand") with Bill Cullen as host and Don Pardo as announcer. The object of the game was to come as close as possible, without going over, to the manufacturer's suggested retail price of a merchandise item.

Four studio contestants were shown a merchandise item. Some items were one-bid items, where each player was given one guess at the actual price. Other items were part of open bidding, where one player bid and the following players had to bid higher than the previous player. The bidding moved through the panel several times before each player had to make a final bid. A player could freeze a bid at any time when feeling that the next guess would put him or her over. The player who came the closest to the price won the item and the player with the greatest dollar amount accumulated returned to play on the next show.

One of the popular features on the show was the weekly home viewer contest, in which viewers sent in postcards with what they believed to be the exact worth of a showcase of prizes.

Nine months after the debut of "The Price Is Right" in daytime, a nighttime edition was added to NBC's schedule.

Sonny Fox became the first of many guest hosts on "The Price Is Right" when he substituted for the vacationing Bill Cullen on June 10, 1957. Other substitute hosts included Jack Clark, Bob Kennedy, Johnny Gilbert, Sam Levenson, Merv Griffin, Robert Q. Lewis, Jack Narz, Arlene Francis, and announcer Don Pardo, who made his debut as a game show host on December 31, 1959. Pardo made one more appearance as host of "The Price Is Right" on December 28, 1962.

Bill Cullen's wife Ann appeared as a model on the August 6, 1957 episode and Bill took a turn at playing the game on December 27, 1963 while Robert Q. Lewis guest hosted.

In September 1963, "The Price Is Right" moved from NBC to ABC and the appearance of a weekly celebrity guest, playing for home viewers or members of the studio audience, became a regular feature. Betsy Palmer, who appeared with

The longest-running daytime game show in television's history, "The Price Is Right." From left to right are Kathleen Bradley, Janice Pennington, Rod Roddy, Bob Barker, Holly Halstrom, and Gena Lee Nolin.

Cullen on I'VE GOT A SECRET, was the first celebrity guest. "The Price Is Right" continued as part of the ABC schedule for two years before being replaced by the talk show "The Young Set."

After a seven-year absence, "The Price Is Right" returned with a new version in September 1972. Bob Barker, who had hosted TRUTH OR CONSEQUENCES since 1956, was selected to host the daytime version for CBS, and Dennis James, whose career in television dated back to the beginning of the medium, hosted the weekly nighttime version.

The show was completely overhauled but the emphasis still remained on pricing merchandise items.

Each show began with four contestants being selected from the studio audience with the announcer (Johnny Olson from 1972 to 1985 and Rod Roddy after 1985) reading their names and giving the now famous cry "Come on down!"

The four players were stationed in "Contestants' Row" and were shown an item of merchandise. The player who came closest to the retail price without going over won the item and a chance to play another pricing game for additional prizes.

Pricing games varied from show to show. The games played on the first program of "The New Price Is Right" series were "Any Number," where numbers were represented on a game board and the player called numbers until he or she filled in the price of a car, a prize, or a cash amount in the piggy bank; "Which Is the Right Price?", where a player selected one price from two possibilities; and "Higher or Lower," where an item was shown with a price and the player had to decide whether the real price was "higher" or "lower."

Other popular pricing games featured on "The Price Is Right" over the years included "The Clock Game," "Hole-in-One," "The Range Game," "Squeeze Play," "Three Strikes," and "Plinko."

After one contestant played a pricing game on stage, the vacancy in "Contestants' Row" was filled with another player called from the audience.

The top-two money winners of the day competed in a "Showcase Showdown Round" Each bid on an assortment of prizes and the player coming closest without going over won his or her showcase. The top-scoring player of the day going into this round had the option of bidding or passing on the first showcase thereby forcing his or her opponent to bid. A rule later added gave a player who came within $100 of the price of his or her showcase, the merchandise in both showcases.

The first "Showcases" offered on "The Price Is Right" were a week's vacation in Acapulco as well as a Kimball organ, a gas range, and floor tiles (actual price was $2,307, the contestant bid $1,750); and a second showcase consisting of roller skates, a stationary bicycle, and a Mazda 808 sedan (actual price $2,504, the player bid $2,500, missing the actual price by only $4).

On November 3, 1975 "The Price Is Right" was expanded to a full hour (from thirty minutes) and a new feature was added. Midway through the show, each of the players who participated in the first three pricing games onstage were given a chance to spin a giant wheel. The wheel was lined with numbers representing "cents" and each player was given up to two spins to reach one dollar. The player coming closest without going over moved on to the Showcase Showdown Round. A player who spun one dollar exactly (in one or two spins) won $1,000. If done again, $10,000 was won. If he or she landed in the adjacent sections $5,000 was won. After three more pricing games were played, a second set of players spun the wheel to determine the second participant in the Showcase Showdown Round.

Bob Barker took over hosting the nighttime edition of "The Price Is Right" in September 1976 and followed Dennis James. That version continued for another three seasons. When the show returned as a daily syndicated series in September 1985, Tom Kennedy became the new emcee. Bob Barker hosted a limited-run primetime version for CBS in the summer of 1986.

Johnny Olson, who had been the announcer on numerous Goodson-Todman game shows since 1958, was the original announcer on "The New Price Is Right." He died on October 6, 1985 and other people, including Charlie O. Donnell, Gene Wood, Johnny Gilbert, and Bob Hilton filled in until Rod Roddy was selected as the new announcer.

On March 27, 1987 "The Price Is Right" became the longest-running daytime network game show in history by breaking the fourteen-and-one-half year record held by CON-CENTRATION. In April 1990 it became television's longest-running game show by passing WHAT'S MY LINE? which had a seventeen-year, seven-month run.

"The Price Is Right" was revived for the third time in syndication in the fall of 1994. The new nighttime edition featured a new host, Doug Davidson of the daytime drama series "The Young and the Restless"; a new announcer, Burton Richardson from "The Arsenio Hall Show"; and three new models (Julie Cialini, Ferrari Farris, and Lisa Stahl). The show was structured differently from the daytime network version. Three contestants were selected from the studio audience to come on stage one at a time and participate in a pricing game, for a prize. Three different games were played on each show.

All contestants competed against each other in a final round for a chance to move on to the "Showcase Showdown Round." One of the featured rounds was called "The Price Was Right." The players were shown a TV commercial from the past and asked to guess the price of the item shown. The player coming closest without going over earned the right to play the showcase.

In the Showcase Showdown Round, the player was shown an assortment of prizes and asked to stop a "price scale" when he or she felt the actual price of the showcase was in a given range. If correct, he or she won the merchandise.

"The Price Is Right" with Bob Barker celebrated its twenty-fifth year on CBS with a primetime one-hour special on August 23, 1996. The show featured special guests and prizes, as well as clips of memorable moments from the first quarter century of shows.

On April 9, 1998 the 5,000th daytime episode of "The Price Is Right" with Bob Barker was broadcast on CBS. In recognition of this achievement, Studio 33 at CBS Television City in Los Angeles, where the show was taped, was dedicated to Bob Barker and "The Price Is Right."

Did you know . . . Bob Barker attended Drury College in Springfield, Missouri, on a basketball scholarship? World War II interrupted his studies and after being discharged he returned to school, graduated Summa Cum Laude, and then began his broadcasting career at KTTS Radio in Springfield. From there his radio career took him to WWPG in Palm Beach, Florida and later to KWIK in Burbank, California. In December 1956 Ralph Edwards hired him to host the new daytime version of TRUTH OR CONSEQUENCES.

The original emcee of "The Price Is Right," Bill Cullen, appeared on the cover of *TV Guide* seven times, the record for a game show emcee. In 1962, he appeared on the cover twice within a four-week period. On the July 28 cover it was for a story on "The Price Is Right" and on August 18 for a story on I'VE GOT A SECRET.

Bill Cullen and producer Bob Stewart teamed up many times after their stint in "The Price Is Right." In 1966, Cullen emceed EYE GUESS, Bob Stewart's first network game show under his own production company. They also worked together on THREE ON A MATCH, WINNING STREAK, PASS THE BUCK, BLANKETY BLANKS, and "The $25,000 Pyramid" (see THE $10,000 PYRAMID).

Game show favorite Dennis James helped get "The Price Is Right" sold to CBS by hosting a demo tape on how "The Price Is Right" would be updated for the 1970s. James would later host the syndicated version of "The Price Is Right" for some four years in the mid-1970s.

Bob Barker has missed only one taping of "The Price Is Right" in over 25 years. On December 2, 1974 Dennis James, who was then hosting the nighttime syndicated version was called on to sub for Barker for a taping of four shows.

Were you watching when . . . "The Price Is Right" producer Jay Wolpert created the first "Showcase Skit," a spoof of Little Red Riding Hood in the spring of 1974?

Mark Goodson made one of his frequent visits to "The Price Is Right" set to congratulate host Bob Barker and his beauties on the anniversary of the show's first CBS broadcast.

Vanna White was a contestant on June 18, 1980. She never made it out of Contestants' Row, but two and a half years later she found her way on stage as the new letter turner on WHEEL OF FORTUNE.

In September 1982 to promote Bill Cullen's new game show CHILD'S PLAY, Cullen made a surprise visit to "The Price Is Right." Johnny Olson called for the next contestant, Bill Cullen, to "come on down!" At that point Bob Barker was shocked to see the original emcee of "The Price Is Right" appear on a little train driven by Janice Pennington. Both Barker and Cullen shared fun moments of "The Price Is Right," and Cullen plugged his new series. This marked Cullen's first and only visit to the set of "The Price Is Right" after he left the show in 1965.

Actress Meg Ryan, then featured in the daytime serial "As the World Turns," appeared on "The Price Is Right" in 1983 as part of a showcase skit.

PRO-FAN

premiere: April 30, 1977   *packager:* Media Masters–Renshar Productions   *broadcast history:* Syndicated April 30, 1977–September 11, 1977   *host:* Charlie Jones   *announcer:* Lloyd Thaxton   *creators:* Sheldon Saltman, Lloyd Thaxton   *producer:* Bud Murphy   *director:* Howard Zuckerman   *set designers:* Henry Lickel, Woodrow Coleman   *origination:* Television Center Studios, Los Angeles

NBC sportscaster Charlie Jones hosted this thirteen-week series, "Pro-Fan," that featured two guest sports celebrities (baseball players Bobby Bonds and Frank Tanana were the debut week guests) teamed with studio contestants. One player on each team tried to answer sports-related trivia questions and if correct that player's partner tried to complete a sports stunt (shoot a basket, sink a putt). The game consisted of three rounds, each four minutes long and worth ten points in round one, twenty points in round two, and forty points in round three. The player attempting the stunt had twenty-four seconds to accomplish the feat.

The high-scoring team played the "Grand Slam" bonus round for over $15,000 in prizes. Both members of the team were asked to complete an athletic stunt and if either one was successful in the allotted time, the studio player won the prizes.

PUBLIC PROSECUTOR

premiere: September 6, 1951   *packager:* Jerry Fairbanks Productions   *broadcast history:* DuMont primetime September 6, 1951–September 27, 1951   *hosts:* John Howard, Warren Hull   *announcer:* Bob Shepard

The DuMont Television Network broadcast "Public Prosecutor" as a four-week mystery quiz featuring detective fiction writers trying to solve a "who done it." Sponsored by Crawford Clothes, the show was also known as "Crawford Mystery Theater." After completing its network run, the show continued on DuMont's New York station WABD until February 28, 1952.

The series consisted of filmed TV dramas, made in 1948, with John Howard playing the prosecuting attorney, Anne Gwynne as his assistant, and Walter Sande as a police lieutenant.

The players tried to guess the outcome of the dramas. The films were stopped before the solutions were revealed and the players had to determine who the culprit was. Players guessing correctly won prizes.

Actor John Howard was host for the first two shows and future STRIKE IT RICH host Warren Hull hosted the last two shows.

PURE INSANITY!

premiere: August 11, 1990   *packager:* Pye-Jaffe Productions   *broadcast history:* Fox primetime special August 11, 1990; Fox primetime special September 2, 1990   *hosts:* Alan Hunter, David Alan Grier, Caroline Schlitt   *executive producers:* Chris Pye, Bob Jaffe   *producer/director:* Kent Weed   *set designers:* Phyllis Hofberg, Chris Hartman   *music:* Bruce Kernohan, Lawrence Tuber   *origination:* Honolulu; Austin

On "Pure Insanity!" six residents from two towns competed to do the craziest stunt for a cash prize of $15,000. Members of a team were selected by disc jockeys from one of the two towns. Some of the people featured on the show included steer-manure divers, human darts, a human wrecking ball, people who let tarantulas crawl over their bodies, and people who fished with their mouths.

Presented as a series of specials, the first program featured teams representing Anchorage, Alaska, and Honolulu, Hawaii, with the Alaska team winning. The second program featured Boston, Massachusetts, playing Austin, Texas, with Austin becoming the champion.

The winning team received $2,500 for the charity of their choice and the individual performing the craziest stunt collected $15,000.

Judges for the first program were baseball umpires from the Pearl City Umpires Association and the second show featured judges who were members of the Royal Air Force.

QED

premiere: April 3, 1951   *broadcast history:* ABC primetime April 3, 1951–October 9, 1951   *hosts:* Doug Browning (first show), Fred Uttal   *producer:* Hal Hackett   *director:* Seymour Robbie   *origination:* New York

"QED" was based on the radio show "Mystery File." A celebrity panel was read a mystery story, submitted by a home viewer, that was stopped just before the solution was revealed. Each member of the panel tried to guess the outcome. The panel for the debut program was comprised of Hy Brown, Nina Foch, and Harold S. Hoffman.

"QED" was also heard on the ABC radio network from April 15, 1951 to October 14, 1951.

QUEEN FOR A DAY

premiere: January 3, 1956   *packagers:* Raymond R. Morgan Company (1956–1958); Queen for a Day Inc. (1958–1964) *broadcast history:* NBC daytime January 3, 1956–September 2, 1960; ABC daytime September 5, 1960–October 2, 1964; Syndicated September 8, 1969–September 18, 1970
1956–1964 version

host: Jack Bailey   *substitute hosts:* Ben Alexander, Steve Dunne, Jack Smith, Dennis Day, Don DeFore, Walter O'Keefe   *announcers:* Gene Baker, John Harlan   *fashion commentator:* Jeanne Cagney   *substitute commentators:* Joan Leslie, Lois January, Jean Bartel, Marilyn Hare   *models:* Barbara Lyon, Beverly Sassoon, Maxine Reeves, Darlene Stuart, Dorene Georgeson   *producers:* Harry Mynatt, Howard Blake, Bill Burch, Edward Kranyak   *directors:* Harry Mynatt, Elbert Walker, James Morgan, Hap Wyman   *set designer:* John Shrum   *origination:* Moulin Rouge, Hollywood
1969–1970 version

host: Dick Curtis   *announcer:* Carl King   *fashion commentator:* Nancy Myers   *executive producer:* Dickson Ward *producers:* Jim Washburn, Bill Martin   *director:* Dick Weinberg   *set designer:* Herman Zimmerman   *origination:* Hollywood Video Center

One of daytime television's most popular tear-jerkers, "Queen for a Day" featured four women chosen each day from the studio audience. They appeared on stage one at a time, and each woman told host Jack Bailey about the great tragedies and misfortunes in her life and if selected "Queen," what she needed to improve her situation. At the end of each program, studio audience applause determined the day's winner, who was proclaimed "Queen for a Day" and showered with gifts.

Broadcast from the Moulin Rouge, a theater-restaurant on Sunset Boulevard near Vine Street in Hollywood, the show also featured a daily fashion show with commentary by Jeanne Cagney, sister of actor James Cagney.

Jack Bailey will soon crown one of these ladies "Queen for a Day."

181

"Queen for a Day" originally began as a radio show on April 30, 1945 on the Mutual Network, where it continued until June 10, 1957. In February 1952 it came to television in the Los Angeles area on station KHJ. Three years later, on January 24, 1955, ABC picked up the show for broadcasts on its six-station Pacific Coast Network. On January 3, 1956 NBC added it to its national daytime schedule. "Queen for a Day" moved from NBC to ABC on September 5, 1960, where it remained until the last Queen was crowned on October 2, 1964.

Jack Bailey, a one-time barker at the San Diego World's Fair in the 1930s and voice of the Walt Disney cartoon character Goofy from 1939 to 1940, was host for the entire network radio and TV run of "Queen for a Day." He began every show staring straight into the TV camera and emitting his famous cry, "Would you like to be Queen for a Day?"

Among the many people who filled in for Jack Bailey during the run of "Queen for a Day" were Ben Alexander, Dennis Day, Don DeFore, Steve Dunne, Adolphe Menjou, Walter O'Keefe, and Jack Smith.

In 1969, Metromedia Producers Corporation mounted a new version of "Queen for a Day" with Dick Curtis as host and Nancy Myers as fashion commentator. This updated edition lasted only one season and featured an electronic voting machine that was used to tabulate the studio audience's votes in selecting the queen.

Did you know . . . the Moulin Rouge, located at 6230 Sunset Boulevard in Hollywood, originally opened in 1938 as "Earl Carroll's Vanities" featuring "Hollywood's Most Beautiful Girls"? It was renamed the Moulin Rouge in 1953 and "Queen for a Day" was telecast from there for most of its TV run. After the show left the air, the club was renamed "The Hullabaloo" in 1965 for Los Angeles radio personality Dave Hull and featured rock and roll music. In 1969 the theater became the Aquarius Theater and during the 1980s "Star Search" called it home. For a brief time in 1993 the theater was known as "The Chevy Chase Theater."

QUICK AS A FLASH

premiere: March 12, 1953 *packagers:* Bernard Prockter Productions (March 1953–July 1953); Moss and Lewis Productions (September 1953–February 1954) *broadcast history:* ABC primetime March 12, 1953–July 2, 1953; ABC primetime September 10, 1953–February 25, 1954 *hosts:* Bobby Sherwood, Bud Collyer *producers:* Dick Lewis, Charles Moss *directors:* Ed Nugent, Harold Loeb *origination:* New York *debut guests:* Eva Gabor, Roger Price

Based on the radio series of the same name that was on the air from July 16, 1944 to June 29, 1951, "Quick as a Flash" featured two teams, each consisting of one celebrity and one contestant. Guest celebrities on the first show were Eva Gabor and Roger Price.

Players viewed a film sequence that hinted at the name of a famous person, place, or thing. A player could stop the film when he or she wanted to give an answer. Celebrities were given one guess, contestants two guesses.

Bobby Sherwood was replaced as host by Bud Collyer in May 1953. "Quick as a Flash" was sponsored by Thor Electric Washing Machines.

QUICK ON THE DRAW

premiere: January 1, 1952 *packager:* Kermit Schafer Productions *broadcast history:* DuMont primetime January 1, 1952–December 9, 1952 *host:* Robin Chandler *cartoonist:* Bob Dunn *producer:* Kermit Schafer *directors:* Bill Warwick, David Lowe *origination:* New York

"Quick on the Draw" began as a local show on New York television station WNBT, debuting on May 27, 1950 and ending its run on December 27, 1951. Eloise McElhone was the hostess for this version and cartoonist Bob Dunn was the artist. The show moved to the DuMont network on January 1, 1952 with a new host, Robin Chandler.

"Quick on the Draw" featured a celebrity panel trying to guess cartoons drawn from ideas sent by home viewers and sketched by Dunn. The panel was given clues in the form of puns to help them guess.

Did you know . . . producer Kermit Schafer was best known for his collection of radio and TV bloopers? Artist Bob Dunn was a long-time artist in the comic art department of King Features, writing the strip "They'll Do It Every Time." He won the Reuben Award in 1976, the comic world's highest award.

QUICKSILVER

premiere: June 27, 1994 *packager:* Stone-Stanley Productions *broadcast history:* USA (cable) June 27, 1994–October 13, 1995 *host:* Ron Maestri *executive producers:* Scott Stone, David Stanley *producer:* David Greenfield *director:* Bob Loudin *set designers:* Joe Stewart, John Shaffner *origination:* Studio 9B, Hollywood Center Studios, Los Angeles

"Quicksilver" was one of two first-run game shows added to the USA cable block of weekday game shows in the summer of 1994 (the other show was FREE 4 ALL). In this show, three contestants competed in a question-and-answer game where four answers were given (some were plays on words), then a question was read and each player rang in, trying to match the question with an answer. Correct answers in the first round were worth twenty-five points and a new series of four answers was revealed after each three questions.

Point values were doubled in the second round. Five answers were revealed on the game board, and the correct answers were replaced by new answers after each question. If a player felt the correct answer was not among the possibilities, he or she could answer by saying "Quicksilver." Giving the correct response earned the player one hundred points. The player who answered the "Quicksilver" question won a bonus prize and a chance to wager up to two hundred points on his or her ability to answer another question on the same subject.

In the third round, contestants could earn seventy-five points for correct answers. The round was played in two parts. In the first half, the players tried to come up with answers to eight questions. The answers revealed were then used to answer a series of one-hundred-point questions in the second half of the round. The "Quicksilver" response could also be used by a player in this round (where the value was two hundred points), in which he or she had the chance to wager up to four-hundred points on a follow-up question. The player with the highest score at the end of this round won the game and played for $500 and a trip in the "Silver Streak" bonus round.

In the bonus round, the winner was shown fifteen answers in a category and he or she tried to match ten questions to those answers within a forty-five-second time limit, winning $50 for each correct answer. Reaching the $500 mark also won the trip for this player.

QUIZ KIDS

premiere: March 1, 1949 *packagers:* Louis Cowan Productions (1949–1956); Bennett-Katleman Productions/Columbia Television (1978); CBS Cable/Quiz Kids Inc. (1981) *broadcast history:* NBC primetime March 1, 1949–October 26, 1951 CBS Sunday afternoons January 13, 1952–April 6, 1952; NBC primetime July 7, 1952–September 1, 1952; CBS Sunday afternoons September 14, 1952–January 11, 1953; CBS primetime January 17, 1953–November 8, 1953; CBS primetime January 12, 1956–September 27, 1956; Syndi-cated April 1978–September 1978; CBS Cable October 12, 1981–December 15, 1982
1949–1956 version
hosts: Joe Kelly, Clifton Fadiman *announcers:* Jack Callaghan, Ed Cooper, Gus Chan, Don Hancock *producers:* Norman Felton, John Lewellen, Rachel Stevenson, Ed Jurist *directors:* Jay Sheridan, Don Meier, Bill Taylor, Scott Young, Ed Jurist, John Lewellen *origination:* Garrick Theater, Chicago (1949–1953); New York (1956)
1978 version
host: Jim McKrell *judge:* Paul Russell *announcer:* Mike Adams *executive producers:* Geoffrey Cowan, Seymour Berns *producer:* Kay Bachman *directors:* Dick Schneider, Seymour Berns *music:* Score Productions *origination:* WNAC–TV, Boston
1981 version
host: Norman Lear *judge:* Jeanne Nolan *executive producers:* Harve Bennett, Geoffrey Cowan *producer:* Kay Bachman *director:* William G. Elliott *set designers:* Don Roberts, Jim Mees *music:* Tom Jenkins *origination:* Studio 2, Chris Craft Television, Los Angeles

"Quiz Kids" began as a radio show on June 28, 1940 and continued on radio until July 5, 1953. Joe Kelly hosted and remained as host when "Quiz Kids" first came to television on NBC's midwest network on January 25, 1949. By the fall of 1949, the show was on the full NBC network.

Are kids smarter than adults? "The Quiz Kids Challenge" featured a team of three kids against a team of three adults in a test of knowledge, hosted by Jonathan Prince.

Each week a panel of five kids answered questions and solved problems that were sent in by home viewers. The children on the panel were under sixteen years of age with IQ's ranging from just above average to over two hundred.

Questions were posed to the kids, who raised their hands to answer. If the panel could not answer a question, the home viewer received a prize. For each question points were awarded based on the difficulty of the question. The three players who answered the most questions correctly, returned on the next show. Each player received a $100 savings bond for each week he or she appeared on the show.

Among the regular panelists on "Quiz Kids" were Pat Conlon, Naomi Cooks, Joel Kupperman, Melvin Miles, Janet Ahern, Harvey Dytch, Vincent Granatelli, Brenda Liebling, Jack Lucal, Robert Strom, Frankie VanderPloeg, and Sallie Ann Wihelm.

"Quiz Kids" bounced back and forth from primetime slots to Sunday afternoon slots and from NBC to CBS. Clifton Fadiman replaced Joe Kelly for the 1956 broadcasts.

"Quiz Kids" returned to television after twenty-two years with a 1978 syndicated version taped in Boston. The weekly show was hosted by Jim McKrell, who had previously emceed THE GAME GAME and CELEBRITY SWEEPSTAKES. Each week five kids appeared, three returning players from the previous show and two new challengers, to compete in a general knowledge quiz.

The game consisted of four rounds of questions, with the first two rounds containing twenty-point jump-in questions. Each player began with two hundred points and added or lost points depending on the answers. The third round consisted of visual questions. In the final round, a category was announced and the player who buzzed in determined its value, from twenty to fifty points. If this person answered correctly, he or she received the points and if not, another player could answer for ten points.

All players received savings bonds for their appearances and the top scorer of the day won a bonus gift.

CBS Cable broadcast a new series of "Quiz Kids" shows in 1981–1982 with TV producer Norman Lear as host.

THE QUIZ KIDS CHALLENGE

premiere: September 10, 1990   *packager:* Guber-Peters Productions/Chilmark   *broadcast history:* Syndicated September 10, 1990–December 28, 1990   *host:* Jonathan Prince   *announcer:* Johnny Gilbert   *executive producers:* Geoffrey Cowan, Scott Sternberg, Julian Fowles   *producer:* Jules Minton   *director:* George Choderker   *set designers:* John Shafner, Joe Stewart   *origination:* Hollywood Center Studios

The popular QUIZ KIDS radio and TV show of the 1940s and 50s was revived as "The Quiz Kids Challenge," a question-and-answer game in 1990, pitting three kids playing as a team against three adults. The kids, usually ranging in age from eleven to fifteen, stayed on the show for a week while the adult team changed daily.

The game began with eight categories revealed, each containing three questions. Correct answers were worth $50 and teams competed against each other to answer the questions. All three questions in one category were played before moving to another category, which was selected by the player correctly answering the last question.

In round two, eight new categories were revealed and the first question was again worth $50. After one player answered correctly, one of the two remaining players on his or her team attempted to answer a second question in that category for $100. If this player answered correctly, the remaining player attempted the third question for $200. The team could stop at any point and an incorrect reply gave the opponents a chance to steal the money.

The final round was a one-hundred-second question round with cash values starting at $50 and doubling every twenty-five seconds to a maximum of $200. Four different categories were played in this round and the player who gave the last correct answer selected the next category.

QUIZZING THE NEWS

premiere: August 16, 1948   *packager:* Robert Brenner Productions   *broadcast history:* ABC primetime August 16, 1948–March 5, 1949   *host:* Allan Prescott   *producer:* Robert Brenner   *directors:* Tom DeHuff, Bob Doyle   *origination:* New York

"Quizzing the News" was one of the first network shows on ABC after they began full network operations in August 1948. This show featured three celebrity panelists trying to identify news events from verbal clues and cartoon sketches. In an audience segment, viewers tried to guess well-known personalities whose pictures were altered with glasses, mustaches, etc.

Among the regular panelists on "Quzzing the News" were Arthur Q. Bryan, Milton Caniff, Mary Hunter, and Ray Joseph.

REACH FOR THE STARS

premiere: January 2, 1967 *packager:* Merv Griffin Productions *broadcast history:* NBC daytime January 2, 1967–March 31, 1967 *host:* Bill Mazer *assistant:* Sandra Douglas *announcers:* Chet Gould, Wayne Howell *producer:* Ron Greenberg *director:* Gil Cates *set designer:* Tom Trimble *origination:* NBC Studio 6A, New York

"Reach for the Stars" was a short-lived game show that had a set designed like a spaceship in which three contestants answered questions and performed stunts.

Each show began with an opening round, where each player had ninety seconds to "reach for the stars" and either perform a stunt or answer a question. The player with the highest score began the challenge round and continued to "reach" until he or she missed a question or failed to complete a stunt. An opposing player could challenge on a missed opportunity and if correct selected the next star.

The player with the most money after the challenge round won the game and played the "Super Star" for a bonus prize.

Host Bill Mazer was a New York sportscaster for many years and also wrote sports trivia books.

READY . . . SET . . . COOK!

premiere: October 2, 1995 *packager:* TV Food Network *broadcast history:* Food Network (cable) October 2, 1995– *hosts:* Robin Young, Sissy Biggers *announcer:* Brian Madden *executive producer:* Marilyn O'Reilly *producer:* Pat O'Gorman *director:* Dini Diskin-Zimmerman *set designer:* Ron Baldwin *origination:* New York

Two nationally acclaimed chefs, each representing different restaurants, compete in a cooking challenge. Before each show, two members of the studio audience are given $10 to purchase ingredients for the chefs to use to prepare a meal.

Each audience member is teamed with a chef. One team is called the "Red Tomato," and the other, the "Green Pepper." The chefs have twenty minutes (later reduced to eighteen) to create a meal out of the purchased ingredients. Both chefs are also supplied with a well-stocked pantry of the essential items found in a kitchen (spices, milk, wine, etc.).

As the chefs prepare their recipes, the host moves back and forth between the teams, quizzing them on what they are preparing. After time has elapsed, the studio audience votes for the winning dish. The audience contestants receive prizes such as cookware or appliances.

Robin Young hosted the first season of "Ready . . . Set . . . Cook!" (October 2, 1995 to September 27, 1996). Sissy Biggers replaced her on September 30, 1996. "Ready . . . Set . . . Cook!" was based on a British show called "Ready . . . Steady . . . Cook!" and seen on the BBC.

Did you know . . . host Sissy Biggers made her TV debut at age sixteen when she appeared as an impostor on "To Tell the Truth"? In that 1973 episode she claimed to be "Abbey Lee Green, a teenage baton twirling magician." While studying for her college degree in English at Barnard College at Columbia University in New York, she worked as an extra on "All My Children." In 1984, Biggers joined NBC as director of late-night and special programming. After a decade behind the scenes, Sissy returned to the other side of the camera as host of a daytime talk series for the Lifetime cable network.

Were you watching when . . . "Ready . . . Set . . . Cook!" presented a zany celebrity cook-off between Dom DeLuise and Jo Anne Worley?

THE REBUS GAME

premiere: March 29, 1965 *packager:* Carl Jampel Productions *broadcast history:* ABC daytime March 29, 1965–September 24, 1965 *host:* Jack Linkletter *announcer:* Wendell Niles *executive producer:* Carl Jampel *producer:* Julian Bercovici *director:* Robin Clark *set designer:* Bob Lee *origination:* Studio D, ABC Television Center, Los Angeles

Two teams of two players competed for a week on this daytime show, "The Rebus Game." A category of the day was revealed (example: science) and all words to be guessed on that day's show were related to that subject.

The words were broken down into syllables and one player from each team had forty-five seconds to draw a syllable for his or her partner to guess. If guessed correctly the team received ten points and a chance to guess the word. The teams alternated drawing syllables of the word until one team guessed the word and received a bonus ten points. If neither

Guess who adds sizzle to this kitchen? It's Sissy Biggers hosting American TV's first cooking game show, "Ready . . . Set . . . Cook!"

team guessed a syllable after two tries the word was tossed out and another played.

The high-scoring team of the day played the "Rebus Race," where they received $50 for each rebus word drawing (broken down by syllables) they could identify in one minute.

Did you know . . .   host Jack Linkletter was part of the only father-and-son combination to host network game shows at the same time? In 1958 Jack was hosting HAGGIS BAGGIS for NBC on Monday nights and his dad Art was the emcee of PEOPLE ARE FUNNY on NBC's Saturday schedule.

THE REEL GAME
premiere: January 18, 1971   *packager:* Jack Barry–Four Star Productions   *broadcast history:* ABC primetime January 18, 1971–May 3, 1971   *host:* Jack Barry   *announcer:* Jack Clark   *producers:* Ken Johnson, John J. Macker   *director:* Marty Pasetta   *set designer:* Bill Morris   *origination:* Studio E, ABC Television Center, Los Angeles

Three studio contestants competed in this quiz show that featured film clips to illustrate the answers. On "The Reel Game," each contestant began the game with $250, betting a portion of his or her money on the possibility of answering a question correctly in a given topic (example: famous marriages). After bets were made, the question was asked and the correct answer was revealed through a film clip on the subject. Each of the four rounds also contained three toss-up questions on the same subject worth $25 if a player answered correctly.

The game concluded with the "grand finale" round, where each player made a final wager before the question was read. The player with the most money at the end of this round won the game and played a bonus film clip round with six additional questions, each worth $50.

"The Reel Game" marked the return of veteran quiz show host Jack Barry to producing shows for network television after a thirteen-year absence resulting from the quiz show scandals.

RELATIVELY SPEAKING

premiere: September 5, 1988   *packager:* Atlantic/Kushner-Locke Inc. and the Maltese Companies (syndicated by Select Media)   *broadcast history:* Syndicated September 5, 1988–June 23, 1989   *host:* John Byner   *assistant:* Stacey Kim Haley   *announcer:* John Harlan   *creators:* David Garber, Bruce Kalish, Michael Poryes   *executive producers:* Peter Locke, Donald Kushner   *producers:* Ken Shapiro, Mitch Gutkowski, Claire Schully, Ray Volpe, Edd Griles, Dawn Tarnofsky   *director:* Kip Walton   *set designer:* Jimmy Cuomo   *music:* Matthew Ender   *origination:* Studio 3, Sunset Gower Studios, Hollywood

A celebrity panel of four tried to determine how a guest contestant was related to a famous person on "Relatively Speaking." The panelists asked questions that required a "yes" or "no" answer and could continue to ask questions until they received a "no" answer. The panel was stumped if they received eight "no" answers before guessing the identity of the guest, who then received a prize.

The last round of the day was played with an in-studio celebrity guest and his or her children, all hidden from the panelists. If they stumped the panel, their winnings were donated to charity.

Were you watching when . . . Dennis James and his son Brad were guest stars or when Gary Owens and his son Chris were guests on "Relatively Speaking"?

REMEMBER THIS?

premiere: October 25, 1996   *packager:* Sande Stewart Productions/MSNBC   *broadcast history:* MSNBC (cable) October 25, 1996–October 5, 1997   *host:* Al Roker   *executive producers:* Robert Mayer, Sande Stewart   *producers:* Molly Gray, Jake Tauber   *directors:* Bruce Burmester, Sande Stewart   *set designer:* James Fenhagen   *origination:* Metropolis Studios, New York; MSNBC Studios, Secaucus

"Today" show weatherman Al Roker was host of this news game show aired three times a week (Fridays, Saturdays, and Sundays) on the cable network MSNBC.

Each show featured two teams of three players representing colleges and universities. The teams tried to answer questions built around news footage from the NBC-TV archives. Teams competed for scholarship money for their schools, with the winning teams from Friday and Saturday facing each other on the Sunday show for the weekly championship. Winning teams on Sunday received a $1,000 scholarship and advanced to the playoffs for a chance at the grand prize, a $20,000 donation to the team's college scholarship fund.

In round one, a film clip was shown and a question asked. The team answering correctly earned ten points and the right

to earn additional points by answering two bonus questions. Point values were doubled in round two with three questions played in each round.

Round three was the "Lightning Round" in which questions were worth thirty points. The team with the most points at the end of this ninety-second round was the winner.

Did you know . . . host Al Roker began his broadcasting career in 1974 as weathercaster and graphic artist with WTVH-TV in Syracuse, New York? He moved on to stations in Cleveland and Washington, D.C. before joining WNBC-TV New York and then the "Today" show on NBC.

REMEMBER THIS DATE

premiere: November 14, 1950   *packager:* Louis Cowan Productions   *broadcast history:* NBC daytime November 14, 1950–June 28, 1951   *host:* Bill Stern   *assistant:* Mary Denny   *featured singer:* Jet McDonald   *announcers:* Don Pardo, Dick Dudley   *producers:* Hal Fimberg, Jean Heaton   *director:* Don Hillman   *music director:* Murray Ross   *origination:* NBC Studio 3B, New York

"Remember This Date," seen on Tuesday and Thursday afternoons, at 3:30 P.M. ("The Bert Parks Show" was on Monday, Wednesday, and Fridays at the same time) was the first daytime game show on NBC.

Contestants answered questions related to a particular date in history. In addition, players also talked about memorable dates in their lives. This show was also known as "Remember the Day."

REMOTE CONTROL

premiere: December 7, 1987   *packager:* MTV Networks   *broadcast history:* MTV (cable) December 7, 1987–November 15, 1990; Syndicated September 23, 1989–September 8, 1990; MTV (cable) April 29, 1991–December 13, 1991   *host:* Ken Ober   *hostesses:* Marisol Massey, Kari Wuhrer, Alicia Coppola, Susan Ashley   *announcer:* Colin Quinn   *creators:* Joe Davola, Michael Dugan   *program consultant:* Howard Blumenthal   *executive producer:* Doug Herzog   *producers:* Joe Davola, Michael Dugan, Lauren Corrao, Jani Barry   *directors:* Dana Calderwood, Scott Fishman, Milton Lage   *set designers:* Byron Taylor, Susan Bolles   *music director:* Steve Treccase   *origination:* Matrix Studios, New York

Cable music video channel MTV premiered its first game show on December 1987 with the offbeat "Remote Control." Set in "the basement at 72 Whooping Cough Lane," the show featured a trio of college-age contestants who sat in oversized leather recliners and used remote control units as their signaling devices to answer questions about music, television, and pop culture.

The players selected from among nine channels (categories). Each channel had three questions worth five, ten, and fifteen points. The player with the last correct answer selected the next category.

Point values doubled in the second round and when the "Zenith TV" went off the air, the player with the lowest score

Your neighbor's basement? No, it's the very hip set of MTV's first game show, "Remote Control." From left to right we have host Ken Ober, announcer Colin Quinn, hostess Marisol Massey, and music director Steve Treccase.

was eliminated from the game and was serenaded by the studio audience singing "Na Na Hey Hey Kiss Him Goodbye" as he or she left the stage. Toward the end of the series, the audience sometimes sang "Hit the Road Jack," instead.

Other distractions that occurred during the game included "Commercial Breaks," which put a player out of the game for thirty seconds, and the "Snack Break," which rewarded a player with either a prize or a practical joke.

The final round consisted of a series of rapid-fire ten-point questions. The player with the highest score won the game and played the bonus round where he or she was strapped into a Craftmatic adjustable bed that was placed in front of nine television monitors. The object was to identify the music videos playing on each monitor within thirty seconds.

A different bonus game, the "Wheel of Jeopardy," was introduced on the 1989 syndicated version of "Remote Con-

trol." The contestant was strapped onto the wheel and tried to answer ten questions while spinning past ten video screens. Each correct answer lit up one screen and if the player's head was pointing at a lighted screen when the game stopped he or she won a grand prize.

During its four-year run, the show added several features including "Sing Along with Colin" (the show's off-key announcer), visits from guest celebrities, and appearances by a regular cast of crazy characters who asked questions of the players.

The set resembled a basement complete with washer, dryer, hot-water heater, and freezer along with unique items such as photos of legendary game show emcees and an oversized "Pez" dispenser with the likeness of Bob Eubanks.

Marisol Massey was the original hostess on the first series of "Remote Control" shows. She was replaced by Kari

Whurer in 1988. Alicia Coppola became the new hostess in June 1989 and Susan Ashley took over the role in February 1990.

Were you watching when . . . Bob Eubanks made a surprise visit to ''Remote Control'' and stood next to the giant ''Pez'' dispenser that was part of the set?

RHYME AND REASON

premiere: July 7, 1975 *packager:* W. T. Naud Productions *broadcast history:* ABC daytime July 7, 1975–July 9, 1976 *host:* Bob Eubanks *announcers:* Jim Thompson, Johnny Jacobs *executive producer:* Steve Friedman *producer:* Walt Case *director:* John Dorsey *set designer:* John C. Mula *music:* Score Productions *origination:* Studio 54, ABC Television Center, Los Angeles *debut guests:* Nipsey Russell, Barbara Feldon, Robert Morse, Mitzi McCall, Charlie Brill, Linda Kaye Henning

She'll win $5,000 if one of the six celebrities completes the rhyming phrase by saying "house," "louse," or "nouse," on "Rhyme and Reason," hosted by Bob Eubanks.

Two contestants and six celebrity ''poets'' were read a root phrase to be used as the first line of a couplet. On ''Rhyme and Reason,'' each contestant secretly selected a final rhyming word to complete the couplet and tried to find a celebrity who had the same rhyming word.

The first player to score three matches won and played a bonus game to try to get the celebrity of his or her choice to say three rhyming words to a bonus phrase in thirty seconds for a grand prize of $5,000.

Were you watching when . . . guest stars Charlie Brill, Pat Harrington Jr., Mitzi McCall, Jaye P. Morgan, and others began destroying the set of ''Rhyme and Reason'' as the show progressed on the last show? They tore up the carpet, broke the lights, and knocked down the emcee's podium. It was one of the more bizarre ways to end a game show.

Bill Cullen, Tom Kennedy, Peter Marshall, and Gary Owens were all guests on the celebrity panel. Regular panel members were Jaye P. Morgan and Nipsey Russell.

RIDDLE ME THIS

premiere: November 20, 1948 *packager:* World Video *broadcast history:* CBS primetime November 20, 1948–March 13, 1949 *hosts:* Douglas Edwards, Paul Gallico, Conrad Nagel *announcer:* Bill Hamilton *producers:* Fred Rosen, Steve Alexander, Larry Algeo, Perry Lafferty *directors:* Ralph Nelson, Alan Dinehart, Ralph Levy, David Rich *origination:* New York

This show, in its first month on the air, went through three titles and three hosts. Originally, it was called THE EYES HAVE IT with Douglas Edwards, then became ''Stop, Look and Listen'' with Paul Gallico, and finally, by December 12, 1948, was called ''Riddle Me This'' with Conrad Nagel.

A male celebrity team played against a female celebrity team by answering questions. Clues were supplied in the form of film clips and live skits performed on stage.

On April 3, 1949, the show changed its title again to CELEBRITY TIME.

RODEO DRIVE

premiere: February 5, 1990 *packager:* Jay Wolpert Productions *broadcast history:* Lifetime (cable) February 5, 1990–August 31, 1990 *host:* Louise Duart *announcer:* Burton Richardson *creators:* Roger Speakman, Jay Wolpert, Randall Neece *producers:* Joel Hecht, Meredith Fox Stewart *director:* Randall Neece *set designers:* Bente Christensen, John Gilles *origination:* Studio 33, CBS Television City, Los Angeles

Three contestants tested their celebrity knowledge and competed for a shopping spree on a set meant to represent the popular Beverly Hills shopping street—Rodeo Drive.

In round one of ''Rodeo Drive,'' a subject and seven clue words were revealed. One player selected a number at random that revealed a clue only to his or her opponents. The opponents then tried to predict whether the first player would mention that word within fifteen seconds. If the opponents predicted correctly they earned fifty points. The player had to say the selected word to earn a pre-determined number of points (one hundred to two hundred fifty). If the player did not say it, he or she got five points for each word said that was on the list of seven clues. The round continued with all three players playing a different subject.

In round two, players earned one hundred points by guessing whether statements about celebrities were fact or rumor. One player kept control until he or she missed a question. The contestant with the most points after this seven-minute round won the game and $500.

The winning contestant received a chance to win merchandise prizes from the shops along "Rodeo Drive" along with a cash jackpot in the bonus round. The value of the jackpot began at $1,000 and the player had to answer five $200 questions to increase the bank. In sixty seconds the player moved along the five shops, listened to gossip and tried to determine who was being talked about. The player won a prize for each successful guess and the cash jackpot if he or she identified who was being talked about at all five stores, in the allotted time. (If time ran out, the player selected a piece of merchandise from one of the stores, as a prize.)

Comedian/impressionist Louise Duart was the host of "Rodeo Drive," one of the first two game shows broadcast on the Lifetime cable channel. (The other was a revised version of the 1960s game show SUPERMARKET SWEEP.)

RUCKUS

premiere: September 9, 1991   *packager:* Merv Griffin Productions/Columbia Pictures Television   *broadcast history:* Syndicated September 9, 1991–January 3, 1992   *host:* "Amazing Jonathan" (Jonathan Szeles)   *assistants:* Helen Incollingo, Charlene Donahue-Wallace   *announcer:* Jim Bradley   *executive producer:* Merv Griffin   *producer:* Burt Wheeler   *director:* James Marcione   *set designers:* Bente Christensen, John Gilles   *music:* Mort Lindsey   *origination:* Merv Griffin's Resorts Casino Hotel, Atlantic City

Contestants, selected from the studio audience, participated in various stunts and magic tricks on this short-lived game show hosted by magician the "Amazing Jonathan."

Some players participated in stunts, like trying to run an obstacle course with one new item added to the course on each run. Another feature was to have members of the studio audience try to predict how a hidden camera stunt involving unsuspecting citizens would turn out.

The final round of the day was called "Reach for a Star," a four-minute round of stunts with three contestants. A toss-up question began the round, and the player who answered correctly got a chance to "reach for a star" and perform the stunt indicated on it for cash or prizes. The player remained at the "Starboard" as long as he or she was successful. When they failed to complete the stunt, another toss-up question was asked to determine who went next to the Starboard.

"Ruckus" received limited exposure when it was first broadcast in 1991. The show was seen only on WNBC, New York, and the hope was to roll it out in syndication. WNBC dropped the show after a few months, and the show remained on the shelf until Game Show Network began running it on a regular basis in October 1997.

RUMOR HAS IT

premiere: June 7, 1993   *packager:* VH-1   *broadcast history:* VH-1 (cable) June 7, 1993–October 28, 1993   *host:* Brian O'Connor   *announcer:* John Ten Eyck   *creators:* Risa Graubard, Carol Jacobs   *executive producer:* Jack Sussman   *supervising producer:* Donna Wolfe   *producers:* Risa Graubard, Carol Jacobs   *director:* Bob Lampel   *production design:* James Fenhagen, Erik Ulfers   *origination:* Chelsea Studios, New York

Three studio contestants tested their knowledge of celebrity hearsay, fact, and innuendo on "Rumor Has It," a cable game show broadcast on music channel VH-1 (Video Hits One).

Each player started the game with one-hundred points. In round one, "Scandalation," players answered toss-up multiple choice questions concerning celebrity scandal and worth ten points. Within the round, the contestants also played a "Scandalation Instant Reflex" segment. Questions were worth twenty points and players chose from two possible choices. The high-scoring player at the end of this round won a prize and the low-scoring player was eliminated.

The remaining two players participated in the "Video Tap" round, where they were shown a clip from a music video and then tried to identify the artist for twenty points. The player who answered correctly was given first choice at answering two questions about the artist. Round two concluded with the rapid fire "Instant Reflex" segment, worth forty points, where each chose from one of two answers to questions in a particular category (example: things Debbie Harry did before she was a member of the rock group "Blondie"). The high-scoring player after this round won the game and a prize.

The day's winner played the "Rumor Mix and Match" bonus game, where he or she tried to match eight statements to celebrity photos in thirty seconds. The player received fifty points for each correct match and a grand prize if all eight matches were correct.

The nine highest-scoring contestants of the season returned to compete in the "Total Trash Tournament."

RUNAROUND

premiere: September 9, 1972   *packager:* Merrill Heatter–Bob Quigley Productions   *broadcast history:* NBC Saturday morning September 9, 1972–September 1, 1973   *host:* Paul Winchell with "Jerry Mahoney" and "Knucklehead Smiff"   *announcer:* Kenny Williams   *executive producers:* Merrill Heatter, Bob Quigley   *producers:* Les Roberts, Art Alisi   *director:* Jerome Shaw   *set designer:* Hub Braden   *music:* Mort Garson   *origination:* NBC Studios, Burbank

Nine children competed in "Runaround," this weekly game show hosted by ventriloquist Paul Winchell and his dummies "Jerry Mahoney" and "Knucklehead Smiff."

After a question was read, three possible answers appeared on stage. Each kid ran to the answer they felt was correct. Kids who selected the correct answer received one token. The others were placed in a penalty box and the game continued until only one player was left. The players with the most tokens at the end of the show received prizes.

Did you know . . . host Paul Winchell won first prize on the ''Major Bowes Amateur Hour'' radio show at age fourteen with his dummy Jerry Mahoney? Originally the dummy was named Terry Mahoney, but everybody called the dummy Jerry, having misunderstood the name. Paul's creative and scientific genius created the artificial heart in 1955, and he was granted the patent in 1963. The heart was later modified and became known as the Jarvik 7.

SALE OF THE CENTURY

premiere: September 29, 1969 *packagers:* Jones-Howard Productions (1969–1974); Reg Grundy Productions (1983–1989) *broadcast history:* NBC daytime September 29, 1969–July 13, 1973; Syndicated September 10, 1973–September 1974; NBC daytime January 3, 1983–March 24, 1989; Syndicated January 1985–September 1986; USA (cable) September 14, 1992–July 29, 1994 (repeats of 1983–1989 series)

1969–1974 version

hosts: Jack Kelly, Joe Garagiola *models:* Barbara Lyon, Kit Dougherty *announcer:* Bill Wendell *executive producer:* Al Howard *producers:* Ron Greenberg, Willie Stein *directors:* Paul Alter, Mike Garguilo *set designers:* Ed Flesh, Carden Bailey, Kathleen Ankers *music:* Al Howard, Irwin Bazelon *origination:* NBC Studio 8H, New York

1983–1989 version

host: Jim Perry *hostesses:* Sally Julian, Lee Menning, Summer Bartholomew *announcers:* Jay Stewart, Don Morrow *executive producers:* Bob Crystal, Al Howard, Robert Noah *producers:* George Vosburgh, Burt Wheeler *directors:* Jerome Shaw, James Marcione *set designer:* Bente Christensen *music:* Ray Ellis, Marc Ellis *origination:* NBC Studios 2 and 3, Burbank

On "Sale of the Century," three contestants competed to answer a rapid-fire series of questions worth $5, $10, and $15. During the game, the players were offered a series of "instant bargains," which could be purchased with the contestant's accumulated cash total. The player with the highest cash total shopped at the "Sale of the Century," where it was possible to purchase luxury items with his or her day's winnings (example: a new car for $250).

On March 26, 1973 the format was changed and two couples competed in two rapid-fire rounds (worth $5 and $10) and a five-question "Century Round" (worth $20). The couple with the highest cash total shopped at the "Sale of the Century."

Jack Kelly, one time costar of the TV series "Maverick," was the original host and was replaced by sportscaster Joe Garagiola on August 23, 1971. Garagiola was a former major league baseball catcher from 1946 to 1955 and played with the St. Louis Cardinals. In 1961 he joined NBC as a play-by-play announcer.

"Sale of the Century" was revised and returned to the NBC daytime schedule on January 3, 1983. In the 1980s version, three contestants again competed in a question-and-answer game with the winner able to purchase luxury prizes at special low prices.

Each player started the game with a bankroll of $20 and received $5 for right answers and lost $5 for wrong answers. From time to time during the game, the player with the most money was offered an "instant bargain" paid for with part of their earnings (example: a color TV for $13).

Also played during the game was a new feature, "The Fame Game," where the first player to solve a "Who Am I?" question selected one number from a board of nine. Behind some of the numbers were merchandise prizes and behind the others were money cards that were added to the player's score.

The game ended with a sixty-second speed round of questions and the player with the most money at the end of this round won the game.

During its six-year run on NBC in the 1980s, several other changes were made to "Sale of the Century." In the main game, an "Instant Cash" feature was added, where the player in the lead could purchase a chance to win a cash jackpot (a minimum of $1,000 plus $1,000 for each day it was not won). The player was given the chance to buy one of three boxes. Two of the boxes contained a $100 bill and the third contained the jackpot. The price for this chance was the amount of the player's lead over the second-place opponent.

The bonus game also changed. By 1987, instead of purchasing prizes with their winnings, the winning contestant played a prize matching game. Using a board of twenty numbered squares, the player called out numbers one at a time, and the player won the first prize that was matched.

The bonus game changed again in 1988 with the winning contestant playing for a cash jackpot (minimum $1,000 plus $1,000 for each day not won) by trying to solve four "six-clue puzzles" in twenty seconds.

Jim Perry hosted the show for its entire run, but his assistants changed three times. During the first months on the air

Here's Jim Perry who took the baton from Jack Kelly and Joe Garagiola to host the most recent version of the classic, "Sale of the Century."

the hostess was Sally Julian. She was replaced by former LAS VEGAS GAMBIT hostess Lee Menning in March 1983. Menning was followed by former Miss USA of 1975, Summer Bartholomew, in December 1984. Summer, a second runner-up in the 1976 Miss Universe contest was also a substitute hostess on WHEEL OF FORTUNE in 1982, and remained with "Sale of the Century" for the rest its the run. Announcer Jay Stewart was replaced by Don Morrow in 1988.

Did you know . . . the original set for "Sale of the Century" had to be sawed in half before it was placed on stage at NBC in New York? The original pilot for the show was taped in Los Angeles, but due to a lack of studio space the show was moved to NBC Studio 8H at Rockefeller Center in New York. According to set designer Ed Flesh, the set was too large for the elevator that would take it to the stage where the show was to be taped.

Host Jim Perry was a straight man to comedian Sid Caesar and was discovered while hosting shows at Grossingers in the Catskill Mountains in New York. Perry also hosted the Canadian game shows DEFINITION, EYE BET, and FRACTURED PHRASES.

SANDBLAST

premiere: December 19, 1994 *packager:* Four Point Entertainment *broadcast history:* MTV (cable) December 19, 1994–September 6, 1996 *hosts:* Summer Sanders and Peter King *announcer:* Kevin James *creators:* Patrick Byrnes, Joe Davola *executive producers:* Ron Ziskin, Shukri Gha-

layini, Patrick Byrnes *producer:* R. Greg Johnston *line producer:* Daniel Goldberg *director:* Ric Lacivita *set designer:* David Morong *origination:* Walt Disney World, Orlando

Two teams of two players (one male, one female) competed in "Sandblast," this sports competition show featuring water- and sand-based stunts such as "Hose Hockey," in which the opponent was sprayed with water from a hose while trying to paddle into a goal; "Sand Slam," a thirty-second round where each team tried to slam dunk baskets in a slowly rising net; and "Dunk This," where the teams challenged each other to see who could slam dunk the highest basket.

Each show consists of five events and the "Crash Course" finale.

Hosting the Florida-based series were 1992 Olympic gold medalist Summer Sanders and surfer Peter King.

SAY IT WITH ACTING

premiere: January 6, 1951 *packager:* West Hooker Productions *broadcast history:* NBC primetime January 6, 1951–May 12, 1951; ABC primetime August 3, 1951–February 22, 1952 *host:* Ben Grauer *substitute host:* Robert Alda *team captains:* Bud Collyer, Maggi McNellis *announcer:* Lionel Ricau *producers:* West Hooker, Wayne Worth *directors:* Warren Jacober, Ralph Nelson, Bob McCahon *set designer:* Phil DeRosier *origination:* NBC Studio 3B, New York

Art James, hosting his first game show back in 1961, "Say When!!"

This celebrity game show featured two teams of actors and actresses from current Broadway shows competing in a game of charades.

"Say It with Acting" began as a local show on WNBT, New York. It was originally called "Look Ma I'm Acting" when it premiered on January 19, 1949. Its title was changed to "Act It Out" on February 20, 1949 and to "Say It with Acting" on May 22, 1949. It completed its local run on October 22, 1950.

SAY WHEN!!

premiere: January 3, 1961 *packager:* Mark Goodson–Bill Todman Productions *broadcast history:* NBC daytime January 3, 1961–March 25, 1965 *host:* Art James *models:* Ruth Halsey, Emily Banks, Gunilla Knutson, Carolyn White, Kristan Johnson, Elizabeth Ames *announcer:* Wayne Howell *substitute announcers:* Roger Tuttle, Fred Collins, Mel Brandt *producer:* S. Robert Rowe *directors:* Dick Schneider, Don Bohl *set designers:* Ted Cooper, Tom Trimble *music director:* Carmen Mastren *origination:* NBC Studio 6B, New York

On "Say When!!" two contestants alternated, picking prizes from four possibilities and attempting to build pots of merchandise that came as close to a predetermined amount as possible without going over. The first player to go over

that amount lost the game while the first player to win two games became the champion and faced another opponent.

A player could "freeze" when he or she felt close to the goal. This forced his or her opponent to try to get closer to the goal or go over the total and lose. One of the frequent prizes was the "blank check," good for one to one-hundred cases of a product.

In October 1961, a "Joke of the Day" contest was started, where viewers sent in a favorite joke and won an encyclopedia if it was used on the air.

Announcer Wayne Howell frequently appeared on camera in the role of a character named "Aunt Hetty Rowe." Howell was the sidekick/announcer on "Broadway Open House," TV's first late-night show (1950) and a staff announcer for NBC from 1946 to 1985.

Did you know . . . long before his game show career, Art James had a tryout with the Yankees in 1946? Also, while serving for two years in the army, Art was stationed in Germany where he was an announcer for the Armed Forces Radio Network.

Were you watching when . . . Art James was doing a live commercial during "Say When!!" for Skippy peanut butter and the jar cracked on camera with the peanut butter dripping all over Art. It has since become a famous commercial blooper seen on several primetime specials.

James sang for the first time on television on the December 24, 1964 episode of "Say When!!"? A bass baritone, James sang "It's Christmas Again."

SCATTERGORIES

premiere: January 18, 1993 *packager:* Reg Grundy Productions *broadcast history:* NBC daytime January 18, 1993–June 10, 1993 *host:* Dick Clark *announcer:* Charlie Tuna *executive producer:* Robert Noah *producer:* Burt Wheeler *director:* James Marcione *set designer:* Bente Christensen *music:* Ray Ellis, Marc Ellis *origination:* The Glendale Studios

Two teams of four contestants (men vs. women) participated in "Scattergories," this game show based on the popular board game. A subject (example: "A place where singles might meet") and a letter of the alphabet were revealed and players on one team were given fifteen seconds to come up with items related to that subject. They scored one point for each acceptable answer and tried to pick up additional points by selecting four celebrities from a group of five who then revealed their answers. The team scored one point for each new answer but lost a point for a repeated answer. After one team played, their opponents played the same category using a different letter.

A second round was played, point values doubled, and the team with the highest score at the end of this round won the game and $500.

The winning team played a bonus round for a potential $4,000. A new category was revealed and a letter was assigned to each of the five celebrities. The team players gave two answers for each letter and then tried to capture three celebrities who had to give an answer that the team had not already mentioned.

Interviews with the celebrities were recorded before the show and different celebrities appeared weekly. The winning team returned to play on the next show.

Were you watching when . . . Phyllis Diller, Wink Martindale, Rip Taylor, Adam West, and Chuck Woolery were all celebrity guests on "Scattergories"? Howard Stern's partner Robin Quivers appeared on the same show with Adam West. Dick Clark teamed the two and called them the team of "Batman and Robin."

SCRABBLE

premiere: July 2, 1984 *packager:* Reg Grundy Productions in association with Exposure Unlimited *broadcast history:* NBC daytime July 2, 1984–March 23, 1990; USA (cable) September 16, 1991–Feb 3, 1995 (repeats of 1984–1990 NBC series); NBC daytime January 18, 1993–June 10, 1993; USA (cable) April 17, 1995–October 13, 1995 (repeats of 1984–1990 series) *host:* Chuck Woolery *announcers:* Jay Stewart, Charlie Tuna *executive in charge of production:* Bill Mason *executive producer:* Robert Noah *supervising producer:* Robert Crystal *producer:* Gary Johnson *director:* Chris Darley *set designer:* Ed Flesh *music:* Ray Ellis, Marc Ellis *origination:* NBC Studio 3, Burbank (1984–1990); NBC Studio 11, Burbank (1993)

On "Scrabble," two contestants competed in guessing words, based on the board game by the same name. A large board was revealed highlighting a specific number of blank spaces for one word. A clue, based on that word, was read. One player then selected two numbered tiles and placed them into an electronic reader to reveal two letters of the alphabet that may have been contained in that word. The player then chose one of those letters and if it was included in the word it showed up in its proper position and the player could then attempt to guess the word. If the letter fell in a blue space, the puzzle was then worth a bonus $500 if the player guessed the word at that moment and $1,000 if the letter fell on a pink space. The player kept control of the board and selected letters until he or she guessed the word or chose a letter not in the word (a "stopper"). The first player to correctly guess three words won the game and $500.

The winner played the reigning champion in the "Scrabble Sprint" round for $1,500 in bonus money. Players, in turn, attempted to guess three words using a clue and letters that made up the word. Only two letters appeared at one time and there were no stoppers in this part of the game. The player who used the least amount of time to guess the words won and became the new reigning champion. Players who won the Sprint round five times won $20,000.

During its six year run NBC changes were made in the Scrabble Sprint round. By 1988, winners of the main game tried to guess four words in the shortest time possible. Once they had established a time, the winner of the second game of the day played the same words in the Sprint round. The fastest time of the day won $1,000 and the chance to play the "Bonus Sprint."

Six out of seven of these celebrities have hosted their own game shows. From left to right we have Jamie Farr, Jim Lange, Jeff MacGregor, Bill Rafferty, Wink Martindale, and down in front Vicki Lawrence and "Scrabble" emcee Chuck Woolery. The odd man out is Jamie Farr; however, he actually substituted for Tom Kennedy on "Wordplay."

In the Bonus Sprint round, the day's overall champion tried to guess two words in ten seconds' for a jackpot that started at $5,000 and increased $1,000 a day until won.

Scrabble was created in 1931 by Alfred M. Butts, who called the game Criss-Cross. James Brunot began manufacturing it in 1948 and renamed it Scrabble. In 1952 Selchow and Righter acquired the rights to market the game.

Did you know . . . before Chuck Woolery hosted game shows, he wrote the song "Naturally Stoned," a top-forty hit in 1968 for the Avant Garde? He was a featured vocalist in the 1974 revival of "Your Hit Parade" and costarred with Cheryl Ladd and Roosevelt Grier in the 1974 motion picture *Treasure of Jamaica Reef.* He also played Mr. Dingle in the syndicated children's series "New Zoo Revue" in 1973.

SCRAMBLE

premiere: September 6, 1993 *packager:* Let's Scramble Inc. *broadcast history:* Syndicated September 6, 1993–January 2, 1994 *host:* Randall Cunningham *referee:* Kat Ashley *assistant referees:* Danny Lopez, Mindy Stover *question judge:* Dale Good *creators:* Jimmie and Freida Hand, Randall Cunningham *executive producer:* Randall Cunningham *producer:* Gary Vautin *director:* John Reither *art director:* Mark Price *origination:* California Image Associates, Rancho Cordova

On "Scramble" two teams (the blue and the gold) of three kids competed in a question-and-answer game in a football game setting. The show was hosted by Philadelphia Eagles quarterback Randall Cunningham.

Teams played one at a time, with the game ball starting on their thirty-yard line. Teams had up to four downs to reach the goal line by answering ten-yard questions ("Run Play," a true or false question), twenty-yard questions ("Pass Play," a multiple choice question), or thirty-yard questions ("Trick Play," questions with one answer).

Reaching the goal line earned a team six points and a chance at an extra point for solving a puzzle or completing a mini-obstacle course. A team could also try a field goal (three points) by having one player answer a general knowledge question. If a team failed to reach the goal line, the opposing team took control of the game.

After three quarters, both teams participated in the final round, "The Two-Minute Scramble," where each team tried to toss footballs through a moving hoop in twenty seconds. Each ball thrown through the hoop earned a team three points and the high-scoring team of the day won the game and prizes that included an encyclopedia and a telescope.

SECOND CHANCE

premiere: March 7, 1977   *packager:* Carruthers Company/Warner Brothers Television   *broadcast history:* ABC daytime March 7, 1977–July 15, 1977   *host:* Jim Peck   *announcers:* Jay Stewart, Jack Clark   *creator:* Bill Carruthers

executive producer: Bill Carruthers   *producer:* Joel Stein   *director:* Chris Darley   *set designer:* Ed Flesh   *music:* Score Productions   *origination:* Studio 54, ABC Television Center, Los Angeles

Three contestants were asked a question. If they kept with their first answer to the question and were correct, they earned three points. On "Second Chance," before the correct answer was revealed, the players were shown three possible answers, one of which was correct. A player could change an answer, but its value was reduced to one point.

After three questions were played, each contestant was given one spin on the big board for each point accumulated. The object was to accumulate as much money (including the retail value of merchandise prizes) without landing on a devil. Any player who landed on a devil lost all he or she had accumulated. Four devils eliminated a player and to avoid landing on a devil, players could give any of their remaining spins to their opponents. The player with the most money won the game.

"Second Chance" was revised in 1983 for CBS under the new title PRESS YOUR LUCK.

Did you know . . . Jim Peck was under contract to the ABC network and "Second Chance" was his third game show that he emceed for ABC, his first being BIG SHOWDOWN in 1974 and his second HOT SEAT in 1976. Jim also filled in on "Good Morning America" for vacationing David Hartman in 1975.

Jim Peck hosting "Second Chance" in 1977 for the ABC network.

SECOND HONEYMOON

premiere: September 2, 1987 *packager:* Wink Martindale–Jerry Gilden Productions *broadcast history:* CBN (cable) September 2, 1987–September 2, 1988 *host:* Wayne Cox *announcer:* Doc Harris *executive producers:* Wink Martindale, Jerry Gilden *producer:* Tony Blake *director:* William Elliot *set designers:* Tony Sabatino, William Harris *origination:* Vancouver, Canada

Three families competed against each other, trying to match answers related to hypothetical situations with the grand prize being a ''second honeymoon'' trip for the parents.

On ''Second Honeymoon,'' each team consisted of a mother, father, and two or three of their children. The kids tried to see how much they knew about their parents by selecting from multiple choice answers to questions such as ''What would your mom do to make your dad feel younger?'' and ''What would your mom do if the phone rang at 4 A.M. and a sexy female asked for your dad?''

The first round had two questions, worth twenty and forty points, with the kids trying to predict how their mothers would react and the second round also had two questions, worth sixty and eighty points, with the fathers being second-guessed.

In the third and final round, the mother and two of her children tried to match the father on one final question. One hundred points were earned for each member of the family who matched the father (three-hundred points possible). The team with the highest score at the end of this round won the second honeymoon.

SECRETS OF THE CRYPTKEEPER'S HAUNTED HOUSE

premiere: September 14, 1996 *packager:* Goldwyn Entertainment/Keller Productions/The Wohl Company *broadcast history:* CBS Saturday morning September 14, 1996–August 23, 1997 *host:* Steve Saunders *voice of the cryptkeeper:* John Kassir *skeleton voice:* Danny Mann *creators/executive producers:* Eytan Keller, Jack Wohl *supervising producer:* Grant Johnson *coproducer:* Julia Gilbert *coordinating producer:* Philip Wallnutt *director:* Eytan Keller *production designer:* Bill Bohnert *music:* Robert J. Walsh *theme:* ''Tales from the Crypt'' by Danny Elfman *origination:* Universal Studios, Orlando

Each week, two teams of two kids each, with team names such as the Amoebas and the Newts, competed in five games or stunts set in a haunted house at Universal Studios in Orlando, Florida.

Games included ''Fireball Alley,'' where one player standing on a suspended bridge tried to protect six ''headstones'' from being knocked down by ''fireballs'' tossed at them by the eyes of a floating head suspended in space; ''The Abyss,'' where one player read a series of five questions in ninety seconds while the other player climbed a series of rope ladders trying to find the correct answer mounted on a wall; and ''Skull Duggery,'' where one player from each team went through the house trying to find as many skulls as he or she could in the allotted time.

Points were awarded for completing events in each game and the team with the most points at the end of the show received a computer, while the runner-up team took home an encyclopedia.

The show's theme music, composed by Danny Elfman, a former member of the pop group Oingo Boingo, was also used on the TV series ''Tales of the Crypt.''

SEVEN KEYS

premiere: April 3, 1961 *packager:* Wellington Productions *broadcast history:* ABC daytime April 3, 1961–March 27, 1964 *host:* Jack Narz *models:* Betty Andrews, Barbara Lyon *announcer:* Jack Powers *creator/executive producer:* Carl Jampel *producer:* Bobbie John *director:* Johnny Stearns *set designer:* Al Wein *theme song:* ''Everything's Coming Up Roses'' *origination:* Studio E, ABC Television Center, Los Angeles

The contestants on ''Seven Keys'' attempted to reach the top of a seventy-space board in fifteen moves to win one of seven keys that unlocked a dream galaxy of prizes. The board was filled with bonus moves, backward moves, stops, and questions that the contestant had to answer. Upon successfully completing the board, the contestant could quit with his or her key or risk that key and try to complete the board again to win a second key. A player could attempt to win as many as seven keys.

''Seven Keys'' began as a local show in the Los Angeles area on TV station KTLA. It was seen from September 12, 1960 to April 28, 1961. After ABC canceled the show in 1964, ''Seven Keys'' returned to KTLA on April 6, 1964 and continued until January 15, 1965.

Jack Narz winces as he informs a lovely contestant she's just landed on a penalty.

Stubby Kaye points the way to fun and games on "Shenanigans."

SHENANIGANS

premiere: September 26, 1964   *packager:* Merrill Heatter–Bob Quigley Productions   *broadcast history:* ABC Saturday morning September 26, 1964–March 20, 1965; ABC Saturday morning September 25, 1965–December 18, 1965   *host:* Stubby Kaye   *announcer:* "Kenny the Cop": Kenny Williams   *"Shenaghoul":* Steve Janos   *producers:* Merrill Heatter, Bob Quigley   *directors:* Hal Cooper, Stuart Phelps   *set designer:* Larry Klein   *music:* Arlo   *origination:* Vine Street Theater, Hollywood

Two children competed on a three-dimensional game board on "Shenanigans." Players' moves were determined by the roll of two dice. The children moved space by space and answered questions or performed whatever was indicated on the square in which they landed. Each correct answer to a question or completed stunt earned "Shenanigans" money. The first player to complete the board won the game and traded his or her money in for prizes.

Host Stubby Kaye appeared in films such as *Guys and Dolls, Lil' Abner, Cat Ballou,* and *Sweet Charity.*

SHOOT FOR THE STARS

premiere: January 3, 1977   *packager:* Bob Stewart Productions   *broadcast history:* NBC daytime January 3, 1977–September 30, 1977   *host:* Geoff Edwards   *announcer:* Bob Clayton   *executive producer:* Bob Stewart   *producer:* Bruce Burmester   *director:* Mike Garguilo   *set designers:* John Robert Lloyd, Herb Andrews   *music:* Bob Cobert   *origination:* NBC Studio 8H, New York   *debut guests:* Anne Meara, Soupy Sales

Two teams, each composed of a celebrity guest and a studio contestant, competed in a word association game on "Shoot for the Stars."

One player selected a box on a game board that contained twenty-four boxes. A clue was read (example: "clever as a lash") and one player had to unscramble the first half of the phrase by providing a synonym for the first portion (example: "smart" for "clever") and his or her teammate had to unscramble the second half (example: "whip" for "lash"). Each phrase was worth money and teams alternated until one team won with $1,500.

The winning team played a one-minute bonus round for a jackpot that began at $1,000 and increased by $500 until time ran out.

Were you watching when . . .   Bill Cullen was often a celebrity guest on "Shoot for the Stars"?

SHOP 'TIL YOU DROP

premiere: July 8, 1991   *packager:* Stone-Stanley Productions   *broadcast history:* Lifetime (cable) July 8, 1991–September 1, 1995; Family Channel (cable) September 30, 1996–August 14, 1998
1991–1995 version
host: Pat Finn   *announcer:* Mark Walberg   *executive producers:* Scott Stone, David Stanley, Heidi Cayn   *producers:* Stephen Brown, Kathy Cotter   *directors:* Jeff Goldstein, Bob Loudin   *set designers:* Joe Stewart, John Shaffner   *origination:* Studio 4, Hollywood Center Studios, Los Angeles
1996–1998 version
host: Pat Finn   *announcers:* Jason Grant Smith, Dee Bradley Baker   *executive producers:* Scott Stone, David Stanley   *producers:* David Greenfield, Dennis Bader   *line producer:* Sue Langham   *director:* Bob Loudin   *production designers:* Joe Stewart, John Shaffner, Rick Bluhm   *music:* Gary Scott   *origination:* Hollywood Center Studios, Los Angeles

Two teams, each consisting of two contestants, competed on "Shop 'Til You Drop," a daily game show that combined shopping knowledge with the ability to complete stunts for the grand prize of a shopping trip and vacation.

Set in a mall-like setting, the show featured teams who first competed in two rounds by attempting to complete stunts within a predetermined time limit. The teams played one at a time and had the option to pass or play. The team that successfully completed the stunt won points (one hundred in the first round, two hundred in the second) and their choice of prizes from one of the mall's stores. Each team performed one stunt in each round.

Round three, the "Shopper's Challenge," consisted of a series of rapid-fire questions, each worth fifty points, that tested a team's knowledge of slogans, merchandise, and shopping. The team with the highest score at the end of this ninety-second round won the game.

In the bonus round, the winning team was given six boxes of prizes. With a ninety-second time limit, they had to open each box and decide if they wished to keep the prizes or exchange them for others in the mall. If they chose to exchange, one team member raced to another store in the mall and selected a replacement box. The goal was to accumulate prizes that totaled over $2,500 in order to win the bonus vacation.

The Family Channel revived "Shop 'Til You Drop" in fall 1996 adding *New* to the title. The game remained the same as it was in the Lifetime version. Dee Bradley Baker took over as announcer in fall 1997 replacing Jason Grant Smith.

SHOPPING SPREE

premiere: September 30, 1996   *package:* Jay Wolpert Enterprises/MTM   *broadcast history:* Family Channel (cable) September 30, 1996–August 14, 1998   *host:* Ron Pearson   *announcer:* Burton Richardson   *creator/executive producer:* Jay Wolpert   *producer:* Shannon Dobson   *line producer:* Rich de Michele   *director:* Chris Darley   *set designer:* Bente Christensen   *theme:* Mark Northam, Al Kasha, Bo Bennike   *music:* Mark Northam   *origination:* Studio 1, Empire Studios, Burbank; Studio 1, CBS Studio Center, Studio City

On this weekday game show, contestants try to second-guess what merchandise a teammate they have never met will preselect. Four players are divided into two teams of two. Each show also features a model, "Denise/Dennis DuJour," who is selected from the studio audience.

Before the show begins, one player from each team secretly selects one of four possible gifts from six different stores on stage. These players then attach clues to their clothes to give their partners hints about their likes and interests.

The other two contestants then run to a store and select the gift that they feel their partner has preselected based on the clues. If they guess correctly, the item goes into the shopping bag, and they move on to the next store. If not, they are given a clue to help identify the proper item. After one team completes this round and establishes a time, the opposing team plays. The team with the best time wins the game.

Before the bonus game, the winning team plays the "Double Up Derby" through which they can double the amount of the jackpot at stake. They try to guess which of four items has been selected by the day's model, Denise/Dennis DuJour. If they are right, they play for a $2,000 shopping spree and trip in the bonus round. Otherwise they play for $1,000.

In the "Birthday Party" bonus round, the winning team tries to match seven different "celebrity" guests (represented by drawings) with items they are most closely associated with in a seventy-five-second time limit. One player goes to the "Birthday Board" and after a celebrity is revealed, picks an item off the board and tosses it to his or her teammate who then puts it in a box and shoves it toward the "celebrity." If correct, they continue on to the next celebrity. If not, the box is rejected and they select again. If they complete the task in the time allotted they win the grand prize shopping spree and trip.

Pat Finn, host of Lifetime cable's "Shop 'Til You Drop."

SHOWDOWN

premiere: July 4, 1966   *packager:* Merrill Heatter–Bob Quigley Productions/Four Star TV   *broadcast history:* NBC daytime July 4, 1966–October 14, 1966   *host:* Joe Pyne   *announcer:* Kenny Williams   *executive producers:* Merrill Heatter, Bob Quigley   *producer:* Larry Klein   *director:* Stuart Phelps   *set designer:* Mary Weaver   *music:* Arlo   *featured band:* The Bantams   *origination:* NBC Studio 3, Burbank

Two teams, each consisting of three contestants, competed in a general information quiz on "Showdown." Each team's members had something in common, such as three being chefs or three being trash collectors.

For each question asked, four possible answers were revealed and each player made his or her choice by pushing a button that locked in his or her answer. The contestants who chose correctly remained standing and any player who answered incorrectly dropped out of sight (using a breakaway seat that dropped them through the floor). When all three players of one team were eliminated, the opposing team won and the players who were still standing received prizes.

The winning team received $100 and the chance to try the "Triple Treat" for a trip. All three players had to answer a question correctly to receive the prize.

During the show, a teenage music combo, "The Bantams," played rock 'n' roll and also provided musical clues for some questions.

Host Joe Pyne was a popular talk radio personality during the 1960s known for his insulting remarks.

SHOWOFFS

premiere: June 30, 1975 *packager:* Mark Goodson–Bill Todman Productions *broadcast history:* ABC daytime June 30, 1975–December 26, 1975 *host:* Bobby Van *announcer:* Gene Wood *producer:* Howard Felsher *director:* Paul Alter *set designer:* Henry Lickel *music:* Score Productions *origination:* Studio 54, ABC Television Center, Los Angeles *debut guests:* Sally Struthers, Dick Gautier, Joyce Bulifant, Ron Masek

On ''Showoffs,'' two teams (two celebrities and one contestant) competed in a game of ''charades.'' Each team was given sixty seconds to communicate (via pantomime or acting) words or phrases to their guessing-partner. The team that guessed the most words won the match and a best two-out-of-three match determined the champion.

In the bonus round, the players again communicated for sixty seconds for a payoff of $1 a word. The contestant was given an additional thirty seconds to guess three more words, with payoffs of ten times his or her sixty-second word score if only one word was guessed; one hundred times for two words; and one thousand times for correctly guessing all three.

Did you know . . . Larry Blyden was the original emcee of ''Showoffs''? Bobby Van replaced Blyden as emcee after Blyden's untimely death in 1975.

Bobby Van played Dobie Gillis in the 1953 motion picture *The Affairs of Dobie Gillis.* Debbie Reynolds and Hans Conreid costarred.

SHUFFLE—THE INTERACTIVE GAME

premiere: March 7, 1994 *packager:* Martindale-Hillier Enterprises/Fiedler-Berlin Productions *broadcast history:* Family Channel (cable) March 7, 1994–June 10, 1994 *host:* Wink Martindale *announcer:* Randy West *executive producers:* Wink Martindale, Bill Hillier *supervising producers:* Peter Berlin, Rob Fiedler *producer:* Gary Johnson *director:* Rob Fiedler *set designer:* Scott Storey *music:* Ed Lojeski *origination:* Glendale Studios, Glendale

Four contestants competed to win a trip in ''Shuffle—The Interactive Game,'' a daily game show that also gave home viewers with touch-tone telephones a chance to compete for prizes.

Each question was played with four answers revealed. Players had ten seconds to choose the correct answer, and were then given five seconds to choose another answer that would be second on the list. Questions like ''Which operatic voice is the lowest?'' were posed. A list of answers (contralto, bass, tenor, and baritone) was revealed and the faster a player picked his or her answer the more points he or she received. Up to one thousand points were awarded for the first answer and a maximum of five hundred points were awarded on the second answer.

Three questions were played in each of three rounds and the low scoring player at the end of each round was eliminated. Scores reverted back to zero at the beginning of each round. The remaining player at the end of the third round won the trip.

SING IT AGAIN

premiere: September 2, 1950 *packager:* Lester Gottlieb Productions *broadcast history:* CBS primetime September 2, 1950–June 23, 1951 *hosts:* Dan Seymour, Jan Murray *announcers:* Hal Simms, Art Hannes, Bern Bennett *producers:* Lester Gottlieb, Herb Moss *directors:* Bob Bleyer, Bruno Zirato Jr. *music director:* Ray Bloch *origination:* CBS Studio 50, New York

''Sing It Again'' was a weekly one-hour Saturday-night music variety quiz show that featured home viewers trying to identify songs with the help of special clues performed by the program's regulars. If the player answered correctly he or she received a chance to identify the ''phantom voice'' for a jackpot prize.

By February 1951, the emphasis shifted to the use of studio contestants to identify the songs and the home viewers participated only in the ''phantom voice'' contest. If the home audience failed to guess the ''voice,'' the studio contestants were given a chance at the end of the show.

''Sing It Again'' began on CBS radio on May 29, 1948 and continued as a simulcast when the show moved to TV in 1950. Comedian Jan Murray replaced original host Dan Seymour on February 24, 1951.

Regular performers on the show included Eugene Baird, Alan Dale, Bob Howard, Betty Luster, Judy Lynn, The Riddlers, and Jack Stanton. Ray Bloch conducted the orchestra.

SINGLED OUT

premiere: June 5, 1995 *packager:* MTV Productions *broadcast history:* MTV (cable) June 5, 1995–May 20, 1998 *host:* Chris Hardwick *cohosts:* Jenny McCarthy, Carmen Electra *piano boy:* Jon Ernst *announcers:* Tami Heide, Royale Watkins *creators:* Burt Wheeler, Sharon Sussman *executive producers:* Lisa Berger, Gary Auerbach *producers:* Nancy McDonald, Mark Cronin, Dean Young, Kallissa Miller *directors:* Milton Lage, Marie NeJame Hack, Joe DeMaio *set designer:* Railton & Associates *art directors:* Kris Bast, Steve Atwell *theme music:* Jon Ernst *origination:* Empire Studios, Burbank

''Singled Out'' was one of the most popular dating game shows of the mid-1990s. It made a celebrity out of cohost Jenny McCarthy, a former *Playboy* magazine centerfold, who moved on to her own comedy series for MTV, ''The Jenny McCarthy Show'' in 1997, and starred in her own sitcom, ''Jenny,'' for NBC in fall 1997. McCarthy left ''Singled Out'' on February 7, 1997 and was replaced on February 10 by Carmen Electra.

''Singled Out'' was first seen during MTV's annual Spring Break Special in 1995. In June of the same year, ''Singled Out'' returned as a daily series, continuing in first-run production until the summer of 1997.

''Singled Out'' featured one hundred young people competing to win a date with a member of the opposite sex.

In the first game, fifty single guys competed for a night on the town with a young woman. With her back to them, she went through several rounds of selection to eliminate most of the players.

In the first round, she picked from one of six categories, such as height, hair length, clothing style, manners, etc. Each category had two choices. She chose one, thus eliminating all of the contestants in the other category. As they paraded by her on their way out of the studio, she could select one to receive the "Golden Ticket" and return to the playing area.

When only a few players remained (usually around six), the game moved on to the second round, where she could keep or dump each contestant after asking them questions or having them perform a stunt. She chose three guys who moved on to the next round.

The three remaining players entered the "Winner's Circle," where they were asked the same question as the female player had been and they tried to match their responses to those of the female player. The first player to match four times won the game and the date. (If two players reached the four matches plateau at the same time, they were asked a question with a numerical answer and the player coming closest won.) The female player finally got to see the man she had singled out after he won the date.

In the second half of the show, the roles were reversed with the male selecting from fifty women. The game was played the same way as in the first half.

Did you know . . . future game show host Annie Wood ("Bzzz!") was a contestant coordinator on "Singled Out" in 1995?

Were you watching when . . . Adam West acted as cohost for an entire show that was themed around his classic series "Batman"? In a fun skit, West had to save both emcee Chris Hardwick and cohost Carmen Electra.

THE $64,000 CHALLENGE

premiere: April 8, 1956 *packager:* Entertainment Productions Inc. *broadcast history:* CBS primetime April 8, 1956–September 7, 1958 *hosts:* Bill "Sonny" Fox, Ralph Story *assistants:* Doris Wiss, Lisa Laughlin, Pat Donovan *announcer:* Bill Rogers *commercials:* Barbara Britton (Revlon), Jonathan Blake (Kent) *executive producers:* Steve Carlin, Harry Fleischman *producers:* Joe Cates, Ed Jurist *directors:* Joe Cates, Seymour Robbie *set designers:* Eddie Gilbert, Charles Lisanby *music director:* Norman Leyden *origination:* CBS Studio 52, New York

"The $64,000 Challenge" was the first successful television game show spin-off. Contestants on this show challenged players who won at least $8,000 on THE $64,000 QUESTION.

The same question was asked of both the challenger and the champion. If a player failed to give the correct answer, he or she was eliminated. The remaining player continued until he or she missed a question or reached the $64,000 limit. The player was guaranteed to win no less than the amount at which he or she defeated his or her opponent.

Teddy Nadler, a civil service clerk from St. Louis, became the biggest money winner in the era of the big-money quiz

Here we see Teddy Nadler (at right) on his way to winning $252,000 on "The $64,000 Challenge" hosted by Ralph Story.

shows by winning $252,000 on "The $64,000 Challenge."

Actors Edward G. Robinson and Vincent Price battled to a tie at the $32,000 level on this show on the subject of art.

Bill "Sonny" Fox was the original host when "The $64,000 Challenge" premiered. He was replaced by Ralph Story on September 2, 1956. Fox went on to host the popular kids series "Wonderama." After "The $64,000 Challenge" left the air, Ralph Story became a Los Angeles TV news personality for over three decades. He was also the off-camera narrator of the TV show "Alias Smith and Jones" during the 1972–1973 season.

THE $64,000 QUESTION

premiere: June 7, 1955 *packager:* Entertainment Productions Inc. *broadcast history:* CBS primetime June 7, 1955–June 24, 1958; CBS primetime September 14, 1958–November 2, 1958 *host:* Hal March *substitute hosts:* Ed Sullivan, Charlton Heston, Gene Kelly, Celeste Holm, Ginger Rogers, Fred MacMurray *assistants:* Lynn Dollar, Pat Donovan, Barbara Britton *announcer:* Bill Rogers *executive producer:* Steve Carlin *producers:* Joe Cates, Mert Koplin *directors:* Joe Cates, Curt Steen, Seymour Robbie *set designers:* Charles Lisanby, Eddie Gilbert *music director:* Norman Leyden *origination:* CBS Studio 52, New York

The era of the big-money quiz shows began on the evening of June 7, 1955 with the premiere of "The $64,000 Question." Contestants who were experts in a particular field played to win huge sums of money. The show became an immediate hit with viewing audiences and became the only primetime quiz show in television history to finish the season as the number-one program, in 1955–1956.

''The $64,000 Question'' was based on the radio show ''Take It or Leave It,'' which offered a grand prize of $64. On the television show, a player started answering questions worth $1 and the value kept doubling on the following questions until a grand prize of $64,000 was reached.

After a player reached the $4,000 level, he or she would be asked only one question per week. If the player answered correctly, he or she was given a week to think about risking all to try to reach the next level. A player was given the chance to quit at any time.

At the $8,000 level, the contestant was placed in an isolation booth on stage to ponder the answer. At this point, a player was given a new Cadillac as a consolation gift if he or she missed an answer.

The first contestant to appear on ''The $64,000 Question'' was Redmond O'Hanlon, a police officer from Staten Island, New York. On the subject of Shakespeare, he won $16,000.

The winning moment! Host Hal March looks on as contestant Dr. Joyce Brothers wins $64,000.

The first contestant to win $64,000 was Richard S. Mc-Cutchen, who accomplished this on September 13, 1955. His subject was cooking and the question for the $64,000 prize was to name and describe five dishes and two wines from the menu of a royal banquet given in 1939 for French president Albert Lebrun by King George VI of England. Mc-Cutchen answered that the five dishes were: consommé, quenelles, filet de truite saumonée, petits pois à la française, sauce maltaise, and corbeille. The two wines were Chateau d'Yquem and Madeira Sercial.

Dr. Joyce Brothers was the second person to reach $64,000 based on her expertise in the subject of boxing.

In June 1957, host Hal March took a six-week leave from the show to film a motion picture. Filling in as guest hosts were Ed Sullivan, Charlton Heston, Gene Kelly, Celeste Holm, Ginger Rogers, and Fred MacMurray. In the summer of 1958, ''The $64,000 Question'' was replaced by another quiz show, BID 'N BUY.

The quiz show scandals that erupted in the fall of 1958 seriously damaged the appeal and credibility of the big-money quiz shows. The audience dwindled, sponsors dropped out, and on November 2, 1958 ''The $64,000 Question'' went off the air.

Did you know . . . assistant Lynn Dollar was the weather girl for WRCA-TV, New York, in the mid-1950s?

Hal March replaced Henry Fonda in the Broadway production of *Two for the Seesaw*. March also appeared on Broadway in *Come Blow Your Horn*.

Where you watching when . . . as a gag, Jack Benny appeared on the October 8, 1957 show as a contestant? He selected the violin as his subject and was asked to give the first name of the Italian violin maker Stradivari and the name of the town where he was born. Jack answered correctly (Antonio was his first name, and he was born in Cremona) and true to his miserly image quit with his winnings of only $64.

SKEDADDLE

premiere: Fall 1988 *packager:* Jay Wolpert Productions/Sunn Classic Pictures Productions *broadcast history:* Syndicated Fall 1988 (six weeks) *host:* Ron Pearson *voice-over talent:* Bill Farmer, Michael Gough *costume characters:* Stacey Koyner, Rick Slaven, Jerry Vogel *creator:* Jay Wolpert *executive producers:* William Hanna, Joe Barbera, Jay Wolpert *director:* Randall Neece *set designers:* Anthony Sabatino, William H. Harris *music:* Walter ''Chip'' Lewis *origination:* Hollywood Center Studios, Los Angeles

Two teams of four kids competed in this six-week game show, a segment on the ''Funtastic World of Hanna-Barbera'' in the fall of 1988.

''Skedaddle'' featured a studio set resembling a sewer occupied by three dinosaurs, ''Slam,'' ''Dunk,'' and ''Seymour.'' A player called on one of the costumed characters who brought out an object and asked a question. The team had fifteen seconds to toss the object around among themselves, earning one point for each time a player caught the object (they could not pass the object back to the person who tossed it to them or in a straight line among their teammates). Before time ran out, one of the players had to run to a horn, ring it, and answer the question. If he or she answered correctly the team won points. If the answer was wrong, the teammates had to face the "Wheel of Terror." Teams took turns tossing objects and answering questions and the team with the most points after four rounds won the game.

In the bonus round, a question was asked of each kid, who selected the answer from among three possibilities. A right answer was worth one point, but a wrong answer eliminated the kid from the round. The team won an assortment of prizes if they earned four points before all of the players were eliminated.

SLIME TIME

premiere: June 11, 1988   *packager:* Hunt-Jaffe Productions/ O.K.T. Productions   *broadcast history:* Syndicated June 11, 1988–September 1988   *host:* Marty Cohen   *announcer:* Dean Goss   *creators:* Barry Jaffe, Gary Hunt   *producers:* Gary Hunt, Barry Jaffe   *director:* Al Roman   *set designers:* William Harris, Fred Duer   *music:* Joey Carbone   *origination:* Chris Craft TV Studios, Los Angeles

Two teams (each representing a school), consisting of a teacher and three of his or her students, tried to earn $1,000 by answering questions and completing stunts in this summertime game series, "Slime Time."

In round one, questions were worth $25 and the team that answered correctly chose a stunt for both teams to perform. Dollar values doubled in round two and again in the final, quick-question round. The first team to reach $1,000 won the game and the opposing team's teacher was "slimed."

SMALL TALK

premiere: September 30, 1996   *packager:* Reg Grundy Productions   *broadcast history:* Family Channel (cable) September 30, 1996–January 31, 1997   *host:* Wil Shriner   *executive producer:* Robert Crystal   *producers:* Gary Johnson, Deb Dittman   *director:* Rob Fiedler   *set designer:* James Agazzi   *music:* Marc Ellis   *origination:* Stage 1, The Production Group, Hollywood

Three adult contestants tried to predict how seven kids had responded to questions like "Do you make your bed in the morning?" and "Would you rather be the president or a movie star?"

Before the first round began, each contestant secretly locked in how they felt the majority of the seven kids had responded. During the round, each contestant selected one of the seven kids and then predicted which choice he or she had made. Each correct prediction was worth ten points, with a twenty-point bonus if they predicted correctly the responses of the majority. Point values were doubled in the second round.

In round three, questions were worth sixty points but no majority prediction was played. The player with the most points at the end of this round won the game and $500.

The day's winner played the bonus game for a chance at $1,000. The player selected kids using a random selector button and then tried to predict how they had answered one final question. They tried to make three correct predictions before making two wrong ones to win the money.

THE SMARTER SEX

premiere: December 18, 1995   *broadcast history:* Syndicated December 18, 1995–December 29, 1995   *host:* David Hirsch   *creator:* Howard Schultz   *executive producers:* Howard Schultz, Brian Frons   *supervising producer:* Michael Maddocks   *coordinating producer:* Linda Lea   *director:* Jerry Kupcinet   *set designers:* John Shaffner, Joe Stewart   *music:* William Anderson   *origination:* Hollywood Center Studios, Hollywood

"The Smarter Sex" received a brief test run that was supposed to be a warm-up to a planned launch into national syndication. The show had only a two-week run in several cities, including Atlanta, Georgia and San Diego, California, before disappearing from the screen.

The studio audience was split into sections of fifty men on one side and fifty women on the other side. From each section, three players were selected to come on stage and participate in a game of determining which sex knew more about the other.

Questions like "Have you ever been naked with a member of the opposite sex?" were asked. One player tried to predict how a member of the opposite sex would respond. If correct, they earned one point. One player from each team, male and female, tried to guess how many people in one section of the studio audience would respond in a particular way. The player coming closest to the actual number earned one point.

In the second round, statements were read about one team with the three players on the other team trying to guess which player said it, scoring one point for each correct guess. Teams alternated guessing about each other.

One player from each team played at a time in round three. A series of questions were read (e.g., "Which sex orders more deep dish pizza?"). The players answered either "men" or "women" and scored three points if correct. If they were wrong, the opposing team added one point to their score.

In the final round, each team picked a question for the other to answer, based on what they thought every man or woman should know. If they answered the question correctly, their score was doubled. If wrong, they lost all of their points. The team with the most points was declared the smarter sex and was given crowns by the other team as they admitted defeat.

SNAP JUDGMENT

premiere: April 11, 1967   *packager:* Mark Goodson–Bill Todman Productions   *broadcast history:* NBC daytime April 11, 1967–March 28, 1969   *host:* Ed McMahon   *announcer:* Johnny Olson   *executive producer:* Robert Noah   *producer:* Ira Skutch   *director:* Franklin Heller   *set designer:* Frank Skinner   *origination:* NBC Studio 8H, New York   *debut guests:* Betsy Palmer, Gene Rayburn

Two studio contestants wrote word associations for a list of words before the day's program began, and their celebrity partners tried to guess those words for cash prizes in this daytime game show that featured "Tonight Show" sidekick Ed McMahon as host.

On "Snap Judgment," the celebrity had three chances to guess the word for ten points. If he or she did not, the opposing celebrity player had a chance to steal the points with one guess. If neither celebrity guessed correctly, the first letter of the concealed word was revealed and both celebrities received a chance to buzz in with an answer.

The winning team of the day had a chance to win $500 playing the "Big Five," where the contestant had to guess the word associations of his or her celebrity partner. The contestant went to a soundproof room and the celebrity was given one word for which he or she made five word associations. The celebrity also selected one word as a bonus word. The contestant then returned to the stage and was given twenty seconds to guess the words. The contestant earned $50 for each correct answer and if the bonus word was guessed, the winnings were doubled.

The format of "Snap Judgment" was changed on December 23, 1968 to resemble that of PASSWORD.

Guests for the debut week were Betsy Palmer and Gene Rayburn. Gene Rayburn returned as a guest host on September 16, 1968 and Ed McMahon played the game.

Bob Hope made a rare appearance as game show celebrity guest on September 7, 1967 and Johnny Carson played the game on March 28, 1968.

Johnny Carson making a rare game show guest appearance on sidekick Ed McMahon's 1967 show "Snap Judgment."

Did you know . . . Ed McMahon first appeared on national television playing a clown in the series "The Big Top" in 1950? In 1957 McMahon became the announcer on TWO FOR THE MONEY and in the fall 1958 became Johnny Carson's sidekick on WHO DO YOU TRUST?

SONGS FOR SALE

premiere: July 7, 1950   *packager:* Lester Gottlieb Productions   *broadcast history:* CBS primetime July 7, 1950–September 1, 1950; CBS primetime February 3, 1951–February 17, 1951; CBS primetime June 30, 1951–June 28, 1952   *hosts:* Jan Murray, Steve Allen   *announcer:* Hal Simms   *producers:* Herb Moss, Al Span   *directors:* Frank Satenstein, Bob Bleyer   *music director:* Ray Bloch   *origination:* New York   *debut guests:* singers Joan Edwards and Johnny Johnston, music publisher Jack Robbins, Mitch Miller

On "Songs for Sale," a weekly musical show, aspiring amateur songwriters submitted their songs to be performed by professional singers. Each week six songs were performed before a judging panel of music experts and the winning song received a $100 cash prize. Every sixth week the winners of the five previous weeks returned to have an opportunity to win additional prizes and cash. The final winner also had his or her song recorded by a top artist from one of the leading record companies.

Among the singers who performed on "Songs for Sale" were Tony Bennett, Rosemary Clooney, Johnny Desmond, Richard Hayes, and Peggy Lee. The judging panel included Duke Ellington and Mitch Miller, then head of A&R (Artists and Repertoire) for Columbia Records.

Jan Murray was host from July 1950 to February 1951 and Steve Allen became host when the show returned in June 1951. "Songs for Sale" was simulcast on CBS radio and television for its first season.

Did you know . . . host Steve Allen was the original host on "The Tonight Show," which premiered on NBC on September 27, 1954. His announcer was future game show host Gene Rayburn. Steve Allen is also a prolific songwriter. His compositions include "This Could Be the Start of Something Big."

SPARRING PARTNERS

premiere: April 8, 1949   *broadcast history:* ABC primetime April 8, 1949–May 6, 1949   *host:* Walter Kiernan   *producer/director:* Sean Dillon   *origination:* New York

"Sparring Partners" was seen on Friday nights on ABC for five weeks in the spring of 1949. A team of three men competed against three women in a game of questions and answers on a set that resembled a boxing arena. The premiere broadcast had three cover girls (including Peggy Kelly, the most photogenic girl of 1949) challenging three male magazine cover models.

SPIN-OFF

premiere: June 16, 1975   *packager:* Nicholson-Muir Productions   *broadcast history:* CBS daytime June 16, 1975–

September 5, 1975   *host:* Jim Lange   *announcer:* Johnny Jacobs   *executive producers:* Nick Nicholson, E. Roger Muir, Barbara Horn   *producer:* Willie Stein   *director:* Bob Schwartz   *set designers:* Jim Ryan, Jack Stewart   *music:* Nick Nicholson   *origination:* Studio 41, CBS Television City, Los Angeles

Two couples, after each answering a question correctly, set in motion a set of spinners, each containing the numbers one through six. On "Spin-Off," each correct answer enabled a team to "roll" one spinner and build the best combination possible. Payoffs were $50 for a pair, $75 for two pairs, $100 for three of a kind, $125 for a straight, $150 for a full house, $175 for four of a kind, and $200 for five of a kind. The first team to win $250 played the "Super Spin-Off" board, where they again rolled their spinners for larger payoffs with a jackpot of $10,000 for five of a kind.

SPIN THE PICTURE

premiere: June 4, 1949   *packager:* Wilbur Stark–Jerry Layton Productions   *broadcast history:* DuMont primetime June 4, 1949–February 4, 1950   *hosts:* Kathi Norris and Carl Caruso   *assistant:* Eddie Dunn   *regulars:* Gordon Dillworth, Shaye Cogan, Bob Dunn   *announcer:* Fred Scott   *producers:* Jerry Layton, Wilbur Stark   *directors:* David Lowe, Nat B. Eisenberg   *music:* Al Logan Trio, Jerry Shad Quartet, Alan Scott Trio   *origination:* New York

On this Saturday evening hour-long show, "Spin the Picture," clues to the identity of a famous person were presented through dramatic sketches, songs, and other entertainment. After each clue was presented a call was made to a viewer at home. A correct guess earned the home viewer a prize.

For the first two weeks on the air, this show was known by the title "Cut."

SPLIT PERSONALITY

premiere: September 28, 1959   *packager:* Mark Goodson–Bill Todman Productions   *broadcast history:* NBC daytime September 28, 1959–February 5, 1960   *host:* Tom Poston   *announcer:* Johnny Olson   *producer:* Robert Rowe   *director:* Paul Alter   *set designer:* Ted Cooper   *origination:* NBC Studio 8H, New York

Two contestants attempted to identify celebrities from biographical clues split between two huge electronic game boards facing them on "Split Personality." Each player chose a clue to give to his or her opponent. Among the possible clues a player could choose from were sex, height and weight, color of hair and eyes, age, place born, number of children, current residence, occupation, and picture of spouse. The first player to correctly guess the identity won the game and the first to win two games won the match and a jackpot of prizes.

In the bonus round, the champion was shown a picture of two celebrities whose images had been combined. If both images were correctly guessed, the champion won a bonus prize.

SPLIT SECOND

premiere: March 20, 1972   *packager:* Stefan Hatos–Monty Hall Productions   *broadcast history:* ABC daytime March 20, 1972–June 27, 1975; Syndicated December 15, 1986–September 1987; Family Channel (cable) August 30, 1993–March 4, 1994; January 2, 1995–September 29, 1995 (repeats of 1986–1987 series)

1972–1975 version

host: Tom Kennedy   *announcer:* Jack Clark   *executive producers:* Stefan Hatos, Monty Hall   *producers:* Stu Billet, Bob Synes   *director:* Kip Walton   *set designer:* Richard James   *music:* Stan Worth   *origination:* Studios D and E, ABC Television Center, Los Angeles

1986–1987 version

host: Monty Hall   *announcer:* Sandy Hoyt   *model:* Sharon Sparrow   *executive producers:* Stefan Hatos, Monty Hall   *producers:* Frank Bluestein, Alan Gilbert   *director:* Henry Pasila   *set designer:* Bob Rappaport   *music:* Todd Thicke   *origination:* Toronto, Canada

Three contestants competed in this daytime question-and-answer game. The game consisted of three quick question rounds. In the first two rounds, questions were read to the players and each question had three possible answers. The players, each with a lock-out button, raced to come up with the first answer in order to leave the more difficult questions to their opponents. If all three players came up with correct answers they each received $5; if only two players came up with correct answers they received $10; and if only one was correct, the payoff was $25. In round two the values were doubled.

In the final round, the "Countdown Round," each contestant had to answer as many questions as necessary to win. The player with the highest cash amount needed to get three right to win the game, the player with the next highest cash amount needed to answer four, and the player with the lowest cash amount needed five. Players could give one, two, or three answers to the multiple choice questions. The first player to answer all questions needed won the game.

The winner of the day was given the opportunity to win one of five new cars on stage if the key he or she chose started the right car. Only one of the five cars was keyed to start. If the car did not start, the player returned to play on the next show and if he or she won again, selected from four keys. Any player who won on five straight shows automatically won a car.

"Split Second" returned as a daily syndicated show at the end of 1986. The main game remained the same and the bonus game still gave the day's champion a chance to win a new car.

The winning player tried to select those three out of the five screens that had the word "car" on it. Finding all three won the player the automobile. The other two screens displayed the name of a merchandise prize and if the player revealed that prize, he or she was given the option of leaving with the prize or returning on the next show to try for the car again.

Monty Hall emceed the syndicated "Split Second," which was taped in Canada and syndicated by Viacom. Repeats

Tom Kennedy's rapid-fire hosting abilities added to ''Split Second,'' the game of split-second decision-making.

aired as part of the Family Channel game show block from August 1993 to March 1994 and again from January to September 1995.

Did you know . . . ''Split Second'' was created by the successful team of Stefan Hatos and Monty Hall, who also created LET'S MAKE A DEAL?

''Split Second'' was the only new game show series that ABC placed on their 1972 and 1973 daytime schedules.

Actress Markie Post (formerly of ''Night Court'') was a staff researcher on ''Split Second'' in 1972. She later worked for Mark Goodson Productions on DOUBLE DARE.

In 1972 Bob Eubanks, Monty Hall, Jim Lange, and Allen Ludden all posed with the ''new kid on the block,'' Tom Kennedy. They were all hosting big hits on ABC at the time and welcomed Tom to the network.

Were you watching when . . . Monty Hall surprised Tom Kennedy with a birthday cake honoring the second season of ''Split Second''?

SPORTS CHALLENGE
premiere: January 23, 1971 *packager:* Gerry Gross Productions for CPM Programs *broadcast history:* Syndicated January 23, 1971–September 1979; CBS weekend May 20,

1973–September 9, 1973 *host:* Dick Enberg *announcers:* Johnny Gilbert, Art James *producers:* Gerry Gross, Gary Brown, Dick Enberg *directors:* Glenn Swanson, Jerry Hughes, Gary Brown *set designers:* Herman Zimmerman, Hub Braden, Anthony Sabatino *theme:* ''Get Back'' by Patrick Williams *origination:* Studio 6, KTLA Television, Los Angeles; Metromedia Studios, Hollywood

In this weekly show, ''Sports Challenge,'' two teams of sports personalities competed in answering the who, what, and where of some of the most memorable moments in sports.

The game consisted of four rounds of three questions (a team had to answer a toss-up question correctly to earn two ''free throws'') and a bonus biography round, where each team tried to guess the identity of a famous sports figure. The winning team received $1,000 to give to a youth group and the runners-up received $500.

The debut week found a New York Yankees team of Joe DiMaggio, Mickey Mantle, and Tommy Heinrich taking on a Brooklyn Dodgers team of Don Drysdale, Don Newcombe, and Duke Snider.

Did you know . . . ''Sports Challenge'' set designer Herman Zimmerman became production designer for the series ''Star Trek: The Next Generation'' in the 1980s?

Dick Enberg was a college professor teaching health science, and was also assistant baseball coach at San Fernando Valley State College (now California State University, Northridge) from 1961 to 1965? He became a sports anchor for KTLA-TV in Los Angeles in the mid-1960s and joined the play-by-play team of both the California Angels baseball team and the Los Angeles Rams football team. He was also the sports announcer in the cartoon series "Where's Huddles?" in 1970.

SPORTS ON TAP

premiere: April 5, 1994   *packager:* Sande Stewart Television *broadcast history:* ESPN (cable) April 5, 1994–September 30, 1994; ESPN January 3, 1995–March 29, 1995   *host:* Tom Green   *assistant:* Shelly Gray as the bar's waitress   *announcer:* Tony Pandolfo   *producer:* Sande Stewart   *director:* Bruce Burmester   *set designer:* Ed Flesh   *origination:* Empire Studios, Burbank

"Sports on Tap" was a daily ESPN quiz show set in a barroom with Tom Green playing bartender and host of the game that featured four contestants competing in a $50,000 sports challenge. The daily winners returned on the Friday show to compete for additional cash and a chance at the grand prize.

Each player started with $50 and, playing one at a time in the first round, selected one of two questions to answer. Correct answers were worth $50. After two questions, players could bet any part of their banks on their ability to answer the third and final question.

Round two was the "Double Play Round," where all four players competed against each other to answer questions worth $50. The player who answered correctly got a chance to earn an additional $50 on a second question and got to choose the next question to be played.

In round three, the value of the questions doubled and the round was played like the previous one.

The final round was the "Playoff Round," where the contestants lined up in the order of their finishes at the end of the third round. The two lowest-scoring players competed first and the first player to answer three questions correctly moved up the next step to play against the next highest-scoring player. The winner of that match challenged the top-scoring player of the day for the championship.

SPORTS SNAPSHOT!

premiere: August 7, 1993   *packager:* GGP   *broadcast history:* Syndicated August 7, 1993–December 1993   *host:* Jimmy Cefalo   *assistant:* Jean Fox   *announcer:* Jerry Gordon   *senior producer:* Ted Griggs   *producer:* Dave Petitto *director:* Jim Dusel   *set designer:* Greg McKee   *music:* Ed Bogas   *origination:* GGP Studios, Corte Madera

Three studio contestants competed in a sports trivia game where the sports-related prizes won by the contestants were also offered to home viewers to purchase via a special 800

Three legendary New York Yankees: (from left to right) Tommy Henrich, Joe DiMaggio, and Mickey Mantle on "Sports Challenge."

phone number. The weekly series, "Sports Snapshot," hosted by former Miami Dolphins football star Jimmy Cefalo, was seen on many stations following sports broadcasts.

Hidden behind a sixteen-panel game board (four rows of four) was a sports photo for the three players to identify. To reveal a portion of the picture, a player chose one of the sixteen categories covering the board. Each category had a sports trivia question and the first player to answer correctly got to see one-sixteenth of the photo. Each question answered correctly earned the player a sports prize (autographed baseball, sports insignia clock), which was placed in his or her locker.

The first player to correctly identify two snapshots was the day's winner who then played the "Sudden Victory" round. In the event of two players each winning one game, the player with the most prizes in his or her locker became champion.

The winning player had forty-five seconds to answer twelve rapid-fire sports trivia questions. For each correct answer, one of twelve squares was uncovered on another sports snapshot and the player won a grand prize if he or she identified the photo.

After several months on the air, the show's format was altered. The three contestants continued to select from sixteen categories on a game board. Each box represented a different category and correct answers were worth $150. Before questions in the center boxes (each worth $300) could be revealed, at least seven of the outer boxes had to be cleared. Also hidden on the board was a secret box that contained a bonus prize to be won if the player answered the question correctly.

The first player to identify the snapshot won the game and used his or her winnings to buy merchandise in the "Sports Snapshot! Showcase."

The winning player also participated in the "Sudden Victory" round for a chance to win a vacation, having thirty-five seconds to answer nine questions. For each correct answer, a piece of a picture was revealed. If the photo was correctly identified the player won the trip.

STARCADE

premiere: September 1983 *packager:* JM Productions *broadcast history:* Syndicated September 1983–September 1984 *host:* Geoff Edwards *announcer:* Kevin McMahon *executive producers:* James Caruso, Mavis Arthur *director:* James Caruso *music:* Mindseed *origination:* San Francisco

"Starcade," seen mostly on Saturday mornings, featured two teams, each composed of a father and son. The teams competed to answer a toss-up question that determined which team would pick one of five arcade games to start the day's match.

One player from each team was given fifty seconds to play the arcade game and earn as many points as possible. The team with the higher score played the "Name the Game" board, where they attempted to identify four games from their graphics for a bonus prize.

Three rounds were played and the highest-scoring team of the day won merchandise prizes and a chance to win an arcade game to take home.

Before its syndicated run, "Starcade" was seen on WTBS, Atlanta, from December 27, 1982 to August 1983 with Mark Richards as host.

STAR GAMES

premiere: September 7, 1985 *packager:* Company III Productions for Viacom *broadcast history:* Syndicated September 7, 1985–September 1986 *hosts:* Bruce Jenner, Pamela Sue Martin, Morgan Brittany *"The Commissioner":* Dick Butkus *play-by-play announcer:* Barry Tompkins *executive producer:* Carolyn Raskin *producers:* Mark Hufnail, Bill Garnet *directors:* Andy Young, David Caldwell, Carolyn Raskin *music:* Kevin Kiner *origination:* University of Santa Barbara; College of the Desert, Palm Springs

"Star Games" was a thirteen-week competition that featured three teams each composed of six cast members from a particular television series. They competed in several athletic events like kayaking, free-style swimming, and track relay-races. Points were awarded for the top three finishes in each activity.

The winning team and the runner-up team of the day moved to the second round of competition. The first-place team each week received $30,000; second place, $21,000; and third place, $12,000.

Twenty-six shows were produced (two sets of thirteen-week competitions) with Pamela Sue Martin and Bruce Jenner hosting the first thirteen. Morgan Brittany replaced Martin on the second set of shows.

The first thirteen shows were taped at the University of Santa Barbara and the second thirteen at the College of the Desert in Palm Springs.

STOP ME IF YOU'VE HEARD THIS ONE

premiere: March 4, 1948 *packager:* Cal Tinney Productions *broadcast history:* NBC primetime March 4, 1948–April 22, 1949 *hosts:* Roger Bower, Leon Janney *announcer:* Radcliff Hall *producers:* Irving Mansfield, Barry Wood, Larry Schwab *directors:* Ira Skutch, Larry Schwab *origination:* NBC Studio 8G, New York *debut guests:* Lew Lehr, Morey Amsterdam, Cal Tinney

The television version of "Stop Me If You've Heard This One" was based on the radio show of the same name that was first heard on NBC radio on October 7, 1939 with Milton Berle as host. It also had a one-year run on the Mutual Radio network in 1947 with Morey Amsterdam as the star.

The television version featured Roger Bower as host, who was replaced by Leon Janney on November 11, 1948, and a panel that included Cal Tinney, Morey Amsterdam, Benny Rubin, and Fox Movietone news commentator Lew Lehr.

Viewers sent in jokes that were read to a panel of three comedians. When one of the panelists recognized the joke he or she would stop the joke and continue it to its conclusion. If the comedian did not give the correct ending, the home viewer won a gift.

STOP THE MUSIC

premiere: May 5, 1949   *packager:* Louis Cowan Productions/Mark Goodson Productions   *broadcast history:* ABC primetime May 5, 1949–April 24, 1952; ABC primetime September 7, 1954–May 31, 1955; ABC primetime September 15, 1955–June 14, 1956
1949–1952 version
host: Bert Parks   *announcers:* Don Hancock, Dennis James, Kenny Williams, Sidney Smith, Paul Luther, Jack Haskell   *producers:* Mark Goodson, Alfred Hollander, Don Appell, Sherman Marks, Charles Henderson   *directors:* Robert Doyle, Ralph Warren, Marshall Diskin, Eddie Nugent   *choreography:* Tony Charmoli   *set designers:* William Lilling, Charles Hawkins, Jim McNaughton, Robert Bright   *music director:* Harry Salter   *origination:* Ritz Theater, New York
1954–1956 version
host: Bert Parks   *announcers:* Kenny Williams, Jimmy Blaine   *producer:* Joe Cates   *directors:* Joe Cates, Matt Harlib   *set designer:* Norman Rock   *music director:* Harry Salter   *featured singers:* Jaye P. Morgan, Felicia Sanders   *origination:* Ritz Theater, New York

"Stop the Music" was the first popular music quiz show on television. It was first heard on radio in March 1948 with Bert Parks as host, made a successful transition to television in May 1949, and was a regular fixture for the next seven years.

A song was performed on the show, frequently using elaborate production numbers, and at some point during the song announcer Kenny Williams would yell "Stop the Music!" A telephone call was then placed to a home viewer who would be asked to identify the song. If the viewer was correct he or she received a merchandise prize and a chance at the "Mystery Melody." If wrong, the player received a consolation prize from the sponsor. Members of the studio audience were then given a chance to identify the song.

The Mystery Melody was a short clip from a song and the viewer who identified it received merchandise prizes.

Songs were performed on the show by a regular cast that included Jimmy Blaine, Betty Ann Grove, Jaye P. Morgan, Marion Morgan, Felicia Sanders, and host Bert Parks.

The show was originally sponsored by Old Gold cigarettes with veteran TV personality Dennis James handling the pitches and a dancing cigarette pack and matchbook providing the entertainment.

"Stop the Music" was broadcast as a sixty-minute live show from the Ritz Theater in New York from 1949 to 1952. When the show returned in the fall of 1954 it was seen as a half-hour series.

Comedian Phil Silvers served as guest host in July 1951 while Bert Parks took a vacation.

Did you know . . .   from 1955 to 1979 Bert Parks was the emcee of "The Miss America Pageant" and helped make the song "There She Is, Miss America" famous?

STORM THE CASTLE

premiere: June 16, 1993   *packager:* Vin Di Bona Productions   *broadcast history:* CBS primetime special June 16, 1993   *hosts:* Michael Burger and Nely Galan   *announcer:* Ernie Anderson   *executive producers:* Vin Di Bona, Howard G. Malley, Eytan Keller   *producers:* Rob Katz, Terry Moore, Craig Golin   *director:* Steven Santos   *set design:* Bill Bohnert   *music:* Dan Slider   *origination:* Universal Studios, Hollywood

This one-hour primetime special, based on the Japanese show "Takeshi's Castle," featured five family members competing in athletic stunts for a shot at $15,000.

The competition began with thirty families searching for tennis balls in a giant mud pit. The first ten teams to find fourteen balls entered the game competition.

The teams competed in nine challenges, each worth a different number of points and following the events the top-two teams went on to "Storm the Castle."

Among the challenges were "Devil's Domain," a honeycomb maze with thirty doors that a player tried to maneuver through while avoiding some of the monsters from Universal Studios. One door led to a safe exit, while the others opened into a pool of water. Other events included "Human Bowling," where a player from each family picked a card to determine his or her position on a bowling lane. Any player left standing after a giant bowling ball was rolled at him or her earned points. Another event was "Dunk Your Parents," where three levers pushed earned points for the team and the fourth lever dropped their parents into the water.

To win the jackpot, the players from the two top-scoring teams were each put into motorized bumper boats and given plastic swords with the goal of trying to be the first team to reach and pop twelve balloons to win the game and $15,000.

STORYBOOK SQUARES

premiere: January 4, 1969   *packager:* Merrill Heatter–Bob Quigley Productions   *broadcast history:* NBC Saturday morning January 4, 1969–August 30, 1969   *host:* Peter Marshall   *announcer:* ("Guardian of the Gate") Kenny Williams   *executive producers:* Merrill Heatter, Bob Quigley   *producer:* Les Roberts   *director:* Jerome Shaw   *set designer:* Ed Flesh   *origination:* NBC Studios, Burbank

"Storybook Squares" was a 1969 Saturday morning series featuring two children playing a junior edition of NBC's popular daytime show, THE HOLLYWOOD SQUARES. The nine celebrities featured on the show were dressed in storybook or TV-character costumes. Among the celebrities who appeared were Marty Allen as Tarzan, Wally Cox as Paul Revere, Soupy Sales as Henry the VIII, Arte Johnson as the soldier from "Laugh-In," Abby Dalton as Little Miss Muffet, Rip Taylor as Custer, Charley Weaver as "Charley Weaver," Barbara Eden as Jeannie, and William Shatner as Captain Kirk.

The kids competed in a game of tic-tac-toe by choosing a square and then deciding if the star had answered the question correctly or not. If a kid's judgement was right, his or her mark was placed in the square; otherwise, the opponent won the box. The first player to put marks in three boxes in a row, either across, up-and-down, or diagonally, won the game and a prize such as a sailboat, color TV, or skis and skiing lessons.

Warren Hull, host of "Strike It Rich." Can you spot that "Heart Line" phone in the background?

Once a show, the "Secret Square" game was played and if the contestant picked a predetermined celebrity and guessed correctly, he or she won an additional prize. The two kids played for the entire show.

STRAIGHT TO THE HEART

premiere: March 20, 1989   *packager:* Jim Rich and Associates/MGM-UA Television   *broadcast history:* Syndicated March 20, 1989–September 8, 1989   *host:* Michael Burger *hostess/announcer:* Barbara Lee Alexander   *executive producer:* Jim Rich   *producer :* Wayne Hackett   *director:* Barry Glazer   *set designers:* Anthony Sabatino, William Harris *music:* Steven Tavani   *origination:* TAV Celebrity Theater, Hollywood

Three men and three women tried to find members of the opposite sex who they were most compatible with in this daily syndicated game show.

The men were asked a question, such as "What is your best romantic move on a date?" Each responded and all three

answers were then revealed to the women, each of whom chose the reply she most preferred. A man earned $50 for each woman who picked his answer. A second question was asked of the women and the men then made their choices.

The two players (one man, one woman) who chose each other most often during the show won the game and played a bonus round to win a possible trip. The remaining players were given a night on the town.

STRIKE IT RICH

premiere: May 7, 1951   *packager:* Walt Framer Productions *broadcast history:* CBS daytime May 7, 1951–January 3, 1958; CBS primetime July 4, 1951–January 12, 1955   *host:* Warren Hull   *announcers:* Ralph Paul, Ron Rawson, John Cannon, Jack Carson, Mort Lawrence   *producer:* Walt Framer   *directors:* Matt Harlib, Paul Alter   *set designers:* Randolph Gunter, Thomas Durkin   *music:* Burt Buhrman *origination:* New York

"Strike It Rich" was known as "The Quiz Show with a Heart" and the contestants who appeared on the show were people in need of money or down on their luck. A player was given $30 and bet part of his or her bank on the ability to answer four general knowledge questions. If unable to answer the questions correctly, the contestant could turn to the "heart line" where viewers would call in and donate money or merchandise.

"Strike It Rich" made its debut on CBS radio on June 29, 1947 with Todd Russell as host. It came to television as a daytime show on May 7, 1951 and two months later a nighttime version was added. Warren Hull, who had played Spiderman and Mandrake the Magician in many "B" film serials of the 1930s was the TV host. Colgate-Palmolive was the longtime TV sponsor.

Among the many people who filled in as guest hosts were Don Ameche, Robert Alda, Monty Hall, Randy Merriman, Todd Russell, and Jack Sterling.

STRIKE IT RICH

premiere: September 15, 1986   *packager:* Kline and Friends/Blair Entertainment   *broadcast history:* Syndicated September 15, 1986–September 1987   *host:* Joe Garagiola *assistant:* Theresa Ring   *announcer:* Bob Hilton   *executive producer/director:* Richard Kline   *producer:* Gary Cox   *set designer:* Rene Lagler   *music:* Hal Hidey   *origination:* Los Angeles

The second game show to use the title "Strike It Rich" appeared as a daily syndicated series in the fall of 1986. Two teams of two (husband and wife or boyfriend and girlfriend) competed in a question-and-answer game.

Each team played their own row of seven screens. Teams played one at a time. A category was revealed (examples: nicknames or folk singers) along with five answers. The playing team chose a "contract" of one, two, or three questions. The number of questions to be answered determined the number of screens to be revealed. Each screen revealed either a prize or "the bandit" who robbed them of all their prizes as well as control of the game board. A wrong answer would also cause a team to lose control to their opponents.

After correctly answering a question, a team could bank their gifts or risk them by going on. The first team to complete their row (seven prize screens) and then one final question won the game.

In the bonus round, each team member played one row of screens and they chose either the top or bottom screen at each stop. The goal was to find five dollar signs before encountering three bandits on the screens. The payoffs were $100 for each dollar sign, $5,000 for five dollar signs, and a $20,000 car for six dollar signs.

STUDS

premiere: March 11, 1991 packager: FTS Productions broadcast history: Syndicated March 11, 1991–September 3, 1993 host: Mark DeCarlo producers: Howard Schultz, Michael Canter, Lois Curren, Jeff Mirkin, George Monas director: Glenn Weiss origination: Studio 6, Fox Television Center, Los Angeles

Two male players attempted to match responses with three women they had both dated, in this syndicated relationship show. "Studs" first appeared on Los Angeles TV station KTTV on March 11, 1991 and was gradually expanded to other stations after its initial success.

In the first part of the show, the women each gave responses to questions like "What do you remember most about your date?" Each male player, in turn, tried to match the statements given to the woman they felt said it. If correct, he was given a "heart."

The second part of the show involved the three women determining which of the two male players best fit a question like "Who is most likely to make love on the beach?" The male players tried to guess whether the question was about them or their opponent. The players received "hearts" for correct guesses.

The final round determined who received an expense-paid date to the location of their choice. Each of the male players selected the woman he would like to go out with again. If she had also picked him and he was the player with the most hearts, they won the date.

STUMP THE STARS

premiere: September 17, 1962 packager: Mike Stokey Productions broadcast history: CBS primetime September 17, 1962–September 16, 1963; Syndicated February 24, 1964–September 2, 1964; Syndicated September 8, 1969–September 25, 1970

1962–1963 version

hosts: Pat Harrington Jr., Mike Stokey announcer: Bill Baldwin producers: Mike Stokey, John Hueners director: Bill Bennington origination: CBS Television City, Los Angeles debut guests: Sebastian Cabot, Beverly Garland, Ross Martin, Jan Clayton, Diana Dors, Mickey Manners, Jayne Mansfield, Jerry Lewis

1964 version

host: Mike Stokey producers: Mike Stokey, Joe Keane director: Paul Fuentes origination: Los Angeles debut guests: Tab Hunter, Mamie VanDoren, Sebastian Cabot, Ross Martin, Richard Long, Stubby Kaye, Connie Stevens, Joyce Jameson

1969–1970 version

host: Mike Stokey announcer: Bob Gilles producer: Burt Wenland director: David Dunn origination: KTLA Studio 6; KTTV Studios, Los Angeles debut guests: Carol Burnett, Harvey Korman, Vicki Lawrence, Roger C. Carmel, Deanna Lund, Dick Patterson

PANTOMIME QUIZ returned to television in 1962 with a new title, "Stump the Stars," and a new host, Pat Harrington Jr. Harrington hosted for thirteen weeks before Mike Stokey returned. Stokey emceed the 1964 and 1969–1970 versions as well.

Two teams of celebrities competed in a game of charades. One member of a team was given a charade and tried to get his or her teammates to identify it within two minutes. The other team then played a charade and the team using the least time overall during the show was the winner.

Charades fell into categories like "Gag Definitions," "Punch Lines," "Quotation Parodies, and "Rhymed Definitions." Members of the viewing audience frequently sent in charades for the panel to perform.

Among the regulars on the 1962 CBS version were Sebastian Cabot, Hans Conreid, Diana Dors, Beverly Garland, Ruta Lee, and Ross Martin. In 1969, the regulars were Roger C. Carmel, Deanna Lund, and Dick Patterson.

"Stump the Stars" took on the new title CELEBRITY CHARADES for another appearance on television in 1979.

STUMPERS

premiere: October 4, 1976 packager: Lin Bolen Productions broadcast history: NBC daytime October 4, 1976–December 31, 1976 host: Allen Ludden announcers: Bill Armstrong, Charlie O'Donnell creators: Bill Barr, Lin Bolen executive producer: Lin Bolen producer: Walt Case directors: Marty Pasetta, Jeff Goldstein set designer: Ed Flesh music: Alan Thicke origination: NBC Studio 3, Burbank debut guests: Dick Gautier, Robert Reed

Two teams consisting of two players and a guest celebrity competed on "Stumpers," this game show. A team picked out one clue (from three possibilities) that they believed was least likely to give away the identity of a "Stumper" phrase, for example: The phrase is "Gomer Pyle" and the clues are *bumpkin, marine, Nabors.*

The other team attempted to guess the answer for fifteen points after one clue, ten points after two clues, and five points after three clues. If the team failed to correctly guess the stumper, the opposing team scored. A second round was played for double point values and the team with the most points won and played the super stumper, where one teammate attempted to guess ten stumpers in sixty seconds at $100 each or $10,000 for all ten. His or her partner gave clues from three possibilities.

SUPER DECADES

premiere: March 17, 1997 packager: Game Show Network broadcast history: Game Show Network (cable) March 17, 1997–October 2, 1998 host: Marianne Curan substitute hosts: Dave Nemeth, Nancy Sullivan, Peter Tomarken announcers: Larry Anderson, Gene Wood, Gary Meeker,

Marianne Curan on the set of "Super Decades" on Game Show Network, the only network devoted twenty-four hours a day to game shows.

Dave Nemeth, Ed MacKay   *executive producer:* Ellie Bendes *supervising producer:* Michael Gilman   *producers:* Susan B. Flanagan, Joel Klein   *interactive game producer:* Maxine Nunes   *director:* Marc Cohen   *virtual set designer:* Jim Sweeney   *music:* Jeff Levin   *origination:* Game Show Network studios, Culver City

"Super Decades" is one of the live interactive game shows featured on Game Show Network, a twenty-four-hour basic cable network that broadcasts classic game shows as well as new first-run productions. Viewers at home are featured as contestants, using the key pads of their touch-tone telephones to participate in the show. "Super Decades" was originally seen as a interstitial segment called "Decades" on the series "Prime Games" on Game Show Network from December 1994 to February 1997.

Two players compete in each game, answering questions based on historical knowledge. Each player has thirty seconds to answer as many questions as he or she can. Three answers are displayed on screen and the player chooses an answer and punches in the corresponding number. The player with the most correct answers moves on to the "Dueling Decades" round, where he or she plays the winner of a second match.

In Dueling Decades, the two players are shown five categories, and each chooses one by pressing the zero button on the telephone to make a random selection. Each player then has thirty seconds to answer questions in the category chosen and the player with the most correct answers becomes the day's winner.

In the event of a tie during any of the rounds, players are asked a question that requires a numerical answer. The player whose guess is closest to the correct answer is the winner.

In the "Final Decades" bonus round, the daily winner played for a jackpot of prizes by selecting one of three possible categories and then trying to correctly answer six questions in a forty-five-second time limit.

SUPER GHOST

premiere: July 27, 1952   *packager:* Louis Cowan Productions   *broadcast history:* NBC primetime July 27, 1952–September 21, 1952; NBC primetime July 19, 1953–September 6, 1953   *host:* Dr. Bergen Evans   *announcers:* Harvey Goldstein, Stewart Greymount   *producers:* Jay Sheridan, John Lewellen, Don Meier   *director:* Paul Robinson   *origination:* Studebaker Theater, Chicago   *debut guests:* Robert Pollack, Sheryl Stern, Gail Compton, Hope Ryder

"Super Ghost" was a summer game show, broadcast from Chicago, that appeared for two seasons on the NBC network. Hosted by Dr. Bergen Evans, a professor of English who would later become the question authority on THE $64,000 QUESTION, "Super Ghost" was based on the parlor games Hangman and Ghosts.

The object of the game was for a celebrity panel to spell and identify a word without the last letter. The panelist who guessed the letter that completed the word earned one-third of a ghost and was eliminated from the game after completing three words. Home viewers received $50 for submitting a word that was used on the show and additional money if the word was correctly guessed by the panel.

Among the regular panelists were model Hope Ryder, columnist Gail Compton, housewife Sheryl Stern, and drama critic of the *Chicago Sun-Times*, Robert Pollack.

SUPER JEOPARDY!

premiere: June 16, 1990   *packager:* Merv Griffin Productions   *broadcast history:* ABC primetime June 16, 1990–September 8, 1990   *host:* Alex Trebek   *announcer:* Johnny Gilbert   *producer:* George Vosburgh   *director:* Dick Schneider   *set designer:* Bob Rang   *origination :* Studio 1, Hollywood TV Center, Los Angeles

JEOPARDY!, under the title "Super Jeopardy!," made its first appearance as a primetime network show with this thirteen-week summertime series that appeared in 1990. Thirty-six past winners, thirty-five from the first six seasons of the syndicated "Jeopardy!" and one from the original 1960s series, were invited to participate in this elimination tournament for a grand prize of $250,000.

The format of the game followed the original program with its "Jeopardy!", "Double Jeopardy!", and "Final Jeopardy!" rounds.

Four contestants competed each week in the quarter final matches with the day's winner moving to the next round. Contestants played for points instead of cash, with the value in the first round ranging from two hundred to one thousand and from five hundred to twenty-five hundred in the "Double Jeopardy!" round.

The three players who competed in the championship match were Dave Traini, who finished third and received $25,000; Bob Verini, who finished second and collected $50,000; and Bruce Seymour, who won the tournament and the $250,000 first prize.

SUPER PASSWORD

premiere: September 24, 1984   *packager:* Mark Goodson Productions   *broadcast history:* NBC daytime September 24, 1984–March 24, 1989   *host:* Bert Convy   *announcers:* Rich

Celebrity guest Pat Sajak joins in on the fun with "Super Password" host Bert Convy.

Jeffries, Gene Wood **executive producers:** Chester Feldman, Howard Felsher, Robert Sherman **producers:** Diane Janaver, Joe Neustein **director:** George Choderker **set designer:** Jack Hart **music:** Score Productions **origination:** NBC Studio 3, Burbank **debut guests:** Pat Sajak, Gloria Loring

In 1984, NBC updated PASSWORD PLUS by giving it a new title, "Super Password," and a new host, Bert Convy, who had previously emceed TATTLETALES.

Two teams, each composed of a celebrity guest and a studio contestant, competed. One member of each team received the "password" and in turn tried to get his or her partner to say the word by using a one-word clue. The player who correctly guessed the word was then given a chance to guess the mystery word or subject, of which each of the five passwords provided clues. The player that solved the puzzle earned $100 for his or her team in the first game, $200 in the second game, and so on. The first team to accumulate $500 won.

The winning team played the "Super Password" round, where one player tried to convey ten words to his or her partner using one-word clues in sixty seconds for $100 a word or $5,000 for all ten.

Did you know . . . Bert Convy was part of the vocal group "The Cheers" that had a top-ten hit in 1955 with "Black Denim Trousers"?

SUPER PAY CARDS!

premiere: September 14, 1981 *packager:* Nicholson-Muir Productions/Champlain Productions *broadcast history:* Syndicated September 14, 1981–April 23, 1982 *host:* Art James *hostess:* Mary Lou Basaraba *executive producers:* Nick Nicholson, Roger E. Muir *producer/director:* Lou Albert *set designer:* Andy Wilson *origination:* CFCF-TV, Montreal, Canada

"Super Pay Cards!" was a one-season revival of the late sixties game show PAY CARDS! Two contestants competed in a card game to build a better hand from a deck of sixteen cards. The payoffs were $20 for a pair, $50 for three of a kind, $100 for a full house, $200 for four of a kind, $300 for five of a kind, and $50 for the player with the highest hand in each round.

The first round was a "Five Card Draw," where four of the sixteen cards were revealed to begin the game. Each player, in turn, called three numbers out and whoever got a pair kept the cards and tried to complete the hand for the highest cash payoff.

The second round was "Four of a Kind," where the deck consisted of four sets of four cards. The third round was a "Wild Card Hand," where wild cards made five of a kind possible.

The top money winner of the day played a bonus round for a possible $5,000. Shown four cards for four seconds, he or she had to correctly remember where one of the cards was located for $50 and, if successful, then studied eight cards for eight seconds to find one card for a possible $500 and finally, sixteen cards for sixteen seconds for $5,000.

SUPERMARKET SWEEP

premiere: December 20, 1965 *packager:* Talent Associates (1965–1967); Al Howard Productions (1990– *broadcast history:* ABC daytime December 20, 1965–July 14, 1967; Lifetime (cable) February 5, 1990–August 14, 1998
1965–1967 version
host: Bill Malone *announcers:* Wally King, Richard Hayes *creator:* Al Howard *producer:* Jerome Schnur *directors:* Peter Molnar, Lloyd Gross *music:* Dave Brubeck, Score Productions *animation:* John Hubley and Storeyboard Inc. *origination:* various locations on the east coast
1990–1998 version
host: David Ruprecht *announcer:* Johnny Gilbert *executive producer:* Al Howard *producer:* Joel Stein *director:* Chris Darley *set designer:* Ed Flesh *origination:* Studio 9, KTLA Television, Los Angeles

"Supermarket Sweep" was a daily game show that gave contestants the chance to run wild through their local supermarkets, gathering up as much as they could in the allotted time.

Three husband-and-wife teams competed in each game. Each team began with a base time of one minute and thirty seconds and tried to earn additional time by playing a pricing game.

The wife was given the chance to earn an additional fifteen seconds by giving the closest guess on the retail price of a food item. Four items were played in the pricing game and

David Ruprecht places his "buns" in a shopping cart to promote his show "Supermarket Sweep."

at the conclusion of this round, the husband used the time won by his wife to run through the market.

Each man raced around the store with a shopping cart gathering a maximum of five of any one item. Bonus items, worth additional cash, were scattered throughout the store. The team with the highest total won the game and returned to face two new challengers.

"Supermarket Sweep" was taped at various food stores on the East Coast. On April 24, 1967 the show began filming exclusively in Miami, Florida. In mid-July, "Supermarket Sweep" evolved into THE HONEYMOON RACE.

"Supermarket Sweep" returned to television after a twenty-three year absence as a first-run cable game show for Lifetime Television. Three teams of two players competed in pricing games to try to build time for a race around the supermarket, which was built in a TV studio in Los Angeles.

Like the original version, teams began with a base time of one minute and thirty seconds and tried to earn additional time by playing different types of pricing games like "higher or lower price?", "guess the product being described," and "which costs more?" Correct guesses added ten seconds to a teams time.

All three teams competed in the sweep. One member of each team raced around the store, gathering up food and bonus items. The team with the highest cash total won the game and played a bonus round for a possible $5,000.

After the winning team was read a clue directing them to look for a specific product in the market, they had one minute to find that item, which contained a clue to the identity of a second item. The second item also contained a clue for a third item and if all three were found they won $5,000. If not, they received $200 for each item they found.

SWAPS

premiere: December 11, 1995 *packager:* Tribune Entertainment *broadcast history:* Syndicated December 11, 1995–February 2, 1996 *host:* Scott St. John *creator:* Scott St. John *executive producers:* Kathy Cotter, Scott St. John *producer:* Dean Young *line producer:* George NeJame *director:* Bob K. Travis *theme:* Craig Marijanian *origination:* The Production Group studios, Hollywood

Three couples who had broken up were the contestants on this short-lived game show. They participated in several rounds of matching answers as each player tried to add to their "date banks." At the end of the show they had to decide if they wanted to get back together with their ex or try a date with one of the other players.

In the first round, the men tried to identify answers given by their former girlfriends prior to the taping of the show. They were read a question with two possible answers to choose from. If their choice matched, they added $100 to their bank.

Round two featured statements made by the women. If the men thought their ex-girlfriend had made the statement, they signaled in by hitting her with a soft, oversized hammer. The guys added $100 to their total if they were correct, but in this round they lost $100 if they were wrong.

The women got their chance to build up their date banks in round three. Here they responded to statements made by their ex-boyfriends. Each woman stood in front of either a "true" or "false" window to answer the questions. Correct answers were worth $100. Then in round four, played the same way as round two, the ladies got to use the "hammers" on the guys.

In round five, one couple played at a time. With a forty-five-second time limit, both players could add to their totals by predicting if statements made by their mates about their attributes were either "cool" or "not cool." Correct guesses were worth $100 and players sat in a revolving set of chairs so that after each three questions the positions were reversed and both could play.

In the final round, each player decided who he or she wanted to date. The guys were asked on camera, and the women positioned themselves behind the door of the guy they chose. If the man picked a woman and she was behind his door, their cash total was combined, and the couple with the most money kept their cash and went out on a date.

SWEETHEARTS

premiere: September 12, 1988 *packager:* Richard Reid Productions/Createl Ltd/Multimedia *broadcast history:* Syndicated September 12, 1988–September 8, 1989 *hosts:*

Charles Nelson Reilly, Richard Kline *announcer:* Jim McKrell *executive producers:* Richard Reid, David Moore, Terry Mardell *producer:* Mary Oberembt *director:* Dennis Rosenblat *set designers:* Anthony Sabatino, William Harris *origination:* Hollywood Center Studios, Los Angeles *debut guests:* Betty White, Sally Struthers, Roger Mosley

This daily comedy game show, "Sweethearts," featured a celebrity panel of three trying to determine, by asking questions, which of three couples was telling the true story of how they met. Contestants won $500 for each celebrity fooled and if the real couple stumped all three celebrities they won a "second honeymoon."

Longtime game show panelist Charles Nelson Reilly made his debut as host of this show. Actor Richard Kline filled in as guest host in December 1988.

Did you know . . . Charles Nelson Reilly received a Tony Award in 1962 for his performance in the Broadway show *How To Succeed in Business Without Really Trying*? He also was Gene Rayburn's understudy while Gene was on Broadway in *Come Blow Your Horn*. Years later they would team up together for THE MATCH GAME.

In 1997 Charles Nelson Reilly portrayed Dr. Jose Chung on the hit series, "The X-Files."

TAG THE GAG

premiere: August 13, 1951   *packager:* Wilbur Stark Productions   *broadcast history:* NBC primetime August 13, 1951–August 20, 1951   *host:* Hal Block   *announcer:* Bob Warren   *producer:* Ray Buffim   *director:* Jac Hein   *origination:* NBC Studio 3B, New York   *debut guests:* Peter Donald, Jackie Miles, Morey Amsterdam, Amanda Sullivan

"Tag the Gag" ran only two weeks. It featured a panel of comedians who tried to guess the punch lines to jokes that were acted out by a group of performers.

The panel on the first show featured Morey Amsterdam, Peter Donald, Jackie Miles, and Amanda Sullivan while the second show included Morey Amsterdam, Jean Carrol, Herkie Stiles, and Harvey Stone.

TAKE A CHANCE

premiere: October 1, 1950   *packager:* Premium Productions   *broadcast history:* NBC primetime October 1, 1950–December 24, 1950   *host:* Don Ameche   *assistant:* Elise Gammon   *announcer:* Bob Shepard   *producers:* Richard Lewis, Peter Arnell   *director:* Grey Lockwood   *music director:* Arlo   *origination:* NBC Studio 6B, New York

Film star Don Ameche emceed "Take a Chance," the Sunday night quiz show that featured contestants selected from the studio audience. A player was given an initial sum of money and to win that money had to answer a question correctly. The player could then risk that money and try to answer another question for more cash or prizes. If the contestant could answer four questions correctly, he or she was given a chance to win a jackpot with the next question. If the player missed a question, the last prize won was forfeited.

TAKE A GOOD LOOK

premiere: October 22, 1959   *packager:* Irving Mansfield–Peter Arnell Productions   *broadcast history:* ABC primetime October 22, 1959–July 21, 1960; ABC primetime October 27, 1960–March 16, 1961   *host:* Ernie Kovacs   *announcer:* Johnny Jacobs   *executive producers:* Irving Mansfield, Peter Arnell   *producers:* Joe Landis, Maury Cohen, Milt Hoffman   *directors:* Barry Shear, Joe Behar   *set designer:* Albert Wein   *origination:* Studio E, ABC Television Center, Los Angeles   *debut guests:* Zsa Zsa Gabor, Cesar Romero, Hans Conreid

Comedian Ernie Kovacs hosted "Take a Good Look," a game show that originally had three contestants competing to identify prominent news figures from film clips and sound recordings. Later the format was changed and a celebrity panel watched sketches while looking for clues and then asking questions as to why a guest was in the news.

Host Ernie Kovacs frequently appeared in the sketches using his various characters. Guests received $50 each time they stumped the panel. Guests who stumped the panel three times won $200.

Among the regular panelists who appeared on "Take a Good Look" were Ernie's wife, Edie Adams, Ben Alexander, Hans Conreid, Carl Reiner, and Cesar Romero.

TAKE A GUESS

premiere: June 11, 1953   *packager:* Peter Arnell Productions   *broadcast history:* CBS primetime June 11, 1953–September 10, 1953   *host:* John K. M. McCaffery   *creator/producer:* Peter Arnell   *director:* Rai Purdy   *origination:* New York   *debut guests:* Margaret Lindsay, Dorothy Hart, Ernie Kovacs, John Crawford

This Thursday night summertime quiz show featured contestants who, aided by a celebrity panel, tried to identify a mystery object. On "Take a Guess," a player started with a bankroll of $150 and lost $5 for each question asked by the panel that resulted in a "yes" answer. The player was given four chances to "Take a Guess" at the identity of the object and won whatever was left of the bank when he or she guessed correctly.

At the end of the show, the three contestants of the day were asked to identify a quotation using the items identified during the program. On one show the items were earmuffs, trash, and a rabbit. The earmuffs were the clue for winter, the trash for can, and the rabbit for spring. The day's quotation was "If winter comes, can spring be far behind?"

During the show's three-month run, Hans Conreid and Robin Chandler were also featured on the panel.

Did you know . . .   John K. M. McCaffery was the 11 P.M. news anchor for WNBC-TV, New York, from 1952 to 1963? He was also formerly a fiction editor for *American Magazine*.

TAKE MY WORD FOR IT

premiere: September 13, 1982 *packager:* Omni Productions/Golden Gate Productions for Worldvision *broadcast history:* Syndicated September 13, 1982–September 1983 *host:* Jim Lange *announcer:* Scott Beach *executive producer:* David Sacks *producers:* Charles and Judith Patterson *director:* Robert Zagone *origination:* KQED Studio A, San Francisco

This syndicated game show, "Take My Word for It," was an updated version of the 1960s program OH MY WORD, in which two contestants tried to decide which of four celebrities was giving an accurate definition for an obscure word.

The game was divided into three rounds with the first two worth one point for correct guesses and the final round worth two points for correct guesses. The player with the most points won the game. In the event of a tie, another word was revealed and a definition given. Each player decided if the definition given was true or false and the first to correctly guess won the game.

In the bonus round, "Turnabout," the player defined the word in such a way as to fool the panelists. The number of celebrities fooled into guessing incorrectly determined the value of the prize won.

TAKE TWO

premiere: May 5, 1963 *packager:* Ray-Eye Productions *broadcast history:* ABC Sunday afternoons May 5, 1963–August 11, 1963 *host:* Don McNeill *announcer:* Fred Kasper *creators:* Fred Olsen, Jack Harris *executive producer:* Fred Olsen *producer:* Jim McLaughlin *director:* Dale Julian *origination:* Evanston *debut guests:* Julie Newmar, Joel Grey, Julie Wilson, Mike McAloney

Four celebrity guests competed on teams of two in this Sunday afternoon show hosted by longtime ABC radio personality Don McNeill. On "Take Two," four pictures were flashed on a screen (examples: Marilyn Monroe, Jayne Mansfield, Amy Vanderbilt, a cat). The first team to ring in and identify the related items (Jayne and Marilyn were actresses) won the round and scored points. The highest-scoring team won prizes for members of the studio audience.

After a few weeks on the air, the format was altered to feature only two celebrity guests each week who were now teamed up with a studio contestant.

Among the celebrities who played, in addition to the premiere guests, were Phyllis Diller, Bob Hope, Hedda Hopper, and Jerry Lester.

Emcee Don McNeil was host of the long-running series "The Breakfast Club" that was heard on the ABC radio network from 1933 to 1969. The June 23 broadcast of "Take Two" featured a thirtieth anniversary salute to "The Breakfast Club."

TALKABOUT

premiere: September 18, 1989 *packager:* Comedia Productions *broadcast history:* Syndicated September 18, 1989–March 16, 1990; USA (cable) June 28, 1993–December 31, 1993 (repeats of 1989 series) *host:* Wayne Cox *announcer:* Dean Hill *creator:* Mark Maxwell-Smith *execu-*tive *producers:* Pat Ferns, Don Taffner *producers:* Mark Maxwell-Smith, Steven Glassman, Chris Paton *director:* Michael Watt *set designer:* Glen Patterson *music:* Bob Buckley *origination:* Vancouver, Canada

On "Talkabout," two teams, each with two players, competed in a game of guessing words and subjects. One team was given a choice of two subjects to talk about. Each member of that team was then given twenty seconds to guess the ten preselected clue words, earning a point for each word spoken. Their opposing team was given the unspoken clue words and could steal the points by correctly guessing the related subjects. Teams reversed positions in each additional round and the first team to reach fifteen points won the game. If a team identified all ten words in a round they won a bonus $500.

The winning team tried to earn up to $2,000 in the bonus game. One player went into a soundproof booth while his or her partner had twenty seconds to guess clue words in a given subject and earned $100 and one second for each word guessed. If the partner identified one word (as yet not spoken) on the list, in the allotted time, the team's winnings were doubled.

TATTLETALES

premiere: February 18, 1974 *packager:* Mark Goodson–Bill Todman Productions *broadcast history:* CBS daytime February 18, 1974–March 31, 1978; Syndicated September 12, 1977–September 1978; CBS daytime January 18, 1982–June 1, 1984 *host:* Bert Convy *guest hosts:* Bob Barker, Jack Narz, Gene Rayburn *announcers:* Jack Clark, Gene Wood, John Harlan, Johnny Olson *executive producer:* Ira Skutch *producer/director:* Paul Alter *set designer:* James Agazzi *music:* Score Productions, Edd Kalehoff *origination:* Studio 31, CBS Television City, Los Angeles *debut guests:* Jerry Stiller and Anne Meara, Bobby Van and Elaine Joyce, Dick Gautier and Barbara Stuart

In "Tattletales," this updated version of the 1969 Goodson-Todman show HE SAID, SHE SAID, three celebrity couples competed, each representing one-third of the studio audience.

In round one, the wives appeared on stage and the husbands were isolated in a soundproof room. A question was read and each wife related a situation that concerned her marriage and a short clue that summarized her answer. The question, along with one of the three clues, was then read to the husbands. The husband who believed that it was his wife's response sounded a bell and tried to relate a similar story. If they matched, they won $100.

Round two reversed round one, with the wives trying to guess what the husbands said. The highest scoring team of the day received an extra $1,000 and all of their winnings were divided among the selected members of the studio audience.

After several months on the air, the format of "Tattletales" was altered to having one mate trying to second-guess the response of the other to questions like "When it comes to your mate are you possessive?" or "Have you ever fallen in love at first sight?" On some questions, they were given a

After careers as a singer and a Broadway actor, Bert Convy played host to celebrity guests and their mates on ''Tattletales.''

choice of several different possibilities. All couples that made a correct match divided the cash pot for that round. The value of the first three rounds was $150 each. The fourth and final round had a cash pot of $300.

The top-scoring team got $1,000 added to their score, and all winnings were divided among the studio audience, with each celebrity couple playing for a particular section (blue, red, or banana).

Did you know . . .   host Bert Convy was born in St. Louis, Missouri, July 23, 1933? After graduating high school, he played minor league baseball for the Philadelphia Phillies. In 1954 he abandoned baseball and with friends Gilbert Garfield and Perry Botkin Jr. formed the vocal group ''The Cheers.'' Among their hit records were ''I Need Your Lovin' '' and ''Black Denim Trousers.'' During the 1960s Convy was in the original Broadway cast productions of *Fiddler on the Roof* and *Cabaret.*

The history of ''Tattletales'' goes back to 1966 when the original pilot, then called ''It Had to Be You,'' was taped with Ed McMahon as host. By 1969, the title was changed to HE SAID, SHE SAID, and Joe Garagiola was the new host. ''He Said, She Said'' had a one-year run in syndication. In January 1973, Gene Rayburn hosted a new pilot, ''Celebrity Match Mates,'' for CBS. The show finally returned for its

most successful run as ''Tattletales'' in 1974. With Gene Rayburn then hosting THE MATCH GAME, Bert Convy was selected as the new host.

Were you watching when . . .   these game show emcees and their wives were on ''Tattletales''? There was Steve Allen, Bob Barker, Bill Cullen, Monty Hall, Dennis James, Tom Kennedy, Allen Ludden, Peter Marshall, Wink Martindale, Jack Narz, Gene Rayburn, Bobby Van, and Chuck Woolery.

Jay Leno, Michael J. Fox, Tommy Lasorda, and Meg Ryan appeared with their respective dates or mates as celebrity guests on ''Tattletales.'' Meg Ryan, then costarring in ''As the World Turns,'' appeared with her love interest from that show.

TEEN WIN, LOSE OR DRAW

premiere: April 29, 1989   *packager:* Buena Vista Entertainment/Stone-Stanley Productions   *broadcast history:* Disney (cable) April 29, 1989–April 28, 1990; Disney (cable) September 10, 1990–September 26, 1992   *host:* Marc Price *announcers:* Brandy Brown, Chase Hampton, Tiffini Hale, Mark Walberg (1990–1992)   *producers:* Jay Wolpert (1989–90), Deborah Williams (1990–92)   *directors:* Dan Diana (1989–90), Jeff Goldstein (1990–92)   *set designers:* Tony Sabatino, William H. Harris, Scott Storey   *music:* Tom Morrison **origination:** Disney-MGM Studios, Orlando, (1989–90); Studio 2, Hollywood Center Studios, Los Angeles (1990–92)

"Teen Win, Lose or Draw" was a junior edition of the popular adult sketchpad charade show that featured two teams, each anchored by a teen celebrity guest. Hosted by actor Marc Price, who played Skippy on the TV series "Family Ties," the show was seen exclusively on the Disney Channel.

The game consisted of three rounds and the team accumulating the most points was the winner. The first round was the clue round, worth two hundred points. Teams had one minute to draw a series of clues (example: teeth, movie, ocean, shark, blood, sherriff were clues for "Jaws") that led to an answer. One player drew while his or her two partners guessed. The other team could steal the points of the first team if they failed to come up with the correct answer.

Round two was the phrase round, also worth two hundred points, where one player of a team had one minute to communicate a phrase to his or her teammates. After thirty seconds he or she could hand-off to another teammate but the value of the phrase was reduced to one hundred points.

The final round was the speed round, where each team tried to guess as many words as they could within ninety seconds. Each correct guess was worth one hundred points.

The first season of "Teen Win, Lose or Draw" was taped at Disney-MGM Studios in Orlando, Florida, and featured members of the Mickey Mouse Club as the show's announcers.

TELE PUN

premiere: July 9, 1948   **packager:** NBC   **broadcast history:** NBC primetime July 9, 1948–August 6, 1948   **host:** Johnny Bradford   **announcer:** Ray Michael   **producers:** Boyce DeGaw, Vance Halleck   **director:** Vance Halleck   **origination:** Washington, D.C.

This offbeat game show was seen for five weeks in the summer of 1948. Broadcast from NBC studios in Washington, D.C., "Tele Pun" featured players performing a "pun" through charades. If the player's performance received the approval of the studio audience, he or she received a prize. A contestant who got thumbs down was "arrested" and "charged." The player was then represented by a comedian posing as his or her attorney and brought before the judge (host Johnny Bradford). If the judge dropped the case, the player received a consolation prize.

TELL IT TO GROUCHO

premiere: January 11, 1962   **packager:** John Guedel Productions   **broadcast history:** CBS primetime January 11, 1962–May 31, 1962   **host:** Groucho Marx   **assistants:** Patty Harmon, Jack Wheeler   **announcer:** Johnny Jacobs   **executive producer:** John Guedel   **producer:** Bernie Smith   **director:** Robert Dwan   **set designer:** Craig Smith   **music director:** Jack Meakin   **origination:** Studio 33, CBS Television City, Los Angeles

"The one, the only Groucho" returned to television with a new series just four months after YOU BET YOUR LIFE left the airwaves. "Tell It to Groucho" featured guests who told interesting stories, or described problems they needed to solve, during their visits with Groucho. Like "You Bet Your Life," the interviews with Groucho were the main thrust of the show, but players were given a chance to win money by playing an identification game.

Contestants could win up to $1,500 by correctly identifying people whose pictures were flashed on a screen for one-quarter of a second. Three pictures were shown, each worth $500. If the contestants missed all three, they could still win $100 by identifying an "easy" picture.

Joining Groucho as his assistants were two former contestants from "You Bet Your Life": eighteen-year-old Jack Wheeler and nineteen-year-old Patty Harmon. Wheeler, an adventurer described as the real-life counterpart of "Jack Armstrong—the All American Boy," was a principal subject on "This Is Your Life" and the youngest person to climb the famed Swiss Matterhorn.

Patty Harmon, a Miss New York, had appeared in off-Broadway productions of *The Tender Trap* and *Susan Slept Here* and in the films *Let's Rock* and *Never Love a Stranger.*

TELL ME SOMETHING GOOD

premiere: September 19, 1988   **packager:** Black Entertainment Television   **broadcast history:** BET (cable) September 19, 1988–May 1989   **host:** Julie Rogers   **executive producer:** Stuart Perkins   **director:** Mike Bruchas   **set design:** Ken Lisbeth   **origination:** Alexandria

Members of the home audience were contestants on "Tell Me Something Good," this live call-in game show. Viewers answered the question of the day (examples: "What is the zaniest or worst thing a member of your family has ever done to discourage your date?" or "What's something you thought was a secret but everybody else knew?") and a celebrity panel of three judges selected the best response for a prize, rating the answers on a scale of zero to five.

TEMPTATION

premiere: December 4, 1967   **packager:** Merrill Heatter–Bob Quigley Productions   **broadcast history:** ABC daytime December 4, 1967–March 1, 1968   **host:** Art James   **model:** Mary Poms   **announcer:** Carl King   **producers:** Merrill Heatter, Bob Quigley   **director:** Marty Pasetta   **set designer:** Romain Johnston   **origination:** The Hollywood Palace Theatre, Los Angeles

Three studio contestants competed against each other in "Temptation," this thirteen-week series, where they tried to outguess one another for merchandise prizes. Players were shown three prizes: a low-value item, a medium-value item, and a big-ticket item. A sample round may have included a shoe collection worth $90, an oven and range worth $380, and a piano worth $1,400. Each player selected a gift and won the merchandise if neither of their opponents selected the same item.

Five rounds were played in each day's game and in the third and fourth rounds, the players could change their minds after they made their first selection. A clue was given about what two of the players had chosen before all three made their final selection.

In the final round, if only one player selected a window of gifts, they won all three windows of gifts. The contestant with the highest total cash score returned to face two new contestants on the next show.

Host Art James and model Mary Poms teamed up again in 1985 on the game show CATCH PHRASE.

Did you know . . . set designer Romain Johnston, in addition to designing sets for numerous game shows and variety programs, also designed the award presented to the inductees into the TV Academy Hall of Fame? During his career, which began with ABC in the early 1950s, he was nominated for sixteen Emmys.

10 SECONDS

premiere: March 29, 1993 *packager:* Reid/Land Productions *broadcast history:* Nashville Network (cable) March 29, 1993–March 25, 1994 *host:* Dan Miller *announcer:* Don Dashiell *executive producers:* Mady Land, Allen Reid *senior producer:* Debbie Mathis *producers:* Donna Nolan, David Gatchell *director:* Ken Vincent *set designers:* Ron Baldwin, Jim Stanley *music:* Mike Johnson, Allen Reid *origination:* Nashville Network Studios, Nashville

On "Ten Seconds," two studio contestants competed in a game of song identification. One player selected the category and his or her opponent picked the amount of time (from one to ten seconds) for the player to guess the song in, after hearing a portion of it.

Round one featured nine categories, each with a value from ten to fifty points. The title of each category was a clue and once a player selected a category and the amount of time had been determined, the player could challenge his or her opponent to guess the song. If a wrong guess was given, the opposing player won the points.

Point values doubled (twenty to one hundred) in the second round of nine categories. The player who was behind at the end of this round was given a chance to catch up. He or she could earn three hundred points by identifying three artists in a ten-second medley. If this was accomplished, the other player was given a chance to win the game back by playing his or her own catch-up round.

The day's winner played for bonus cash by trying to identify nine song titles from short audio clips in sixty seconds. The value of the bonus round started at $2,500 with $500 added each day until won.

THE $10,000 PYRAMID

premiere: March 26, 1973 *packager:* Bob Stewart Productions *broadcast history:* CBS daytime March 26, 1973–March 29, 1974; ABC daytime May 6, 1974–June 27, 1980; Syndicated September 9, 1974–September 1979; Syndicated January 26, 1981–September 1981; CBS daytime September 20, 1982–December 31, 1987; Syndicated September 9, 1985–September 2, 1988; CBS daytime April 4, 1988–July 1,

Two ageless classics: Dick Clark and "The $10,000 Pyramid!"

1988; USA (cable) October 17, 1988–November 4, 1994 (repeats of 1982–1987 CBS version); Syndicated January 7, 1991–March 6, 1992; USA (cable) December 28, 1992–September 8, 1995 (repeats of 1985–1988 version)
1973–1980 versions
hosts: Dick Clark, Bill Cullen *announcers:* Bob Clayton, Steve O'Brien, Fred Foy, John Causier, Alan Kalter, Dick Heatherton, Scott Vincent, Ed Jordan *executive producer:* Bob Stewart *producer:* Anne Marie Schmidt *director:* Mike Garguilo *set designer:* Jim Ryan *theme:* "Tuning Up" by Ken Aldin *debut guests:* Rob Reiner, June Lockhart *origination:* Ed Sullivan Theater, New York (1973–1974); Studio 31, CBS Television City, Los Angeles (Fall 1973); ABC Studio TV-15, New York (1974–1980)
1981 version
host: Dick Clark *announcer:* Steve O'Brien *executive producer:* Bob Stewart *producers:* Anne Marie Schmidt, Sande Stewart *director:* Mike Garguilo *set designer:* Jim Ryan *music:* Bob Cobert *origination:* ABC Studio TV-15, New York *debut guests:* Jo Anne Worley, Sal Viscuso
1982–1988 version
host: Dick Clark *announcers:* Jack Clark, Johnny Gilbert, Charlie Tuna, Dean Goss, Charlie O'Donnell, Jerry Bishop, Rod Roddy, Bob Hilton *executive producer:* Bob Stewart

producers: Anne Marie Schmidt, Sande Stewart, Francine Bergman, David Michaels *directors:* Bruce Burmester, Dennis Rosenblatt *set designer:* Ed Flesh *music:* Bob Cobert *origination:* Studio 33, CBS Television City, Los Angeles *debut guests:* Constance McCashin, Robert Mandan
1991–1992 version
host: John Davidson *announcers:* Johnny Gilbert, Dean Goss *producers:* David Michaels, Erin Perry *director:* Bruce Burmester *set designer:* Ed Flesh *music:* Bob Cobert *origination:* Studio 31, CBS Television City, Los Angeles *debut guests:* Vicki Lawrence, Clifton Davis

"The $10,000 Pyramid" was one of the most successful game shows introduced in the 1970s. The show was a staple on the ABC daytime schedule in the 1970s and on the CBS schedule in the 80s. Repeats of "The $25,000 Pyramid" have been one of the most popular shows on the USA cable network.

"Pyramid" also received sixteen nominations for Emmys for "Outstanding Game Show" and won the award nine times.

The value of the Pyramid increased during its TV history. When the show premiered in March 1973, it was called "The $10,000 Pyramid." On January 19, 1976 the value (and title) increased to $20,000 and when the show returned in 1982 it became "The $25,000 Pyramid." The nighttime edition began as "The $25,000 Pyramid" in 1974 and prize money increased to $50,000 in 1981 and $100,000 in 1985.

Dick Clark is the host most associated with "Pyramid," but Bill Cullen emceed the nighttime version during the 1970s and John Davidson hosted the 1991–1992 edition.

The object of the game was to communicate words and subjects by describing them in a predetermined time limit. Each of two teams was composed of a celebrity guest and a studio contestant.

One team played at a time, with one player trying to describe seven items in a related category to his or her partner in thirty seconds. The other team then played another category and the team with the highest score after three rounds won the game and was given the opportunity to play the Pyramid for a grand prize.

In the bonus round, one team member attempted to describe to his or her partner six categories, by listing elements of that category in a maximum of sixty seconds. The partner had to guess the category and if he or she correctly guessed all six in the allotted time the player won the grand prize of $10,000.

When the show returned in 1982, a player could win up to $25,000 by returning to the Winner's Circle twice in the same show. Other new features added in the 1980s editions were the "Mystery Seven," where a player could win a bonus prize by guessing the seven items without being given the category and the "7–11," introduced in April 1983, where the contestant could win $1100 for guessing seven answers in thirty seconds in a special predetermined category.

The 1981 version, "The $50,000 Pyramid," had the players trying for $5,000 on the first trip to the Winner's Circle and $10,000 on the second visit. The players with the fastest time in a several week period returned to compete for $50,000.

The 1985 syndicated version, "The $100,000 Pyramid," had the three players with the fastest time in the Winner's Circle returning at a later date to play for $100,000.

The 1991 edition added another new feature to the main game, "Double Trouble," where each team had forty-five seconds to convey two-word phrases and if successful won an additional $500.

The all-time speed record for clearing all six categories on the Pyramid was set by celebrity guest Billy Crystal in 1978 with a time of twenty-six seconds.

Did you know . . . Dick Clark played a teacher in the 1960 motion picture *Because They're Young,* which starred Michael Callan, James Darren, Doug McClure, and Tuesday Weld? Clark also appeared with Eddie Albert in the 1961 movie *The Young Doctor.*

Announcer Charlie O'Donnell was Dick Clark's announcer/sidekick on "American Bandstand" from 1958 to 1968.

Were you watching when . . . one "Pyramid" week was billed as "Kirk vs. Spock"? The reason? Both William Shatner and Leonard Nimoy were the celebrity guests for that week.

Bill Cullen often guest-starred on Dick's "$10,000" and "$20,000 Pyramids," and Dick Clark, in turn, was a guest on Bill's "$25,000 Pyramid."

Billy Crystal and David Letterman were often celebrity players. At the time Billy was on ABC's "Soap" and David was a headliner comic at many top comedy clubs.

TEXACO STAR NATIONAL ACADEMIC CHAMPIONSHIP

premiere: July 1, 1989 *packager:* Texaco *broadcast history:* Discovery Channel (cable) July 1, 1989–August 19, 1989; Discovery Channel (cable) July 7, 1990–August 25, 1990; Syndicated July 3, 1991–September 4, 1991; Syndicated June 22, 1992–September 21, 1992; Syndicated June 19, 1993–September 11, 1993; Bravo (cable) March 4, 1994–May 27, 1994 *host:* Chip Beall *announcer:* Don Armstrong *creator:* Chip Beall *executive producers:* Andrea Black, Frank W. Miller *producers:* Lynn Schultz, Ted Shaw, Ron Putterman *director:* Ron Putterman *origination:* KPRC-TV, Rice University, Houston

"Texaco Star National Academic Championship" was an annual tournament featuring university teams competing in a quiz show format. Beginning in 1989, Texaco distributed the championship series of shows free to stations that wished to carry them.

Two four-member teams competed each week in four rounds of questioning, with each round called a "quarter." The first quarter (the warm-up round) had teams answering toss-up questions worth either five or ten points.

The second quarter began with a ten-point toss-up question. The team answering correctly could then answer four bonus questions, worth from five to twenty points. The team kept answering until they missed a question.

The third quarter had each team choosing one of four subjects and then trying to answer ten questions in a sixty-second time limit. If they got all ten right they received a twenty-point bonus. The opposing team could steal points by answering any missed questions.

The final quarter was a four-minute round called "Stump the Experts" with questions worth fifteen and twenty points.

The high-scoring team moved to the next round in a single elimination tournament.

THAT **** QUIZ SHOW

premiere: September 1982   *packager:* JSC Productions/Metromedia Producers Corp.   *broadcast history:* Syndicated September 1982–December 1982   *hosts:* Greg and John Rice   *announcer:* Mario Machado   *executive producers:* John Barbour, Bob Mages   *producer:* Keith Burns   *director:* Larry Shulman   *set designer:* Visual Productions   *origination:* Studio 7, KTTV–Television, Los Angeles

Twin midgets, Greg and John Rice, hosted this short-lived series that featured two teams of two players who each had unusual jobs or backgrounds. On "That **** Quiz Show," each team started with $500 and could wager between $50 and $200 on their ability to answer multiple choice trivia questions. The teams played separately, were each asked four questions, and the team with the most money played a bonus question submitted by a home viewer for a prize.

Did you know . . . both Greg and John Rice were featured on "Real People," a show that John Barbour, who created "That **** Quiz Show," cohosted on NBC?

THAT REMINDS ME

premiere: February 27, 1952   *broadcast history:* NBC primetime February 27, 1952 (one broadcast)   *host:* Arlene Francis   *producer:* Richard Lewis   *director:* Craig Allen   *origination:* International Theater, New York

A panel of four tried to identify a guest celebrity through the use of objects associated with the celebrities in this game show that was seen as a one-time special.

The panel on "That Reminds Me" was divided into two teams of two, composed of Nina Foch, Roger Price, Robert Coote, and a member of the studio audience. The studio player received money and the same amount was donated to the American Red Cross. A different audience member was selected for each game.

A curtain divided the stage with the panel seated on one side and the guest, seen only by the studio and home audience, on the other side.

Three different objects were shown to the panel, one at a time, each one connecting the celebrity guest to his or her profession or to a famous role that he or she played. The prize money started at $50 and decreased to $25 when the next object was shown and $15 when the final object was revealed.

When Boris Karloff guested on the show, his objects were "a piece of lace," "a bridal veil," and "a frightened girl screaming." Other actors who guested on the telecast were Lex Barker of *Tarzan* fame, boxer Joe Louis, and Lassie.

THAT'S AMORE

premiere: September 14, 1992   *packager:* Four Point Entertainment, for Group W Productions   *broadcast history:* Syndicated September 14, 1992–September 10, 1993   *host:* Luca Barbareschi   *announcer:* Bill Ratner   *executive producers:* Ron Ziskin, Shukri Ghalayini   *supervising producer:* Mack Anderson   *producer:* Walt Case   *director:* Rob Fiedler   *set designer:* Scott Storey   *theme:* "That's Amore" by Dean Martin   *origination:* The Production Group, Los Angeles

Italian TV personality Luca Barbareschi hosted "That's Amore," a relationship show that featured both a husband and wife airing their gripes about each other and letting the studio audience decide who was right. Both the husband and wife had friends to support them in their defenses.

Each mate presented three complaints about the other, who tried to defend himself or herself. The winning player received an "Amore" ring and the couple was sent on a second honeymoon trip.

THAT'S MY DOG!

premiere: September 1, 1991   *packager:* Albert Wallace Enterprises/North Star Entertainment Group   *broadcast history:* Family Channel (cable) September 1, 1991–September 30, 1995   *hosts:* Steve Skrovan, Wil Shriner   *assistants:* Roxie Stice, Susan Pari   *announcer:* Dean Miuccio   *creators:* Derek Hobson, John Viner   *executive producers:* S. Harry Young, Albert Wallace   *producers:* Paul Pieratt, Jerry Cardwell, Robert Sherman   *directors:* John Wolf, George Choderker   *set designer:* Tim Duffy   *music:* Scott V. Smith   *origination:* Universal Studios, Orlando

Two families and their dogs competed in this weekly cable game show, "That's My Dog!" that was based on a British series of the same name. The teams competed in five events, earning points if the stunt was completed in the allotted time. The high-scoring team of the day won a year's supply of dog food for their pet and merchandise prizes for the family.

Events varied from week to week and included "Hound Hurdles," a thirty-second marathon where the dog followed its owner's commands by jumping over different sets of hurdles (low height was worth one point; medium height, two points; and high height, five points) without knocking the bar off. "Tricky Trail" was a forty-five-second event where the dog tried to find its way through a maze loaded with distractions while attempting to find its master. The team received twenty points if the dog made it through the maze and if both teams completed the event, the team with the fastest time received an extra ten points.

The final event of the day was the "Doggie Decathlon," where the dog and its owner had to make their way through a seven-item obstacle course in sixty seconds, earning ten points for each obstacle passed and one hundred points if they finished the course before time ran out.

Taped at Universal Studios in Orlando, Florida, the first two seasons of "That's My Dog!" were hosted by Steve Skrovan. He was assisted by Roxie Stice for the first shows and

Susan Pari for the remainder of his two seasons. Comedian Wil Shriner, whose father Herb had emceed TWO FOR THE MONEY in the 1950s, became the new host in the third season, and the role of assistant was dropped. Additional games have been introduced as part of the show's format each season.

THERE'S ONE IN EVERY FAMILY

premiere: September 29, 1952 *packager:* CBS Television *broadcast history:* CBS daytime September 29, 1952–June 12, 1953; CBS Saturday morning November 15, 1952–June 13, 1953
New York version
hosts: John Reed King, Mike Wallace *announcer:* Hal Simms *creator:* Marlo Lewis *producer:* Richard Lewine *directors:* James Sheldon, Rai Purdy
Los Angeles version
host: Dean Miller *announcer:* Roy Rowan *producer/director:* Stefan Hatos *origination:* Studio 41, CBS Television City, Los Angeles

This daytime quiz show, "There's One in Every Family," spotlighted three contestants whose families as well as themselves would receive cash and prizes after they had demonstrated that their specialties rightfully entitled their kin to be proud of them. Their accomplishments included anything from the ability to play an unusual musical instrument to holding the record for blood donations. After being interviewed by the emcee, the contestants were asked a series of questions that related to the reason for their selection.

After six weeks on the air, a Saturday morning version was added on November 16, 1952 with Mike Wallace as host. Wallace had been hosting a daytime talk-variety show on CBS with his wife Buff Cobb.

On March 9, 1953 CBS moved the show from New York City to its studios at the new CBS Television City in Hollywood, which had opened in the fall of 1952. Dean Miller became the new host replacing both John Reed King and Mike Wallace. Roy Rowan took over as announcer and Stefan Hatos as producer. The show ran another three months before ending its run in June 1953.

The show was broadcast live at 8 A.M. in the morning and the studio audience was given coffee and donuts at 7:30 A.M. as well as a tour of CBS Television City.

THEY'RE OFF

premiere: June 30, 1949 *broadcast history:* DuMont primetime June 30, 1949–August 18, 1949 *host:* Tom Shirley

Films of famous horse races provided the subject matter for questions on "They're Off." Byron Field was the caller for this Thursday night DuMont show.

THINK FAST

premiere: March 26, 1949 *packager:* Robert Jennings Productions *broadcast history:* ABC primetime March 26, 1949–October 8, 1950 *hosts:* Dr. Mason Gross, Gypsy Rose Lee *substitute host:* Rex Stout *producers:* Robert Jennings, Charles Harrell *directors:* Howard Cordery, Cort Steen *music:* David Broekman Orchestra *origination:* New York

On "Think Fast," a weekly show, members of a celebrity panel tried to outtalk each other on various topics and then challenge each other with questions in an effort to "ascend a throne" and be the "King of the Table."

Dr. Mason Gross, Dean of Rutgers University, was the original host. Gypsy Rose Lee, whose autobiography inspired the Broadway musical *Gypsy*, became the new host in 1950.

The debut week panel consisted of music director David Broekman, Lois Wilson, Eloise McElhone, Leon Janney, and Vivian della Chiesa.

THINK FAST

premiere: May 1, 1989 *packager:* Games Productions Inc./ MTV Networks *broadcast history:* Nickelodeon (cable) May 1, 1989–June 29, 1991 *hosts:* Michael Carrington, Skip Lackey *announcers:* James Eoppolo, Henry J *creators:* Michael Klinghoffer, Robert Mittenthal *producers:* Robert Mittenthal, Marjorie Cohn *directors:* Lexi Rae, Bob Lampel *set designer:* Byron Taylor *origination:* Universal Studios, Orlando

On "Think Fast," two teams of two players competed in a variety of events that tested mental ability and physical skill. Each event that the team won earned cash and a chance to solve the "Brain Bender," entailing an enlarged photo of an everyday object that was revealed one section at a time. The team that solved the "Brain Bender" won an additional $200 and a chance to win more money in the "Mad Dash for Cash in the Locker Room."

Up to six events were played on each show with the first three worth $50 to the winning team and the remaining events valued at $100. One event was called "Altered States," where each team tried to fill in the missing states on a very large map on the floor, representing the United States. "Close Calls" was an event where one player from each team pushed a number on an oversized telephone keypad and the next player repeated that number adding one more to the sequence until one of the two made a mistake. Another event entailed guessing the identities of celebrities through items associated with them.

The winning team played the Mad Dash for Cash on a set with fifteen lockers. The goal was to match seven pairs of lockers in one minute, with the first four matches worth $100 each and the remaining three worth bonus prizes.

Players took turns and after one-half of the match was revealed, they both tried to find each other by opening the different lockers. An unmatched object was called the "red herring" and if encountered, the player had to pull a special cord to close the locker door.

THINK TWICE

premiere: October 10, 1994 *packager:* WGBH Television *broadcast history:* PBS (primetime) October 10, 1994–December 26, 1994 *host:* Monteria Ivey *announcer:* Chris Zito *creators:* Mark Maxwell-Smith, Michael Bevan, Bob Boden *executive producers:* Paula S. Apsell, Nancy Linde *producers:* Susan Dangel, Gary Johnson, Lin Schreiber *director:* Hugh Martin   *set designers:* James Fenhagen, Eric Ulfers, Mark Solan   *music:* Pat Hollenbeck, John Pinter (vocals by Ellis Hall)   *origination:* WGBH-TV, Boston

Two teams of two players were tested on their information, imagination, and intuition on "Think Twice," a weekly quiz show broadcast on PBS (Public Broadcasting System). Comedian Monteria Ivey was host of the series that was taped at WGBH-TV in Boston.

Round one was a test of the players' store of information. Every question had two answers and if one player came up with the first answer, his or her teammate had to come up with the second answer. Correct responses were worth ten points. If a team couldn't answer both parts, their opponents could answer the remaining segments for the points.

Round two was the imagination round, where each player on one team had thirty seconds to incorporate nine clue words into a made-up story. After hearing the story, the opposing team tried to guess the subject, scoring fifty points if they were correct. If not, the story tellers got the points. Teams traded positions for the second half of this round.

A player's intuition was tested in round three. A subject, such as "the six most watched films of all time" was given. Each player answered with the films they thought were on the list. The players on the opposing team could either accept or challenge that answer. The player giving the answer scored ten points. If the answer was the number-one response in the subject, it was worth fifty points.

The winning team played the bonus round, where they tried to come up with six correct answers to general knowledge questions within sixty seconds. Each question required two answers and if a team was successful within the time limit, each player received a $2,500 mutual fund investment.

Did you know . . . "Think Twice" cocreator Bob Boden was involved in launching Sony's Game Show Network. A game show junkie since he attended his first taping at age five (PASSWORD, with Allen Ludden), Bob appeared as a contestant on THE DATING GAME in 1980 and was a subject on "Real People," which profiled him as a game show ticket-collecting fan.

3RD DEGREE

premiere: September 11, 1989   *packager:* Burt and Bert Productions/Kline and Friends   *broadcast history:* Syndicated September 11, 1989–September 7, 1990   *host:* Bert Convy   *announcer:* Bob Hilton   *producers:* Richard Kline, Howard Schultz   *director:* Richard Kline   *set designer:* John C. Mula   *music:* Perry Botkin   *origination:* Studio 41, CBS Television City, Los Angeles

Two teams, one composed of two male celebrities and the other composed of two female celebrities, competed. Each team had one minute in round one to question a pair of guests, in order to figure out the relationship between them. At the end of each team's questioning the guests collected $250 if neither celebrity team came up with the connection. A second round of questioning was played with each team being allowed thirty seconds to answer in. If both teams were

stumped after two rounds the guests won $1,000 plus a $1,000 bonus.

Did you know . . . game show great Peter Marshall hosted the pilot for "3rd Degree"?

THIS IS THE MISSUS

premiere: November 17, 1948   *broadcast history:* CBS daytime November 17, 1948–January 12, 1949   *hosts:* Bud Collyer, Warren Hull   *assistant:* Tom Mahoney   *producers:* Lelia Swift, Walter Ware   *director:* Ralph Levy   *origination:* New York

In this revised version of MISSUS' GOES-A-SHOPPING, female contestants competed in various humorous stunts, including blowing up balloons until they burst and having a blindfolded man kiss three women and then pick his wife out from among them.

Warren Hull became host of "This Is the Missus" in December 1948, replacing Bud Collyer.

THREE FOR THE MONEY

premiere: September 29, 1975   *packager:* Stefan Hatos–Monty Hall Productions   *broadcast history:* NBC daytime September 29, 1975–November 28, 1975   *host:* Dick Enberg   *announcer:* Jack Clark   *producer:* Stu Billet   *director:* Hank Behar   *set designer:* Ed Flesh   *origination:* NBC Studio 4, Burbank   *debut guests:* Dick Gautier, Linda Kaye Henning

Two teams of three players competed for a week in a question-and-answer game called "Three for the Money," where one team chose the number of opponents they wished to challenge in various general knowledge categories.

If one team member beat one challenger in answering a split-second identification question, the question was worth $100; correctly answering a question against two challengers was worth $200; and against all three, $300. The trailing team was given a chance to catch up in the second round. The top-scoring team of the day tried for a cash jackpot that increased $1,000 a day until it was won.

THREE ON A MATCH

premiere: August 2, 1971   *packager:* Bob Stewart Productions   *broadcast history:* NBC daytime August 2, 1971–June 28, 1974   *host:* Bill Cullen   *substitute host:* Larry Blyden   *announcers:* Don Pardo, Bob Clayton, Roger Tuttle, Wayne Howell   *executive producer:* Bob Stewart   *producers:* Anne Marie Schmidt, Bruce Burmester   *director:* Mike Garguilo   *set designer:* Don Shirley   *music:* Bob Cobert   *origination:* NBC Studio 6A, New York

On "Three on a Match," three contestants were shown three general knowledge categories and each player secretly selected the number of questions they wished to answer (between one and four). The player with the highest number won the right to answer that number of true-false questions in the category of their choice. The value of the cash jackpot was determined by adding the number of questions bid by all three players and multiplying it by ten. To win the cash, the player had to answer his questions correctly. If he didn't, the player with the next highest number got to choose from

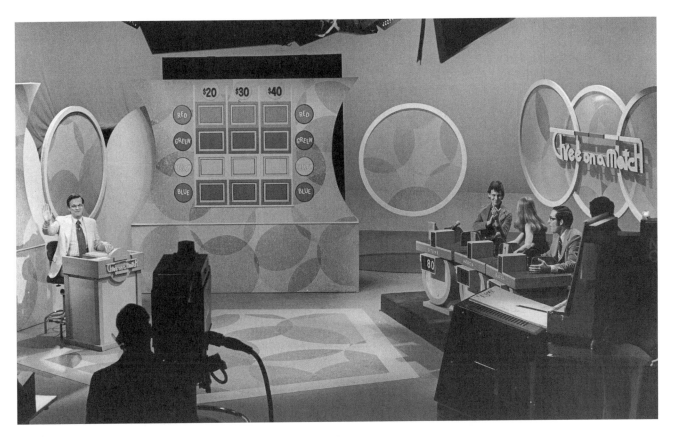

Bill Cullen invites America to join in on the fun on ''Three on a Match.''

the remaining two categories. If all three players selected the same number in their bid, the bids were erased and each player bid again.

The questions segment continued until one player decided he or she had enough cash to purchase $20, $30, and $40 squares on a game board. The player attempted to match identical gifts in all three columns to win that gift, the game, and the right to meet two new challengers.

The format of ''Three on a Match'' was changed on April 23, 1973. Under the new format, contestants had to match symbols on the game board, one in each of three columns. A player who matched the same symbol in each column won the game, and the first player to win three games won the match and $5,000. Winners faced two new opponents in the next match, and any player who won five matches retired as an ''undefeated champion.''

A player who made an ''instant match,'' finding the same symbol in each column using only three picks, won a new car.

Did you know . . . Bill Cullen began his broadcasting career in 1939 as an unpaid announcer for radio station WWSW in Pittsburgh, Pennsylvania? Cullen later moved to KDKA, Pittsburgh, and in 1944 joined CBS radio as a staff announcer.

While hosting ''Three on a Match,'' Bill Cullen was also hosting ''Monitor,'' where he was one of several hosts for

the NBC radio network. Bill was also a regular panelist on TO TELL THE TRUTH and emceed a weekly nighttime version of THE $25,000 PYRAMID.

THREE'S A CROWD
premiere: September 17, 1979   *packager:* Chuck Barris Productions   *broadcast history:* Syndicated September 17, 1979–February 1980   *host:* Jim Peck   *announcer:* Johnny Jacobs   *executive producer:* Chuck Barris   *producer:* Mike Metzger   *director:* John Dorsey   *set designer:* Mark Batterman   *music:* Lee Ringuette   *origination:* Television Center Studios, Los Angeles

The object of ''Three's a Crowd'' was to determine who knew a husband better—his wife or his secretary. Three husbands were asked three questions relating to either their wives or their secretaries. The secretaries then joined their employers and were asked the same questions. Each secretary's response that matched his or her boss's earned a point. The wives then returned and to score points they had to match the answers of both their husbands and the secretaries. The team (secretaries or wives) with the most points split $1,000.

TIC TAC DOUGH
primetime: July 30, 1956   *packager:* Jack Barry and Dan Enright Productions   *broadcast history:* NBC daytime July 30,

Wink Martindale poses in front of the "Tic Tac Dough" logo.

1956–October 23, 1959; NBC primetime September 12, 1957–December 29, 1958; CBS daytime July 3, 1978–September 1, 1978; Syndicated September 18, 1978–September 1986; USA (cable) October 12, 1987–September 7, 1990 (repeats of 1978–1986 syndicated series); Syndicated September 10, 1990–March 8, 1991; USA (cable) March 29, 1993–June 24, 1994 (repeats of 1990–1991 syndicated series)
1956–1959 version
daytime hosts: Jack Barry, Gene Rayburn, Bill Wendell
primetime hosts: Jay Jackson, Win Elliott **substitute host:** Johnny Olson **announcers:** Bill Wendell, Bill McCord, Johnny Olson **executive producers:** Hudson Fausett, Robert Noah, John Goetz, Bob Aaron, Ed Pierce, Joe Cates **producer:** Howard Felsher **directors:** Edward King, Hudson Fausett, Garry Simpson, Richard Auerbach **set designers:** Willis Conner, Frank Schneider, Ted Cooper **music director:** Paul Taubman **origination:** Ziegfeld Theater, Colonial Theater, NBC Studio 6B, New York
1978–1986 version
hosts: Wink Martindale, Jim Caldwell **announcers:** Jay Stewart, Charlie O'Donnell, Art James, Mike Darrow **executive producer:** Dan Enright **producers:** Ron Greenberg, Allen Koss, Chris Sohl **directors:** Richard Kline, D. A. Diana **set designers:** John C. Mula, Dennis Roof **music:** Hal Hidey **origination:** Studio 31, CBS Television City; KCOP TV Studios, Los Angeles; The Production Group, Hollywood
1990–1991 version
host: Patrick Wayne **announcers:** Larry Van Nuys, Art James **executive producer:** Dan Enright **producer:** Chris Sohl **director:** Michael Dimich **set designers:** John C. Mula, Kevin Pfieffer **music:** Henry Mancini **origination:** Studio 6, Hollywood Center Studios, Los Angeles

The children's game of tic-tac-toe was turned into the question-and-answer "Tic Tac Dough," which enjoyed three successful TV runs. The first version of "Tic Tac Dough" was seen on NBC in the late 1950s. Jack Barry was the original host of the daytime version. Barry was also hosting the nighttime show TWENTY-ONE, which was seen on Thursdays, and for several months during the 1956–1957 season Gene Rayburn emceed "Tic Tac Dough" on Fridays. In February 1957, "Twenty-One" moved to Monday nights and Jack Barry began hosting on Fridays. Barry remained as emcee of the daytime version until October 6, 1958 when announcer Bill Wendell became the permanent host.

A primetime version of "Tic Tac Dough" was added in the fall of 1957 with Jay Jackson as host. Win Elliott replaced him as host on October 2, 1958.

The object of the game was for a player to be the first to put his or her mark, "X" or "O," in three boxes, either across, up, down, or diagonally. Two players alternated selecting a box and answering a question from the category indicated on the box in order to be able to place their mark in the box. The center box was worth $200 and the others $100. Each correct answer added to the game's jackpot, which was won by the player making tic-tac-toe. After each round of questions, one for each player, the nine categories were rotated to different boxes.

After an nineteen-year absence from television, "Tic Tac Dough" returned in the summer of 1978 with a nine-week run on CBS, followed by an eight-year run in first-run syndication. Wink Martindale emceed the new version and the game remained the same except for an increase in the value of the boxes and the addition of a bonus game. The value of the center box was $500 and the outside boxes increased to $300.

In the bonus game, six boxes contained cash amounts ranging from $50 to $500. Behind the other boxes were either the words "tic" or "tac," or the face of a dragon. The object was to accumulate $1,000 before hitting the dragon, which stopped the bonus round. If the player found both the tic and tac boxes, he or she automatically won the game. The player could quit at any time in the bonus round and keep his or her cash winnings or risk all by going on.

Players continued on "Tic Tac Dough" until defeated and, in 1980, Thomas McKee became one of the biggest winners in game show history by winning $312,750 on forty-five consecutive shows.

Wink Martindale left the show in September 1985 and Jim Caldwell emceed the final season.

"Tic Tac Dough" was revived for a third time in the fall of 1990. Patrick Wayne (son of movie legend John Wayne) emceed this one-season edition that featured a theme song composed by Henry Mancini, best known for his film music.

The value of the center box was increased to $1,000 and the surrounding boxes were valued at $500. Categories now rotated after each question was asked.

The winning contestant still played a bonus game for additional cash and prizes. Behind each of seven boxes were either "X" or "O." The remaining two boxes had either a dragon or a dragonslayer. The goal was for the player to get tic-tac-toe in the letter of his or her choice ("X" or "O") or find the dragonslayer before finding the dragon. The player earned $500 for finding the first mark and the cash jackpot was doubled with each additional mark. Finding the dragon caused the player to lose all he or she had accumulated in the bonus game.

Did you know . . . "Tic Tac Dough" announcer/host Bill Wendell joined NBC as a staff announcer in 1955? Prior to his NBC work, he had worked as an announcer on the DuMont Television Network. Among his first assignments for NBC was the job of announcer for Ernie Kovacs on Kovac's morning show. In 1982, Wendell became the announcer on "Late Night with David Letterman" and stayed with the show when it moved to CBS in August 1993.

While hosting "Tic Tac Dough," original emcee Jack Barry hosted TWENTY-ONE and HIGH LOW in the same year and all for NBC.

Wink Martindale would find "Tic Tac Dough" to be his most successful game show. Wink emceed "Tic Tac Dough" for almost eight years and, prior to "Tic Tac Dough," Wink had a four-year hit with CBS's GAMBIT.

Throughout the late 1970s and the mid-80s "Tic Tac Dough," with Wink Martindale, and THE JOKER'S WILD, with Jack Barry, would prove to be two of the most successful syndicated game shows of that period.

While hosting "Tic Tac Dough" for television, Wink Martindale also kept very busy in radio. On the national scene he hosted several top-rated syndicated radio specials. The most memorable and successful was a fifteen-hour salute to the life and times of Wink's friend, Elvis Presley. Wink and Elvis were boyhood friends beginning in the early 1950s.

Wink Martindale made the cover of the national *TV Guide* in the January 21–27 issue in 1984. He shared the cover with fellow friends and emcees: Bob Barker, Jack Barry, Bill Cullen, Monty Hall, and then newcomer Pat Sajak.

TIME MACHINE
premiere: January 7, 1985 *packager:* Reg Grundy Productions *broadcast history:* NBC daytime January 7, 1985–April 26, 1985 *host:* John Davidson *announcer:* Charlie Tuna *creator:* Bill Barr *executive in charge of production:* Bill Mason *executive producer:* Robert Noah *producers:* Caryn Lucas, Roger Speakman *directors:* Chris Darley, James Marcione *set designers:* Ed Flesh, Molly Joseph, Dennis Roof *music:* Ray Ellis, Marc Ellis *origination:* NBC Studio 2, Burbank

"Time Machine," a short-lived daytime game show, went through two formats in just four months. From January 7 to February 8, the show had three contestants playing one at a time, answering questions about people and events of the past. Among the games played were "The Tube Game," where players answered questions about television; "Main Event," where the questions covered the events of a particular year; "Jukebox Game," where the players were given four different years and attempted to match songs to each of those years; and "Before or After," where a player was given

the date an event occurred and then had to identify another event, placing it either before or after the original date given.

All three players competed in the final round, "The Time Capsule." From a series of clues like "Kermit the Frog," "Does She or Doesn't She," "Ducktail Haircut," and "Hound Dog," each player tried to guess the year in question. The player coming closest to the year in his or her guess won $1,000 and a chance at a jackpot question for additional prizes.

To try for the jackpot, the champion was given four headlines and attempted to pick out the one which described an event that had happened in the Time Capsule year.

On February 11, the format was changed to one where two contestants played against one another and the winner then played against the previous day's champion.

To determine who would be the new champion, five clues were given and each player attempted to guess the years that related to those clues. The player coming closest won and was given a chance to win a new car.

To win the car, the player was given a base year and had to decide if four different events happened before or after that year.

Did you know . . . John Davidson costarred with Sally Field in the 1973 TV series "The Girl with Something Extra"?

TIME WILL TELL
premiere: August 27, 1954 *packager:* Adams-Davis Productions *broadcast history:* DuMont primetime August 27, 1954–October 15, 1954 *host:* Ernie Kovacs *announcer:* Don Russell *producer:* Robert Adams *director:* Harry Coyle *origination:* New York

"Time Will Tell" was a show whose main feature was Ernie Kovacs' clowning around with the contestants. The quiz segment had three players competing against each other by trying to answer questions before time ran out on a ninety-second, five-foot-high hour glass.

TO SAY THE LEAST
premiere: October 3, 1977 *packager:* Merrill Heatter–Bob Quigley Productions *broadcast history:* NBC daytime October 3, 1977–April 21, 1978 *host:* Tom Kennedy *announcer:* Kenny Williams *executive producers:* Merrill Heatter, Bob Quigley *producer:* Robert Noah *director:* Jerome Shaw *set designer:* Ed Flesh *music:* Stan Worth *origination:* NBC Studio 3, Burbank *debut guests:* Robert Fuller, Jamie Farr, Lee Meriwether, Rita Moreno

Two teams, each composed of three members, competed on "To Say the Least." Two players from each team were isolated backstage. A phrase was then shown to the on-stage players, who alternated in eliminating words from it. On any turn, a contestant could challenge his or her opponents to guess the phrase from the remaining words. If they could recognize the phrase, they scored one point, and if not the challenging team scored.

The first team to win two games played the bonus round. The contestants were shown a statement and eliminated all but three words. Each celebrity was given a chance to guess the phrase for cash. If the first celebrity was successful, the second celebrity attempted a guess with another word eliminated and the round continued until all celebrities had guessed the phrase.

TO TELL THE TRUTH

premiere: December 18, 1956　*packager:* Mark Goodson–Bill Todman Productions (1956–1981); Mark Goodson Productions (1990–1991)　*broadcast history:* CBS primetime December 18, 1956–September 25, 1966; CBS daytime June 18, 1962–September 6, 1968; CBS primetime December 12, 1966–May 22, 1967; Syndicated September 8, 1969–September 1978; Syndicated September 8, 1980–September 4, 1981; NBC daytime September 3, 1990–May 31, 1991

1956–1968 version

host: Bud Collyer　*substitute hosts:* Jack Clark, Sonny Fox, Jim Fleming, Ralph Bellamy, John Cameron Swayze, Robert Q. Lewis, Merv Griffin, Gene Rayburn, Mark Goodson　*announcers:* Bern Bennett (December 1956–June 1960); Roger Forster (1960); Johnny Olson (October 1960–September 1968)　*substitute announcer:* Hal Simms, Jack Clark, Warren Moran　*commercial announcers:* Dwight Weist, Bob Shepard, James Daly　*executive producer:* Gil Fates　*producers:* Bob Stewart, Willie Stein, Bruno Zirato Jr.　*directors:* Franklin Heller, Paul Alter, Lloyd Gross　*theme:* ''Peter Pan'' by Dolf van der Linden (1956–1962); Bob Colbert (1962–1968).　*set designers:* Carl Kent (original), Nelson Baume, Robert Rowe Paddock　*origination:* CBS Studio 59, New York (December 1956–June 9, 1960); CBS Studio 52, New York (June 16, 1960–September 1968)　*debut panelists:* Primetime (1956): Hildy Parks, Polly Bergen, Dick Van Dyke, John Cameron Swayze; daytime (1962): Sam Levenson, Sally Ann Howes, Barry Nelson, Mimi Benzell

1969–1978 version

hosts: Garry Moore, Bill Cullen, Joe Garagiola　*announcers:* Johnny Olson, Bill Wendell, Alan Kalter, Don Pardo　*executive producer:* Gil Fates　*producer:* Bruno Zirato Jr.　*directors:* Paul Alter, Lloyd Gross　*set designer:* Ted Cooper　*origination:* Ed Sullivan Theater, New York; Studio 6A, NBC, New York　*debut week panel:* Orson Bean, Kitty Carlisle, Peggy Cass, Bill Cullen

1980–1981 version

host: Robin Ward　*announcer:* Alan Kalter, Bill Wendell　*producer:* Mimi O'Brien　*director:* Lloyd Gross　*set designer:* Ron Baldwin　*origination:* NBC Studios 8H and 6A, New York　*debut week panel:* Pat Collins, Nipsey Russell, Margaret Trudeau, John Wade

Remember "To Tell the Truth's" mod 1969 set? Longtime Goodson-Todman art director Ted Cooper created this updated set. From left to right are Bill Cullen, Peggy Cass, Gene Rayburn, Kitty Carlisle, and new host Garry Moore.

1990–1991 version
hosts: Gordon Elliott, Lynn Swann, Alex Trebek **substitute host:** Mark Goodson **announcers:** Burton Richardson, Charlie O'Donnell **producer:** Mimi O'Brien **director:** Paul Alter **set designer:** Anthony Sabatino **music:** Score Productions **origination:** NBC Studio 3, Burbank **debut week panel:** Kitty Carlisle, Gloria Loring, David Niven Jr, Lynn Swann

"To Tell the Truth" had a run on both network and syndicated television of over thirty years.

A panel of four celebrities attempted to guess which of three people were associated with a previously told story of an unusual event. All three people claimed to be the same person and each show began with the announcer (Bern Bennett was the first) asking the question, "Number one, what is your name?"

The panel, originally called "cross examiners," questioned the contestants and then voted for the person they felt was telling the truth. The host then asked the fateful question, "Will the real 'John Doe' please stand up?" The contestants won cash based on their ability to fool the panel and the cash amount was determined by the number of wrong votes. The amount paid per incorrect vote varied during the run of "To Tell the Truth." When the show premiered in 1956, guests received $250 for each wrong vote by the panel. If the guests got no wrong votes, they split $150.

Originally, the show was supposed to be called "Nothing But the Truth," but the title was changed due to a conflict with a movie of the same name. Future "60 Minutes" anchor Mike Wallace emceed the original pilot but was replaced by Bud Collyer when the show became a series.

The guests on the first telecast were Cecil H. Underwood, governor of West Virginia, and Jean Hoffman, sportswriter. Kitty Carlisle made her first appearance as a panelist on March 19, 1957, and continued as a regular through 1991. Other regulars included Don Ameche, Orson Bean, Ralph Bellamy, Johnny Carson, Peggy Cass, Hy Gardner, and Tom Poston.

Among the "central subjects" featured on "To Tell the Truth" during its network run were Los Angeles Dodger pitcher Don Drysdale, author Ted Geisel (Dr. Seuss), *Dennis the Menace* creator Hank Ketcham, John Scopes of the Scopes trial of the 1920s, TV personality Shirley Dinsdale, who received the first Emmy Award, and singers Adam Wade, Brian Hyland, Bonnie Guitar, and Hank Ballard.

Some of the people who appeared as imposters on the show included TV personality Mitch Miller, actresses Cicely Tyson and Lauren Hutton, baseball stars Jerry Coleman and Ralph Houk, and future football coach Tom Landry.

To celebrate the fifth anniversary of "To Tell the Truth," on December 18, 1961, the show featured Cecil Underwood, former governor of West Virginia, as the subject of the first round. Underwood had appeared on the very first program. James Pickering, an astronomer at the Hayden Planeterium in New York, also encored as an imposter.

"To Tell the Truth" moved from network to first-run syndication in the fall of 1969. Former I'VE GOT A SECRET host Garry Moore emceed the new daily version for eight seasons before retiring. Sports personality Joe Garagiola hosted the final year, in 1977–1978.

Two years later "To Tell the Truth" was back for another season in syndication with Canadian actor Robin Ward as host and regular panelists Peggy Cass and Soupy Sales.

A new feature added to this version was the "one-on-one" segment. All of the day's imposters returned at the end of the show for a chance to earn more money. An additional fact about one of the imposters was held back earlier in the show and each of the four panelists was given time to question one of the imposters. At the end of that time the panelists decided if that imposter was telling the truth or not. After all four imposters were questioned the real person stood up. The team of imposters was paid $100 for each incorrect answer and $500 if they foiled the entire panel.

On September 3, 1990, "To Tell the Truth" returned to network television after an absence of over twenty years. The new version featured reporter Gordon Elliott as host, Burton Richardson as announcer, and Kitty Carlisle as a regular panelist. However, on its premiere broadcast, the network fed out the wrong episode to the East Coast and Midwest. Viewers who tuned in saw the pilot episode of the new version that featured a different host (actor Richard Kline) and a slightly different format.

A new "one-on-one" segment was introduced giving members of the studio audience a chance to win $500. A guest was introduced who made two statements, only one of which was true. Each member of the panel asked a question about each claim before the audience player decided which statement was the truth. The player received the money if his or her judgment was correct; otherwise, the guest won the cash.

After two months on the air, Gordon Elliott left the show and was replaced by former football star Lynn Swann on October 29, 1990. Veteran game show host Alex Trebek replaced Swann as emcee on February 4, 1991. Trebek also hosted the program preceding "To Tell the Truth" on NBC, CLASSIC CONCENTRATION, giving him a full hour on daytime television.

Original "To Tell the Truth" announcer Bern Bennett became the subject on the January 29, 1991 broadcast. It was his first appearance in front of the camera in thirty-four years, the last coming on BEAT THE CLOCK when he was the subject of a "Draw the Masked Announcer" contest. Bennett was the announcer on "To Tell the Truth" from December 18, 1956 to June 30, 1960. Roger Forster replaced him from July to October 1960. On October 31, 1960, Johnny Olson took over and remained with the show until 1972. Longtime NBC staff announcer Bill Wendell replaced Olson in 1972 and continued as announcer until 1978.

Did you know . . . Mark Goodson produced game shows for over forty years but only appeared as a host twice, both times on "To Tell the Truth"? First, in 1967 Goodson filled in for host Bud Collyer, and twenty-four years later, on February 19, 1991, he filled in for Alex Trebek, who had rushed to the hospital when his wife gave birth to their first child.

Other people being considered as host when Bud Collyer got the job were Vincent Price and Don Ameche.

Kitty Carlisle costarred with The Marx Brothers in the 1935 film classic *A Night at the Opera*.

Were you watching when . . . these game show hosts were all guest panel members on "To Tell the Truth": Johnny Carson, Dick Clark, Burt Convy, Bill Cullen, Hugh Downs, Merv Griffin, Art James, Tom Kennedy, Art Linkletter, Allen Ludden, Gene Rayburn, and Gene Wood?

TOP CARD

premiere: April 3, 1989   *packager:* Reid-Land Productions *broadcast history:* Nashville Network (cable) April 3, 1989– March 26, 1993   *hosts:* Jim Caldwell, Dan Miller   *hostesses:* Blake Pickett, Paige Brown   *announcers:* Don Dashiell, Brad Staggs   *creators:* Allen Reid, Mady Land   *producers:* Diane Duvall, Debbie Mathis, Donna Carter   *director:* Ken Vincent *set designers:* Ron Baldwin, Jim Stanley   *music:* Mike Johnson, Allen Reid   *origination:* Opryland USA, Nashville

In 1989 the Nashville Network replaced their six-year-old country music game show FANDANGO with the more entertainment-oriented series "Top Card."

Based on the popular card game "21," the show featured three contestants who answered toss-up questions with each correct answer revealing a card on a game board (aces worth one point; picture cards, ten points; and all others, the number indicated on them) with the goal of coming closest to twenty-one without going over. Players had the option of keeping the card on the game board or taking an unseen top card from a deck.

The winner of the first game earned the right to move on to the championship game and play the winner of the second game. The third game determined the day's winner. Both the second and third games were played like the first game.

The winner of the day played a bonus round for a chance to win merchandise prizes. To win a grand prize, the champion had four chances to select merchandise prizes from the game board. Behind each prize was a card with a value. Again the player had the choice to keep the card or take the top card off the deck. If the player hit twenty-one within the four chances he or she won the grand prize and also kept the other prizes if he or she stayed under twenty-one.

TOP DOLLAR

premiere: March 29, 1958   *packager:* Entertainment Productions Inc./Harry Fleischman   *broadcast history:* CBS primetime March 29, 1958–August 30, 1958; CBS daytime August 18, 1958–October 16, 1959   *host (primetime):* Toby Reed   *hosts (daytime):* Warren Hull, Jack Narz   *assistant:* Joanne Copeland   *spelling authority:* Dr. Bergen Evans *announcers:* Ralph Paul, Jack Clark   *executive producer:* Steve Carlin   *producer:* Merrill Heatter   *directors:* Seymour Robbie (primetime), Cort Steen (daytime)   *set designer:* Eddie Gilbert   *music director:* Bob Nicholson   *origination:* CBS Studio 52 and 62, New York

That's model Blake Pickett and host Jim Caldwell of "Top Card," for The Nashville Network.

Jack Narz was top banana on "Top Dollar."

"Top Dollar" was based on the parlor game "Ghosts." The object was for three contestants to add letters to a potential word without adding the letter that completed the word. After the first three letters were revealed, each additional letter added $100 to the jackpot. Any player who added the final letter to a word was eliminated and the game continued until only one player remained who then won the pot.

In the home viewer portion of the game, the first eight letters of the top dollar (longest) word of the day were matched to a telephone dial and converted to digits. Any viewer who could match those numbers to the serial number on a $1 bill won $5,000.

Radio personality Toby Reed emceed the primetime version with Dr. Bergen Evans, a professor of English at Northwestern University, serving as spelling authority.

On August 18, 1958, a daytime version of "Top Dollar" with Warren Hull as host was quickly added to the CBS schedule, to replace DOTTO.

One month later, on September 22, daytime "Top Dollar" was given a new format based on the parlor game "Hangman." Two contestants tried to guess a mystery word as they alternated filling in a given number of blank spaces. Each word was related to a prize (example: if the mystery word was "Aladdin," the prize might have been a set of lamps) and the player who identified the word won the gift.

In November 1958, Jack Narz replaced Warren Hull as host of "Top Dollar."

TOP OF THE WORLD

premiere: January 17, 1982 *packager:* WPBT-TV, South Florida/Thames Television/ABC Channel 2, Sydney, Australia *broadcast history:* PBS primetime January 17, 1982–April 11, 1982 *host:* Eamonn Andrews *executive producers:* Shep Morgan, Philip Jones *producers:* Malcolm Morris and Philip Jones (for Thames TV), Shep Morgan (WPBT), Barry Crook (Australia) *director:* Malcolm Morris *set designers:* Grover Cole, Rod Stratfold

On "Top of the World," three contestants competed, each representing the United States, the United Kingdom, or Australia. Broadcast via satellite, each contestant played from his or her home country and the host was based in London. In round one, each contestant was required to answer twelve questions, four based on his or her own country and eight based on his or her challenger's countries. Each correct response earned one point.

In round two, contestants were quizzed for two minutes on a subject of their own choosing. Each correct answer was worth two points.

Players were tested on world knowledge in round three, with each correct answer worth three points. (An incorrect answer deducted three points from a players score.)

The top-scoring player won the game and the highest-scoring players from each country returned to play in a championship game for the grand prize: a rare 1924 Rolls-Royce.

TRASHED

premiere: February 14, 1994 *packager:* MTV Networks *broadcast history:* MTV (cable) February 14, 1994–July 23,

1994 *host:* Chris Hardwick *hostess:* Andrea Wagner *"The Trasher":* Mark Fite *creators:* Juliette Blake, Trevor Hopkins *executive producer:* Joel Stillerman *producer:* Leslie Kolins *line producer:* David J. Hudson *director:* Glenn Weiss *set designer:* Tom Buderwitz *theme music:* Dweezil Zappa *origination:* The Production Group, Los Angeles

Two teams of two friends competed for a chance at a vacation trip to Europe and also merchandise prizes by risking their prized possessions in "Trashed," this offbeat game show. The losing team earned the privilege of helping various community organizations with ten hours of service.

The game began with a toss-up question and the team that answered correctly gained control of the game. They selected a possession of the opposing team's that they wished to see "trashed."

The opposing team could save their possession if they answered two questions correctly in the next category played. Each category had three pop trivia questions, each worth fifty points. If the other team responded with correct answers, the possession was destroyed by "The Trasher." The team that won the round determined their opponent's next item to be trashed.

After three fifty-point rounds, point values doubled for the next rounds. The final round was "the survival round," where questions were worth one hundred fifty points. One member of each team was put in a "jeopardy" situation while their partners answered questions within a thirty-nine-second time limit.

Three categories were revealed and statements were read to the players. Players buzzed in and tried to match the statements to the right categories. The team with the most points at the end of this round won the game.

The winning team played the grand prize round for a trip and other prizes. The goal was to name the recording artists on six video screens. Each player described three of the artists to his or her partner for the partner to identify. They were given a time limit of thirty seconds plus a five-second bonus time for each of their six possessions that were not trashed earlier in the program.

TREASURE HUNT

premiere: September 7, 1956 *packagers:* Jantone Productions (1956–1959); Chuck Barris Productions (1973–1982) *broadcast history:* ABC primetime September 7, 1956–May 31, 1957; NBC daytime August 12, 1957–December 4, 1959; NBC primetime December 24, 1957–June 17, 1958; Syndicated September 10, 1973–September 1977; Syndicated September 14, 1981–September 1982
1956–1959 version
host: Jan Murray *substitute hosts:* Mel Allen, Bob Kennedy, Keefe Braselle, Dennis James, Buddy Hackett, Tom Reddy, Johnny Johnston, "Buffalo" Bob Smith *announcers:* Tom Reddy, Bill Wendell, Bob Williams, Carl King *pirate girls:* Marian Stafford, Pat White, Greta Thyssen, Jackie Johnson *producer:* Bud Granoff *directors:* Phil Levens, Dave Brown *set designers:* Romain Johnston, Norman Davidson *music*

director: Milton DeLugg, Nicky Tagg   *origination:* Century Theater, New York; Studio 6B, NBC, New York

1973–1977 version

host: Geoff Edwards   *models:* Sivi Aberg, Jane Nelson, Tanya Morgan, Nome DeVargas, Pamela Hensley *announcer:* Johnny Jacobs *executive producers:* Chuck Barris, Walt Case *producer:* Mike Metzger *director:* John Dorsey *art director:* Spencer Davies *music coordinator:* Lee Ringuette *origination:* The Burbank Studios

1981–1982 version

host: Geoff Edwards   *model:* Jan Speck *announcer:* Tony McClay *executive producers:* Chuck Barris, Budd Granoff *producer:* Mike Metzger *director:* John Dorsey *art director:* John C. Mula *music coordinator:* Lee Ringuette *origination:* The Burbank Studios

In the original version of "Treasure Hunt," hosted by Jan Murray, two contestants were asked a series of four questions, in categories that they chose for each other. Players received $50 for each correct answer and the player with the most money at the end of the round of questioning won the game and chose from among thirty treasure chests on stage. The chests contained everything from a head of cabbage to a jackpot of up to $25,000 on the ABC version and $10,000

Host Jan Murray seems to enjoy peeking at the chest brought to him by pirate girl Marian Stafford.

plus another $1,000 for each week it was not found, on the NBC version. Before a chest was opened, the player was offered a predetermined cash amount to sell the chest back. When both players tied in the question game, each was given a chance to select a treasure chest.

Assisting host Jan Murray was the "Pirate Girl." Greta Thyssen was the original Pirate Girl on the primetime "Treasure Hunt," with Pat White as her daytime counterpart. Marian Stafford replaced White in December 1957 and Thyssen on January 28, 1958.

Chuck Barris Productions acquired the rights to produce a new version of "Treasure Hunt," with the show returning as a weekly syndicated series in September 1973. Geoff Edwards served as host.

In this version, three contestants selected from the studio audience each received a gift box on stage. Two of the boxes were empty while the third contained a "surprise." The player choosing the box with the surprise continued and was given the opportunity to select from among thirty boxes. Each of the thirty boxes contained a prize ranging from expensive gifts to worthless objects. One box contained the grand prize, a check for $25,000. Before the box selected was opened, the player was offered a cash amount to take as a substitute before the contents were revealed.

The first syndicated version of "Treasure Hunt" had a four-year run. In 1981, the show was brought back again, this time as a daily syndicated series. The new version featured sixty-six boxes instead of thirty and a grand prize jackpot that began at $50,000 and increased by $1,000 a day until it was selected. Only two players were featured in the game, one a returning champion and the other selected from the studio audience.

Did you know . . . Geoff Edwards, host of the 1970s version of "Treasure Hunt," had to memorize over thirty skits for each taping? Due to the security system on the set no cue cards were provided for Edwards to read. Each taping day was a crash course in memory. Did he ever forget a line? According to producer Steve Friedman (who also played the role of "diaper baby"), Edwards never did.

Do you remember the name of the show's security guard? His name was Emile Aturi, and he was the bonded security agent on the show. In real life he was a security guard at the studio where "Treasure Hunt" was taped. One day Barris asked if he'd like to be on one of his new shows. The result was his appearance on "Treasure Hunt."

TREASURE ISLE

premiere: December 18, 1967   *packager:* John MacArthur–Paul Alter Productions   *broadcast history:* ABC daytime December 18, 1967–December 27, 1968   *host:* John Bartholomew Tucker   *assistants:* Julia Hayes, Pat Minor, Renee Hampton, Bonnie Maudaley   *announcer:* "The Sage" (Bill Templeton)   *creator:* Paul Alter   *executive producer:* Bill Templeton   *producers:* Paul Alter, Roy Kammerman   *directors:* Paul Alter, Peter Calabrasse   *set designer:* Grover Cole   *origination:* Colonnades Beach Hotel, Palm Beach Shores

Julia Hayes and Pat Minor assist host John Bartholomew Tucker on daytime television's first outdoor game show, "Treasure Isle."

In "Treasure Isle," three couples competed by answering questions, solving puzzles, and completing stunts in the hopes of reaching a specially constructed island to hunt for buried treasure.

In round one, contestants tried to complete an oversized jigsaw puzzle and then decipher it. The second round consisted of solving various puzzles. In round three, each team attempted to cross from one island to another in an inflatable raft with the wives directing their blindfolded mates. The first team to reach the island won.

The winning team was given three minutes to unscramble clues and dig for miniature treasure chests, each of which contained a prize.

The lagoon and island cost $800,000 to build and the set was built at the Colonnades Beach Hotel in Palm Beach Shores, Florida.

TREASURE MALL

premiere: June 11, 1988 *packager:* Saban Productions/ Fiedler-Berlin Productions/O.K.T. Productions *broadcast history:* Syndicated June 11, 1988–September 1988 *host:* Hal Sparks *announcer:* Ed MacKay *creator:* Ellen Levy *executive producers:* Haim Saban, Robert Unkel, Peter R. Berlin, Rob Fiedler *producer:* Peter R. Berlin *director:* Rob Fiedler *set designer:* Jimmy Cuomo *music:* Andrew Dimitroff *origination:* Chris Craft TV, Los Angeles

Set in a shopping mall, "Treasure Mall" featured teams as they tried to win points to earn the opportunity to hunt for prizes among booby-trapped boxes.

Two teams, each composed of two kids, tried to pick the most likely answers to questions based on a survey of other kids. Each player picked one of three possible choices to questions like "What would third grade boys do for $100?" Possible choices included (a) shave their heads, (b) eat earthworms, or (c) kiss girls. If the right answer was chosen, the player scored a point for his or her team. The first team to reach five points won the game.

The winning team was given the opportunity to find coins hidden in one of the stores of the treasure mall. The two players alternated, with twenty-five-second searches, to find up to four coins hidden in four places (a total of sixteen possible).

Two rounds were played and the team with the most coins earned a chance to crack the treasure chest. The winning team tried to find keys that were hidden in gift-wrapped boxes. They were given thirty seconds to find as many as possible and if any of the keys found opened the lock on the chest, the team won an assortment of prizes.

TREASURE QUEST

premiere: April 24, 1949 *broadcast history:* ABC primetime April 24, 1949–September 2, 1949 *host:* John Weigel *announcer:* Jack Lester *producer:* Alan Fishburn *director:* Greg Garrison *origination:* WENR-TV, Chicago

Two contestants on this Chicago-based quiz show tried to identify geographical locations through photos and clues. The player with the most correct identifications won a trip to the place of his or her choosing.

The original title of the show was "Bon Voyage" and the name "Treasure Quest" was adopted on May 8, 1949.

TRIPLE THREAT

premiere: October 8, 1988 *packager:* Television Program Enterprises *broadcast history:* Syndicated October 8, 1988–October 1, 1989; BET (cable) September 14, 1992–September 17, 1993

1988–1989 version

hosts: Jim Lange, Alan Hunter *announcer:* Sam Riddle *producers:* Sam Riddle, Walt Case *director:* Bruce Burmester *set designer:* Ed Flesh *music:* Joey Carbone, Wil Shriner *consultant:* Steve Resnik *origination:* The Aquarius Theater, Hollywood

1992–1993 version

host: Spencer Christian *announcer:* John Walker *concept/ executive producer:* Al Masini *producers:* Noreen Donovan, Robert Hess, Laurie Rich *director:* Bruce Burmester *set designers:* John Shaffner, Joe Stewart *theme:* Kenni Hairston *music clearance:* Evan Greenspan *consultant:* Tommy Haynes *origination:* NBA Entertainment Studios Secaucus

Two teams, each composed of three members from different generations, competed in "Triple Threat," this game show that tested their knowledge of music, movies, and television, past and present. Each team consisted of a celebrity guest, a member of his or her family, and a studio contestant playing for cash.

The game consisted of three rounds of questions, with the first round featuring one player from each team facing off against a member of his or her own generation by attempting to guess songs from their generation. As a song was played, four possible answers were revealed. Players rang in when they felt the right answer was revealed and a correct response was worth $50. Each member of the team competed in this round.

In round two, the value of each question was $100 and players tried to identify songs not related to their own generation. Questions were worth $200 in round three, the "free for all," where any player could buzz in to answer. The team with the highest score at the end of this round won the game.

The winning team could triple the money in the "Triple Threat Relay Round." They were given sixty seconds to place thirteen song titles into one of four categories. The categories represented three musical artists and an "out of play" section. Players, in turn, attempted to place three correct hits under each artist.

Jim Lange was the host of "Triple Threat" with MTV "VJ" Alan Hunter guest-hosting one show. "Triple Threat" was conceived by Al Masini, who was also responsible for "Star Search" and "Entertainment Tonight."

"Triple Threat" was revived in 1992 for the Black Entertainment Television cable network. Spencer Christian, weatherman of ABC's early morning talk show "Good Morning America," became the new host.

The game was played the same way as the syndicated version, except that contestants played for points instead of cash (five points in round one, ten points in round two, and twenty points in round three) and bonus prizes in the "Triple Threat Reality Round." The show featured three members of a family (instead of celebrity guests) and was seen daily.

TRIVIA TRACK

premiere: March 17, 1997   *packager:* Game Show Network *broadcast history:* Game Show Network (cable) March 17, 1997–October 2, 1998   *hosts:* Larry Anderson, Marianne Curan   *substitute hosts:* Peter Tomarken, Nancy Sullivan, Dave Nemeth   *announcers:* Gene Wood, Ed MacKay   *executive producer:* Ellie Bendes   *supervising producer:* Michael Gilman   *producers:* Susan B. Flanagan, Joel Klein *interactive game producer:* Maxine Nunes   *director:* Marc Cohen   *virtual set designer:* Intermetrics   *music:* Jeff Levin *origination:* Game Show Network studios, Culver City

Contestants compete in a question-and-answer game using telephone keypads to enter their answers on this live, interactive series with a horse race setting.

Five contestants are randomly selected to play in each game with two games featured on each show.

Each game is a ten-furlong race, with each player using their telephone keypad to select one of the answers on the screen. The first question is worth one furlong for a correct answer; the second question, two furlongs, etc.; and all questions from the fifth on have a value of five furlongs. The first player to cross the finish line (at the ten-furlong mark) wins the game and moves on to the "Triple Crown" round to face the winner of the second game.

The object of the "Triple Crown" round is to be the first player to accumulate three crowns. Players alternate hitting the number zero on their keypad to stop a random sequence on a game board that contains nine boxes with either one crown, two crowns, a free crown, or lose a turn. Landing on the center box earns an automatic win for the player. To win the value of a box, a player has to answer a multiple choice question correctly.

Larry Anderson, who had hosted a revival of TRUTH OR CONSEQUENCES in 1987, was the host of "Trivia Track" for the first six months. He was replaced by Marianne Curan, who also hosts SUPER DECADES, another interactive game show on Game Show Network.

TRIVIA TRAP

premiere: October 8, 1984   *packager:* Mark Goodson Productions   *broadcast history:* ABC daytime October 8, 1984– April 5, 1985   *host:* Bob Eubanks   *announcers:* Bob Hilton, Charlie O'Donnell, Gene Wood   *executive producer:* Chester Feldman   *producer:* Jonathan Goodson   *director:* Marc Breslow   *set designer:* Dennis Roof   *music:* Edd Kalehoff *origination:* Studio 55, ABC Television Center, Los Angeles

Two teams, one with three members over the age of thirty and the other with three members under the age of thirty, competed against each other in this trivia quiz show, "Trivia Trap."

The first team to earn $1,000 won the game. In round one, four possible answers to a question were shown. Players had to eliminate all the wrong answers. They earned $50 for eliminating the first wrong answer, $100 for eliminating the second, and $300 for eliminating all three. If they chose the answer that was correct, they lost control of the board to their opponents. In round two, teams chose trivia-related categories and tried to answer questions for $50.

The winning team played the trivia ladder for a possible $10,000. The members of the team then played against their own teammates. Four possible answers were shown and a player could play, or pass the first question to his or her partners. A correct answer was worth $1,000. If any of the three players survived the first part of the bonus game, they could try to answer one more trivia question for a possible $10,000.

During its six-month run, some of the trivia games during the main portion of the show were changed.

TRIVIAL PURSUIT

premiere: June 7, 1993   *packager:* Martindale-Hillier Enterprises/The Family Channel   *broadcast history:* Family Channel (cable) June 7, 1993–July 14, 1995   *host:* Wink Martindale   *announcer:* Randy West   *executive producers:* Wink Martindale, Bill Hillier   *producers:* Peter Berlin, Rob Fiedler   *director:* Rob Fiedler   *set designer:* Scott Storey *music:* Ed Lojeski   *origination:* Oakridge Studios, Glendale

"Trivial Pursuit," the world-famous board game that sold more than thirty million copies since it was introduced in 1982, finally made it to the small screen as the first interactive game show, when it premiered as part of The Family Channel's game show block on June 7, 1993.

The three-hour block included two hours of vintage shows (LET'S MAKE A DEAL, SPLIT SECOND, and "The $100,000 Name That Tune" [see NAME THAT TUNE]), ten "Trivial Pursuit" playbreaks per day, and a one-hour studio version in which twelve players competed against each other to answer multiple choice questions. The top-three scoring players in the first half of the show, determined by their speed in selecting right answers, moved on to a half-hour standard game show format to compete for $1,000 and a grand prize.

The object of the game was to be the first to light up all six color wedges (categories) on a game board, with two correct answers needed to complete a color. The players picked a category and if they missed, their opponents got a chance to win the point. Categories played were sports and leisure, art and literature, geography, history, science, and entertainment.

In round one, six categories were played, with each player allowed two chances at the question board. Six new categories were revealed in round two along with bonus questions that could earn a player cash and an additional wedge on the game board. The third round was a toss-up question round where all three players competed against each other to try to complete their game boards. The first player to collect all twelve wedges won the game and $500.

The winning player played a bonus round and tried to answer one question from each of the six categories in forty-five seconds, for a bonus prize.

Wink Martindale appears to be quite pleased about hosting television's first hour-long interactive game show.

Home viewers with touch-tone telephones could participate in the daily playbreaks by calling a special number. A series of multiple choice questions were flashed on the TV screen and the top-ten scorers of the day, as determined by accuracy of answers and speed, competed in the daily "Playoff" at the end of the daily game show block.

The Family Channel celebrated New Year's Day 1994 with a day-long marathon of "Trivial Pursuit" playbreaks and it was the first game show marathon in TV history.

"Trivial Pursuit: The Interactive Game" aired for the last time on March 4, 1994 and was replaced the following Monday with two new interactive games, SHUFFLE and BOGGLE. The studio version of "Trivial Pursuit" continued as part of the Family Channel's game show block.

Did you know . . . announcer Randy West got interested in game show announcing when he first met the legendary Johnny Olson on the classic WHAT'S MY LINE? back in 1969? West was also on several game shows as a contestant before becoming an announcer. Those included ALL STAR BLITZ, HIT MAN (the last episode), PRESS YOUR LUCK, TO TELL THE TRUTH, and SWEETHEARTS.

TRUMP CARD

premiere: September 10, 1990 *packager:* Fiedler-Berlin Productions/Createl Ltd. *broadcast history:* Syndicated September 10, 1990–September 6, 1991 *host:* Jimmy Cefalo *hostess:* Debi Massey *announcer:* Chuck Reilly *creator:* Terry Mardell *producers:* Rob Fiedler, Peter Berlin *director:* Bill Carruthers *set designer:* Tony Sabatino *origination:* Trump Castle Hotel and Casino, Atlantic City

Celebrated entrepreneur Donald Trump lent his name to this syndicated game show that was taped at Trump Castle and Casino in Atlantic City, New Jersey.

In "Trump Card" three contestants answered questions and each correct response enabled a player to cover up a space on a bingo-like playing card. The first player to cover all fifteen spaces won the game.

In round one, players tried to cover the four corner boxes on their game cards by answering questions from four possible categories. The player giving the correct answer selected the next category and the first player to cover his or her corner boxes won $750.

Players competed for $1,500 in round two by trying to be the first to cover the five boxes across the center line of their game board. Incorrect responses blocked the players from the next question. Each player also had a trump card which could be used to stop the progress of an opposing player. That player then had to answer a question to remove the trump card.

In the final round all three players answered more questions and the first player to complete his or her card won the game and $3,000.

The winning contestant played a bonus round for a $10,000 jackpot. Within forty-five seconds, this person had to complete a row on a game board of five rows of five. The

"Truth or Consequences" creator and original host Ralph Edwards helps current host Bob Barker hold a twenty-fifth birthday banner back in 1965.

player could move up, down, or diagonally. Missing a question meant that he or she had to start another row.

TRUTH OR CONSEQUENCES

premiere: September 7, 1950 *packager:* Ralph Edwards Productions *broadcast history:* CBS primetime September 7, 1950–May 31, 1951; NBC primetime May 18, 1954–September 28, 1956; NBC daytime December 31, 1956–September 25, 1959; NBC primetime December 13, 1957–June 6, 1958; NBC daytime October 26, 1959–September 24, 1965; Syndicated September 19, 1966–September 1975; Syndicated September 19, 1977–September 1978; Syndicated September 14, 1987–February 26, 1988
1950–1951 version
host: Ralph Edwards *announcer:* Frank Barton *producer:* Ralph Edwards *director:* Phil Davis *music director:* Buddy Cole *origination:* Los Angeles
1954–1956 version
host: Jack Bailey *announcers:* Jerry Lawrence, Ken Carpenter *producer:* Ed Bailey *director:* Stuart Phelps *music director:* Buddy Cole *origination:* NBC Studio D, Hollywood
1956–1965 daytime version
host: Bob Barker *assistant:* Dresser Dahlstead *announcer:* Charles Lyon *producer:* Ed Bailey *director:* Bob Lehman *set designer:* John Shrum *music director:* Don Isham

theme: "Merrily We Roll Along" *origination:* NBC Studio D, Hollywood NBC Studio 1, Burbank
1957–1958 primetime version
host: Steve Dunne *announcer:* Wendell Niles *producers:* Ed Bailey, Bill Burch *director:* Stuart Phelps *music director:* Jack Fasinato *origination:* NBC studios, Hollywood
1966–1975 version
host: Bob Barker *assistant:* Dresser Dahlstead *announcer:* Charles Lyon *producer:* Ed Bailey *directors:* Jack Scott, Bill Chesnut *set designers:* Cyril Jones, Anthony Sabatino *music:* Hal Hidey *theme:* "Stop Gap" by Wilfred Burns *origination:* KTTV Television Studios, Hollywood
1977–1978 version
host: Bob Hilton *announcer:* John Harlan *executive producers:* Ralph Edwards, Ed Bailey, Jon Ross, Bruce Belland *producers:* George Vosburgh, Mark Maxwell-Smith *set designers:* Anthony Sabatino, William H. Harris *music:* Hal Hidey *theme:* Bruce Belland, Gary Edwards, Gary Mandell *origination:* KTTV Television Studios, Hollywood
1987–1988 version
host: Larry Anderson *hostess:* Hillary Safire *costar:* Murray Langston *announcer:* Ted Zigler *executive producers:* Ralph Edwards, Stu Billett, Chris Bearde, Jay Feldman *producers:* Bianca Pino, Molly Miles, Jeffrey Barron, Don Segall *director:* Joe Carolei *set designers:* Anthony Sabatino, William H. Harris *music:* Don Felder *origination:* Hollywood Center Studios

Television's long-running comedy-stunt game, "Truth or Consequences," made its first appearance on TV on July 1, 1941, the day commercial television began operating. The broadcast, seen on New York station WNBT, featured creator-host Ralph Edwards.

"Truth or Consequences" began as a radio series on March 23, 1940 with Edwards as host. The show began a network television run on CBS in the fall of 1950 with Ralph Edwards again hosting the first year. During its seventeen-year run on radio, which lasted until August 30, 1957, "Truth or Consequences" became one of the most popular audience participation shows.

"Truth or Consequences" was derived from the parlor games "Fine or Superfine" and "Forfeits." Players who gave incorrect answers to ridiculous questions or who failed to answer before "Beulah the Buzzer" sounded had to pay the consequences by completing an often humorous or embarrassing stunt. Frequently mixed in with the stunts were reunions of friends and relatives long separated.

The more serious side of "Truth or Consequences" had begun on radio during World War II when the show won the Eisenhower Award for selling the most war bonds. A "Mrs. Hush" contest brought in over $800,000 for the March of Dimes and the "Walking Man" contest resulted in over $1,600,000 in contributions to the fight against heart disease. ("Mrs. Hush" was actress Clara Bow and the "Walking Man" was Jack Benny.)

The Ralph Edwards–hosted edition of "Truth or Consequences" ran only one season, but the show returned for two other primetime runs, one in 1954 with QUEEN FOR A DAY host

Jack Bailey as emcee and another in 1957 with Steve Dunne hosting.

The best-remembered television version of ''Truth or Consequences'' was the daytime edition that introduced radio personality Bob Barker to a national audience. Just prior to the show's debut in December 1956, producer Ralph Edwards heard Barker on Burbank radio station KWIK and invited him to audition for the job. Barker remained as host of ''Truth or Consequences'' for the next nineteen years. Assisting Barker on many of the stunts were announcer Charles Lyon and assistant Dresser Dahlstead.

Two later versions of ''Truth or Consequences'' did not enjoy long runs. During the 1977–1978 season longtime TV announcer Bob Hilton took the helm and comedian Larry Anderson emceed a 1987–1988 version. Anderson was joined by hostess Hillary Safire, daughter of LET'S MAKE A DEAL model Carol Merrill.

Did you know . . . Ralph Edwards graduated from the University of California at Berkeley with a B.A. in English? During the 1930s he was a staff announcer for CBS and once roomed with ''Your Hit Parade'' announcer Andre Baruch and baseball broadcaster Mel Allen.

''Truth or Consequences'' is the only game show to have a town in the United States named after it. On March 31, 1950 the town of Hot Springs, New Mexico officially changed its name to Truth or Consequences, New Mexico. To celebrate the tenth anniversary of the radio show, host Ralph Edwards asked, on air, for a town that was willing to change its name to honor the program. In return, ''Truth or Consequences'' would originate its tenth anniversary show from that city. The city of Hot Springs voted 1,294 to 295 to change its name. On April 1, 1950, the first ''Truth or Consequences Fiesta'' was staged, bringing approximately 10,000 people to the town. The annual fiesta continues to be celebrated the first weekend in May.

TRY AND DO IT

premiere: July 4, 1948 *broadcast history:* NBC primetime July 4, 1948–September 5, 1948 *host:* Jack Bright *assistant:* Eloise McElhone *announcer:* Ken Roberts *producer:* Herb Leder *music:* Thomas Lender Jones Brass Band *origination:* NBC Studio 8G, New York

''Try and Do It,'' an audience participation show seen during the summer of 1948, featured contestants selected from the studio audience who tried to perform stunts in a picnic ground setting. Home viewers submitted ideas for stunts and received prizes if their stunts were used on the program.

Eloise McElhorne joined the show as cohost on August 8. Sponsored by Maxwell House coffee, ''Try and Do It'' was seen on the seven-station NBC network (New York; Washington, D.C.; Philadelphia; Schenectady; Baltimore; Boston; and Richmond).

TURN IT UP!

premiere: June 30, 1990 *packager:* Chauncey Street Productions *broadcast history:* MTV (cable) June 30, 1990–December 7, 1990 *host:* Jordan Brady *announcer:* Stuffy Shmitt *creators:* Alan Goodman, Albie Hecht, Lauren Corrao *producers:* Albie Hecht, Shirley Abraham *director:* Dana Calderwood *set designer:* Susan Bolles *music producer:* Rob Stevens for One Stone Productions *music:* Stuffy Shmitt and the Zombo Combo *origination:* New York

Testing a player's knowledge of rock and roll music was the object of ''Turn It Up!'', the second game show series broadcast by MTV (REMOTE CONTROL was the first). Three players selected questions worth either ten, twenty, or thirty points from four possible categories in round one. The player with the last correct answer controlled the next choice from the board.

In round two all three contestants challenged the ''Wall of Video,'' which showed audio and video clips to illustrate the clues for all the questions in the four categories. Only the two top-scoring players in this round moved to the final round.

The final round, called ''Add-a-Track,'' featured a song played by only one musical instrument. Every five seconds (within a thirty-second time period) another instrument was added to the song until one player correctly identified the song. Four songs were played in this round, with the first, worth twenty-five points and a prize; the second, fifty points; the third, seventy-five points; and the final song, one hundred points. If either player guessed all four songs correctly he or she won a bonus prize.

TWENTY-ONE

premiere: September 12, 1956 *packager:* Jack Barry and Dan Enright Productions *broadcast history:* NBC primetime September 12, 1956–October 16, 1958 *host:* Jack Barry *substitute host:* Monty Hall (summer 1958) *hostesses:* Arlene and Ardell Terry, Terry Ford and Marlene Manners *announcer:* Bill McCord *executive producers:* Robert Noah, Joe Cates *producers:* Howard Merrill, Al Freedman *directors:* Charles Dubin, Al Freedman *set designer:* Jack Landau *music director:* Paul Taubman *origination:* NBC Studio 6B, New York

On ''Twenty-One,'' two contestants, each in an isolation booth, competed in a quiz show to test their knowledge with an unlimited cash prize possible. The object of the game was to score twenty-one points by answering general knowledge questions. The degree of difficulty of the questions determined the point value, from one to eleven. Each round was based on a different category, with each player choosing the amount of points he or she wished to play for. The winner of the game received $500 for each point difference between the scores. If the game ended in a tie, the point value was doubled in the next game. After two rounds of questions, either player who thought that he or she was winning, could stop the game. Winners played until they were defeated.

The first champ was Tom Hendrick, a Brooklyn longshoreman who won $10,500. On November 28, 1956, college professor Charles Van Doren made his first appearance on ''Twenty-One.'' He became a celebrity overnight and in his four months on the show won $129,000 before losing to Vivian Nearing on March 11, 1957.

A historic moment in game show history: Charles Van Doren and Herbert Stempel square off for the classic competition whose outcome was already predetermined!

The biggest winner on "Twenty-One" was Elfrida Von Nardoff who won $220,500 in the spring of 1958. "Twenty-One" was dropped by NBC in the fall of 1958 amid charges that the program was fixed. Van Doren later admitted that he had been given the answers to questions used on the show.

Did you know . . . "Twenty-One" host Jack Barry met partner Dan Enright in 1946 at radio station WOR New York? Barry was an announcer for the station and Enright an audio engineer. In 1947 they teamed to produce the children's series "Juvenile Jury." They went on to produce "Winky Dink and You," DOUGH RE MI, CONCENTRATION, and "The Joe DiMaggio Show."

Dan Enright began his career as an audio engineer at New York radio station WNYC. In 1947 he teamed up with Jack Barry to form Barry and Enright Productions. In 1951 he reorganized Israel's radio network and returned in 1971 at the request of Prime Minister Golda Meir to analyze Israel's television network. In 1990 he won an Emmy Award for "Caroline?", a CBS Hallmark Hall of Fame presentation.

"Twenty-One" was featured in the 1994 motion picture *Quiz Show.* The film dramatized the congressional investigation in the late 1950s, of the rigging of "Twenty-One." The movie starred Rob Morrow as investigator Richard Goodwin, Ralph Fiennes as Charles Van Doren, and John Turturro as Herbert Stempel. Host Jack Barry was played by Christopher McDonald and producer Dan Enright by David Paymer. Robert Redford, who had appeared on PLAY YOUR HUNCH in the late 1950s, was the producer/director of *Quiz Show,* which was nominated for an Academy Award for both best picture and best director.

Were you watching when . . . coauthor Fred Wostbrock was a guest on "The Joan Rivers Show" along with famed "Twenty-One" contestant Herbert Stempel? They both discussed the quiz show scandals.

TWENTY QUESTIONS

premiere: November 26, 1949   *packager:* Fred Van De Venter Productions/Mutual Broadcasting   *broadcast history:* NBC primetime November 26, 1949–December 24, 1949; ABC primetime March 17, 1950–June 29, 1951; DuMont primetime July 6, 1951–May 30, 1954; ABC primetime July 6, 1954–May 3, 1955   *hosts:* Bill Slater, Jay Jackson   *announcers:* Frank Waldecker, John Gregson, Bob Shepard *creator:* Fred Van De Venter   *producers:* Norman Livingston, Jack Wyatt, Duane McKinney, George Elber, Gary Stevens   *directors:* Roger Bower, Dick Sandwick, Harry Coyle, Bill McCarthy   *origination:* New Amsterdam Theater, New York   *debut guests:* Herb Polesie, Florence Renard, Johnny McPhee, Fred Van De Venter, Albert E. Driscoll, governor of New Jersey

On this weekly quiz show, "Twenty Questions," based on the parlor game "Animal, Vegetable or Mineral," a panel of five were permitted to ask up to twenty questions to guess the identity of a mystery subject. Topics were sent in by home viewers who received prizes (originally Ronson pocket lighters) if their entries were used and hostess smoking sets if their subjects stumped the panel.

The panel consisted of four regulars (creator Fred Van De Venter, his wife Florence Renard, motion picture producer Herb Poleise, and teenager Johnny McPhee) and a weekly guest. At different times during the TV run, the teenage chair was also occupied by Dickie Harrison and Bobby McGuire.

Bill Slater was the original TV host with Frank Waldecker as announcer. Jay Jackson replaced Slater as emcee in 1952. Among the directors assigned to the show was Harry Coyle, who later established a notable career as a sports director for NBC for over thirty years.

Originally broadcast from studios on the roof of the New Amsterdam Theatre in New York, "Twenty Questions" was simulcast on both WOR-TV, New York and the NBC television network.

"Twenty Questions" was heard on the Mutual radio network from February 2, 1946 to March 27, 1954.

TWO FOR THE MONEY

premiere: September 30, 1952   *packager:* Mark Goodson–Bill Todman Productions   *broadcast history:* NBC primetime September 30, 1952–August 11, 1953; CBS primetime August 15, 1953–September 22, 1956; CBS primetime March 23, 1957–September 7, 1957
1952–1956 version
host: Herb Shriner   *substitute hosts:* Walter O'Keefe, Sam Levenson, Fred Allen   *announcers:* Kenny Williams, Dennis James, Ralph Paul   *judges:* Dr. Mason Gross of Rutgers University, Walter Cronkite   *producers:* Mark Goodson, Gil Fates, Ira Skutch   *directors:* Jerome Schnur, Paul Alter   *set designer:* Jac Venza   *music director:* Milton DeLugg   *origi-*

nation: International Theater, New York (1952–1953); Studio 52, CBS, New York (1953–1956)
1957 version
host: Sam Levenson   *announcers:* Ed McMahon, Carl King   *producer:* Ira Skutch   *directors:* Ira Skutch, Lloyd Gross   *set designer:* John Ward   *origination:* Biltmore Theater, New York

The quiz show, "Two for the Money," was designed more as a humorous showcase for its host, comedian Herb Shriner, than as a question-and-answer show. In round one, players received $5 for every correct answer given within fifteen seconds to questions like "Can you name fictional detectives?" Rounds two and three were played in the same way. Cash values in round two were determined by multiplying the number of right answers given in round one by $5. Round three was played in a similar way.

"Two for the Money" was originally designed for comedian Fred Allen, who had filmed the pilot in 1952, but bowed out due to illness when the show became a series. On January 9, 1954 Fred Allen finally got his chance to host "Two for the Money" when he filled in for regular host Herb Shriner.

Herb Shriner was the original host of "Two for the Money" and stayed with the show through 1956. Walter O'Keefe filled in as guest host during the summer of 1954 and Sam Levenson hosted in the summers of 1955 and 1956. When the show returned in March 1957, Sam Levenson became the new host and Ed McMahon made his network debut as the new announcer.

Did you know . . . Sam Levenson taught Spanish in the New York City high school system for ten years?

Kenny Williams was the off-camera announcer and Dennis James was the on-camera announcer for "Two for the Money." He was also the on-camera spokesman for Old Gold Cigarettes, which sponsored the show.

TWO IN LOVE

premiere: June 19, 1954   *packager:* Robert Jennings Productions   *broadcast history:* CBS primetime June 19, 1954–September 11, 1954   *host:* Bert Parks   *producer:* Herb Moss   *director:* Rai Purdy   *music director:* Alfredo Antonini   *origination:* New York

A weekly romantic quiz party for devoted couples was the idea behind "Two in Love," a summer show seen on CBS on Saturday nights in 1954. Contestants on the show were engaged, newly married, or celebrating an anniversary. They were joined onstage by relatives and friends who talked about the couple and participated in a quiz segment designed to build up a "nest egg" for the lucky pair.

Did you know . . . host Bert Parks left his native Atlanta at age nineteen to try his luck at network radio in New York? He wound up as a singer and straightman for comedian Eddie Cantor and an announcer on the Benny Goodman and Xavier Cugat radio shows.

ULTRA QUIZ

premiere: November 10, 1981 *packager:* Dick Clark Productions/20th Century Fox TV *broadcast history:* NBC primetime November 10, 1981–November 17, 1981 *hosts:* Dan Rowan and Dick Martin *assistants:* Jayne Kennedy, Richard Simmons *announcer:* John Harlan *executive producers:* Dick Clark, George Paris *producers:* Dee Baker, Chris Darley *director:* Bill Carruthers *games developer:* Bill Mitchell *set designers:* Anthony Sabatino, William H. Harris *music:* Ron Pendergast *origination:* NBC Studios, Burbank and on location

TV comedy stars Dan Rowan and Dick Martin ("Laugh-In") emceed this two-week game show special, "Ultra Quiz," based on a Japanese game show that started with 932 contestants competing in an elimination game at Dodger Stadium in Los Angeles. From there, eighty-four players moved to other contests conducted in various cities around the world (Washington, D.C.; London; Paris; Rome; and Athens). The winners in each city were flown with all expenses paid to the next destination while the losers paid their own way home. When only two players remained, they returned to NBC studios in Burbank to compete against each other for a grand prize of $100,000. The winner was Craig Powers.

Did you know . . . Dan Rowan and Dick Martin met at a party in 1952? They were discovered by columnist Walter Winchell and made their film debut in the 1957 movie *Once Upon a Horse*. Years later they would make television history with "Rowan and Martin's Laugh-In."

UP TO PAAR

premiere: July 28, 1952 *broadcast history:* NBC early evening July 28, 1952–September 26, 1952 *host:* Jack Paar *costars:* Alice Adams (scrubwoman), Bob Bye (janitor) *announcer:* Ed King *producers:* Hugh Wedlock, Howard Snyder, Bob Henry, W. A. Bennington *director:* Dick McDonough *origination:* El Capitan Theater, Hollywood

Jack Paar made his network television debut hosting "Up to Paar," seen Mondays, Wednesdays, and Fridays at 7 P.M. After interviewing members of the studio audience, Paar asked questions based on stories taken from the pages of daily newspapers. The first question was worth $5 and the following questions $10, $15, $25, and $50, with winnings paid in silver dollars.

At the end of the show all of the day's players returned for the jackpot question. The winner of that round received $100 and all of the money not won by the other players earlier in the show.

This show was also known as "I've Got News for You."

Did you know . . . Jack Paar costarred with Marilyn Monroe in the 1951 film *Love Nest*? Paar also made appearances in other films including *Variety Time*, *Easy Living*, and *Walk Softly Stranger*.

USA GONZO GAMES

premiere: October 6, 1991 *packager:* Stone-Stanley Productions *broadcast history:* USA (cable) October 6, 1991–March 29, 1992 *host:* Mark Walberg *executive producers:* David G. Stanley, Scott A. Stone *producers:* Kurt Brendlinger, Brady Connell *director:* Phil Martino *set designer:* Deborah Dawson *music:* Gary Scott *origination:* Universal Studios, Orlando

"USA Gonzo Games" was a weekly first-run cable series featuring contestants who were tested for endurance by participating in embarrasing stunts. Some of the stunts included having contestants hold fifteen-pound torches up as long as they could, and having contestants try to hold their balance while standing on a board over a pool as fire hoses sprayed water at them to knock them into the water.

Five players competed in the first round with the top-two players moving to the second round. The winner of the day received a trip.

THE VIDEO GAME

premiere: September 1984 *packager:* JM Productions *broadcast history:* Syndicated September 1984–September 1985 *host:* Greg Winfield *assistant:* Karen Lea *announcer:* Christopher Kriesa *producers:* James Caruso, Mavis Arthur *directors:* James Caruso, Phil Martino *set designer:* Tho. E. Azzari *origination:* Six Flags Magic Mountain, Valencia

"The Video Game," usually seen on Saturday mornings, featured two contestants who competed in three rounds of playing video arcade games. The first player to reach a predetermined point score won the game and played for bonus prizes in the second half of the show by answering questions related to video game characters and by playing additional games.

VIDEO POWER

premiere: October 1, 1990 *packager:* Bohbot Productions/ Saban Entertainment *broadcast history:* Syndicated October 1, 1990–September 4, 1992 *host:* Stivi Paskoski *cohost/announcer:* Terry Lee Torok *creator/executive producer:* Allen Bohbot *producer:* Terry Lee Torok *supervising producer:* Charles Cody-Leveridge *line producer:* Larry Dell *director:* Kevin S. Murray *set designers:* Lou Martin, Barry Goldberg *music:* Steve Treccase *theme:* Noam Kaniel, Shuki Levy *origination:* Telecraft Studios, New York

"Video Power" was a daily syndicated game show that previewed the latest in video games and gave four kids a chance to play arcade games.

After playing a "Stump the Host" segment by asking questions about video games, the four players competed in a video arcade game round. After two minutes of play, the two top-scoring players advanced to round two.

Round two consisted of five questions about video games with point values of either ten or twenty points. Round three was another video game challenge worth fifty points, where the two players tried to collect the highest score within sixty-one-seconds. The player with the highest score at the end of this round won the game.

The winner played a bonus game where he or she had thirty seconds to visit the "Video Game Mall" and gather up

The "Video Village" gang: announcer Kenny Williams, assistant Eileen Barton, and the "Mayor" of "Video Village," Monty Hall.

as many games as possible. If the player located a predetermined game he or she won a bonus prize.

VIDEO VILLAGE

premiere: July 1, 1960 *packager:* Merrill Heatter–Bob Quigley Productions *broadcast history:* CBS primetime July 1, 1960–September 16, 1960; CBS daytime July 11, 1960–June 15, 1962; CBS Saturday morning September 30, 1961–June 16, 1962 *hosts:* ("the mayor") Jack Narz, Red Rowe, Monty Hall *assistants:* ("assistant mayor") Joanne Copeland,

Eileen Barton   *announcer:* ("town crier") Kenny Williams *executive producer:* Robert Quigley   *producer:* Merrill Heatter   *director:* Jerome Shaw   *set designers:* Marvin Chomsky, Larry Eggleton *music director:* Sid Wayne *origination:* CBS Studio 52, New York (July 1960–March 10, 1961); CBS Studio 43, Los Angeles (March 13, 1961–June 1962)

On "Video Village," a TV studio was transformed into a game board on which two contestants moved about as "pieces" competing for merchandise and cash by answering questions and performing stunts as indicated by their positions on the board.

The players tried to move through the village as quickly as possible, with their moves determined by the roll of a die in a "chuck-a-luck" cage. The cage was turned by each contestant's "second" (a friend or relative), and the move was announced by the town crier (announcer Kenny Williams).

The village consisted of three streets. The first two, "Money Street" and "Bridge Street," had squares that offered cash, posed questions, and indicated setbacks, like "lose a turn" and "go to jail."

The third street, "The Magic Mile," offered merchandise prizes for players who landed on certain squares and bigger hazards, like "1, 2, 3, Go! 4, 5, 6, No!" and "Exchange Places." The first player to go all the way through the village won the game.

The studio audience, called the "Town Council," was sometimes called upon to give opinions on nonserious questions. If the council agreed with the player's answer, the player received a small cash prize.

Jack Narz was the original host of "Video Village." He left after two months and Red Rowe became temporary emcee on the final nighttime shows. Monty Hall became host of the daytime version on September 19, 1960.

"Video Village" moved from New York City to Television City in Los Angeles on March 13, 1961, with Eileen Barton replacing Joanne Copeland (who became Mrs. Johnny Carson).

In September 1961, a Saturday morning version for children was added to the CBS lineup. "Video Village" was the first network television game show from Merrill Heatter–Bob Quigley Productions.

Did you know . . .   "Video Village" was the first hit show for game show legend Monty Hall? After "Video Village," Monty Hall achieved his greatest success with LET'S MAKE A DEAL.

WAIT 'TIL YOU HAVE KIDS!!

premiere: September 30, 1996 *packager:* Jay Wolpert Enterprises/MTM *broadcast history:* Family Channel (cable) September 30, 1996–January 31, 1997 *host:* Tom Parks *announcer:* Burton Richardson *parenting expert:* Dr. Ellen Winters *executive producer:* Jay Wolpert *producer:* Shannon Dobson *creator/supervising producer:* Gary Jonke *line producer:* Rich de Michele *director:* Randall Neece *set designer:* Bente Christensen *origination:* Stage 1, Empire Studios, Glendale; CBS Studio Center, Studio City

"Wait 'Til You Have Kids!!" was an updated version of the 1972 game show THE PARENT GAME and featured three couples trying to match their answers with those of a licensed family therapist on the subject of parenting.

Topics on the show ranged from sibling rivalry and peer pressure to keeping secrets. For each question asked, three possible responses were shown, and each couple selected the answer that they felt was the correct solution. The show's expert, Dr. Ellen Winters, then went over the answers and explained which made the best solution.

Four questions were played on each show, with the couples working as a team on the first three questions and then as individuals on the final question. The first question was worth one point; the second, two points; the third, three points; and the fourth, four points.

The team with the most points won the game and played a bonus round in which they were given situations involving children and had to decide if it was a "Problem" or "OK." If their choices matched those of the therapist seven times in sixty seconds, they won the bonus prize.

WANNA BET?

premiere: April 21, 1993 *packager:* Four Point Entertainment/Gary H. Grossman Productions *broadcast history:* CBS primetime special April 21, 1993 *host:* Mark McEwen *cohost:* Gordon Elliott *announcer:* Mark Elliott *executive producers:* Gary H. Grossman, Ron Ziskin, Shukri Ghalayini *producer:* Mack Anderson *director:* Morris Abraham *set designer:* Bill Bohnert *music:* Ray Bunch, Mark Leggett *origination:* Studio 36, CBS Television City, Los Angeles *debut guests:* Marsha Warfield, Martin Mull, Victoria Jackson, Evander Holyfield

Tom Parks hosts "Wait 'Til You Have Kids!!" on the Family Channel.

"Wanna Bet?" had four celebrity panelists betting on whether or not guests could perform feats.

The feats attempted included changing a tire on a car going twenty-five miles per hour, supporting an armored truck on four Wedgewood tea cups, parallel parking a car while traveling at sixty miles an hour, challenging pro basketball player Kiki Vandeweghe to a free-throw contest, and identifying water from the five Great Lakes by taste and smell.

WAY OUT GAMES

premiere: September 11, 1976 **packager:** Jack Barry and Dan Enright Productions/MGM Television **broadcast history:** CBS Saturday morning September 11, 1976–September 4, 1977 **host:** Sonny Fox **assistant:** Mark Maxwell-Smith **producers:** Jack Barry, Dan Enright **director:** Richard Kline **set designer:** Anthony Sabatino **music:** Mort Lindsay **origination:** Magic Mountain Amusement Park, Valencia

Fifty-one teams, each composed of six children and each representing one of the fifty states and Puerto Rico, competed in a series of athletic games with the emphasis on humor and the unexpected on "Way Out Games."

The participants, ranging in age from twelve to fifteen, represented different schools selected with the aid of the American Alliance for Health, Physical Education, and Recreation (AAHPER).

Each week three teams competed in three events, with the first worth one point; the second, two points; and the third, three points. Events were played against the clock and the team with the best time won the points.

Events included obstacle courses and physical stunts with the winning teams moving to the championship round. The twenty-sixth show was the championship match featuring the team from Oregon representing students from Sivslaw Junior High defeating Zionsville Junior High of Indiana. Teams received trophies for their accomplishments.

The entire series was taped at Magic Mountain Amusement Park in Valencia, California, and was broadcast twice during its one season on the air.

Did you know . . . host Sonny Fox began his broadcasting career working for Allen Funt Productions ("Candid Camera") in 1947? He emceed many children's TV shows during the 1950s and 60s including "Let's Take a Trip," ON YOUR MARK, and the Emmy-nominated "Wonderama." From 1976 to 1977 he was vice president of children's programming for NBC.

Were you watching when . . . two Saturday morning children's game shows premiered on September 11, 1976? They were "Jr. Almost Anything Goes" (see ALMOST ANYTHING GOES) on ABC and WAY OUT GAMES on CBS.

WE INTERRUPT THIS WEEK

premiere: October 6, 1978 **packager:** Cadogan Productions/WNET Television **broadcast history:** PBS primetime October 6, 1978–December 29, 1978; PBS primetime February 2, 1979–March 2, 1979 **host:** Ned Sherrin **executive producer:** Tom Seldin **producer:** John Gilroy **directors:** David Heely, Jon Meredin **set designer:** Ron Baldwin **origination:** Studio 55, WNET Television, New York **debut guests:** Carrie Nye, Marshall Brickman, Richard Reeves, Barbara Howar, Robert Newman, Robin MacNeil

"We Interrupt This Week" was the first game show to be produced for the Public Broadcasting System (PBS). Two teams of three panelists competed in a tongue-in-cheek quiz based on the past week's news. Points were awarded arbitrarily to players who gave correct answers that were also inventive, charming, or provocative. The winning player of the day received a tasteless gift.

Host Ned Sherrin was producer/director of "That Was the Week That Was" for the BBC in the 1960s and appeared as the on-stage narrator of Broadway's "Side by Side by Sondheim," where he received a Tony nomination for his performance.

WE TAKE YOUR WORD

premiere: April 1, 1950 **packager:** CBS **broadcast history:** CBS primetime April 1, 1950–April 22, 1950; CBS primetime June 9, 1950–January 23, 1951; CBS primetime March 9, 1951–June 1, 1951 **hosts:** ("wordmasters") John K. M. McCaffery, John Daly **"voice of authority":** Tony Marvin **announcer:** Bill Shipley **producers:** Werner Michel, Sam Abelow, Gil Fates **directors:** Fred Rickey, Lloyd Gross **set designer:** Edward Mitchell **origination:** CBS Studio 41, Grand Central Studios, New York **debut guests:** Lyman Bryson, Abe Burrows, Jan Struthers

In this quiz show, a celebrity panel tried to guess the definitions of words submitted by home viewers. Regular panelists Lyman Bryson and Abe Burrows were joined by Jan Struthers, author of *Mrs. Miniver,* on the first telecast.

On "We Take Your Word," viewers sent in categories containing three words and the panel tried to guess the definitions and origins of the words. The viewer received a prize if his or her entry was used and $50 if the panel was stumped.

Members of the panel were fined $10 each for bad puns, tampering with the word in play, or otherwise offending the judgement of the host. A panelist had the chance to cancel the fine by correctly defining a word or answering a question posed by the "voice of authority."

"We Take Your Word" began as a series on the CBS radio network on January 29, 1950 with John K. M. McCaffery as host and Tony Marvin as the "voice of authority." They continued their roles in a four-week trial run on CBS television in April 1950. John Daly took over as host when "We Take Your Word" returned as a regular weekly series in June 1950. On March 9, 1951 McCaffery returned to host the TV version.

Did you know . . . John Daly was the host of the first "Miss America" pageant broadcast on television? Joining Daly on the 1954 broadcast was cohost Bess Myerson and Lee Ann Meriweather was crowned Miss America 1955.

WEDDING PARTY

premiere: April 1, 1968 **packager:** Ralph Andrews–Art Stark Productions **broadcast history:** ABC daytime April 1, 1968–July 12, 1968 **host:** Alan Hamel **announcer:** Chet Gould, Charlie O'Donnell **models:** Elaine Fulkerson, Mary Anne Ellis **executive producer:** Art Stark **producers:** Roy

Kammerman, Fred Tatashore *director:* Mike Garguilo *origination:* Colonial Theater, New York

Young engaged couples were the focus of this daytime game show, "Wedding Party," which presented the stories of their meetings and courtships. The couples also played games to win prizes for their new homes.

One member of a couple was taken off-stage while the other was shown three sets of three prizes. After the on-stage player selected one gift from each group, his or her mate returned and tried to guess what had been selected. Each time a correct match was made the gift was won and if the couple agreed on all three gifts, they won a honeymoon trip.

WHAT DO YOU HAVE IN COMMON?

premiere: July 1, 1954   *packager:* John Guedel Productions *broadcast history:* CBS primetime July 1, 1954–September 23, 1954   *host:* Ralph Story   *assistant:* Fran Bennett   *announcer:* Johnny Jacobs   *creator:* James Fonda   *producer:* Bill Brennan   *directors:* Seymour Berns, John Claar   *origination:* Studio 31, CBS Television City, Los Angeles

Popular Los Angeles TV personality Ralph Story made his network television debut as a game show host on the Thursday night summer replacement series "What Do You Have in Common?"

Three studio contestants had three minutes to question each other to determine what they all had in common with an unseen fourth person. The fourth person ranged from a girl who had dated the three guys, to a photographer who had taken baby pictures of the contestants. Clues to the common bond had a money value that was paid out of the potential winnings, which started at $500. The contestant who discovered the connection was the winner.

The player with the best time of the day returned at the end of the show for a chance at a $1,000 bonus. Three pictures were flashed on a screen and the player had to determine what they had in common.

Assisting host Ralph Story was Fran Bennett, who later appeared with James Dean in the movie *Giant.* Story went on to host THE $64,000 CHALLENGE in 1956 before turning to news, joining Los Angeles station KNXT as one of the original anchors of television's first hour-long newscast, "The Big News." On January 14, 1964 he became one of the pioneers of the TV magazine show format with the premiere of "Ralph Story's Los Angeles."

WHAT HAPPENED?

premiere: August 7, 1952   *packager:* Frank Cooper Productions   *broadcast history:* NBC primetime August 7, 1952–August 21, 1952   *host:* Ben Grauer   *announcer:* Jack Costello   *off-stage voice:* Wayne Howell   *producer:* Art Stark   *director:* Alan Neuman   *origination:* New Amsterdam Theater, New York   *debut guests:* Roger Price, Maureen Stapleton, Lisa Ferraday, Frank Gallop

On "What Happened?", a celebrity panel tried to determine in what news event a guest contestant had recently participated. The panelists asked questions that solicited "yes" or "no" answers from the contestants. Each time the contestant replied with a no answer, he or she received $5

and filled in one letter of the show's title. The player who filled in all the letters stumped the panel and won $60.

Regular panelists included Lisa Ferraday, "Lights Out" announcer Frank Gallop, Roger Price, and actress Maureen Stapleton. Scheduled for only a three-week run on Thursday nights, the show was known as "Guess What Happened?" during its premiere broadcast.

WHAT IN THE WORLD?

premiere: October 7, 1951   *packager:* Charles Vanda Productions/WCAU-TV   *broadcast history:* CBS weekends October 7, 1951–April 2, 1955   *hosts:* Dr. Froelich Rainey, Dr. Alfred Kidder   *announcer:* Barry Cassell   *producer:* Robert Forrest   *directors:* Joseph Tinney Jr., Glenn Bernard   *origination:* WCAU-TV, Philadelphia

A panel of three professors tried to identify works of art from the University of Pennsylvania Museum on "What in the World?" Panelists were also asked to describe the origins and original uses of the works. Dr. Froelich Rainey, director of the museum, and Dr. Alfred Kidder alternated as emcees of this live show.

The show was seen in various time periods on both Saturday and Sunday afternoons on CBS.

Regular panelists on the show included Dr. Schuyler Cammann, Dr. Carleton Coon, and Dr. Wilton Krogman.

WHAT WOULD YOU DO?

premiere: August 31, 1991   *packager:* Woody Fraser Productions/Reeves Entertainment   *broadcast history:* Nickelodeon (cable) August 31, 1991–   *host:* Marc Summers   *assistant:* Robin Marrella   *executive producers:* Woody Fraser, Andy Bamberger, Bo Kaprall   *producers:* Bonnie Karrin, Dave Garrison, Margaret Weber, Tim Street   *directors:* Aaron B. Coleman, Milton Lage   *set designers:* Byron Taylor, David Ellis   *theme:* Wendy Fraser   *music:* Allan Ett, Terry Esau   *origination:* Universal Studios, Orlando

Selected members of the studio audience were asked to participate in sometimes messy or embrassing stunts and demonstrations in "What Would You Do?", an audience participation show.

Some of the sample stunts included having two twelve-year-olds dressed in sumo wrestling suits, trying to push each other out of a ring, a father and his daughter being taught how to belly dance by a professional dancer, and two teams of parents and their children competing in a contest to see who could knock an object off the top of a straw hat worn by the parents. The kids used tubes that squirted pie filling at the parents.

Emcee Marc Summers was also the host of the long-running DOUBLE DARE and FAMILY DOUBLE DARE shows for Nickelodeon.

WHAT'S GOING ON?

premiere: November 28, 1954   *packager:* Mark Goodson–Bill Todman Productions   *broadcast history:* ABC primetime November 28, 1954–December 26, 1954   *host:* Lee Bowman   *announcer:* Jimmy Blaine   *commercials:* Midge Ware (for Revlon)   *executive producer:* Allan Sherman *assistant producer:* Frank Wayne   *program supervisor:* Barbara Olson   *director:* Jerome Schnur   *origination:* Elysee Theater, New York   *debut guests:* Kitty Carlisle, Hy Gardner, Jayne Meadows, Cliff Norton, Susan Oakland, Gene Raymond

A panel of three celebrities in the studio of "What's Going On?" tried to guess where other celebrities were and what they were doing at remote locations, in this short-lived series. Each member of the studio panel could ask questions requiring a "yes" or "no" answer of the celebrity on location.

Regular panelists included Kitty Carlisle, Hy Gardner, Audrey Meadows, Jayne Meadows, Cliff Norton, Susan Oakland, and Gene Raymond.

Some examples included Gene Raymond washing windows eighty-six stories up on the outside of the Empire State Building; Audrey Meadows burning $1 million in worn-out dollar bills at the Federal Reserve Bank in Chicago; and Hy Gardner eating a Chinese dinner with chopsticks in Chinatown, New York City.

Did you know . . .   host Lee Bowman played the title role in the TV series "The Adventures of Ellery Queen" in the early 1950s?

WHAT'S IN A WORD?

premiere: July 22, 1954   *packager:* Peter Arnell Productions   *broadcast history:* CBS primetime July 22, 1954–September 9, 1954   *host:* Clifton Fadiman   *announcer:* Bern Bennett   *producer:* Peter Arnell   *director:* Lamar Caselli   *origination:* New York   *debut guests:* Faye Emerson, Mike Wallace, Audrey Meadows, Jim Moran, Charles Coburn

"What's in a Word?" was a word association game in which a celebrity panel participated by trying to guess simple rhymes made up by studio contestants. The panel members were given one-word clues until they came up with the nouns in the rhymes (example: fickle pickle). Contestants received $5 for each clue given to the panel and another $5 for each wrong guess by the panel.

Clifton Fadiman, a Phi Beta Kappa from Columbia University, served as host.

"What's in a Word?" was seen Thursday nights as a summer replacement for the comedy series "Meet Mr. McNutley."

WHAT'S IT FOR?

premiere: October 12, 1957   *packager:* Entertainment Productions Inc.   *broadcast history:* NBC primetime October 12, 1957–January 4, 1958   *host:* Hal March   *announcer:* Wayne Howell   *creator:* Merrill Heatter   *producers:* Ed Jurist, Ronald Dubin   *director:* Seymour Robbie   *set designer:* Eddie Gilbert   *origination:* Studio 6A, NBC, New York   *debut guests:* Betsy Palmer, Abe Burrows, Cornelia Otis Skinner, Hans Conreid

A celebrity panel attempted to guess the use of an unusual invention by asking the inventor questions on "What's It For?" Each player was given one minute to cross-examine the guest. If the panel could not come up with the correct

answer, the inventor received $100. If the panel guessed correctly, the inventor received $50.

The debut week panel tried to guess such inventions as a "pair of half slacks," "a fruit picker's jacket," and "a janitor's alarm bed."

Emcee Hal March hosted both "What's It For?" on Saturday nights for NBC and THE $64,000 QUESTION on Tuesday nights for CBS at the same time.

Did you know . . .   Hal March appeared in the films *It's Always Fair Weather* and *The Eddie Cantor Story?*

WHAT'S MY LINE?

premiere: February 2, 1950   *packager:* Mark Goodson–Bill Todman Productions   *broadcast history:* CBS primetime February 2, 1950–September 3, 1967; Syndicated September 9, 1968–September 1975; ABC late night May 28, 1975 (special)

1950–1967 version

host: John Daly   *substitute hosts:* Bennett Cerf, Eamonn Andrews, Clifton Fadiman   *announcers:* Lee Vines, Bern Bennett, John Briggs, Dick Stark, Hal Simms, Jack Clark, Johnny Olson, Ralph Paul   *producers:* Gil Fates, Bob Bach   *directors:* Paul Monroe, Franklin Heller, Frank Satenstein   *set designers:* Manuel Essman, John Ward, Robert Rowe Paddock, Willard Levitas   *closing theme:* "Roller Coaster" by Milton DeLugg and Lou Burch   *origination:* Grand Central Studios, New York; Studios 52, 59, and 50, CBS, New York   *debut panelists:* Louis Untermeyer, Dorothy Kilgallen, Harold Hoffman, Dr. Richard Hoffman, and—first mystery guest—Phil Rizzuto

1968–1975 version

hosts: Wally Bruner, Larry Blyden   *announcers:* Johnny Olson, Chet Gould, Wayne Howell, Dennis Wholey, Bob Williams, Jack Haskell   *producer:* Gil Fates   *director:* Lloyd Gross   *set designers:* Ron Baldwin, Ted Cooper   *music:* Score Productions   *origination:* Ed Sullivan Theater, New York (1968–1971); NBC Studios 8H and 6A, New York (1971–1975)

"What's My Line?" was network television's longest-running primetime game show, with a broadcast run of over seventeen-and-one-half years. For seventeen of those years the show aired Sunday nights at 10:30 P.M. The game, which remained unchanged throughout its long run, consisted of four panelists trying to guess either the unusual occupation of a guest contestant or a product associated with them.

A panel member asked questions and the guest would answer either yes or no. The panelist remained in control of the questioning until he or she received a no answer. The next member of the panel could then ask questions. A contestant received $5 for each no answer and ten no's ended the game in favor of the contestant. In the last round of the evening, the panelists put on blindfolds and tried to guess the identity of a celebrity mystery guest. (On the first broadcast, model Madeline Tyler made her only appearance passing out the blindfolds.) The mystery guest would frequently disguise his or her voice to avoid identification. During the first years

These celebrities were also mystery guests on "What's My Line?": Desi Arnaz, Lucille Ball, Warren Beatty, Jack Benny, Marlon Brando, George Burns and Gracie Allen, James Cagney, Jimmy Carter, Montgomery Clift, Ty Cobb, Nat King Cole, Joan Collins, Sean Connery, Gary Cooper, Joan Crawford, Salvador Dali, Bobby Darin, Bette Davis, Sammy Davis Jr., Cecil B. DeMille, Phyllis Diller, Walt Disney, Howdy Doody, Clint Eastwood, Errol Flynn, Henry Fonda, Jane Fonda, Gerald Ford, Judy Garland, Jackie Gleason, Benny Goodman, Frank Gorshin, Hugh Hefner, Charlton Heston, Alfred Hitchcock, Dustin Hoffman, Bob Hope, Boris Karloff, Lassie, Jack Lemmon, Jerry Lewis, Liberace, Sophia Loren, Jayne Mansfield, Mickey Mantle, Ann-Margaret, Dean Martin, Steve McQueen, Roger Moore, Edward R. Murrow, Paul Newman, Ronald Reagan, Burt Reynolds, Joan Rivers, Norman Rockwell, Richard Rogers and Oscar Hammerstein II, Eleanor Roosevelt, Soupy Sales, Frank Sinatra, Jimmy Stewart, Barbra Streisand, Ed Sullivan, Diana Ross and the Supremes, Elizabeth Taylor, Tiny Tim, Barbara Walters, John Wayne, Raquel Welch, Betty White, Walter Winchell, Natalie Wood, and Frank Zappa.

Among the celebrities who made guest appearances as panelists were Woody Allen, Red Barber, Johnny Carson, Errol Flynn, Ernie Kovacs, Jerry Lewis, Groucho Marx, Ozzie Nelson, Jack Paar, William Shatner, Orson Welles, and Jonathan Winters.

WHAT'S MY NAME?

premiere: September 18, 1950 *packager:* Louis Cowan Productions *broadcast history:* NBC primetime September 18, 1950–June 29, 1953 *hosts:* Paul Winchell with "Jerry Mahoney" and "Knucklehead Smiff" *costars:* Patricia Bright, Sid Raymond *announcers:* Jimmy Blaine, Ted Brown, Norman Brokenshire *creator:* Ed Byron *executive producer:* Sherman Marks *producers:* Louis Cowan, Ed Byron *directors:* Sidney Smith, Harold Eisenstein *set designers:* Mabel Buell, Lee Aronson, Perry Watkins *music directors:* John Gart, Milton DeLugg *origination:* International Theater, New York

"What's My Name?" was the quiz segment of the "Paul Winchell–Jerry Mahoney Show," a popular variety show seen from 1950 to 1954. The quiz segment was shown once a week for the first three seasons.

Contestants, selected from the studio audience, tried to identify famous people from clues in sketches performed by Paul, his dummies, and weekly guest stars. If the player guessed correctly, they won a $100 savings bond. If they were incorrect, they received a $25 savings bond, and the $100 bond was added to the home viewer jackpot.

Each week a home viewer was called after a sketch was performed and given a chance to identify the famous person and win the jackpot.

The show was also known as "The Speidel Show" for its sponsor, Speidel watches and watchbands.

Did you know . . . Paul Winchell was the voice of Tigger in Disney's "Winnie the Pooh," as well as Dick Dastardly on "The Wacky Racers."

WHAT'S THE STORY?

premiere: July 25, 1951 *packager:* DuMont Television *broadcast history:* DuMont primetime July 25, 1951–September 23, 1955 *hosts:* Walter Raney, Walter Kiernan, Al Capp, John K. M. McCaffery *announcer:* Fred Scott *producers:* James Caddigan, David Lowe, Paul Rosen *director:* David Lowe *origination:* New York

A panel of four news reporters tried to identify news stories with clues supplied by "reporters" who telephoned in their clues, on "What's the Story?" Viewers who submitted ideas that were used received prizes if their stories stumped the panel.

Among the first panelists to appear on the show were Bob Cooke of the New York *Herald Tribune,* Betty Forsling of *Newsweek* magazine, Aileen Keller of the New York *World Telegram,* and Nancy Thompson of *Look* magazine.

DuMont newscaster Walter Raney was the original host when "What's the Story?" premiered in July 1951. He was replaced by Walter Kiernan in September 1951. Cartoonist Al Capp took over as emcee on June 27, 1953 and later in 1953, John K. M. McCaffery replaced him.

In its four-year run, "What's the Story?" aired in eleven different time slots and was the last entertainment series to go off the DuMont network when the network folded in September 1955.

Did you know . . . "What's the Story?" announcer Fred Scott joined the DuMont network as a staff announcer in 1948? He was heard as the announcer on "Captain Video" and after the network folded he continued with New York flagship station WNEW-TV.

WHAT'S THIS SONG?

premiere: October 26, 1964 *packager:* Stuart Phelps–Jack Reeves–Jesse Martin Productions *broadcast history:* NBC daytime October 26, 1964–September 24, 1965 *host:* Wink Martindale *announcer:* Steve Dunne *producer/director:* Stuart Phelps *set designers:* Wes Cook, John Shrum *music director:* Bobby Hammack *origination:* NBC Studio 3, Burbank *debut guests:* Beverly Garland, Lorne Greene

"What's This Song?" began in the 1930s as a radio show with the title "What's the Name of That Song?" The show moved to television in 1949, with Bill Gwinn as host, airing on several Los Angeles stations during a ten-year run.

In February 1964, the show was revived by Los Angeles TV station KTLA and eight months later NBC picked it up for their daytime schedule to replace WORD FOR WORD.

Radio personality Wink Martindale (using the name "Win Martindale") made his debut as a game show host with this program.

Two teams, each composed of a celebrity guest and a studio contestant, attempted to identify songs. If a team guessed correctly, they earned twenty points and an opportunity to collect twenty more points by singing the first four opening bars. If the opposing team thought the lyrics were sung incorrectly they could challenge and if correct could win the points by singing the correct lyrics. The first team to collect one hundred points won the game.

Wink Martindale, who was known as Win Martindale in 1964 when he hosted his very first network game show, "What's This Song?" for NBC.

The winning team played the bonus round, called the "Minute Medley," where they attempted to guess ten songs in sixty seconds, earning $20 for each correct response.

Celebrities who tried singing on the show included Walter Brennan, Dick Clark, Andy Devine, Angie Dickinson, Phyllis Diller, Michael Landon, Ryan O'Neal, and Betty White.

"What's This Song?" was revived in 1968 as WIN WITH THE STARS, with Allen Ludden as host.

Did you know . . . Wink Martindale sang on camera in the 1958 motion picture *Let's Rock?* Other musical performers featured in the film were Paul Anka, Danny and the Juniors, Roy Hamilton, Della Reese, and The Royal Teens. The movie starred Julius LaRosa, Phyllis Newman, and Conrad Janis.

In 1959 Wink Martindale had a top-ten hit record with the song "Deck of Cards," which he introduced on "The Ed Sullivan Show."

WHAT'S YOUR BID

premiere: February 14, 1953 *packager:* RKR Productions/ Charles Antell Productions *broadcast history:* ABC primetime February 14, 1953–April 18, 1953; DuMont primetime May 3, 1953–June 29, 1953 *host (auctioneer):* Liberal Bill *assistants:* Robert Alda, John Reed King *model:* Roslyn Woods *announcer:* Dick Shepard *producers:* Frank Bunetta, Leonard Rosen, Charles Kasher *directors:* Frank Bunetta, Robert Doyle, Sonny Diskin *set designers:* James Trittipo, Norman Davidson *origination:* New York

The excitement of an auction was staged weekly on this live television show called "What's Your Bid." Members of the studio audience used their own money to bid for merchandise items, with all the proceeds donated to the charity of the week. Hosting the proceedings was auctioneer Liberal Bill, who frequently added additional merchandise to the original items in the bid.

A weekly feature on the show also enabled home viewers to participate in a special auction with show announcers John Reed King and Dick Shepard relaying the bids to the host.

The show was sponsored by Charles Antell Inc., makers of Formula 9 and Liquid Creme shampoo, and all participants received samples of the products.

WHEEL OF FORTUNE

premiere: October 3, 1952 *packager:* Peter Arnell Productions *broadcast history:* CBS daytime October 3, 1952–December 25, 1953; CBS primetime July 7, 1953–September 15, 1953 *host:* Todd Russell *model:* Betsy Palmer *announcer:* Hal Simms *producer:* Peter Arnell *directors:* Lloyd Gross, Frances Buss, Judd Whiting *set designer:* John Ward *music director:* Milton Kaye *origination:* CBS Studio 50, New York

To be eligible as a contestant on this show, a person must have done a good deed. Heroes, good Samaritans, and other benefactors received rewards for outstanding good deeds and they, along with the people they helped, appeared as guests. The subject who had been done a favor played for the good Samaritan. A wheel was spun to determine a cash amount to play for ($30 to $1,000) and the number of questions needed to be answered correctly (one, two, or three) to win that amount. The beneficiary received a gold watch for his or her appearance.

Host Todd Russell had emceed radio's STRIKE IT RICH and DOUBLE OR NOTHING as well as the kids' show "Rootie Kazootie" for television.

WHEEL OF FORTUNE

premiere: January 6, 1975 *packager:* Merv Griffin Productions *broadcast history:* NBC daytime January 6, 1975–June 30, 1989; Syndicated September 19, 1983– ; CBS daytime July 17, 1989–January 11, 1991; NBC daytime January 14, 1991–September 20, 1991 *hosts:* Chuck Woolery, Pat Sajak, Rolf Benirschke, Bob Goen *substitute host:* Alex Trebek *hostesses:* Susan Stafford, Vanna White *substitute hostesses:* Summer Bartholomew, Cynthia Washington, Arte Johnson, Vicky McCarty, Tricia Gist *announcers:* Charlie O'Donnell, Don Morrow, Jack Clark, Johnny Gilbert, M. G. Kelly, Don Pardo *producers:* John Rhinehart, Nancy Jones, Harry Friedman *directors:* Jeff Goldstein, Dick Carson *set designers:* Ed Flesh, Dick Stiles *theme song:* "Changing Keys" by Merv Griffin *origination:* NBC Studio 4, Burbank (1975–1989); Studio 33, CBS Television City, Los Angeles (1989–1995); Stage 11, Sony Studios, Culver City (1995–)

One of the most popular game shows in television history, "Wheel of Fortune" was based on the parlor game hangman. "Wheel" was a successful daytime game show on NBC in the 1970s. It exploded in popularity in the 80s with the introduction of a syndicated version in September 1983. Host

The original team for "Wheel of Fortune," Susan Stafford and emcee Chuck Woolery.

Pat Sajak had been added in December 1981 (replacing original host Chuck Woolery) and hostess Vanna White had been added on December 13, 1982 (replacing Susan Stafford).

"Wheel of Fortune," which had premiered on only fifty-nine stations in the fall of 1983, replaced FAMILY FEUD as the number-one syndicated show by 1984 and remained in that spot for over ten years.

The game consisted of three contestants, who, in turn, spun a giant wheel containing various cash amounts and penalty segments (bankrupt, lose a turn). The contestant who spun a cash amount guessed a consonant to see if it would fill a blank in a word puzzle, which had to be completed in order to win the round. Players retained control of the wheel as long as they successfully filled in the blanks. A player could purchase a vowel for $250 to help solve the puzzle.

Originally, the player who correctly guessed the puzzle used his or her earnings to buy merchandise, but that was changed to players building a cash bank.

The top money winner of the day played a bonus round where he or she attempted to win a jackpot prize by guessing a phrase or a name within ten seconds. They were given five consonants (R, S, T, L, N) and one vowel (E) and got to select an additional three consonants and another vowel. The bo-

nus game was not added to the show until December 28, 1981.

Chuck Woolery and Susan Stafford were the original host and hostess when "Wheel of Fortune" premiered on January 6, 1975. Alex Trebek filled in as host for a week in August 1980 and Arte Johnson appeared as "letter turner" for one game in September 1977.

Woolery was replaced by Pat Sajak on December 28, 1981. Sajak turned the network version of "Wheel of Fortune" over to ex-football star Rolf Benirschke on January 10, 1989. When the show moved to CBS on July 17, 1989, Bob Goen became the new host.

Susan Stafford left on October 22, 1982, and Summer Bartholomew filled in as hostess for three weeks, followed by Vicky McCarty and Vanna White. On December 13, 1982, Vanna became the new permanent hostess.

Charlie O'Donnell was the original announcer when the show started in 1975. He was followed by Jack Clark in 1982. O'Donnell returned after the death of Clark in 1988. During a visit to New York City for two weeks of shows in 1988, "Wheel of Fortune" used the legendary voice of NBC, Don Pardo, as announcer.

From December 11, 1975 to January 19, 1976, "Wheel of Fortune" was seen as a daily sixty-minute show on the NBC daytime schedule.

Pat Sajak and Vanna White have snuggled up to a career that has brought them fame and more fortune than all of the "Wheel of Fortune" contestants combined.

The original pilot for "Wheel of Fortune" was called "Shoppers Bazaar" and featured Edd Byrnes, best known as Kookie on "77 Sunset Strip," as host.

Did you know . . .   Vanna White was a contestant on THE PRICE IS RIGHT in 1980? Pat Sajak was a disc jockey with the Armed Forces Radio Network in Vietnam from 1968 to 1972 and a local weatherman for KNBC in Los Angeles in the 1970s and 1980s. Charlie O'Donnell was the announcer on "American Bandstand" from 1958 to 1968. Producer Nancy Jones was a chaperone on THE DATING GAME and director Dick Carson is the brother of "The Tonight Show" host Johnny Carson.

By 1987 Vannamania was sweeping the country, with Vanna appearing on the cover of *Newsweek* magazine, starring in the TV movie *Goddess of Love,* and writing a best-selling autobiography, *Vanna Speaks.* Vanna White played herself in the 1994 movie *Naked Gun 33⅓—The Final Insult.*

In 1992, the *Guinness Book of World Records* listed Vanna White as the world's most frequent clapper. Vanna puts her hands together for contestants some 140,000 times a season, an average of 720 times per show.

Were you watching when . . .   a puzzle actually came to life on February 2, 1998? The answer was The Oak Ridge Boys and when the contestant solved the puzzle, out walked Duane Allen, Joe Bonsall, William Lee Golden, and Richard Sterban of the Grammy Award–winning band.

On April Fool's Day, 1997, "Jeopardy!" emcee Alex Trebek filled in as host while Pat Sajak and Vanna White were contestants. Pat's wife, Leslie, took over Vanna's duties as letter-turner.

Vanna White made her debut as letter-turner/hostess on December 13, 1982. The first letter she turned was a *t* in a puzzle that turned out to be *General Hospital.*

WHEEL OF FORTUNE 2000

premiere: September 13, 1997   *packager:* Scott Sternberg Productions/Columbia Tri Star TV   *broadcast history:* CBS Saturday morning September 13, 1997–   ; Game Show Network (cable) October 11, 1997–   *host:* David Sidoni   *cohost:* "Cyber Lucy" (performed by Tanika Ray; designed by Don Shank)   *executive producer:* Scott Sternberg   *producers:* Adam Tyler, Pamela Covais   *director:* James Marcione   *production designer:* Tom Buderwitz   *music:* Dan Sawyer   *origination:* Stage 11, Sony Studios, Culver City

Three contestants, mostly seventh graders, compete in this kids' version of WHEEL OF FORTUNE. The basic game is played like the adult version, but with a few new elements added. One change is the addition of a spot on the wheel that challenges players with a physical game or stunt in the first round. Another notable change is an "animated" cohost, Cyber Lucy, who turns the letters and interacts with host David Sidoni and contestants.

The object of the game is to solve a puzzle by guessing letters that might be in the puzzle. Players spin a wheel to determine the point value of each letter they guess.

In the first round, a player who lands on the physical stunt can earn up to three possible letters by successfully completing the stunt. Other spots on the wheel include "Loser," where a player loses a turn; "Double Up," where a player who answers a question can double the points received after correctly guessing a letter in the puzzle; "Prize Box," where a player receives a small prize if the letter he or she selects is in the puzzle; and "The Creature," who takes away all of a player's points accumulated in the game.

Maximum point value on the wheel in round one is one thousand; in round two it's two thousand, and five thousand in round three. Players who solve the puzzle receive a prize, and the player with the most points when time runs out plays the bonus round.

In the bonus round, the player selects either the "A" or "B" prize, which he or she wins if the person solves the final puzzle. A category is revealed along with the letters *r, s, t, l, n,* and *e* if they appear in the puzzle. The player then selects three more consonants and one vowel and has ten seconds to solve the puzzle.

"Wheel of Fortune 2000," also known as "Wheel 2000," was first seen as part of the CBS Saturday morning schedule. Episodes were broadcast a month later on the Kids Zone schedule on Game Show Network.

WHERE IN THE WORLD IS CARMEN SANDIEGO?

premiere: September 30, 1991   *packager:* WGBH Television/QED Communications   *broadcast history:* PBS daytime September 30, 1991–October 4, 1996   *host:* Greg Lee   *"The Chief":* Lynne Thigpen   *voices:* Christine Sockol (Carmen), Doug Preis, Chris Phillips, Barry Carl, Laura Dean   *creators:* Howard Blumenthal, Dorothy Curley, Dana Calderwood   *executive producers:* Jay Rayvid, Kate Taylor   *senior producer:* Howard Blumenthal   *producers:* Ariel Schwartz, Jonathan G. Meath   *directors:* Dana Calderwood, Hugh Martin   *set designers:* James Fenhagen, Laura Brock   *music:* Rockapella (Sean Altman, tenor; Barry Carl, bass; Scott Leonard, high tenor; Elliott Kerman, baritone)   *theme:* Sean Altman, David Yazbek   *origination:* Lifetime Studios, New York

Based on the popular Broderbund computer game of the same name, "Where in the World Is Carmen Sandiego?" became the first daily game show on PBS (Public Broadcasting System). The show's contestants were junior gumshoes, ages eight to thirteen, who answered geography questions as they tried to trap Carmen Sandiego and her band of thieves.

Designed like a 1940s Hollywood-style detective agency, the show starred actress Lynne Thigpen as The Chief, who appeared on a video screen to give clues and encouragement to the players. Greg Lee was her assistant and host of the game show.

Three players competed, beginning each game with fifty points and earning ten points for each correct answer selected from multiple choice questions in the first part of the game. Five-point questions were played in a lightning round to increase the scores.

The final clue gave the players a chance to secretly wager from zero to fifty points, based on the ability to answer a final question. The top-two players moved to the final round.

In the final round, the two remaining players used a game board of fifteen locations to attempt to find "the loot," "the

Here we see members of the Acme Crimenet. That's Lynn Thigpen up front with host Greg Lee and the group Rockapella in the background on "Where in the World Is Carmen Sandiego?"

warrant," and "the crook" in that order. The players competed, in turn, calling out locations. Each time they found one item, it gave them a chance to call another location. The first player to locate all three in the correct order won the game and a chance to play for a bonus prize.

The winning player of the day was given forty-five seconds to locate eight places on a huge map that covered the studio floor and then identify them with a flashing marker. If the player accomplished this feat in the given time, Carmen Sandiego was captured and the contestant won a trip to any place he or she chose in the continental United States

Each season sixty-five new episodes were produced and shown four times in a year. Celebrity guests made appearances beginning in the second season, to give special clues to the players. Guests included model Kim Alexis, Levar Burton, former First Lady Barbara Bush, Olympic silver medal winners Kitty and Peter Carruthers, Lou Ferrigno, and Maury Povich.

Music from the show was performed by the acapella group "Rockapella" and was released on compact disc by BMG Records in 1992.

In 1993, "Where in the World Is Carmen Sandiego?" received the prestigious George Foster Peabody Award for excellence.

The Fox Television Network added an animated version of "Carmen Sandiego" to their Saturday morning schedule on February 5, 1994, under the title "Where on Earth Is Carmen Sandiego?" The cartoon series featured the voice of Rita Moreno as "Carmen," the world's most notorious thief, as she tried to avoid "Ivy" and "Zack," teenaged sleuths from the Acme Detective Agency. Clues were provided on screen for the home audience to play along with the show. The series was produced by DIC Productions.

Did you know . . . "The Chief," Lynne Thigpen was an original cast member of the Broadway production of *Godspell?* She was also nominated for a Tony Award for *Tintypes* in 1981 and was a semi-regular on the TV show "L.A. Law."

WHERE IN TIME IS CARMEN SANDIEGO?
premiere: October 7, 1996 *packager:* WGBH Boston/ WQED Pittsburgh *broadcast history:* PBS October 7, 1996– *host ("Squadron Leader"):* Kevin Shinick *"The Chief":* Lynne Thigpen *"Engine Crew":* Alaine Kashian, Jamie Gustis, John Lathan *cast:* James Greenberg, Janine LaManna, Paula Leggett Chase, Owen Taylor, Brenda Bruce *executive producers:* Kate Taylor, Jay Rayvid *senior producer:* Shirley Abraham *supervising producer:* Howard Lee *producers:* Charles Nordlander, James Greenberg *contributing producer:* Dana Calderwood *director:* David Turner *set designers:* James Fenhagen, Erik Ulfers *art director:* Laura Brock *theme sung by:* Jamie Gustis, Alaine Kashian, John Latham *music:* D. Norman Yazbeck, Sean Altman *music director:* Robert Agnello *origination:* Lifetime Studios, New York (1996); Metropolis Studios, New York (1997)

After five seasons of chasing Carmen Sandiego around the world in the geography-based "Where in the World Is Carmen Sandiego?", the show was revised in the fall of 1996 for a trip through history with the new title "Where in Time Is Carmen Sandiego?"

Lynne Thigpen returned as "The Chief," who gives out assignments, and new host Kevin Shinick replaced Greg Lee. The three contestants are now called "Time Pilots"; their mission is to track Carmen and her gang through time in an attempt to retrieve stolen historical items. Some are serious like the Declaration of Independence; some are whimsical, like the world's first sewer system.

Players begin the game with one hundred power points, and questions are based on the day's theme as determined by the stolen item. Players are given clues in skits and then shown three possible answers. Correct guesses are worth ten points. Players can also earn additional points in the "Data Boost" (five-point questions) and the "Ultimate Data Boost" (ten points). The low-scoring player at the end of this round is eliminated from the game.

In the second round, the remaining two players attempt to place eight items from history in correct chronological order, from the most recent to the furthest back in the past. Players alternate control of the board, and the first to successfully complete the board wins the game.

The day's champion plays a bonus round and chases Carmen Sandiego through the "Trail of Time" by trying to answer six history questions correctly in ninety seconds. The player stands in a "time portal" (under an archway) to trigger the question. If the answer is correct, the gate opens and he or she proceeds to the next time portal; if not, the person has to manually open the gate and uses up time. A player who completes this round in the allotted time captures Carmen and wins a multimedia computer system.

The show also features a three-member performance group, called "The Engine Crew," who perform on the show and "power" the time travel machine, which is called the "Chronoskimmer."

WHERE WAS I?

premiere: September 2, 1952   *packager:* White-Rosenberg Productions   *broadcast history:* DuMont primetime September 2, 1952–October 6, 1953   *hosts:* Dan Seymour, Eddie Dunn, Ken Roberts, John Reed King   *announcer:* Bob Williams   *producers:* Larry White, Manny Rosenberg, Mike Dutton   *directors:* Harry Coyle, Martin Magner   *origination:* Ambassador Theater, New York   *debut guests:* Peter Donald, Nancy Guild, David Ross, Joey Adams

This weekly game show, "Where Was I?", went through three hosts and at least two formats during its year on the air. Dan Seymour was the original host. Ken Roberts replaced him on September 16, 1952, and John Reed King became host in December 1952.

One of the formats of "Where Was I?" had a celebrity panel trying to guess where a contestant was at a certain time, and in another format the panel tried to guess the nature of a photograph that was shown only to the viewers. When the panel was stumped, money was donated to the Damon Runyon Cancer Fund.

WHEW!

premiere: April 23, 1979   *packager:* Bud Austin Company/Jay Wolpert Productions/Burt Sugarman Productions   *broadcast history:* CBS daytime April 23, 1979–May 30, 1980   *host:* Tom Kennedy   *announcer:* Rod Roddy   *executive producers:* Bud Austin, Burt Sugarman   *creator/producer:* Jay Wolpert   *directors:* William Carruthers, Tom Trbovich, Chris Darley   *set designer:* James Agazzi   *music:* Alan Thicke   *origination:* Studio 33, CBS Television City, Los Angeles

On this show, "Whew!", two players competed, one called the "charger" and the other the "blocker." A game board with five rows of five boxes and one row of three boxes was used. The boxes in the five-box rows had values from $10 to $50 and the boxes in the three-box row had values of $200, $350, and $500. The blocker selected any six boxes on the board, which then became five-second penalty boxes. The charger then attempted to answer six questions, one in each row, within sixty seconds. The charger won the game if the questions were answered in the set time; otherwise, the blocker won. The two players reversed positions in the second game and the first player to win two games became the champion.

In the bonus round, the champion tried to correct ten "bloopers" (which were mistated facts such as: Lyndon B. Johnson chopped down a cherry tree) in under one minute for $100 a correct answer or $25,000 for all ten.

Starting in November 1979, celebrities were used as teammates for the players.

WHO DO YOU TRUST?

premiere: September 30, 1957   *packager:* Don Fedderson Productions   *broadcast history:* ABC daytime September 30, 1957–December 27, 1963   *hosts:* Johnny Carson, Woody Woodbury   *assistant:* Cindy Lindt   *announcers:* Del Sharbutt, Todd Russell, Ed McMahon, Bill Nimmo   *producers:* Jim Morgan, Art Stark, Jim Landis   *directors:* Al Burton, David Lowe   *set designer:* Romain Johnston   *music director:* John Gart   *origination:* Little Theater, New York

Like "You Bet Your Life," "Who Do You Trust?" was played more for the banter between host and guests than for the game. Couples, usually a husband and wife, chosen for their unusual background, competed. After being interviewed by the emcee, each couple was asked a series of three questions and the men, after hearing what each category was, made the decision to answer or let the woman answer.

Three couples participated on each show and the couple with the most correct answers returned at the end of the show to play for a $500 cash jackpot against the previous day's winning couple.

If two or three couples had the same number of correct answers, one member of each team played a tiebreaker question, which required a numerical answer. The player whose answer was closest to the correct answer had his or her team move on to the jackpot round.

In the jackpot round, one member of each team (usually the man) was placed in his own isolation booth and was given the same question. The question required him to give a list of items in a specified time limit (example: in ten seconds list the capitals of South American countries). The player with the most correct answers won $500 for his team and the chance to appear on the next show.

The show premiered under the title "Do You Trust Your Wife?" and the "Who Do You Trust?" title was adopted on July 14, 1958. Johnny Carson was the original host and Del Sharbutt the original announcer. When "Who Do You Trust?" moved to a new time period on November 18, 1957, Bill Nimmo replaced Del Sharbutt. In 1958 Nimmo was replaced by Todd Russell. On October 13, 1958, Carson was joined by a new sidekick/announcer, Ed McMahon.

Carson and McMahon left "Who Do You Trust?" in September 1962 to become host and announcer on NBC's "The Tonight Show." On September 10, 1962, Woody Woodbury became the new host of "Who Do You Trust?" and Bill Nimmo returned as announcer.

Did you know . . . Johnny Carson started his broadcasting career on radio station KFAB Lincoln, Nebraska? He became a staff announcer on Los Angeles TV station KNXT in

Tom Kennedy gives a contestant last-minute directions as she prepares to run the gauntlet on "Whew!"

1950. Four years later he made his national TV debut as emcee of "Earn Your Vacation" for CBS.

WHO PAYS?

premiere: July 2, 1959   *packager:* Lester Lewis Productions
broadcast history: NBC primetime July 2, 1959–September 24, 1959   *host:* Mike Wallace   *announcer:* Pat Hernon
producer/director: Jerome Schnur   *associate producer:* Barbara Olson   *concept:* based on an idea by Allan Kalmus and Irving Settel   *consultant:* Bob Wald   *set designer:* Frank Schneider   *origination:* NBC studio 6B, New York   *debut panel:* Celeste Holm, Gene Klavin, Sir Cedric Hardwicke
debut guests: Red Buttons, Carol Channing

On this Thursday night summer replacement series "Who Pays?", a panel of three celebrities (Sir Cedric Hardwicke, Celeste Holm, and Gene Klavin) tried to identify a guest celebrity by questioning two people who worked for that celebrity. As the first clue, each employee identified the job he or she did for the celebrity (hair dresser, cook, butler, etc.). Each panelist was alotted one minute to question the guests. Questions required specific and detailed answers.

If the panel did not correctly guess the person's identity, a second clue was given and another round of questioning began. The guest celebrity could make comments from an offstage booth using a disguised voice.

A guest received $100 after one round if he or she stumped the panel and $200 after two rounds.

Did you know . . . this was the last game show Mike Wallace emceed in his ten-year career as a game show host? In 1961 he became narrator on "Biography" and in 1963 joined CBS news. He was one of the original hosts of "60 Minutes" when it premiered in September 1968.

Future game show announcer Gene Wood was a writer on "Who Pays?" During the 1960s, Wood also did some writing for Captain Kangaroo. He didn't begin his game show announcing career on a regular basis until 1969, when he was heard on BEAT THE CLOCK.

WHO SAID THAT?

premiere: December 9, 1948   *packager:* NBC Television (1948–1954); ABC Television (1955)   *broadcast history:*

NBC primetime December 9, 1948–July 19, 1954; ABC primetime February 2, 1955–July 26, 1955
1948–1954 version
hosts: Robert Trout, Walter Kiernan **announcers:** Kenneth Banghart, Rex Marshall, Bill Cochran, Peter Roberts, Dick Dudley **creator:** Fred Friendly **producers:** Fred Friendly, Herb Leder **directors:** Mark Hawley, Garry Simpson, Dick Goode, Roger Muir, Martin Hoade, Clarence Thoman, Warren Wade **set designer:** Joseph Kirby **origination:** NBC Studio 3A, New York **debut guests:** Elsa

Zippy the Chimp tells host Mike Wallace, "You take the blonde, and I'll take the brunette," on the 1959 show "Who Pays?"

Life and television were so simple back in 1948. No bells, no flashing lights, no neon . . . just a huge dry cleaning bill. From left to right, Elliot Roosevelt, Faye Emerson, Earl Wilson, John Cameron Swayze, and Ken Banghart, with emcee Robert Trout, test their knowledge of news quotes on the game show "Who Said That?"

Maxwell, George Allen, H. V. Kaltenborn, John Cameron Swayze

1955 version

host: John Daly   *announcer:* Durwood Kirby   *producer:* Anne Gillis   *director:* Eddie Nugent   *origination:* New York

"Who Said That?" was a news quiz featuring a panel composed of journalists and guest celebrities who tried to guess the author of a quotation that was recently in the news. Panelists also had to describe the circumstances surrounding the quote. They were each penalized $5 if they did not come up with the correct answers. Home viewers submitted "All-time Quotes" and, if the quotes were used on the show, the viewers won $50 bonds.

Robert Trout was host from 1948 to 1951, Walter Kiernan from 1951 to 1954, and John Daly in 1955. The panelists on the first show were George Allen, unofficial adviser to President Harry Truman, commentator H. V. Kaltenborn, columnist Elsa Maxwell, and newsman John Cameron Swayze. Other regular panelists on "Who Said That?" included Morey Amsterdam, John Mason Brown, Bob Considine, Bill Henry, and June Lockhart.

Did you know . . . "Who Said That?" producer Fred Friendly went on to a more distinguished career in broadcast journalism? He teamed up with journalist Edward R. Murrow to create and produce "See It Now" from 1951 to 1958 and became president of CBS News from 1964 to 1966.

THE WHO WHAT OR WHERE GAME

premiere: December 29, 1969   *packager:* Ron Greenberg Productions   *broadcast history:* NBC daytime December 29, 1969–January 4, 1974   *host:* Art James   *announcer:* Mike Darrow   *executive producer:* Ron Greenberg   *producer:* John Rhinehart   *director:* Dick Schneider   *set design:* Alan Kimmel   *music:* George David Weiss   *origination:* NBC Studios 6A and 8H, New York

On "The Who What or Where Game," three contestants competed against each other by risking money on their ability to answer "who," "what," and "where" questions related to a specified subject.

Each contestant was given a bankroll of $125 and could bet up to $50 on any one question. More difficult questions paid off in higher odds. If two contestants declared for the same question, the $50 limit was waived and an auction was held. The highest bidder got the question he or she wanted to answer.

To determine the day's winner, contestants risked any or all of their winnings on the ability to answer one final question. The top money winner of the day returned to play again.

Did you know . . . game show veteran Jack Narz hosted the original pilot for "The Who What or Where Game" in 1966? Three years later, when NBC added the show to their daytime schedule, Art James became its emcee.

Were you watching when . . . these emcees were guest contestants: Bob Clayton (CONCENTRATION), Joe Garagiola (JOE GARAGIOLA'S MEMORY GAME), Art Fleming (JEOPARDY!), Jack Kelly (SALE OF THE CENTURY), and Gene Rayburn (THE MATCH GAME)?

WHODUNNIT?

premiere: April 12, 1979 *packager:* Marble Arch Productions *broadcast history:* NBC primetime April 12, 1979–May 17, 1979 *host:* Ed McMahon *announcer:* John Harlan *creators:* Jeremy Lloyd, Lance Percival *executive producer:* Martin Starger *producers:* Bill Carruthers (game), Doris Quinlan (drama) *directors:* Bill Carruthers (game), Don Wallace (drama) *set designer:* Ed Flesh *music:* Fred Werner *origination:* NBC Studio 3, Burbank *debut guests:* Jim Conway, Yvonne Braithwaite Burke, F. Lee Bailey

Three contestants and a panel of three experts, including attorneys, detectives, and court reporters, were part of the mystery game show "Whodunnit?"

Each program began with a crime segment that featured a celebrity guest in a dramatic sketch. Celebrities who appeared on the six episodes of "Whodunnit?" were Loni Anderson, Mike Connors, Erik Estrada, Jack Klugman, Audra Lindley, and Vic Tayback.

Just before the villain was revealed, the action was stopped and all the subjects were brought before the panel to be interrogated. At this point, the contestants could choose to play for $10,000 and decide who the culprit was, or wait for more information to be revealed.

The panel of experts cross-examined the suspects and then all six participants made their final selections. The contestant who correctly identified the suspect won $5,000. If the contestant and the expert both selected the right suspect, the contestant won $1,000.

Experts who appeared on the show included Melvin Belli, Los Angeles Police Chief Ed Davis, and *New York Times* crime reporter Lacey Fosburgh.

WHO'S THE BOSS?

premiere: February 19, 1954 *packager:* Lester Lewis Productions *broadcast history:* ABC primetime February 19, 1954–August 27, 1954 *hosts:* Walter Kiernan, Mike Wallace *creators:* Allan Kallmus, Irving Settel *producer:* Lester Lewis *director:* Charles Dubin *set designer:* Romain Johnston *origination:* Elysee Theater, New York *debut guests:* Dick Kollmar, Polly Rowles, Sylvia Lyons, Horace Sutton

On "Who's the Boss?", four celebrity panelists quizzed secretaries to determine who their famous bosses were. The secretaries could win $100 for each wrong vote by the panel.

The panel for the first program included actor Dick Kollmar, actress Polly Rowles, *Saturday Review* travel editor Horace Sutton, and Sylvia Lyons, wife of *New York Post* columnist Leonard Lyons. They quizzed the secretaries of Betty Furness, hotel magnate Conrad Hilton, and Robert F. Wagner, mayor of New York City.

Walter Kiernan was the host through July and Mike Wallace replaced him beginning July 16, 1954.

"Who's the Boss?" was revived in 1959 as WHO PAYS?, with Mike Wallace returning as host.

WHO'S THERE

premiere: July 14, 1952 *packager:* Benton and Bowles *broadcast history:* CBS primetime July 14, 1952–September 15, 1952 *host:* Arlene Francis *announcer:* Rex Marshall *producer/director:* Richard Lewis *origination:* New York *debut guests:* Bill Cullen, Robert Coote, Paula Stone

On "Who's There," a celebrity panel attempted to guess the identity of a famous person through clues from props, apparel, and other items associated with that person.

Guests who were to be identified were Gertrude Ederle, George Jessel, and Phil Rizutto. The props shown to the panel so they could identify Jessel included a portrait of Whistler's Mother (for Jessel's "Mom" monologues), a picture of a fox (his association with 20th Century-Fox), and a telephone booth (for his telephone monologues).

WHO'S WHOSE

premiere: June 25, 1951 *packager:* Lester Lewis Productions *broadcast history:* CBS primetime June 25, 1951 (one broadcast) *host:* Phil Baker *announcer:* "Gunga" *producer:* Lester Lewis *director:* Alex Leftwich *origination:* New York *debut guests:* Basil Rathbone, Robin Chandler, Art Ford, Emily Kimbrough

On this game show, "Who's Whose," a celebrity panel of three regular players and one guest attempted to match a woman with her spouse from among three possibilities. The panel was given the opportunity to question each of the four people involved to help make their decision. Three groups of contestants were each presented on the show. As an added feature, the panel tried to pick a celebrity's wife from among a group of three contestants.

Regulars on the panel were Robin Chandler, hostess of CBS-TV's "Meet Your Cover Girl"; Basil Davenport, head of the Book of the Month club; and radio personality Art Ford. They were joined by guest panelist Emily Kimbrough. Dizzy Dean appeared as the celebrity guest.

"Who's Whose" was canceled by sponsor General Foods after only one broadcast and replaced by IT'S NEWS TO ME.

Did you know . . . host Phil Baker was the emcee of radio's "Take It or Leave It," the forerunner of TV's THE $64,000 QUESTION?

WHOSE LINE IS IT ANYWAY?

premiere: May 1, 1990 *packager:* Hat Trick Productions for Channel Four *broadcast history:* Ha! (cable) May 1, 1990–Mar 31, 1991; Comedy Central (cable) April 1, 1991–June 21, 1998 *host:* Clive Anderson *creators:* Dan Patterson, Mark Leveson *executive producer:* Denise O'Donoghue *producer:* Dan Patterson *directors:* Paul O'Dell, John Northover, Chris Bould *set designers:* Pip Gardner, Graeme Story *music:* Philip Pope (theme), Richard Vranch (improvised music) *origination:* London, England

Four stand-up comedians competed in this comedy improvisation show to win the grand prize, a chance to read the closing credits. "Whose Line Is It Anyway?" was first seen on Channel Four in England in 1988 and made its American debut on the cable channel Ha! in May 1990. Ha! merged with Comedy Channel to form Comedy TV (CTV) on April 1, 1991. Several months later the cable channel changed its name to Comedy Central.

The panel performed skits based on a general topic determined by host Clive Anderson and the further suggestions from the studio audience. Each show consisted of several rounds in which the players were awarded points based on their performances. The player with the most points at the end of the show was declared the winner.

Games featured on the show included "Film and Theater Styles," where players pair up to act out a situation in the style of a particular film; "Sound Effects," in which two players team up with one acting out a situation while the other provides the effects; "Props," where the players split into teams of two with each given a different prop and come up with different uses for it; and "March," where all four panelists create a song based on a subject suggested by the studio audience.

The player with the most points at the end of the show was the winner and earned the right to read the closing credits in the manner of a celebrity selected by the host.

WHY?

premiere: December 29, 1952 *packager:* John Reed King Productions *broadcast history:* ABC primetime December 29, 1952–April 20, 1953 *host:* John Reed King *announcer/assistant:* Bill Cullen *producer:* Bill Cullen *director:* Roger Sharpe *origination:* New York

On this weekly show, the first four "W"'s (who, what, when, and where) of a situation were given and a panel tried to come up with the "why."

The first two shows were seen only on WJZ, New York before the program was fed to ABC.

Regular panelists included Lillian Bailey, Clara Dechart, and Frank Fox.

WILD & CRAZY KIDS

premiere: July 8, 1990 *packager:* Woody Fraser Productions/Reeves Entertainment Group *broadcast history:* Nickelodeon (cable) July 8, 1990– ; *hosts:* Annette Chavez, Omar Gooding, Donnie Jeffcoat *executive producer:* Woody Fraser *producer:* Richard Crystal *directors:* Steve Feld, David Lowe *theme music:* Wendy Fraser and Todd Sharp *music:* Don Great Music *origination:* varies from show to show

This Nickelodeon series featured kids competing in various wild and wacky sporting events. Each program was taped at a different location, including Wild Rivers Water Amusement Park in Irvine, California, and Huish Family Fun Center in Anaheim, California. Each show featured three different events with teams of children participating.

Among the events featured, which changed from show to show, were "Bumper Boat Lacrosse," "Go-Cart Ring Toss," "Bombay Blaster Challenge," and "Congo River Rapids Throw and Catch," where players tried to catch frisbees while going down a water slide.

WILD ANIMAL GAMES

premiere: October 2, 1995 *packager:* Woody Fraser Productions *broadcast history:* Family Channel (cable) October 2, 1995–September 21, 1996 *host:* Ryan Seacrest *announcer:* Randy West *animal voices:* Charles Fleisher *executive producer:* Woody Fraser *supervising producer:* Marty Tenney *producer:* Damian Sullivan *director:* Jerry Kupcinet *production designer:* Gene Macavoy *art director:* Henry L. Cota *music:* Wendy DeAugustine *origination:* Glendale Studios, Glendale

Members of a studio audience composed mostly of kids participated in various types of stunts and games in this game show with an animal theme. In addition, live animals were brought on stage and used in some of the stunts.

Stunts and games varied from show to show. Among the many stunts featured were two teams competing to clean the frosting off an elephant using hoses, and players trying to toss a ball through a swinging tire suspended from the ceiling while sliding down a ramp into a pool. The top-scoring player in each game received prizes.

WILD GUESS

premiere: October 1, 1996 *packager:* Keg Productions in association with CFCN-TV/YTV Canada *broadcast history:* Animal Planet (cable) October 1, 1996–March 28, 1997; Animal Planet (cable) July 1, 1997–September 26, 1997 *host (guessmaster):* Neil Crone *team captains:* Marilyn Smith, Linda Verry *executive producer:* Stephen Ellis *producer/director:* Brian Purdy *art director:* Peter Baran *music:* Denis Keldie *origination:* CFCN-TV, Calgary, Alberta, Canada

Two teams of players competed in a test of animal knowledge in this Canadian produced game show. Recorded in 1988 for Canadian television, it didn't appear on American television until the Animal Planet cable channel picked it up in 1996.

Each team was named after an animal and consisted of two kids and an adult team captain (Marilyn Smith or Linda Verry).

The teams answered multiple choice questions from six categories, which included "Living Proof," "Trivology," "Monkey Business," "Creature Feature," "Catnip," and "Call of the Wild," where players tried to identify an animal from recorded sounds.

Questions in each category were worth thirty points, with teams given their choice of four possible answers. One team played each question, and if the answer was wrong, the team could then "Wild Guess" and play for twenty points. If the answer was wrong again, the opposing team could choose one of the two remaining answers for a possible ten points.

The final round of the day was Catnip, in which two questions were asked and teams could buzz in to answer. If the answer was right, the team earned thirty points; if wrong, it lost ten points. The team with the most points at the end of this round won.

WILD WEST SHOWDOWN

premiere: October 1, 1994 *packager:* Four Point Entertainment/Samuel Goldwyn Company *broadcast history:* Syndicated October 1, 1994–March 1995 *hosts:* Alex Cord ("West") and Lisa Coles ("K. C. Coles") *announcer:* Joe Fowler *outlaws:* Sandy Berumen, Craig Branham, Tremel James, Lynn Jonckowski, Cheryl Lawson, Juddson Keith Linn, Jeff Manzanares, Kerry Maureen Mellin, Randall Oliver, Jason Reins Rodriguez, Con Schell *concept:* based on an idea by Stu Schreiberg, Charles Segars *executive producers:* Ron Ziskin, Shukri Ghalayini, Stu Schreiberg, Charles Segars *producer:* Burt Wheeler *coordinating producer:* Dan Goldberg *director:* Joseph Carolei *production designers:* Gerry Hariton, Vicki Barl *music:* John Arrias, Richard Freeman Davis, Craig Safan *origination:* Santa Clarita

This weekly syndicated series, "Wild West Showdown," featured three contestants living out their fantasies as "cowboys" in the Old West while competing for cash prizes. The show starred actor Alex Cord as "West," who narrated the action, and Lisa Coles as K. C. Clark, the newspaper reporter who interviewed the players.

Set in the fictitious western town of Broken Neck, the cowboys competed in six events. The first three rounds were each worth $100 and the second three, $200. The player with the most money moved on to the "Final Showdown" for a possible $5,000.

Events included "Rawhide," in which a cowboy was dragged behind an outlaw's horse and attempted to reach a release rope to break away in the fastest time; "Stagecoach," where the cowboy rode a galloping horse, trying to catch up to a runaway stagecoach, mount it, and stop it; and "Saloon Brawl," where a player had forty-five seconds to pull an outlaw out of the saloon in a one-on-one tug-of-war.

The "Final Showdown" bonus round was a run through the town, climbing over buildings to reach a bag of cash to get to a horse, to make a getaway through town within a two-minute time limit without getting hit by outlaws shooting "paint bullets" at them.

WIN BEN STEIN'S MONEY

premiere: July 28, 1997 *packager:* Valleycrest Productions *broadcast history:* Comedy Central (cable) July 28, 1997– *host:* Ben Stein *announcer:* Jimmy Kimmel *executive producers:* Andrew J. Golder, Al Burton, Byron Glore *producer:* Terrence McDonnell *director:* Dennis Rosenblatt *production designer:* Jimmy Cuomo *origination:* Studio 2, Hollywood Center Studios

Three contestants compete in a general knowledge quiz for the chance to win the $5,000 daily paycheck of host Ben Stein. In the first round, the players compete against each other, drawing money from the $5,000 put up by Stein. Five

Ben Stein says, "You'll have to work pretty hard to win my money."

categories are revealed; category topics range from "Things more phony than a sorority girl" to "Rock older than Chuck Berry." Values of questions in each category go from $50 to $150 with no penalty for a wrong guess. As each category is played, it is replaced by a new one. At the end of the round, the player with the lowest score is eliminated from the game.

Host Ben Stein becomes a contestant in round two to defend his money against the two remaining players, and announcer Jimmy Kimmel takes over as emcee. Again, five possible categories are available to choose from, with question values now ranging from $200 to $500. At the end of this round, the player with the most money takes on Ben Stein for a possible $5,000.

In the final round, Ben and the remaining player compete in a test of knowledge. Each player is placed in his or her own isolation booth and has sixty seconds to answer ten questions. If the contestant answers more questions correctly than Ben, he or she wins $5,000. Otherwise, the person receives the amount he or she had at the end of the second round. In the event of a tie, the player wins the $5,000 paycheck.

Various classical compositions are used as theme music on "Win Ben Stein's Money," including Ludwig Van Beethoven's "Ode to Joy" in the show's opening and "Ride of the Valkyries" by Richard Wagner in the closing.

Did you know . . . host Ben Stein was a speechwriter for President Richard M. Nixon and law professor at Pepperdine University before entering the world of show business? He has appeared in over twenty movies since 1980, including

Ferris Bueller's Day Off, Ghostbusters II, and *Dennis the Menace.*

WIN, LOSE OR DRAW

premiere: September 7, 1987 *packager:* Burt and Bert Productions/Kline and Friends *broadcast history:* NBC daytime September 7, 1987–September 1, 1989; Syndicated September 7, 1987–August 30, 1990; USA (cable) December 31, 1990–December 24, 1992 (repeats of syndicated series) *hosts:* Vicki Lawrence, Bert Convy, Robb Weller *substitute host:* Sally Struthers *announcers:* Gene Wood, Bob Hilton *executive producers:* Bert Convy, Burt Reynolds *producer/ director:* Richard Kline *set designer:* John C. Mula *origination:* Studios 33 and 41, CBS Television City, Los Angeles *debut guests:* Burt Reynolds, Debbie Reynolds, Loretta Swit, Jason Bateman

On the popular game show "Win, Lose or Draw," two teams, each composed of two celebrity guests and one contestant, competed in a game of "sketch pad charades." The object of the game was to get one's partners to guess the correct names or phrases from drawings made on a sketch pad.

To begin, a player went up to the easel and had sixty seconds to draw pictures that would help his or her teammates guess the subject. Correct guesses earned $200 for the team if they came up with the answer in the first thirty seconds, or $100 if they guessed it before time ran out. If they didn't come up with the correct answer, the opposing team got a chance to guess.

In the second round, the "Speed Round," each team had ninety seconds to convey as many words as possible. One player sketched while his or her teammates guessed. Each correct guess earned a team $100. The team with the most money at the end of this round won the game and an additional $1,000.

By the third year of the show, the time limit of the speed round was reduced to sixty seconds, and correct answers

Emmy winner Vicki Lawrence hosts and sometimes referees "Win, Lose or Draw." Here she is with guest celebrities Burt Reynolds and pal Dom DeLuise.

were worth $50. A bonus game was added to allow a player the chance to win up to $5,000. One player tried to get his or her teammates to guess seven words from sketches in ninety seconds. The first word was worth $50 and the value doubled on each succeeding word, with the last word worth $5,000.

Vicki Lawrence hosted the NBC network version, and Bert Convy emceed the first two years of the syndicated edition. Robb Weller took over as host for the final year of the syndicated version. Sally Struthers filled in for Vicki Lawrence during February 1988.

Did you know . . . Bert Convy was a baseball player for two years in the Philadelphia Phillies organization?

Vicki Lawrence was a member of the singing group "The Young Americans" during the mid-1960s. In 1973 she had a number-one hit with "The Night the Lights Went Out in Georgia."

The original set of "Win, Lose or Draw," designed by John C. Mula, was modeled after Burt Reynolds's living room.

Were you watching when . . . these favorites were guest celebrities: Tony Danza, Phyllis Diller, Charles Durning, Peter Marshall, Gary Owens, Charles Nelson Reilly, Burt Reynolds, Rip Taylor, and Chuck Woolery.

WIN WITH A WINNER

premiere: June 24, 1958 *packager:* Win Elliott–Peg Mayer Productions *broadcast history:* NBC primetime June 24, 1958–September 9, 1958 *hosts:* Sandy Becker, Win Elliott *assistants (postcard girls):* Marilyn Toomey, Rita Hayes *announcer:* Bill Wendell *producers:* Win Elliott, Peg Mayer *director:* Alan Beaumont *set designer:* Peter Dohanos *music director:* Arlo *origination:* New York

On "Win with a Winner," five contestants played a question-and-answer game on a set resembling a race track. The object of the game was to try and be the first player to reach the finish line. To achieve that goal, players chose questions with different point values. The higher the point value, the more difficult the question. Point values also corresponded to the number of places players could move if they answered correctly.

Contestants for the following show were introduced at the end of each show. Home viewers sent in postcards with the names of the contestants they thought would win. Cards were drawn during the show, and all the players who picked the day's winner divided the same amount of money won by the studio contestant.

Original hosts Sandy Becker and Marilyn Toomey were replaced by Win Elliott and Rita Hayes on July 22.

Did you know . . . announcer Bill Wendell made his motion picture debut in the 1992 Billy Crystal motion picture *Mr. Saturday Night,* playing an announcer?

Host Sandy Becker played "Young Doctor Malone" on the radio series of the same name. Postcard girl Marilyn Toomey was NBC-TV's "Color Girl" in the 1950s.

WIN WITH THE STARS

premiere: September 18, 1968 *packager:* Stuart Phelps–Jesse Martin *broadcast history:* Syndicated September 18, 1968–September 1969 *host:* Allen Ludden *announcer:* Jay Stewart *executive producer:* Arthur E. Picken Jr. *producer:* Reinald Werrenwrath *director:* Stuart Phelps *set designer:* Herman Zimmerman *music director:* Bobby Hammack *origination:* NBC Studios, Burbank *debut guests:* Peter Marshall, Barbara McNair

On "Win With the Stars," two teams, consisting of a celebrity guest and a studio contestant, competed to identify songs and sing the first verse in this weekly musical game show. Producers Stuart Phelps and Jesse Martin derived this show from their earlier series WHAT'S THIS SONG? and "What's the Name of That Song?"

Each team played against a clock of 45 seconds to guess as many songs and then sing the first two lines of lyrics. They score five points for correctly guessing the title and one point for each word they correctly sing. After each team plays, the high-scoring contestant returned to play in the final round against the winner of the second round that featured two new contestants.

The winner of the third round had their total winnings of the day doubled.

Other personalities who appeared on the show were Bill Bixby, Judy Carne, George Jessel, Dorothy Lamour, Shari Lewis, Cliff Robertson, and Mel Torme.

Did you know . . . in 1964 RCA Victor records released an album with Allen Ludden singing his favorite songs including "I've Grown Accustomed to Her Face," "Call Me Irresponsible," and "The Nearness of You?"

WINDOW SHOPPING

premiere: April 2, 1962 *packager:* Wolf Productions *broadcast history:* ABC daytime April 2, 1962–June 29, 1962 *host:* Bob Kennedy *announcer:* Dirk Fredericks *judge:* Professor William Wood (professor of journalism at Columbia University) *creators:* Herbert Wolf, Frank Wayne, H. Richard Silver, Donald E. Degnan *executive producer:* Herbert Wolf *producer:* Alan Gilbert *director:* Lloyd Gross *set designer:* Romain Johnston *music director:* Bobby Rosengarden *origination:* Little Theater, New York

On "Window Shopping," three contestants were given only fifteen seconds to study a photo and remember what they saw. The players accrued points by describing the details they remembered that constituted new information. The game continued until only one player remained.

The winner was allowed to look at a window full of merchandise, for as many seconds as he or she had piled up points, then received the merchandise he or she could accurately describe. The winner got everything if one of the items described was in a preselected envelope.

WINGO

premiere: April 1, 1958 *packager:* Jantone Productions *broadcast history:* CBS primetime April 1, 1958–May 6, 1958 *host:* Bob Kennedy *hostess:* Lois O'Brien *announcer:* Ken Roberts *producer:* Dave Brown *director:* Kevin Joe Jonson *set designer:* Richard Senie *music director:* Elliott

Three window shoppers with emcee Bob Kennedy.

Lawrence   *origination:* Maxine Elliott Theater (Studio 51), New York

Contestants tried to combine knowledge and luck to win a jackpot of $250,000 on "Wingo," this live Tuesday night quiz show that lasted only six weeks.

Two players competed in a general knowledge quiz with the winner receiving $1,000 and a chance at the jackpot. Prior to the quiz, each player blindly selected five letters from a giant Wingo board that contained six of each letter used to spell "Wingo." One letter was placed under each letter of "Wingo" but was not revealed till the bonus round. Before the letters were turned over, the champ was given the option of a cash buyout.

If he or she chose to play the Wingo board, it was possible to receive $1,000 for matching one letter, $5,000 for matching two letters, $25,000 for three letters, $75,000 for four matching letters, and the grand prize of $250,000 if all five letters matched. The odds of that happening were one in 2,200.

After two weeks on the air the stakes were raised on matching one letter to $5,000, and two letters to $10,000. Other prize values stayed the same. Nobody won the grand prize in "Wingo's" brief run.

Did you know . . . "Wingo" quizmaster Bob Kennedy played "Curly" in the Broadway production of *Oklahoma!* in 1945?

WINNER TAKE ALL

premiere: July 1, 1948   *packager:* Mark Goodson–Bill Todman Productions   *broadcast history:* CBS primetime July 1, 1948–October 3, 1950; CBS daytime February 12, 1951– April 20, 1951; NBC daytime February 25, 1952–April 25, 1952

1948–1950 version

host: Bud Collyer   *assistant ("Glamour Girl"):* Roxanne Arlen   *announcer:* Bern Bennett   *producers:* Gil Fates, Alice Polver   *directors:* Roland Gillett, Ralph Levy, Paul Monroe, Hugh Rogers, Fred Rickey, Alex Leftwich   *set designers:* Mason Arvold, Richard Rychtorik   *music director:* Bernard Leighton   *origination:* Maxine Elliott Theater (CBS Studio 51), New York

1951 version

host: Barry Gray   *costars:* Betty Jane Watson, Jerry Austen, Howard Malone   *announcer:* Harry Kramer   *producer:* Nat Eisenberg   *director:* Frances Buss   *music director:* Bernard Leighton   *origination:* Maxine Elliott Theater, New York

1952 version

host: Bill Cullen   *assistants:* Shelia Connolly, Marion James, Frank Wayne   *announcer:* Don Pardo   *producer:* Peter Arnell   *director:* Frank Jacoby   *music director:* Arlo   *origination:* New Amsterdam Theater, New York

"Winner Take All" was the first Mark Goodson–Bill Todman game show on television. It was also the first CBS network game show after they began full network operations in the spring of 1948. Other innovations included being the first game show to feature two contestants competing against each other using a "lock-out" device, and having a returning champion continue to face new challengers until defeated.

"Winner Take All" had previously been heard on the CBS radio network. Its debut on radio was on June 3, 1946 with host Bill Cullen.

The format of the show had two contestants competing against each other in a question-and-answer game. One player had a bell, the other a buzzer, and the first to signal could answer. A correct answer was worth one point and three points won a game. The winner received a prize and the right to face a new challenger.

In CBS's 1951 daytime version, some of the questions were illustrated through songs and sketches. New York radio personality Barry Gray emceed and featured performers included songstress Betty Jane Watson, vocalist Jerry Austen, and dancer Howard Malone.

Bill Cullen made his network debut as a TV game show host on the 1952 daytime version of "Winner Take All" for NBC. He and announcer Don Pardo would team up again in

the mid-1950s on the long-running THE PRICE IS RIGHT and in the 70s with WINNING STREAK.

From June 9, 1952 to September 5, 1952, "Winner Take All" was also seen as a segment on the daytime series "Matinee in New York."

Did you know . . . announcer Bern Bennett began his career on the staff of CBS on May 1, 1944? In 1948 he moved over to the TV side of CBS when they began network operations on a continuing basis. Among the shows he announced were "CBS Television News" with Douglas Edwards, "To the Queen's Taste," "Toast of the Town," and "This Is Show Business." During the 1950s he was heard on many game shows as well as "The Phil Silvers Show" and "Rock and Roll Dance Party" with Alan Freed. In 1960 Bennett was transferred to Los Angeles and since then his voice has been heard on "The Danny Kaye Show," "The Jonathan Winters Show," "The Young and the Restless," "The Bold and the Beautiful," and, for over thirty years, the annual "Tournament of Roses Parade" on New Year's Day.

WINNING STREAK

premiere: July 1, 1974   *packager:* Bob Stewart Productions **broadcast history:** NBC daytime July 1, 1974–January 3, 1975   *host:* Bill Cullen   *announcer:* Don Pardo **executive producer:** Bob Stewart   *producer:* Bruce Burmester   *director:* Mike Garguilo   *set designer:* Merrill Sindler   *origination:* Studio 6A, NBC, New York

On "Winning Streak" two contestants competed against each other to spell words in a designated category from a pool of sixteen letters of the alphabet. Each letter had a different point value. A player won the points and the letter by successfully answering a question. The first person to complete a word won the game and advanced to the money board, where he or she formed words using letters chosen at random. The prize money doubled as each letter was selected and continued until the player quit (keeping his or her winnings) or failed to form a word using all the letters selected.

Did you know . . . Studio 6A, where "Winning Streak" was taped, was also the home of other Bill Cullen–hosted shows ("Eye Guess" and "Three on a Match")? Today it's the home of "Late Night with Conan O'Brien."

WIPEOUT

premiere: September 12, 1988   *packager:* Dames-Fraser Productions/Paramount Television   **broadcast history:** Syndicated September 12, 1988–September 8, 1989; USA (cable) September 11, 1989–September 13, 1991 (repeats of 1988 series)   *host:* Peter Tomarken   *announcers:* Jim Hackett, Bob Ridgely, John Harlan   *supervising producer:* Peter Tomarken   *producer:* Bill Mitchell   *director:* Jerome Shaw *set designers:* Anthony Sabatino, William H. Harris   *music:* Otis Conner   *origination:* Stage 30, Paramount Studios, Hollywood

Three contestants competed for a chance to win a new car on "Wipeout," this daily game show that was taped at Paramount Studios in Hollywood. Using a game board of sixteen answers in a particular category, the players tried to find

Announcer Bern Bennett and host Bud Collyer teamed up on three different Goodson-Todman game shows, beginning with "Winner Take All" in 1948. They joined forces again in the 1950s on "Beat The Clock" and "To Tell The Truth."

Bill Cullen at his emcee podium on "Winning Streak," in 1974.

didn't find all six could go back and keep trying until he or she found them, or until time ran out.

WITH THIS RING

premiere: January 28, 1951 *broadcast history:* DuMont primetime January 28, 1951–March 11, 1951 *hosts:* Bill Slater, Martin Gabel *producer:* Charles Adams *director:* Pat Fay *music:* Lew White *origination:* New York

This Sunday night quiz show, "With This Ring," featured contestants who had recently become engaged. Couples were selected and their opinions asked on how to handle a marriage situation. After they responded a pair of married celebrity judges evaluated the answers. The winning couple received a free honeymoon trip.

Martin Gabel replaced Bill Slater as host on the last two broadcasts.

Did you know . . . host Martin Gabel was married to longtime "What's My Line?" panelist Arlene Francis? He frequently joined his wife on the panel of that classic show.

THE WIZARD OF ODDS

premiere: July 17, 1973 *packager:* Burt Sugarman Productions *broadcast history:* NBC daytime July 17, 1973–June 28, 1974 *host:* Alex Trebek *assistant:* Mary Poms *announcers:* Sam Riddle, Charlie O'Donnell, Jerry Dexter

Alex Trebek in a candid pose at NBC in 1973 to promote his first American game show, "The Wizard of Odds."

eleven correct answers without coming across the five wrong answers. The first correct answer found was worth $25; the second, $50; on up to $275 for the eleventh answer.

Playing alone, the contestant kept picking answers and building a bankroll until he or she selected a wrong answer. This person could also pass control of the board to his or her opponent. A wrong answer eliminated all money won by the player. The game continued until all eleven answers were found. The two top-scoring players moved on to the second round.

In the second round, the "Challenge Round," the game board consisted of twelve answers, eight of them being correct responses. One player bid for the number of answers he or she believed could be found on the board. The other player could bid higher or challenge the first player. The challenged player who picked all the correct answers won the game. If not, the challenger could steal the game by picking one of the remaining correct answers.

The winning contestant played the bonus round for a new car, using a game board of twelve answers, six correct, six incorrect, in a particular category (examples: English rulers, game shows hosted by Bill Cullen). The player tried to find all six correct answers in sixty seconds, for the grand prize, by touching six screens and then hitting a plunger to determine the number of correct answers found. The player who

Word for word, it goes without saying that Merv Griffin and a microphone proved to be a winning combination on any show.

pick a group of items whose average added up to exactly the target number. If the contestant was right, he or she won gifts, including a new car.

WORD FOR WORD

premiere: September 30, 1963   *packager:* Milbarn Productions (Merv Griffin)   *broadcast history:* NBC daytime September 30, 1963–October 23, 1964   *host:* Merv Griffin   *substitute host:* Bill Wendell   *model:* Maureen Reynolds   *word authority:* Dr. Francis X. Connolly   *announcers:* Frank Simms, Bill Wendell, Bill McCord   *producers:* Bobby Lane, Ron Greenberg   *director:* Dick Schneider   *set designer:* Rene D'Auriac   *theme:* Merv Griffin   *master word portion:* created by Bill Derman   *origination:* Studio 8H, NBC, New York

"Word for Word" was based on the word game anagrams. Two contestants competed for cash and merchandise by making as many short words as they could out of one big word. Words could be three or more letters, but no proper names or foreign words were accepted. The round continued until one player could not come up with a new word. The other player continued to add words for as long as he or she could.

Players received two seconds' worth of time for each word they created, plus an additional ten seconds if their lists contained a predetermined bonus word. After two rounds, the player with the most words won the game and $100.

In the bonus round, the winning player used the time accumulated in the main game and was shown five prizes. To win that prize, the player tried to unscramble letters that made up a word.

executive producer: Burt Sugarman   *producers:* Perry Cross, Alan Thicke, Neal Marshall   *director:* Terry Kyne   *set designer:* Dick Stiles   *music director:* Stan Worth   *theme song:* written and sung by Alan Thicke   *origination:* NBC Studio 4, Burbank

Veteran game show host Alex Trebek made his American debut as host of "The Wizard of Odds." Contestants were selected from the studio audience and asked questions based on statistical information, for cash and prizes.

The "Wizard" (Alex) began the show by choosing three contestants and asking questions based on the law of averages. The next players selected were given a series of words or phrases and told to pick the one that didn't match. The person with the most correct answers was given the chance to pick one of five prizes that were behind windows which were either "open" or "locked." This person could continue to play, or stop at any time, keeping the prizes; however, picking a window that was locked lost the player all his or her prizes. Every contestant picked to participate on the show had his or her name added to the "Wizard's Wheel of Fortune."

At the end of the show, the wheel was spun and the person picked was eligible for bonus gifts. A list of averages was then brought out, with a number above it. The contestant had to

WORDPLAY

premiere: December 29, 1986   *packager:* Scotti Brothers–Syd Vinneage Productions in association with Fiedler-Berlin Productions and Rick Ambrose Productions   *broadcast history:* NBC daytime December 29, 1986–September 4, 1987   *host:* Tom Kennedy   *substitute host:* Jamie Farr   *announcer:* Charlie O'Donnell   *executive producers:* Syd Vinneage, Tony Scotti, Peter Berlin, Rob Fiedler   *supervising producer:* John Vinneage   *producer:* Howard Kuperberg   *director:* Rob Fiedler   *set designer:* Ed Flesh   *music:* Level 22   *origination:* NBC Studio 4, Burbank   *debut guests:* Richard Moll, Dick Shawn, Dorothy Lyman

On "Word Play," two contestants playing in turn, chose one word from nine possibilities on a game board (examples: fantasia, turgid, avuncular, cudgel, hoodoo, germane). Each of the three guest celebrities gave a definition. The player tried to choose the correct definition and if successful won a cash amount (this varied) associated with the word. The player with the most money after six words were played won the game.

In the bonus round (called "Speedword" on the first show only), the day's champion tried to go from one side of the game board to the other by guessing words from two definitions associated with that word in forty-five seconds. The player earned $100 for each word correctly guessed or a bo-

Game show great Tom Kennedy hosting his fifteenth national game show, "Wordplay," for NBC back in 1986.

Wink Martindale gets ready to explain the rules on his 1970 musical game, "Words and Music."

nus that started off at $5,000 and was increased by $2,500 each time it was not won. Players could stay on for a maximum of three days.

WORDS AND MUSIC

premiere: September 28, 1970 *packager:* Jack Quigley–Winter Rosen Productions *broadcast history:* NBC daytime September 28, 1970–February 12, 1971 *host:* Wink Martindale *announcer:* Johnny Gilbert *creator:* Jack Quigley *producers:* Armand Grant, Howard Felsher *director:* Lou Tedesco *set designer:* Bob Inkelas *music director:* Jack Quigley *featured singers:* Peggy Connelly, Katie Gran, Bob Marlo, Don Minter, Pat Henderson *origination:* NBC Studio 1, Burbank

Three contestants competed using a game board of sixteen squares in this musical quiz show, "Words and Music." Each square contained a clue that was associated with a word in a song (example: the clue was "right between the eyes" and the word the players were listening for was "nose"). The first player to correctly guess the word after it was sung won cash and the opportunity to select the next clue. The game consisted of four rounds of four songs. The cash values increased from round to round. The person with the highest cash score at the end of the day won, returned to play the next day, and if able to continue winning for three straight days, won a new car.

YAHTZEE

premiere: January 11, 1988 *packager:* Bernstein-Hovis Productions/Ralph Andrews Productions *broadcast history:* Syndicated January 11, 1988–September 1988 *host:* Peter Marshall *dice girls:* Kelly Grant, Denise DiRenzo, Theresa Ganzel *announcers:* Larry Hovis, John Content *executive producer:* Ralph Andrews *director:* Lou Tedesco *set designer:* Don Wallschlaeger *music:* Jet 88 *origination:* Trump's Castle, Atlantic City

The popular dice game Yahtzee was turned into a daily game show that featured five guest celebrities and two teams of three contestants. The object of "Yahtzee," the TV game, was to gain control of the dice and be the first team to accumulate five of one particular number.

The game began with the celebrities answering questions like "Give a reason why a young bride would call her mother." Each of the members of one team tried to come up with the same answers that the celebrities gave. The team with the most matches earned the chance to toss five dice.

One side of each die was marked "wild" and could be used as any number. The first team to collect five of any number won the game.

The winning team played the bonus round for additional cash. Behind each of the letters of the word "Yahtzee" were cash amounts. The team chose one of the letters, which determined the amount they played for. They tried to earn as many as five rolls of the five dice by matching as many celebrities as they could on one question. The team earned one roll of the dice for each celebrity they matched and if they collected five of one number they won the jackpot.

YOU BET YOUR LIFE

premiere: October 5, 1950 *packager:* Filmcraft Productions for John Guedel Productions *broadcast history:* NBC primetime October 5, 1950–September 21, 1961; Syndicated September 1961– (repeats of NBC series) *host:* Groucho Marx *announcer:* George Fennaman *producer:* John Guedel *directors:* Robert Dwan, Bernie Smith *music directors:* Jerry Fielding, Jack Meakin *theme song:* "Hooray for Captain Spaulding" by Bert Kalmar and Harry Ruby *origination:* NBC Studio D, Hollywood

"You Bet Your Life" was played more for the comedy of host Groucho Marx's conversations with the contestants than for the quiz segments. The show began on radio in 1947 and moved to television in the fall of 1950. An hour of show material was filmed in front of a studio audience at the old NBC studios in Hollywood at Sunset and Vine Streets (now the home of a bank) and edited down to a half-hour show.

The show began with Groucho interviewing the contestants. Afterwards the contestants played a quiz game. The games, all question and answer, varied from season to season. In one of the games the team selected a category of questions and was given $100 for betting money. Questions ranged in value from $10 to $100, depending on the difficulty, and four questions were asked. If the players gave correct answers they added to their bankroll, if not they lost money. A second set of contestants then played a round, and the high-scoring teams from each round returned to play for a bonus prize at the end of the show.

The one . . . the only . . . Groucho!

268

In one of the other quizzes, the two players were asked to answer four questions in a row correctly to win $1,000. Two wrong answers would eliminate a player from the game. After two teams played, one couple returned to try to answer one more question for big money. They chose two numbers, from one to ten, one for $10,000 and the other for $5,000. A wheel was spun and if their number came up they could go for the big money, otherwise they played for $2,000.

At the start of each show, the audience was informed of the night's secret word. If any contestant said the word during the show, a stuffed duck dropped down and they won $100 in cash. On the first show the secret word was "wall."

Jerry Fielding was the music director on "You Bet Your Life" from 1950 to 1954, with Jack Meakin taking over for the rest of the series.

When the show began its eleventh season, on September 22, 1960, the title was changed to "The Groucho Show." On December 8, 1960 the show was seen in color for the only time in its run. The five hundred twenty-eighth, and final, first-run show was seen on June 29, 1961.

Since "You Bet Your Life" was a filmed show, not a live broadcast, summer reruns of the past season were seen under the title "The Best of Groucho." (In the summer of 1951 "You Bet Your Life" was replaced by IT PAYS TO BE IGNORANT.) During its run, the show was seen on Thursday nights, and after going off NBC, the show was syndicated on local stations. In the 1980s the CBN cable network aired repeats of "You Bet Your Life" as did the Comedy Central cable network in the early 90s.

In 1950 Groucho Marx received an Emmy Award for his duties as host.

Did you know . . . funny lady Phyllis Diller was a contestant on "You Bet Your Life"? Less than ten years later she was a comedy superstar and pioneer.

Were you watching when . . . Groucho would often glance heavenward during a joke? He was really reading his next funny line or "ad-lib" . . . you see, the show was fully scripted. Jokes were printed on well-placed cue cards projected onto a small television screen placed just above Groucho's head.

Harpo Marx made a guest appearance on his brother's show. He was lowered down to Groucho like the duck was always lowered to Groucho. Why? He was the suprise duck for that memorable show.

YOU BET YOUR LIFE
premiere: September 8, 1980 *packager:* Hill-Eubanks Productions/MCA Television *broadcast history:* Syndicated September 8, 1980–September 1981 *host:* Buddy Hackett *announcer:* Ron Husmann *executive producers:* Mike Hill, Bob Eubanks *producer:* Walt Case *director:* Chris Darley *set designer:* Ed Flesh *music:* Lee Ringuette *origination:* TAV Studios, Hollywood

In this 1980s revival of the old Groucho Marx show of the same name, "You Bet Your Life," contestants were interviewed by comedian Buddy Hackett. The players then competed in a general knowledge quiz to win money. The first correct answer was worth $25 and winnings doubled with each additional correct response to a maximum of $400 (five questions). The players then had the option of tripling their winnings on a sixth question, but if they were incorrect they lost half of the earnings.

The top-scoring team of the day returned at the end of the show to meet "Leonard the Duck," and the team picked one of his eggs for a bonus prize.

YOU BET YOUR LIFE
premiere: August 31, 1992 *packager:* Carsey-Werner Productions in association with Bill Cosby *broadcast history:* Syndicated August 31, 1992–September 3, 1993 *host:* Bill Cosby *assistant:* Renfield (Robbi Chong) *announcer:* Buster Jones *executive producers:* Marcy Carsey, Tom Werner, Caryn Mandabach *producers:* Bob Davis, Henry Chan *directors:* Bill Carruthers, Chuck Vinson *set designer:* Garvin Eddy *music:* Shirley Scott sextet *origination:* Studio C, WHYY-TV, Philadelphia

Comedian Bill Cosby made the second attempt to bring back the Groucho Marx classic YOU BET YOUR LIFE with this 1992 syndicated series. Taped in Philadelphia, the show reunited Cosby with Marcy Carsey and Tom Werner, who had produced his highly successful comedy show of the 1980s, "The Cosby Show."

Each show began with a black goose, dressed in a Temple University sweatshirt (Cosby's alma mater), dropping down to reveal the "Secret Word" of the day. Any player who said the word during the show was awarded $500.

After an interview designed to reveal the often humorous and interesting aspects of the guests, a simple question-and-answer game was played. The team began with $750 and could bet any part of their bank on their ability to answer a series of three questions in a predetermined category.

The top-scoring team of the day returned at the end of the show to try for bonus cash. Three cards were placed on a table. Two of the cards had pictures of "The Black Goose" and if the team selected one of those cards, they played for double their winnings. The third card was worth $10,000 for a correct answer.

Did you know . . . Bill Cosby has a doctorate in education, which he achieved during the 1970s? Cosby's first TV show was the adventure/espionage show "I Spy" in 1965. He followed that with "The Bill Cosby Show" in 1969, playing a school teacher. In 1976 he was host of the variety show "Cos" and during the 1980s "The Cosby Show" enjoyed an eight-year run on NBC.

YOU DON'T SAY!
premiere: April 1, 1963 *packagers:* Ralph Andrews–Bill Yagemann Productions (1963–1967); Ralph Andrews Productions (1967–1979) *broadcast history:* NBC daytime April 1, 1963–September 26, 1969; NBC primetime January 7, 1964–May 12, 1964; ABC daytime July 7, 1975–November 26, 1975; Syndicated September 18, 1978–March 1979

1963–1969 version

host: Tom Kennedy   **announcers:** Jay Stewart, John Harlan **substitute host:** Jack Narz   **producers:** Ralph Andrews, Bill Yagemann, Dick McDonough   **directors:** Stuart Phelps, Bill Yagemann, Dick McDonough, Tom Belcher   **set designers:** John Shrum, Robert Kelly   **music director:** Rex Koury **origination:** NBC Studios 4 and 9, Burbank   **debut guests:** Betty White, Barry Sullivan (daytime); Ida Lupino, Howard Duff (primetime)

1975–1978 versions

hosts: Tom Kennedy (1975), Jim Peck (1978)   **announcer:** John Harlan   **producers:** Bill Carruthers, Gary Hunt   **director:** Bill Carruthers   **set designer:** John C. Mula   **music:** Stan Worth   **origination:** The Burbank Studios (1975), KHJ-TV Los Angeles (1978)

"You Don't Say!" began its broadcast run as a local show in the Los Angeles area on November 25, 1962 on KTLA. Jack Barry was the original emcee, but when it was picked up by NBC in 1963, Tom Kennedy became the host.

From 1963 to 1969 the game was played with two teams, each composed of a celebrity guest and a studio contestant, trying to guess names of famous people and places using incomplete sentences as clues. The last word, which sounded like a portion of the name, was left blank for his or her teammate to guess. Teams alternated with clues until the name

was guessed. The first team to guess three names won the game, $100, and a chance to play the bonus round for additional cash.

During the bonus round, contestants were given three incomplete words that were revealed one at a time. If they correctly guessed the subject after one clue, they won $500. If they needed a second clue, the value dropped to $200, and if they used all three clues they won $100. Guests for the first week, in April 1963, were Betty White and Barry Sullivan.

Host Tom Kennedy appeared as a celebrity panelist on his own show once a year in 1964, 1965, and 1966, with his brother Jack Narz subbing as emcee. Announcer John Harlan appeared as a panelist for one week in September 1966. In March 1968 "You Don't Say!" went on location to Cypress Gardens in Florida to tape shows.

In the 1970s version of "You Don't Say!" two players received clues from four guest celebrities. Guessing the name after one clue was worth $200; after two clues, $150; and after three clues, $100. Players alternated, and the first contestant to win $500 played a bonus round, receiving a maximum of five clues to guess as many names as possible. The prize money started at $500 and doubled with each correct guess.

Were you watching when . . . all these game show emcees were guest celebrities: Bill Cullen, Monty Hall, Dennis James, Allen Ludden, Peter Marshall, Tom Kennedy's brother Jack Narz, and Gene Rayburn?

From time to time "You Don't Say!" would do television theme shows. Remember when John Astin and Carolyn Jones were on an "Addam's Family" show or when June Lockhart ("Lost in Space") and Leonard Nimoy ("Star Trek") were on a week's worth of shows dealing with space shows?

Remember when game show favorite Wink Martindale guest-starred as a celebrity contestant on "You Don't Say!", and when he filled in for host Tom Kennedy for two weeks?

YOU WRITE THE SONGS

premiere: September 5, 1986   **packager:** Bob Banner Associates   **broadcast history:** Syndicated September 5, 1986– September 1987   **host:** Ben Vereen   **creator:** Al Masini **producer:** Sam Riddle   **directors:** Tim Kiley, Tony Charmoli **set designer:** John Shafner   **music director:** Joey Carbone **featured singers:** Monica Page, Cat Adams, Kenny James **origination:** The Aquarius Theater, Hollywood

Three songwriters, either amateur or professional, competed on "You Write the Songs," this weekly series for a cash prize worth $1,000. Each contestant had a song performed by one of the show's regular singers and was judged on a scale from one to ten by a panel of five judges, including a singer, a record company executive, a record producer, and a disc jockey and one of his listeners. The winning song was brought back to compete on the next show against two new songs.

The five songs with the highest scores after twelve weeks competed for a grand prize of $100,000. The songs that competed for the championship were "Am I Losing You?" (Larry Hart), "Jericho" (Susan Pomeranz), "First Time on a Ferris

Do these two game show favorites look like brothers? Well, they should. They are! That's "You Don't Say!" emcee Tom Kennedy and his famous brother Jack Narz with guest June Lockhart.

Wheel'' (Harriet Schock, Mischa Segal), ''For So Long'' (Chris McCollum, Monroe James), and the winner, ''Everybody Needs a Dream'' (Tom Grose).

Each program also included a musical salute and chats with popular songwriters like Donna Summer, Stevie Wonder, Kenny Loggins, and Burt Bacharach.

YOU'RE IN THE PICTURE

premiere: January 20, 1961 *packager:* Steve Carlin Productions/Solar Enterprises/Idees Grandes Inc. *broadcast history:* CBS primetime January 20, 1961 (one broadcast) *host:* Jackie Gleason *announcer:* Johnny Olson *creators:* Bob Synes, Don Lipp *producer:* Steve Carlin *director:* Seymour Robbie *set designer:* Eddie Gilbert *original music:* Jackie Gleason *music director:* Norman Leyden *origination:* CBS Studio 52, New York *debut guests:* Arthur Treacher, Pat Harrington Jr., Pat Carroll, Jan Sterling

Comedian Jackie Gleason returned to the small screen after a two-year absence to host this weekly panel show, ''You're in the Picture,'' which turned out to be one of the biggest bombs in TV history.

In ''You're in the Picture,'' four celebrity panelists (Pat Carroll, Pat Harrington Jr., Jan Sterling, and Arthur Treacher) were situated behind a picture frame seven feet high and ten feet wide. The players put their heads through porthole cutouts, making them part of a picture, which they themselves could not see. The goal was to identify the content of the picture.

After a clue was given, each of the panelists was given time to question host Jackie Gleason about what he or she was doing in the picture. The five pictures enacted on the only telecast of ''You're in the Picture'' were ''Pocahontas rescues John Smith,'' ''Itsy Bitsy Teenie Weenie Yellow Polka Dot Bikini,'' ''The Metropolitan Museum of Art,'' ''The Burlesque Beef Trust Girls,'' and ''Goldilocks and the Three Bears.''

''You're in the Picture'' was sponsored by Kelloggs of Battle Creek, with veteran pitchman Dennis James handling the commercials.

Did you know . . . instead of presenting the second telecast of ''You're in the Picture'' a week later, host Jackie Gleason, sitting in a chair on a empty stage, apologized for the first broadcast and spent the rest of the program just talking to the audience?

YOU'RE ON YOUR OWN

premiere: December 22, 1956 *packager:* Jack Barry and Dan Enright Productions *broadcast history:* CBS primetime December 22, 1956–March 16, 1957 *host:* Steve Dunne *announcer:* Hal Simms *commercials:* Joann Jordan for Hazel Bishop *executive producers:* Jack Barry, Dan Enright, Robert Noah *producer:* Howard Merrill *director:* Tom

Getting ready for their big debut, panelists Jan Sterling, Pat Carroll, and Arthur Treacher try to guess who they are in this rehearsal shot from ''You're in the Picture,'' with host Jackie Gleason.

Donovan *music director:* Paul Taubman *origination:* Mansfield Theater, New York

On this game show contestants could win money not only for how much they knew, but for how fast they could find the answer. The stage of "You're on Your Own" was filled with all sorts of reference material, and the faster a player could find an answer to a question the more money could be won, with a grand prize of $25,000 possible.

By the end of the show's run, the game was changed to one in which a player who answered questions incorrectly had to perform a stunt.

Did you know . . . Steve Dunne began a movie career in the 1946 Vincent Price film *Shock?* His final film appearance was in the 1974 movie *Superdad* with Bob Crane and Kurt Russell.

YOU'RE PUTTING ME ON
premiere: June 30, 1969   *packager:* Bob Stewart Productions   *broadcast history:* NBC daytime June 30, 1969–December 26, 1969   *hosts:* Bill Leyden, Larry Blyden   *announcer:* Jack Clark   *executive producer:* Bob Stewart   *producer:* Anne Marie Schmidt   *director:* Lou Tedesco   *set designer:* Rex Fluty Jr.   *music:* Bob Cobert   *origination:* NBC Studio 6A, New York   *debut guests:* Totie Fields, Betsy Palmer, Orson Bean

On this show, three teams of two celebrities each competed against each other to guess which of four famous people their teammate was pretending to be. On "You're Putting Me On," each team played for members of the studio audience.

Each week three regular celebrities (Larry Blyden, Peggy Cass, and Bill Cullen) were joined by three guest celebrities. One member of a team tried to get the other person to guess who he or she was pretending to be, by responding to certain questions the way that person thought the real celebrity would respond.

The team with the most points played a bonus game.

Host Bill Leyden left the show after thirteen weeks and panelist Larry Blyden moved to the emcee's chair for the final thirteen weeks.

Did you know . . . Larry Blyden was nominated for a Tony Award, honoring the best in Broadway theater, three times, finally winning in 1972 for his performance in *A Funny Thing Happened on the Way to the Forum?*

YOUR BIG MOMENT
premiere: May 19, 1953   *packager:* Bernard Shubert Productions   *broadcast history:* DuMont primetime May 19, 1953–June 2, 1953   *host:* Melvyn Douglas   *announcer:* Ken Roberts   *producer:* Mike Dutton   *director:* Don Hillman   *origination:* New York

Movie actor Melvyn Douglas hosted "Your Big Moment," this 1953 revised version of BLIND DATE. Contestants on the show were viewers who wrote in wanting a date with a certain type of person or wanting to go with a date to a special event.

On the first telecast, one viewer was featured on a date with a singer sounding like Don Cornell. On the date, she met the real singer at the Copacabana Club. Another viewer wanted a portrait done by a famous artist.

After three weeks, this Tuesday night show changed back to "Blind Date," and Jan Murray replaced Douglas as host.

YOUR FIRST IMPRESSION
premiere: January 2, 1962   *packager:* Monty Hall–Art Stark Productions   *broadcast history:* NBC daytime January 2, 1962–June 26, 1964   *host:* Bill Leyden   *substitute host:* Monty Hall   *announcer:* Wendell Niles   *producers:* Fred Stettner, Stefan Hatos   *director:* H. Wesley Kenney   *music director:* Ivan Ditmars   *theme:* "Three Blind Mice"   *origination:* NBC Studio 2, Burbank   *debut guests:* Linda Darnell, George Kirgo, Dennis James

On "Your First Impression," celebrity panelists attempted to guess the identity of an in-studio guest on the basis of the guest's initial reaction to single words or clauses. Each guest sat behind the members of the celebrity panel in a sound-proof room. Before the questioning began, the panel was shown five pictures, one of which was the guest. The guest's responses were relayed to the panel by host Bill Leyden. The panel was given two rounds of questioning before making their guesses.

From left to right are regular panelist Dennis James, guest panelist Helen O'Connell, and "Your First Impression" emcee Bill Leyden.

On March 30, 1964, the format was changed. Members of the studio audience tried to identify a famous star's relatives from three candidates appearing on the show, or they tried to guess the identity of a mystery celebrity concealed in a booth behind the celebrity panel.

"Your First Impression" frequently featured celebrity guests, with Walter Brennan and Gisele McKenzie visiting on the first program.

In June 1962, Stefan Hatos joined the show as producer and began a long association with packager Monty Hall. Their production company went on to produce such shows as LET'S MAKE A DEAL and SPLIT SECOND.

Were you watching when . . . Richard M. Nixon, then running for governor of California, made an appearance in 1962, or when actors Charles Bronson, Buster Keaton, and Rod Serling guested in 1963? Johnny Carson made a rare appearance in 1962.

YOUR LUCKY CLUE

premiere: July 13, 1952   *packager:* BBD&O/MCA   *broadcast history:* CBS primetime July 13, 1952–August 31, 1952   *host:* Basil Rathbone   *announcer:* Andre Baruch   *producer/director:* Perry Lafferty   *music director:* John Gart   *origination:* Maxine Elliott Theater, New York   *debut guests:* detectives W. Sherman Burns, Patrick King, Walter Greaza of NBC's "T-Men in Action," radio's Perry Mason, John Larkin

On this game show, "Your Lucky Clue," two professional detectives competed against two amateur sleuths in trying to discover the guilty party in various fictional crimes. "Your Lucky Clue" was a summer replacement for "This Is Show Business" on Sunday nights on CBS and was sponsored by Lucky Strike cigarettes.

Host Basil Rathbone, best known for his movie portrayal of Sherlock Holmes, gave the contestants clues and answered their questions. Andre Baruch, the longtime announcer for "Your Hit Parade" and "The Shadow," as well as play-by-play broadcaster for the Brooklyn Dodgers in the mid-1950s, was the show's announcer.

Detectives on the premiere show were W. Sherman Burns, Walter Greaza, Patrick King, and John Larkin.

Did you know . . . during World War II, Andre Baruch helped create the Armed Forces Radio Network?

YOUR NUMBER'S UP

premiere: September 23, 1985   *packager:* Sande Stewart Productions   *broadcast history:* NBC daytime September 23, 1985–December 20, 1985   *host:* Nipsey Russell   *hostess:* Lee Menning   *announcers:* John Harlan, Gene Wood, Johnny Haymer   *producer:* Sande Stewart   *director:* Bruce Burmester   *set designer:* Ed Flesh   *music:* Bob Cobert   *origination:* NBC Studio 2, Burbank

In this short-lived game show, "Your Number's Up," three contestants competed on stage while the studio audience played along for possible prizes. Numbers, from zero to nine, were selected by a random wheel that put two numbers into

Nipsey Russell measures up as the host with the most in the 1985 show "Your Number's Up."

play at any one time. The contestant who did not have a number in each round chose a phrase (from two possibilities) for his or her opponents to fill out correctly. (Example: "When *T. O.* speaks everyone in the house listens." To solve the problem, the person had to guess that T. O. stood for Tip O'Neill.) The first player to guess correctly received a point; five points won the game.

Members of the studio audience used the last four digits of their telephone numbers to play, and as the contestant on stage solved a phrase, the "number" by that player could be eliminated from the telephone number. If any member of the audience could eliminate all four numbers, the audience member came on stage and selected one of the three players he or she believed would win the game. Guessing correctly won this person a prize.

YOUR SURPRISE PACKAGE

premiere: March 13, 1961   *packager:* Singer Productions   *broadcast history:* CBS daytime March 13, 1961–February 23, 1962   *host:* George Fennaman   *model:* Carol Merrill   *announcer:* Bern Bennett   *creator/executive producer:* Al Singer   *producer:* Allan Sherman   *director:* Hal Cooper   *set designer:* William Craig Smith   *music:* Alvin Stoller, Veryle Mills   *origination:* Studio 43, CBS Television City, Los Angeles

"Your Surprise Package" was one of a trio of game shows introduced by CBS in the spring of 1961 as the network tried to build a game show block on their daytime schedule. The others in this block were DOUBLE EXPOSURE and FACE THE FACTS.

In this game, three contestants competed to identify and win the contents of a box aided by a series of clues and questions.

At the beginning of each game, the players were credited with money equal to the value of the contents of the box. After a clue was given, a player could use some of the money to buy time in order to question the emcee about the contents of the package. Each questioning period lasted forty-five seconds. Up to five clues were given per game and if nobody guessed correctly, the prize was given to a member of the studio audience.

Did you know . . . host George Fennaman was the narrator on the TV version of "Dragnet" during the 1950s and 1960s? He also appeared in the classic science fiction film *The Thing.* Model Carol Merrill achieved greater fame after this show with her work on LET'S MAKE A DEAL, and announcer Bern Bennett has been the announcer on "The Young and the Restless" since its debut in 1973.

YOUR SURPRISE STORE

premiere: May 12, 1952   *packager:* CBS Television   *broadcast history:* CBS daytime May 12, 1952–June 27, 1952   *host:* Lew Parker   *hostess:* Jacqueline Susann   *announcer:* Bern Bennett   *creator:* Irving Mansfield   *producer:* Hal Fimberg   *director:* Frank Satenstein   *set designer:* Randy Gunter   *music director:* Chet Kingsberry   *origination:* New York

A short-lived daytime series, "Your Surprise Store" had a format in which studio contestants got the chance to swap personal possessions for valuable merchandise off the counters, shelves, and racks of the store in the studio. To make the swap, a player had to advance through several levels of brain teasers, stunts, and games of skill.

Actor Lew Parker, a veteran of vaudeville, stage, screen, radio, and night clubs hosted "Your Surprise Store." During the 1960s he became familiar to TV audiences as Marlo Thomas' father in "That Girl."

Assisting Parker was actress Jacqueline Susann who achieved greater fame as the author of the best-selling book *Valley of the Dolls.*

Originally called "Your Super Store," "Your Surprise Store" was intended as a primetime show. It was given daytime exposure in the hopes of selling it to sponsors, but "Your Surprise Store" closed after a seven-week run.

Did you know . . . announcer Bern Bennett was CBS's announcer on the network New Year's Day coverage of the Tournament of Roses Parade from 1961 to 1996? His voice was also heard on the CBS serial "The Clear Horizon," "The Danny Kaye Show," and "The Phil Silvers Show." In 1976 he filled in for Johnny Olson for a week on "Match Game '76."

YOURS FOR A SONG

premiere: November 14, 1961   *packager:* Robert R. Russell Productions   *broadcast history:* ABC primetime November 14, 1961–September 18, 1962; ABC daytime December 4, 1961–March 29, 1963   *host:* Bert Parks   *scoreboard girl:* Michaelina Martel   *announcer:* Johnny Gilbert   *creator:* Robert Russell   *producer:* Harry Salter   *directors:* Seymour Robbie, Garth Dietrick   *set designer:* Fred Stover   *music directors:* Ted Rapf, Arch Koty   *origination:* TV-2, ABC Studios West 66th Street, New York

"Yours for a Song" was a game show and also an audience sing-a-long, with TV personality Bert Parks then hosting his third musical game show (STOP THE MUSIC and HOLD THAT NOTE were the others).

Two contestants competed against each other by recalling lyrics to popular songs. Players were asked to fill in the missing words as the songs were sung. On the primetime version each player received $20 for each word, while on the daytime version each player was awarded $10. Each song had six words missing from different spots in its first chorus and each game had two songs. The high scorer won the game and faced a new challenger.

"Yours for a Song" was the last game show hosted by Bert Parks, whose career as an emcee on television began in 1946.

Did you know . . . Bert Parks was the host on the original pilot of the game show THE HOLLYWOOD SQUARES, which was produced for CBS? When NBC picked up the show in 1966, Peter Marshall got the nod as emcee.

APPENDIX A
Broadcast Networks

abbreviation	network	date TV service began	abbreviation	network	date TV service began
ABC	American Broadcasting Company	Apr 19, 1948		Network (network discontinued in September 1955)	
CBS	Columbia Broadcasting System	May 3, 1948	PBS	Public Broadcasting System	Oct 5, 1970
NBC	National Broadcasting Company	May 9, 1946	FOX	Fox Broadcasting Company	Oct 9, 1986
DuMont	DuMont Television	Apr 13, 1946			

Cable Networks

abbreviation	network	date	abbreviation	network	date
AMC	American Movie Classics	Oct 1, 1984	FOOD	Food Network	Nov 23, 1993
	Animal Planet	Jun 1, 1996	FX	FX Cable	Jun 1, 1994
BET	Black Entertainment Television	Jan 25, 1980	GSN	Game Show Network	Dec 1, 1994
BRAVO	Bravo Cable	Dec 1, 1980	HA!	Ha! (an MTV comedy network) (merged with Comedy Channel on April 1, 1991 to form Comedy Central)	Apr 1, 1990
CBN	Christian Broadcasting Network (name changed to The Family Channel)	Apr 29, 1977	LIFETIME	Lifetime Television	Feb 1, 1984
CBS Cable	CBS Cable (network ceased operation December 17, 1982)	Oct 12, 1981	MSNBC		Jul 15, 1996
			MTV	Music Television	Aug 1, 1981
			TNN	The Nashville Network	Mar 7, 1983
			NICK	Nickelodeon	Apr 1, 1979
COM	Comedy Central (formed by the merger of Ha! and The Comedy Channel)	Apr 1, 1991	NOST	The Nostalgia Network	May 1, 1985
			ODYSSEY	Odyssey	Sep 19, 1988
			PLAYBOY	The Playboy Channel (originally a pay channel, became pay-per-view on December 1, 1989)	Nov 1, 1982
DISC	The Discovery Channel	Jun 17, 1985			
DISNEY	The Disney Channel	Apr 18, 1983			
ESPN	Entertainment & Sports Program Network	Sep 7, 1979	TRAVEL	The Travel Channel	Feb 1, 1987
ESPN-2	Entertainment & Sports Program Network 2	Oct 1, 1993	USA	USA Network	Apr 9, 1980
FAMILY	The Family Channel	Apr 29, 1977	VH-1	Video Hits One	Jan 1, 1985

APPENDIX B
Chronology of Game Shows

program	network	first–last broadcast	program	network	first–last broadcast
TRUTH OR CONSE-QUENCES*	NBC	Jul 1, 1941 (special)	MOVIELAND QUIZ	ABC	Aug 12, 1948– Nov 9, 1948
UNCLE JIM'S QUESTION BEE*	NBC	Jul 1, 1941 (special)	QUIZZING THE NEWS	ABC	Aug 16, 1948– Mar 5, 1949
CBS TELEVISION QUIZ*	CBS	Jul 2, 1941– late 1942	PLAY THE GAME	ABC	Aug 20, 1948– Nov 6, 1948
MISSUS' GOES-A-SHOPPING*	CBS	Aug 3, 1944– Jan 22, 1946	BREAK THE BANK	ABC	Oct 22, 1948– Sep 23, 1949
IT'S A GIFT*	CBS	Jan 29, 1946– Jul 6, 1946	THIS IS THE MISSUS	CBS	Nov 17, 1948– Jan 12, 1949
FACE TO FACE**	NBC	Jun 9, 1946– Jan 26, 1947	THE EYES HAVE IT	NBC	Nov 20, 1948– Jan 27, 1949
CASH AND CARRY	DuMont	Jun 20, 1946– Jul 1, 1947	RIDDLE ME THIS	CBS	Nov 20, 1948– Mar 13, 1949
KING'S PARTY LINE*	CBS	Jul 13, 1946– Dec 28, 1946	MESSING PRIZE PARTY	CBS	Dec 6, 1948– Jun 17, 1949
PLAY THE GAME	DuMont	Sep 24, 1946– Dec 17, 1946	WHO SAID THAT?	NBC	Dec 9, 1948– Jul 19, 1954
LET'S CELEBRATE*	NBC	Dec 15, 1946 (special)	DRAW ME A LAUGH	ABC	Jan 15, 1949– Feb 5, 1949
PARTY LINE*	NBC	Jun 8, 1947– Aug 31, 1947	IDENTIFY	ABC	Feb 14, 1949– May 9, 1949
MISSUS' GOES-A-SHOPPING*	CBS	Nov 19, 1947– Nov 10, 1948	QUIZ KIDS	NBC	Mar 1, 1949– Oct 26, 1951
CHARADE QUIZ	DuMont	Dec 4, 1947– Jun 23, 1949	THE EYES HAVE IT	NBC	Mar 13, 1949– Jun 19, 1949
AMERICANA	NBC	Dec 8, 1947– Jul 4, 1949	THINK FAST	ABC	Mar 26, 1949– Oct 8, 1950
STOP ME IF YOU'VE HEARD THIS ONE	NBC	Mar 4, 1948– Apr 22, 1949	CELEBRITY TIME	ABC	Apr 3, 1949– Mar 26, 1950
WINNER TAKE ALL	CBS	Jul 1, 1948– Oct 3, 1950	SPARRING PARTNERS	ABC	Apr 8, 1949– May 6, 1949
TRY AND DO IT	NBC	Jul 4, 1948– Sep 5, 1948	LADIES BE SEATED	ABC	Apr 22, 1949– Jun 10, 1949
TELE PUN	NBC	Jul 9, 1948– Aug 6, 1948	TREASURE QUEST	ABC	Apr 24, 1949– Sep 2, 1949
			BLIND DATE	ABC	May 5, 1949– Jun 8, 1950
			STOP THE MUSIC	ABC	May 5, 1949– Apr 24, 1952
			HOLD IT PLEASE	CBS	May 8, 1949– May 22, 1949

*By definition, a show considered network must be carried on at least two stations. These shows were produced by networks but only carried on one station.

**"Face to Face" was not seen on the full NBC network when it began, but it was before it completed its run.

program	network	first–last broadcast	program	network	first–last broadcast
SPIN THE PICTURE	DuMont	Jun 4, 1949–Feb 4, 1950	TRUTH OR CONSEQUENCES	CBS	Sep 7, 1950–May 31, 1951
FUN AND FORTUNE	ABC	Jun 6, 1949 (one broadcast)	WHAT'S MY NAME?	NBC	Sep 18, 1950–Jun 29, 1953
IT PAYS TO BE IGNORANT	CBS	Jun 6, 1949–Sep 19, 1949	CELEBRITY TIME	CBS	Oct 1, 1950–Sep 21, 1952
FUN FOR THE MONEY	ABC	Jun 17, 1949–Dec 9, 1949	TAKE A CHANCE	NBC	Oct 1, 1950–Dec 24, 1950
THEY'RE OFF	DuMont	Jun 30, 1949–Aug 18, 1949	CAN YOU TOP THIS?	ABC	Oct 3, 1950–Mar 26, 1951
HEADLINE CLUES	DuMont	Jul 4, 1949–May 4, 1951	KAY KYSER'S COLLEGE OF MUSICAL KNOWLEDGE	NBC	Oct 5, 1950–Dec 28, 1950
BROADWAY TO HOLLY-WOOD HEADLINE CLUES	DuMont	Jul 20, 1949–Jul 15, 1954	YOU BET YOUR LIFE	NBC	Oct 5, 1950–Sep 21, 1961
MAJORITY RULES	ABC	Sep 2, 1949–Jul 30, 1950	LIFE WITH LINKLETTER	ABC	Oct 6, 1950–Apr 25, 1952
AUCTION-AIRE	ABC	Sep 30, 1949–Jun 23, 1950	REMEMBER THIS DATE	NBC	Nov 14, 1950–Jun 28, 1951
BREAK THE BANK	NBC	Oct 5, 1949–Jan 9, 1952	LIVE LIKE A MILLIONAIRE	CBS	Jan 5, 1951–Mar 14, 1952
TWENTY QUESTIONS	NBC	Nov 26, 1949–Dec 24, 1949	SAY IT WITH ACTING	NBC	Jan 6, 1951–May 12, 1951
KAY KYSER'S COLLEGE OF MUSICAL KNOWLEDGE	NBC	Dec 1, 1949–Jun 29, 1950	WITH THIS RING	DuMont	Jan 28, 1951–Mar 11, 1951
WHAT'S MY LINE?	CBS	Feb 2, 1950–Sep 3, 1967	SONGS FOR SALE	CBS	Feb 3, 1951–Feb 17, 1951
TWENTY QUESTIONS	ABC	Mar 17, 1950–Jun 29, 1951	BILL GWINN SHOW	ABC	Feb 5, 1951–Apr 21, 1952
BEAT THE CLOCK	CBS	Mar 23, 1950–Feb 23, 1958	WINNER TAKE ALL	CBS	Feb 12, 1951–Apr 20, 1951
WE TAKE YOUR WORD	CBS	Apr 1, 1950–Apr 22, 1950	WE TAKE YOUR WORD	CBS	Mar 9, 1951–Jun 1, 1951
CELEBRITY TIME	CBS	Apr 2, 1950–Jun 27, 1950	QED	ABC	Apr 3, 1951–Oct 9, 1951
ANSWER YES OR NO	NBC	Apr 30, 1950–Jun 23, 1950	STRIKE IT RICH	CBS	May 7, 1951–Jan 3, 1958
WE TAKE YOUR WORD	CBS	Jun 9, 1950–Jan 23, 1951	DOWN YOU GO	DuMont	May 30, 1951–May 20, 1955
BY POPULAR DEMAND	CBS	Jul 2, 1950–Sep 22, 1950	GUESS AGAIN	CBS	Jun 14, 1951–Jun 21, 1951
PANTOMIME QUIZ	CBS	Jul 3, 1950–Sep 25, 1950	WHO'S WHOSE	CBS	Jun 25, 1951 (one broadcast)
SONGS FOR SALE	CBS	Jul 7, 1950–Sep 1, 1950	SONGS FOR SALE	CBS	Jun 30, 1951–Jun 28, 1952
HOLD THAT CAMERA	DuMont	Aug 27, 1950–Dec 15, 1950	GENERAL ELECTRIC GUEST HOUSE	CBS	Jul 1, 1951–Aug 26, 1951
BLIND DATE	ABC	Aug 31, 1950–Sep 20, 1951	IT'S NEWS TO ME	CBS	Jul 2, 1951–Sep 12, 1953
SING IT AGAIN	CBS	Sep 2, 1950–Jun 23, 1951	PANTOMIME QUIZ	CBS	Jul 2, 1951–Aug 20, 1951
CHANCE OF A LIFETIME	ABC	Sep 6, 1950–Nov 28, 1951	STRIKE IT RICH	CBS	Jul 4, 1951–Jan 12, 1955

program	network	first–last broadcast	program	network	first–last broadcast
IT PAYS TO BE IGNORANT	NBC	Jul 5, 1951–Sep 27, 1951	I'VE GOT A SECRET	CBS	Jun 19, 1952–Apr 3, 1967
TWENTY QUESTIONS	DuMont	Jul 6, 1951–May 30, 1954	THE BIG PAYOFF	NBC	Jun 29, 1952–Sep 14, 1952
GO LUCKY	CBS	Jul 15, 1951–Sep 2, 1951	INFORMATION PLEASE	CBS	Jun 29, 1952–Sep 21, 1952
WHAT'S THE STORY	DuMont	Jul 25, 1951–Sep 23, 1955	ASK ME ANOTHER	NBC	Jul 3, 1952–Sep 25, 1952
THE ART FORD SHOW	NBC	Jul 28, 1951–Sep 15, 1951	PANTOMIME QUIZ	CBS	Jul 4, 1952–Sep 26, 1952
THE AD-LIBBERS	CBS	Aug 3, 1951–Aug 31, 1951	ARE YOU POSITIVE	NBC	Jul 6, 1952–Aug 24, 1952
SAY IT WITH ACTING	ABC	Aug 3, 1951–Feb 22, 1952	QUIZ KIDS	NBC	Jul 7, 1952–Sep 1, 1952
TAG THE GAG	NBC	Aug 13, 1951–Aug 20, 1951	GUESS WHAT?	DuMont	Jul 8, 1952–Aug 26, 1952
PUBLIC PROSECUTOR	DuMont	Sep 6, 1951–Sep 27, 1951	YOUR LUCKY CLUE	CBS	Jul 13, 1952–Aug 31, 1952
HAIL THE CHAMP	ABC	Sep 22, 1951–Jun 14, 1952	MASQUERADE PARTY	NBC	Jul 14, 1952–Aug 25, 1952
WHAT IN THE WORLD	CBS	Oct 7, 1951–Apr 2, 1955	WHO'S THERE	CBS	Jul 14, 1952–Sep 15, 1952
THE NAME'S THE SAME	ABC	Dec 5, 1951–Aug 31, 1954	SUPER GHOST	NBC	Jul 27, 1952–Sep 21, 1952
THE BIG PAYOFF	NBC	Dec 31, 1951–Mar 27, 1953	UP TO PAAR	NBC	Jul 28, 1952–Sep 26, 1952
BATTLE OF THE AGES	DuMont	Jan 1, 1952–Jun 17, 1952	WHAT HAPPENED?	NBC	Aug 7, 1952–Aug 21, 1952
PANTOMIME QUIZ	NBC	Jan 2, 1952–Mar 26, 1952	MEET YOUR MATCH	NBC	Aug 25, 1952–Sep 5, 1952
IT'S IN THE BAG	NBC	Jan 7, 1952–Feb 22, 1952	WHERE WAS I?	DuMont	Sep 2, 1952–Oct 6, 1953
QUICK ON THE DRAW	DuMont	Jan 8, 1952–Dec 9, 1952	BATTLE OF THE AGES	CBS	Sep 6, 1952–Nov 29, 1952
BREAK THE BANK	CBS	Jan 13, 1952–Feb 1, 1953	QUIZ KIDS	CBS	Sep 14, 1952–Nov 8, 1953
QUIZ KIDS	CBS	Jan 13, 1952–Apr 6, 1952	THERE'S ONE IN EVERY FAMILY	CBS	Sep 29, 1952–Jun 13, 1953
WINNER TAKE ALL	NBC	Feb 25, 1952–Apr 25, 1952	TWO FOR THE MONEY	NBC	Sep 30, 1952–Aug 11, 1953
THAT REMINDS ME	NBC	Feb 27, 1952 (special)	WHEEL OF FORTUNE	CBS	Oct 3, 1952–Dec 25, 1953
GIVE AND TAKE	CBS	Mar 20, 1952–Jun 12, 1952	DOUBLE OR NOTHING	CBS	Oct 6, 1952–Jul 2, 1954
DRAW TO WIN	CBS	Apr 22, 1952–Jun 10, 1952	BALANCE YOUR BUDGET	CBS	Oct 18, 1952–May 2, 1953
CHANCE OF A LIFETIME	ABC	May 8, 1952–Aug 20, 1953	LIVE LIKE A MILLIONAIRE	ABC	Oct 18, 1952–Feb 7, 1953
YOUR SURPRISE STORE	CBS	May 12, 1952–Jun 27, 1952	THE GREATEST MAN ON EARTH	ABC	Dec 3, 1952–Feb 19, 1953
MIDWAY	DuMont	May 28, 1952–Sep 3, 1952	HAIL THE CHAMP	ABC	Dec 27, 1952–Jun 20, 1953
BLIND DATE	NBC	Jun 7, 1952–Jul 19, 1952	WHY?	ABC	Dec 29, 1952–Apr 20, 1953

program	network	first–last broadcast	program	network	first–last broadcast
WHAT'S YOUR BID	ABC	Feb 14, 1953–Apr 18, 1953	PLACE THE FACE	CBS	Aug 27, 1953–Aug 26, 1954
FREEDOM RINGS	CBS	Mar 2, 1953–Aug 27, 1953	ON YOUR WAY	DuMont	Sep 9, 1953–Jan 20, 1954
QUICK AS A FLASH	ABC	Mar 12, 1953–Jul 2, 1953	QUICK AS A FLASH	ABC	Sep 10, 1953–Feb 25, 1954
PERSONALITY PUZZLE	ABC	Mar 19, 1953–Jun 25, 1953	CHANCE OF A LIFETIME	DuMont	Sep 11, 1953–Jun 24, 1955
THE BIG PAYOFF	CBS	Mar 30, 1953–Oct 16, 1959	DOLLAR A SECOND	DuMont	Sep 20, 1953–Jun 14, 1954
BREAK THE BANK	NBC	Mar 30, 1953–Sep 18, 1953	PANTOMIME QUIZ	DuMont	Oct 20, 1953–Apr 13, 1954
WHAT'S YOUR BID	DuMont	May 3, 1953–Jun 29, 1953	BACK THAT FACT	ABC	Oct 22, 1953–Nov 26, 1953
YOUR BIG MOMENT	DuMont	May 19, 1953–Jun 2, 1953	DOCTOR I.Q.	ABC	Nov 4, 1953–Oct 17, 1954
DOUBLE OR NOTHING	NBC	Jun 5, 1953–Jul 3, 1953–	ON YOUR WAY	ABC	Jan 23, 1954–Apr 17, 1954
ON YOUR ACCOUNT	NBC	Jun 8, 1953–Jul 2, 1954	BREAK THE BANK	ABC	Jan 31, 1954–Jun 20, 1956
BLIND DATE	DuMont	Jun 9, 1953–Sep 15, 1953	WHO'S THE BOSS?	ABC	Feb 19, 1954–Aug 27, 1954
TAKE A GUESS	CBS	Jun 11, 1953–Sep 10, 1953	IT'S ABOUT TIME	ABC	Mar 4, 1954–May 2, 1954
I'LL BUY THAT	CBS	Jun 15, 1953–Jul 2, 1954	BANK ON THE STARS	NBC	May 15, 1954–Aug 21, 1954
BANK ON THE STARS	CBS	Jun 20, 1953–Aug 8, 1953	TRUTH OR CONSEQUENCES	NBC	May 18, 1954–Sep 28, 1956
THE BIG PAYOFF	NBC	Jun 21, 1953–Sep 27, 1953	EARN YOUR VACATION	CBS	May 23, 1954–Sep 5, 1954
MASQUERADE PARTY	CBS	Jun 22, 1953–Sep 14, 1953	TWO IN LOVE	CBS	Jun 19, 1954–Sep 11, 1954
BREAK THE BANK	NBC	Jun 23, 1953–Sep 1, 1953	DROODLES	NBC	Jun 21, 1954–Sep 17, 1954
PLACE THE FACE	NBC	Jul 2, 1953–Aug 20, 1953	MASQUERADE PARTY	CBS	Jun 21, 1954–Sep 27, 1954
GLAMOUR GIRL	NBC	Jul 6, 1953–Jan 8, 1954	WHAT DO YOU HAVE IN COMMON?	CBS	Jul 1, 1954–Sep 23, 1954
NAME THAT TUNE	NBC	Jul 6, 1953–Jun 14, 1954	COLLEGE OF MUSICAL KNOWLEDGE	NBC	Jul 4, 1954–Sep 12, 1954
FOLLOW THE LEADER	CBS	Jul 7, 1953–Aug 18, 1953	DOLLAR A SECOND	NBC	Jul 4, 1954–Aug 22, 1954
WHEEL OF FORTUNE	CBS	Jul 7, 1953–Sep 15, 1953	ON YOUR ACCOUNT	CBS	Jul 4, 1954–Mar 30, 1956
PANTOMIME QUIZ	CBS	Jul 10, 1953–Aug 28, 1953	ONE MINUTE PLEASE	DuMont	Jul 6, 1954–Feb 17, 1955
ANYONE CAN WIN	CBS	Jul 14, 1953–Sep 1, 1953	TWENTY QUESTIONS	ABC	Jul 6, 1954–May 3, 1955
SUPER GHOST	NBC	Jul 19, 1953–Sep 6, 1953	IT'S NEWS TO ME	CBS	Jul 9, 1954–Aug 27, 1954
TWO FOR THE MONEY	CBS	Aug 15, 1953–Sep 22, 1956	PANTOMIME QUIZ	CBS	Jul 9, 1954–Aug 27, 1954
JUDGE FOR YOURSELF	NBC	Aug 18, 1953–May 11, 1954	GAMBLE ON LOVE	DuMont	Jul 16, 1954–Aug 13, 1954

program	network	first–last broadcast	program	network	first–last broadcast
WHAT'S IN A WORD	CBS	Jul 22, 1954– Sep 9, 1954	DOLLAR A SECOND	ABC	Sep 2, 1955– Aug 31, 1956
TIME WILL TELL	DuMont	Aug 27, 1954– Oct 15, 1954	DOWN YOU GO	ABC	Sep 15, 1955– Jun 14, 1956
NAME THAT TUNE	CBS	Sep 2, 1954– Mar 24, 1955	STOP THE MUSIC	ABC	Sep 15, 1955– Jun 14, 1956
STOP THE MUSIC	ABC	Sep 7, 1954– May 31, 1955	NAME THAT TUNE	CBS	Sep 27, 1955– Oct 19, 1959
PLACE THE FACE	NBC	Sep 18, 1954– Dec 25, 1954	THE BIG SURPRISE	NBC	Oct 8, 1955– Jun 9, 1956
PEOPLE ARE FUNNY	NBC	Sep 19, 1954– Apr 16, 1961	LOVE STORY	CBS	Oct 24, 1955– Mar 30, 1956
COME CLOSER	ABC	Sep 20, 1954– Dec 13, 1954	DO YOU TRUST YOUR WIFE?	CBS	Jan 3, 1956– Mar 26, 1957
MASQUERADE PARTY	ABC	Sep 29, 1954– Dec 29, 1956	QUEEN FOR A DAY	NBC	Jan 3, 1956– Sep 2, 1960
DOLLAR A SECOND	ABC	Oct 1, 1954– Jun 24, 1955	CHOOSE UP SIDES	NBC	Jan 7, 1956– Mar 31, 1956
FEATHER YOUR NEST	NBC	Oct 4, 1954– Jul 27, 1956	QUIZ KIDS	CBS	Jan 12, 1956– Sep 27, 1956
THE NAME'S THE SAME	ABC	Oct 25, 1954– Oct 7, 1955	THE $64,000 CHALLENGE	CBS	Apr 8, 1956– Sep 7, 1958
FUNNY BONERS	NBC	Nov 20, 1954– Jul 9, 1955	IT COULD BE YOU	NBC	Jun 4, 1956– Dec 29, 1961
WHAT'S GOING ON?	ABC	Nov 28, 1954– Dec 26, 1954	DOWN YOU GO	NBC	Jun 16, 1956– Sep 8, 1956
PANTOMIME QUIZ	ABC	Jan 22, 1955– Mar 6, 1955	PANTOMIME QUIZ	CBS	Jul 6, 1956– Sep 7, 1956
WHO SAID THAT?	ABC	Feb 2, 1955– Jul 26, 1955	HIGH FINANCE	CBS	Jul 7, 1956– Dec 15, 1956
HAVE A HEART	DuMont	May 3, 1955– Jun 21, 1955	TIC TAC DOUGH	NBC	Jul 30, 1956– Oct 23, 1959
PENNY TO A MILLION	ABC	May 4, 1955– Oct 19, 1955	TREASURE HUNT	ABC	Sep 7, 1956– May 31, 1957
THE $64,000 QUESTION	CBS	Jun 7, 1955– Jun 24, 1958	TWENTY-ONE	NBC	Sep 12, 1956– Oct 16, 1958
DOWN YOU GO	CBS	Jun 11, 1955– Sep 3, 1955	THE BIG SURPRISE	NBC	Sep 18, 1956– Apr 2, 1957
PLACE THE FACE	NBC	Jun 28, 1955– Sep 13, 1955	BREAK THE $250,000 BANK	NBC	Oct 9, 1956– Jan 15, 1957
CHANCE OF A LIFETIME	ABC	Jul 3, 1955– Jun 23, 1956	GIANT STEP	CBS	Nov 7, 1956– May 29, 1957
IT PAYS TO BE MARRIED	NBC	Jul 4, 1955– Oct 28, 1955	CAN DO	NBC	Nov 26, 1956– Dec 31, 1956
DOLLAR A SECOND	NBC	Jul 5, 1955– Aug 30, 1955	THE PRICE IS RIGHT	NBC	Nov 26, 1956– Sep 6, 1963
MAKE THE CONNECTION	NBC	Jul 7, 1955– Sep 29, 1955	TO TELL THE TRUTH	CBS	Dec 18, 1956– Sep 25, 1966
PANTOMIME QUIZ	CBS	Jul 8, 1955– Sep 30, 1955	YOU'RE ON YOUR OWN	CBS	Dec 22, 1956– Mar 16, 1957
MUSICAL CHAIRS	NBC	Jul 9, 1955– Sep 17, 1955	TRUTH OR CONSEQUENCES	NBC	Dec 31, 1956– Sep 25, 1959
LET'S SEE	ABC	Jul 14, 1955– Aug 25, 1955	HOLD THAT NOTE	NBC	Jan 22, 1957– Apr 2, 1957

program	network	first–last broadcast	program	network	first–last broadcast
MASQUERADE PARTY	NBC	Mar 6, 1957–Sep 4, 1957	HAGGIS BAGGIS	NBC	Jun 30, 1958–Jun 19, 1959
TWO FOR THE MONEY	CBS	Mar 23, 1957–Sep 7, 1957	LUCKY PARTNERS	NBC	Jun 30, 1958–Aug 22, 1958
IT'S A HIT	CBS	Jun 1, 1957–Sep 21, 1957	PLAY YOUR HUNCH	CBS	Jun 30, 1958–Jan 2, 1959
DOLLAR A SECOND	NBC	Jun 22, 1957–Sep 28, 1957	BID 'N' BUY	CBS	Jul 1, 1958–Sep 23, 1958
HIGH LOW	NBC	Jul 4, 1957–Sep 19, 1957	DOTTO	NBC	Jul 1, 1958–Aug 12, 1958
PANTOMIME QUIZ	CBS	Jul 5, 1957–Sep 6, 1957	IT COULD BE YOU	NBC	Jul 2, 1958–Sep 17, 1958
TREASURE HUNT	NBC	Aug 12, 1957–Dec 4, 1959	ANYBODY CAN PLAY	ABC	Jul 6, 1958–Dec 8, 1958
TIC TAC DOUGH	NBC	Sep 12, 1957–Dec 29, 1958	E.S.P.	ABC	Jul 11, 1958–Aug 22, 1958
BEAT THE CLOCK	CBS	Sep 16, 1957–Sep 12, 1958	KEEP TALKING	CBS	Jul 15, 1958–Oct 28, 1958
THE PRICE IS RIGHT	NBC	Sep 23, 1957–Sep 6, 1963	MASQUERADE PARTY	CBS	Aug 4, 1958–Sep 15, 1958
WHO DO YOU TRUST?	ABC	Sep 30, 1957–Dec 27, 1963	TOP DOLLAR	CBS	Aug 18, 1958–Oct 16, 1959
KEEP IT IN THE FAMILY	ABC	Oct 12, 1957–Feb 8, 1958	CONCENTRATION	NBC	Aug 25, 1958–Mar 23, 1973
WHAT'S IT FOR?	NBC	Oct 12, 1957–Jan 4, 1958	BRAINS AND BRAWN	NBC	Sep 13, 1958–Dec 27, 1958
TRUTH OR CONSEQUENCES	NBC	Dec 13, 1957–Jun 6, 1958	THE $64,000 QUESTION	CBS	Sep 14, 1958–Nov 2, 1958
TREASURE HUNT	NBC	Dec 24, 1957–Jun 17, 1958	COUNTY FAIR	NBC	Sep 22, 1958–Sep 25, 1959
DOTTO	CBS	Jan 6, 1958–Aug 15, 1958	MASQUERADE PARTY	NBC	Oct 2, 1958–Sep 24, 1959
DOUGH RE MI	NBC	Feb 24, 1958–Dec 30, 1960	BEAT THE CLOCK	ABC	Oct 13, 1958–Jan 30, 1961
MAKE ME LAUGH	ABC	Mar 20, 1958–Jun 12, 1958	CHANCE FOR ROMANCE	ABC	Oct 13, 1958–Dec 5, 1958
TOP DOLLAR	CBS	Mar 29, 1958–Aug 30, 1958	MOTHER'S DAY	ABC	Oct 13, 1958–Jan 2, 1959
HOW DO YOU RATE?	CBS	Mar 31, 1958–Jun 26, 1958	CONCENTRATION	NBC	Oct 30, 1958–Nov 20, 1958
WINGO	CBS	Apr 1, 1958–May 6, 1958	KEEP TALKING	CBS	Nov 9, 1958–Sep 2, 1959
PANTOMIME QUIZ	ABC	Apr 8, 1958–Sep 2, 1958	IT COULD BE YOU	NBC	Nov 27, 1958–Mar 12, 1959
MUSIC BINGO	NBC	May 29, 1958–Sep 11, 1958	MUSIC BINGO	ABC	Dec 8, 1958–Jan 1, 1960
THE BIG GAME	NBC	Jun 13, 1958–Sep 19, 1958	DOCTOR I.Q.	ABC	Dec 15, 1958–Mar 23, 1959
HAGGIS BAGGIS	NBC	Jun 20, 1958–Sep 29, 1958	G.E. COLLEGE BOWL	CBS	Jan 4, 1959–Jun 28, 1959
WIN WITH A WINNER	NBC	Jun 24, 1958–Sep 9, 1958	PLAY YOUR HUNCH	ABC	Jan 5, 1959–May 8, 1959
FOR LOVE OR MONEY	CBS	Jun 30, 1958–Jan 30, 1959	JACKPOT BOWLING	NBC	Jan 9, 1959–Jun 24, 1960

program	network	first–last broadcast	program	network	first–last broadcast
LAUGH LINE	NBC	Apr 16, 1959–Jun 11, 1959	CAMOUFLAGE	ABC	Jan 9, 1961–Nov 16, 1962
PANTOMIME QUIZ	ABC	May 18, 1959–Oct 9, 1959	YOU'RE IN THE PICTURE	CBS	Jan 20, 1961 (one broadcast)
ACROSS THE BOARD	ABC	Jun 1, 1959–Oct 9, 1959	NUMBER PLEASE	ABC	Jan 31, 1961–Dec 29, 1961
PANTOMIME QUIZ	ABC	Jun 8, 1959–Sep 28, 1959	DOUBLE EXPOSURE	CBS	Mar 13, 1961–Sep 29, 1961
WHO PAYS?	NBC	Jul 2, 1959–Sep 24, 1959	FACE THE FACTS	CBS	Mar 13, 1961–Sep 29, 1961
IT COULD BE YOU	NBC	Sep 5, 1959–Jan 23, 1960	YOUR SURPRISE PACKAGE	CBS	Mar 13, 1961–Feb 23, 1962
SPLIT PERSONALITY	NBC	Sep 28, 1959–Feb 5, 1960	SEVEN KEYS	ABC	Apr 3, 1961–Mar 27, 1964
G.E. COLLEGE BOWL	CBS	Oct 4, 1959–Jun 26, 1960	CONCENTRATION	NBC	Apr 24, 1961–Sep 18, 1961
TAKE A GOOD LOOK	ABC	Oct 22, 1959–Jul 21, 1960	IT COULD BE YOU	NBC	Jun 7, 1961–Sep 27, 1961
MASQUERADE PARTY	CBS	Oct 26, 1959–Jan 18, 1960	ON YOUR MARK	ABC	Sep 23, 1961–Dec 16, 1961
TRUTH OR CONSEQUENCES	NBC	Oct 26, 1959–Sep 24, 1965	G.E. COLLEGE BOWL	CBS	Sep 24, 1961–Jun 17, 1962
KEEP TALKING	ABC	Oct 29, 1959–May 3, 1960	VIDEO VILLAGE JR.	CBS	Sep 30, 1961–Jun 16, 1962
PLAY YOUR HUNCH	NBC	Dec 7, 1959–Sep 27, 1963	MAKE A FACE	ABC	Oct 2, 1961–Mar 30, 1962
ABOUT FACES	ABC	Jan 4, 1960–Jun 30, 1961	PASSWORD	CBS	Oct 2, 1961–Sep 15, 1967
MASQUERADE PARTY	NBC	Jan 29, 1960–Sep 23, 1960	YOURS FOR A SONG	ABC	Nov 14, 1961–Sep 18, 1962
HOME RUN DERBY	SYN	Apr 1960–Oct 1960	YOURS FOR A SONG	ABC	Dec 4, 1961–Mar 29, 1963
PLAY YOUR HUNCH	NBC	Apr 15, 1960–Sep 23, 1960	PASSWORD	CBS	Jan 2, 1962–Sep 9, 1965
VIDEO VILLAGE	CBS	Jul 1, 1960–Sep 16, 1960	YOUR FIRST IMPRESSION	NBC	Jan 2, 1962–Jun 26, 1964
VIDEO VILLAGE	CBS	Jul 11, 1960–Jun 15, 1962	TELL IT TO GROUCHO	CBS	Jan 11, 1962–May 31, 1962
CELEBRITY GOLF	NBC	Sep 2, 1960–May 21, 1961	WINDOW SHOPPING	ABC	Apr 2, 1962–Jun 29, 1962
JAN MURRAY SHOW	NBC	Sep 5, 1960–Sep 28, 1962	TO TELL THE TRUTH	CBS	Jun 18, 1962–Sep 6, 1968
QUEEN FOR A DAY	ABC	Sep 5, 1960–Oct 2, 1964	PLAY YOUR HUNCH	NBC	Jun 20, 1962–Sep 26, 1962
JACKPOT BOWLING	NBC	Sep 19, 1960–Mar 13, 1961	STUMP THE STARS	CBS	Sep 17, 1962–Sep 16, 1963
G.E. COLLEGE BOWL	CBS	Oct 2, 1960–Jun 11, 1961	G.E. COLLEGE BOWL	CBS	Sep 23, 1962–Jun 16, 1963
MAKE THAT SPARE	ABC	Oct 8, 1960–Jun 30, 1962	MAKE A FACE	ABC	Sep 29, 1962–Dec 22, 1962
TAKE A GOOD LOOK	ABC	Oct 27, 1960–Mar 16, 1961	MAKE THAT SPARE	ABC	Oct 6, 1962–Sep 11, 1964
SAY WHEN!!	NBC	Jan 3, 1961–Mar 25, 1965	THE MATCH GAME	NBC	Dec 31, 1962–Sep 26, 1969

program	network	first–last broadcast	program	network	first–last broadcast
ALUMNI FUN	ABC	Jan 20, 1963– Apr 28, 1963	ALUMNI FUN	CBS	Jan 10, 1965– Mar 28, 1965
ART LINKLETTER SHOW	NBC	Feb 18, 1963– Sep 16, 1963	EVERYTHING'S RELATIVE	SYN	Feb 1, 1965– Aug 27, 1965
YOU DON'T SAY!	NBC	Apr 1, 1963– Sep 26, 1969	CALL MY BLUFF	NBC	Mar 29, 1965– Sep 24, 1965
TAKE TWO	ABC	May 5, 1963– Aug 11, 1963	I'LL BET	NBC	Mar 29, 1965– Sep 24, 1965
PICTURE THIS	CBS	Jun 25, 1963– Sep 17, 1963	THE REBUS GAME	ABC	Mar 29, 1965– Sep 24, 1965
PEOPLE WILL TALK	NBC	Jul 1, 1963– Dec 27, 1963	CELEBRITY GAME	CBS	Apr 8, 1965– Sep 9, 1965
MISSING LINKS	NBC	Sep 9, 1963– Mar 27, 1964	PDQ	SYN	Aug 30, 1965– Sep 26, 1969
THE PRICE IS RIGHT	ABC	Sep 9, 1963– Sep 3, 1965	G.E. COLLEGE BOWL	NBC	Sep 19, 1965– Jun 12, 1966
100 GRAND	ABC	Sep 15, 1963– Sep 29, 1963	SHENANIGANS	ABC	Sep 25, 1965– Dec 18, 1965
THE PRICE IS RIGHT	ABC	Sep 18, 1963– Sep 11, 1964	FRACTURED PHRASES	NBC	Sep 27, 1965– Dec 31, 1965
G.E. COLLEGE BOWL	NBC	Sep 22, 1963– Jun 14, 1964	LET'S PLAY POST OFFICE	NBC	Sep 27, 1965– Jul 1, 1966
WORD FOR WORD	NBC	Sep 30, 1963– Oct 23, 1964	THE DATING GAME	ABC	Dec 20, 1965– Jul 6, 1973
DO YOU KNOW?	CBS	Oct 12, 1963– Apr 25, 1964	SUPERMARKET SWEEP	ABC	Dec 20, 1965– Jul 14, 1967
LET'S MAKE A DEAL	NBC	Dec 30, 1963– Dec 27, 1968	EYE GUESS	NBC	Jan 3, 1966– Sep 26, 1969
THE OBJECT IS	ABC	Dec 30, 1963– Mar 27, 1964	ALUMNI FUN	CBS	Jan 23, 1966– May 1, 1966
ALUMNI FUN	CBS	Jan 5, 1964– Apr 5, 1964	THE FACE IS FAMILIAR	CBS	May 7, 1966– Sep 3, 1966
YOU DON'T SAY!	NBC	Jan 7, 1964– May 5, 1964	CHAIN LETTER	NBC	Jul 4, 1966– Oct 14, 1966
STUMP THE STARS	SYN	Feb 24, 1964– Sep 2, 1964	SHOWDOWN	NBC	Jul 4, 1966– Oct 14, 1966
GET THE MESSAGE	ABC	Mar 30, 1964– Dec 25, 1964	THE NEWLYWED GAME	ABC	Jul 11, 1966– Dec 20, 1974
JEOPARDY!	NBC	Mar 30, 1964– Jan 3, 1975	OH MY WORD	SYN	Sep 1966– Sep 1967
MISSING LINKS	ABC	Mar 30, 1964– Dec 25, 1964	G.E. COLLEGE BOWL	NBC	Sep 18, 1966– Jun 4, 1967
CELEBRITY GAME	CBS	Apr 5, 1964– Sep 13, 1964	TRUTH OR CONSEQUENCES	SYN	Sep 19, 1966– Sep 1975
MADE IN AMERICA	CBS	Apr 5, 1964– May 3, 1964	THE DATING GAME	ABC	Oct 6, 1966– Jan 17, 1970
G.E. COLLEGE BOWL	NBC	Sep 20, 1964– Jun 13, 1965	THE HOLLYWOOD SQUARES	NBC	Oct 17, 1966– Jun 20, 1980
SHENANIGANS	ABC	Sep 26, 1964– Mar 20, 1965	TO TELL THE TRUTH	CBS	Dec 12, 1966– May 22, 1967
WHAT'S THIS SONG?	NBC	Oct 26, 1964– Sep 24, 1965	DREAM GIRL OF '67	ABC	Dec 19, 1966– Dec 29, 1967
CELEBRITY GAME	CBS	Dec 20, 1964– Jan 24, 1965	PASSWORD	CBS	Dec 25, 1966– May 22, 1967

program	network	first–last broadcast	program	network	first–last broadcast
REACH FOR THE STARS	NBC	Jan 2, 1967–Mar 31, 1967	G.E. COLLEGE BOWL	NBC	Sep 28, 1968–Jun 8, 1969
THE NEWLYWED GAME	ABC	Jan 7, 1967–Aug 30, 1971	FUNNY YOU SHOULD ASK!!	ABC	Oct 28, 1968–Jun 27, 1969
EVERYBODY'S TALKING	ABC	Feb 6, 1967–Dec 29, 1967	BEAT THE ODDS	SYN	Dec 16, 1968–Sep 1969
MATCHES 'N MATES	SYN	Mar 20, 1967–Sep 1968	LET'S MAKE A DEAL	ABC	Dec 30, 1968–Jul 9, 1976
ONE IN A MILLION	ABC	Apr 10, 1967–Jun 16, 1967	THE STORYBOOK SQUARES	NBC	Jan 4, 1969–Aug 30, 1969
SNAP JUDGMENT	NBC	Apr 11, 1967–Mar 28, 1969	LIARS CLUB	SYN	Jan 20, 1969–Jun 13, 1969
LET'S MAKE A DEAL	NBC	May 21, 1967–Sep 3, 1967	THE ANNIVERSARY GAME	SYN	Jan 27, 1969–Sep 5, 1970
THE FAMILY GAME	ABC	Jun 19, 1967–Dec 29, 1967	THE GENERATION GAP	ABC	Feb 7, 1969–May 23, 1969
PERSONALITY	NBC	Jul 3, 1967–Sep 26, 1969	LET'S MAKE A DEAL	ABC	Feb 7, 1969–Aug 30, 1971
HONEYMOON RACE	ABC	Jul 17, 1967–Dec 1, 1967	MONEY MAKERS	SYN	Mar 3, 1969–May 30, 1969
IT'S YOUR MOVE	SYN	Sep 18, 1967–Dec 1967	IT TAKES TWO	NBC	Mar 31, 1969–Jul 31, 1970
THE PERFECT MATCH	SYN	Sep 18, 1967–Sep 1968	YOU'RE PUTTING ME ON	NBC	Jun 30, 1969–Dec 26, 1969
G.E. COLLEGE BOWL	NBC	Sep 23, 1967–Jun 9, 1968	THE MOVIE GAME	SYN	Sep 8, 1969–Feb 1, 1972
CELEBRITY BILLIARDS	SYN	Sep 27, 1967–Sep 1968	QUEEN FOR A DAY	SYN	Sep 8, 1969–Sep 18, 1970
CELEBRITY GAME (repeats)	CBS	Oct 1, 1967–Jan 7, 1968	STUMP THE STARS	SYN	Sep 8, 1969–Sep 25, 1970
HOW'S YOUR MOTHER-IN-LAW?	ABC	Dec 4, 1967–Mar 1, 1968	TO TELL THE TRUTH	SYN	Sep 8, 1969–Sep 1978
TEMPTATION	ABC	Dec 4, 1967–Mar 1, 1968	BEAT THE CLOCK	SYN	Sep 15, 1969–Sep 20, 1974
TREASURE ISLE	ABC	Dec 18, 1967–Dec 27, 1968	HE SAID, SHE SAID	SYN	Sep 15, 1969–Aug 21 1970
THE BABY GAME	ABC	Jan 1, 1968–Jul 12, 1968	THE GAME GAME	SYN	Sep 29, 1969–Sep 1970
THE HOLLYWOOD SQUARES	NBC	Jan 12, 1968–Sep 13, 1968	IT'S YOUR BET	SYN	Sep 29, 1969–Sep 1973
DREAM HOUSE	ABC	Mar 27, 1968–Sep 19, 1968	LETTERS TO LAUGH-IN	NBC	Sep 29, 1969–Dec 26, 1969
DREAM HOUSE	ABC	Apr 1, 1968–Jan 2, 1970	NAME DROPPERS	NBC	Sep 29, 1969–Mar 27, 1970
WEDDING PARTY	ABC	Apr 1, 1968–Jul 12, 1968	SALE OF THE CENTURY	NBC	Sep 29, 1969–Jul 13, 1973
FAST DRAW	SYN	May 25, 1968–Sep 1968	G.E. COLLEGE BOWL	NBC	Oct 11, 1969–Jun 14, 1970
PAY CARDS!	SYN	Sep 9, 1968–Sep 1969	THE WHO WHAT OR WHERE GAME	NBC	Dec 29, 1969–Jan 4, 1974
WHAT'S MY LINE?	SYN	Sep 9, 1968–Sep 1975	CAN YOU TOP THIS?	SYN	Jan 26, 1970–Sep 1970
WIN WITH THE STARS	SYN	Sep 18, 1968–Sep 1969	WORDS AND MUSIC	NBC	Sep 28, 1970–Feb 12, 1971

program	network	first–last broadcast	program	network	first–last broadcast
CELEBRITY BOWLING	SYN	Jan 16, 1971–Sep 1978	CONCENTRATION	SYN	Sep 10, 1973–Sep 1978
THE REEL GAME	ABC	Jan 18, 1971–May 3, 1971	THE DATING GAME	SYN	Sep 10, 1973–Sep 1974
SPORTS CHALLENGE	SYN	Jan 23, 1971–Sep 1979	IT PAYS TO BE IGNORANT	SYN	Sep 10, 1973–Sep 1974
JOE GARAGIOLA'S MEMORY GAME	NBC	Feb 15, 1971–Jul 30, 1971	SALE OF THE CENTURY	SYN	Sep 10, 1973–Sep 1974
PASSWORD	ABC	Apr 5, 1971–Jun 27, 1975	TREASURE HUNT	SYN	Sep 10, 1973–Sep 1977
THREE ON A MATCH	NBC	Aug 2, 1971–Jun 28, 1974	JACKPOT	NBC	Jan 7, 1974–Sep 26, 1975
ALL ABOUT FACES	SYN	Aug 30, 1971–Sep 1972	DEALER'S CHOICE	SYN	Jan 21, 1974–Dec 12, 1975
ANYTHING YOU CAN DO	SYN	Sep 13, 1971–Sep 1973	TATTLETALES	CBS	Feb 18, 1974–Mar 31, 1978
LET'S MAKE A DEAL	SYN	Sep 13, 1971–Sep 1977	CELEBRITY SWEEPSTAKES	NBC	Apr 1, 1974–Oct 1, 1976
THE HOLLYWOOD SQUARES	SYN	Nov 1, 1971–Sep 1981	NOW YOU SEE IT	CBS	Apr 1, 1974–Jun 13, 1975
GOLF FOR SWINGERS	SYN	Jan 15, 1972–Sep 1972	THE $10,000 PYRAMID	ABC	May 6, 1974–Jun 27, 1980
SPLIT SECOND	ABC	Mar 20, 1972–Jun 27, 1975	HIGH ROLLERS	NBC	Jul 1, 1974–Jun 11, 1976
AMATEUR'S GUIDE TO LOVE	CBS	Mar 27, 1972–Jun 23, 1972	WINNING STREAK	NBC	Jul 1, 1974–Jan 3, 1975
GAMBIT	CBS	Sep 4, 1972–Dec 10, 1976	NAME THAT TUNE	NBC	Jul 29, 1974–Jan 3, 1975
THE JOKER'S WILD	CBS	Sep 4, 1972–Jun 13, 1975	THE $25,000 PYRAMID	SYN	Sep 9, 1974–Sep 1979
THE PRICE IS RIGHT	CBS	Sep 4, 1972–	CELEBRITY SWEEPSTAKES	SYN	Sep 9, 1974–Sep 1975
THE PARENT GAME	SYN	Sep 4, 1972–Sep 1973	JEOPARDY!	SYN	Sep 9, 1974–Sep 7, 1975
RUNAROUND	NBC	Sep 9, 1972–Sep 1, 1973	MASQUERADE PARTY	SYN	Sep 9, 1974–Sep 1975
I'VE GOT A SECRET	SYN	Sep 11, 1972–Sep 1973	NAME THAT TUNE	SYN	Sep 9, 1974–Sep 1981
THE PRICE IS RIGHT	SYN	Sep 11, 1972–Sep 1979	THE BIG SHOWDOWN	ABC	Dec 23, 1974–Jul 4, 1975
THE $10,000 PYRAMID	CBS	Mar 26, 1973–Mar 29, 1974	THE MONEYMAZE	ABC	Dec 23, 1974–Jul 4, 1975
BAFFLE	NBC	Mar 26, 1973–Mar 29, 1974	BLANK CHECK	NBC	Jan 6, 1975–Jul 4, 1975
HOLLYWOOD'S TALKING	CBS	Mar 26, 1973–Jun 22, 1973	THE DIAMOND HEAD GAME	SYN	Jan 6, 1975–Sep 1975
SPORTS CHALLENGE	CBS	May 20, 1973–Sep 9, 1973–	WHEEL OF FORTUNE	NBC	Jan 6, 1975–Jun 30, 1989
MATCH GAME	CBS	Jul 2, 1973–Apr 20, 1979	BLANKETY BLANKS	ABC	Apr 21, 1975–Jun 27, 1975
WIZARD OF ODDS	NBC	Jul 17, 1973–Jun 28, 1974	WHAT'S MY LINE?	ABC	May 28, 1975 (special)
CELEBRITY TENNIS	SYN	Sep 1973–Sep 1974	MUSICAL CHAIRS	CBS	Jun 16, 1975–Oct 31, 1975

program	network	first–last broadcast	program	network	first–last broadcast
SPIN-OFF	CBS	Jun 16, 1975–Sep 5, 1975	CELEBRITY SWEEPSTAKES	SYN	Sep 20, 1976–Sep 1977
SHOWOFFS	ABC	Jun 30, 1975–Dec 26, 1975	50 GRAND SLAM	NBC	Oct 4, 1976–Dec 31, 1976
THE MAGNIFICENT MARBLE MACHINE	NBC	Jul 7, 1975–Jan 2, 1976	STUMPERS	NBC	Oct 4, 1976–Dec 31, 1976
RHYME AND REASON	ABC	Jul 7, 1975–Jul 9, 1976	DOUBLE DARE	CBS	Dec 13, 1976–Apr 29, 1977
YOU DON'T SAY!	ABC	Jul 7, 1975–Nov 26, 1975	NAME THAT TUNE	NBC	Jan 3, 1977–Jun 10, 1977
ALMOST ANYTHING GOES	ABC	Jul 31, 1975–Aug 28, 1975	SHOOT FOR THE STARS	NBC	Jan 3, 1977–Sep 30, 1977
DON ADAMS' SCREEN TEST	SYN	Sep 8, 1975–Sep 19, 1976	SECOND CHANCE	ABC	Mar 7, 1977–Jul 15, 1977
GIVE-N-TAKE	CBS	Sep 8, 1975–Nov 26, 1975	PRO-FAN	SYN	Apr 30, 1977–Sep 11, 1977
HIGH ROLLERS	SYN	Sep 8, 1975–Sep 19, 1976	IT'S ANYBODY'S GUESS	NBC	Jun 13, 1977–Sep 30, 1977
MATCH GAME PM	SYN	Sep 8, 1975–Sep 1982	THE BETTER SEX	ABC	Jul 18, 1977–Jan 13, 1978
THREE FOR THE MONEY	NBC	Sep 29, 1975–Nov 28, 1975	THE JOKER'S WILD	SYN	Sep 1977–Sep 1986
CROSS WITS	SYN	Dec 15, 1975–Sep 1980	THE HOLLYWOOD CONNEC-TION	SYN	Sep 5, 1977–Apr 1978
THE NEIGHBORS	ABC	Dec 29, 1975–Apr 9, 1976	THE NEWLYWED GAME	SYN	Sep 5, 1977–Sep 1980
THE MAGNIFICENT MARBLE MACHINE	NBC	Jan 19, 1976–Jun 11, 1976	TATTLETALES	SYN	Sep 12, 1977–Sep 1978
ALMOST ANYTHING GOES	ABC	Jan 24, 1976–May 2, 1976	ALL STAR ALMOST ANY-THING GOES	SYN	Sep 16, 1977–Sep 1978
BREAK THE BANK	ABC	Apr 12, 1976–Jul 23, 1976	FAMILY FEUD	SYN	Sep 19, 1977–Sep 1985
THE FUN FACTORY	NBC	Jun 14, 1976–Oct 1, 1976	TRUTH OR CONSEQUENCES	SYN	Sep 19, 1977–Sep 1978
THE GONG SHOW	NBC	Jun 14, 1976–Jul 21, 1978	KNOCKOUT	NBC	Oct 3, 1977–Apr 21, 1978
I'VE GOT A SECRET	CBS	Jun 15, 1976–Jul 6, 1976	TO SAY THE LEAST	NBC	Oct 3, 1977–Apr 21, 1978
FAMILY FEUD	ABC	Jul 12, 1976–Jun 14, 1985	QUIZ KIDS	SYN	Apr 1978–Sep 1978
HOT SEAT	ABC	Jul 12, 1976–Oct 22, 1976	PASS THE BUCK	ABC	Apr 3, 1978–Jun 30, 1978
THE GONG SHOW	SYN	Sep 1976–Sep 1980	CARD SHARKS	NBC	Apr 24, 1978–Oct 23, 1981
THE LIARS CLUB	SYN	Sep 1976–Sep 1979	HIGH ROLLERS	NBC	Apr 24, 1978–Jun 20, 1980
JUNIOR ALMOST ANYTHING GOES	ABC	Sep 11, 1976–Sep 4, 1977	ALL STAR FAMILY FEUD SPECIALS	ABC	May 8, 1978–May 23, 1984
WAY OUT GAMES	CBS	Sep 11, 1976–Sep 4, 1977	COLLEGE BOWL	SYN	Jun 3, 1978 (Special)
THE $128,000 QUESTION	SYN	Sep 18, 1976–Sep 1978	TIC TAC DOUGH	CBS	Jul 3, 1978–Sep 1, 1978
BREAK THE BANK	SYN	Sep 18, 1976–Sep 11, 1977	THE $1.98 BEAUTY SHOW	SYN	Sep 1978–Sep 1980

program	network	first–last broadcast	program	network	first–last broadcast
THE CHEAP SHOW	SYN	Sep 1978–Sep 1979	BULLSEYE	SYN	Sep 29, 1980–Sep 24, 1982
THE DATING GAME	SYN	Sep 4, 1978–Sep 1980	BLOCKBUSTERS	NBC	Oct 27, 1980–Apr 23, 1982
THE LOVE EXPERTS	SYN	Sep 18, 1978–Sep 1979	LAS VEGAS GAMBIT	NBC	Oct 27, 1980–Nov 27, 1981
TIC TAC DOUGH	SYN	Sep 18, 1978–Sep 1986	THE $50,000 PYRAMID	SYN	Jan 26, 1981–Sep 1981
YOU DON'T SAY!	SYN	Sep 18, 1978–Mar 1979	THE KRYPTON FACTOR	ABC	Aug 7, 1981–Sep 4, 1981
JEOPARDY!	NBC	Oct 2, 1978–Mar 2, 1979	EVERYTHING GOES	PLAY-BOY	Sep 12, 1981–Sep 28, 1988
WE INTERRUPT THIS WEEK	PBS	Oct 6, 1978–Dec 29, 1978	PITFALL	SYN	Sep 14, 1981–Sep 1982
CELEBRITY CHARADES	SYN	Jan 1979–Sep 1979	SUPER PAY CARDS!	SYN	Sep 14, 1981–Apr 23, 1982
ALL STAR SECRETS	NBC	Jan 8, 1979–Aug 10, 1979	TREASURE HUNT	SYN	Sep 14, 1981–Sep 1982
PASSWORD PLUS	NBC	Jan 8, 1979–Mar 26, 1982	QUIZ KIDS	CBS Cable	Oct 12, 1981–Dec 15, 1982
MAKE ME LAUGH	SYN	Jan 15, 1979–Feb 29, 1980	BATTLESTARS	NBC	Oct 26, 1981–Apr 23, 1982
WE INTERRUPT THIS WEEK	PBS	Feb 2, 1979–Mar 2, 1979	ULTRA QUIZ	NBC	Nov 10, 1981–Nov 17, 1981
WHODUNNIT?	NBC	Apr 12, 1979–May 17, 1979	TOP OF THE WORLD	PBS	Jan 17, 1982–Apr 11, 1982
WHEW!	CBS	Apr 23, 1979–May 30, 1980	TATTLETALES	CBS	Jan 18, 1982–Jun 1, 1984
BEDTIME STORIES	SYN	Jun 18, 1979–Jul 27, 1979	THAT **** QUIZ SHOW	SYN	Sep 1982–Dec 1982
MINDREADERS	NBC	Aug 13, 1979–Jan 11, 1980	TAKE MY WORD FOR IT	SYN	Sep 13, 1982–Sep 1983
JOKER! JOKER! JOKER!	SYN	Sep 1979–Sep 1980	THE $25,000 PYRAMID	CBS	Sep 20, 1982–Dec 31, 1987
BEAT THE CLOCK	CBS	Sep 17, 1979–Feb 1, 1980	CHILD'S PLAY	CBS	Sep 20, 1982–Sep 16, 1983
THE GUINNESS GAME	SYN	Sep 17, 1979–Sep 1980	GRAND PRIX ALL STAR SHOW	SYN	Sep 25, 1982–Sep 17, 1983
THREE'S A CROWD	SYN	Sep 17, 1979–Feb 1980	HIT MAN	NBC	Jan 3, 1983–Apr 1, 1983
PLAY THE PERCENTAGES	SYN	Jan 7, 1980–Sep 12, 1980	JUST MEN!	NBC	Jan 3, 1983–Apr 1, 1983
CHAIN REACTION	NBC	Jan 14, 1980–Jun 20, 1980	SALE OF THE CENTURY	NBC	Jan 3, 1983–Mar 24, 1989
FACE THE MUSIC	SYN	Jan 14, 1980–Sep 11, 1981	FANDANGO	TNN	Mar 8, 1983–Mar 31, 1989
CAMOUFLAGE	SYN	Feb 4, 1980–Apr 1980	BATTLESTARS	NBC	Apr 4, 1983–Jul 1, 1983
TO TELL THE TRUTH	SYN	Sep 8, 1980–Sep 4, 1981	DREAM HOUSE	NBC	Apr 4, 1983–Jun 29, 1984
YOU BET YOUR LIFE	SYN	Sep 8, 1980–Sep 1981	CONTRAPTION	DISNEY	Apr 18, 1983–Jan 9, 1988
LET'S MAKE A DEAL	SYN	Sep 22, 1980–Sep 1981	DUELING FOR PLAYMATES	PLAY-BOY	Aug 7, 1983–Aug 30, 1988

program	network	first–last broadcast	program	network	first–last broadcast
STARCADE	SYN	Sep 1983– Sep 1984	ALL STAR BLITZ	ABC	Apr 8, 1985– Dec 20, 1985
POP 'N' ROCKER GAME	SYN	Sep 17, 1983– Sep 1984	STAR GAMES	SYN	Sep 7, 1985– Sep 1986
LOVE CONNECTION	SYN	Sep 19, 1983– Sep 1994	THE $100,000 PYRAMID	SYN	Sep 9, 1985– Sep 2, 1988
PRESS YOUR LUCK	CBS	Sep 19, 1983– Sep 26, 1986	HEADLINE CHASERS	SYN	Sep 9, 1985– Sep 1986
WHEEL OF FORTUNE	SYN	Sep 19, 1983–	THE PRICE IS RIGHT	SYN	Sep 9, 1985– Sep 5, 1986
GO	NBC	Oct 3, 1983– Jan 20, 1984	BREAK THE BANK	SYN	Sep 16, 1985– Sep 12, 1986
THE MATCH GAME– HOLLYWOOD SQUARES HOUR	NBC	Oct 31, 1983– Jul 27, 1984	CATCH PHRASE	SYN	Sep 16, 1985– Jan 10, 1986
HOT POTATO	NBC	Jan 23, 1984– Jun 29, 1984	THE NEWLYWED GAME	SYN	Sep 16, 1985– Sep 8, 1989
THE NEWLYWED GAME	ABC	Feb 13, 1984– Feb 17, 1984	YOUR NUMBER'S UP	NBC	Sep 23, 1985– Dec 20, 1985
PEOPLE ARE FUNNY	NBC	Mar 24, 1984– Jul 21, 1984	GO! (repeats)	CBN	Sep 30, 1985– Aug 29, 1986
COLLEGE BOWL	NBC	May 23, 1984 (special)	JACKPOT	USA	Sep 30, 1985– Dec 30, 1988
BODY LANGUAGE	CBS	Jun 4, 1984– Jan 3, 1986	THE $1,000,000 CHANCE OF A LIFETIME	SYN	Jan 6, 1986– Sep 11, 1987
SCRABBLE	NBC	Jul 2, 1984– Mar 23, 1990	BRUCE FORSYTH'S HOT STREAK	ABC	Jan 6, 1986– Apr 4, 1986
VIDEO GAME	SYN	Sep 1984– Sep 1985	CARD SHARKS	CBS	Jan 6, 1986– Mar 31, 1989
THE $100,000 NAME THAT TUNE	SYN	Sep 10, 1984– Sep 1985	PERFECT MATCH	SYN	Jan 13, 1986– Sep 12, 1986
ANYTHING FOR MONEY	SYN	Sep 17, 1984– Sep 1985	ALL STAR BLITZ (repeats)	USA	Mar 31, 1986– Dec 26, 1986
EVERY SECOND COUNTS	SYN	Sep 17, 1984– Sep 1985	THE PRICE IS RIGHT	CBS	Aug 14, 1986– Sep 18, 1986
JEOPARDY!	SYN	Sep 17, 1984–	DOUBLE TALK	ABC	Aug 18, 1986– Dec 19, 1986
LET'S MAKE A DEAL	SYN	Sep 17, 1984– Sep 1986	YOU WRITE THE SONGS	SYN	Sep 5, 1986– Sep 1987
GUILTY OR INNOCENT	SYN	Sep 24, 1984– Dec 1984	DREAM GIRL USA	SYN	Sep 6, 1986– Sep 1987
SUPER PASSWORD	NBC	Sep 24, 1984– Mar 24, 1989	CARD SHARKS	SYN	Sep 8, 1986– Sep 1987
THE GONG SHOW (repeats)	USA	Oct 1, 1984– Oct 9, 1987	CROSSWITS	SYN	Sep 8, 1986– Sep 1987
MAKE ME LAUGH (repeats)	USA	Oct 2, 1984– Sep 26, 1986	THE DATING GAME	SYN	Sep 15, 1986– Sep 8, 1989
TRIVIA TRAP	ABC	Oct 8, 1984– Apr 5, 1985	HOLLYWOOD SQUARES	SYN	Sep 15, 1986– Sep 8, 1989
SALE OF THE CENTURY	SYN	Jan 1985– Sep 1986	STRIKE IT RICH	SYN	Sep 15, 1986– Sep 1987
TIME MACHINE	NBC	Jan 7, 1985– Apr 26, 1985	ANYTHING FOR MONEY (repeats)	USA	Sep 29, 1986– Jun 24, 1988
BULLSEYE (repeats)	USA	Apr 1, 1985– Jun 26, 1987	CHAIN REACTION	USA	Sep 29, 1986– Dec 27, 1991
THE JOKER'S WILD (repeats)	USA	Apr 1, 1985– Apr 24, 1987			

program	network	first–last broadcast	program	network	first–last broadcast
LOVE ME, LOVE ME NOT	USA	Sep 29, 1986–Sep 11, 1987	BLACKOUT	CBS	Jan 4, 1988–Apr 1, 1988
DOUBLE DARE	NICK	Oct 6, 1986–Mar 15, 1991	YAHTZEE	SYN	Jan 11, 1988–Sep 1988
SPLIT SECOND	SYN	Dec 15, 1986–Sep 1987	BOARDWALK & BASE-BALL'S SUPER BOWL OF SPORTS TRIVIA	ESPN	Jan 28, 1988–May 16, 1988
LET'S MAKE A DEAL (repeats)	USA	Dec 29, 1986–Dec 30, 1988	DOUBLE DARE	SYN	Feb 22, 1988–Sep 8, 1989
WORDPLAY	NBC	Dec 29, 1986–Sep 4, 1987	MAKE THAT SPARE	ABC	Mar 12, 1988 (special)
BLOCKBUSTERS	NBC	Jan 5, 1987–May 1, 1987	FAMILY DOUBLE DARE	FOX	Apr 3, 1988–Jul 23, 1988
PLAY THE PERCENTAGES (repeats)	USA	Apr 27, 1987–Jun 23, 1989	THE $25,000 PYRAMID	CBS	Apr 4, 1988–Jul 1, 1988
CLASSIC CONCENTRATION	NBC	May 4, 1987–Sep 20, 1991	SLIME TIME	SYN	Jun 11, 1988–Sep 1988
HOME SHOPPING GAME	SYN	Jun 15, 1987–Sep 11, 1987	TREASURE MALL	SYN	Jun 11, 1988–Sep 1988
BUMPER STUMPERS	USA	Jun 29, 1987–Dec 28, 1990	FAMILY FEUD	CBS	Jul 4, 1988–Sep 10, 1993
HOT POTATO (repeats)	USA	Jun 29, 1987–Jun 23, 1989	GRANDSTAND	SYN	Jul 9, 1988–Jul 1989
BARGAIN HUNTERS	ABC	Jul 6, 1987–Sep 4, 1987	KING PINS	NICK	Jul 29, 1988 (special)
ANIMAL CRACK-UPS	ABC	Aug 8, 1987–Sep 12, 1987	FUN HOUSE	SYN	Sep 5, 1988–Sep 9, 1990
SECOND HONEYMOON	CBN	Sep 2, 1987–Sep 2, 1988	NFL TRIVIA GAME	ESPN	Sep 5, 1988–Jan 21, 1989
WIN, LOSE OR DRAW	NBC	Sep 7, 1987–Sep 1, 1989	RELATIVELY SPEAKING	SYN	Sep 5, 1988–Jun 23, 1989
WIN, LOSE OR DRAW	SYN	Sep 7, 1987–Aug 30, 1990	FINDERS KEEPERS	SYN	Sep 12, 1988–Mar 10, 1989
ANIMAL CRACK-UPS	ABC	Sep 12, 1987–Dec 30, 1989	THE GONG SHOW	SYN	Sep 12, 1988–Sep 15, 1989
I'M TELLING	NBC	Sep 12, 1987–Aug 27, 1988	SWEETHEARTS	SYN	Sep 12, 1988–Sep 8, 1989
COLLEGE BOWL	DISNEY	Sep 13, 1987–Dec 20, 1987	WIPEOUT	SYN	Sep 12, 1988–Sep 8, 1989
HIGH ROLLERS	SYN	Sep 14, 1987–Sep 9, 1988	FAMILY FEUD	SYN	Sep 19, 1988–Sep 1995
MATCHMAKER	SYN	Sep 14, 1987–Sep 1988	HIGH ROLLERS (repeats)	USA	Sep 19, 1988–Sep 13, 1991
PRESS YOUR LUCK (repeats)	USA	Sep 14, 1987–Feb 3, 1995	TELL ME SOMETHING GOOD	BET	Sep 19, 1988–May 1989
TRUTH OR CONSEQUENCES	SYN	Sep 14, 1987–Feb 26, 1988	LIARS CLUB	SYN	Oct 3, 1988–Jun 30, 1989
LINGO	SYN	Sep 28, 1987–Sep 1988	TRIPLE THREAT	SYN	Oct 8, 1988–Oct 1, 1989
TIC TAC DOUGH (repeats)	USA	Oct 12, 1987–Sep 7, 1990	THE $25,000 PYRAMID (repeats)	USA	Oct 17, 1988–Nov 4, 1994
FINDERS KEEPERS	NICK	Nov 2, 1987–Sep 11, 1988	HOME RUN DERBY (repeats)	ESPN	Dec 17, 1988–Dec 28, 1988
REMOTE CONTROL	MTV	Dec 7, 1987–Nov 15, 1990			

program	network	first–last broadcast
$100,000 NAME THAT TUNE (repeats)	USA	Jan 2, 1989–Sep 13, 1991
FACE THE MUSIC (repeats)	USA	Jan 2, 1989–Sep 8, 1989
COUCH POTATOES	SYN	Jan 23, 1989–Sep 8, 1989
CONTRAPTION (repeats)	DISNEY	Mar 8, 1989–Oct 25, 1989
FINDERS KEEPERS (repeats)	NICK	Mar 13, 1989–Jun 30, 1990
STRAIGHT TO THE HEART	SYN	Mar 20, 1989–Sep 8, 1989
BOARDWALK & BASE-BALL'S SUPER BOWL OF SPORTS TRIVIA	ESPN	Apr 3, 1989–Sep 18, 1989
NOW YOU SEE IT	CBS	Apr 3, 1989–Jul 14, 1989
TOP CARD	TNN	Apr 3, 1989–Mar 26, 1993
TEEN WIN, LOSE OR DRAW	DISNEY	Apr 29, 1989–Apr 28, 1990
THINK FAST	NICK	May 1, 1989–Jun 29, 1991
PICTIONARY	SYN	Jun 12, 1989–Sep 8, 1989
TEXACO STAR NATIONAL ACADEMIC CHAMPIONSHIP	DISCOV-ERY	Jul 1, 1989–Aug 19, 1989
HOME RUN DERBY (repeats)	ESPN	Jul 10, 1989–Oct 28, 1989
WHEEL OF FORTUNE	CBS	Jul 17, 1989–Jan 11, 1991
MOVIE MASTERS	AMC	Aug 2, 1989–Jan 19, 1990
AMERICAN GLADIATORS	SYN	Sep 9, 1989–Sep 14, 1997
COLLEGE MAD HOUSE	SYN	Sep 9, 1989–Sep 1, 1990
I'M TELLING (repeats)	FAMILY	Sep 9, 1989–Sep 8, 1990
3RD DEGREE	SYN	Sep 11, 1989–Sep 7, 1990
COUCH POTATOES (repeats)	USA	Sep 11, 1989–Mar 23, 1990
HOLLYWOOD SQUARES (repeats)	USA	Sep 11, 1989–Jun 25, 1993
NFL TRIVIA GAME	ESPN	Sep 11, 1989–Dec 25, 1989
WIPEOUT (repeats)	USA	Sep 11, 1989–Sep 13, 1991
JACKPOT	SYN	Sep 18, 1989–Mar 16, 1990
THE LAST WORD	SYN	Sep 18, 1989–Jan 5, 1990
TALKABOUT	SYN	Sep 18, 1989–Mar 16, 1990
REMOTE CONTROL	SYN	Sep 23, 1989–Sep 8, 1990
MAKE THE GRADE	NICK	Oct 2, 1989–Dec 29, 1991
RODEO DRIVE	LIFE-TIME	Feb 5, 1990–Aug 31, 1990
SUPERMARKET SWEEP	LIFE-TIME	Feb 5, 1990–Aug 14, 1998
FACE THE MUSIC (repeats)	USA	Mar 26, 1990–Sep 14, 1990
CAMPUS ALL-STAR CHAL-LENGE	BET	Apr 14, 1990–Jun 2, 1990
WHOSE LINE IS IT ANY-WAY?	HA!/COM	May 1, 1990–Jun 21, 1998
CLASH	HA!/COM	May 1, 1990–Dec 28, 1991
THE GREAT GETAWAY GAME	TRAVEL	Jun 1, 1990–Apr 1991
ANIMAL CRACK-UPS (repeats)	ABC	Jun 2, 1990–Sep 1, 1990
ARE YOU KIDDING?	CBS	Jun 8, 1990 (special)
MONOPOLY	ABC	Jun 16, 1990–Sep 1, 1990
SUPER JEOPARDY!	ABC	Jun 16, 1990–Sep 8, 1990
ALL ABOUT THE OPPOSITE SEX	SYN	Jun 18, 1990–Aug 17, 1990
HOLD EVERYTHING!	SYN	Jun 18, 1990–Aug 17, 1990
TURN IT UP!	MTV	Jun 30, 1990–Dec 7, 1990
TEXACO STAR NATIONAL ACADEMIC CHAMPIONSHIP	DISCOV-ERY	Jul 7, 1990–Aug 25, 1990
WILD & CRAZY KIDS	NICK	Jul 8, 1990
LET'S MAKE A DEAL	NBC	Jul 9, 1990–Jan 11, 1991
MATCH GAME	ABC	Jul 16, 1990–Jul 12, 1991
KING OF THE MOUNTAIN	FOX	Jul 28, 1990 (special)
PURE INSANITY!	FOX	Aug 11, 1990 (special)
FAMILY DOUBLE DARE	NICK	Aug 13, 1990
PURE INSANITY!	FOX	Sep 2, 1990 (special)
THE CHALLENGERS	SYN	Sep 3, 1990–Aug 31, 1991
TO TELL THE TRUTH	NBC	Sep 3, 1990–May 31, 1991
FOX FUN HOUSE	FOX	Sep 10, 1990–Apr 13, 1991
HOT POTATO (repeats)	USA	Sep 10, 1990–Dec 28, 1990

program	network	first–last broadcast	program	network	first–last broadcast
THE JOKER'S WILD	SYN	Sep 10, 1990–Sep 13, 1991	CLASSIC CONCENTRATION (repeats)	NBC	Oct 28, 1991–Dec 31, 1993
QUIZ KIDS CHALLENGE	SYN	Sep 10, 1990–Dec 28, 1990	THE JOKER'S WILD (repeats)	USA	Dec 30, 1991–Sep 11, 1992
TEEN WIN, LOSE OR DRAW	DISNEY	Sep 10, 1990–Sep 26, 1992	NICKELODEON ARCADE	NICK	Jan 3, 1992–Sep 28, 1997
TIC TAC DOUGH	SYN	Sep 10, 1990–Mar 8, 1991	LIP SERVICE	MTV	Feb 22, 1992–Jan 3, 1993
TRUMP CARD	SYN	Sep 10, 1990–Sep 6, 1991	LOVE AT FIRST SIGHT	SYN	Jun 1, 1992–Aug 14, 1992
THE KRYPTON FACTOR	SYN	Sep 15, 1990–Sep 7, 1991	CAMPUS ALL-STAR CHALLENGE	BET	Jun 6, 1992–Jul 25, 1992
VIDEO POWER	SYN	Sep 24, 1990–Sep 4, 1992	A PERFECT SCORE	CBS	Jun 15, 1992–Dec 8, 1992
FAMILY FIGURES	BET	Oct 16, 1990–Dec 29, 1990	THE HOLLYWOOD GAME	CBS	Jun 19, 1992–Jul 10, 1992
WIN, LOSE OR DRAW (repeats)	USA	Dec 31, 1990–Dec 24, 1992	TEXACO STAR NATIONAL ACADEMIC CHAMPIONSHIP	SYN	Jun 22, 1992–Sep 28, 1992
THE $100,000 PYRAMID	SYN	Jan 7, 1991–Mar 6, 1992	PLAYBOY'S LOVE & SEX TEST	PLAY-BOY	Aug 7, 1992–Sep 26, 1994
WHEEL OF FORTUNE	NBC	Jan 14, 1991–Sep 20, 1991	BEDROOM BUDDIES	SYN	Aug 10, 1992–Sep 18, 1992
STUDS	SYN	Mar 11, 1991–Sep 3, 1993	YOU BET YOUR LIFE	SYN	Aug 31, 1992–Sep 3, 1993
GET THE PICTURE	NICK	Mar 18, 1991–Mar 13, 1993	DOUBLE UP	NBC	Sep 5, 1992–Oct 17, 1992
FANTASY PARK	FOX	Apr 13, 1991 (special)	CAMPUS ALL-STAR CHALLENGE (repeats)	BET	Sep 5, 1992–Oct 24, 1992
REMOTE CONTROL (repeats)	MTV	Apr 29, 1991–Dec 31, 1991	SALE OF THE CENTURY (repeats)	USA	Sep 14, 1992–Jul 29, 1994
CAMPUS ALL-STAR CHALLENGE	BET	Jun 1, 1991–Jul 20, 1991	THAT'S AMORE	SYN	Sep 14, 1992–Sep 10, 1993
TEXACO STAR NATIONAL ACADEMIC CHAMPIONSHIP	SYN	Jul 3, 1991–Sep 4, 1991	TRIPLE THREAT	BET	Sep 14, 1992–Sep 17, 1993
LET'S GO BACK	NOSTAL-GIA	Jul 6, 1991–May 31, 1993	LOVE BETWEEN THE SEXES	BET	Sep 15, 1992–Jan 16, 1993
SHOP 'TIL YOU DROP	LIFE-TIME	Jul 8, 1991–Sep 1, 1995	NICKELODEON GUTS	NICK	Sep 19, 1992–Sep 2, 1995
WHAT WOULD YOU DO?	NICK	Aug 31, 1991–	KNIGHTS & WARRIORS	SYN	Sep 19, 1992–Sep 11, 1993
THAT'S MY DOG!	FAMILY	Sep 1, 1991–Sep 30, 1995	BORN LUCKY	LIFE-TIME	Oct 5, 1992–Apr 2, 1993
THE GRUDGE MATCH	SYN	Sep 7, 1991–Sep 6, 1992	THE $100,000 PYRAMID (repeats)	USA	Dec 28, 1992–Sep 8, 1995
RUCKUS	SYN	Sep 9, 1991–Jan 3, 1992	AMERICAN GLADIATORS (repeats)	USA	Jan 4, 1993–Oct 8, 1993
PERSONALS	CBS	Sep 16, 1991–Dec 23, 1992	SCATTERGORIES	NBC	Jan 18, 1993–Jun 10, 1993
SCRABBLE (repeats)	USA	Sep 16, 1991–Feb 3, 1995	SCRABBLE	NBC	Jan 18, 1993–Jun 10, 1993
WHERE IN THE WORLD IS CARMEN SANDIEGO?	PBS	Sep 30, 1991–Oct 4, 1996	DREAM LEAGUE	ESPN	Feb 1, 1993–May 27, 1993
USA GONZO GAMES	USA	Oct 6, 1991–Mar 29, 1992	CONQUER FORT BOYARD	ABC	Mar 20, 1993 (special)
NIGHT GAMES	CBS	Oct 14, 1991–Jun 12, 1992			

program	network	first–last broadcast	program	network	first–last broadcast
FAMILY SECRETS	NBC	Mar 22, 1993–Jun 11, 1993	BOARDWALK & BASEBALL'S SUPER BOWL OF SPORTS TRIVIA (repeats)	ESPN-2	Oct 4, 1993–Jan 7, 1994
10 SECONDS	TNN	Mar 29, 1993–Mar 25, 1994	DESIGNATED HITTER	ESPN	Dec 1, 1993–Mar 31, 1994
THE JOKER'S WILD (repeats)	USA	Mar 29, 1993–Jun 24, 1994	TRASHED	MTV	Feb 14, 1994–Jul 23, 1994
TIC TAC DOUGH (repeats)	USA	Mar 29, 1993–Jun 24, 1994	TEXACO STAR NATIONAL ACADEMIC CHAMPIONSHIP	BRAVO	Mar 4, 1994–May 27, 1994
WANNA BET?	CBS	Apr 21, 1993 (special)	SHUFFLE: THE INTERACTIVE GAME	FAMILY	Mar 7, 1994–Jun 10, 1994
LIP SERVICE	MTV	May 10, 1993–Dec 17, 1994	BOGGLE: THE INTERACTIVE GAME	FAMILY	Mar 7, 1994–Nov 18, 1994
THE $100,000 NAME THAT TUNE (repeats)	FAMILY	Jun 7, 1993–Mar 29 1996	SPORTS ON TAP	ESPN	Apr 5, 1994–Sep 30, 1994
CROSSWITS (repeats)	FAMILY	Jun 7, 1993–Aug 27, 1993	CAMPUS ALL-STAR CHALLENGE	BET	Jun 11, 1994–Jul 30, 1994
LET'S MAKE A DEAL (repeats)	FAMILY	Jun 7, 1993–Mar 29, 1996	JUMBLE: THE INTERACTIVE GAME	FAMILY	Jun 13, 1994–Sep 2, 1994
RUMOR HAS IT	VH-1	Jun 7, 1993–Oct 28, 1993	QUICKSILVER	USA	Jun 27, 1994–Oct 13, 1995
TRIVIAL PURSUIT	FAMILY	Jun 7, 1993–Jul 14, 1995	FREE 4 ALL	USA	Jun 27, 1994–Nov 4, 1994
TRIVIAL PURSUIT: THE INTERACTIVE GAME	FAMILY	Jun 7, 1993–Mar 4, 1994	CAESARS CHALLENGE (repeats)	USA	Jun 27, 1994–Nov 4, 1994
CAMPUS ALL-STAR CHALLENGE	BET	Jun 12, 1993–Aug 7, 1993	AMERICAN GLADIATORS (repeats)	USA	Jun 27, 1994–Sep 8, 1995
CAESARS CHALLENGE	NBC	Jun 14, 1993–Jan 14, 1994	ILLINOIS INSTANT RICHES	WGN	Jul 9, 1994–
STORM THE CASTLE	CBS	Jun 16, 1993 (special)	I'M TELLING (repeats)	FAMILY	Aug 29, 1994–Sep 30, 1995
TEXACO STAR NATIONAL ACADEMIC CHAMPIONSHIP	SYN	Jun 19, 1993–Sep 11, 1993	MAXIMUM DRIVE	FAMILY	Aug 29, 1994–Sep 30, 1995
TALKABOUT (repeats)	USA	Jun 28, 1993–Dec 31, 1993	MASTERS OF THE MAZE	FAMILY	Aug 29, 1994–Sep 22, 1996
BORN LUCKY (repeats)	LIFE-TIME	Jul 5, 1993–Dec 31, 1993	TRIVIAL PURSUIT: INTERACTIVE GAME	FAMILY	Sep 6, 1994–Dec 30, 1994
BRAINS & BRAWN	NBC	Jul 10, 1993–Oct 16, 1993	CAMPUS ALL-STAR CHALLENGE (repeats)	BET	Sep 10, 1994–Oct 29, 1994
SPORTS SNAPSHOT!	SYN	Aug 7, 1993–Dec 1993	THE PRICE IS RIGHT	SYN	Sep 12, 1994–Jan 27, 1995
SPLIT SECOND (repeats)	FAMILY	Aug 30, 1993–Mar 4, 1994	GLADIATORS 2000	SYN	Sep 17, 1994–Sep 14, 1997
DREAM LEAGUE	ESPN	Sep 1, 1993–Sep 29, 1994	BEACH CLASH	SYN	Sep 19, 1994–Sep 1995
CAMPUS ALL-STAR CHALLENGE (repeats)	BET	Sep 4, 1993–Oct 23, 1993	WILD WEST SHOWDOWN	SYN	Oct 1, 1994–Mar 1995
SCRAMBLE	SYN	Sep 6, 1993–Dec 31, 1993	BLADE WARRIORS	SYN	Oct 1, 1994–Apr 30, 1995
LEGENDS OF THE HIDDEN TEMPLE	NICK	Sep 11, 1993–	PERFECT MATCH	ESPN	Oct 3, 1994–Dec 30, 1994
BABY RACES	FAMILY	Sep 12, 1993–Aug 27, 1994	THINK TWICE	PBS	Oct 10, 1994–Dec 26, 1994
PICK YOUR BRAIN	SYN	Sep 18, 1993–Sep 1994	GATERS	ESPN	Nov 1, 1994–Dec 30, 1994

program	network	first–last broadcast	program	network	first–last broadcast
THE NEWS HOLE	COM	Oct 26, 1994– Nov 19, 1994	GRILL ME	USA	Sep 9, 1996– Sep 15, 1996
JUMBLE: INTERACTIVE GAME (repeats)	FAMILY	Nov 21, 1994– Dec 30, 1994	BZZZ!	SYN	Sep 9, 1996– Sep 5, 1997
SANDBLAST	MTV	Dec 19, 1994– Sep 6, 1996	THE DATING GAME	SYN	Sep 9, 1996–
			THE NEWLYWED GAME	SYN	Sep 9, 1996–
FACE THE MUSIC (repeats)	FAMILY	Jan 2, 1995– Sep 29, 1995	SECRETS OF THE CRYPT- KEEPER'S HAUNTED HOUSE	CBS	Sep 14, 1996– Aug 23, 1997
SPLIT SECOND (repeats)	FAMILY	Jan 2, 1995– Sep 29, 1995	KWIK WITZ	SYN	Sep 20, 1996–
SPORTS ON TAP	ESPN	Jan 3, 1995– Mar 29, 1995	SHOPPING SPREE	FAMILY	Sep 30, 1996– Aug 14, 1998
PRESS YOUR LUCK (repeats)	USA	Apr 17, 1995– Oct 13, 1995	THE NEW SHOP 'TIL YOU DROP	FAMILY	Sep 30, 1996– Aug 14, 1998
SCRABBLE (repeats)	USA	Apr 17, 1995– Oct 13, 1995	SMALL TALK	FAMILY	Sep 30, 1996– Jan 31, 1997
SINGLED OUT	MTV	Jun 5, 1995– May 20, 1998	WAIT 'TIL YOU HAVE KIDS	FAMILY	Sep 30, 1996– Jan 31, 1997
CAMPUS ALL-STAR CHAL- LENGE	BET	Jun 24, 1995– Aug 12, 1995	WILD GUESS	ANIMAL PLANET	Oct 1, 1996– Mar 28, 1997
LIARS	SYN	Jul 10, 1995– Sep 29, 1995	WHERE IN TIME IS CAR- MEN SANDIEGO?	PBS	Oct 7, 1996–
GLOBAL GUTS	NICK	Sep 5, 1995–	REMEMBER THIS?	MSNBC	Oct 25, 1996– Oct 5, 1997
INSPIRATION, PLEASE!	ODYS- SEY	Oct 1, 1995–	IDIOT SAVANTS	MTV	Dec 9, 1996– Apr 25, 1997
WILD ANIMAL GAMES	FAMILY	Oct 2, 1995– Sep 21, 1996	IT TAKES TWO	FAMILY	Mar 10, 1997– May 30, 1997
FAMILY CHALLENGE	FAMILY	Oct 2, 1995– Sep 7, 1997	TRIVIA TRACK	GSN	Mar 17, 1997– Oct 2, 1998
READY . . . SET . . . COOK!	FOOD	Oct 2, 1995–	SUPER DECADES	GSN	Mar 17, 1997– Oct 2, 1998
LOVE CONNECTION (repeats)	USA	Oct 16, 1995– Jun 6, 1997	ANIMAL PLANET ZOOVEN- TURE	ANIMAL PLANET	Mar 31, 1997–
I'M TELLING (repeats)	FAMILY	Oct 30, 1995– Mar 29, 1996	ANIMAL PLANET ZOOVEN- TURE	DISC	Apr 6, 1997–
SWAPS	SYN	Dec 11, 1995– Feb 2, 1996	MAKE ME LAUGH	COM	Jun 2, 1997–
THE SMARTER SEX	SYN	Dec 18, 1995– Dec 29, 1995	WILD GUESS	ANIMAL PLANET	Jul 1, 1997– Sep 26, 1997
BZZZ!	SYN	Jan 22, 1996– Mar 8, 1996	FIGURE IT OUT	NICK	Jul 7, 1997–
DEBT	LIFE- TIME	Jun 3, 1996– Aug 14, 1998	WIN BEN STEIN'S MONEY	COM	Jul 28, 1997–
			CLICK	SYN	Sep 6, 1997–
THE BIG DATE	USA	Jun 17, 1996– Sep 19, 1997	PEER PRESSURE	SYN	Sep 6, 1997–
			WHEEL OF FORTUNE 2000	CBS	Sep 13, 1997–
AMERICAN GLADIATORS (repeats)	USA	Jul 1, 1996– Sep 13, 1996	PICTIONARY	SYN	Sep 22, 1997– Sep 1998
MAJORITY RULES	SYN	Aug 5, 1996– Jan 1997	WHEEL OF FORTUNE 2000	GSN	Oct 11, 1997–
NO RELATION	FX	Aug 12, 1996– Feb 8, 1998	THE DATING GAME	GSN	Oct 11, 1997–
			THE NEWLYWED GAME	GSN	Oct 11, 1997–
BIG DEAL	FOX	Sep 1, 1996– Oct 6, 1996	JEP!	GSN	Jan 30, 1998–
			MY GENERATION	VH-1	Mar 8, 1998–
			DEBT	SYN	Mar 9, 1998–

APPENDIX C

TV Game Shows by Network

(Only first-run shows are listed.)

Program	Network			Program	Network
$10,000 PYRAMID	ABC	ABC . . .		DREAM HOUSE	ABC
100 GRAND	ABC	AMERICAN		E.S.P.	ABC
ABOUT FACES	ABC	BROADCASTING		EVERYBODY'S TALK-	ABC
ACROSS THE BOARD	ABC	COMPANY		ING!	
ALL STAR BLITZ	ABC			FAMILY FEUD	ABC
ALMOST ANYTHING	ABC			FAMILY GAME	ABC
GOES				FUN AND FORTUNE	ABC
ALUMNI FUN	ABC			FUN FOR THE MONEY	ABC
ANIMAL CRACK-UPS	ABC			FUNNY YOU SHOULD	ABC
ANYBODY CAN PLAY	ABC			ASK!!	
AUCTION-AIRE	ABC			THE GENERATION	ABC
THE BABY GAME	ABC			GAP	
BACK THAT FACT	ABC			GET THE MESSAGE	ABC
BARGAIN HUNTERS	ABC			THE GREATEST MAN	ABC
BEAT THE CLOCK	ABC			ON EARTH	
BETTER SEX	ABC			HAIL THE CHAMP	ABC
BIG SHOWDOWN	ABC			THE HONEYMOON	ABC
BILL GWINN SHOW	ABC			RACE	
BLANKETY BLANKS	ABC			HOT SEAT	ABC
BLIND DATE	ABC			HOW'S YOUR MOTHER-	ABC
BREAK THE BANK	ABC			IN-LAW?	
BRUCE FORSYTH'S	ABC			IDENTIFY	ABC
HOT STREAK				IT'S ABOUT TIME	ABC
CAMOUFLAGE	ABC			JUNIOR ALMOST ANY-	ABC
CAN YOU TOP THIS?	ABC			THING GOES	
CELEBRITY TIME	ABC			KEEP IT IN THE FAM-	ABC
CHANCE FOR RO-	ABC			ILY	
MANCE				KEEP TALKING	ABC
CHANCE OF A LIFE-	ABC			THE KRYPTON FACTOR	ABC
TIME				LADIES BE SEATED	ABC
COME CLOSER	ABC			LET'S MAKE A DEAL	ABC
CONQUER FORT BOY-	ABC			LET'S SEE	ABC
ARD (special)				LIFE WITH LINKLETTER	ABC
THE DATING GAME	ABC			LIVE LIKE A MILLION-	ABC
DOCTOR I.Q.	ABC			AIRE	
DOLLAR A SECOND	ABC			MAJORITY RULES	ABC
DOUBLE TALK	ABC			MAKE A FACE	ABC
DOWN YOU GO	ABC			MAKE ME LAUGH	ABC
DRAW ME A LAUGH	ABC			MAKE THAT SPARE	ABC
DREAM GIRL OF '67	ABC			MASQUERADE PARTY	ABC

Program	Network	Program	Network
MATCH GAME	ABC	WHY?	ABC
MISSING LINKS	ABC	WINDOW SHOPPING	ABC
THE MONEYMAZE	ABC	YOU DON'T SAY!	ABC
MONOPOLY	ABC	YOURS FOR A SONG	ABC
MOTHER'S DAY	ABC		
MOVIELAND QUIZ	ABC	THE MOVIE MASTERS	AMC
MUSIC BINGO	ABC		
THE NAME'S THE SAME	ABC		
NEIGHBORS	ABC		
THE NEWLYWED GAME	ABC	ANIMAL PLANET ZOOVENTURE WILD GUESS	
NUMBER PLEASE	ABC		
THE OBJECT IS	ABC		
ON YOUR MARK	ABC	CAMPUS ALL-STAR CHALLENGE	BET
ON YOUR WAY	ABC		
ONE IN A MILLION	ABC	FAMILY FIGURES	BET
PANTOMIME QUIZ	ABC	LOVE BETWEEN THE SEXES	BET
PASSWORD	ABC		
PENNY TO A MILLION	ABC	TELL ME SOMETHING GOOD	BET
PERSONALITY PUZZLE	ABC		
PLAY THE GAME	ABC	TRIPLE THREAT	BET
PLAY YOUR HUNCH	ABC		
THE PRICE IS RIGHT	ABC	TEXACO STAR NA- TIONAL ACADEMIC CHAMPIONSHIP	BRAVO
QED	ABC		
QUEEN FOR A DAY	ABC		
QUICK AS A FLASH	ABC		
QUIZZING THE NEWS	ABC	SECOND HONEYMOON	CBN
THE REBUS GAME	ABC		
THE REEL GAME	ABC		
RHYME AND REASON	ABC		
SAY IT WITH ACTING	ABC		
SECOND CHANCE	ABC		
SEVEN KEYS	ABC	THE $10,000 PYRAMID	CBS
SHENANIGANS	ABC	THE $25,000 PYRAMID	CBS
SHOWOFFS	ABC	THE $64,000 CHAL- LENGE	CBS
SPARRING PARTNERS	ABC		
SPLIT SECOND	ABC	THE $64,000 QUESTION	CBS
STOP THE MUSIC	ABC	A PERFECT SCORE	CBS
SUPER JEOPARDY!	ABC	AD-LIBBERS	CBS
SUPERMARKET SWEEP	ABC	ALUMNI FUN	CBS
TAKE A GOOD LOOK	ABC	AMATEUR'S GUIDE TO LOVE	CBS
TAKE TWO	ABC		
TEMPTATION	ABC	ANYONE CAN WIN	CBS
THINK FAST	ABC	ARE YOU KIDDING	CBS
TREASURE HUNT	ABC	BALANCE YOUR BUD- GET	CBS
TREASURE ISLE	ABC		
TREASURE QUEST	ABC	BANK ON THE STARS	CBS
TRIVIA TRAP	ABC	BATTLE OF THE AGES	CBS
TWENTY QUESTIONS	ABC	BEAT THE CLOCK	CBS
WEDDING PARTY	ABC	BID 'N' BUY	CBS
WHAT'S GOING ON?	ABC	BIG PAYOFF	CBS
WHAT'S YOUR BID?	ABC	BLACKOUT	CBS
WHO DO YOU TRUST?	ABC	BODY LANGUAGE	CBS
WHO SAID THAT?	ABC	BREAK THE BANK	CBS
WHO'S THE BOSS?	ABC	BY POPULAR DEMAND	CBS

AMC . . . AMERICAN MOVIE CLASSICS (CABLE)

ANIMAL PLANET

BET . . . BLACK ENTERTAIN- MENT TELEVISION (CABLE)

BRAVO (CABLE)

CHRISTIAN BROADCASTING NETWORK (CABLE)

CBS . . . COLUMBIA BROADCASTING SYSTEM

Program	Network	Program	Network
CARD SHARKS	CBS	MISSUS' GOES-A-SHOPPING	CBS
CBS TELEVISION QUIZ	CBS		
CELEBRITY GAME	CBS	MUSICAL CHAIRS	CBS
CELEBRITY TIME	CBS	NAME THAT TUNE	CBS
CHILD'S PLAY	CBS	NIGHT GAMES	CBS
DO YOU KNOW?	CBS	NOW YOU SEE IT	CBS
DO YOU TRUST YOUR WIFE?	CBS	ON YOUR ACCOUNT	CBS
		PANTOMIME QUIZ	CBS
DOTTO	CBS	PASS THE BUCK	CBS
DOUBLE DARE	CBS	PASSWORD	CBS
DOUBLE EXPOSURE	CBS	PERSONALS	CBS
DOUBLE OR NOTHING	CBS	PICTURE THIS	CBS
DOWN YOU GO	CBS	PLACE THE FACE	CBS
DRAW TO WIN	CBS	PLAY YOUR HUNCH	CBS
EARN YOUR VACA-TION	CBS	PRESS YOUR LUCK	CBS
		THE PRICE IS RIGHT	CBS
THE FACE IS FAMILIAR	CBS	QUIZ KIDS	CBS
FACE THE FACTS	CBS	RIDDLE ME THIS	CBS
FAMILY FEUD	CBS	SECRETS OF THE CRYPTKEEPER'S HAUNTED HOUSE	CBS
FOLLOW THE LEADER	CBS		
FOR LOVE OR MONEY	CBS		
FREEDOM RINGS	CBS	SING IT AGAIN	CBS
G.E. COLLEGE BOWL	CBS	SONGS FOR SALE	CBS
GAMBIT	CBS	SPIN-OFF	CBS
GENERAL ELECTRIC GUEST HOUSE	CBS	SPORTS CHALLENGE	CBS
		STORM THE CASTLE	CBS
GIANT STEP	CBS	STRIKE IT RICH	CBS
GIVE AND TAKE	CBS	STUMP THE STARS	CBS
GIVE-N-TAKE	CBS	TAKE A GUESS	CBS
GO LUCKY	CBS	TATTLETALES	CBS
GUESS AGAIN	CBS	TELL IT TO GROUCHO	CBS
HIGH FINANCE	CBS	THERE'S ONE IN EVERY FAMILY	CBS
HOLD IT PLEASE	CBS		
THE HOLLYWOOD GAME	CBS	THIS IS THE MISSUS	CBS
		TIC TAC DOUGH	CBS
HOLLYWOOD'S TALK-ING	CBS	TO TELL THE TRUTH	CBS
		TOP DOLLAR	CBS
HOW DO YOU RATE?	CBS	TRUTH OR CONSE-QUENCES	CBS
I'LL BUY THAT	CBS		
I'VE GOT A SECRET	CBS	TWO FOR THE MONEY	CBS
INFORMATION PLEASE	CBS	TWO IN LOVE	CBS
IT PAYS TO BE IGNO-RANT	CBS	VIDEO VILLAGE	CBS
		WANNA BET?	CBS
IT'S A GIFT	CBS	WAY OUT GAMES	CBS
IT'S A HIT	CBS	WE TAKE YOUR WORD	CBS
IT'S NEWS TO ME	CBS	WHAT DO YOU HAVE IN COMMON?	CBS
THE JOKER'S WILD	CBS		
KEEP TALKING	CBS	WHAT IN THE WORLD?	CBS
KING'S PARTY LINE	CBS	WHAT'S IN A WORD?	CBS
LIVE LIKE A MILLION-AIRE	CBS	WHAT'S MY LINE?	CBS
		WHEEL OF FORTUNE	CBS
LOVE STORY	CBS	WHEEL OF FORTUNE 2000	CBS
MADE IN AMERICA	CBS		
MASQUERADE PARTY	CBS	WHEW!	CBS
MATCH GAME	CBS	WHO'S THERE	CBS
MESSING PRIZE PARTY	CBS	WHO'S WHOSE	CBS

Program	Network		Program	Network	
WINGO	CBS		SPIN THE PICTURE	DUM	
WINNER TAKE ALL	CBS		THEY'RE OFF	DUM	
YOU'RE IN THE PIC-TURE	CBS		TIME WILL TELL	DUM	
			TWENTY QUESTIONS	DUM	
YOU'RE ON YOUR OWN	CBS		WHAT'S THE STORY	DUM	
			WHAT'S YOUR BID	DUM	
YOUR LUCKY CLUE	CBS		WHERE WAS I?	DUM	
YOUR SURPRISE PACK-AGE	CBS		WITH THIS RING	DUM	
			YOUR BIG MOMENT	DUM	
YOUR SURPRISE STORE	CBS				
			BOARDWALK & BASE-BALL'S . . .	ESPN	ESPN (CABLE)
QUIZ KIDS	CBSC	CBS CABLE	DESIGNATED HITTER	ESPN	
			DREAM LEAGUE	ESPN	
CLASH	COM	COM . . .	GATERS	ESPN	
MAKE ME LAUGH	COM	COMEDY	NFL TRIVIA GAME	ESPN	
THE NEWS HOLE	COM	CENTRAL	THE PERFECT MATCH	ESPN	
WHOSE LINE IS IT ANYWAY?	COM	(CABLE)	SPORTS ON TAP	ESPN	
WIN BEN STEIN'S MONEY	COM		BABY RACES	FAMILY	FAMILY . . .
			BOGGLE—THE INTER-ACTIVE GAME	FAMILY	THE FAMILY CHANNEL
ANIMAL PLANET ZOO-VENTURE	DISC	DISC . . . DISCOVERY	FAMILY CHALLENGE	FAMILY	(CABLE)
			IT TAKES TWO	FAMILY	
TEXACO STAR NA-TIONAL ACADEMIC THE CHAMPIONSHIP	DISC	CHANNEL (CABLE)	JUMBLE—THE INTER-ACTIVE GAME	FAMILY	
			MASTERS OF THE MAZE	FAMILY	
COLLEGE BOWL	DISN	DISN . . .	MAXIMUM DRIVE	FAMILY	
CONTRAPTION	DISN	THE DISNEY	THE NEW SHOP 'TIL YOU DROP	FAMILY	
TEEN WIN, LOSE OR DRAW	DISN	CHANNEL (CABLE)	SHOPPING SPREE	FAMILY	
			SHUFFLE—THE INTER-ACTIVE GAME	FAMILY	
BATTLE OF THE AGES	DUM	DUM . . .	SMALL TALK	FAMILY	
BLIND DATE	DUM	DuMONT	THAT'S MY DOG	FAMILY	
BROADWAY TO HOL-LYWOOD HEADLINE	DUM	TELEVISION NETWORK	TRIVIAL PURSUIT	FAMILY	
			WAIT 'TIL YOU HAVE KIDS!!	FAMILY	
CASH AND CARRY	DUM				
CHANCE OF A LIFE-TIME	DUM		WILD ANIMAL GAMES	FAMILY	
CHARADE QUIZ	DUM				
DOLLAR A SECOND	DUM		READY . . . SET . . . COOK!	FOOD	FOOD . . . FOOD NET-WORK (CABLE)
DOWN YOU GO	DUM				
GAMBLE ON LOVE	DUM				
GUESS WHAT?	DUM				
HAVE A HEART	DUM				
HEADLINE CLUES	DUM		BIG DEAL!	FOX	FOX . . .
HOLD THAT CAMERA	DUM		FAMILY DOUBLE DARE	FOX	FOX
IT'S IN THE BAG	DUM		FANTASY PARK	FOX	TELEVISION
MIDWAY	DUM		FOX FUN HOUSE	FOX	NETWORK
ON YOUR WAY	DUM		KING OF THE MOUNTAIN	FOX	
ONE MINUTE PLEASE	DUM				
PANTOMIME QUIZ	DUM		PURE INSANITY!	FOX	
PLAY THE GAME	DUM				
PUBLIC PROSECUTOR	DUM		NO RELATION	FX	FX . . .
QUICK ON THE DRAW	DUM				FX CABLE

Program	Network		Program	Network
THE DATING GAME	GSN	GSN . . .	BREAK THE BANK	NBC
JEP!	GSN	GAME SHOW	CAESARS CHALLENGE	NBC
THE NEWLYWED GAME	GSN	NETWORK (CABLE)	CALL MY BLUFF	NBC
SUPER DECADES	GSN		CAN DO	NBC
TRIVIA TRACK	GSN		CARD SHARKS	NBC
WHEEL OF FORTUNE 2000	GSN		CELEBRITY GOLF	NBC
			CELEBRITY SWEEP-STAKES	NBC
BORN LUCKY	LIFE	LIFETIME	CHAIN LETTER	NBC
DEBT	LIFE	(CABLE)	CHAIN REACTION	NBC
RODEO DRIVE	LIFE		CHOOSE UP SIDES	NBC
SHOP 'TIL YOU DROP	LIFE		CLASSIC CONCENTRA-TION	NBC
SUPERMARKET SWEEP	LIFE		COLLEGE OF MUSICAL KNOWLEDGE	NBC
REMEMBER THIS?	MSNBC	MSNBC	CONCENTRATION	NBC
			COUNTY FAIR	NBC
IDIOT SAVANTS	MTV	MTV . . . MU-SIC TELEVISION	DOLLAR A SECOND	NBC
LIP SERVICE	MTV	NETWORK	DOTTO	NBC
REMOTE CONTROL	MTV	(CABLE)	DOUBLE OR NOTHING	NBC
			DOUBLE UP	NBC
SANDBLAST	MTV		DOUGH RE MI	NBC
SINGLED OUT	MTV		DOWN YOU GO	NBC
TRASHED	MTV		DREAM HOUSE	NBC
TURN IT UP!	MTV		DROODLES	NBC
			EYE GUESS	NBC
			THE EYES HAVE IT	NBC
FANDANGO	TNN	TNN . . . THE NASHVILLE	FACE TO FACE	NBC
TOP CARD	TNN	NETWORK	FAMILY SECRETS	NBC
10 SECONDS	TNN	(CABLE	FEATHER YOUR NEST	NBC
			FRACTURED PHRASES	NBC
			FUN FACTORY	NBC
50 GRAND SLAM	NBC	NBC . . .	FUNNY BONERS	NBC
ALL STAR SECRETS	NBC	NATIONAL	G.E. COLLEGE BOWL	NBC
AMERICANA	NBC	BROADCASTING	GLAMOUR GIRL	NBC
ANSWER YES OR NO	NBC	COMPANY	GO	NBC
ARE YOU POSITIVE	NBC		THE GONG SHOW	NBC
ART FORD SHOW	NBC		HAGGIS BAGGIS	NBC
ART LINKLETTER SHOW	NBC		HIGH LOW	NBC
			HIGH ROLLERS	NBC
ASK ME ANOTHER	NBC		HIT MAN	NBC
BAFFLE	NBC		HOLD THAT NOTE	NBC
BANK ON THE STARS	NBC		THE HOLLYWOOD SQUARES	NBC
BATTLESTARS	NBC		HOT POTATO	NBC
BIG GAME	NBC		I'LL BET	NBC
BIG PAYOFF	NBC		I'M TELLING	NBC
BIG SURPRISE	NBC		IT COULD BE YOU	NBC
BLANK CHECK	NBC		IT PAYS TO BE IGNO-RANT	NBC
BLIND DATE	NBC			
BLOCKBUSTERS	NBC		IT PAYS TO BE MAR-RIED	NBC
BRAINS & BRAWN	NBC			
BRAINS AND BRAWN	NBC		IT TAKES TWO	NBC
BREAK THE $250,000 BANK	NBC		IT'S ANYBODY'S GUESS	NBC
			IT'S IN THE BAG	NBC

Program	Network
JACKPOT	NBC
JACKPOT BOWLING	NBC
THE JAN MURRAY SHOW	NBC
JEOPARDY!	NBC
JOE GARAGIOLA'S MEMORY GAME	NBC
JUDGE FOR YOURSELF	NBC
JUST MEN!	NBC
KNOCKOUT	NBC
LAS VEGAS GAMBIT	NBC
LAUGH LINE	NBC
LET'S CELEBRATE	NBC
LET'S MAKE A DEAL	NBC
LET'S PLAY POST OFFICE	NBC
LETTERS TO LAUGH-IN	NBC
LUCKY PARTNERS	NBC
MAGNIFICENT MARBLE MACHINE	NBC
MAKE THE CONNECTION	NBC
MASQUERADE PARTY	NBC
THE MATCH GAME	NBC
MATCH GAME-HOLLYWOOD SQUARES HOUR	NBC
MEET YOUR MATCH	NBC
MINDREADERS	NBC
MISSING LINKS	NBC
MUSIC BINGO	NBC
MUSICAL CHAIRS	NBC
NAME DROPPERS	NBC
NAME THAT TUNE	NBC
ON YOUR ACCOUNT	NBC
PANTOMIME QUIZ	NBC
PARTY LINE	NBC
PASSWORD PLUS	NBC
PEOPLE ARE FUNNY	NBC
PEOPLE WILL TALK	NBC
PERSONALITY	NBC
PLACE THE FACE	NBC
PLAY YOUR HUNCH	NBC
THE PRICE IS RIGHT	NBC
QUEEN FOR A DAY	NBC
QUIZ KIDS	NBC
REACH FOR THE STARS	NBC
REMEMBER THIS DATE	NBC
RUNAROUND	NBC
SALE OF THE CENTURY	NBC
SAY IT WITH ACTING	NBC
SAY WHEN!!	NBC
SCATTERGORIES	NBC

Program	Network
SCRABBLE	NBC
SHOOT FOR THE STARS	NBC
SHOWDOWN	NBC
SNAP JUDGMENT	NBC
SPLIT PERSONALITY	NBC
STOP ME IF YOU'VE HEARD THIS ONE	NBC
THE STORYBOOK SQUARES	NBC
STUMPERS	NBC
SUPER GHOST	NBC
SUPER PASSWORD	NBC
TAG THE GAG	NBC
TAKE A CHANCE	NBC
TELE PUN	NBC
THAT REMINDS ME	NBC
THREE FOR THE MONEY	NBC
THREE ON A MATCH	NBC
TIC TAC DOUGH	NBC
TIME MACHINE	NBC
TO SAY THE LEAST	NBC
TO TELL THE TRUTH	NBC
TREASURE HUNT	NBC
TRUTH OR CONSEQUENCES	NBC
TRY AND DO IT	NBC
TWENTY QUESTIONS	NBC
TWENTY-ONE	NBC
TWO FOR THE MONEY	NBC
ULTRA QUIZ	NBC
UP TO PAAR	NBC
WHAT HAPPENED?	NBC
WHAT'S IT FOR?	NBC
WHAT'S MY NAME?	NBC
WHAT'S THIS SONG?	NBC
WHEEL OF FORTUNE	NBC
WHO PAYS?	NBC
WHO SAID THAT?	NBC
WHO WHAT OR WHERE GAME	NBC
WHODUNNIT?	NBC
WIN WITH A WINNER	NBC
WIN, LOSE OR DRAW	NBC
WINNER TAKE ALL	NBC
WINNING STREAK	NBC
WIZARD OF ODDS	NBC
WORD FOR WORD	NBC
WORDPLAY	NBC
WORDS AND MUSIC	NBC
YOU BET YOUR LIFE	NBC
YOU DON'T SAY!	NBC
YOU'RE PUTTING ME ON	NBC

Program	Network		Program	Network
YOUR FIRST IMPRESSION	NBC		ALL ABOUT THE OPPOSITE SEX	SYN
YOUR NUMBER'S UP	NBC		ALL STAR ALMOST ANYTHING GOES	SYN
DOUBLE DARE	NICK	NICK . . .	AMERICAN GLADIATORS	SYN
FAMILY DOUBLE DARE	NICK	NICKELODEON (CABLE)	ANNIVERSARY GAME	SYN
FINDERS KEEPERS	NICK		ANYTHING FOR MONEY	SYN
GET THE PICTURE	NICK			
KING PINS	NICK		ANYTHING YOU CAN DO	SYN
LEGENDS OF THE HIDDEN TEMPLE	NICK		BEACH CLASH	SYN
			BEAT THE CLOCK	SYN
MAKE THE GRADE	NICK		BEAT THE ODDS	SYN
NICKELODEON ARCADE	NICK		BEDROOM BUDDIES	SYN
			BEDTIME STORIES	SYN
NICEKLODEON GUTS	NICK		BLADE WARRIORS	SYN
THINK FAST	NICK		BREAK THE BANK	SYN
WHAT WOULD YOU DO?	NICK		BULLSEYE	SYN
			BZZZ!	SYN
			CAESARS CHALLENGE	SYN
LET'S GO BACK	NOST	NOST . . .	CAMOUFLAGE	SYN
		NOSTALGIA NETWORK (CABLE)	CAN YOU TOP THIS?	SYN
			CARD SHARKS	SYN
			CATCH PHRASE	SYN
			CELEBRITY BILLIARDS	SYN
INSPIRATION, PLEASE!	ODY	ODY . . .	CELEBRITY BOWLING	SYN
		ODYSSEY CHANNEL (CABLE)	CELEBRITY CHARADES	SYN
			CELEBRITY SWEEPSTAKES	SYN
			CELEBRITY TENNIS	SYN
THINK TWICE	PBS	PBS . . .	THE CHALLENGERS	SYN
TOP OF THE WORLD	PBS	PUBLIC BROADCASTING SYSTEM	CHEAP SHOW	SYN
WE INTERRUPT THIS WEEK	PBS		CLICK	SYN
			COLLEGE BOWL	SYN
WHERE IN THE WORLD IS CARMEN SANDIEGO?	PBS		COLLEGE MADHOUSE	SYN
			CONCENTRATION	SYN
			COUCH POTATOES	SYN
WHERE IN TIME IS CARMEN SANDIEGO?	PBS		CROSS WITS	SYN
			THE DATING GAME	SYN
			DEALER'S CHOICE	SYN
DUELING FOR PLAYMATES	PLAY	PLAY . . .	DEBT	SYN
		PLAYBOY CABLE	THE DIAMOND HEAD GAME	SYN
EVERYTHING GOES	PLAY			
PLAYBOY'S LOVE & SEX TEST	PLAY		THE $1.98 BEAUTY SHOW	SYN
			DON ADAMS' SCREEN TEST	SYN
THE $100,000 PYRAMID	SYN	SYN . . .		
		SYNDICATION	DOUBLE DARE	SYN
THE $128,000 QUESTION	SYN		DREAM GIRL USA	SYN
THE $1,000,000 CHANCE OF A LIFETIME			EVERY SECOND COUNTS	SYN
			EVERYTHING'S RELATIVE	SYN
THE $25,000 PYRAMID	SYN		FACE THE MUSIC	SYN
ALL ABOUT FACES	SYN		FAMILY FEUD	SYN
			FAST DRAW	SYN

Program	Network	Program	Network
THE $50,000 PYRAMID	SYN	THE NEWLYWED GAME	SYN
FINDERS KEEPERS	SYN	OH MY WORD	SYN
FUN HOUSE	SYN	THE PARENT GAME	SYN
THE GAME GAME	SYN	PAY CARDS!	SYN
GLADIATORS 2000	SYN	PDQ	SYN
GOLF FOR SWINGERS	SYN	PEER PRESSURE	SYN
THE GONG SHOW	SYN	THE PERFECT MATCH (Enberg)	SYN
GRAND PRIX ALL STAR SHOW	SYN	PERFECT MATCH (Goen)	SYN
GRANDSTAND	SYN	PICK YOUR BRAIN	SYN
GRUDGE MATCH	SYN	PICTIONARY	SYN
GUILTY OR INNOCENT	SYN	PITFALL	SYN
THE GUINNESS GAME	SYN	PLAY THE PERCENT-AGES	SYN
HE SAID, SHE SAID	SYN	THE POP 'N' ROCKER GAME	SYN
HEADLINE CHASERS	SYN	THE PRICE IS RIGHT	SYN
HIGH ROLLERS	SYN	PRO-FAN	SYN
HOLD EVERYTHING!	SYN	QUEEN FOR A DAY	SYN
HOLLYWOOD CON-NECTION	SYN	QUIZ KIDS	SYN
HOLLYWOOD SQUARES	SYN	THE QUIZ KIDS CHAL-LENGE	SYN
HOME RUN DERBY	SYN	RELATIVELY SPEAKING	SYN
HOME SHOPPING GAME	SYN	REMOTE CONTROL	SYN
I'VE GOT A SECRET	SYN	RUCKUS	SYN
IT PAYS TO BE IGNO-RANT	SYN	SALE OF THE CENTURY	SYN
IT'S YOUR BET	SYN	SCRAMBLE	SYN
IT'S YOUR MOVE	SYN	SKEDADDLE	SYN
JACKPOT	SYN	SLIME TIME	SYN
JEOPARDY!	SYN	THE SMARTER SEX	SYN
JOKER! JOKER! JOKER!	SYN	SPLIT SECOND	SYN
THE JOKER'S WILD	SYN	SPORTS CHALLENGE	SYN
KNIGHTS AND WARRI-ORS	SYN	SPORTS SNAPSHOT	SYN
THE KRYPTON FACTOR	SYN	STAR GAMES	SYN
KWIK WITZ	SYN	STARCADE	SYN
THE LAST WORD	SYN	STRAIGHT TO THE HEART	SYN
LET'S MAKE A DEAL	SYN	STRIKE IT RICH	SYN
LIARS	SYN	STUMP THE STARS	SYN
LIARS CLUB	SYN	SUPER PAY CARDS!	SYN
LINGO	SYN	SWAPS	SYN
LOVE AT FIRST SIGHT	SYN	SWEETHEARTS	SYN
LOVE CONNECTION	SYN	TAKE MY WORD FOR IT	SYN
LOVE EXPERTS	SYN	TALKABOUT	SYN
MAJORITY RULES	SYN	TATTLETALES	SYN
MAKE ME LAUGH	SYN	TEXACO STAR NA-TIONAL ACADEMIC CHAMPIONSHIP	SYN
MASQUERADE PARTY	SYN	THAT **** QUIZ SHOW	SYN
MATCH GAME	SYN	THIRD DEGREE	SYN
MATCHES 'N MATES	SYN	THAT'S AMORE	SYN
MATCHMAKER	SYN	THREE'S A CROWD	SYN
MONEY MAKERS	SYN	TIC TAC DOUGH	SYN
THE MOVIE GAME	SYN		
NAME THAT TUNE	SYN		

Program	Network
TO TELL THE TRUTH	SYN
TREASURE HUNT	SYN
TREASURE MALL	SYN
TRIPLE THREAT	SYN
TRUMP CARD	SYN
TRUTH OR CONSE-QUENCES	SYN
THE VIDEO GAME	SYN
VIDEO POWER	SYN
WHAT'S MY LINE?	SYN
WHEEL OF FORTUNE	SYN
WILD WEST SHOW-DOWN	SYN
WIN WITH THE STARS	SYN
WIN, LOSE OR DRAW	SYN
WIPEOUT	SYN
YAHTZEE	SYN
YOU BET YOUR LIFE (Hackett)	SYN
YOU BET YOUR LIFE (Cosby)	SYN
YOU DON'T SAY!	SYN

Program	Network	
YOU WRITE THE SONGS	SYN	
GREAT GETAWAY GAME	TRAV	TRAV . . . TRAVEL CHANNEL (CABLE)
THE BIG DATE	USA	USA . . .
BUMPER STUMPERS	USA	USA NETWORK
CHAIN REACTION	USA	(CABLE)
FREE 4 ALL	USA	
GRILL ME	USA	
JACKPOT	USA	
LOVE ME, LOVE ME NOT	USA	
QUICKSILVER	USA	
USA GONZO GAMES	USA	
MY GENERATION	VH-1	VH-1
RUMOR HAS IT	VH-1	(CABLE)
ILLINOIS INSTANT RICHES	WGN	WGN

APPENDIX D

Longest-Running Television Game Shows

(Includes first-run shows only.)

1. THE PRICE IS RIGHT* CBS daytime 26 years (Mark Goodson Productions debut: September 1972)
2. WHAT'S MY LINE? CBS primetime 17 years 7 months (Goodson-Todman Productions debut: February 1950)
3. WHEEL OF FORTUNE NBC/CBS daytime 16 years 9 months (Merv Griffin Productions debut: January 1975)
4. WHEEL OF FORTUNE* syndicated 15 years (Merv Griffin Productions debut: September 1983)
5. I'VE GOT A SECRET CBS primetime 14 years 10 months (Goodson-Todman Productions debut: June 1952)
6. CONCENTRATION NBC daytime 14 years 7 months (NBC Productions debut: August 1958)
7. JEOPARDY!* syndicated 14 years (Merv Griffin Productions debut: September 1984)
8. THE HOLLYWOOD SQUARES NBC daytime 13 years 8 months (Heatter-Quigley Productions debut: October 1966)
9. LET'S MAKE A DEAL NBC/ABC daytime 12 years 6 months (Hatos-Hall Productions debut: December 1963)
10. G.E. COLLEGE BOWL** CBS/NBC weekend 11 years 5 months (Don Reid Productions debut: January 1959)
11. LOVE CONNECTION syndicated 11 years (Eric Leiber Productions debut: September 1983)
12. YOU BET YOUR LIFE NBC primetime 11 years (John Guedel Productions debut: October 1950)
13. JEOPARDY! NBC daytime 10 years 9 months (Merv Griffin Productions debut: March 1964)
14. TO TELL THE TRUTH CBS primetime 10 years 5 months (Goodson-Todman Productions debut: December 1956)
15. PANTOMIME QUIZ** CBS/NBC/ABC/Dumont 9 years 3 months (Mike Stokey Productions debut: July 1950)
16. TO TELL THE TRUTH syndicated 9 years (Goodson-Todman Productions debut: September 1969)
17. TRUTH OR CONSEQUENCES syndicated 9 years (Ralph Edwards Productions debut: September 1966)
18. THE JOKER'S WILD syndicated 9 years (Barry & Enright Productions debut: September 1977)
19. FAMILY FEUD ABC daytime 8 years 11 months (Goodson-Todman Productions debut: July 1976)
20. THE PRICE IS RIGHT NBC/ABC daytime 8 years 9 months (Goodson-Todman Productions debut: November 1956)
21. QUEEN FOR A DAY NBC/ABC daytime 8 years 9 months (Queen for a Day Inc. debut: January 1956)
22. TRUTH OR CONSEQUENCES NBC daytime 8 years 9 months (Ralph Edwards Productions debut: December 1956)
23. THE NEWLYWED GAME ABC daytime 8 years 5 months (Chuck Barris Productions debut: July 1966)
24. BREAK THE BANK NBC/CBS/ABC primetime 8 years 3 months (Wolf Productions debut: October 1948)
25. MASQUERADE PARTY** NBC/CBS/ABC primetime 8 years 2 months (Wolf Productions debut: July 1952)
26. THE PRICE IS RIGHT syndicated 8 years (Mark Goodson Productions debut: September 1972)
27. FAMILY FEUD syndicated 8 years (Goodson-Todman Productions debut: September 1977)
28. TIC TAC DOUGH syndicated 8 years (Barry & Enright Productions debut: September 1978)
29. BEAT THE CLOCK CBS primetime 7 years 11 months (Goodson-Todman Productions debut: March 1950)
30. THE BIG PAYOFF NBC/CBS daytime 7 years 10 months (Walt Framer Productions debut: December 1951)

*Show still on the air.
**Seasonal show.
Game shows included on this list are broken down into individual work, syndication, or cable broadcast runs of at least five years. Information complied through September 1998.

31. THE DATING GAME   ABC daytime   7 years 6 months (Chuck Barris Productions   debut: December 1965)
32. THE $10,000 PYRAMID/THE $20,000 PYRAMID   CBS/ABC daytime   7 years 3 months (Bob Stewart Productions   debut: March 1973)
33. THE PRICE IS RIGHT   NBC/ABC primetime   7 years (Goodson-Todman Productions   debut: September 1957)
34. WHAT'S MY LINE?   syndicated   7 years (Goodson-Todman Productions   debut: September 1968)
35. SPORTS CHALLENGE   syndicated   7 years (Gerry Gross Productions   debut: January 1971)
36. NAME THAT TUNE   syndicated   7 years (Ralph Edwards Productions   debut: September 1974)
37. CELEBRITY BOWLING   syndicated   7 years (7-10 Productions   debut: January 1971)
38. FAMILY FEUD   syndicated   7 years (Mark Goodson Productions   debut: September 1988)
39. THE MATCH GAME   NBC daytime   6 years 9 months (Goodson-Todman Productions   debut: December 1962)
40. AMERICAN GLADIATORS   syndicated   7 years (Four Point Entertainment–TransWorld International–Samuel Goldwyn Television   debut: September 1989)
41. STRIKE IT RICH   CBS daytime   6 years 8 months (Walt Framer Productions   debut: May 1951)
42. PEOPLE ARE FUNNY   NBC primetime   6 years 7 months (John Guedel Productions   debut: September 1954)
43. CLASSIC CONCENTRATION   NBC daytime   6 years 7 months (Mark Goodson Productions   debut: May 1987)
44. YOU DON'T SAY!   NBC daytime   6 years 6 months (Ralph Andrews Productions   debut: April 1963)
45. TO TELL THE TRUTH   CBS daytime   6 years 3 months (Goodson-Todman Productions   debut: June 1962)
46. WHO DO YOU TRUST?   ABC daytime   6 years 3 months (Don Fedderson Productions   debut: September 1957)
47. NAME THAT TUNE   NBC/CBS primetime   6 years 3 months (Harry Salter Productions   debut: July 1953)
48. SALE OF THE CENTURY   NBC daytime   6 years 3 months (Reg Grundy Productions   debut: January 1983)
49. PASSWORD   CBS daytime   6 years (Goodson-Todman Productions   debut: October 1961)
50. LET'S MAKE A DEAL   syndicated   6 years (Hatos-Hall Productions   debut: September 1971)
51. MATCH GAME PM   syndicated   6 years (Goodson-Todman Productions   debut: September 1975)
52. FANDANGO   Nashville Network   6 years (Reid-Land Productions   debut: March 1983)
53. MATCH GAME   CBS daytime   5 years 10 months (Goodson-Todman Productions   debut: July 1973)
54. SCRABBLE   NBC daytime   5 years 9 months (Reg Grundy Productions   debut: July 1984)
55. THE $25,000 PYRAMID   CBS daytime   5 years 9 months (Bob Stewart Productions   debut: September 1982)
56. WHO SAID THAT?   NBC primetime   5 years 7 months (NBC Productions   debut: December 1948)
57. IT COULD BE YOU   NBC daytime   5 years 6 months (Ralph Edwards Productions   debut: June 1956)
58. TWENTY QUESTIONS   NBC/ABC/Dumont primetime   5 years 6 months (Fred Van Deventer Productions   debut: November 1949)
59. DOWN YOU GO   Dumont/CBS/ABC/NBC primetime   5 years 4 months (Louis Cowan Productions-debut: May 1951)
60. CHAIN REACTION   USA Cable   5 years 3 months (Bob Stewart Productions   debut: September 1986)
61. PLAY YOUR HUNCH   CBS/ABC/NBC daytime   5 years 3 months (Goodson-Todman Productions debut: June 1958)
62. FAMILY FEUD   CBS daytime   5 years 2 months (Mark Goodson Productions   debut: July 1988)
63. CONCENTRATION   syndicated   5 years (Goodson-Todman Productions   debut: September 1973)
64. BEAT THE CLOCK   syndicated   5 years (Goodson-Todman Productions   debut: September 1969)
65. WHERE IN THE WORLD IS CARMEN SANDIEGO?   PBS 5 years   (WGBH/WQED   debut: October 1991)

APPENDIX E
Game Show Award Winners and Nominees

I. CABLEACE AWARD WINNERS AND NOMINEES

The CableAce Awards were established in 1979 as the "Ace Awards" in recognition of outstanding achievement in original programs for cable television, by the National Academy of Cable Television. In 1992, the awards were renamed "CableAce." In 1989, at the tenth annual ceremony, cable game shows were given their own category.

Winners are capitalized.

Tenth Annual Ace Awards   (presented in January 1989)
DOUBLE DARE   (Nickelodeon)
Remote Control   (MTV)
Second Honeymoon   (CBN)

Eleventh Annual Ace Awards   (presented in January 1990)
TOP CARD   (The Nashville Network)
Think Fast   (Nickelodeon)
Texaco Star National Academic Championship   (Discovery)

Twelfth Annual Ace Awards   (presented in January 1991)
TURN IT UP!   (MTV)
Remote Control   (MTV)
Family Double Dare   (Nickelodeon)

Thirteenth Annual Ace Awards   (presented January 12, 1992)
SUPERMARKET SWEEP   (Lifetime)
Be a Star   (The Nashville Network)
Get the Picture   (Nickelodeon)
Shop 'til You Drop   (Lifetime)
In addition, "Whose Line Is It Anyway?" received the Ace Award as Best International Series or Special.

Fourteenth Annual CableAce Awards   (presented January 17, 1993)
(the name of the award was changed effective this year)
LIP SERVICE   (MTV)
Double Dare   (Nickelodeon)
Nick Arcade   (Nickelodeon)

Fifteenth Annual CableAce Awards   (presented January 16, 1994)

SUPERMARKET SWEEP   (Lifetime)
Rumor Has It   (VH-1)
That's My Dog!   (The Family Channel)

Sixteenth Annual CableAce Awards   (presented January 15, 1995)
LEGENDS OF THE HIDDEN TEMPLE   (Nickelodeon)
Nickelodeon Guts   (Nickelodeon)
Supermarket Sweep   (Lifetime)
In addition, "Whose Line Is It Anyway?" received the CableAce Award as Best International Dramatic or Comedy Series or Special, movie or mini-series.

Seventeenth Annual CableAce Awards   (presented December 1, 1995)
THE NEWS HOLE   (Comedy Central)
Legend of the Hidden Temple   (Nickelodeon)
Nickelodeon Guts   (Nickelodeon)
In addition, "Whose Line Is It Anyway?" received the CableAce Award for the second year in a row as Best International Comedy Series or Special.

Eighteenth Annual CableAce Awards   (presented October 16, 1996)
DEBT   (Lifetime)
Legends of the Hidden Temple   (Nickelodeon)

Nineteenth Annual CableAce Awards   (presented November 15, 1997)
IDIOT SAVANTS (MTV)
Animal Planet Zooventure   (Animal Planet)
Win Ben Stein's Money   (Comedy Central)

II. DAYTIME EMMY AWARD WINNERS AND NOMINEES

The Daytime Emmy Awards were established as a separate broadcast from the Primetime Emmy Awards in the 1973–1974 season. Categories honoring "Outstanding Game Show," "Best Host or Hostess in a Game Show," and "Best Individual Director for a Game Show" were introduced that year.

Winners are capitalized.

First Annual Daytime Emmy Awards   (1973–1974) for daytime programs telecast between March 19, 1973 and March 17, 1974 . . . presented May 28, 1974

Outstanding Game Show
PASSWORD   (Goodson-Todman Productions)
The Hollywood Squares   (Heatter-Quigley Productions)
Jeopardy!   (Merv Griffin Productions)

Best Game Show Host or Hostess
PETER MARSHALL   (The Hollywood Squares)
Allen Ludden   (Password)
Art Fleming   (Jeopardy!)

Best Individual Director for a Game Show
MIKE GARGUILO   (Jackpot)
Jerome Shaw   (The Hollywood Squares)
Stuart Phelps   (Password)

Second Annual Daytime Emmy Awards   (1974–1975) for daytime programs telecast between March 18, 1974 and March 10, 1975 . . . presented May 15, 1975

Outstanding Game Show
THE HOLLYWOOD SQUARES   (Heatter-Quigley Productions)
The $10,000 Pyramid   (Bob Stewart Productions)
Jeopardy!   (Merv Griffin Productions)
Let's Make a Deal   (Hatos-Hall Productions)

Best Host or Hostess in a Game Show
PETER MARSHALL   (The Hollywood Squares)
Monty Hall   (Let's Make a Deal)
Gene Rayburn   (The Match Game)

Best Individual Director for a Game Show
JEROME SHAW   (The Hollywood Squares)
Joe Behar   (Let's Make a Deal)

Third Annual Daytime Emmy Awards   (1975–1976) for daytime programs telecast between March 11, 1975 and March 15, 1976 . . . presented May 11, 1976

Outstanding Game Show
THE $20,000 PYRAMID   (Bob Stewart Productions)
The Price Is Right   (Goodson-Todman Productions)
Match Game   (Goodson-Todman Productions)
The Hollywood Squares   (Heatter-Quigley Productions)
Let's Make a Deal   (Hatos-Hall Productions)

Best Host or Hostess in a Game Show
ALLEN LUDDEN   (Password)
Peter Marshall   (The Hollywood Squares)
Geoff Edwards   (Jackpot)

Best Individual Director for a Game Show
MIKE GARGUILO   (The $20,000 Pyramid)
Jerome Shaw   (The Hollywood Squares)

Fourth Annual Daytime Emmy Awards   (1976–1977) for daytime programs telecast between March 16, 1976 and March 13, 1977 . . . presented May 12, 1977

Outstanding Game Show
FAMILY FEUD   (Goodson-Todman Productions)
The $20,000 Pyramid   (Bob Stewart Productions)
The Hollywood Squares   (Heatter-Quigley Productions)
Match Game   (Goodson-Todman Productions)
Tattletales   (Goodson-Todman Productions)

Best Host or Hostess in a Game Show
BERT CONVY   (Tattletales)
Dick Clark   (The $20,000 Pyramid)
Gene Rayburn   (Match Game)

Best Individual Director for a Game Show
MIKE GARGUILO   (The $20,000 Pyramid)
Joe Behar   (Let's Make a Deal)

Fifth Annual Daytime Emmy Awards   (1977–1978) for daytime programs telecast between March 14, 1977 and March 21, 1978 . . . presented June 7, 1978

Outstanding Game Show
THE HOLLYWOOD SQUARES   (Heatter-Quigley Productions)
Family Feud   (Goodson-Todman Productions)
The $20,000 Pyramid   (Bob Stewart Productions)

Best Host or Hostess in a Game Show
RICHARD DAWSON   (Family Feud)
Dick Clark   (The $20,000 Pyramid)
Gene Rayburn   (Match Game)
Chuck Woolery   (Wheel of Fortune)
Susan Stafford   (Wheel of Fortune)

Best Individual Director for a Game Show
MIKE GARGUILO   (The $20,000 Pyramid)
Paul Alter   (Family Feud)

Sixth Annual Daytime Emmy Awards   (1978–1979)
for daytime programs telecast between March 22, 1978 and
March 5, 1979 . . . presented May 17, 1979

Outstanding Game Show
THE HOLLYWOOD SQUARES   (Heatter-Quigley Productions)
Family Feud   (Goodson-Todman Productions)
The $20,000 Pyramid   (Bob Stewart Productions)

Best Host or Hostess in a Game Show
DICK CLARK   (The $20,000 Pyramid)
Bob Barker   (The Price Is Right)
Peter Marshall   (The Hollywood Squares)

Best Individual Director for a Game Show
JEROME SHAW   (The Hollywood Squares)
Mike Garguilo   (The $20,000 Pyramid)
Dick Schneider   (Jeopardy!)

Seventh Annual Daytime Emmy Awards   (1979–1980)
for daytime programs telecast between March 6, 1979 and
March 5, 1980 . . . presented June 4, 1980

Outstanding Game Show
(tie for the winners)
THE HOLLYWOOD SQUARES   (Heatter-Quigley Productions)
THE $20,000 PYRAMID   (Bob Stewart Productions)
Family Feud   (Goodson-Todman Productions)

Best Host or Hostess in a Game Show
PETER MARSHALL   (The Hollywood Squares)
Richard Dawson   (Family Feud)

Best Individual Director for a Game Show
JEROME SHAW   (The Hollywood Squares)
Paul Alter   (Family Feud)

Eighth Annual Daytime Emmy Awards   (1980–1981)
for daytime programs telecast between March 6, 1980 and
March 5, 1981 . . . presented May 21, 1980

Outstanding Game Show
THE $20,000 PYRAMID   (Bob Stewart Productions)
Family Feud   (Goodson-Todman Productions)
The Hollywood Squares   (Heatter-Quigley Productions)

Best Host or Hostess in a Game Show
PETER MARSHALL   (The Hollywood Squares)
Dick Clark   (The $20,000 Pyramid)
Richard Dawson   (Family Feud)

Best Individual Director for a Game Show
MIKE GARGUILO   (The $20,000 Pyramid)
Paul Alter   (Family Feud)

Ninth Annual Daytime Emmy Awards   (1981–1982)
for daytime programs telecast between March 6, 1981 and
March 5, 1982 . . . presented June 8, 1982

Outstanding Game Show
PASSWORD PLUS   (Goodson-Todman Productions)
Family Feud   (Goodson-Todman Productions)
The Price Is Right   (Goodson-Todman Productions)
Wheel of Fortune   (Merv Griffin Productions)

Best Host or Hostess in a Game Show
BOB BARKER   (The Price Is Right)
Bill Cullen   (Blockbusters)
Richard Dawson   (Family Feud)

Best Individual Director for a Game Show
PAUL ALTER   (Family Feud)
Dick Carson   (Wheel of Fortune)

Tenth Annual Daytime Emmy Awards   (1982–1983)
for daytime programs telecast between March 6, 1982 and
March 5, 1983 . . . presented June 6, 1983

Outstanding Game Show
THE $25,000 PYRAMID   (Bob Stewart Productions)
The Price Is Right   (Mark Goodson Productions)
Family Feud   (Mark Goodson Productions)

Best Host or Hostess in a Game Show
BETTY WHITE   (Just Men!)
Dick Clark   (The $25,000 Pyramid)
Richard Dawson   (Family Feud)

Best Individual Director for a Game Show
MARC BRESLOW   (The Price Is Right)
Paul Alter   (Family Feud)
Bruce Burmester   (The $25,000 Pyramid)

Eleventh Annual Daytime Emmy Awards   (1983–1984)
for daytime programs telecast between March 6, 1983 and
March 5, 1984 . . . presented June 27, 1984

Outstanding Game Show
THE $25,000 PYRAMID   (Bob Stewart Productions)
Family Feud   (Mark Goodson Productions)
The Price Is Right   (Mark Goodson Productions)
Wheel of Fortune   (Merv Griffin Productions)

Best Host or Hostess in a Game Show
BOB BARKER   (The Price Is Right)
Richard Dawson   (Family Feud)
Betty White   (Just Men!)

Best Individual Director for a Game Show
MARC BRESLOW   (The Price Is Right)
Paul Alter   (Family Feud)

Twelfth Annual Daytime Emmy Awards   (1984–1985)
for daytime programs telecast between March 6, 1984 and
March 5, 1985 . . . presented August 1, 1985

Outstanding Game Show
THE $25,000 PYRAMID   (Bob Stewart Productions)
Family Feud   (Mark Goodson Productions)
Jeopardy! (Merv Griffin Productions)
The Price Is Right   (Mark Goodson Productions)
Wheel of Fortune   (Merv Griffin Productions)

Best Host or Hostess in a Game Show
DICK CLARK   (The $25,000 Pyramid)
Bob Barker   (The Price Is Right)
Bill Cullen   (Hot Potato)
Richard Dawson   (Family Feud)
Pat Sajak   (Wheel of Fortune)

Best Individual Director for a Game Show
MARC BRESLOW   (The Price Is Right)
Dick Carson   (Wheel of Fortune)
Dick Schneider   (Jeopardy!)

Thirteenth Annual Daytime Emmy Awards   (1985–1986)
for daytime programs telecast between March 6, 1985 and
March 5, 1986 . . . presented July 17, 1986

Outstanding Game Show
THE $25,000 PYRAMID   (Bob Stewart Productions)
Family Feud   (Mark Goodson Productions)
Jeopardy! (Merv Griffin Productions)
The Price Is Right   (Mark Goodson Productions)
The Wheel of Fortune   (Merv Griffin Productions)

Best Host or Hostess in a Game Show
DICK CLARK   (The $25,000 Pyramid)
Bob Barker   (The Price Is Right)
Pat Sajak   (Wheel of Fortune)

Best Individual Director for a Game Show
DICK CARSON   (Wheel of Fortune)
Joe Behar   (Let's Make a Deal)
Marc Breslow   (The Price Is Right)
Bruce Burmester   (The $25,000 Pyramid)
George Choderker   (Super Password)

Fourteenth Annual Daytime Emmy Awards   (1986–1987)
for daytime programs telecast between March 6, 1986 and
March 5, 1987 . . . presented June 30, 1987

Outstanding Game Show
THE $25,000 PYRAMID   (Bob Stewart Productions)
Jeopardy! (Merv Griffin Productions)
The Price Is Right   (Mark Goodson Productions)
Wheel of Fortune   (Merv Griffin Productions)

Best Host or Hostess in a Game Show
BOB BARKER   (The Price Is Right)
Dick Clark   (The $25,000 Pyramid)

Pat Sajak   (Wheel of Fortune)
Alex Trebek   (Jeopardy!)

Best Individual Director for a Game Show
MARC BRESLOW   (The Price Is Right)
Paul Alter   (The Price Is Right)
Dick Carson   (Wheel of Fortune)
Dick Schneider   (Jeopardy!)

Fifteenth Annual Daytime Emmy Awards   (1987–1988)
for daytime programs telecast between March 6, 1987 and
March 5, 1988 . . . presented June 29, 1988

Outstanding Game Show
THE PRICE IS RIGHT   (Mark Goodson Productions)
The $25,000 Pyramid   (Bob Stewart Productions)
Wheel of Fortune   (Merv Griffin Productions)
Win, Lose or Draw   (Burt & Bert Productions)

Best Host or Hostess in a Game Show
BOB BARKER   (The Price Is Right)
Dick Clark   (The $25,000 Pyramid)
Vicki Lawrence   (Win, Lose or Draw)
Alex Trebek   (Classic Concentration)

Best Individual Director for a Game Show
BRUCE BURMESTER   (The $25,000 Pyramid)
Dick Carson   (Wheel of Fortune)
Richard Kline   (Win, Lose or Draw)

Sixteenth Annual Daytime Emmy Awards   (1988–1989)
for daytime programs telecast between March 6, 1988 and
March 5, 1989 . . . presented June 29, 1989

Outstanding Game Show
THE $25,000 PYRAMID   (Bob Stewart Productions)
Jeopardy! (Merv Griffin Productions)
The Price Is Right   (Mark Goodson Productions)
Wheel of Fortune   (Merv Griffin Productions)
Win, Lose or Draw   (Burt & Bert Productions)

Best Host or Hostess in a Game Show
ALEX TREBEK   (Jeopardy!)
Dick Clark   (The $25,000 Pyramid)
Pat Sajak   (Wheel of Fortune)
Vicki Lawrence Schultz   (Win, Lose or Draw)

Best Individual Director for a Game Show
DICK SCHNEIDER   (Jeopardy!)
Dick Carson   (Wheel of Fortune)
Richard Kline   (Win, Lose or Draw)

Seventeenth Annual Daytime Emmy Awards   (1989–1990)
for daytime programs telecast between March 6, 1989 and
March 5, 1990 . . . presented June 28, 1990

Outstanding Game Show
JEOPARDY! (Merv Griffin Productions)
The Price Is Right   (Mark Goodson Productions)

Wheel of Fortune   (Merv Griffin Productions)
Win, Lose or Draw   (Burt & Bert Productions)

Best Host or Hostess in a Game Show
(tie for winner)
BOB BARKER   (The Price Is Right)
ALEX TREBEK   (Jeopardy!)
Alex Trebek   (Classic Concentration)

Best Individual Director for a Game Show
JOE BEHAR   (Fun House)
Paul Alter   (The Price Is Right)
Dick Schneider   (Jeopardy!)

Eighteenth Annual Daytime Emmy Awards   (1990–1991)
for daytime programs telecast between March 6, 1990 and
March 5, 1991 . . . presented June 27, 1991

Outstanding Game Show
JEOPARDY!   (Merv Griffin Productions)
The $100,000 Pyramid   (Bob Stewart Productions)
The Price Is Right   (Mark Goodson Productions)
Wheel of Fortune   (Merv Griffin Productions)

Best Host or Hostess in a Game Show
BOB BARKER   (The Price Is Right)
Alex Trebek   (Jeopardy!)
Alex Trebek   (Classic Concentration)

Best Individual Director for a Game Show
DICK SCHNEIDER   (Jeopardy!)
Paul Alter   (The Price Is Right)
Joe Behar   (Fun House)

Nineteenth Annual Daytime Emmy Awards   (1991–1992)
for daytime programs telecast between March 1991 and
March 1992 . . . presented June 23, 1992

Outstanding Game Show
JEOPARDY!   (Merv Griffin Productions)
The $100,000 Pyramid   (Bob Stewart Productions)
Family Feud   (Mark Goodson Productions)
The Price Is Right   (Mark Goodson Productions)

Best Host or Hostess in a Game Show
BOB BARKER   (The Price Is Right)
Dom DeLuise   (Candid Camera)
Alex Trebek   (Jeopardy!)

Best Individual Director for a Game Show
DICK SCHNEIDER   (Jeopardy!)
Paul Alter   (The Price Is Right)

Annual Daytime Emmy Awards (1992–1993) for daytime
programs telecast between March 1992 and March
1993 . . . presented May 26, 1993

Outstanding Game Show
JEOPARDY!   (Merv Griffin Productions)

Family Feud Challenge   (Mark Goodson Productions)
The Price Is Right   (Mark Goodson Productions)
Wheel of Fortune   (Merv Griffin Productions)

Best Host or Hostess in a Game Show
PAT SAJAK   (Wheel of Fortune)
Bob Barker   (The Price Is Right)
Ray Combs   (Family Feud)
Alex Trebek   (Jeopardy!)

Best Individual Director for a Game Show
KEVIN McCARTHY   (Jeopardy!)
DICK SCHNEIDER   (Jeopardy!)
Paul Alter   (The Price Is Right)
Dick Carson   (Wheel of Fortune)

Twenty-first Annual Daytime Emmy Awards (1993–1994)
for daytime programs telecast between March 1993 and
March 1994 . . . presented May 26, 1994

Outstanding Game Show
JEOPARDY!   (Merv Griffin Productions)
The Price Is Right   (Mark Goodson Productions)
Wheel of Fortune   (Merv Griffin Productions)

Outstanding Game Show Host
BOB BARKER   (The Price Is Right)
Alex Trebek   (Jeopardy!)

Outstanding Direction in a Game/Audience Participation Show
BOB LEVY   (American Gladiators)
Paul Alter   (The Price Is Right)
Kevin McCarthy   (Jeopardy!)

Twenty-second Annual Daytime Emmy Awards (1994–
1995) for daytime programs telecast between February 1994
and February 1995 . . . presented May 15, 1995

Outstanding Game/Audience Participation Show
JEOPARDY!   (Syndicated/Merv Griffin Productions)
American Gladiators (Syndicated/Four Point–Samuel
Goldwyn)
MTV's Fourth Annual Rock 'n' Jock B-Ball Jam   (Cable/
MTV)
The Price Is Right   (CBS/Mark Goodson Productions)
Wheel of Fortune   (Syndicated/Merv Griffin Productions)

Outstanding Game Show Host
BOB BARKER   (The Price Is Right)
Alex Trebek   (Jeopardy!)

Outstanding Directing in a Game/Audience Participation Show
KEVIN McCARTHY   (Jeopardy!)
Bob Levy   (American Gladiators)
Paul Alter   (The Price Is Right)

Twenty-third Annual Daytime Emmy Awards (1995–
1996) for daytime programs telecast between February 1995
and February 1996 . . . presented May 22, 1996

Outstanding Game/Audience Participation Show
THE PRICE IS RIGHT   (CBS/Mark Goodson Productions)
Jeopardy!   (Syndicated/Merv Griffin Productions)

Outstanding Game Show Host
BOB BARKER   (The Price Is Right)
Alex Trebek   (Jeopardy!)

Outstanding Directing in a Game/Audience Participation Show
KEVIN McCARTHY   (Jeopardy!)
Paul Alter   (The Price Is Right)

Twenty-fourth Annual Daytime Emmy Awards (1996–1997) for daytime programs telecast between February 1996 and February 1997 . . . presented May 21, 1997

Outstanding Game/Audience Participation Show
THE PRICE IS RIGHT   (CBS/Mark Goodson Productions)
Debt (Lifetime Cable/Faded Denim Productions/Buena Vista Television)
Jeopardy! (Syndicated/Columbia/Tri Star Television)
Secrets of the Cryptkeeper's Haunted House   (CBS/Goldwyn Entertainment/Keller Productions/The Wohl Company)

Outstanding Game Show Host
PAT SAJAK   (Wheel of Fortune)
Bob Barker   (The Price Is Right)

Al Roker   (Remember This?)
Alex Trebek   (Jeopardy!)

Outstanding Directing in a Game Show Series
DICK CARSON   (Wheel of Fortune)
Paul Alter   (The Price Is Right)
Kevin McCarthy   (Jeopardy!)

Twenty-fifth Annual Daytime Emmy Awards (1997) for daytime programs telecast between February 8, 1997 and December 31, 1997 . . . presented May 15, 1998

Outstanding Game/Audience Participation Show
JEOPARDY!   (Columbia/Tri Star Television)
Pictionary   (Kline & Friends)
The Price Is Right   (Mark Goodson/All American Television)
Wheel of Fortune   (Columbia/Tri Star Television)
Win Ben Stein's Money   (Valleycrest Productions)

Outstanding Game Show Host
PAT SAJAK   (Wheel of Fortune)
Bob Barker   (The Price Is Right)
Alex Trebek   (Jeopardy!)

Outstanding Directing in a Game/Audience Participation Show
DENNIS ROSENBLATT   (Win Ben Stein's Money)
Kevin McCarthy (Jeopardy!)
Dick Carson (Wheel of Fortune)

III. PRIMETIME EMMY AWARD WINNERS AND NOMINEES

The first Emmy Awards for television programs were presented on January 25, 1949, honoring programs aired in 1948. In the first two years, game shows were part of the category covering "Most Popular Television Program" (1948) and "Best Live Show" (1949). In 1950, a separate category was created for game, quiz, and audience-participation shows. Emmy Awards for this category were not given every year and none were given after the 1962–1963 season.

1948 Emmy Awards (presented January 25, 1949)
"Pantomime Quiz" won the Emmy as "Most Popular Television Program." No other game shows were nominated. Mike Stokey, host of "Pantomime Quiz" was nominated as "Most Outstanding Television Personality."

1949 Emmy Awards (presented January 27, 1950)
"Pantomime Quiz" was nominated but did not win in the category of "Best Live Show." Mike Stokey was again nominated as "Outstanding Live Personality."

1950 Emmy Awards (presented January 23, 1951)
Best Game and Audience-Participation Show (new category)
TRUTH OR CONSEQUENCES (winner)
Kay Kyser's College of Musical Knowledge

Life With Linkletter
Pantomime Quiz
You Bet Your Life
Groucho Marx won the Emmy for "Most Outstanding Personality"

1951 Emmy Awards (presented February 18, 1952)
There was no game show category this year, but "You Bet Your Life" was nominated as "Best Comedy Show."

1952 Emmy Awards (presented February 5, 1953)
Best Audience Participation, Quiz, or Panel Program (new title)
WHAT'S MY LINE?
Down You Go
This Is Your Life

Two for the Money
You Bet Your Life

1953 Emmy Awards (presented February 11, 1954)
Best Audience Participation, Quiz, or Panel Program
(tie for the Emmy)
THIS IS YOUR LIFE
WHAT'S MY LINE?
I've Got a Secret
Two for the Money
You Bet Your Life

1954 Emmy Awards (presented March 7, 1955)
Best Audience Participation, Quiz, or Panel Program
THIS IS YOUR LIFE
Masquerade Party
People Are Funny
What's My Line?
You Bet Your Life

1955 Emmy Awards (presented March 17, 1956)
Best Audience Participation, Quiz, or Panel Program
THE $64,000 QUESTION
I've Got a Secret
People Are Funny
What's My Line?
You Bet Your Life

There were no game show Emmys presented in 1956 or 1957.

1958 Emmy Awards (presented May 6, 1959)
Best Panel, Quiz, or Audience Participation Series

WHAT'S MY LINE?
I've Got a Secret
Keep Talking
The Price Is Right
This Is Your Life
You Bet Your Life

There were no Emmy Awards given for game shows in 1959–1960, 1960–1961, and 1961–1962 seasons.

1962–1963 Emmy Awards (presented May 26, 1963)
Outstanding Program Achievement in the Field of Panel, Quiz, or Audience Participation
G.E. COLLEGE BOWL
Password
To Tell the Truth

No Emmy Awards were given for game shows from 1963–1964 season through 1971–1972 season.

1972–1973 Emmy Awards (presented May 20, 1973)
Outstanding Achievement in Daytime Programs
DINAH'S PLACE
The Hollywood Squares
Jeopardy!
The Mike Douglas Show
Password

(category included game shows and talk shows)

Beginning in the 1973–1974 season, game show Emmys were presented as part of the Daytime Emmy Award ceremonies.

IV. MOST DAYTIME EMMY AWARDS FOR OUTSTANDING GAME SHOW

9 The $10,000 Pyramid/The $25,000 Pyramid/The $100,000 Pyramid
(1976, 1980, 1981, 1983, 1984, 1985, 1986, 1987, 1989)
7 Jeopardy!
(1990, 1991, 1992, 1993, 1994, 1995, 1998)
4 The Hollywood Squares
(1975, 1978, 1979, 1980)

3 The Price Is Right
(1988, 1996, 1997)
2 Password/Password Plus
(1974, 1982)
1 Family Feud
(1977)

V. MOST DAYTIME EMMY NOMINATIONS FOR OUTSTANDING GAME SHOW

17 The Price Is Right
16 The $10,000 Pyramid/The $25,000 Pyramid/The $100,000 Pyramid
14 Jeopardy!

13 Wheel of Fortune
12 Family Feud
 8 The Hollywood Squares
 3 Win, Lose or Draw

2 Let's Make a Deal
2 Match Game
2 Password/Password Plus
1 American Gladiators
1 Debt

1 Pictionary
1 Secrets of the Cryptkeeper's Haunted House
1 Tattletales
1 Win Ben Stein's Money

VI. MOST DAYTIME EMMY AWARDS FOR OUTSTANDING GAME SHOW HOST

9 Bob Barker   (1982, 1984, 1987, 1988, 1990, 1991, 1992, 1994, 1996)
4 Peter Marshall   (1974, 1975, 1980, 1981)
3 Dick Clark   (1979, 1985, 1986)
3 Pat Sajak   (1993, 1997, 1998)

2 Alex Trebek   (1989, 1990)
1 Bert Convy   (1977)
1 Richard Dawson   (1978)
1 Allen Ludden   (1976)
1 Betty White   (1983)

VII. MOST DAYTIME EMMY NOMINATIONS FOR OUTSTANDING GAME SHOW HOST

15 Bob Barker
13 Alex Trebek
10 Dick Clark
 7 Richard Dawson
 6 Peter Marshall
 6 Pat Sajak
 3 Gene Rayburn
 2 Bill Cullen
 2 Vicki Lawrence
 2 Allen Ludden

2 Betty White
1 Ray Combs
1 Bert Convy
1 Dom DeLuise
1 Geoff Edwards
1 Art Fleming
1 Monty Hall
1 Al Roker
1 Susan Stafford
1 Chuck Woolery

APPENDIX F

Top-Rated Game Shows

I. TOP-RATED DAYTIME NETWORK GAME SHOWS
Information courtesy of A. C. Nielsen.
Information not available prior to 1952–1953 season.

OCTOBER 1952–APRIL 1953
1. STRIKE IT RICH   (CBS)
2. THE BIG PAYOFF   (NBC)
3. DOUBLE OR NOTHING   (CBS)

OCTOBER 1953–APRIL 1954
1. STRIKE IT RICH   (CBS)
2. THE BIG PAYOFF   (CBS)
3. ON YOUR ACCOUNT   (NBC)

OCTOBER 1954–APRIL 1955
1. STRIKE IT RICH   (CBS)
2. THE BIG PAYOFF   (CBS)
3. ON YOUR ACCOUNT   (CBS)

OCTOBER 1955–APRIL 1956
1. QUEEN FOR A DAY   (NBC)
2. STRIKE IT RICH   (CBS)
3. THE BIG PAYOFF   (CBS)

OCTOBER 1956–APRIL 1957
1. QUEEN FOR A DAY   (NBC)
2. THE BIG PAYOFF   (CBS)
3. STRIKE IT RICH   (CBS)

OCTOBER 1957–APRIL 1958
1. DOTTO   (CBS)
2. THE PRICE IS RIGHT   (NBC)
3. TREASURE HUNT   (NBC)

OCTOBER 1958–APRIL 1959
1. CONCENTRATION   (NBC)
2. THE PRICE IS RIGHT   (NBC)
3. TIC TAC DOUGH   (NBC)

OCTOBER 1959–APRIL 1960
1. CONCENTRATION   (NBC)
2. THE PRICE IS RIGHT   (NBC)
3. PLAY YOUR HUNCH   (NBC)

OCTOBER 1960–APRIL 1961
1. CONCENTRATION   (NBC)
2. THE PRICE IS RIGHT   (NBC)
3. PASSWORD   (CBS)

OCTOBER 1961–APRIL 1962
1. CONCENTRATION   (NBC)
2. THE PRICE IS RIGHT   (NBC)
3. PASSWORD   (CBS)

OCTOBER 1962–APRIL 1963
1. PASSWORD   (CBS)
2. TO TELL THE TRUTH   (CBS)
3. CONCENTRATION   (NBC)

OCTOBER 1963–APRIL 1964
1. PASSWORD   (CBS)
2. TO TELL THE TRUTH   (CBS)
3. THE MATCH GAME   (NBC)

OCTOBER 1964–APRIL 1965
1. PASSWORD   (CBS)
2. TO TELL THE TRUTH   (CBS)
3. YOU DON'T SAY!   (NBC)

OCTOBER 1965–APRIL 1966
1. PASSWORD   (CBS)
2. TO TELL THE TRUTH   (CBS)
3. YOU DON'T SAY!   (NBC)

OCTOBER 1966–APRIL 1967
1. TO TELL THE TRUTH   (CBS)
2. PASSWORD   (CBS)
3. YOU DON'T SAY!   (NBC)

OCTOBER 1967–APRIL 1968
1. YOU DON'T SAY!   (NBC)
2. TO TELL THE TRUTH   (CBS)
3. THE MATCH GAME   (NBC)

OCTOBER 1968–APRIL 1969
1. LET'S MAKE A DEAL   (ABC)
2. THE NEWLYWED GAME   (ABC)
3. YOU DON'T SAY!   (NBC)

OCTOBER 1969–APRIL 1970
1. THE NEWLYWED GAME   (ABC)
2. JEOPARDY!   (NBC)
3. THE HOLLYWOOD SQUARES   (NBC)

OCTOBER 1970–APRIL 1971
1. THE HOLLYWOOD SQUARES   (NBC)
2. JEOPARDY!   (NBC)
3. THE NEWLYWED GAME   (ABC)

OCTOBER 1971–APRIL 1972
1. THE HOLLYWOOD SQUARES   (NBC)
2. THE NEWLYWED GAME   (ABC)
3. JEOPARDY!   (NBC)

OCTOBER 1972–APRIL 1973
1. THE HOLLYWOOD SQUARES   (NBC)
2. THE NEWLYWED GAME   (ABC)
3. LET'S MAKE A DEAL   (ABC)

OCTOBER 1973–APRIL 1974
1. MATCH GAME '74   (CBS)
2. THE HOLLYWOOD SQUARES   (NBC)
3. LET'S MAKE A DEAL   (ABC)

OCTOBER 1974–APRIL 1975
1. MATCH GAME '75   (CBS)
2. THE PRICE IS RIGHT   (CBS)
3. THE HOLLYWOOD SQUARES   (NBC)

OCTOBER 1975–APRIL 1976
1. MATCH GAME '76   (CBS)
2. BREAK THE BANK   (ABC)
3. THE $20,000 PYRAMID   (ABC)

OCTOBER 1976–APRIL 1977
1. MATCH GAME '77   (CBS)
2. FAMILY FEUD   (ABC)
3. THE $20,000 PYRAMID   (ABC)

OCTOBER 1977–APRIL 1978
1. FAMILY FEUD   (ABC)
2. MATCH GAME '78   (CBS)
3. THE $20,000 PYRAMID   (ABC)

OCTOBER 1978–APRIL 1979
1. FAMILY FEUD   (ABC)
2. THE PRICE IS RIGHT   (CBS)
3. WHEEL OF FORTUNE   (NBC)

OCTOBER 1979–APRIL 1980
1. THE PRICE IS RIGHT   (CBS)
2. FAMILY FEUD   (ABC)
3. WHEEL OF FORTUNE   (NBC)

OCTOBER 1980–APRIL 1981
1. THE PRICE IS RIGHT   (CBS)
2. FAMILY FEUD   (ABC)
3. WHEEL OF FORTUNE   (NBC)

OCTOBER 1981–APRIL 1982
1. THE PRICE IS RIGHT   (CBS)
2. FAMILY FEUD   (ABC)
3. WHEEL OF FORTUNE   (NBC)

OCTOBER 1982–APRIL 1983
1. THE PRICE IS RIGHT   (CBS)
2. FAMILY FEUD   (ABC)
3. WHEEL OF FORTUNE   (NBC)

OCTOBER 1983–APRIL 1984
1. THE PRICE IS RIGHT   (CBS)
2. WHEEL OF FORTUNE   (NBC)
3. DREAM HOUSE   (NBC)

OCTOBER 1984–APRIL 1985
1. THE PRICE IS RIGHT   (CBS)
2. WHEEL OF FORTUNE   (NBC)
3. SCRABBLE   (NBC)

OCTOBER 1985–APRIL 1986
1. THE PRICE IS RIGHT   (CBS)
2. WHEEL OF FORTUNE   (NBC)
3. SCRABBLE   (NBC)

OCTOBER 1986–APRIL 1987
1. THE PRICE IS RIGHT   (CBS)
2. WHEEL OF FORTUNE   (NBC)
3. SCRABBLE   (NBC)

OCTOBER 1987–APRIL 1988
1. THE PRICE IS RIGHT   (CBS)
2. WHEEL OF FORTUNE   (NBC)
3. WIN, LOSE OR DRAW   (NBC)

OCTOBER 1988–APRIL 1989
1. THE PRICE IS RIGHT   (CBS)
2. WHEEL OF FORTUNE   (NBC)
3. SCRABBLE   (NBC)

OCTOBER 1989–APRIL 1990
1. THE PRICE IS RIGHT   (CBS)
2. FAMILY FEUD   (CBS)
3. WHEEL OF FORTUNE   (CBS)

OCTOBER 1990–APRIL 1991
1. THE PRICE IS RIGHT   (CBS)
2. FAMILY FEUD   (CBS)
3. CLASSIC CONCENTRATION   (NBC)

OCTOBER 1991–APRIL 1992
1. THE PRICE IS RIGHT   (CBS)
2. FAMILY FEUD   (CBS)
3. CLASSIC CONCENTRATION   (NBC)

OCTOBER 1992–APRIL 1993
1. THE PRICE IS RIGHT   (CBS)
2. FAMILY FEUD   (CBS)
3. SCRABBLE   (NBC)

OCTOBER 1993–APRIL 1994
1. THE PRICE IS RIGHT   (CBS)
2. CLASSIC CONCENTRATION   (NBC)
3. CAESARS CHALLENGE   (NBC)
After the 1993–1994 season, "The Price Is Right" was the
only game show on network daytime television.

II. TOP-RATED PRIMETIME NETWORK GAME SHOWS
Information courtesy of A. C. Nielsen.
Complete ratings are not available for the years 1950–1951
through 1956–1957 seasons.

OCTOBER 1950–APRIL 1951
1. YOU BET YOUR LIFE   (NBC)
2. STOP THE MUSIC   (ABC)

OCTOBER 1951–APRIL 1952
1. YOU BET YOUR LIFE   (NBC)
2. STRIKE IT RICH   (CBS)

OCTOBER 1952–APRIL 1953
1. YOU BET YOUR LIFE   (NBC)
2. WHAT'S MY LINE?   (CBS)
3. STRIKE IT RICH   (CBS)

OCTOBER 1953–APRIL 1954
1. YOU BET YOUR LIFE   (NBC)

OCTOBER 1954–APRIL 1955
1. YOU BET YOUR LIFE   (NBC)
2. I'VE GOT A SECRET   (CBS)
3. TWO FOR THE MONEY   (CBS)

OCTOBER 1955–APRIL 1956
1. THE $64,000 QUESTION   (CBS)
2. YOU BET YOUR LIFE   (NBC)
3. I'VE GOT A SECRET   (CBS)

OCTOBER 1956–APRIL 1957
1. THE $64,000 QUESTION   (CBS)
2. I'VE GOT A SECRET   (CBS)
3. YOU BET YOUR LIFE   (NBC)

OCTOBER 1957–APRIL 1958
1. I'VE GOT A SECRET   (CBS)
2. YOU BET YOUR LIFE   (NBC)
3. THE $64,000 QUESTION   (CBS)

OCTOBER 1958–APRIL 1959
1. I'VE GOT A SECRET   (CBS)
2. THE PRICE IS RIGHT   (NBC)
3. NAME THAT TUNE   (CBS)

OCTOBER 1959–APRIL 1960
1. THE PRICE IS RIGHT   (NBC)
2. YOU BET YOUR LIFE   (NBC)
3. WHAT'S MY LINE?   (CBS)

OCTOBER 1960–APRIL 1961
1. THE PRICE IS RIGHT   (NBC)
2. WHAT'S MY LINE?   (CBS)
3. I'VE GOT A SECRET   (CBS)

OCTOBER 1961–APRIL 1962
1. THE PRICE IS RIGHT   (NBC)
2. TO TELL THE TRUTH   (CBS)
3. WHAT'S MY LINE?   (CBS)

OCTOBER 1962–APRIL 1963
1. WHAT'S MY LINE?   (CBS)
2. I'VE GOT A SECRET   (CBS)
3. TO TELL THE TRUTH   (CBS)

OCTOBER 1963–APRIL 1964
1. I'VE GOT A SECRET   (CBS)
2. WHAT'S MY LINE?   (CBS)
3. TO TELL THE TRUTH   (CBS)

OCTOBER 1964–APRIL 1965
1. I'VE GOT A SECRET   (CBS)
2. TO TELL THE TRUTH   (CBS)
3. WHAT'S MY LINE?   (CBS)

OCTOBER 1965–APRIL 1966
1. I'VE GOT A SECRET   (CBS)
2. TO TELL THE TRUTH   (CBS)
3. WHAT'S MY LINE?   (CBS)

OCTOBER 1966–APRIL 1967
1. WHAT'S MY LINE?   (CBS)
2. THE DATING GAME   (ABC)
3. THE NEWLYWED GAME   (ABC)

OCTOBER 1967–APRIL 1968
1. THE NEWLYWED GAME   (ABC)
2. THE DATING GAME   (ABC)
3. THE HOLLYWOOD SQUARES   (NBC)

OCTOBER 1968–APRIL 1969
1. THE NEWLYWED GAME   (ABC)
2. THE DATING GAME   (ABC)
3. LET'S MAKE A DEAL   (ABC)

OCTOBER 1969–APRIL 1970
1. THE NEWLYWED GAME   (ABC)
2. LET'S MAKE A DEAL   (ABC)
3. THE DATING GAME   (ABC)

OCTOBER 1970–APRIL 1971
1. THE NEWLYWED GAME   (ABC)
2. LET'S MAKE A DEAL   (ABC)
3. THE REEL GAME   (ABC)

No regularly scheduled game shows in primetime after the 1970–1971 season.

APPENDIX G
TV Game Shows That Began on Radio

show (radio host)	network	first–last broadcast	show (radio host)	network	first–last broadcast
Beat the Clock (Bill Cullen)	CBS	Jan 5, 1949–May 4, 1949	Meet Your Match (Jan Murray)	Mutual, NBC	May 5, 1949–Jan 18, 1953
Blind Date (Arlene Francis)	ABC, NBC	Jul 8, 1943–Jan 18, 1946	Missus Goes-A-Shopping (John Reed King)	CBS	Feb 17, 1941–Dec 21, 1951
Break the Bank (John Reed King, Johnny Olson, Bud Collyer, Bert Parks)	Mutual, ABC, NBC	Oct 20, 1945–Jul 15, 1955	Name That Tune (Red Benson)	NBC	Dec 20, 1952–Apr 10, 1953
Can You Top This? (Ward Wilson)	Mutual, NBC, ABC	Dec 9, 1940–Jul 9, 1954	People Are Funny (Art Baker, Art Linkletter)	CBS, NBC	Apr 3, 1942–1959
Chance of a Lifetime (John Reed King)	ABC	Sep 4, 1949–Jan 19, 1952	QED	ABC	Apr 15, 1951–Oct 14, 1951
College Bowl (Allen Ludden)	NBC	Oct 10, 1953–May 6, 1955	Queen for a Day (Jack Bailey)	Mutual	Apr 30, 1945–Jun 10, 1957
County Fair (Peter Donald, Win Elliott, Jack Bailey)	CBS	Jul 10, 1945–Apr 1, 1950	Quick as a Flash (Ken Roberts, Win Elliott, Bill Cullen)	ABC, Mutual	Jul 16, 1944–Jun 29, 1951
Double or Nothing (Walter Compton, Todd Russell, Walter O'Keefe, John Reed King)	Mutual, CBS, NBC, ABC	Sep 29, 1940–Jan 15, 1954	Quiz Kids (Joe Kelly)	ABC, CBS, NBC	Jun 28, 1940–Jul 5, 1953
Doctor I. Q. (James McClain, Lew Valentine)	NBC, ABC	Apr 10, 1939–Nov 29, 1950	Sing It Again (Dan Seymour)	CBS	May 29, 1948–Jun 23, 1951
Earn Your Vacation (Jay C. Flippen)	CBS	Jun 5, 1949–Jul 2, 1950	Songs for Sale (Jan Murray, Richard Hayes)	CBS	Jun 30, 1950–Oct 6, 1951
Give and Take (John Reed King)	CBS	Aug 25, 1945–Dec 26, 1953	Stop Me If You've Heard This One (Milton Berle, Morey Amsterdam)	NBC, Mutual	Oct 7, 1939–Feb 24, 1940 Sep 13, 1947–Oct 9, 1948
Information Please (Clifton Fadiman)	NBC, Blue, CBS, Mutual	May 17, 1938–Apr 22, 1951	Stop the Music (Bert Parks)	ABC, CBS	Mar 21, 1948–Feb 15, 1955
It Pays to Be Ignorant (Tom Howard)	Mutual, CBS, NBC	Jun 25, 1942–Sep 26, 1951	Strike It Rich (Todd Russell, Warren Hull)	CBS, NBC	Jun 29, 1947–Dec 27, 1957
Kay Kyser's College of Musical Knowledge (Kay Kyser)	ABC, Mutual, NBC	Mar 30, 1938–Jul 29, 1949	Think Fast (Mason Gross)	ABC	May 29, 1949–May 7, 1950
			Truth or Consequences (Ralph Edwards)	CBS, NBC	Mar 23, 1940–Aug 30, 1957
Ladies Be Seated (Johnny Olson, Penny Olson)	ABC	Jun 26, 1944–Jul 29, 1949	Twenty Questions (Bill Slater, Jay Jackson)	Mutual	Feb 2, 1946–Mar 27, 1954

show (radio host)	network	first–last broadcast	show (radio host)	network	first–last broadcast
Two for the Money (Herb Shriner)	NBC, CBS	Sep 30, 1952–Sep 23, 1956	Who Said That? (Robert Trout)	NBC	Jul 2, 1948–Aug 22, 1950
We Take Your Word	CBS	Feb 5, 1950–Jul 6, 1951	Winner Take All (Bill Cullen)	CBS	Jun 14, 1946–Feb 1, 1952
What's My Line?* (John Daly)	CBS	May 20, 1952–Jul 1, 1953	You Bet Your Life (Groucho Marx)	ABC, CBS, NBC	Oct 27, 1947–Sep 19, 1956

*The radio version of ''What's My Line?'' premiered two years after the debut of the TV version.

APPENDIX H
Game Shows That Have Had Multiple Runs

Beat the Clock	1950–1961 1969–1974 1979–1980	I'll Bet/ It's Your Bet	1965 1969–1973
Blockbusters	1980–1982 1987	It Pays to Be Ignorant	1949–1951 1973–1974
Camouflage	1961–1962 1980	It Takes Two	1969–1970 1997
Can You Top This?	1950–1951 1970	I've Got a Secret	1952–1967 1972–1973 1976
Card Sharks	1978–1981 1986–1989	Jackpot!	1974–1975 1985–1988 1989–1990
Chain Reaction	1980 1986–1991	Jeopardy!	1964–1975 1978–1979 1984– present
Concentration/ Classic Concentration	1958–1978 1987–1993		
College Bowl/Campus All Star Challenge	1959–1970 1987 1990–1995	The Joker's Wild	1972–1975 1977–1986 1990–1991
Crosswits	1975–1980 1986–1987	The Krypton Factor	1981 1990–1991
The Dating Game	1965–1974 1978–1980 1986–1989 1996–	Let's Make a Deal	1963–1977 1980–1981 1984–1986 1990–1991
Doctor I.Q.	1953–1954 1958–1959	Liars Club	1969 1976–1979 1988–1989
Dream House	1968–1970 1983–1984		
Family Feud	1976–1985 1988–1995	Make Me Laugh	1958 1979–1980 1997–
Gambit/ Las Vegas Gambit	1972–1976 1980–1981	Make That Spare	1960–1964 1988
The Gong Show	1976–1980 1988–1989	Masquerade Party	1952–1960 1974–1975
High Rollers	1974–1976 1978–1980 1987–1988	Match Game	1962–1969 1973–1982 1990–1991
The Hollywood Squares	1966–1981 1986–1989		

Name That Tune	1953–1959	Split Second	1972–1975
	1974–1981		1987
	1984–1985	Supermarket Sweep	1965–1967
The Newlywed Game	1966–1974		1990–present
	1977–1980	Tattletales	1974–1978
	1985–1989		1982–1984
	1996–	The $10,000 Pyramid/	1973–1980
Now You See It	1974–1975	The $50,000 Pyramid/	1981
	1989	The $25,000 Pyramid/	1982–1988
Oh My Word/	1966–1967	The $100,000 Pyramid	1991–1992
Take My Word for It	1982–1983	Tic Tac Dough	1956–1959
The $64,000 Question/	1955–1958		1978–1986
The $128,000 Question	1976–1978		1990–1991
Pantomime Quiz/	1950–1959	To Tell the Truth	1956–1968
Stump the Stars/Celebrity Charades	1962–1963		1969–1978
	1969–1970		1980–1981
	1979		1990–1991
Password/	1961–1967	Treasure Hunt	1956–1959
	1971–1975		1973–1977
Password Plus/	1979–1982		1981–1982
Super Password	1984–1989	Truth or Consequences	1950–1951
Pay Cards!/	1968–1969		1954–1965
Super Pay Cards!	1981–1982		1966–1975
People Are Funny	1954–1961		1977–1978
	1984		1987–1988
Pictionary	1989	What's My Line?	1950–1967
	1997–		1968–1975
The Price Is Right	1956–1965	Winner Take All	1948–1950
	1972–present		1951
Queen for a Day	1956–1964		1952
	1969–1970	You Bet Your Life	1950–1961
Quiz Kids	1949–1956		1980–1981
	1978		1992–1993
	1981–1982	You Don't Say!	1963–1969
Sale of the Century	1969–1974		1975
	1983–1989		1978–1979
Shop 'Til You Drop	1991–1995		
	1996–		

APPENDIX I

Twenty Game Show Hosts Who Had Hit Songs

artist	biggest hit	year released	peak position on Billboard pop charts
Steve Allen	"Autumn Leaves"	1955	35
Bill Anderson	"Still"	1963	8
Jon Bauman (As a member of Sha Na Na)	"(Just Like) Romeo and Juliet"	1975	55
Bert Convy (as a member of The Cheers)	"Black Denim Trousers"	1955	6
Bill Cosby	"Little Ole Man (Uptight— Everything's Alright)"	1967	4
Tennessee Ernie Ford	"Sixteen Tons"	1955	1
Jackie Gleason (with his orchestra)	"Autumn Leaves"	1955	50
Merv Griffin (with Freddy Martin and his orchestra)	"I've Got A Lovely Bunch of Coconuts"	1949	8
Buddy Hackett	"Chinese Rock & Egg Roll"	1956	87
Richard Hayes	"The Old Master Painter"	1949	2
Clint Holmes	"Playground in My Mind"	1973	2
Gabe Kaplan	"Up Your Nose"	1977	91
Kay Kyser	"Jingle Jangle Jingle"	1942	1
Vicki Lawrence	"The Night the Lights Went Out in Georgia"	1973	1
Robert Q. Lewis	"Where's-a Your House"	1951	22
Art Linkletter	"We Love You, Call Collect"	1969	42
Wink Martindale	"Deck of Cards"	1959	7

artist	biggest hit	year released	peak position on Billboard pop charts
Paul Peterson	"My Dad"	1962	6
Jack Smith	"Cruising Down the River"	1949	3
Adam Wade	"The Writing on the Wall"	1961	5

Sources: *Joel Whitburn's Top Pop Singles 1955–1993*
Joel Whitburn's Pop Hits 1940–1954

APPENDIX J

Six Catchy Game Show Phrases That Became Part of Our Vocabulary

1. "Come on down!" (The Price Is Right)

2. "Enter and sign in please!" (What's My Line?)

3. "I'd like to buy a vowel." (Wheel of Fortune)

4. "Is it bigger than a breadbox?" (What's My Line?)

5. "Say the secret word." (You Bet Your Life)

6. "Will the real (John Doe) please stand up?" (To Tell the Truth)

Johnny Olson made "Come on down!" a household phrase more than 25 years ago . . . *and Rod Roddy will carry on the tradition into the twenty-first century.*

APPENDIX K
Index of Game Show Personalities

personality	game show	personality	game show
Aames, Willie	Krypton Factor (host)	Anderson, Ernie	Break the Bank (announcer), Dream Girl USA (announcer) Storm the Castle (announcer)
Abercrombie, Judy	All Star Almost Anything Goes (score girl)	Anderson, Larry	Truth or Consequences (host), Super Decades (announcer), Trivia Track (host)
Aberg, Siv	The Gong Show (assistant), Treasure Hunt (assistant)		
Adamle, Mike	American Gladiators (host)		
Adams, Don	Don Adams' Screen Test (host)	Andrews, Betty	Double Exposure (model), Mother's Day (assistant), Seven Keys (model)
Adams, Joey	Back That Fact (host)		
Adams, Mike	Quiz Kids (announcer)		
Addotta, Kip	Everything Goes (host)	Andrews, Eamonn	Top of the World (host), What's My Line? (substitute host), Lingo (host)
Alaskey, Joe	Couch Potatoes (announcer)		
Albert, Steve	The Grudge Match (host)	Andrews, Ralph	
Alda, Robert	By Popular Demand (host), Can Do (host), Personality Puzzle (host), What's Your Bid (assistant)	Ansbro, George	Across the Board (announcer), Doctor I.Q. (assistant), Penny to a Million (announcer)
		Appleton, Cindee	All New Beat the Clock (model)
Aletter, Kyle	The Price Is Right (substitute model)	Archerd, Army	The Movie Game (assistant)
		Areno, Lois	Card Sharks (assistant)
Alexander, Barbara Lee	Straight to the Heart (announcer/cohost)	Arlen, Roxanne	Beat the Clock (assistant), Winner Take All (assistant)
Alexander, Ben	About Faces (host), Queen for a Day (substitute host)	Armstrong, Bill	Celebrity Sweepstakes (announcer), The Liars Club (announcer/host), Matchmaker (announcer), Stumpers (announcer)
Alexander, Eddie	Junior Almost Anything Goes (host)		
Ali, Tatyana	Brains & Brawn (cohost)		
Allan, Jed	Celebrity Bowling (host), Celebrity Tennis (host)	Armstrong, Don	Texaco Star National Academic Championship (announcer)
Allen, Dayton	Dough Re Mi (substitute host)	Arthur, Maureen	Jan Murray Show (assistant)
Allen, Fred	Judge for Yourself (host), Two for the Money (substitute host)	Ashley, Kat	Scramble (referee)
		Ashley, Susan	Remote Control (assistant)
Allen, Herb	Hail the Champ (host)	Attell, Dave	Idiot Savants ("Savant Player")
Allen, Laurie	Lip Service (announcer)	Babbitt, Harry	Glamour Girl (host)
Allen, Mel	Jackpot Bowling (host), Let's Celebrate (host), Treasure Hunt (substitute host)	Bailey, Jack	Place the Face (host), Queen for a Day (host), Truth or Consequences (host)
Allen, Steve	I've Got a Secret (host), Songs for Sale (host)	Baker, Dee	Legends of the Hidden Temple (announcer), Shop 'til You Drop (announcer)
Ameche, Don	Strike It Rich (substitute host), Take a Chance (host)		
		Baker, Gene	Queen for a Day (announcer)
Ames, Elizabeth	Say When!! (model)	Baker, Janice	Card Sharks (assistant)
Amsterdam, Morey	Battle of the Ages (host)	Baker, Joe	The Cheap Show (assistant)
Andelin, Jim	Hail the Champ (assistant)	Baker, Phil	Who's Whose (host)
Anderson, Bill	The Better Sex (host), Fandango (host)	Baldwin, Bill	Beat the Odds (announcer), Stump the Stars (announcer)

personality	game show	personality	game show
Bamber, Judy	Anybody Can Play (assistant)		Match Game (substitute announcer), Sing It Again (announcer), To Tell the Truth (announcer), What's in a Word (announcer), What's My Line? (announcer), Winner Take All (announcer), Your Surprise Package (announcer), Your Surprise Store (announcer)
Banghart, Kenneth	Who Said That? (announcer)		
Banks, Emily	Say When!! (model)		
Barber, Bill	Illinois Instant Riches (announcer)		
Barbareschi, Luca	That's Amore (host)		
Barker, Bob	Dream Girl of '67 (host), The Family Game (host), The Price Is Right (host), Truth or Consequences (host)		
		Bennett, Fran	What Do You Have in Common? (assistant)
Barkley, Roger	Bedtime Stories (host), Name Droppers (host)	Benson, Hugh	Messing Prize Party (assistant)
		Benson, Red	Name That Tune (host)
Barnes, Binnie	Blind Date (substitute host)	Bentley, Beverly	Beat the Clock (assistant), The Price Is Right (model)
Barris, Chuck	The Gong Show (host)		
Barry, Jack	The Big Surprise (host), Break the Bank (host), Concentration (host), Dough Re Mi (substitute host), The Generation Gap (host), High Low (host), Joker! Joker! Joker! (host), The Joker's Wild (host), The Reel Game (host), Tic Tac Dough (host), Twenty-One (host)	Bergen, Bob	Jep! (host)
		Bergen, Edgar	Do You Trust Your Wife? (host)
		Berle, Milton	Jackpot Bowling (host)
		Berman, Chris	Boardwalk & Baseball's Super Bowl of Sports Trivia (host), Conquer Fort Boyard (host)
		Bernheim, Shirl	The Cheap Show (assistant)
		Berns, Alan	G.E. College Bowl (announcer)
Bartel, Jean	Queen for a Day (substitute commentator)	Berry, Bill	Liars Club (announcer), Make Me Laugh (announcer)
Bartholomew, Summer	Sale of the Century (hostess), Wheel of Fortune (substitute hostess)	Biggers, Sissy	Ready. . .Set . . . Cook! (host)
Bartlett, Debbie	50 Grand Slam (assistant), Animal Crack-ups (assistant) Dream House (assistant), Every Second Counts (assistant), Home Shopping Game (assistant)	Bishop, Jerry	The $25,000 Pyramid (announcer), Cross Wits (announcer)
		Bjorklund, Kristin	Card Sharks (substitute assistant)
		Blackman, Rob	Gaters (host)
		Blacknell, Steve	Playboy's Love and Sex Test (assistant)
Barton, Eileen	Video Village (assistant)		
Barton, Frank	Glamour Girl (announcer	Blaine, Jimmy	The Big Payoff (substitute host), Hold That Camera (host), Pantomime Quiz (announcer), Stop the Music (announcer), What's Going On? (announcer), What's My Name? (announcer)
Barton, John	Pitfall (announcer)		
Baruch, Andre	Americana (substitute host), Your Lucky Clue (announcer)		
Basaraba, Mary Lou	Super Pay Cards! (assistant)		
Bauman, Jon	Match Game–Hollywood Squares Hour (host), Pop 'n' Rocker Game (host)	Blaze, Heather	Idiot Savants ("Savant Player")
		Bleu, Don	The Gong Show (host)
Beach, Scott	Take My Word for It (announcer)	Block, Hal	Tag the Gag (host)
Beal, John	Freedom Rings (host)	Blu, Susan	Animal Crack-ups (voices)
Beall, Chip	Texaco Star National Academic Championship (host)	Blumer, Kati	Blade Warriors (warrior)
		Blyden, Larry	The Movie Game (host), Personality (host), Three on a Match (substitute host), What's My Line? (host), You're Putting Me On (host)
Beauchamp, Lee	Anything You Can Do (assistant)		
Beck, Billy	The Cheap Show (assistant)		
Becker, Sandy	Win with a Winner (host)		
Bellamy, Ralph	To Tell the Truth (substitute host)		
Belli, Melvin	Guilty or Innocent (host)	Boardman, Eric	Liars Club (host)
Benirschke, Rolf	Wheel of Fortune (host)	Bob & Ray (Bob Elliot & Ray Goulding)	The Name's the Same (hosts)
Bennett, Bern	Beat the Clock (announcer), By Popular Demand (announcer), I've Got a Secret (announcer), Keep Talking (announcer),		
		Boggs, Bill	All Star Almost Anything Goes (host)
		Bojanowski, Jamie	Double Dare (assistant)

personality	game show	personality	game show
Boland, Joe	Ask Me Another (host)	Buneta, Bill	Celebrity Bowling (assistant)
Bonasso, Amber	Click (cohost/announcer)	Burger, Michael	Family Challenge (host), Personals (host), Straight to the Heart (host)
Bower, Roger	Stop Me if You've Heard This One (host)		
Bowie, Kim	Blade Warriors (warrior)	Burns, Monica	Name That Tune (singer)
Bowman, Lee	What's Going On? (host)	Butkus, Dick	Star Games (commissioner)
Bracken, Eddie	Masquerade Party (host)	Buxton, Frank	Get the Message (host)
Bradford, Johnny	Tele Pun (host)	Byner, John	Relatively Speaking (host)
Bradley, Kathleen	The Price Is Right (model)	Byron, Carol	Doctor I.Q. (assistant)
Brady, Jim	Ruckus (announcer)	Cabot, Shirley	Anyone Can Win (assistant)
Brady, Jordan	Grill Me (host), Turn It Up! (host)	Cagney, Jeanne	Queen for a Day (fashion commentator)
Brady, Laurie	Jackpot Bowling (assistant)	Caldwell, Jim	Tic Tac Dough (host), Top Card (host)
Brandt, Mel	G.E. College Bowl (announcer), Say When!! (substitute announcer)		
		Callaghan, Jack	Quiz Kids (announcer)
		Calvin, Betty	Beat the Clock (assistant)
Braselle, Keefe	County Fair (substitute host), Dough Re Mi (substitute host), Treasure Hunt (substitute host)	Cameron, Cindy	Chance of a Lifetime (assistant)
		Campbell, Tom	Camouflage (host)
		Canning, Lisa	Knights and Warriors (host)
Brennan, Ed	Everything's Relative (announcer)	Cannon, John	I've Got a Secret (announcer), Strike It Rich (announcer)
Briggs, John	What's My Line? (announcer)	Capp, Al	Anyone Can Win (host), What's the Story (host)
Bright, Jack	Try and Do It (host)		
Bright, Patricia	Draw Me a Laugh (host), Movieland Quiz (assistant)	Carpenter, Ken	Truth or Consequences (announcer)
Briley, Connie	Love Between the Sexes (assistant)	Carrington, Michael	Personals (announcer), Think Fast (host)
Brittany, Morgan	Star Games (host)	Carson, Jack	Strike It Rich (announcer)
Britton, Barbara	The $64,000 Question (assistant)	Carson, Jim	Everything Goes (announcer)
Brock, Claudia	Let's Make a Deal (substitute model)	Carson, Johnny	Earn Your Vacation (host), Who Do You Trust? (host)
Brokenshire, Norman	Battle of the Ages (announcer), Masquerade Party (announcer), What's My Name? (announcer)	Carter, Janis	Feather Your Nest (assistant)
		Caruso, Carl	Back That Fact (announcer), Spin the Picture (host)
Brooke, Carol	Down You Go (announcer)	Caruso, Chris	Video Game (announcer)
Brophy, Bill	Mother's Day (announcer)	Case, Nelson	Masquerade Party (announcer)
Brown, Brandy	Teen Win, Lose or Draw (announcer)	Casey, Angel	Hail the Champ (assistant)
		Cash, Annette	Concentration (model)
Brown, Jim	King's Party Line (assistant), Missus Goes-A-Shopping (assistant)	Cassell, Barry	What in the World (announcer)
		Casson, Mel	Draw Me a Laugh (artist)
Brown, Joe E.	Strike It Rich (substitute host)	Cates, Challen	Perfect Match (cohost)
Brown, John Mason	Americana (host)	Causier, John	The $10,000 Pyramid (announcer)
Brown, Paige	Top Card (assistant)		
Brown, Ted	Across the Board (host), College of Musical Knowledge (announcer), The Greatest Man on Earth (host), What's My Name? (announcer)	Cavett, Dick	College Bowl (host)
		Cefalo, Jimmy	Sports Snapshot! (host), Trump Card (host)
		Cervenka, John	Love Connection (announcer)
		Chalabois, Rod	Chain Reaction (announcer)
Browning, Doug	Q.E.D. (host)	Chambers, Michael	Fun House (announcer)
Bruner, Wally	What's My Line? (host)	Chan, Gus	Quiz Kids (announcer)
Bryan, Arthur Q.	Movieland Quiz (host)	Chandler, Chuck	Let's Make a Deal (announcer)
Buffer, Michael	The Grudge Match (ring announcer)	Chandler, Ed	Anybody Can Play (announcer)
		Chandler, Robin	Quick on the Draw (host)
Bullard, Pat	Hold Everything! (host)	Chaplin, Curt	Designated Hitter (host), Grandstand (host)
Bullock, Jim J.	Hollywood Squares (substitute host)		
		Chong, Robbi (Renfield)	You Bet Your Life (assistant)

personality	game show	personality	game show
Christensen, Todd	American Gladiators (host)	Cohen, Marty	Slime Time (host)
Christian, Spencer	Triple Threat (host)	Cohen, Tom	Idiot Savants ("Savant Player")
Christopher, Kay	Doctor I.Q. (assistant)	Cole, Judy	King of the Mountain (cohost)
Cialini, Julie	The Price Is Right (model)	Coleman, Jonathan	Born Lucky (announcer)
Cipriano, Joe	Pictionary (announcer)	Coles, Lisa	Wild West Showdown (host)
Circosta, Bob	Home Shopping Game (announcer)	Collins, Fred	Lucky Partners (announcer), Pay Cards! (announcer), Say When!! (substitute announcer)
Claire, Julie	Debt (announcer)		
Clark, Dan "Nitro"	American Gladiators (cohost)	Collyer, Bud	Beat the Clock (host), Break the Bank (host), Feather Your Nest (host), Masquerade Party (host), Number Please (host), On Your Way (host), Quick as a Flash (host), This Is the Missus (host), To Tell the Truth (host), Truth or Consequences (announcer), Winner Take All (host)
Clark, Dick	The $10,000 Pyramid (host), The $20,000 Pyramid (host), The $25,000 Pyramid (host), The $50,000 Pyramid (host), The $100,000 Pyramid (host), Challengers (host), It Takes Two (host), The Krypton Factor (host), Missing Links (host), The Object Is (host), Scattergories (host)		
		Colon, Mercedes	Maximum Drive (cohost)
Clark, Jack	The $25,000 Pyramid (announcer), 100 Grand (host), The Big Surprise (announcer), Cross Wits (host), Dealer's Choice (host), Eye Guess (announcer), The Face Is Familiar (announcer), How Do You Rate? (announcer), The Love Experts (announcer), Password (announcer/substitute host), Personality (announcer), The Price Is Right (announcer/substitute host), The Reel Game (announcer), Second Chance (announcer), Split Second (announcer), Tattletales (announcer), Three for the Money (announcer), To Tell the Truth (announcer/substitute host), Top Dollar (announcer), What's My Line? (announcer), Wheel of Fortune (announcer), You're Putting Me On (announcer)	Combs, Ray	Family Challenge (host), Family Feud (host)
		Coniff, Frank	Are You Positive (host)
		Conklin, Joe	Finders Keepers (announcer)
		Conlon, Pat	The Big Payoff (model)
		Connolly, Dr. Francis	Word for Word (authority)
		Connor, Lynn	Balance Your Budget (assistant)
		Conreid, Hans	Made in America (host)
		Conte, John	Personality Puzzle (host)
		Content, John	Yahtzee (announcer)
		Convy, Bert	3rd Degree (host), Super Password (host), Tattletales (host), Win, Lose or Draw (host)
		Conway, Pat	The Big Payoff (model), Greatest Man on Earth (assistant)
		Cook, Lou	Bill Gwinn Show (announcer)
		Cooper, Bobby	Celebrity Bowling (assistant)
		Cooper, Ed	Down You Go (announcer), Quiz Kids (announcer)
		Copeland, Joanne	Top Dollar (assistant), Video Village (assistant)
		Coppola, Alicia	Remote Control (assistant)
		Cord, Alex	Wild West Showdown (host)
Clawson, Connie	Live Like a Millionaire (assistant)	Cordell, Carl	Lucky Partners (host)
Clayton, Bob	The $10,000 Pyramid (announcer), The $20,000 Pyramid (announcer), The $25,000 Pyramid (announcer), Blankety Blanks (announcer), Concentration (announcer/host), Make a Face (host), Pass the Buck (announcer), Shoot for the Stars (announcer), Three on a Match (announcer)	Cosby, Bill	You Bet Your Life (host)
		Costello, Jack	Art Ford Show (announcer), What Happened? (announcer)
		Cox, Wayne	Second Honeymoon (host), Talkabout (host)
		Coy, Jim	Down You Go (announcer)
		Crager, Joel	Chance for Romance (announcer)
		Cramer, John	Big Deal! (announcer), The Dating Game (announcer), Hollywood Game (announcer), The Newlywed Game (announcer)
Clooney, Nick	Money Maze (host)		
Cochran, Bill	Who Said That? (announcer)		
Cody, Laura	The Krypton Factor (announcer)	Cristal, Linda	County Fair (assistant)
Cohen, Mark	Make Me Laugh (host)	Crone, Neil	Wild Guess (host)

personality	game show	personality	game show
Cronkite, Walter	It's News to Me (host)	Davis, Nelson	College Bowl (announcer)
Crosby, Cathy Lee	Conquer Fort Boyard (host)	Dawson, Richard	Family Feud (host), Masquerade Party (host)
Csonka, Larry	American Gladiators (host)		
Cullen, Bill	The $25,000 Pyramid (host), Bank on the Stars (host), Blankety Blanks (host), Blockbusters (host), Break the Bank (substitute host), Chain Reaction (host), Child's Play (host), Down You Go (host), Eye Guess (host), Give and Take (announcer), Hot Potato (host), I've Got a Secret (host), The Joker's Wild (host), Love Experts (host), Name That Tune (host), Pass the Buck (host), Password Plus (host), Place the Face (host), The Price Is Right (host), Three on a Match (host), To Tell the Truth (host), Why? (assistant), Winner Take All (host), Winning Streak (host)	Day, Dennis	Queen for a Day (substitute host)
		Day, Steve	Caesars Challenge (announcer), Just Men! (announcer)
		Dayton, Danny	County Fair (substitute host)
		DeCarlo, Mark	Big Deal! (host), Studs (host)
		Defore, Don	Queen for a Day (substitute host)
		Dennis, Donna	Blade Warriors (warrior)
		Denny, Mary	Remember This Date (assistant)
		DeVargas, Nome	Treasure Hunt (model)
		Dewitt, George	Name That Tune (host)
		Dexter, Jerry	The Wizard of Odds (announcer)
		Dimaggio, Lou	Perfect Match (announcer)
		DiRenzo, Denise	Yahtzee ("Dice Girl")
		Diva, Paola	Concentration (model)
		Dixon, Bob	It's News to Me (announcer), On Your Account (announcer)
		Doherty, Dan	Casesars Challenge (assistant)
		Dollar, Lynn	The $64,000 Question (assistant), Lucky Partners (assistant)
Cummings, Brian	Let's Make a Deal (announcer)		
Cunningham, Arlene	Art Ford Show (assistant)	Dombeck, Reggie	Number Please (assistant)
Cunningham, Bob	Fun for the Money (announcer)	Donahue-Wallace, Charlene	Ruckus (assistant)
Cunningham, Heather	Big Showdown (assistant)		
Cunningham, Randall	Scramble (host)		
Curan, Marianne	Super Decades (host), Trivia Track (host)	Donald, Peter	Ad-Libbers (host), Masquerade Party (host)
Curtis, Dick	Queen for a Day (host)	Donovan, Pat	The $64,000 Challenge (assistant), The $64,000 Question (assistant)
Dahlstead, Dresser	Truth or Consequences (assistant)		
Dalton, Lynn	Play Your Hunch (assistant)	Dougherty, Kit	Sale of the Century (model)
Daly, John	It's News to Me (host), We Take Your Word (host), What's My Line? (host), Who Said That? (host)	Douglas, Melvyn	Your Big Moment (host)
		Douglas, Sandra	Reach for the Stars (assistant)
		Downs, Hugh	Concentration (host)
Damon, Jerry	G.E. College Bowl (announcer), Haggis Baggis (announcer), Jan Murray Show (announcer)	Driscoll, John	Fantasy Park (announcer)
		Driscoll, Mark	Now You See It (announcer)
		Duart, Louise	Rodeo Drive (host)
Daniels, Dan	Big Showdown (announcer)	Dubay, Chantel	The Price Is Right (model)
Darcel, Denise	Gamble on Love (host)	Dubois, Al	Bumper Stumpers (host)
Dark, Danny	Dream Girl USA (announcer)	Dudley, Dick	Americana (announcer), Are You Positive (announcer), The Price Is Right (substitute announcer), Remember This Date? (announcer), Who Said That? (announcer)
Darrow, Mike	The $128,000 Question (host), Dream House (host), Jackpot (host), The Who What or Where Game (announcer)		
Dashiell, Don	10 Seconds (announcer), Top Card (announcer)	Dumas, Jeffrey	Figure It Out (announcer)
		Dumke, Ralph	Movieland Quiz (host)
Davidson, Doug	The Price Is Right (host)	Dunbar, Dixie	Judge for Yourself (dancing cigarette pack)
Davidson, Jim	Blade Warriors (host)		
Davidson, John	The $100,000 Pyramid (host), Hollywood Squares (host), Time Machine (host)	Duncan, Dr. Carolyn	Password (word authority)
		Dunham, John	Hail the Champ (announcer), It's About Time (announcer)
Davis, Dave	Celebrity Bowling (assistant)	Dunn, Bob	Face to Face (host), Quick on the Draw (cartoonist)
Davis, Fred	Brains and Brawn (host)		
Davis, Kathy	Monopoly (assistant)	Dunn, Eddie	Face to Face (host), Where Was I? (host)

personality	game show	personality	game show
Dunne, Steve	Double Exposure (host), Queen for a Day (substitute host), Truth or Consequences (host), What's This Song? (announcer), You're on Your Own (host)		Same (host), Quiz Kids (host), What's in a Word (host)
		Farago, Joe	Break the Bank (host)
		Farr, Jamie	Wordplay (substitute host)
Durocher, Leo	Jackpot Bowling (host)	Farr, Shonda	Idiot Savants ("Savant Player")
Dwyer, Virginia	Pantomime Quiz (assistant)	Farris, Ferrari	The Price Is Right (model)
Earhard, Bernard	Knights and Warriors (announcer/Lord of the Rules)	Faso, Laurie	I'm Telling (host)
		Fates, Gil	Hold It Please (host), Missus Goes-A-Shopping (substitute host)
Earle, Robert	G.E. College Bowl (host)	Felton, Happy	It's a Hit (host)
Easy Marvin	Funny Boners (announcer)	Fennaman, George	Anybody Can Play (host), You Bet Your Life (announcer), Your Surprise Package (host)
Edwards, Allyn	One Minute Please (host)		
Edwards, Douglas	Masquerade Party (host), Riddle Me This (host)		
		Ferguson, June	The Price Is Right (model)
Edwards, Geoff	Chain Reaction (host), Hollywood's Talking (host), Jackpot (host), Let's Make a Deal (substitute host), Play the Percentages (host), Shoot for the Stars (host), Starcade (host), Treasure Hunt (host)	Ferrer, Vivian	Americana (cohost)
		Fiala, Jerri	Cross Wits (assistant)
		Fields, Linda	County Fair (assistant)
		Finn, Pat	The Joker's Wild (host), Shop 'til You Drop (host)
		Firestone, Lauren	High Rollers (assistant)
		Fite, Mark	Trashed (trasher)
Edwards, Ralph	Truth or Consequences (host)	Fitzmaurice, Michael	Giant Step (announcer), Live Like a Millionaire (announcer)
Ekman, Kirstin	Beach Clash (hard body)		
Electra, Carmen	Singled Out (cohost)	Fitzsimmons, Greg	Idiot Savants (host)
Elliott, Gordon	To Tell the Truth (host)	Fleming, Art	College Bowl (host), Doctor I.Q. (assistant), Jeopardy! (host), Pantomime Quiz (announcer)
Elliott, Win	Beat the Clock (substitute host), Break the Bank (announcer), Make That Spare (host), On Your Account (host), Tic Tac Dough (host), Win with a Winner (host)		
		Fleming, Jim	To Tell the Truth (substitute host)
		Fogg, Kirk	Legends of the Hidden Temple (host)
Ellis, Mary Anne	Wedding Party (model)	Ford, Anitra	The Price Is Right (model)
Elson, Bob	Identify (host)	Ford, Art	Art Ford Show (host)
Ely, Ron	Face the Music (host)	Ford, Janie	Chance of a Lifetime (assistant)
Emmons, Blake	Chain Reaction (host)	Ford, Tennessee Ernie	College of Musical Knowledge (host)
Enberg, Dick	Bafle (host), The Perfect Match (host), Sports Challenge (host), Three for the Money (host)		
		Ford, Terry	Twenty-One (assistant)
England, Sue	Doctor I.Q. (assistant)	Forman, Shana (Mary Poms)	Catch Phrase (assistant)
Engstrom, Kurt	Debt (security guard)	Forrest, Jacqueline	Fun House (assistant)
Eoppolo, James	Think Fast (announcer)	Forrest, Samantha	Fun House (assistant)
Epstein, Donald	Inspiration, Please! (announcer)	Forster, Roger	To Tell the Truth (announcer)
Ernst, Jon	Singled Out ("Piano Boy")	Forsyth, Bruce	Bruce Forsyth's Hot Streak (host)
Eubanks, Bob	All Star Secrets (host), Card Sharks (host), The Diamond Head Game (host), Dream House (host), Family Secrets (host), The Newlywed Game (host), Rhyme and Reason (host), Trivia Trap (host)	Fowler, Joe	Knights and Warriors (host), Maximum Drive (host), Wild West Showdown (announcer)
		Fox, Jean	Sports Snapshot! (assistant)
		Fox, Sonny	The $64,000 Challenge (host), Beat the Clock (substitute host), The Movie Game (host), On Your Mark (host), The Price Is Right (substitute host), To Tell the Truth (substitute host), Way Out Games (host)
Eure, Wesley	Finders Keepers (host)		
Evans, Dr. Bergen	Down You Go (host), It's About Time (host), Superghost (host), Top Dollar (authority)		
Ewing, Bill	Doctor I.Q. (announcer)	Foy, Fred	The $20,000 Pyramid (announcer), The Generation Gap (announcer)
Fadiman, Clifton	Alumni Fun (host), Information Please (host), The Name's the		

personality	game show	personality	game show
Francis, Arlene	Blind Date (host), By Popular Demand (host), The Price Is Right (substitute host), That Reminds Me (host), Who's There (host)		Laugh (announcer), The Movie Game (announcer), Music Bingo (host), Perfect Match (announcer), The Price Is Right (substitute host/announcer), Quiz Kids Challenge (announcer), Sports Challenge (announcer), Super Jeopardy! (announcer), Supermarket Sweep (announcer), Wheel of Fortune (announcer), Words and Music (announcer), Yours for a Song (announcer)
Frederick, Miranda	Contraption (announcer)		
Fredericks, Dirk	Beat the Clock (announcer), Doctor I.Q. (assistant), It's Your Move (announcer), Make a Face (announcer), Window Shopping (announcer)		
Friedman, Ellen	The Dating Game (dancer)		
Friedman, Julie	Pictionary ("Felicity")		
Fulkerson, Elaine	Wedding Party (model)	Gilles, Bob	Stump the Stars (announcer)
Gabel, Martin	With This Ring (host)	Gilmore, Art	Pantomime Quiz (announcer)
Gallico, Paul	Riddle Me This (host)	Gist, Tricia	Wheel of Fortune (substitute assistant)
Galloway, Don	The Guinness Game (host)		
Gammon, Elise	Take a Chance (assistant)	Gleason, Jackie	You're in the Picture (host)
Ganzel, Theresa	Yahtzee ("Dice Girl")	Godfrey, Arthur	I've Got a Secret (substitute host)
Garagiola, Joe	He Said She Said (host), Joe Garagiola's Memory Game (host), Sale of the Century (host), Strike It Rich (host), To Tell the Truth (host)	Godfrey, Kathy	On Your Way (host)
		Goen, Bob	Blackout (host), Born Lucky (host), Hollywood Game (host), Home Shopping Game (host), Perfect Match (host), Wheel of Fortune (host)
Gardner, Liz	Concentration (model), Play Your Hunch (assistant)		
Gardner, Mary	The Big Surprise (assistant)	Gold, Bruce	Playboy's Love and Sex Test (host)
Garnet, Sylvie	The $128,000 Question (assistant)	Goldstein, Harvey	Super Ghost (announcer)
		Goodman, Lee	The Name's the Same (commercial announcer)
Gautier, Dick	It's Your Bet (host)		
Georgeson, Dorene	Queen for a Day (model)	Goodman, Mark	Illinois Instant Riches (host)
Gilbert, Janice	Break the Bank (assistant), Hold That Note (assistant)	Goodson, Mark	To Tell the Truth (substitute host)
		Goodson-Cutt, Marjorie	Classic Concentration (model)
Gilbert, Johnny	$1,000,000 Chance of a Lifetime (announcer), The $25,000 Pyramid (announcer), The $100,000 Pyramid (announcer), Anything for Money (announcer), Beat the Odds (host), Blackout (announcer), Blank Check (announcer), Camouflage (announcer/substitute host), Chain Reaction (announcer), Child's Play (announcer), Double Talk (announcer), Dream House (announcer), Every Second Counts (announcer), Family Feud (announcer), Fast Draw (host), Go (announcer), Headline Chasers (announcer), Hollywood Connection (announcer), Jackpot (announcer), Jeopardy! (announcer), The Joker's Wild (announcer), Love Connection (announcer), Magnificent Marble Machine (announcer), Make a Face (announcer), Make Me	Goodwin, Bill	It Pays to Be Married (host), I've Got a Secret (substitute host), Penny to a Million (host)
		Goodwin, Dr. Reason A.	Password (word authority)
		Gordon, Jerry	Sports Snapshot! (announcer)
		Goss, Dean	The $25,000 Pyramid (announcer), Bargain Hunters (announcer), High Rollers (announcer), I'm Telling (announcer), Let's Make a Deal (announcer), Slime Time (announcer)
		Gosselaar, Mark-Paul	Brains & Brawn (host)
		Gould, Chet	The Baby Game (announcer), Camouflage (announcer), Dream House (announcer), Get the Message (announcer), Money Maze (announcer), One in a Million (announcer), Reach for the Stars (announcer), To Tell the Truth (announcer), Wedding Party (announcer), What's My Line? (announcer)

personality	game show	personality	game show
Grant, Kelly	Yahtzee ("Dice Girl")	Hamilton, Jillian	Kwik Witz (host)
Grauer, Ben	Americana (host), College of Musical Knowledge (announcer), Say It with Acting (host), What Happened? (host)	Hampton, Chase	Teen Win, Lose or Draw (announcer)
		Hampton, Renee	Treasure Isle (assistant)
		Hancock, Don	Down You Go (announcer), Quiz Kids (announcer), Stop the Music (announcer)
Gray, Barry	Winner Take All (host)		
Gray, Shelley	Sports on Tap (assistant)		
Green, Tom	Sports on Tap (host)	Hanks, Michael	Break the Bank (announcer)
Greene, Professor David	Password (word authority)	Hannes, Art	Draw to Win (announcer), Guess Again (announcer), Sing It Again (announcer)
Greenfield, David	A Perfect Score (announcer)		
Gregson, Jack	Auction-Aire (host), High Finance (announcer), Live Like a Millionaire (announcer),	Hannold, Marilyn	Jan Murray Show (model)
		Hardwick, Chris	Singled Out (host), Trashed (host)
Gregson, John	Twenty Questions (announcer)		
Grey, Marilyn	Concentration (model)	Hare, Marilyn	Queen for a Day (substitute fashion commentator)
Greymount, Stuart	Super Ghost (announcer)		
Grier, David Alan	Pure Insanity! (host)	Hargis, Autumn	All New Beat the Clock (model)
Griffin, Merv	Keep Talking (host), Play Your Hunch (host), The Price Is Right (substitute host), To Tell the Truth (substitute host), Word for Word (host)	Harlan, John	50 Grand Slam (announcer), All Star Blitz (announcer), American Gladiators (announcer), Are You Kidding (announcer), Catch Phrase (announcer), Celebrity Sweepstakes (announcer), Cross Wits (announcer), Dueling for Playmates (announcer), Face the Music (announcer), It Takes Two (announcer), It's Your Bet (announcer), Jackpot (announcer), Jeopardy! (announcer), Knockout (announcer), The Krypton Factor (announcer), Name That Tune (announcer), Password (announcer), Password Plus (announcer), Press Your Luck (announcer), Queen for a Day (announcer), Relatively Speaking (announcer), Tattletales (announcer), Truth or Consequences (announcer), Ultra Quiz (announcer), Whodunnit? (announcer), Wipeout (announcer), You Don't Say (announcer), Your Number's Up (announcer)
Griffin, Wayne	Identify (announcer)		
Gross, Dr. Mason	Think Fast (host), Two for the Money (judge)		
Grove, Betty Ann	The Big Payoff (singer)		
Guardolo, Bill	Gaters (host)		
Gustis, Jamie	Where in Time Is Carmen Sandiego? ("Engine Crew")		
Gwinn, Bill	Bill Gwinn Show (host)		
Hackett, Buddy	You Bet Your Life (host)		
Hackett, Jim	Wipeout (announcer)		
Haeffor, Edward	The Price Is Right (substitute announcer)		
Hale, Tiffini	Teen Win, Lose or Draw (announcer)		
Haley, Stacey Kim	Relatively Speaking (assistant)		
Hall, Monty	The All New Beat the Clock (host), It's Anybody's Guess (host), Keep Talking (host), Let's Make a Deal (host), Password (substitute host), Split Second (host), Strike It Rich (substitute host), Twenty-One (substitute host), Video Village (host), Your First Impression (substitute host)		
		Harmon, Patty	Tell It to Groucho (assistant)
		Harrington Jr., Pat	County Fair (substitute host), Stump the Stars (host)
Hall, Pat	Art Ford Show (assistant)		
Hall, Radcliff	Stop Me if You've Heard This One (announcer)	Harris, Danielle	Brains & Brawn (cohost)
		Harris, Doc	Second Honeymoon (announcer)
Hallstrom, Holly	The Price Is Right (model)		
Halsey, Ruth	Say When!! (model)	Harris, John	Jackpot (announcer)
Hamel, Alan	Anniversary Game (host), Wedding Party (host)	Harris, Ralph	Contraption (host)
		Harron, Don	Anything You Can Do (host)
Hamilton, Bill	Celebrity Time (announcer), It's News to Me (announcer), Riddle Me This (announcer)	Hart, Bill	Beat the Clock (substitute host)
		Hart, Moss	Answer Yes or No (host)
		Hartman, Phil	Pop 'N' Rocker Game (announcer)
Hamilton, Gene	Are You Positive (announcer)		

personality	game show	personality	game show
Harvey (John Harvey)	Double Dare (announcer), Finders Keepers (announcer)	Hirsch, David	Beach Clash (host), The Smarter Sex (host)
Haskell, Jack	Stop the Music (announcer), What's My Line? (substitute announcer)	Hite, Bob	General Electric Guest House (announcer)
Hastings, Bob	Dealer's Choice (host)	Hocks, Linda	Card Sharks (assistant)
Hayek, Julie	Break the Bank (assistant)	Hoffer, Neil	Dream League (referee)
Hayes, Julie	Treasure Isle (assistant)	Holenreich, Nick	Beat the Clock (announcer)
Hayes, Peter Lind	Alumni Fun (host)	Holliday, Doc	Family Double Dare (announcer)
Hayes, Richard	All About Faces (host), The Baby Game (host), Honeymoon Race (announcer), Play Your Hunch (host), Supermarket Sweep (announcer)	Holm, Celeste	The $64,000 Question (substitute host)
		Holmes, Clint	Campus All-Star Challenge (host)
Hayes, Rita	Win with a Winner (assistant)	Hovis, Larry	Yahtzee (announcer)
Haymer, Johnny	Your Number's Up (announcer)	Howard, John	Public Prosecutor (host)
Haymes, Bob	The Big Payoff (substitute host)	Howard, Ken	Dream Girl USA (host)
Healy, Jim	All Star Almost Anything Goes (cohost)	Howard, Tom	It Pays to Be Ignorant (host)
Hearn, Chick	Jackpot Bowling (host)	Howell, Wayne	Call My Bluff (announcer), Concentration (announcer), Dotto (announcer), Dough Re Mi (announcer), Fractured Phrases (announcer), Jackpot (announcer), Let's Play Post Office (announcer), Match Game (substitute announcer), Meet Your Match (announcer), Music Bingo (announcer), Name That Tune (announcer), Play Your Hunch (announcer), Reach for the Stars (announcer), Say When!! (announcer), What's It For? (announcer), What's My Line? (announcer)
Heatherton, Dick	The $20,000 Pyramid (announcer)		
Heide, Tami	Singled Out (announcer)		
Henry, Bill	Who Said That? (substitute host)		
Henry, Chuck	Now You See It (host)		
Hensley, Pamela	Treasure Hunt (model)		
Herlihy, Ed	Americana (substitute host)		
Herlihy, Walter	Blind Date (announcer)		
Herman, Dave	Grandstand (announcer)		
Hernon, Pat	Musical Chairs (announcer), Who Pays? (announcer)		
Heston, Charlton	The $64,000 Question (substitute host)		
Hicks, Johnny	Come Closer (announcer)	Hoyt, Sandy	The $128,000 Question (announcer), Split Second (announcer)
Hill, Dean	Talkabout (announcer)	Hull, Dave	Matchmaker (host)
Hilton, Bob	3rd Degree (announcer), Blockbusters (announcer), Body Language (announcer), Card Sharks (announcer), Challengers (announcer), Child's Play (announcer), The Dating Game (announcer), Double Talk (announcer), The Guinness Game (host), The Joker's Wild (announcer), Let's Make a Deal (host), Match Game (substitute announcer), The Newlywed Game (announcer), Password Plus (announcer), Play the Percentages (announcer), The Price Is Right (announcer), Strike It Rich (announcer), Super Password (announcer), Trivia Trap (announcer), Truth or Consequences (host), Win, Lose or Draw (announcer)	Hull, Warren	The Big Payoff (substitute host), Public Prosecutor (host), Strike It Rich (host), This Is the Missus (host), Top Dollar (host)
		Hunt, Lou	Matchmaker (announcer)
		Hunt, Phyllis	The Greatest Man on Earth (assistant)
		Hunter, Alan	Pure Insanity! (host), Triple Threat (substitute host)
		Hunter, Melinda	Card Sharks (model)
		Hurley, John "Tiny"	Fun House (announcer)
		Hurley, Walter	Draw Me a Laugh (host)
		Husman, Ron	You Bet Your Life (announcer)
		Hutton, Jim	Everything's Relative (host)
		Incollingo, Helen	Ruckus (assistant)
		Isaics, Jim	Liars Club (announcer)
		Ivey, Monteria	Think Twice (host)
		J, Henry	Get the Picture (announcer), Think Fast (announcer)
		Jackson, A. J.	Blade Warriors (warrior)

personality	game show	personality	game show
Jackson, Jay	Tic Tac Dough (host), Twenty Questions (host)		tute host), Two for the Money (commercial announcer)
Jacobs, Johnny	$1.98 Beauty Show (announcer), The Big Game (announcer), Blank Check (announcer), Break the Bank (announcer), Camouflage (announcer), The Dating Game (announcer), Dream Girl of '67 (announcer), Face the Facts (announcer), The Family Game (announcer), The Game Game (announcer), Give-n-Take (announcer), The Gong Show (announcer), Hollywood's Talking (announcer), How's Your Mother-in-Law (announcer), The Joker's Wild (announcer), The Newlywed Game (announcer), Rhyme and Reason (announcer), Spin-Off (announcer), Take a Good Look (announcer), Tell It to Groucho (announcer), Three's a Crowd (announcer), Treasure Hunt (announcer), What Do You Have in Common? (announcer)	James, Hugh	Americana (announcer)
		James, Kevin	Sandblast (announcer)
		James, Marion	The Big Payoff (model)
		James, Maryann	The Price Is Right (model)
		Janney, Leon	Stop Me if You've Heard This One (host)
		Janos, Steve	Shenanigans ("Shenaghoul")
		January, Lois	Queen for a Day (substitute fashion commentator)
		Jeffreys, Allan	Music Bingo (announcer)
		Jeffries, Rich	Blockbusters (announcer), Love Connection (announcer), Password Plus (announcer), Super Password (announcer), The Price Is Right (announcer)
		Jenkin, Deron	Beach Clash ("hard body")
		Jenner, Bruce	Star Games (host)
		Jensen, Gretchen	Dream League (field reporter)
		Johnson, Arte	Knockout (host)
		Johnson, Deborah	Grandstand (assistant)
		Johnson, Gary	Challengers (judge)
James, Art	Blank Check (host), Catch Phrase (host), Classic Concentration (announcer), Concentration (announcer/substitute host), Face the Music (announcer), Family Feud (substitute announcer), Fractured Phrases (host), The Joker's Wild (announcer), Magnificent Marble Machine (host), Matches 'n Mates (host), NFL Trivia Game (announcer), Pay Cards! (host), Say When!! (host), Sports Challenge (announcer), Super Pay Cards! (host), Temptation (host), Tic Tac Dough (announcer), The Who What or Where Game (host)	Johnson, Jackie	Treasure Hunt (pirate girl)
		Johnson, Jay	Celebrity Charades (host)
		Johnson, Kathie Lee	Name That Tune (singer)
		Johnson, Kristian	Say When!! (model)
		Johnston, Johnny	Make That Spare (host), Treasure Hunt (substitute host)
		Jones, Buster	You Bet Your Life (announcer)
		Jones, Charlie	Almost Anything Goes (host), Pro-Fan (host)
		Jordan, Ed	The $10,000 Pyramid (announcer), The Price Is Right (substitute announcer)
		Jordan, Joanne	Beat the Clock (assistant)
		Joyce, Elaine	The Dating Game (host)
		Julian, Sally	Sale of the Century (assistant)
		K, Ellen	The Newlywed Game (announcer)
		Kalter, Alan	The $10,000 Pyramid (announcer), The $128,000 Question (announcer), Money Maze (announcer), To Tell the Truth (announcer)
James, Dennis	Cash and Carry (host), Chance of a Lifetime (host), Dollar a Second (substitute host), Haggis Baggis (host), High Finance (host), Judge for Yourself (commercial announcer), Let's Make a Deal (substitute host), Name That Tune (host), The Name's the Same (host), On Your Account (host), PDQ (host), People Will Talk (host), The Price Is Right (host), Stop the Music (announcer), Treasure Hunt (substi-	Kamer, Steve	Dream League (announcer)
		Kaplan, Gabe	NFL Trivia Game (host)
		Karges, Kathy	Monopoly (assistant)
		Karsten, Adrian	Dream League (assistant)
		Kashian, Alaine	Where in Time Is Carmen Sandiego? ("Engine Crew")
		Kasper, Fred	Take Two (announcer)
		Kassir, John	Secrets of the Cryptkeeper's Haunted House (voice of the Cryptkeeper)
		Kaye, Jeff	NFL Trivia Game (announcer)

personality	game show	personality	game show
Kaye, Stubby	Shenanigans (host)	King, Wally	Supermarket Sweep (announcer)
Kelly, Al	Back That Fact (assistant)	Kinnear, Greg	College Madhouse (host)
Kelly, Gene	The $64,000 Question (substitute host)	Kirby, Durward	General Electric Guest House (host), Make the Connection (announcer), Who Said That? (announcer)
Kelly, Jack	Sale of the Century (host)		
Kelly, Joe	Quiz Kids (host)		
Kelly, M. G.	Pop 'N' Rocker Game (announcer), Wheel of Fortune (announcer)	Kirshner, Claude	Ladies Be Seated (announcer)
		Klimaszewski, Diane	Let's Make a Deal (model)
		Klimaszewski, Elaine	Let's Make a Deal (model)
Kelly, Tom	Let's Make a Deal (substitute host)	Kline, Richard	Sweethearts (substitute host)
		Knutson, Gunilla	Say When!! (model)
Kennedy, Bob	Beat the Clock (substitute host), Feather Your Nest (substitute host), Name That Tune (announcer), Password (substitute announcer), The Price Is Right (substitute host), Treasure Hunt (substitute host), Window Shopping (host), Wingo (host)	Kohlmeyer, Linda	Illinois Instant Riches (cohost)
		Kollmar, Dick	Guess What? (host)
		Kominsky, Sherry	Celebrity Bowling (assistant)
		Kovack, Nancy	Beat the Clock (assistant)
		Kovacs, Ernie	Gamble on Love (host), Take a Good Look (host), Time Will Tell (host)
		Kozlowski, Paul	Idiot Savants ("Savant Player")
Kennedy, Jayne	Ultra Quiz (assistant)	Kraft, Randy	Feather Your Nest (announcer)
Kennedy, Tom	50 Grand Slam (host), Body Language (host), Break the Bank (host), Doctor I.Q. (host), It's Your Bet (host), Name That Tune (host), Password Plus (host), The Price Is Right (host), Split Second (host), To Say the Least (host), Whew! (host), Wordplay (host), You Don't Say! (host)	Kramer, Harry	Winner Take All (announcer)
		Kroeger, Gary	The Newlywed Game (host)
		Kyser, Kay	College of Musical Knowledge (host)
		Lackey, Skip	Think Fast (host)
		Lamond, Bob	Do You Trust Your Wife? (announcer)
		Lange, Hope	Back That Fact (assistant)
Kidder, Dr. Alfred	What in the World (host)	Lange, Jim	$1,000,000 Chance Of A Lifetime (host), Bullseye (host), The Dating Game (host), Give-n-Take (host), Hollywood Connection (host), $100,000 Name That Tune (host), The Newlywed Game (host), Oh My Word (host), Spin-off (host), Take My Word for It (host), Triple Threat (host)
Kiernan, Walter	Sparring Partners (host), What's the Story (host), Who Said That? (host), Who's the Boss? (host)		
Kimball, Billy	Clash (host)		
Kimmel, Jimmy	Win Ben Stein's Money (announcer)		
King, Carl	Queen for a Day (announcer), Temptation (announcer), Two for the Money (announcer)		
King Ed,	Up to Paar (announcer)	Langston, Murray	Truth or Consequences (assistant)
King, Joe	Alumni Fun (announcer)	Lapierre, Karen	Let's Make a Deal (model)
King, John Reed	Battle of the Ages (host), Beat the Clock (substitute host), Chance of a Lifetime (host), Give and Take (host), Have a Heart (host), It's a Gift (host), King's Party Line (host), Let's See (host), Missus' Goes-A-Shopping (host), The Name's the Same (commercial announcer) On Your Way (host), There's One in Every Family (host), What's Your Bid (assistant), Where Was I? (host), Why? (host)	Lathan, John	Where in Time Is Carmen Sandiego? ("Engine Crew")
		Laughlin, Lisa	The $64,000 Challenge (assistant)
		Laurence, Mike	Funny You Should Ask!! (announcer), The Object Is (announcer)
		Lawrence, Jerry	Truth or Consequences (announcer)
		Lawrence, Mort	The Big Payoff (announcer), Strike It Rich (announcer)
		Lawrence, Steve	Jan Murray Show (substitute host)
King, Louise	Beat the Clock (assistant)	Lawrence, Vicki	Win, Lose or Draw (host)
King, Perry	Sandblast (host)	Laybourne, Emmy	Idiot Savants ("Savant Player")

personality	game show	personality	game show
Lazar, William	Answer Yes or No (announcer)	Ludden, Allen	G. E. College Bowl (host), Liars Club (host), Password (host), Password Plus (host), Stumpers (host), Win with the Stars (host)
Lea, Karen	Video Game (assistant)		
Lear, Norman	Quiz Kids (host)		
Lee, Greg	Where in the World Is Carmen Sandiego? (host)		
		Luther, Paul	Stop the Music (announcer)
Lee, Gypsy Rose	Think Fast (host)	Luxton, Bill	Anything You Can Do (announcer)
Lee, Luann	Night Games (announcer)		
Lee, Patti	The $128,000 Question (assistant)	Lyall, Jennifer	The Last Word (announcer)
		Lynn, Judy	The Big Payoff (singer)
Lee, Robert G.	Inspiration, Please! (host)	Lyon, Barbara	Let's Make a Deal (model), Queen for a Day (model), Sale of the Century (model), Seven Keys (model)
Lee, Ruta	High Rollers (assistant)		
Lescoulie, Jack	Brains and Brawn (host), Fun and Fortune (host)		
Leslie, Joan	Queen for a Day (substitute fashion commentator)		
		Lyon, Charles	Truth or Consequences (announcer)
Lester, Jack	Majority Rules (announcer), Treasure Quest (announcer)	MacDonald, Rich	Beach Clash ("hard body")
		MacDonnell, Kyle	Feather Your Nest (substitute assistant), Hold That Camera (host)
Levant, Oscar	General Electric Guest House (host)		
		MacGregor, Jeff	The Dating Game (host), Love at First Sight (host)
Levenson, Sam	The Price Is Right (substitute host), Two for the Money (host)		
		MacGregor, Richard	College Madhouse (assistant)
Levin, Dave	Clash (announcer)	Machado, Mario	That **** Quiz Show (announcer)
Lewis, Robert Q.	Get the Message (host), Make Me Laugh (host), Masquerade Party (host), The Name's the Same (host), Play Your Hunch (host), The Price Is Right (substitute host), To Tell the Truth (substitute host)	Mack, Dotty	Mother's Day (assistant)
		MacMurray, Fred	The $64,000 Question (substitute host)
		MacPherson, Lori	Movie Masters (assistant)
		Madden, Brian	Ready . . . Set . . . Cook! (announcer)
		Maestri, Ron	Quicksilver (host)
Leyden, Bill	Call My Bluff (host), It Could Be You (host), Let's Make a Deal (substitute host), Musical Chairs (host), You're Putting Me On (host), Your First Impression (host)	Mahoney, Tom	This Is the Missus (assistant)
		Maki, Mac	Blade Warriors (host)
		Malden, Beverly	Las Vegas Gambit (card dealer)
		Mallow, John	Down You Go (announcer)
		Malone, Bill	Honeymoon Race (host), Supermarket Sweep (host)
Liberal Bill	What's Your Bid? (host)		
Lindt, Cindy	Who Do You Trust? (assistant)	Mann, Anita	The Dating Game (dancer)
Linkletter, Art	Art Linkletter Show (host), Life with Linkletter (host), People Are Funny (host)	Mann, Danny	Secrets of the Cryptkeeper's Haunted House (skeleton voice)
		Mann, Stuart	Dollar a Second (assistant)
Linkletter, Jack	Haggis Baggis (host), Rebus Game (host)	Manners, Fred	Greatest Man on Earth (assistant)
		Manners, Marlene	Twenty-One (assistant)
Linn, Teri Ann	Grand Prix All Star Show (cohost)	Marcato, Bob	Password (announcer)
		March, Hal	The $64,000 Question (host), I've Got a Secret (substitute host), It's Your Bet (host), Jan Murray Show (substitute host), What's It For? (host)
Lively, Andrea	Nick Arcade (announcer)		
Locke, Lauri	The $128,000 Question (assistant)		
Logan, Christy	County Fair (assistant)	March, Steve	Name That Tune (singer)
Lohman Jr., Al	Bedtime Stories (host), Namedroppers (host)	Marder, Jeff	A Perfect Score (host), Night Games (host)
Lopez, Mario	Masters of the Maze (host)	Maren, Jerry	The Gong Show ("Little Man")
Lor, Denise	The Big Payoff (singer)	Marlo, Micki	Jan Murray Show (assistant)
Lougherty, Jackie	Earn Your Vacation (assistant)	Marrella, Robin	Double Dare (assistant), What Would You Do? (assistant)
Lucas, Jim	Concentration (announcer/substitute host), Jan Murray Show (substitute host)		
		Marshall, Peter	All Star Blitz (host), The Hollywood Squares (host), Yahtzee (host)

personality	game show	personality	game show
Marshall, Rex	Blind Date (announcer), Masquerade Party (announcer), Who Said That? (announcer), Who's There (announcer)	McCoo, Harold	Love Between the Sexes (host)
		McCord, Bill	Bank on the Stars (announcer), Concentration (announcer), Tic Tac Dough (announcer), Twenty-One (announcer), Word for Word (announcer)
Martel, Michaelina	Yours for a Song (scoreboard girl)		
Martell, Dusty	Lingo (assistant)		
Martin, Bernard	Dollar a Second (assistant)	McCoy, Jack	Glamour Girl (host), Live Like a Millionaire (host)
Martin, Betty	County Fair (assistant)		
Martin, Dick	Cheap Show (host), Mindreaders (host), Ultra Quiz (host)	McElhone, Eloise	Try and Do It (assistant)
		McElwee, Bob	American Gladiators (referee)
Martin, Jennifer	No Relation (announcer), Personals (announcer)	McGeehan, Pat	People Are Funny (announcer)
		McKay, Ed	The Joker's Wild (announcer), Super Decades (announcer), Treasure Mall (announcer), Trivia Track (announcer)
Martin, Pamela Sue	Star Games (cohost)		
Martindale, Wink	Boggle—The Interactive Game (host), Can You Top This? (host), Debt (host), Dream Girl of '67 (host), Everybody's Talking (announcer), Gambit (host), The Great Getaway Game (host), Headline Chasers (host), High Rollers (host), How's Your Mother-in-Law? (host), Jumble—The Interactive Game (host), Las Vegas Gambit (host), The Last Word (host), Shuffle—The Interactive Game (host), Tic Tac Dough (host), Trivial Pursuit (host), What's This Song? (host), Words and Music (host), You Don't Say! (substitute host)	McKay, Jim	Make the Connection (host)
		McKenzie, Margaux	Lingo (assistant)
		McKrell, Jim	Celebrity Sweepstakes (host), College Bowl (announcer), Couch Potatoes (announcer), The Game Game (host), Quiz Kids (host), Sweethearts (announcer)
		McMahon, Ed	Concentration (host), Missing Links (host), Snap Judgment (host), Two for the Money (announcer), Who Do You Trust? (announcer)
		McMahon, Kevin	Starcade (announcer)
		McNair, Ralph	The Eyes Have It (host)
		McNeill, Don	I've Got a Secret (substitute host), Take Two (host)
Marvin, Tony	We Take Your Word (announcer)		
Marx, Groucho	Tell It to Groucho (host), You Bet Your Life (host)	Meeker, Gary	Super Decades (announcer)
		Meikle, Pat	Love Story (assistant)
Massey, Debi	Trump Card (assistant)	Meinch, Joan	Double or Nothing (assistant)
Massey, Marisol	Remote Control (assistant)	Menning, Lee	Las Vegas Gambit (card dealer), Sale of the Century (assistant), Your Number's Up (assistant)
Matheny, Andi	Kwik Witz (host)		
Mattis, Fred	Greatest Man on Earth (announcer)		
Maudaley, Bonnie	Treasure Isle (assistant)	Merrill, Carol	Let's Make a Deal (model), Your Surprise Package (model)
Maxwell, Bob	Do You Know? (host)		
Mazer, Bill	Concentration (substitute host), Reach for the Stars (host)	Merriman, Randy	The Big Payoff (host), Strike It Rich (substitute host)
McCaffery, John K.M.	Alumni Fun (host), Americana (substitute host), One Minute Please (host), Take a Guess (host) We Take Your Word (host), What's the Story (host)	Michael, Ray	Tele Pun (announcer)
		Michaels, Dave	Matches 'n Mates (announcer)
		Michaels, Ed	Can You Top This? (announcer), Doctor I.Q. (assistant)
		Michener, James	What's the Story (substitute host)
McCarthy, Jenny	Singled Out (cohost)	Miles, Chris	Family Double Dare (assistant)
McCarty, Vicki	Wheel of Fortune (substitute hostess)	Milito, Maria	Make the Grade (announcer)
		Miller, Cory	Blade Warriors (warrior)
McClain, Bob	Matches 'n Mates (announcer)	Miller, Dan	10 Seconds (host), Top Card (host)
McClain, James	Doctor I.Q. (host)		
McClay, Tony	All Star Secrets (announcer), The Guinness Game (announcer), The Newlywed Game (announcer)	Miller, Dean	There's One in Every Family (host)
		Miller, Valarie	Gladiators 2000 (cohost), Peer Pressure (cohost)
McClure, Paula	The Grudge Match (assistant)	Mills, Vicki	Name That Tune (singer)

personality	game show	personality	game show
Minor, Pat	Treasure Isle (assistant)		nouncer), Concentration (host), Dotto (host), I'll Bet (host), Now You See It (host), Password Plus (substitute host), Place the Face (announcer), The Price Is Right (substitute host), Seven Keys (host), Top Dollar (host), Video Village (host), You Don't Say! (substitute host)
Mitchell, Cory	Blade Warriors (warrior)		
Mitchell, Kathy	Make a Face (assistant)		
Mitchell, Roy	I'll Bet (announcer)		
Mitchell, Spring	Pantomime Quiz (assistant)		
Miuccio, Dean	Family Secrets (announcer), Let's Make a Deal (announcer), That's My Dog! (announcer)		
Mohr, Jay	Lip Service (host)		
Montville, Clea	Masters of the Maze (cast member)	Nelson, Jane	Dealer's Choice (assistant), The Diamond Head Game (assistant), Give-n-take (assistant), The Neighbors (assistant), Treasure Hunt (assistant)
Moore, Garry	I've Got a Secret (host), To Tell the Truth (host)		
Moore, Phil	Nick Arcade (host)		
Moore, Tom	Ladies Be Seated (host), Majority Rules (host)	Nelson, Jimmy	Bank on the Stars (host), Come Closer (host)
Moran, Warren	To Tell the Truth (substitute announcer)	Nelson, John	Live Like a Millionaire (announcer/host)
Morgan, Henry	Draw to Win (host), I've Got a Secret (substitute host)	Nemeth, Dave	Super Decades (announcer), Trivia Track (substitute host)
Morgan, Jaye P.	Stop the Music (singer)	Neville, Arthel	Majority Rules (host)
Morgan, Ray	It Pays to Be Ignorant (announcer)	Nicholas, Michelle	Monopoly (assistant)
		Niles, Ken	Pantomime Quiz (announcer)
Morgan, Tanya	Treasure Hunt (model)	Niles, Wendell	The Big Game (announcer), Chain Letter (announcer), It Could Be You (announcer), The Rebus Game (announcer), Truth or Consequences (announcer), Your First Impression (announcer)
Morris, Robb Edward	Make the Grade (host)		
Morrow, Don	Camouflage (host), Challengers (announcer), E.S.P. (announcer), G.E. College Bowl (announcer), Let's Play Post Office (host), Masquerade Party (announcer), Now You See It (announcer), On Your Way (announcer), Pantomime Quiz (announcer), Personality Puzzle (announcer), Quick as a Flash (announcer), Sale of the Century (announcer)	Nimmo, Bill	For Love or Money (host), Keep It in the Family (host), Who Do You Trust? (announcer)
		Nolin, Gina Lee	The Price Is Right (model)
		Norris, Kathi	Spin the Picture (host)
		North, Zeme	County Fair (assistant)
		Oakland, Sue	The Big Surprise (assistant)
Morse, Wayne	Jeopardy! (substitute announcer)	Ober, Ken	Make Me Laugh (host), Perfect Match (host), Remote Control (host)
Mueller, Rita	Make a Face (assistant)		
Mulrooney, John	Are You Kidding (host), King of the Mountain (host)	O'Brien, Joe	Anyone Can Win (announcer), Messing Prize Party (announcer), Play the Game (host)
Murray, Jan	Blind Date (host), Chain Letter (host), Dollar a Second (host), Go Lucky (host), Jan Murray Show (host), Meet Your Match (host), Sing It Again (host), Songs for Sale (host), Treasure Hunt (host)		
		O'Brien, Kerry	Anything You Can Do (assistant)
		O'Brien, Lois	Wingo (hostess)
		O'Brien, Steve	The $10,000 Pyramid (announcer), To Tell the Truth (announcer)
Myers, Nancy	Queen for a Day (commentator)		
Myerson, Bess	The Big Payoff (hostess)	O'Connell, Kevin	Go (host)
Naber, John	Dream League (host)	O'Connor, Brian	Rumor Has It (host)
Nagel, Conrad	Broadway to Hollywood Headline Clues (host), Celebrity Time (host), Riddle Me This (host)	O'Donnell, Charlie	The $25,000 Pyramid (announcer), All Star Secrets (announcer), Bullseye (announcer), Card Sharks (announcer), The Cheap Show (announcer), The Dating Game (announcer), Ev-
Narz, Jack	Beat the Clock (announcer/host), Card Sharks (announcer) College of Musical Knowledge (an-		

personality	game show	personality	game show
	erybody's Talking (announcer), The Gong Show (announcer), The Guinness Game (announcer), Hot Potato (announcer), The Joker's Wild (announcer), Let's Go Back (announcer), Monopoly (announcer), The Newlywed Game (announcer), The Parent Game (announcer), Stumpers (announcer) Tic Tac Dough (announcer), To Tell the Truth (announcer), Trivia Trap (announcer), Wedding Party (announcer), Wheel of Fortune (announcer), The Wizard of Odds (announcer), Wordplay (announcer)	O'Malley, Mike	Get the Picture (host), Nickelodeon Guts (host)
		O'Neill, Danny	One in a Million (host)
		O'Rourke, Michael	The $128,000 Question (security guard)
		O'Sullivan, Terry	Blind Date (announcer), Dollar a Second (announcer), Pantomime Quiz (announcer)
		Ovitz, Judy	50 Grand Slam (assistant)
		Owen, Al	Let's See (announcer)
		Owen, Jay	Doctor I.Q. (host)
		Owens, Crystal	High Rollers (assistant)
		Owens, Gary	The Gong Show (host), Letters to Laugh-In (host)
		Owens, Wendy	Anything You Can Do (assistant)
O'Halloran, Michael	Live Like a Millionaire (assistant)	Paar, Jack	Bank on the Stars (host), Up to Paar (host)
O'Keefe, Dennis	I've Got a Secret (substitute host)	Paige, Robert	The Big Payoff (host)
O'Keefe, Walter	Queen for a Day (substitute host), Two for the Money (host)	Palmer, Betsy	I'll Buy That (model), I've Got a Secret (substitute host), Wheel of Fortune (model)
Olson, Johnny	Blockbusters (announcer), Body Language (announcer), Break the Bank (announcer), Call My Bluff (announcer), Card Sharks (announcer), Concentration (announcer), Double Dare (announcer), Fun for the Money (host), Get the Message (announcer), He Said She Said (announcer), Hold That Note (announcer), I've Got a Secret (announcer), Joe Garagiola's Memory Game (announcer), Keep It in the Family (announcer), Keep Talking (announcer), Masquerade Party (announcer), Match Game (announcer), Mindreaders (announcer), Missing Links (announcer), Name That Tune (announcer), Now You See It (announcer), On Your Mark (announcer), Password Plus (announcer), Play Your Hunch (announcer/substitute host), The Price Is Right (announcer), Snap Judgment (announcer), Split Personality (announcer), Tattletales (announcer), Tic Tac Dough (announcer), To Tell the Truth (announcer), What's My Line? (announcer), You're in the Picture (announcer)	Palmer, Bud	Jackpot Bowling (host)
		Palmer, June	Double Exposure (model)
		Pandolfo, Tony	Sports on Tap (announcer)
		Paolella, Joe	Liars (polygraph expert)
		Pardo, Don	Choose Up Sides (announcer/Mr. Mischief), Concentration (announcer), Droodles (announcer), Eye Guess (announcer), High Low (announcer), It's in the Bag (announcer), Jackpot (announcer), Jan Murray Show (announcer), Jeopardy! (announcer), Judge for Yourself (announcer), The Price Is Right (announcer/substitute host), Remember This Date (announcer), Three on a Match (announcer), Wheel of Fortune (announcer), Winner Take All (announcer), Winning Streak (announcer)
		Pardo, Paula	Jan Murray Show (model)
		Pari, Susan	That's My Dog! (assistant)
		Parker, Lew	Your Surprise Store (host)
		Parkes, Lisa	All New Beat the Clock (model)
		Parkinson, Dian	The Price Is Right (model)
		Parks, Bert	Balance Your Budget (host), Bid 'n' Buy (host), The Big Payoff (host), Break the Bank (host), County Fair (host), Double or Nothing (host), Giant Step (host), Hold That Note (host), Masquerade Party (host), Party Line (host), Stop the Music (host), Two in Love (host), Yours for a Song (host)

personality	game show	personality	game show
Parks, Tom	Wait 'til You Have Kids! (host)	Putnam, George F.	Broadway to Hollywood Headline Clues (host)
Parnell, Pat	Blade Warriors (warrior)	Pyne, Joe	Showdown (host)
Passarella, Art	Home Run Derby (umpire)	Quinn, Colin	Remote Control (announcer)
Patrick, Evelyn	Dollar a Second (assistant)	Quirk, Moira	Nickelodeon Guts (referee)
Patterson, Dick	Celebrity Charades (announcer)	Race, Clark	The Parent Game (host)
Patton, Phil	Ladies Be Seated (assistant)	Rafferty, Bill	Blockbusters (host), Card Sharks (host), Every Second Counts (host)
Paul, Ralph	The Big Payoff (announcer/substitute host), Dotto (announcer), Number Please (announcer), Strike It Rich (announcer), Top Dollar (announcer), Two for the Money (announcer), What's My Line? (announcer)	Rainey, Dr. Froelich	What in the World (host)
		Randall, Rebel	Auction-Aire (assistant)
		Raney, Walter	On Your Way (announcer), What's the Story (host)
Pearson, Ron	Shopping Spree (host)	Rashad, Ahmad	Caesars Challenge (host)
Peck, Jim	The Big Showdown (host), Hot Seat (host), The Joker's Wild (substitute host), Second Chance (host), Three's a Crowd (host), You Don't Say! (host)	Rathbone, Basil	Your Lucky Clue (host)
		Rawlins, Judith	Double Exposure (assistant)
		Rawson, Ron	Strike It Rich (announcer)
		Ray, Tanika	Wheel of Fortune 2000 ("Cyber Lucy")
Pemberton, Lacey	Card Sharks (assistant)	Rayburn, Gene	Amateur's Guide to Love (host), Break the Bank (host), Choose Up Sides (host), Dough Re Mi (host), Make the Connection (host), The Match Game (host), Match Game–Hollywood Squares Hour (host), Movie Masters (host), Play Your Hunch (host), Snap Judgment (substitute host), Tattletales (substitute host), Tic Tac Dough (host), To Tell the Truth (substitute host),
Pennington, Ann	Card Sharks (assistant)		
Pennington, Janice	The Price Is Right (model)		
Perry, Jim	Card Sharks (host), It's Your Move (host), Money Makers (host), Sale of the Century (host)		
Peterson, Paul	Dream Girl of '67 (host)		
Peterson, Penny	Make Me Laugh (assistant)		
Philbin, Regis	Almost Anything Goes (host), The Neighbors (host)		
Phillips, Chris	Where in the World Is Carmen Sandiego? (voices)		
Pickett, Blake	Fandango (assistant), Top Card (assistant)	Reagan, Michael	Lingo (host)
Pinette, John	Grudge Match (referee)	Reddy, Tom	Doctor I.Q. (assistant), Dollar a Second (assistant), How Do You Rate? (host), Laugh Line (announcer), Treasure Hunt (announcer)
Polic II, Henry	Double Talk (host)		
Poms, Mary (Shana Forman)	The Price Is Right (substitute model), Temptation (model), The Wizard of Odds (model)		
		Reed, Toby	Top Dollar (host)
Post, Markie	Card Sharks (assistant)	Reeves, Maxine	Queen for a Day (model)
Poston, Tom	Split Personality (host)	Reilly, Charles Nelson	Sweethearts (host)
Powers, Jack	Seven Keys (announcer)	Reilly, Chuck	Trump Card (announcer)
Pratt, Peter	Movie Masters (announcer)	Reilly, Mike	Monopoly (host)
Preis, Doug	Where in the World Is Carmen Sandiego? (voices)	Reimers, Ed	Do You Trust Your Wife? (announcer), Pantomime Quiz (announcer)
Prentiss, Ed	Majority Rules (host)		
Presby, Arch	Musical Chairs (announcer)	Reiner, Carl	Celebrity Game (host), Keep Talking (host)
Prescott, Allan	Quizzing the News (host)		
Price, Becky	High Rollers (assistant)	Reynolds, Cyndi	The $128,000 Question (assistant)
Price, Cynthia	Bank on the Stars (assistant)		
Price, Janelle	The Cheap Show (assistant)	Reynolds, Maureen	Word for Word (model)
Price, Marc	Teen Win, Lose or Draw (host)	Ricau, Lionel	Say It with Acting (announcer)
Price, Matt	Idiot Savants (announcer)	Rice, Greg & John	That **** Quiz Show (host)
Price, Roger	Droodles (host)	Rich, Judy	Blank Check (assistant)
Price, Vincent	E.S.P. (host)	Richardson, Burton	Campus All-Star Challange (announcer), It Takes Two (announcer), The Price Is Right
Prince, Jonathan	Quiz Kids Challenge (host)		
Purcell, Sarah	The Better Sex (host)		

personality	game show	personality	game show
	(announcer), Rodeo Drive (announcer), Shopping Spree (announcer), To Tell the Truth (announcer), Wait 'til You Have Kids! (announcer)	Roth, Michelle	Cross Wits (announcer)
		Rowan, Dan	Ultra Quiz (host)
Rickman, Al	King Pins (announcer)	Rowan, Roy	Earn Your Vacation (announcer), Family Game (announcer), Follow the Leader (announcer), How's Your Mother-in-Law? (announcer), There's One in Every Family (announcer)
Riddle, Sam	Almost Anything Goes (announcer), Triple Threat (announcer), The Wizard of Odds (announcer)		
		Rowe, Mike	No Relation (host)
Ridgely, Bob	Wipeout (announcer)	Rowe, Red	Face the Facts (host), Video Village (host)
Riggs, Bobby	Celebrity Tennis (cohost)		
Riggs, Glenn	Auction-Aire (announcer), Make Me Laugh (announcer)	Ruby, Zack	Caesars Challenge (assistant)
		Ruprecht, David	Supermarket Sweep (host)
Ring, Theresa	The Grudge Match (ring girl), Strike It Rich (assistant)	Russell, Bob	It's in the Bag (host)
Rivers, Bobby	Bedroom Buddies (host)	Russell, Don	Broadway to Hollywood Headline Clues (host), Midway (host), One Minute Please (announcer), Pantomime Quiz (announcer), Time Will Tell (announcer)
Robbins, Brian	Pictionary (host)		
Robbins, Fred	Dough Re Mi (substitute host), Haggis Baggis (host)		
Roberts, Howard	Hail the Champ (host)		
Roberts, Ken	Blind Date (announcer), Chance of a Lifetime (announcer), Dollar a Second (announcer), Make Me Laugh (announcer), Music Bingo (announcer), Truth or Consequences (announcer), Try and Do It (announcer), Where Was I? (host), Wingo (announcer)	Russell, Nipsey	Your Number's Up (host)
		Russell, Todd	Strike It Rich (substitute host), Wheel of Fortune (host), Who Do You Trust? (announcer)
		Ryan, Ken	Bumper Stumpers (announcer), Jackpot (announcer)
		Ryle, Glenn	Pay Cards! (announcer)
		Safire, Hillary	Truth or Consequences (assistant)
Roberts, Peter	Who Said That? (announcer)		
Roby, Vic	Concentration (substitute announcer), The Price Is Right (substitute announcer)	Sajak, Pat	College Bowl (host), Wheel of Fortune (host)
		Sales, Soupy	Junior Almost Anything Goes (host)
Roddy, Rod	The $25,000 Pyramid (announcer), Battlestars (announcer), Dream House (announcer), Hit Man (announcer), The Newlywed Game (announcer), Press Your Luck (announcer), The Price Is Right (announcer), Whew! (announcer)	Sam, Mary Lou	Grand-Prix All Star Show (announcer)
		Sanders, Felicia	Stop the Music (singer)
		Sanders, Steve	Secrets of the Cryptkeeper's Haunted House (host)
		Sanders, Summer	Figure It Out (host), Sandblast (host)
		Sansone, Maria	Gladiators 2000 (host)
Rodriguez, Paul	The Newlywed Game (host)	Sassoon, Beverly	Queen for a day (model)
Rogers, Bill	The $64,000 Challenge (announcer), The $64,000 Question (announcer), Bid 'n' Buy (announcer), On Your Account (announcer)	Sattelle, Georgia	Let's Make a Deal (model)
		Sawyer, Stan	Name That Tune (announcer)
		Saxon, Fred	Child's Play (announcer)
		Sayers, Susan	The Big Payoff (model)
		Schackelford, Lynn	Almost Anything Goes (host)
Rogers, Buddy	Break the Bank (substitute host)	Schenkel, Chris	Make That Spare (host)
Rogers, Ginger	The $64,000 Question (substitute host)	Schlitt, Caroline	Pure Insanity! (host)
		Schmitter, Morgan	Jan Murray Show (judge)
Rogers, Julie	Tell Me Something Good (host)	Schneider, Lew	Make the Grade (host)
Rogers, Lorraine	The Big Surprise (assistant), Jan Murray Show (assistant)	Scott, Fred	Fast Draw (announcer), Spin the Picture (announcer), What's the Story (announcer)
Roker, Al	Remember This? (host)		
Roth, JD	Double Up (host), Fun House (host), Masters of the Maze (host)	Scott, Mark	Home Run Derby (host)
		Scott, Molly	King Pins (assistant)
		Scully, Vin	It Takes Two (host)

personality	game show	personality	game show
Seacrest, Ryan	Click (host), Gladiators 2000 (host), Wild Animal Games (host)		nouncer), Songs for Sale (announcer), To Tell the Truth (substitute announcer), What's My Line? (announcer), Wheel of Fortune (announcer), You're on Your Own (announcer)
Seiter, Joe	Liars Club (announcer), The Neighbors (announcer)		
Serling, Rod	Liars Club (host)		
Seymour, Dan	Sing It Again (host), Where Was I? (host)	Simms, Hank	Dream Girl of '67 (announcer), How's Your Mother-in-Law? (announcer)
Shafer, Ross	Love Me, Love Me Not (host), Match Game (host)	Simms, Jay	High Finance (announcer)
Sharbutt, Del	Who Do You Trust? (announcer)	Sinclair, Millie	Earn Your Vacation (assistant)
Shearer, Harry	The News Hole (host)	Skrovan, Steve	That's My Dog! (host)
Shearin, John	Guilty or Innocent (jury moderator)	Slater, Bill	Broadway to Hollywood Headline Clues (host), Charade Quiz (host), Messing Prize Party (host), Twenty Questions (host), With This Ring (host)
Sheldon, Gail	Beat the Clock (assistant), The Price Is Right (model)		
Shepard, Bob	Beat the Clock (announcer) Break the Bank (announcer), Doctor I.Q. (announcer), The Name's the Same (announcer), Public Prosecutor (announcer), Take a Chance (announcer), To Tell the Truth (announcer), Twenty Questions (announcer)	Slattery, Jack	Art Linkletter Show (announcer), Life with Linkletter (announcer)
		Smith, "Buffalo" Bob	Treasure Hunt (substitute host)
		Smith, Jack	Love Story (host), Place the Face (host), Queen for a Day (substitute host)
Shepard, Dick	What's Your Bid (announcer)	Smith, Jason Grant	Shop 'til You Drop (announcer)
Sherrin, Ned	We Interrupt This Week (host)	Smith, Marilyn	Love Me, Love Me Not (announcer)
Sherry, Bob	It's News to Me (announcer)		
Sherwood, Bobby	The Big Payoff (substitute host), Quick as a Flash (host)	Smith, Mark	Way Out Games (assistant)
		Smith, Sidney	Stop the Music (announcer)
Sherwood, Brad	The Dating Game (host)	Smith, Sydney	The Big Payoff (substitute assistant)
Shikiar, Dave	Double Dare (assistant)		
Shinick, Kevin	Where in Time Is Carmen Sandiego? (host)	Smith, Verne	College of Musical Knowledge (announcer)
Shipley, Bill	Alumni Fun (announcer), Beat the Clock (commercial announcer), We Take Your Word (announcer)	Snead, Sam	Celebrity Golf (host)
		Snyder, Jay	Oh My Word (announcer)
		Sokol, Christine	Where in the World Is Carmen Sandiego? (voices)
Shirley, Tom	They're Off (host)	Solomita, Fran	Liars (host)
Shmitt, Stuffy	Turn It Up! (announcer)	Sommers, Rick	The Great Getaway Game (announcer)
Shoemaker, Craig	My Generation (host)		
Shorr, Lonnie	Dueling for Playmates (host)	Spano, Nick	Peer Pressure (host)
Shriner, Herb	Judge for Yourself (substitute host), Two for the Money (host)	Sparks, David	All About the Opposite Sex (host), Cross Wits (host), NFL Trivia Game (host)
Shriner, Wil	Small Talk (host), That's My Dog! (host)		
		Sparks, Hal	Treasure Mall (host)
Sidoni, David	Wheel of Fortune 2000 (host)	Sparrow, Sharron	Split Second (model)
Siegal George	King Pins (host)	Speck, Jan	Treasure Hunt (model)
Silvers, Phil	Stop the Music (substitute host)	Spence, Sandra	Pantomime Quiz (assistant)
Simmons, Richard	Ultra Quiz (assistant)	Spencer, Larry	The $1.98 Beauty Show (assistant)
Simms, Frank	For Love Or Money (announcer), Word for Word (announcer)		
		Stafford, Marian	Treasure Hunt (pirate girl)
Simms, Hal	Beat the Clock (substitute announcer), Go Lucky (announcer), I'll Buy That (announcer), Made in America (announcer), Sing It Again (an-	Stafford, Susan	Wheel of Fortune (assistant)
		Staggs, Brad	Top Card (announcer)
		Stahl, Lisa	The Price Is Right (model)
		Stanley, Don	Glamour Girl (announcer)

personality	game show	personality	game show
Stark, Dick	Down You Go (announcer), It Pays to Be Ignorant (announcer), What's My Line? (announcer)	Sullivan, Nancy	Super Decades (substitute host), Trivia Track (substitute host)
		Summers, Marc	Couch Potatoes (host), Double Dare (host), Majority Rules (host), Pick Your Brain (host), What Would You Do? (host)
Stein, Ben	Win Ben Stein's Money (host)		
Steinfeld, Andy	The Grudge Match (corner man)		
Steinfeld, Pete	The Grudge Match (corner man)	Susann, Jacqueline	Your Surprise Store (assistant)
Sterling, Jack	Strike It Rich (substitute host)	Swann, Lynn	To Tell the Truth (host)
Stern, Bill	Are You Positive (host), Remember This Date (host)	Swayze, John Cameron	Chance for Romance (host), To Tell the Truth (substitute host)
Stern, Rick	Designated Hitter (announcer)	Szeles, Amazing Jonathan	Ruckus (host)
Sternberg, Scott	Let's Go Back (host)		
Stevens, Harry	Finders Keepers (announcer), Pictionary (announcer)	Tadlock, Thelma	Play Your Hunch (assistant)
		Taylor, Deems	Americana (host)
Stevens, Richard	Hollywood Squares (announcer)	Taylor, Diana	Classic Concentration (model)
Stevens, Shadoe	Hollywood Squares (announcer)	Taylor, Rip	The $1.98 Beauty Show (host)
Stewart, Dick	Dream Girl of '67 (host)	Templeton, Bill	Treasure Isle (announcer)
Stewart, Elaine	Gambit (assistant), High Rollers (assistant)	Ten Eck, John	Rumor Has It (announcer)
		Terry, Arlene & Ardell	Twenty-One (assistants)
Stewart, Jay	Blackout (announcer), Bullseye (announcer), Card Sharks (announcer), Cross Wits (announcer), Hollywood Connection (announcer), It Could Be You (announcer), It Pays to Be Married (announcer), It's Anybody's Guess (announcer), The Joker's Wild (announcer), Knockout (announcer), Let's Make a Deal (announcer), Love Experts (announcer), Masquerade Party (announcer), Penny to a Million (announcer), Play the Percentages (announcer), Sale of the Century (announcer), Scrabble (announcer), Second Chance (announcer), Tic Tac Dough (announcer), Win with the Stars (announcer), You Don't Say! (announcer)	Thaxton, Lloyd	Everybody's Talking (host), Funny You Should Ask!! (host), Pro-Fan (announcer)
		Theismann, Joe	American Gladiators (host)
		Thicke, Alan	Animal Crack-ups (host), Pictionary (host)
		Thigpen, Lynne	Where in the World Is Carmen Sandiego? ("The Chief"), Where in Time Is Carmen Sandiego? ("The Chief")
		Thomas, Jerry	Pay Cards! (announcer)
		Thomas, Karen	The $1,000,000 Chance of a Lifetime (assistant)
		Thompson, Jim	Dealer's Choice (announcer), The Diamond Head Game (announcer), The Fun Factory (announcer), Rhyme and Reason (announcer)
Stice, Roxie	That's My Dog! (assistant)	Thompson, Larry	American Gladiators (referee)
Stockwell, Dr. Robert	Password (word authority)	Thompson, Mark	Fantasy Park (host)
Stoddart, Lindsey	My Generation (announcer)	Thorsell, Karen	Lucky Partners (assistant)
Stokey, Mike	Pantomime Quiz (host), Stump the Stars (host)	Thyssen, Greta	Treasure Girl (pirate girl)
		Tice, Olin	Bank on the Stars (announcer)
Stones, Dwight	Dream League (referee/host)	T-Money	Lip Service (DJ)
Storrs, Suzanne	Number Please (assistant), Play Your Hunch (assistant)	Toffler, Larry	Finders Keepers (host)
		Tom, Kiana	Blade Warriors (host)
Story, Ralph	The $64,000 Challenge (host), What Do You Have in Common (host)	Toman, Jerry	It's in the Bag (host)
		Tomarken, Peter	Bargain Hunters (host), Hit Man (host), Press Your Luck (host), Super Decades (substitute host), Trivia Track (substitute host), Wipeout (host)
Stout, Rex	Think Fast (substitute host)		
Stroupe, Carolyn	The Price Is Right (model)		
Struthers, Sally	Win, Lose or Draw (substitute host)	Tompkins, Barry	Star Games (announcer)
		Toomey, Marilyn	Win with a Winner (assistant)
Stuart, Darlene	Queen for a Day (model)	Trabert, Tony	Celebrity Tennis (cohost)
Sullivan, Ed	The $64,000 Question (substitute host)	Travalena, Fred	Anything for Money (host), Baby Races (host)

personality	game show	personality	game show
Travers, Ted	Celebrity Billiards (host)	Vincent, Scott	The $10,000 Pyramid (announcer), 100 Grand (announcer)
Trebek, Alex	The $128,000 Question (host), Battlestars (host), Classic Concentration (host), Double Dare (host), High Rollers (host), Jeopardy! (host), Pitfall (host), Super Jeopardy! (host), To Tell the Truth (host), Wheel of Fortune (substitute host), The Wizard of Odds (host)	Vincz, Melanie	Let's Make a Deal (model)
		Vines, Lee	Balance Your Budget (announcer), Beat the Clock (announcer), The Big Surprise (announcer), Fractured Phrases (announcer), Make the Connection (announcer), The Name's the Same (announcer), Password (announcer), Picture This (announcer), What's My Line? (announcer)
Trevino, Lee	Golf for Swingers (host)		
Trout, Robert	Who Said That? (host)	Von Zell, Harry	Celebrity Golf (host)
Tucker, John Bartholomew	Treasure Isle (host)	Wade, Adam	Musical Chairs (host)
		Waggoner, Lyle	It's Your Bet (host)
Tufeld, Dick	Celebrity Sweepstakes (announcer), Don Adams' Screen Test (announcer), People Are Funny (announcer)	Wagner, Andrea	Trashed (hostess)
		Walberg, Mark	The Big Date (host), Free 4 All (host), Shop 'til You Drop (announcer), Teen Win, Lose or Draw (announcer), USA Gonzo Games (host)
Tuna, Charlie	The $25,000 Pyramid (announcer), Battlestars (announcer), Scattergories (announcer), Scrabble (announcer), Time Machine (announcer)		
		Waldecker, Frank	Twenty Questions (announcer)
		Waldecker, Fred	Love Story (announcer)
		Walker, John	Triple Threat (announcer)
Tuttle, Roger	Dough Re Mi (announcer/substitute host), Jan Murray Show (announcer), Play Your Hunch (announcer), The Price Is Right (substitute announcer), Say When!! (announcer), Three on a Match (announcer)	Wallace, Mike	The Big Surprise (host), Guess Again (host), I'll Buy That (host), Majority Rules (host), There's One in Every Family (host), Who Pays? (host), Who's the Boss? (host)
		Wallace, Toni	The Price Is Right (model)
Tyler, Madeline	Beat the Clock (assistant)	Walters, Mimi	Doctor I.Q. (assistant), Party Line (assistant)
Uttal, Fred	Q.E.D. (host)		
Vague, Vera	Follow the Leader (host), The Greatest Man on Earth (host)	Walters, Nancy	The Big Payoff (model)
		Wanderone Jr., Rudolph	Celebrity Billiards (host)
Van, Bobby	The Fun Factory (host), Make Me Laugh (host), Showoffs (host)		
Van De Venter, Fred	Twenty Questions (substitute host)	Ward, Robin	To Tell the Truth (host)
		Warren, Bob	On Your Account (announcer), Place the Face (announcer), Tag the Gag (announcer)
Van Dyke, Dick	Laugh Line (host), Mother's Day (host)		
Van Dyke, Jerry	Picture This (host)	Washington, Cynthia	Wheel of Fortune (substitute hostess)
Van Horn, Arthur	Battle of the Ages (announcer)		
Van Nuys, Larry	All About the Opposite Sex (announcer), Hold Everything! (announcer), Tic Tac Dough (announcer)	Watkins, Royale	Singled Out (announcer)
		Watson, Virginia	The Dating Game (announcer)
		Wayne, Frank	Beat the Clock (substitute host), Password (announcer)
Vano, Alan	Blade Warriors (warrior)		
Van Peebles, Mario	Family Figures (host)	Wayne, Patrick	Tic Tac Dough (host)
Van Peebles, Melvin	Family Figures (host)	Weaver, Beau	College Mad House (announcer)
Ventura, Jesse	The Grudge Match (host)	Webber, Dean	The Anniversary Game (announcer)
Vereen, Ben	You Write the Songs (host)		
Vermiere, Brian	Maximum Drive (cohost)	Weigel, John	Treasure Quest (host)
Vestoff, Floria	Judge for Yourself (dancing cigarette pack)	Weist, Dwight	To Tell the Truth (commercial announcer)
		Weldon, Jimmy	Funny Boners (host)

personality	game show	personality	game show
Weller, Robb	Win, Lose or Draw (host)		Talk (announcer), Runaround (announcer), Shenanigans (announcer), Showdown (announcer), Stop the Music (announcer), To Say the Least (announcer), Two for the Money (announcer), Video Village (announcer)
Wells, John	Guilty or Innocent (announcer)		
Wendell, Bill	Brains and Brawn (announcer), Can Do (announcer), Haggis Baggis (announcer), Jan Murray Show (announcer/substitute host), Let's Play Post Office (announcer), Personality (announcer), Sale of the Century (announcer), Tic Tac Dough (announcer/host), To Tell the Truth (announcer), Treasure Hunt (announcer), Win with a Winner (announcer), Word for Word (announcer/substitute host)		
		Williams, Suzanna	Card Sharks (assistant)
		Williams, Vince	Freedom Rings (announcer)
		Wilshire, Deanna	Blade Warriors (warrior)
		Wilson, Donna	College Mad House (assistant)
		Wilson, Flip	People Are Funny (host)
		Wilson, Ward	Can You Top This? (host)
		Winchell, Paul	Runaround (host), What's My Name? (host)
West, Randy	Boggle—The Interactive Game (announcer), Jumble—The Interactive Game (announcer), Shuffle—The Interactive Game (announcer), Trivial Pursuit (announcer), Wild Animal Games (announcer)		
		Winfield, Greg	Video Game (host)
		Winkler, KC	High Rollers (assistant)
		Wirth, Sandra	County Fair ("Miss County Fair")
Wheeler, Jack	Tell It to Groucho (assistant)	Wiss, Doris	The $64,000 Challenge (assistant), Lucky Partners (assistant)
Whitaker, Jack	The Face Is Familiar (host)	Wolf, Renee	Masquerade Party (timekeeper)
White, Betty	Just Men! (host), Password (substitute host)	Wood, Annie	Bzzz! (host)
White, Carolyn	Say When!! (model)	Wood, Gene	Anything You Can Do (host), Baby Races (announcer), Beat the Clock (announcer/host), The Better Sex (announcer), Body Language (announcer), Bruce Forsyth's Hot Streak (announcer), Card Sharks (announcer), Child's Play (announcer), Classic Concentration (announcer), Double Dare (announcer), Family Challenge (announcer), Family Feud (announcer), Love Connection (announcer), Match Game (announcer), Match Game–Hollywood Squares Hour (announcer), Now You See It (announcer), Password (announcer), Password Plus (announcer), The Price Is Right (announcer), Showoffs (announcer), Super Decades (announcer), Super Password (announcer), Tattletales (announcer), That's My Dog! (announcer), Trivia Track (announcer), Trivia Trap (announcer), Win, Lose Or Draw (announcer), Your Number's Up (announcer)
White, Pat	Concentration (model), Treasure Hunt (pirate girl), Dollar a Second (assistant)		
White, Vanna	Wheel of Fortune (hostess)		
Whittington, Dick	Almost Anything Goes (cohost)		
Wholey, Dennis	The Generation Gap (host), What's My Line? (announcer)		
Wicker, Irene	Play the Game (host)		
Williams, Bob	Double or Nothing (announcer), Treasure Hunt (announcer), What's My Line? (announcer), Where Was I? (announcer)		
Williams, Dave	Face the Music (announcer)		
Williams, Dave	Dream League (referee)		
Williams, Jean	Feather the Nest (assistant)		
Williams, Kenny	Amateur's Guide to Love (announcer), Auction-Aire (announcer), Baffle (announcer), Bedtime Stories (announcer), Celebrity Game (announcer), County Fair (announcer), Double Exposure (announcer), Funny You Should Ask!! (announcer), Gambit (announcer), The Hollywood Squares (announcer), Hot Seat (announcer), Las Vegas Gambit (announcer), Name Droppers (announcer), PDQ (announcer), People Will		
		Wood, Professor William	Window Shopping (judge)

personality	game show	personality	game show
Woodbury, Woody	Who Do You Trust? (host)	Young, Robin	Ready . . . Set . . . Cook! (host)
Woods, Charles	Pantomime Quiz (announcer)		
Woods, Roslyn	What's Your Bid (model)	Zigler, Ted	Truth or Consequences (announcer)
Woolery, Chuck	The Dating Game (host), Love Connection (host), Scrabble (host), Wheel of Fortune (host)	Zito, Chris	Think Twice (announcer)
		Zobeck, Margaret	Anything You Can Do (assistant)
Wuhrer, Kari	Remote Control (assistant)	Zorbaugh, Dr. Harvey	Play the Game (host)
Wylie, Eric	Blade Warriors (warrior)	Zumwalt, Rick	Pictionary (judge)
Young, Michael	Grand-Prix All Star Show (host)		

BIBLIOGRAPHY

Anderson, Kent A. *Television Fraud: The History and Implications of the Quiz Show Scandals.* Westport, Conn.: Greenwood Press, 1978.

Barnouw, Erik. *A Tower in Babel: A History of Broadcasting in the United States.* Volume 1. New York: Oxford, 1966.

———. *The Golden Web: A History of Broadcasting in the United States.* Volume 2. New York: Oxford, 1968.

———. *The Image Empire: A History of Broadcasting in the United States.* Volume 3. New York: Oxford, 1970.

Barris, Chuck. *The Game Show King, a Confession.* New York: Carroll & Graf, 1993.

Blumenthal, Norman. *The TV Game Shows.* New York: Pyramid, 1975.

Brooks, Tim, and Earl Marsh. *The Complete Directory to Prime-time Network TV Shows.* Sixth edition. New York: Ballantine, 1995.

Brown, Les. *Les Brown's Encyclopedia of Television.* Third edition. Detroit, Mich.: Visible Ink Press, 1992.

Buxton, Frank, and Bill Owen. *The Big Broadcast: 1920–1950.* New York: Flare Books/Avon Books, 1972.

Campbell, Robert. *The Golden Years of Broadcasting, A Celebration of the First Fifty Years of Radio and TV on NBC.* New York: Rutledge Book/Scribners, 1976.

Castleman, Harry, and Walter J. Podrazik. *The TV Schedule Book: Four Decades of Network Programming from Sign-on to Sign-off.* New York: McGraw-Hill Book Company, 1984.

———. *Watching TV: Four Decades of American Television.* New York: McGraw-Hill Book Company, 1982.

David, Nina. *TV Season 1974–1975; 1975–1976; 1976–1977; 1977–1978.* Phoenix, Ariz.: Oryx Press, 1976, 1977, 1978, 1979.

DeLong, Thomas: *Quiz Craze: America's Infatuation with the Radio and Television Game Show.* Westport, Conn.: Praeger Publishers, 1991.

Downs, Hugh. *On Camera, My Ten Thousand Hours on Television.* New York: G.P. Putnam's Sons, 1986.

Dunning, John. *Tune in Yesterday: The Ultimate Encyclopedia of Old-Time Radio 1925–1976.* Englewood Cliffs, N.J.: Prentice-Hall, 1976.

Editors of Broadcasting Magazine. *The First Fifty Years of Broadcasting.* Washington, D.C.: Broadcasting Publications, 1982.

Erickson, Hal. *Syndicated Television: The First Forty Years 1947–1987.* Jefferson, N.C.: McFarland & Company, 1989.

Fabe, Maxene. *TV Game Shows.* New York: Doubleday, 1979.

Fates, Gil. *What's My Line? The Inside History of TV's Most Famous Panel Show.* Englewood Cliffs, N.J.: Prentice-Hall, 1978.

Fischer, Stuart. *Kid's TV: The First Twenty-five Years.* New York: Facts On File, Inc., 1983.

Goldenson, Leonard H., with Marvin J. Wolf. *Beating the Odds.* New York: Charles Scribner's Sons, 1991.

Goldstein, Fred, and Stan Goldstein. *Prime-Time Television, A Pictorial History from Milton Berle to "Falcon Crest."* New York: Crown Books, 1983.

Grossman, Gary H. *Saturday Morning TV.* New York: Dell Publishing, 1981.

Hall, Monty, and Bill Libby. *Emcee Monty Hall.* New York: Ballantine, 1973.

Hyatt, Wesley. *The Encyclopedia of Daytime Television.* New York: Billboard Books, 1997.

Inman, David. *The TV Encyclopedia.* New York: Perigee Books, 1991.

Kaplan, Mike (editor), and Daily Variety. *Variety Who's Who in Show Business.* Revised edition. New York: Garland Publishing, 1985.

Linkletter, Art (as told to George Bishop). *I Didn't Do It Alone, The Autobiography of Art Linkletter.* Ottawa, Illinois: Caroline House Publishers, 1980.

MacDonald, J. Fred. *One Nation Under Television.* New York: Pantheon Books, 1990.

Marx, Groucho (with Hector Arce). *The Secret Word Is Groucho.* New York: Berkeley Medallion Books, 1976.

McNeil, Alex. *Total Television, A Comprehensive Guide to Programming from 1948 to the Present.* Fourth edition. New York: Penguin Books, 1996.

Norback, Craig T., and Norback Peter G., eds. *TV Guide Almanac.* New York: Ballantine Books, 1980.

O'Neil, Thomas. *The Emmys; Star Wars, Showdowns and the Supreme Test of TV's Best.* New York: Penguin Books, 1992.

Polizzi, Rick, and Fred Schaefer. *Spin Again. Board Games from the Fifties and Sixties.* San Francisco: Chronicle Books, 1991.

Ryan, Steve. *Classic Concentration: The Game, the Show, the Puzzles.* New York: Sterling Publishing, 1991.

Sackett, Susan. *Prime Time Hits. Television's Most Popular Network Programs 1950 to the Present.* New York: Billboard Books, 1993.

Sackett, Susan, and Cheryl Blythe. *You Can Be a Game Show Contestant and Win.* New York: Dell Books, 1982.

Sams, David R., and Robert L. Shook. *Wheel of Fortune.* New York: St. Martin's Press, 1987.

Shulman, Arthur, and Roger Youman. *How Sweet It Was. Television: A Pictorial Commentary.* New York: Bonanza Books, 1966.

Slater, Robert. *This . . . Is CBS, A Chronicle of Sixty Years.* Englewood Cliffs, N.J.: Prentice Hall, 1988.

Slide, Anthony. *The Television Industry, A Historical Dictionary.* Westport, Conn.: Greenwood Press, 1991.

Stone, Joseph, and Tim Yohn. *Prime Time and Misdemeanors: Investigating the 1950s TV Quiz Scandal—a D.A.'s Account.* New Brunswick, N.J.: Rutgers University Press, 1992.

Tamerius, Steve. *How to Make a Fortune on TV Game Shows.* New York: Zebra Books, 1987.

Terrace, Vincent. *Television 1970–1980.* San Diego: A.S. Barnes and Company, 1981.

Terrace, Vincent. *Encyclopedia of TV Series, Pilots and Specials, 1937–1973; 1974–1984.* New York: New York Zoetrope, 1986.

———. *Fifty Years of Television, A Guide to Series and Pilots, 1937–1988.* New York: Cornwall Books, 1991.

Trebek, Alex, and Peter Barsocchini. *The Jeopardy! Book.* New York: HarperCollins, 1990.

Whitburn, Joel. *Top Pop Singles 1955–1990.* Menomonee Falls, Wis.: Record Research, 1991.

Winship, Michael. *Television.* New York: Random House, 1988.

Woolery, George. *Children's Television: The First Thirty-five Years, 1946–1981. Part II: Live, Film and Tape Series.* Metuchen, N.J.: Scarecrow Press, 1985.

Magazines
Billboard Magazine
Broadcasting Magazine
Daily Variety
Electronic Media
The Hollywood Reporter
Spin Again Magazine
Television Forecast
Television Index
TV Guide
TV-Radio Age
TV-Radio Daily
TV-Radio Life
Variety

Almanacs
International Television Almanac
Quigley Publications, New York
Radio Annual, Television Yearbook
Radio Daily Television Daily

Newspapers
Bergen Record, New Jersey
Chicago Tribune
Las Vegas Sun
Los Angeles Daily News
Los Angeles Herald Examiner
Los Angeles Times
New York Daily News
New York Times

ABOUT THE AUTHORS

DAVID SCHWARTZ

Game show history is just one of the many areas of expertise of author David Schwartz. He has also done extensive research in the areas of television history, daytime TV, and popular music.

A graduate of California State University, Northridge, with a B.A. in radio-TV-film, Schwartz was assistant music director for KIIS-FM, Los Angeles, from 1979 to 1982. In 1982, he joined KRLA-AM, Los Angeles, as "oldies but goodies" authority and programming assistant.

In September 1994, David left the world of radio to join Game Show Network, television's first cable network devoted exclusively to classic game shows of the past and present.

STEVE RYAN

Steve Ryan is recognized as the most prolific creator of puzzles in the world, with more than eleven thousand brain-busting bafflers to his credit. This virtuoso of vexation has been inventing games and puzzles since childhood. Early in his career he found a market for his creations through Copley News Service, where his Puzzles & Posers and Zig-Zag features have appeared for nearly twenty-five years and currently challenge readers in more than 150 newspapers across the United States and Canada.

Ryan's creativity also catapulted him into television, where he cocreated and developed the TV game show "Blockbusters" for television's most prestigious game show packager, Mark Goodson. Ryan has also written for "Password Plus," "Trivia Trap," "Body Language," and "Catch Phrase," and created all the rebus puzzles for TV's "Classic Concentration." Currently, Ryan heads the development of new games for the Goodson lottery division, creating lottery games such as Force Field, Splashdown, Stack-Up, Vortex, and Wrecking Ball that have aired in Illinois, New York, Florida, Massachusetts, Hungary, South Africa, and Brazil.

Ryan is the author of more than a dozen popular books, including *Brain Busters, Pencil Puzzlers, Test Your Puzzle IQ, Test Your Math IQ, Mystifying Math Puzzles,* and *Classic Concentration.* His puzzles have also appeared in *Games* magazine and *Games & Puzzles* magazine in the United Kingdom. His puzzle books have been translated into Dutch, French, Portuguese, and Spanish and have also surfaced in India, Pakistan, and Indonesia.

FRED WOSTBROCK

One of the leading historians of game shows, Wostbrock has been a game show fan since the age of twelve when he attended his first game show taping in New York City and met the legendary Bill Cullen. Throughout his high school years, Wostbrock visited countless game show sets in New York.

A graduate of Syracuse University, Wostbrock majored in television broadcasting and communications law. Since moving to Los Angeles in 1982, he has worked on more than ten national network and syndicated game shows. In the summer of 1987, he produced a five-part special on the history of game shows for "Good Morning America."

Wostbrock has been featured on E!, "Entertainment Tonight," "Good Morning America," and ABC News. He has also guest-starred on "Donahue," "Geraldo," FOX's "The Late Show," "Marilu," "The Joan Rivers Show," and "Rolanda," where he has shared the stage at various times with such game show greats as Chuck Barris, Monty Hall, Art James, Dennis James, Tom Kennedy, Jim Lange, Peter Marshall, Wink Martindale, Gary Owens, and Gene Rayburn.

In 1990, Cynthia Kazarian, Pammela Spencer, and Don Pitts, owners of the prestigious and multifaceted Joseph, Heldfond and Rix talent agency in Hollywood, welcomed Fred to their successful business as a game show, infomercial, and broadcasting agent.

In 1995, the agency was renamed Kazarian Spencer and Associates, Inc., and Wostbrock currently works in Studio City, California.

Wostbrock was a regular contributor in 1997 for Game Show Network, where he was known as "Mr. Game Show." As Mr. Game Show, Fred answered viewer questions on the world of game shows and highlighted a certain celebrity or classic game show each week. Among the celebrity guests of Mr. Game Show were Phyllis Diller, Bob Eubanks, Tom Kennedy, Wink Martindale, Jack Narz, Gene Rayburn, Adam West, and Gene Wood.

Among his clients are giants in the game show world, from America's favorite emcees and announcers to Emmy-winning creators and executive producers, to television's favorite celebrities.

Wostbrock has the largest collection of game show memorabilia and rare game show photos in the United States.

GAME SHOW INDEX

This game show index is designed to be used in conjunction with the A-to-Z entries. The main A-to-Z entries are indicated by **boldface** page references. *Italicized* page references indicate illustrations. Entries in the appendices are indicated by a letter following the page number: "a" indicates awards; "c" indicates chronology; "l" indicates longest-runs; "m" indicates multiple runs; "n" indicates networks: "r" indicates radio origins and "t" indicates top ratings. Entries are filed letter by letter.

NAME INDEX

This name index is designed to be used in conjunction with the A-to-Z entries. The names are alphabetized letter by letter. *Italicized* page references indicate illustrations. The appendices entries are indicated by a letter following the page number: "a" indicates awards and "h" indicates host or announcer.